FINAL JUDGEMENT AND THE DEAD IN MEDIEVAL JEWISH THOUGHT

THE LITTMAN LIBRARY OF
JEWISH CIVILIZATION

Life Patron
COLETTE LITTMAN

Dedicated to the memory of
LOUIS THOMAS SIDNEY LITTMAN
who founded the Littman Library for the love of God
and as an act of charity in memory of his father
JOSEPH AARON LITTMAN
and to the memory of
ROBERT JOSEPH LITTMAN
who continued what his father Louis had begun
יהא זכרם ברוך

'Get wisdom, get understanding:
Forsake her not and she shall preserve thee'
PROV. 4: 5

The Littman Library of Jewish Civilization is a registered UK charity
Registered charity no. 1000784

FINAL JUDGEMENT AND THE DEAD IN MEDIEVAL JEWISH THOUGHT

SUSAN WEISSMAN

London
The Littman Library of Jewish Civilization
in association with Liverpool University Press

The Littman Library of Jewish Civilization
Registered office: 14th floor, 33 Cavendish Square, London W1G 0PW

in association with Liverpool University Press
4 Cambridge Street, Liverpool L69 7ZU, UK
www.liverpooluniversitypress.co.uk/littman

Managing Editor: Connie Webber

Distributed in North America by Longleaf Services
116 S Boundary St, Chapel Hill, NY 27514, USA

First published in hardback 2020
First published in paperback 2025

Catalogue records for this book are available from the British Library and the Library of Congress
ISBN 978-1-802071-99-3

Publishing co-ordinator: Janet Moth
Copy-editing: Agnes Erdos
Proof-reading: Andrew Kirk
Index: Sarah Ereira
Designed and typeset by Pete Russell, Faringdon, Oxon.

The manufacturer's authorised representative in the EU for product safety is:
Easy Access System Europe, Mustamäe tee 50, 10621 Tallinn, Estonia
https://easproject.com (gpsr.requests@easproject.com)

To my husband
ALLAN

In memory of my dear parents
NORMAN AND DINA MOSKOWITZ
May their souls be bound in everlasting life

לעלוי נשמת אבי מורי
נחמן יונה בן שמעון
ואמי מורתי
דינה בת דוד אריה
תהיינה נפשותיהם צרורות בצרור החיים

ACKNOWLEDGEMENTS

IT WOULD BE AN UNDERSTATEMENT to say that this book would not have been possible without the tutelage and guidance of my thesis supervisor, Haym Soloveitchik. His vast erudition and wise counsel inspired and enlightened me. His critical eye and consistent encouragement benefited and sustained me. His inexhaustible patience and unfailing dedication carried me through this long endeavour.

I also wish to acknowledge the support of David Berger in his role as professor and dean. His classes in Jewish–Christian relations sparked my interest in this field many years ago, and his careful evaluation of my thesis served as an invaluable aid. I also wish to thank the Bernard Revel Graduate School and its former dean, Arthur Hyman, as well as Mordechai Katz, the chairman of the board, for providing many years of financial support and an outstanding faculty from whose members I had the privilege of learning. As important as the necessary funds, if not more so, were the understanding and patience that both men displayed in allowing me, a mother of young children, to work at my own pace; had they limited me to the normal term of support I would never have completed this project. At a time when flexible options for women in the workplace were not nearly as common as they are now, I truly appreciate how forward-thinking and magnanimous this act was. Lastly, I would like to express my gratitude to Ezra Merkin and his wife Lauren for their generosity, via the Tehillah Foundation grant, which helped fund the conclusion of this project.

I was also fortunate to have the aid of several scholars at various phases in the formulation of this work. In its earliest stages, Talya Fishman, Ephraim Shoham-Steiner, and the late Valerie Flint offered valuable advice and suggestions. I owe a debt of gratitude to Robert Graham Edwards for sending me his hard-to-acquire thesis on posthumous purgation, Diarmuid O' Riain for his chapter on the monastery at Regensburg, Eva Haverkamp for her map of Regensburg and other related material, Elisabeth Hollender for her expertise in Ashkenazi *piyut*, Naomi Feuchtwanger-Sarig for help with illuminated manuscripts, and Dalia Gross for sharing her Master's thesis with me. At a much later stage, Sylvie Anne Goldberg, whose work opened up the entire field of death studies in Jewish life, and Jean-Claude Schmitt, the pre-eminent scholar of ghost tales in the Middle Ages, were kind enough to review the entire manuscript and comment upon it. I wish to sincerely thank Robert Chazan for serving as the third reader of my dissertation and for sharing his insights and various recommendations for publication. Undoubtedly my work would not be the same without the input of all these people.

I would also like to thank the librarians at the Pollack and Mendel Gottesman libraries of Yeshiva University for their invaluable help in procuring many a book and article for me. I am particularly grateful to John Moryl for his efforts in tracking down the microfiches of Jean-Pierre Deregnaucourt's doctorate (for which, at the time, there was no other copy in the USA, UK, or France) and to Mary Ann Linahan for obtaining a vast amount of material through inter-library loan in the most efficient and amicable way imaginable. I wish to express my appreciation to Eleanor Yadin, librarian at the Dorot Jewish Division of the New York Public Library, for her aid in securing the image printed on the front cover of this book.

My feelings of gratitude towards my dear parents, Dina and Norman Moskowitz, of blessed memory, are impossible to convey in words. From my earliest years, my mother instilled in me a love of learning and a thirst for knowledge that have continued unabated ever since. This has been a great gift to me, only to be surpassed by my parents' steadfast love and unwavering support for my work all through the years. My father modelled for me the values of honesty, integrity, loyalty, and generosity and possessed a genuine love of life. With his passing at the final stages of the editing of this book, it is a source of great pain to me that he and my mother did not live to see it in print. May their memory be a blessing.

I would also like to thank my dear in-laws, Joseph and Sonia Weissman, for their commitment to my achievements. May they be rewarded with health and longevity.

My dear children, Bracha, Simcha and Omrit, Shimon and Adina, Hindi and Daniel, Sara and Maor, Rachel and Sammy, Miri, David, and Chezky, deserve much credit for their patience, understanding, and devotion. My love for them held me aloft during difficult days and seemingly endless nights. My prayer for them is that they may live long, healthy, and God-fearing lives filled with meaningful accomplishment.

Last, but certainly not least, I would like to publicly express my gratitude to my husband Allan, whose guidance, wisdom, and love served as both my anchor and my inspiration. His boundless dedication to my work manifested itself in so many ways, large and small. I could think of no better role model or life partner than him. I am truly blessed.

S.W.

CONTENTS

Note on Sources x

Note on Transliteration xi

Introduction 1

PART I

THE DEAD OF *SEFER ḤASIDIM*

1. The Dangerous Dead 17
2. The Sinful Dead 59
3. The Holy Dead 85
4. The Neutral Dead and the Pietist Dead 115

PART II

THE AFTERLIFE IN *SEFER ḤASIDIM*

5. Status in the Hereafter 151
6. On Sin, Penance, and Purgation 208
7. Bonds Between the Living and the Dead I 267
8. Bonds Between the Living and the Dead II 307
9. Conclusion 373

Bibliography 395

Index 423

NOTE ON SOURCES

References to *Sefer ḥasidim* (*SḤ*) are to section, followed where noted 'p.' by page number in cases where the section is so long that it occupies more than one page.

While there exists a shorter edition of *Sefer ḥasidim* (Bologna, 1538), unless otherwise noted the edition referred to throughout is that of Judah Wistinetzky (Berlin, 1891; repr. Jerusalem: Mekitsei Nirdamim, 1998), based on MS Parma H 3280. All readings were checked against the parallel manuscripts collected in the Princeton University Sefer Hasidim Database (PUSHD), <https://etc.princeton.edu/sefer_hasidim/>. Any significant variant readings are signalled in the footnotes.

Translations from the Babylonian Talmud are taken, with some minor modifications, from the *Hebrew–English Edition of the Babylonian Talmud*, trans. Maurice Simon, ed. Isidore Epstein (London: Soncino Press, 1972).

Abbreviations

BL	British Library, London
Bodl.	Bodleian Library, Oxford
Bologna	*Sefer ḥasidim* (Bologna, 1538; repr. Jerusalem: Mosad Harav Kook, 1957, ed. R. Margaliot)
CUL	Cambridge University Library
JTS	Jewish Theological Seminary, New York
SḤ	*Sefer ḥasidim*

NOTE ON TRANSLITERATION

The transliteration of Hebrew in this book reflects consideration of the type of book it is, in terms of its content, purpose, and readership. The system adopted therefore reflects a broad approach to transcription, rather than the narrower approaches found in the *Encyclopaedia Judaica* or other systems developed for text-based or linguistic studies. The aim has been to reflect the pronunciation prescribed for modern Hebrew, rather than the spelling or Hebrew word structure, and to do so using conventions that are generally familiar to the English-speaking reader.

In accordance with this approach, no attempt is made to indicate the distinctions between *alef* and *ayin*, *tet* and *taf*, *kaf* and *kuf*, *sin* and *samekh*, since these are not relevant to pronunciation; likewise, the *dagesh* is not indicated except where it affects pronunciation. Following the principle of using conventions familiar to the majority of readers, however, transcriptions that are well established have been retained even when they are not fully consistent with the transliteration system adopted. On similar grounds, the *tsadi* is rendered by 'tz' in such Anglicized words as barmitzvah. Likewise, the distinction between *ḥet* and *khaf* has been retained, using *ḥ* for the former and *kh* for the latter; the associated forms are generally familiar to readers, even if the distinction is not actually borne out in pronunciation, and for the same reason the final *heh* is indicated too. As in Hebrew, no capital letters are used, except that an initial capital has been retained in transliterating titles of published works (for example, *Shulḥan arukh*).

Since no distinction is made between *alef* and *ayin*, they are indicated by an apostrophe only in intervocalic positions where a failure to do so could lead an English-speaking reader to pronounce the vowel-cluster as a diphthong—as, for example, in *ha'ir*—or otherwise mispronounce the word. An apostrophe is also used, for the same reason, to disambiguate the pronunciation of other English vowel clusters, as for example in *mizbe'aḥ*.

The *sheva na* is indicated by an *e*—*perikat ol*, *reshut*—except, again, when established convention dictates otherwise.

The *yod* is represented by *i* when it occurs as a vowel (*bereshit*), by *y* when it occurs as a consonant (*yesodot*), and by *yi* when it occurs as both (*yisra'el*).

Names have generally been left in their familiar forms, even when this is inconsistent with the overall system.

INTRODUCTION

THIS BOOK is, in actuality, two books. Although not formally structured as such, it contains two distinct studies, which conceptually, although not thematically, divide it into two. One study assesses the degree of cultural embeddedness that was manifest among the Jews of medieval Ashkenaz with regard to their beliefs and practices surrounding the dead and their world. This first study seeks to contribute to the general research on death and the afterlife in medieval Europe by showing how some of the current beliefs and rituals were cross-culturally shared by neighbours, Jews and Christians alike. It compares medieval Jewish beliefs regarding the dead and their world to those of an earlier period, the great midrashic, talmudic thought-world of the rabbis which medieval Jews inherited. The portrait that emerges will hopefully contribute to a clearer conception of the unique cultural and religious history of medieval Ashkenaz.

The second study presented in this book pertains specifically to the German Pietists (Hasidei Ashkenaz), an elitist group of twelfth- and thirteenth-century Ashkenazi Jews that was heir to a mystical tradition, and whose leader, R. Judah the Pious, proposed a radical religious and social programme. The subjects of many studies, the Pietists have been examined for their mystical beliefs,[1] social theories, and models of communal organization,[2] as well as their supra-legal system of law entitled *retson haboré* and their religious programme,[3] their doctrine of penance,[4]

[1] The references that follow are not meant to serve as an exhaustive list of the rich literature on *Sefer ḥasidim*; they are only representative samples. For a comprehensive and recent bibliography, see Marcus, *Sefer Ḥasidim and the Ashkenazic Book*. Among the first historians to discuss the esoteric thought of the Pietists were Abraham Epstein ('The History of Ashkenazic Kabbalah' (Heb.)), Yekutiel Kamelhar (*The First Pietists* (Heb.)), and Gershom Scholem (*Major Trends in Jewish Mysticism*, ch. 3). An abundance of further research has been conducted by Joseph Dan, Moshe Idel, and Daniel Abrams; see e.g. Dan, *The Esoteric Theology of Ashkenazi Hasidim*; id., *The 'Unique Cherub' Circle*; Idel, 'Gazing at the Head in Ashkenazi Hasidism'; and Abrams, 'The Literary Emergence of Esotericism in German Pietism'.

[2] Among the first to explore this question was Baer, 'The Social-Religious Programme of *Sefer ḥasidim*' (Heb.). For a more recent example, see Marcus, *Piety and Society*.

[3] See e.g. Soloveitchik, 'Three Themes in *Sefer Ḥasidim*'.

[4] See n. 13 below.

attitude towards women,[5] and views on martyrdom,[6] among others. Their very existence as a movement,[7] or a sect,[8] has been debated as well as the relative impact they had on their contemporaries and later generations.[9] This study seeks to evaluate the particular views of the Pietists on matters pertaining to the dead and the afterlife. In its exploration of the theories of sin and punishment, doctrines of atonement and penance, and attitudes towards prayer for the dead and Divine judgement that R. Judah puts forth, this second study arrives at conclusions regarding the very nature of Pietism—its influences, its origins, and even possible reasons for its swift dissolution.

These two books intersect through the medium of another book, the great religious-ethical work of the Pietists, *Sefer ḥasidim* (Book of the Pious).[10] In the 1930s, Joshua Trachtenberg produced a study of the huge infiltration of non-Jewish popular notions and practices into Judaism as lived by Franco-German and east European Jewry from the eleventh to the sixteenth centuries.[11] Among other works, he used *Sefer ḥasidim* as a valuable resource. Even before that, in the previous century, Moritz Güdemann detected the influence of Christian currents upon the thinking of R. Judah the Pious.[12] Since then, scholars have argued about the question of outside influence upon *Sefer ḥasidim*, specifically in relation to its doctrine of penance, and have taken extreme positions at either end of the spectrum as well as compromise positions in between.[13]

[5] See e.g. Baskin, 'From Separation to Displacement', and 'Women and Sexual Ambivalence in *Sefer Ḥasidim*'.

[6] See e.g. Chazan, 'The Early Development of Hasidut Ashkenaz'; Dan, 'The Problem of Martyrdom' (Heb.).

[7] See Dan, '*Ashkenazi Hasidim*, 1941–1991'.

[8] Marcus, *Piety and Society*.

[9] See e.g. Soloveitchik, 'Piety, Pietism and German Pietism', and Elbaum, *Repentance and Self-Flagellation*.

[10] On the structure and redaction of *Sefer ḥasidim*, see Marcus, 'The Recensions and Structure of "Sefer Ḥasidim"', and most recently id., *Sefer Ḥasidim and the Ashkenazic Book*; on its dating, see Soloveitchik, 'On Dating *Sefer ḥasidim*'.

[11] Trachtenberg, *Jewish Magic and Superstition*.

[12] Güdemann, *The Torah and Life in Western Lands*.

[13] The first to ascribe Christian influence to the penitential doctrine of the Pietists was Yitshak Baer, in 'The Social-Religious Programme of *Sefer ḥasidim*' (Heb.), followed soon after by Gershom Scholem, in *Major Trends in Jewish Mysticism*. An important study which advanced the argument was A. Rubin, 'The Concept of Repentance among the *Hasidey 'Ashkenaz*'. Others, however, wished to perpetuate internal Jewish sources (earlier rabbinic examples of extreme penances which *Sefer ḥasidim* itself mentions) as the source of the Pietist doctrine: see Marcus, *Piety and Society*, 150 n. 54, and Schäfer, 'The Ideal of Piety of the Ashkenazi Hasidim', 10, 18. On the general role of asceticism in rabbinic literature, see Urbach, 'Asceticism and Afflictions in the Teachings of the Rabbis' (Heb.). More recently, Talya Fishman, in her essay 'The

In this book I explore the nature of this influence, and assess how far death-related beliefs and practices that circulated in the Germano-Christian environment of the time penetrated *Sefer ḥasidim*. This thirteenth-century work is a rich storehouse of information on popular notions, practices, and sensibilities reflective of high medieval German Jewish society. Although the German Pietists appear to have had little influence even in their own time,[14] and despite the clear pietistic programme of its author, *Sefer ḥasidim* contains a multitude of descriptions of everyday situations which present a realistic portrayal of late twelfth- to thirteenth-century German Jewish life. Add to this the fact that the book is clearly popular in its reach and it becomes legitimate to assume that the images, ideas, and practices regarding the dead and the hereafter which it records were popularly known or imagined. It is the working hypothesis of this study that *Sefer ḥasidim* can be successfully mined to detect such attitudes and practices, which were the common property of Pietist and non-Pietist alike.

In particular, I have employed the ghost tales in *Sefer ḥasidim* to explore the larger issue of the role that the dead and beliefs about the afterlife play in the book and in medieval Ashkenazi society in general. Termed 'the invasion of ghosts' by Jean-Claude Schmitt,[15] a flood of stories involving the dead inundated western Christendom during the high Middle Ages. I propose that, although few in number compared to those prevalent in non-Jewish sources, the ghost tales of *Sefer ḥasidim* are outgrowths of this larger phenomenon. By comparing these tales with external contemporary sources, such as Icelandic sagas, ancient Germanic tales, high medieval exempla (illustrative or moralizing tales), early medieval visionary accounts, historical and literary chronicles, miracle stories, saints' lives, and monumental church art, I conceptualize the role that the dead and beliefs about the afterlife played in the society of the living. I have tried to uncover the nature and extent of the outside influence upon these conceptualizations by contrasting the material contained in *Sefer ḥasidim* with internal Jewish sources, both antecedent—rabbinic, post-rabbinic, and geonic literature—

Penitential System of *Ḥasidei Ashkenaz*', again champions the argument for Christian influence. Denying that the evidence from rabbinic literature is sufficient to serve as a 'proximate cause', she instead points to the many close similarities between prevalent Christian and Pietist penitential doctrines. See also the comments of David Berger on the matter in 'Judaism and General Culture', 121–2, and in his book *Persecution, Polemic, and Dialogue*, 46.

14 Joseph Dan notes the almost total lack of references in Ashkenazi literature to the unique ideas or practices of the Pietists; see '*Ashkenazi Hasidim*, 1941–1991', 96. See also Soloveitchik, 'Piety, Pietism and German Pietism'. Possible reasons why this is so will be suggested at the conclusion of the book.

15 This phrase forms the title of a chapter in Schmitt's *Ghosts in the Middle Ages*, 59–71.

and contemporary—tosafist commentary, halakhic literature, *piyut* commentaries, illuminated manuscripts, and Pietist writings. All this with the goal of enriching our understanding of Ashkenazi Jewish culture in general, and the unique world-view of the Pietists in particular.

In establishing the specific outlook of the Pietists, I have only used material that stems from the writings of R. Judah the Pious, a leader of the movement, and those in his circle, not sources that merely report on them. Thus, I have not included the cycle of miracle stories that surround the persona of R. Judah and his father, R. Samuel the Pious, contained in the *Ma'aseh bukh*, a Jewish hagiographical work of the early modern period.[16] Eli Yassif has argued that, although the stories surrounding R. Judah are found in a sixteenth-century manuscript, they form part of the earliest strand of tales and originate from around the year 1300.[17] Even granting the early date of these stories (a contested matter), it is still an open question whether wonder tales of holy men reflect what a holy man was or the mind of the people who composed the tales. I maintain that, with a few exceptions,[18] these stories are unlike those found in *Sefer ḥasidim*. They differ totally from the unique atmosphere of *Sefer ḥasidim*, not to speak of the values expressed and endorsed there. Universal consent has it that R. Judah is one of three major figures that led the Hasidei Ashkenaz (R. Judah, his father, and his pupil, R. Eleazar of Worms) and that *Sefer ḥasidim* reflects the Pietist *Weltanschauung*, so I find it implausible that one figure could generate two sharply different ideological images. If someone wishes to insist that such is the case, they are entitled to their view; I am analysing the corpus that has for centuries been seen as the work of this famous figure and that is sufficient for me. Since, in their descriptions of the dead and the afterlife, the miracle stories of the *Ma'aseh bukh* paint a very different portrait of R. Judah the Pious than the one that emerges from the

[16] See Gaster, *Ma'aseh Book*. See also Dan, *R. Judah the Pious* (Heb.), 163–76. An isolated tale about R. Judah is cited in Raspe, 'A Medieval Sage in Early Modern Folk Narrative', 140; thanks to Ephraim Shoham-Steiner for this last reference. For a mid-fourteenth-century report regarding R. Judah the Pious and recorded by R. Isaac, son of R. Eleazar of Worms, reputed author of the *Sefer hagan*, see the Appendix to Ch. 8 below.

[17] See Yassif, *Ninety-Nine Tales* (Heb.), 9. Ivan Marcus has championed this claim, dating the stories to as early as the thirteenth century in his *Sefer Ḥasidim and the Ashkenazic Book*, 46 and n. 2.

[18] Stories 4, 8, and 59 (a version of Hellequin's Hunt—a genre that I discuss in Ch. 2) in Yassif's *Ninety-Nine Tales* are true exempla relating to the dead and the afterlife, and could belong within the pages of *Sefer ḥasidim*. Stories 1 and 16 contain versions of the R. Akiva tale (a story discussed in Ch. 8 below) that were widely known in Pietist and Ashkenazi circles in the thirteenth century.

pages of *Sefer ḥasidim*,[19] I feel the miracle stories reflect the opinions of their redactors (and their intended audience) rather than offer a true description of the man and his views.[20]

When dealing with material from *Sefer ḥasidim* itself, it, too, remains an open question whether or not the book reflects a unified outlook. Given its aggregate nature and the tangled question of authorship, one might conclude that it is a composite work. In fact, some isolated passages within it have been shown to be contradictory and may be the work of editors and compilers who freely inserted their own or others' material into the texts.[21] The bewildering variety of topics covered in the book supports the supposition that one author may not be responsible for every single passage in it. Inbal Gur has gone so far as to argue that R. Judah's authorship can never be established with absolute certainty since nothing currently exists that was penned by him.[22] On the other hand, Ivan Marcus points out the segmented nature of the book and attributes it to the distinctive features of its composition. An 'open book', *Sefer ḥasidim* results from the combination of a multitude of parallel editions (rather than one original) built upon shorter units of texts disjunctively combined.[23] Despite this multi-layered structural characterization, Marcus marshals a host of evidence which connects R. Judah the Pious with many passages within the otherwise anonymously written *Sefer ḥasidim* and establishes him as its primary author.[24]

While I agree that a sole individual is not the author of every section of the book, I argue, on the basis of thematic evidence presented in this study with regard to matters of death and the afterlife, that there exists a consistency of opinion in *Sefer ḥasidim* on these issues that points to a single prominent voice. Of the three leaders of the German Pietists, two main figures stand behind *Sefer ḥasidim*—R. Judah the Pious and R. Eleazar of Worms.[25] Since the opinion I find in *Sefer ḥasidim* does not always align

19 Many of the stories in *Ninety-Nine Tales* that relate to the dead contain midrashic elements and themes that are absent from *Sefer ḥasidim*. See e.g. nos. 5, 64, 66, 72, 78, 80, and 91.

20 See *Ninety-Nine Tales*, nos. 2, 3, 5, 27, 28, 29, 30, 32, 33, 34, 35, 36, 85, 86, 87, 92, 94, and 95 for examples of this phenomenon, and the discussion in Ch. 9., n. 27 below.

21 In response to Ivan Marcus's lecture entitled 'Sefer Hasidim, its Author, and Hasidei Ashkenaz in Historical Context', which he delivered at the 'Sefer Ḥasidim in Context' conference (Jerusalem, March 2017), David Shyovitz pointed to the presence of specific passages, such as *SḤ* 1031, which express an anti-Pietist view.

22 Inbal Gur has advanced this claim in a lecture entitled 'The Complexity of the Book of Angels in Various Manuscripts', delivered at the March 2017 conference 'Sefer Ḥasidim in Context'.

23 See Marcus, *Sefer Ḥasidim and the Ashkenazic Book*, 5.

24 Ibid. 45–64.

25 This contention excludes the first thirteen paragraphs of the book, which may be the work of R. Judah's father, R. Samuel the Pious. A. Epstein attributes them to R. Samuel on the basis

with the view of R. Eleazar, by elimination it stands to reason that it reflects that of R. Judah. I will therefore speak of R. Judah as the author of the work when citing passages that relate to these matters, and even in areas where his views are in consonance with those of R. Eleazar. However, should someone insist that the major voice speaking in *Sefer ḥasidim* is that of another Pietist, I would not argue with them as it would not affect my basic argument about the views of the book on the dead and the afterlife, sin and punishment, or ghosts and final judgement. Personally, I feel it is highly improbable that major themes in the work are the making of an anonymous hasid; but if someone wishes to substitute all my mentions of R. Judah with 'the hasid', he or she should feel free to do so; I will ascribe that voice to R. Judah. I would argue further that the best way to address this problem is not by scouring medieval sources for attributions of authorship, but rather by testing, through a series of thematic studies such as this one, the unity of its thought on specific issues.

Medieval Ashkenaz as a cultural milieu included the Jewish communities of Germany (the empire north of the Alps), France north of the Loire, and England—a French community dating from the Norman conquest in 1066. The temporal contours of the study reflect the period in which Ashkenaz flourished as a creative Jewish centre; its first literary traces date from around the year 1000, while its intellectual creativity came to an end in the late thirteenth century in northern France and England, and in the early years of the fourteenth century in Germany.

Historians of western Europe have documented major transformations in attitudes and practices related to death and the hereafter which took place in that period.[26] One such transformation consisted of a movement away from the perception of death as a generalized, objective experience and towards a more subjective, individualized notion of it. Belief in personal judgement after the death of the individual similarly became widespread at the time.[27] The rise of the Cluniac cult of the dead, with its annual commemoration of all Christians who have passed on, can be dated back to around the year 1000. The following two centuries produced an abundance of works of varying genre, each of which contains myriads of tales of the

of a gematria cited by R. Margeshet: the gematria (numerical value) of the name Shemuel is equivalent to that of the phrase *sod yirei elohim*—the opening heading of *Sefer ḥasidim*. See *SḤ*, ed. Wistinetzky, 490, bottom of Notes section. Even so, R. Judah's views, as outlined in the rest of the book, are not at odds with the views expressed in these first paragraphs.

[26] Prominent among them are Ariès, *Western Attitudes toward Death*; Vovelle, *Ideologies and Mentalities*; and Le Goff, *The Birth of Purgatory*.

[27] See Ariès, *Western Attitudes toward Death*.

ordinary dead who return to the world of the living. In the realm of the hereafter, the twelfth and thirteenth centuries witnessed the rise to prominence of Purgatory as a distinct locus, separate from Heaven and Hell. Historians of popular culture point to ancient pre-Christian notions of the dead, still extant in high medieval Europe, that played no small role in the widespread acceptance of Purgatory and in the promotion of the idea of reciprocal relations between the living and the dead.[28] This study builds upon the work of historical anthropologists who have laboured in the field of the study of death and the afterlife.[29]

Historians of medieval Jewry have also pointed to the primacy of the high medieval period in the shaping of Jewish practices and attitudes regarding the dead. That period was particularly fertile in this regard as it gave rise to the Yizkor service, the Jewish ceremony of commemorating souls,[30] and parallels between the *memorbukh*s of Ashkenaz and medieval

[28] See e.g. Gurevich, *Historical Anthropology of the Middle Ages*, and id., *Medieval Popular Culture*.

[29] See Gurevich, 'Popular and Scholarly Medieval Cultural Traditions', and N. Davis's review of *The Birth of Purgatory*, 31. Jean-Claude Schmitt highlights the popular elements to be found in medieval conceptions of the hereafter in his study *Ghosts in the Middle Ages*. In some excellent comparative studies, Eli Yassif and Tamar Alexander successfully integrate the findings of the school of historical anthropology into their research of medieval Jewish texts. Yassif, 'The Exempla Tale in *Sefer ḥasidim*' (Heb.) demonstrates that the hundreds of stories recorded by R. Judah the Pious parallel those found in contemporary collections of medieval exempla in terms of content, style, technique, or function. Joseph Dan, in 'Rabbi Judah the Pious and Caesarius of Heisterbach', has attempted to correlate some specific stories in *Sefer ḥasidim* with those of the thirteenth-century exempla collection *Dialogue on Miracles* (*Dialogus miraculorum*) by Caesarius of Heisterbach. Alexander, 'Neighbour in Paradise in *Sefer ḥasidim*' (Heb.), analyses from a narrative perspective stories in *Sefer ḥasidim* that concern the afterlife, focusing on changed elements that reflect a pietistic world-view within a common motif found in popular folklore. Most recently Kushelevsky, *Penalty and Temptation* (Heb.), has placed various narratives circulating in Ashkenaz within the specific social and religious context of medieval Christendom. Perez, 'The Dead in the World of the Living' (Heb.), focuses on Jewish tales of the returning dead within that same milieu.

[30] Goldberg, 'The Contribution of the Study of Death to Jewish Studies', 162, notes that 'the essential turning point in Jewish attitudes to death occurred around the time of the Crusades'. Eric Zimmer, in 'The Persecutions of 1096' (Heb.), views the *memorbukh* as a product of the 1096 massacres. Israel Lévi, in 'La Commémoration des âmes dans le Judaïsme', was the first to make the connection between Jewish memorialization and the Crusades, viewing the Yizkor service as a direct outgrowth of the latter. This linkage was contested by Galinsky, 'Charity and Prayer in the Ashkenazi Synagogue' (Heb.), a lecture delivered at the sixteenth World Congress of Jewish Studies in 2013 and printed in Dagan (ed.), *Essays in Jewish Studies* (Heb.), 163–74, esp. 166–7. Elisheva Baumgarten follows Galinsky's approach and points to the Christian model of *pro anima* donations as the primary impetus; see Baumgarten, *Practicing Piety in Medieval Ashkenaz*, 108–15. Nati Barak, however, in his dissertation 'Time of Rage' (Heb.), has argued again for a causal link between the Crusades and both the *memorbukh* and

monastic necrologies, *libri vitae* (books of lives) and *libri memoriales* (books of commemoration), have been documented.[31] In terms of the hereafter, the practice of reciting the mourners' Kaddish—a prayer performed by the living for the benefit of the dead—emerged in medieval Ashkenaz.[32] Apart from the Kaddish, liturgical practices rooted in an ancient belief in the sabbath rest of souls in Gehenna sprouted and flourished in the communities of Ashkenaz at this time.[33]

Bearing in mind these simultaneous shifts in consciousness and praxis within both the dominant culture of Christian Europe and the subculture of medieval Ashkenaz, I have sought to discover whether these changes were related or merely coincidental. Even though the Jews of medieval Christendom strictly adhered to traditional rabbinic norms and practices, and maintained cultural boundaries with the surrounding society, the small size of their communities and the socio-economic ties they developed with their Christian neighbours often brought them into close contact with those neighbours' beliefs and practices.[34] My general readings in the areas of death and the afterlife showed enough similarity to lead me to suspect that there was some degree of influence of the general environment upon the beliefs and practices of medieval Ashkenazi Jewry. What I had not realized was just how massive that influence actually was, and who, of all people, was most receptive to it. I discovered that the significant developments in attitudes to death and the hereafter that took place in western Europe at this time had an enormous impact upon Jewish attitudes. After my research was completed, I began to see that my findings of cultural influence were shared by other scholars in the field.[35]

the Yizkor service: see pp. 217–34 of his study. Despite the argument surrounding the impetus behind their emergence, Jewish historians agree that both originated at some point during the high medieval period.

[31] Lévi, 'La Commémoration des âmes', and Baumgarten, *Practicing Piety in Medieval Ashkenaz*, 110–15.

[32] See Roth, 'Memorial Prayer' (Heb.), and Ta-Shma, *Early Franco-German Ritual and Custom* (Heb.), 299–310. Most recently see Shyovitz, '"You Have Saved Me from the Judgment of Gehenna"'.

[33] See Lévi, 'Le Repos sabbatique des âmes damnées'.

[34] On the close proximity of Jews and Christians in the urban communities of the Middle Ages, see A. Haverkamp, 'Jews and Urban Life'.

[35] Study of the dead and their role in medieval Jewish life has come to the foreground of scholarship. Avriel Bar-Levav, for example, has defined the role of the cemetery in Jewish life, as well as burial and mourning practices, in 'A Separate Place' (Heb.) and 'Death, Burial, and Mourning' (Heb.). Barak, 'Time of Rage' (Heb.), documents the changes in Ashkenazi burial customs and memorial practices over the course of the high medieval period. In a recent volume, Reif, Lehnardt, and Bar-Levav (eds.), *Death in Jewish Life*, particular attention is paid to the strong influence of the Christian environment upon Jewish belief and practice.

Since my intent was to reveal information regarding Jewish customs and beliefs about the dead that were uniquely medieval, I compared the beliefs found in *Sefer ḥasidim* with those prevalent in talmudic and midrashic literature. What I uncovered was a major transformation in Jewish attitudes towards and practices regarding the dead and the afterlife that had occurred from the rabbinic period to medieval times. A huge influx of Germano-Christian beliefs, customs, and fears had seeped into Ashkenazi society, which shared, even if unwittingly, the mental and cultural structures of high medieval Europe in this area of great theological import.[36]

Even more surprising to me in the course of my research was to find a significant divide between the ideas and practices that impressed themselves upon Ashkenazi Jews and those that penetrated Pietist thinking and praxis. *Sefer ḥasidim* bears witness to the cultural infusion of Germano-Christian beliefs on two levels: first, when it reflects those of Ashkenazi society in general, and second, on a deeper level, when it communicates the doctrines specific to Pietism. Here, too, the objectives of the 'two books' within this study collide.

With my interest piqued, I sought to evaluate the particular position of R. Judah the Pious on the topic of the hereafter in light of the tradition he had received. As heir to an authoritative corpus of halakhic and aggadic texts, R. Judah encountered an entire body of rabbinic literature with its own set of teachings on the matter of the dead and the afterlife. My question was whether he perpetuated these traditional teachings or whether he advocated a new stance, one more consonant with the regnant views of his host society. If, in fact, the latter was found to be true, then the further question arose as to how he dealt with those traditional Jewish teachings and texts that were in conflict with his innovative stance. After first comparing R. Judah's views with those of his halakhic predecessors, I proceeded to examine them alongside those of his contemporaries: the great masters of talmudic dialectics, the tosafists. As heirs to the same legal and narrative corpus, I wondered, did the tosafists interpret these texts in the same way as R. Judah did?

My findings revealed that there was a profound influence of Christian

36 There has been a growing body of research, by such scholars as Ivan Marcus, Jeremy Cohen, Elisheva Baumgarten, and Ephraim Shoham-Steiner, that underscores Jewish cultural embeddedness within Christian society in medieval Europe. Scholars have shown that, in ritual and praxis, during life-cycle events, and in everyday life, Ashkenazi Jews mimicked, even while reacting against, their host society's religious beliefs and practices. See Marcus, *Rituals of Childhood*; Cohen, *Sanctifying the Name of God*; Baumgarten, *Mothers and Children* and *Practicing Piety in Medieval Ashkenaz*; and Shoham-Steiner, *On the Margins of a Minority* (Heb.).

attitudes upon Pietist ideology in areas I had not imagined were susceptible in this way. While traditional texts may have been the source of R. Judah's views on matters pertaining to the dead and the hereafter, I argue that, though he may not have intended it, outside influence had infiltrated his thinking. This infiltration was so strong as to effect a radical departure in Pietist thinking from rabbinic thought, and to spur outright contradiction of talmudic principles. In the areas of sin and posthumous punishment in particular, the degree of penetration into the world-view of R. Judah was enormous, such that, in this realm, he had absorbed entire narratives from Christian teaching.

This unconscious absorption of fundamental Christian dogma came to isolate R. Judah from his contemporaries. His unique views on the ubiquitous nature of sin and on the harsh character and inescapability of posthumous punishment were totally at variance with those held in the tosafist academies,[37] and ran against the elevated Ashkenazi self-image and the notion of the *kehilah kedoshah* (holy community) portrayed by Haym Soloveitchik, and which also animated tosafist thought in the thirteenth century.[38] Additionally, R. Judah parted company on these matters with key members of his own movement. R. Eleazar of Worms disagreed with him in matters of sin and posthumous punishment, as did R. Eleazar's student, R. Abraham b. Azriel, author of a liturgical commentary that bears the influence of the mystical tradition of the Pietists.[39] This difference of approach between R. Judah and R. Eleazar, first noted by Haim Hillel Ben-Sasson in 1971 in matters of social reform,[40] and confirmed by Ivan Marcus ten years later in that arena as well as in the cardinal hasidic doctrine of penance,[41] I have now extended to the realm of the afterlife. R. Judah's radical, sectarian Pietism, with the sage-confessor at its helm, as formulated by Marcus, is consonant with R. Judah's extreme stance on matters of Divine judgement as portrayed in this book. Similarly, R. Eleazar's more moderate and mainstream views on posthumous judgement, which are reflective of medieval Ashkenaz as a whole, also match Marcus's characterization of his

[37] This holds true of both the academy of R. Isaac of Dampierre (Ri) and that of Evreux. On the various tosafist academies, see Urbach, *The Tosafists* (Heb.). On the difference of the Evreux academy from that of Ri, see Kanarfogel, *Jewish Education and Society*, 75–6, 78–9.

[38] See Soloveitchik, 'Religious Law and Change', *AJS Review*, 12 (1987), 205–23 (repr. in a newly edited form in id., *Collected Essays*, i (Oxford, 2013), 239–57); id., *Pawnbroking* (Heb.), 111–12, 118–19. It also forms a leitmotif of his *Wine in Ashkenaz* (Heb.).

[39] See Soloveitchik, 'Piety, Pietism and German Pietism', 469.

[40] See Ben-Sasson, 'The German Pietists' (Heb.).

[41] See Marcus, *Piety and Society*, 55–106.

position regarding social melioration and private penitence—both areas where R. Eleazar expressed a more conventional type of Pietism.[42] This alignment in the patterning of the views of each of the two rabbis on social reform, penance, and aspects of the afterlife strengthens the argument for seeing a unified approach, expressive of a single voice, that of R. Judah the Pious, in *Sefer ḥasidim*.

I find the Christian origins of R. Judah's thinking in doctrinal matters to be both shocking and ironic, considering the great antipathy and palpable revulsion he expressed towards that religion, its symbols, its institutions, and its proponents.[43] What could have compelled him, even if unconsciously, to adopt such foreign elements? In the process of seeking answers to this question, I uncovered an ideology that stretched far beyond matters of the dead and their world to include several other key aspects of Pietist thought. This ideological tendency was, in fact, so fundamental to Pietism as possibly to have spurred its very creation, while, at the same time, serving as a catalyst for the movement's early demise.

Although this book is primarily a study of the culture of a medieval Jewish enclave, it seeks to demonstrate how the seminal beliefs of medieval Christendom could penetrate beyond their place of origin and take root in a society of competing religious values—even in the realm of doctrinal belief. It opens a window on a parallel universe, or, more accurately, it shows how shared Germano-Christian conceptions of ghosts and the afterlife played themselves out in parallel universes. By bringing these concepts into sharp focus and examining them in the context of the beliefs of the surrounding Christian society, I hope to shed light on the importance of the dead and their world within the society of the living in the Middle Ages.

*

The book is divided into two parts. The first, entitled 'The Dead of *Sefer Ḥasidim*', comprises Chapters 1 to 4. It identifies who the 'characters' of the dead are in *Sefer ḥasidim*: the dangerous dead (Chapter 1), the sinful dead (Chapter 2), the holy dead (Chapter 3), and the neutral and Pietist dead (Chapter 4). The focus of this section is to highlight the disparity between the nature and role of these characters as they appear in rabbinic sources and as we encounter them in *Sefer ḥasidim*. Ideas that surround the dead

42 Moshe Idel has suggested that R. Eleazar did not fully share R. Judah's radical anti-anthropomorphism, thus isolating R. Judah even more. See Idel, 'Regarding the Identity of the Authors of Two Ashkenazi Commentaries' (Heb.), 156 n. 352.

43 Jacob Katz noted this phenomenon as early as 1961 in his book *Exclusiveness and Tolerance*.

in that work are examined in the context of notions that were current in Germany at the time. Such a correlation reveals that notions of the nature of the dead, as well as of the type of interaction that took place between the dead and the living, drew upon ancient Germanic ideas, which were first Christianized and then Judaized as they made their way onto the pages of *Sefer ḥasidim*.

Chapter 1 analyses the fear of the dead in Ashkenazi society as depicted in *Sefer ḥasidim* and other, non-Pietist, sources. Chapter 2 focuses on the way the sinful dead are punished in Pietist sources as opposed to talmudic ones. Chapter 3 identifies the heightened value assigned to martyrdom in the medieval period as an example of appropriation of Christian concepts involving the holy dead. Chapter 4 examines the role of the neutral dead in *Sefer ḥasidim* and shows how the concern for clothing the dead, in its various stages of existence, assumed specifically medieval forms. It concludes with an examination of the Pietist practice of burial in a *talit* with *tsitsit*, which highlights the singularity of the Pietists' unusually strong attachment to burial in such a garment and reveals an affinity with an ancient Germanic belief and custom regarding the afterlife.

Part II, entitled 'The Afterlife in *Sefer Ḥasidim*', comprises Chapters 5 to 8. It deals with matters pertaining to the world of the dead, both in Paradise and in Gehenna, as well as with the relationship between the worlds of the dead and the living. It speaks of the way the afterlife is envisioned and presented in medieval sources—both Jewish and non-Jewish—in contrast to rabbinic ones, and highlights the uniqueness of R. Judah's position in relation to his peers—both Jewish and non-Jewish—and his predecessors. Finally, it seeks to locate the origin of the unique doctrines and practices documented in *Sefer ḥasidim* within the environment of medieval Germany, in which the work was produced.

Chapter 5, entitled 'Status in the Hereafter', analyses R. Judah's selection of ghost tales that pertain to the individual's status in the afterlife. I contrast elements of his tales with rabbinic notions of the afterlife and compare them with those found in tales that circulated in the Germano-Christian environment. In Chapter 6, 'On Sin, Penance, and Purgation', I examine R. Judah's position on posthumous punishment as compared with rabbinic tradition and tosafist commentary. I assess his views on the matter in light of the changes that occurred within the Christian doctrine of penance and the rise of Purgatory in the high medieval period. Chapters 7 and 8, 'Bonds Between the Living and the Dead', look at two aspects of a single subject and discuss the different ways in which the dead and the living aided each other in rabbinic times in contrast to medieval times. These chapters focus on R. Judah's position regarding prayer and alms for the dead and evaluate it against the geonic stance he inherited, contemporary Jewish sentiment and practice, and various streams of Christian positions. The chapters conclude with a study of R. Judah's theories of sin and accountability in Divine judgement relative to contemporary Jewish views, and with an exploration of his conception of God as depicted in *Sefer ḥasidim*.

Chapter 9 concludes this 'double' book: I summarize my findings and main points while attempting to deepen and sharpen them, and draw a sketch of the Pietist aspirations that emerge when one ties together the various strands of Pietist teaching on many of the subjects touched upon in earlier chapters. These aspirations lay at the very heart of the Pietist movement.

*

In this introduction, I have spoken about my study of the dead and their world. I will now allow the dead of *Sefer ḥasidim* to speak for themselves.

PART I

THE DEAD OF *SEFER ḤASIDIM*

CHAPTER ONE

THE DANGEROUS DEAD

ON THE SECOND FOLIO of tractate *Berakhot*, the rabbis relate the following encounter between the dead prophet Elijah[1] and the tannaitic sage R. Yosi:

It has been taught: R. Yosi said, 'I was once travelling on the road, and I entered into one of the ruins of Jerusalem in order to pray. Elijah, of blessed memory, appeared and waited for me at the door till I finished my prayer. After I finished my prayer, he said to me, "Peace be with you, my master!" And I replied, "Peace be with you, my master and teacher!" And he said to me, "My son, why did you go into this ruin?" I replied, "To pray." He said to me, "You ought to have prayed on the road." I replied, "I feared lest passers-by might interrupt me." He said to me, "You ought to have said an abbreviated prayer." Thus I then learned from him three things: One must not go into a ruin; one may say the prayer on the road; and if one does say one's prayer on the road, one recites an abbreviated prayer.'[2]

The following passage in *Sefer ḥasidim* details what one ought to do when one encounters the dead:

And some say, when he sees the dead [person], he should bind him by oath in the name of God, in the same language that the dead [person] speaks [spoke] when he was alive,[3] and he should say, 'I am binding you, harmful one [*mazik*], by oath, that you will not harm me nor harm any of my loved ones.' And if he binds him by oath [so] that he cannot leave from there, [then] he [the deceased] will not be permitted to leave, so long as he has not changed [his form], [since it is possible] that he [can] make himself appear like a wild beast or like a man or like a cat that

[1] Although the Talmud (BT *MK* 26*a*) records the opinion of Reish Lakish that Elijah never died (according to the account in 2 Kgs 2, his body ascended heavenward in a chariot of fire), the conclusion of the passage is that Elijah is considered as if he is dead by his student Elisha, who has witnessed the event. Irrespective of his actual status, however, we can assume that Elijah's appearance to a living person during the rabbinic period would have elicited the same reaction as that of a dead person.

[2] BT *Ber.* 3*a*.

[3] Although the printed edition contains the present tense, *keshehu baḥayim*, the manuscript on which Wistinetzky's edition is based, MS Parma H 3280, records the past-tense form of the verb, *keshehayah baḥayim*.

comes to bite or harm . . . And if the man does not have the courage to bind him by oath, he should ask him, for the sake of the Holy One, blessed be He, not to harm him. And some say, he should fall before him to the ground, [with the logic that] since he has shown submission, he will not harm him. And he should not flee, rather he should ask him, in the name of God, and for the sake of God, not to harm him . . . And when he falls before him, he should ask of the Holy One, blessed be He, that he should not harm him.[4]

The cordial encounter between R. Yosi and Elijah bespeaks a bond of affection between the two men, despite the centuries that separate them and the boundary of death that divides them. Elijah's status in the Bible as a miracle-working prophet, true defender of the faith, and harbinger of the messiah undoubtedly contributes to his favourable reception.[5] However, his stormy personality and his spirited accusations against the idol-worshipping Israelites of his day could surely have garnered for him a more punitive posthumous role.[6] The Talmud, in one place, reflects on Elijah's 'hot-tempered' nature,[7] yet it overwhelmingly casts his posthumous appearances in a positive light.[8] It is as an authority on halakhah that the dead Elijah appears on the scene here.[9] Despite the reverence he accords R. Yosi (by patiently waiting at the door until he has finished his prayer), he proves to be the latter's superior by instructing him in matters of Jewish law previously unknown to him. R. Yosi is grateful for the gentle rebuke; the teachings of the dead prophet have enlightened the living sage.

Far from being friendly, however, any anticipated meeting with the dead that *Sefer ḥasidim* recounts is pervaded by a sense of fear. The dead man is identified as a *mazik*, who clearly has the capacity (and the will) to inflict bodily harm upon the person to whom he appears, as well as upon his loved ones. The intensity of the fear is apparent in the fact that R. Judah the Pious advocates swearing in the name of God as the prime means of protection from the dead. Given the immense power ascribed to oaths in medieval society and the fact that swearing in God's name is a major sin in the Pietist canon,[10] the use of the Divine name here is not to be taken lightly. It is no wonder that R. Judah offers an alternative method: if one is afraid to invoke God's name then he recommends the less preferred avenues of supplication before the ghost and prayer to God.

4 *SḤ* 327.

5 See 1 Kgs 17–18; Mal. 3: 23.

6 See 1 Kgs 18–19, esp. 19: 10 and 19: 14.

7 *Eliyahu kapdan hu*; see BT *San.* 113*a–b*.

8 Talmudic examples of encounters with Elijah are recorded below.

9 On Elijah's role as an authority on halakhah, see e.g. BT *Men.* 45*a*.

10 See *SḤ* 1386, 1393, 1394. See also Shoham-Steiner, 'From Speyer to Regensburg' (Heb.), 172–3.

Not only has the tone of the encounter changed, but so have the characters and their respective roles. Instead of the dead prophet of the talmudic story, an anonymous dead person (who can change from human to animal form at will[11]) is expected, and an ordinary medieval Jew replaces the rabbinic sage. In the medieval version, then, average people are substituted for men of importance. Furthermore, whereas Elijah's interaction with R. Yosi has a didactic function, the aim of the encounter in the Pietist passage is to neutralize the malevolence of the dead. An ordinary dead man, armed with supernatural ability and the intent to harm the living? We have traversed a great distance from the wise prophet of the talmudic account. We have come face to face with a medieval ghost.

Encounters with the Dead in Rabbinic Sources

Elijah's visit to R. Yosi is not an exceptional occurrence; the Talmud records numerous other posthumous appearances of the prophet.[12] He answers a query from Rabah son of Avuha in Jewish law,[13] and solves rabbinic disputes in matters of aggadah.[14] Descending from the heavenly sphere, Elijah reveals to the living what God is concerned with at any specific moment,[15] and identifies who among them is destined to inherit a portion in the World to Come.[16] While he does offer rebuke at times,[17] he overwhelmingly appears for a benign purpose. On no fewer than ten separate occasions, the Talmud mentions him as engaging in friendly conversation with the rabbis[18] and with the pious.[19] For some, he is even a frequent visitor.[20] For others, he acts as guardian: several times, Elijah intervenes to save the living from harm.[21]

[11] See n. 29 below.

[12] For a thorough list of the sources mentioning Elijah in rabbinic literature and beyond, see Visfish, *Book of Ramot Gilad* (Heb.), vol. i, and Klapholz, *Stories of Elijah the Prophet*.

[13] BT *BM* 114*a*; see also *Ber.* 29*b*.

[14] BT *Meg.* 15*b*.

[15] BT *Ḥag.* 15*b*, *Git.* 6*b*, *Ta'an.* 24*b*, *BM* 59*b*.

[16] BT *Ta'an.* 22*a* and *San.* 98*a*.

[17] See BT *BM* 84*a*.

[18] According to BT *Ta'an.* 22*a*, Elijah 'frequently appeared' to R. Beroka in the marketplace at Bei Lapat, and according to BT *Ket.* 106*a*, he 'was a frequent visitor' of R. Anan. See also JT *Ber.* 9: 2, 64*a*, where Elijah asks a question of R. Nehorai; BT *Yoma* 19*b*, where he asks one of R. Judah; BT *Ḥag.* 9*b*, where he converses with Bar Hei Hei; BT *BM* 85*b*, in which he frequents R. Judah Hanasi's academy; BT *San.* 113*a–b*, where he is wont to visit R. Yosi; and BT *Mak.* 11*a*, where he decides not to appear to R. Joshua b. Levi on account of his inappropriate action.

[19] See BT *BB* 7*b*. BT *Tem.* 16*b* identifies the pious man as either R. Judah b. Bava or R. Judah b. Ilai, both *tana'im*. See also BT *Ket.* 61*a*.

[20] See n. 18 above.

[21] He serves as a witness to save R. Sheila (BT *Ber.* 58*a*); he saves a man who swallows a snake (BT *Shab.* 109*b*); he saves R. Huna from throwing himself off a roof (BT *Kid.* 40*a*); he saves

In one isolated passage, the Talmud recounts a situation in which Elijah's appearance causes harm to the living. According to *Berakhot 6b*, disguised as an Arab merchant, he stabs a Jew to death for committing a crime that the rabbis label as evil. However, some manuscript editions record that an Arab passer-by, not Elijah, kills the Jew.[22] There is also a lone talmudic account (*Ket.* 106*a*) in which Elijah, who has been a frequent visitor to and teacher of R. Anan,[23] ceases to visit the rabbi on account of the latter's connection with an impropriety relating to legal judgement. After much fasting and prayer on R. Anan's part, Elijah reappears to him. This time, however, R. Anan greatly fears the dead prophet's presence and listens to him while hiding in a box. Has the prophet's anger changed his visage or has R. Anan's misconduct placed him on a lower spiritual level? In either case, it is not Elijah's appearance as a dead person that frightens the rabbi; rather, it is the changed circumstance of their encounter.

Elijah is not the only deceased holy personage in rabbinic literature to appear bodily to the living. The Talmud reports that R. Judah the Prince, redactor of the Mishnah, would return posthumously to his house every Friday night, study at his place at the table, and sleep in his own bed. This practice continued until his maid, who was not startled at all by his presence, let the secret out. The Talmud explains why R. Judah's visitations ceased: once his posthumous appearances were known beyond his own household, they would cause dishonour to other righteous dead before him who were unable to return.[24]

Apart from these cases of the special dead, encounters with the ordinary dead also find a place in the Talmud. Here, too, the element of fear is absent. *Berakhot* recounts a string of episodes in which rabbis go to the 'courtyard of death' (*ḥatser hamavet*) in order to extract information from the deceased: Ze'iri seeks the whereabouts of money he had deposited with his landlady, who then died, and Samuel wishes to know the location of some money that his father had set aside for charity before he passed away.[25] Although the Talmud fails to explain how these encounters take

R. Eleazar b. Perata from punishment by the Roman authorities (BT *AZ* 17*b*); he saves R. Meir from being captured by the Romans (BT *AZ* 18*b*); and he announces to R. Shimon b. Yohai and his son that it is safe for them to emerge from hiding (BT *Shab.* 33*b*).

22 *Sefer dikdukei soferim*, i: *Berakhot*, ed. Rabinowitz, 20.

23 See also JT *Ter.* 8: 12.

24 BT *Ket.* 103*a*.

25 BT *Ber.* 18*b*. This narrative in its entirety has been studied by Aryeh Cohen in '"Do the Dead Know?"', where he argues that the *ḥatser hamavet* referred to in the passage above describes a 'space of death'. He defines this as a 'somewhat fluid space in which the dead and living can interact and affect one another'. The 'space of death' is modelled after the geograph-

place, in each case the living person is able to communicate with the deceased and, in two of the three cases, actually see him; Samuel sees his father 'weeping and laughing', and he observes Levi sitting outside the Academy of Heaven. Although he is puzzled by what he sees, at no time is he discomfited by it. The episodes conclude with the dead revealing to the living the location of the sums in question. Characteristic of all these talmudic encounters is that the living seek out the physical presence of the dead, and the dead dutifully respond to their queries.

In only one case in the Babylonian Talmud does the bodily appearance of the ordinary dead elicit fear. In *Mo'ed katan*, the sage R. Huna is about to be buried in the family cave of R. Hiya. As R. Haga enters the cave with R. Huna's body, one of R. Hiya's dead sons urges his twin brother to arise from his grave in honour of R. Huna. As the twin does so, a column of fire rises up with him, and R. Haga is 'overcome with fear'. He quickly sets down the coffin and leaves.[26] Interestingly, even where the Talmud does record fear in association with the physical presence of the ordinary dead, it is the fire that accompanies the dead body and not the body itself that provokes the fear.

In *Sefer ḥasidim*, however, the physical appearance of the ordinary dead is precisely the phenomenon that instils fear. Contrary to talmudic precedent, the dead who appear bodily in *Sefer ḥasidim* do not rescue or heal; they return to inflict harm and endanger life. The comforting presence of holy dead personages such as Elijah the prophet and R. Judah the Prince is gone; anonymous ghosts who are easily mistaken for demons take their place.[27] Although ghost and demon are classified by *Sefer ḥasidim* as two separate entities, they share common characteristics.[28] Both are dangerous

ical 'space of the dead' in which burial took place at that time—i.e. an ossuary with a courtyard in front of it. See Cohen, 45, 67.

26 BT *MK* 25*a*.

27 *SḤ* 326. According to no. 324, in order to determine if the dead person who appears before one is a demon (*shed*), and whether he comes with harmful intent (*mazik*) or is benevolent, one should demand that he utter an oath. The benevolent ghost will refrain from doing so as he will be careful not to utter God's name in vain.

28 *SḤ* 326 distinguishes between a true ghost (*met*) and a demon—'who appears to him like a dead person but he is a *shed*'. Christian literary sources also record an initial confusion between ghost and demon. A fifteenth-century manuscript of sermons, for example, tells how the inhabitants of a certain town in Brittany, when confronted by a ghost, ask if he is 'a dead man or an evil spirit'. See Schmitt, *Ghosts in the Middle Ages*, 147. While many ecclesiastical writers make the same distinction as *Sefer ḥasidim* between ghosts and demons, some do not. Thomas of Cantimpré, for example, in an attempt to deny the body any 'life' of its own, explains the phenomenon of ghosts as a product of demonic possession of the corpse. He thus merges the two

beings who can assume varying forms at will, and one must follow a specific procedure in order to protect oneself from them.[29] Who are the ghosts of *Sefer ḥasidim* and why do they come with evil intent?

Belief in the Dangerous Dead

Fear is the most ancient, most widespread reaction to an encounter with the returning dead. As far back as Roman times, the dead were viewed as impure and dangerous; special conciliatory rites were performed to pacify them.[30] It is a belief common to all Indo-European peoples that those who have suffered an abnormal death, having met a violent end, died prematurely, or been denied proper burial, are unable to rest in peace; they will wander and reappear among the living.[31] Some, especially the 'bad dead', such as criminals, suicides, and enemies, will become violent and vengeful as well.[32]

Although a belief in the return of the violent dead existed in our period in northern France, Germany, and England, it was in Iceland that it was most clearly articulated and most elaborately discussed. The Icelandic sagas are a rich and invaluable resource for the study of popular beliefs about ghosts since they record centuries-old customs and practices of people who lived in relative isolation from the rest of Europe and its ongoing Christianization.[33] These sagas tell story after story of *draugar* (sing. *draugr*; the Old

entities into one. See Caciola, 'Wraiths, Revenants and Ritual', 14–15. Early medieval exorcism rites (the sprinkling of holy water and salt while reciting a formula of conjuration) are identical for both demons and ghosts. See Schmitt, *Ghosts in the Middle Ages*, 29. For a fuller discussion of the role of demons in *Sefer ḥasidim*, see Dan, 'Demonological Stories from the Writings of R. Judah' (Heb.).

[29] According to *SḤ* 326 and 327, one should spit at the demon repeatedly and shout at him, 'Leave, impure one; impure one, flee!' The notion that the ghost can change from human into animal form is not unknown in medieval exempla. Several tales from the Yorkshire collection of around 1400 mention ghosts that assume the form of a horse, dog, or raven, for example. See James, 'Twelve Medieval Ghost Stories', 414, 415. According to Lecouteux, *Fantômes et revenants*, 111–14, these were originally pagan elements. The notion that demons can appear in various animal forms (donkeys, wolves, lions, tigers, etc.) exists in rabbinic literature, and Jewish artifacts from the late antique period contain such images. See Bohak, 'Conceptualizing Demons in Late Antique Judaism', 115–16, and id., 'Expelling Demons and Attracting Demons', 179. I wish to thank Professor Bohak for these references.

[30] Lecouteux, *Fantômes et revenants*, 20–1.

[31] Ibid. 22.

[32] Ibid. 20–1. Schmitt, *Ghosts in the Middle Ages*, 12.

[33] Lecouteux, *Fantômes et revenants*, 11–12. See also Caciola, 'Wraiths, Revenants and Ritual', 15. While the sagas most often reflect pagan beliefs and customs, they sometimes tell of practices that contain a mixture of pagan and Christian elements. Either the Christian elements coexist with the pagan ones or they replace certain pagan elements while still expressing

Icelandic term for the returning dead), who haunt, horrify, and wreak havoc upon the living. One saga tells of the *draugr* Glam, who, after having been violently murdered, proceeds to scare local townspeople, and even kills two of them. His marauding ceases only when he is beheaded and reburied.[34] Similarly in two other sagas, the *draugar* Thorolf and Hrapp, both very disagreeable men during their lifetimes, return and kill many people. Thorolf kills so many that the remaining villagers leave the area; Hrapp's murderous rage ends when his body is exhumed and reburied far away.[35] The *Eyrbyggja Saga* tells of a malevolent dead man, Þórólfr, a cheat and murderer during his lifetime, who returns to kill his former townspeople indiscriminately. Cremation of his corpse stops the carnage.[36]

Apart from literary sources, archaeological evidence gathered from excavations of ancient north German cemeteries attests to various apotropaic measures taken to prevent the return of the dead.[37] These include crushing the skull, folding up and tying the arms and legs across the chest, weighing down the cadaver with branches, logs, or stones,[38] and decapitation.[39] Burchard of Worms, in his *Decretum* written in the early eleventh century, speaks out against the 'devilish' practice of some women, who pierce the dead bodies of their unbaptized newborn babies before burial. He records that they feel compelled to do this; otherwise, their children will return to harm the living.[40] Archaeological excavations at Sutton Hoo in England uncovered what are believed to be the bodies of executed criminals of the eleventh century; these had been decapitated, crushed under boulders, bound, dismembered, and buried face down.[41] According to twelfth-century north European burial rites, the body was to be sewn into a shroud and then nailed into a coffin.[42] As late as the thirteenth century, Norman law retained the ancient custom of burying criminals in pits

an underlying pagan belief. See e.g. Lecouteux, *Fantômes et revenants*, 105–6. Martin, 'Law and the (Un)Dead', argues for a greater Christian influence in the sagas. Yet they reflect the particular high medieval Christian corporeal model of the undead rather than the 'official' Augustinian model of a demonic/angelic apparition.

34 *La Saga de Grettir*, chs. 32–5, quoted in Lecouteux, *Fantômes et revenants*, 102–6, and Caciola, 'Wraiths, Revenants and Ritual', 15.

35 *Eyrbyggja Saga*, chs. 33–4; *Laxdaela Saga*, ch. 17, quoted in Caciola, 'Wraiths, Revenants and Ritual', 16.

36 See Martin, 'Law and the (Un)Dead', 74.

37 Lecouteux, *Fantômes et revenants*, 29.

38 Tacitus, *Germania*, XII, mentions this as one of the customs of the Germans; cited in Lecouteux, *Fantômes et revenants*, 28.

39 Lecouteux, *Fantômes et revenants*, 25–9.

40 Burchard, *Decretum*, XIX, 5, 179 ff., quoted in Lecouteux, *Fantômes et revenants*, 43–4.

41 Simpson, 'Repentant Soul or Walking Corpse?', 390.

42 Caciola, 'Wraiths, Revenants and Ritual', 33.

filled with mud and weighted down by an 'obstacle' of wood or stone, labelling it *bèche* or *becca*.[43] The fifteenth-century communal laws of Riga regulated the fixation in the grave, by means of nails or stakes, of the bodies of suicides, while in some towns in northern Germany their cadavers were burned.[44] The custom in southern Germany was to set the corpse of a suicide adrift in a flowing body of water.[45] The Salian Franks decapitated the bodies of their enemies so that none could return to avenge their death.[46] One function of the late medieval custom of bell-ringing at the time of a funeral was apotropaic—to prevent the return of the dead.[47]

Other north European burial practices aimed to hasten the decomposition of the body in an attempt to forestall the bodily reappearance of the dead. Bodies were boiled and dismembered immediately before burial in order to remove the flesh from the bones; small amounts of 'flesh-eating soil' were deposited in the grave during burial.[48] One Icelandic saga describes the process of removal of the corpse from the house: the wall of the house was pierced, the cadaver removed, and the hole then blocked up so that the deceased could not return by the same way that he or she left the house.[49] After the body had been removed, the bed in which the deceased had slept or the straw upon which the body had lain was burned. This custom was intended to speed up the process of decay: just as the bed or straw was destroyed immediately, so the body of the deceased should decompose quickly.[50]

A common feature of the tales of the violent and vengeful dead found in the Icelandic sagas and north European literary sources is the corporeal nature of ghosts.[51] The sagas are filled with violent stories of certain 'bad dead' who appear bodily to harm the living. The dead Hrapp, for example, uses a metal sword he holds in his hand to fight with the living Olaf. Olaf

[43] Lecouteux, *Fantômes et revenants*, 28. [44] Ibid. [45] Ibid.

[46] Ibid. As recently as the First World War, English soldiers stated that they would bury dead German soldiers face down in order to prevent them from taking a post-mortem 'walk'. By burying them in this manner, they reasoned, if the body moved 'it [would] only dig [its] way deeper into the ground'. See Simpson, 'Repentant Soul or Walking Corpse?'

[47] See Davis, 'Ghosts, Kin, and Progeny', 93.

[48] See Caciola, 'Wraiths, Revenants and Ritual', 33–4.

[49] *La Saga de Snorri le Godi*, 112, quoted in Lecouteux, *Fantômes et revenants*, 38. This practice continued until as late as the thirteenth century. A Franciscan preacher, Berthold de Ratisbonne, prescribes this very method of removal for the body of one who dies in a state of mortal sin: see *Fantômes et revenants*, 44.

[50] Lecouteux, *Fantômes et revenants*, 42; Barbar, *Vampires, Burial, and Death*, 192.

[51] Davidson, 'The Restless Dead', 167. Lecouteux, *Fantômes et revenants*, 134, cites linguistic evidence which further attests to belief in the corporeal nature of ghosts. See also Chadwick, 'Norse Ghosts', 50.

defeats him, burns his corpse, and throws his ashes into the sea.[52] Thorolf l'Estropié, who has risen from his grave with a body as big as an ox, proceeds to kill man and beast until his corpse is burned and the ashes are dispersed in the wind.[53] The sagas recount that at the same time that these dead are harming the living, their cadavers are still found intact in their graves.[54] This 'double body' phenomenon is based on the concept of multiple souls, widespread among shamanistic peoples, and explains the corporeal nature of the Germanic ghost. One soul departs at the time of death, while another remains to reanimate the body. Only when the physical remains are annihilated can the living be assured that the animating soul is gone and the dead can no longer return and harm them.[55]

The corporeal Germanic ghost has no antecedent in early Christianity. The nascent Church, in the face of an existing pagan Roman cult of the dead, frowned on the belief in the returning dead. St Augustine, while acknowledging that the dead may appear to the living in a dream, stresses that they do so without any knowledge of it, in the same way that the living appear in the dreams of others without being aware of any such appearance.[56] Angels, both good and evil, control these apparitions, using them as vehicles to impart messages to the living.[57] The only waking visions of the returning dead that are possible, argues Augustine, are those of the special dead, that is, saints. Even then, only 'semblances of bodies' are visible within the 'spirit' of the viewer via the imaginative faculty.[58]

Gregory the Great, in the sixth century, used illustrative stories and exempla (moral tales meant to inspire imitation) in his *Dialogues* to recount details about the dead who are conscious of their return to the world of the living. While the wide popularity enjoyed by Gregory's work helped to disseminate the idea of the ghost tale throughout western Christendom, stories about the ordinary dead were rare in that period. The appearance of saints and demons predominated in the early medieval consciousness.[59]

52 *La Laxdoela Saga*, chs. 17 and 24, cited in Lecouteux, *Fantômes et revenants*, 95.

53 *La Saga de Snorri le Godi*, chs. 33–4 and 63, quoted in Lecouteux, *Fantômes et revenants*, 98–9.

54 See Lecouteux, *Fantômes et revenants*, p. iii; Barbar, *Vampires, Burial, and Death*, 190–1.

55 Barbar, *Vampires, Burial, and Death*, 191.

56 Schmitt, *Ghosts in the Middle Ages*, 21; Lecouteux, *Fantômes et revenants*, 54.

57 Schmitt, *Ghosts in the Middle Ages*, 21; Lecouteux, *Fantômes et revenants*, 55. The early Church was suspicious of dreams for this very reason. Dreams could either empower a commoner by imparting to him hidden truths from the other world without the scrutiny of the Church or could subject him to the dangerous machinations of the Devil. See Le Goff, 'Dreams in the Culture and Collective Psychology of the Medieval West'.

58 Schmitt, *Ghosts in the Middle Ages*, 22–4, and Baschet, *Corps et âmes*, 28.

59 Schmitt, *Ghosts in the Middle Ages*, 29–33.

Despite the theological difficulties that the corporeal return of the dead posed for Christianity,[60] elements of this corporeality were present in west European literature of the high medieval period. This retention of a theologically problematic belief is an example of what Nancy Caciola has termed a 'pagan survival': something that was 'consciously and actively chosen' by the members of medieval Christian society.[61] Similarly, Jérôme Baschet has noted that outside the 'scholarly discourse of the clerical elite', which consistently maintained a belief in the 'complete incorporeality of the soul' from the fourth to the thirteenth centuries, a 'corporeal dimension to the soul' persisted.[62] Evidence of encounters with the violent dead, similar to those found in the Icelandic sagas, exists in the writings of learned men of various north European countries.[63] In the thirteenth century William of Auvergne, bishop of Paris, despite his lack of any personal belief in the returning dead, admitted that he had heard many tales 'about certain dead men who kill other men from among the living'.[64] A thirteenth-century German chronicle, *Historiae memorabiles*, records a tale about a man named Henry, who is violently assaulted and nearly killed by three dead men on horseback near a riverbank.[65] It is significant that Henry recognizes one of the assailants as a recently deceased knight who has suffered a violent end himself.[66] Two other tales, from the *Dialogus miraculorum* of the Cistercian Caesarius of Heisterbach, speak of malevolent men—one an unscrupulous and promiscuous knight, the other a usurer[67]—who return

[60] According to Christian teaching (and in consonance with the position put forth by the thirteenth-century scholastic theologian St Thomas Aquinas), the immaterial, incorporeal soul, rather than the material body, is the vital force of life, and only the soul lives on after death, awaiting its reunification with the body at the time of the resurrection of the dead. See Livingstone (ed.), *Concise Oxford Dictionary of the Christian Church*, s.v. 'resurrection of the dead'; 'soul'. See also Schmitt, *Ghosts in the Middle Ages*, 196–7.

[61] Caciola, *Afterlives*, 15. Jean-Claude Schmitt argues that the corporeality of ghosts in the literature of this period was less a pagan inheritance and more a factor of the 'telling over' process. The dead, who were in essence imaginary, were actualized and made real, i.e. physical, when stories about them were communicated orally and then written down. See Schmitt, *Ghosts in the Middle Ages*, 8–9.

[62] Baschet, *Corps et âmes*, 26–8.

[63] See Swanson, 'Ghosts and Ghostbusters in the Middle Ages', 155–6.

[64] William of Auvergne, *De universo*, ii. 3. 24, quoted in Caciola, 'Wraiths, Revenants and Ritual', 17.

[65] Water was considered a divide between this world and the hereafter (Lecouteux, *Fantômes et revenants*, 33). In ancient journey literature, as well as in early medieval visionary literature, the soul that travels to the other world most often crosses a sea or river. See Patch, *The Other World*, 26, 29, 60–1, 62, 74, 79, 128.

[66] Rudolf von Schlettstadt, *Historiae memorabiles*, ch. 47, esp. pp. 110–11, quoted in Caciola, 'Wraiths, Revenants and Ritual', 17–18. See also Schmitt, *Ghosts in the Middle Ages*, 139.

[67] The usurer is commonly depicted in medieval exempla as an archetypal sinner whose true nature is revealed through posthumous punishment.

from the dead to haunt the homes of their surviving children. Although the ghosts do not commit any actual crimes, the children clearly fear their fathers' return and try to rid themselves of them.[68]

A tale that enjoyed wide diffusion in western Europe emanates from the *Sermones vulgares* of the French preacher and prelate Jacques de Vitry.[69] According to this tale, a usurer who had bribed certain monks to have him buried in the church rises from his grave and, with a candelabrum in his hand, attacks those very monks while they are at prayer. Having hoped for salvation, he seeks revenge on them for having been condemned to eternal damnation instead. According to a variant story found in another manuscript,[70] the usurer's ghost continues to haunt the neighbourhood, despite the removal and reburial of his corpse in unconsecrated ground. A thirteenth-century Scottish chronicle tells of a clergyman who dies excommunicate and reappears in the habit of a black monk. Described as a 'deadly thing' who 'savagely batter[s] those who attempt to fight him as nearly to shatter all their joints', the ghost attacks a certain family 'with missiles and blows' until it murders the family's heir.[71]

The English chroniclers Walter Map and William of Newburgh record several ghost tales that contain all the elements found in stories of the Icelandic *draugar*. The subjects are men who fall into the category of the 'bad dead' (they were either evil in life or died 'irreligiously'): they return to wander at night, attack the living, and strike fear into the hearts of their townspeople, and their acts of terror can only be stopped by the dismemberment or cremation of their corpse.[72] William of Newburgh remarks that 'such things often happened in England . . . cadavers of the dead [get] out of their graves . . . to terrorize or injure the living . . . [and it] would not easily be accepted as true if there were not so many examples at hand from our own time, and if testimony were not so abundant'.[73]

68 *Dialogus miraculorum*, 327 no. 15; 328 no. 18, quoted in Caciola, 'Wraiths, Revenants and Ritual', 18–19.

69 Jacques de Vitry, *Exempla*, no. 176. The tale appears (sometimes with slight variations) ten times in five different manuscripts of the *Catalogue of Romances*, vol. iii, ed. Herbert, as well as in several other exempla collections.

70 MS BL Arundel 506 fo. 27, col. 2 (*Catalogue of Romances*, iii. 551 no. 143). The manuscript dates from the first half of the fourteenth century.

71 *Chronicon de Lanercost*, 163–4, quoted in Caciola, 'Wraiths, Revenants and Ritual', 23–4.

72 Map, *De nugis curialium*, 202–4, and William of Newburgh, *Historia rerum Anglicarum*, ii. 476–82, quoted in Caciola, 'Wraiths, Revenants and Ritual', 19–21.

73 William of Newburgh, *Historia rerum Anglicarum*, ii. 475, 477, quoted in Caciola, 'Wraiths, Revenants and Ritual', 19–21. See also Schmitt, *Ghosts in the Middle Ages*, 61–2.

The Dangerous Dead in *Sefer Ḥasidim*

It is this fear of the dangerous dead—a remnant of the pre-Christian *draugr* transformed into a medieval ghost—that found its way into *Sefer ḥasidim*. Having absorbed the notion from its Germano-Christian environment, the book presents an encounter with the dead as a terrifying event. Believed to be violent and harmful, these dead must be warded off by prescribed measures and procedures, particularly invocation of the Divine name. This remedy again reflects ideas found in the surrounding culture.

Documented in the exempla literature of western Europe, invocation of the Divine name in order to protect oneself from the dead is mentioned in two tales from a small Yorkshire collection of ghost stories, dating from around the year 1400.[74] In one tale, a dead man, Robert, who terrorizes the local townspeople nightly, is stopped only when the parish priest, after having been seized by two living men, 'came quickly and conjured him in the name of the Holy Trinity'.[75] Likewise, in the other story, a certain tailor, confronting a ghost who appears to him in the form of a dog, proclaims the following: 'I will conjure him in the name of the Holy Trinity and by virtue of the blood of the five wounds of Christ that he speak to me and do me no harm.'[76]

In a similar spirit, the compilation of legal rulings and customs of the fourteenth-century Rabbi Shalom of Neustadt in Austria contains the text of a conjuration that was administered in the presence of a quorum of males as part of an actual funeral ceremony. In it, the deceased was adjured to 'cause them [the living] no harm either with your body or your spirit or your soul'. Reflecting awareness and fear of the possibility of the physical return of the dangerous dead, the oath, which included 'sanctions from now until the end of days', proceeded to bind the dead to 'remain in the grave until the resurrection of the dead'.[77] In another example, about a century and a half after the redaction of *Sefer ḥasidim* in Germany, R. Jacob b. Moses Moelin (Maharil) is recorded as having pronounced a similar oath over a grave to prevent the dead person from returning to endanger the living. The oath, which adjures the deceased 'not to wander in this world . . .

[74] James, 'Twelve Medieval Ghost Stories', 418.

[75] The translation is by Caciola, 'Wraiths, Revenants and Ritual', 23.

[76] James, 'Twelve Medieval Ghost Stories', 415. The translation follows that in Lecouteux, *Fantômes et revenants*, 113.

[77] *Hilkhot uminhagei rabenu shalom minoyshtat*, 159–60 no. 544, quoted in Schur, 'When the Grave Was Searched', 183.

to harm or to see any Jew or Jewess', is to be taken early in the morning and in the presence of a quorum of males. To ensure that the deceased understands, the oath is to be recited both in Hebrew and 'in the language that the deceased was familiar with when he was alive'.[78]

In light of this, the Pietist ghost tale cited at the beginning of this chapter becomes understandable. Medieval ghosts, unlike those of the rabbinic period, needed to be warded off by means of the Divine name, which neutralized their malevolence. Moreover, a belief similar to the idea of the 'double body' characteristic of the corporeal Germanic ghost is attributed to R. Judah the Pious in a fourteenth-century Ashkenazi source. R. Menahem ben Meir Tsiyon, in his *Sefer tsiyuni*, relates in the name of Judah ben Samuel of Regensburg that the dead possess two souls—an 'animal spirit' (*nefesh behemit*), which lingers in the grave, and a 'soul' (*neshamah*), which ascends to Heaven and remains there. It is the 'animal spirit' which makes bodily reanimation after death possible, such that 'if one were to search inside the grave, no corporeal remains would be found'.[79]

An anonymous text issuing from the circle of Hasidei Ashkenaz (German Pietists) illustrates the type of harm that a returning ghost can inflict. Entitled 'The Testament of R. Judah the Pious', the text suggests: 'When burying a woman who was wont to devour children during her lifetime, if you see that her mouth is open, it is certain [*beyadua*] that she will do so after her death for one year, and [so] one should fill her mouth with dirt so that she can no longer cause harm.'[80] Apart from her gender, this woman fits the basic description of the Icelandic *draugr*. Malevolent and dangerous while alive, she is certain to continue her destructive behaviour after death. While Jewish law forbids any form of mutilation of a dead body,[81] a non-violent form of preventing the return of the 'bad dead' replaces mutilation: by neutralizing the dangerous body part (her mouth), this woman's posthumous attacks can be prevented.

A later illustration of a Jewish burial custom that may have apotropaic intent is cited in *Sefer leket yosher*. The author of the work, Joseph ben Moses (late fourteenth to early fifteenth centuries) records the custom in Wiener Neustadt of constructing whole coffins for *kohanim* and for women who died in childbirth, whereas all the other dead of the community were

78 See Yuval, *Sages in Their Time* (Heb.), 89.

79 Menahem Tsiyon, *Sefer tsiyuni*, 10c, quoted in Schur, 'When the Grave Was Searched', 178.

80 'The Testament of R. Judah the Pious' (Heb.), no. 5, p. 12. On the later diffusion of this text, see Kahana, 'Sources of Knowledge and the Vicissitudes of Time' (Heb.).

81 This prohibition is based on Deut. 21: 23.

buried in coffins with one bottom plank missing.[82] While the reason for the deviation from this custom for *kohanim* may have had to do with containment of the ritual impurity of the deceased,[83] Yechiel Schur attributes the deviation with regard to women who died in childbirth to a fear of the dangerous dead. Having died prematurely, these women qualify as having experienced a 'bad death'; burying them in whole coffins served to seal their bodies inside so that they could not return to cause harm.[84]

Sefer ḥasidim records another funerary practice which is related to belief in the violent dead. R. Judah writes: 'And why does it say, "God is good to all" [Ps. 145: 9]? Rather, "good to all" [includes] even the dead, that they putrefy. For this reason, they are quick to bury them. And also, that they are fearful of the dead [*mitpaḥadim min hametim*]. . . . all this [occurs] so that they will hasten to bury them.'[85] According to this interpretation of the biblical verse, the putrefaction of the corpse reflects God's goodness, as it prompts a quick burial. This has two benefits. The first accrues to the dead and is well documented in Jewish legal sources: the Torah states that it is forbidden to leave the dead unburied overnight, as it will disgrace and dishonour them.[86] The second benefit accrues to the living: an unburied body is open to reanimation and can potentially harm the living.[87] Being in the presence of the dead was thought to hasten one's own death. Quick burial and subsequent putrefaction are thus a blessing as they serve to protect the living and put fear to rest.

Despite the prohibition on leaving a corpse unburied overnight, the Mishnah attests to a practice, current in rabbinic times, of carrying the body through the community in order to publicize the death and in so doing

[82] Schur, 'The Care for the Dead in Medieval Ashkenaz', 102. On the basis of Gen. 3: 19, 'Dust you are and to dust shall you return', Jewish law dictates that the body of the deceased must come into contact with the earth in which it is buried. Removal of a bottom plank of the coffin made this contact possible.

[83] While Schur is uncertain of the reason for this practice with regard to *kohanim* (see n. 61 ibid.), I would suggest that it may serve to insulate the ritual impurity associated with the dead body, so that the relatives of the deceased who are also *kohanim* would be allowed to visit the grave. (Jewish law generally prohibits *kohanim* from exposing themselves to dead bodies and becoming ritually impure.)

[84] Ibid.

[85] *SḤ* 305, p. 96. *SḤ* 336 also stresses the importance of a quick burial. Just as the patriarch Abraham immediately consented to the exorbitant price demanded for the site where he wished to bury his wife, so too, 'when the dead lie before us, we do not delay'.

[86] Deut. 21: 23.

[87] Nancy Caciola has argued that the possibility of a dead person returning as a ghost is directly tied to the amount of flesh that remains on the corpse: 'the fresher the cadaver, the more dangerous it is'. Total decay of the body eliminates the possibility of the reanimation of the corpse; an unburied body, denied access to 'flesh-eating soil', decays more slowly. See 'Wraiths, Revenants and Ritual', 31, 33.

honour the deceased.[88] In this period, exposure of the dead to the community of the living was considered an act that comforted the living rather than terrorize them. *Sefer ḥasidim*, however, documents hasty burial and a fearful assembly of the living as customary in its day.

Specific mention of the 'bad dead' who return to harm the living can be found in a work written by another Pietist, a student of R. Judah. R. Eleazar of Worms, in his *Sefer ḥokhmat hanefesh*, offers the following explanation for the unusual frequency of illness on the sabbath:

> And why do the spirits [do] harm on the sabbath eve? Because the spirits are not in Gehenna [then], for the spirits of the wicked cause harm [*mazikin*] even in their death like the descendants of Cain, on whose influence their souls became harmful and permission was given them to harm those who desecrate the sabbath, if they are sad [on the sabbath] or do not delight in it. For this reason, most illnesses caused by spirits [occur] on the sabbath.[89]

Sickness on the sabbath is common because it is the only day of the week on which the wicked dead are released from Gehenna.[90] Freed from their abode in the afterlife, they are permitted to return to the world of the living. Still malevolent in their nature, however, they wish to harm the living. R. Eleazar makes it explicit that the harmful dead were evil when they lived. His use of the descendants of Cain—the first murderer and who was murdered in turn[91]—as examples of this phenomenon strengthens their association with the *draugar* of the Icelandic sagas, themselves evil men who have suffered unnatural deaths. In contrast to the sagas and exempla literature, however, where the dangerous dead strike their former townspeople indiscriminately, according to R. Eleazar the harmful souls released from Gehenna on the sabbath are restricted in their malevolence: they only attack those who violate the sabbath. Further, this means violation by Pietistic standards. The guilty have not transgressed the normative rules of sabbath observance; their sole crime is being sad on, or failing to delight in the holiness of, the day—a supra-legal matter punishable only in a system

88 Mishnah *Kel.* 1: 7. N. Rubin, *The End of Life* (Heb.), 132.

89 Eleazar of Worms, *Sefer ḥokhmat hanefesh*, 24*b*. The Lemberg edition of the work, although identical, has some different pagination; unless otherwise noted, the edition cited is Safed, 1913.

90 The sabbath repose of souls in Gehenna is a belief which medieval Jews and Christians shared. See Lévi, 'Le Repos sabbatique des âmes damnées', and see my discussion in Ch. 6 below.

91 According to a midrashic tradition that was widely known in medieval Ashkenaz, Cain was killed accidentally by his descendant Lemekh. See Rashi's commentary on Gen. 4: 23, s.v. *shema'an koli*.

which holds the individual accountable for more than what is prescribed by normative law.[92]

As well as causing illness on the sabbath, the dead are considered responsible for bringing plague. One passage in *Sefer ḥasidim* authorizes the exhumation of the dead, despite the prohibition of doing so in other cases,[93] in order to determine 'who was responsible for the catastrophe [*ra'ah*]—this dead [person] or [others'] graves'.[94] Another passage in *Sefer ḥasidim* expresses a similar attitude: a grave may be opened and the corpse manipulated, for example by straightening the limbs or replacing a worn-out shroud, in order to rectify any possible improprieties of burial, which are seen as the cause of the plague.[95] The language ('when there is a plague in the city and they search the dead') seems to suggest that this practice was current at the time, or at least was known to be the proper procedure in such a situation. Fixing these improprieties would serve to stop the spread of the disease by preventing the return of the dead, in much the same way that the burning of corpses does in the sagas. Belief that the returning dead spread disease was widespread in early medieval culture,[96] and found its way into high medieval literature: William of Newburgh, in his *Historia rerum Anglicarum*, tells of ghosts who cause epidemics, among other evils.[97]

The Vengeful Dead in *Sefer Ḥasidim*

Fear of the violent dead in the specific form of the vengeful dead is also present in *Sefer ḥasidim*, though these vengeful figures appear in a more muted form here than they do in the passage cited above from *Sefer ḥokhmat hanefesh*. One passage relates how a certain dying rabbi suspects his student of making plans to marry his wife in anticipation of his im-

[92] The notion of a larger will of God, which includes an additional, unwritten Pietist law and is termed by the Pietists *retson haboré*, forms a cornerstone of Pietist theology. See Soloveitchik, 'Three Themes in *Sefer Ḥasidim*', 311–17.

[93] *Sefer ḥasidim* refers to one such case where one wishes to check if a person was a minor at the time of his death in order to invalidate an inheritance that person distributed prior to his death; exhumation is not permitted. See BT *BB* 154*a*.

[94] *SḤ* 330. The original source has 'his graves' in the plural. I have corrected it to refer to others' graves. Another possibility is that 'his grave' is meant in the singular and it was a copyist's error. While it could be possible that an improperly kept grave was the cause of a plague, it seems more plausible that people were searching different graves to find out which dead person was responsible, especially in light of the evidence below from *Sefer ḥasidim* and of known practice during times of plague. A variant reading in the Bologna print edn., no. 730, records *kovrav*, which means 'those who buried him'.

[95] *SḤ* 1542.

[96] See Dunn, *The Christianization of the Anglo-Saxons*, where the author documents this phenomenon.

[97] See Schmitt, *Ghosts in the Middle Ages*, 82.

minent demise. The student, in an attempt to thwart this suspicion and clear his standing in the eyes of his teacher, engages himself to another woman. R. Judah approves of the student's action and makes the following declaration:

> A man must be very careful that the sick person does not suspect him, even though, after death, the sick person will know that he did not have bad intentions. [Still] he needs to be careful, because the sick, when they die in the midst of pain that was inflicted upon them, even in [their] death, will seek revenge.[98]

Although this rabbi dies a normal (that is, non-violent and not too premature) death, his intense mental anguish relegates him to the category of those who have suffered a bad death. Just as the *draugr* Glam, who has been murdered, and the dead knight who attacks Henry on the riverbank, and who has himself suffered a violent end, return to harm the living in the tales mentioned above, so too, according to *Sefer ḥasidim*, anyone who suffers a difficult death will exact posthumous revenge.[99] Unlike the vengeful dead in the Icelandic sagas and in many German and English tales, however, the rabbi in this story is not portrayed as a negative character—he is neither evil nor sinful. His vengeful wrath is averted by the precautionary measures adopted by the student while his master is alive.

The 'Testament of R. Judah the Pious' prohibits the placing of one coffin upon another, because 'if this is done, certainly one resident of the city will die within nine days'.[100] While the text offers no reason for this assumption, one cannot rule out the possibility of revenge. Angry at those who committed this affront to his honour, the dead person in the bottom coffin will take murderous revenge upon a member of the community.[101]

In marked contrast to the belief recorded in Pietist sources, the Talmud recounts an actual situation of verbal abuse hurled at the deceased, which

98 *SḤ* 1885.

99 While R. Judah's story of the master and student ends happily (the master does not suspect his student and therefore dies a peaceful death), William of Newburgh's similar tale involving a husband and wife has a violent end. The husband, while spying on his wife, who is together with another man, falls from the roof of his house and dies. He then returns nightly to attack and kill the living. See Caciola, 'Wraiths, Revenants and Ritual', 21.

100 'The Testament of R. Judah the Pious' (Heb.), no. 3, p. 11.

101 A similar rationale might explain another prohibition mentioned in 'The Testament of R. Judah the Pious' (Heb.). In *SḤ* 11, p. 13, the author does not permit burial of a dead body in another city if there is a cemetery in the city in which the person died. Rather than it being an indignity to the dead body to be transferred from place to place, the reason supplied for the prohibition is that 'the dead that lie there [in that city's cemetery] are angry, for it is a disgrace to them'. Although this is unstated, the author of the 'Testament' may fear a vengeful reprisal, similar to the one indicated above, on the part of the disgraced dead.

suggests that vengeance does not come from the dead person:

R. Isaac said: If one makes remarks about the deceased, it is like making remarks about a stone. Some say [the reason is that] they do not know, others that they know but do not care. Can that be so? Has not R. Papa said: A certain man made derogatory remarks about Mar Samuel and a log fell from the roof and broke his skull? A rabbinic student is different, because the Holy One, blessed be He, avenges his insult.[102]

As the rabbis see it, it is not the dead who are vengeful; it is God—but he only avenges the honour of those who study his Torah.

In another passage in *Sefer ḥasidim*,[103] a story is told of a dead man who seeks revenge, not for an affront to his honour but for a violation of his property, specifically an object that was used for his burial. A certain Jew wishes to fashion for himself a harp out of the wood remaining from another's coffin. When the Jew disregards the cautionary words of others, the dead man appears to him in a dream, warning him that if he carries through his intentions 'he will exact vengeance upon him'. The Jew ignores the threat and fashions the musical instrument. The dead man thereupon threatens that if he does not break it, 'it will be dangerous'. Ignoring the warning yet again, the man becomes gravely ill, only to be cured when his son breaks the harp over the grave of the dead man and leaves the pieces upon it. R. Judah concludes by citing two biblical verses.[104] The first, Proverbs 17: 5, denounces anyone who mocks the dead, while the second, Ecclesiastes 9: 5, denies that the dead can have any knowledge. While the rabbis of the Talmud debate the latter verse, and also the passage from *Berakhot* quoted above, to decide whether the dead have knowledge of the actions of the living,[105] R. Judah is certain that they do, and he qualifies and reinterprets the verse from Ecclesiastes, saying that the statement that 'the dead know nothing at all' refers exclusively to their knowledge and authority regarding the commandments; in all other matters their knowledge is solid and the pronouncements they make in dreams are truthful and binding—a crucial distinction as such pronouncements play a central role in *Sefer ḥasidim*.[106] It is clear from this passage that R. Judah feels that the Jew who fashions a harp from the leftover wood of a coffin acts recklessly, foolishly endangering his life. The dead seek revenge for stolen property (including even the remnants thereof!) and zealously guard their burial

102 BT *Ber.* 19*a*.

103 *SḤ* 323.

104 This is not unique to *Sefer ḥasidim*. Any traditional work will seek to ground its doctrines in the authority of the biblical text.

105 BT *Ber.* 17*b*–19*a*. See A. Cohen, '"Do the Dead Know?"'

106 See Ch. 5 below.

sites.[107] Everyone knows that. The admonitions of anonymous acquaintances in the story make it clear that the Jew has acted against common opinion. Secondly, R. Judah's manipulation of the verse in Ecclesiastes suggests that a firm belief in the vengeful nature of the dead was widely held. Since he offers no textual support for his novel reading, it would appear that common knowledge dictated it.

The Pietist tale does not directly involve the body of the dead, for Jewish law prohibits making personal use of, or deriving benefit from, a dead body.[108] Instead, it revolves around articles used in handling or burying the body (*tashmishei hamet*).[109] However, for the Jewish reader this focus would naturally be accompanied by the mental echo of *hazmanah milta*—a halakhic principle stating that anything set aside for use in the performance of a *mitsvah* assumes the status of the *mitsvah* object itself even prior to its use.[110] Such an association would render using the material for the coffin as forbidden as using the body itself. What the tale tells the reader, then, is that deriving benefit from the leftover material of the coffin may not only be forbidden but is also dangerous.

While expressing a belief in the vengeance of the dead upon the living, the tale modifies the type of violence that the dead commit. Instead of the direct face-to-face physical encounter with the living that was characteristic of the Icelandic sagas, the dead man in this tale attacks the Jew only indirectly, striking him with a deathly sickness and hurling repeated threats of vengeance and danger at him, but only in a dream. The introduction of the dream as a medium for communication between the dead and the living means that the corporeality of the ghost has here disappeared. Dreams are especially suited for such contact as they bridge the gap between the 'twilight zones of life—past and present, physical and spiritual, private and public'.[111] Dreams are linked with death in Jewish tradition, as 'sleep constitutes one-sixtieth of death'.[112] The etymology of the word in Germanic languages, however, testifies to its origin in encounters with the dead in a live, wakeful, corporeal experience: both the German *Traum* and the English 'dream' stem from the ancient root *draugr*.[113]

107 The fear of deadly vengeance as stated clearly in this passage surpasses mere violation of the talmudic precept enunciated in BT *Men.* 99*a*, 'One ascends in holiness and never descends.' On the gravesite as a sacred place, see Lichtenstein, *From Impurity to Sanctity* (Heb.), 444–6.

108 BT *AZ* 29*b*.

109 See BT *San.* 47*b*. On the concept of *tashmishim* in general, see BT *Meg.* 26*b*.

110 See BT *Ber.* 23*b*. On the application of the concept of *hazmanah milta* to objects pertaining to the burial of the dead, see BT *San.* 47*b*.

111 Hazan-Rokem, *Web of Life*, 91–2.

112 BT *Ber.* 57*b*.

113 Schmitt, 'The Liminality and Centrality of Dreams in the Medieval West', 281.

Fear of the vengeful dead is evident in another passage in *Sefer ḥasidim*, which precedes the aforementioned tale.[114] It contains a rather lengthy account of an encounter between a dead father and his living son. A certain *ḥakham* (Pietist master) sees in a dream a figure that is 'taller than a house' but has the countenance of a man, and who takes him to see his father's grave.[115] The figure opens the grave and instructs him to speak to his father. But the father is angry and refuses to speak to his son. The figure explains why: first, certain Gentiles have disturbed his grave by removing two stones from among those that encircled it, and the son has not replaced them; second, the son has failed to complete repayment of a debt that the father had incurred before he died. On waking, the son turns to his mother for verification of these claims. When he learns that his father had, in fact, repaid the full amount of the debt, he informs his mother of his intent to fulfil the first of his father's wishes—to replace the missing stones as well as to add some earth on top of the grave. His acquaintances[116] attempt to dissuade him: 'Don't do it! It is a life-threatening danger [*sakanat nefesh hi*]!' At first, he listens to them and refrains.[117] Many days later, however, he sees some Gentiles removing earth from their home and, remembering the dream, he pays them to dump it in the cemetery. He fills his father's grave with earth and replaces the stones. He then proceeds to fill other sunken graves with earth as well, intending to do so for all the graves in the cemetery, but has to stop as the Gentiles no longer want to transport earth for him. In the end, the *ḥakham*'s own son and daughter die. R. Judah offers the following rationale: 'And some in the community said, "[it is] because he started [to fulfil] a commandment and did not complete it, as in [the case of] Judah, [whose

[114] *SḤ* 322. This is a significant fact because ideas tend to be clustered in *Sefer ḥasidim*, with the same theme occupying several consecutive passages. Therefore the juxtaposition of these two tales solidifies the common theme that unites them.

[115] Such a figure seems to resemble closely the angelic guides who lead the souls of the living on a tour of the other world in Jewish and Christian apocalyptic literature. Apart from directing the soul on its journey, the angel also explains to it the meaning and purpose behind the various sights and events it witnesses (see Himmelfarb, *Tours of Hell*). Perhaps a more direct source of influence is to be found in 3 Enoch. Part of the *heikhalot/merkavah* tradition of mysticism studied by the Pietists, 3 Enoch records, using identical language (*bo ve'areka*), how Metatron, the supreme angel and prince of the Divine Presence, takes R. Ishmael by the hand and conducts him to the other world. There the rabbi sees the abodes of the righteous, average, and wicked dead, with Metatron acting as his guide and instructor. See Odeberg (ed.), *3 Enoch*, 132–7.

[116] The anonymous 'they said' is used in the text.

[117] This translation follows MS Parma H 3280 against Wistinetzky's edition of *Sefer ḥasidim* and the Bologna print edn., no. 727, as this reading is found in all other parallel passages of manuscript provenance.

sons] Er and Onan died [on account of] him".'[118] According to the claim of this segment of the community, one is obligated to care for the gravesites of the dead. Whereas the son succeeded in replacing the missing stones and filled his father's grave with earth, his failure to restore the graves of all the Jewish dead in the cemetery (even though they had not called upon him to do so) was considered a serious crime, punishable by the death of his offspring. The rationale offered for the son's misfortunes is based on the rabbinic principle, 'Whoever starts [fulfilling] a commandment and does not complete it buries his wife and children.'[119] This principle originally referred to the performance of a biblically mandated commandment, but here members of the Jewish community had extended its application.

Another manuscript of *Sefer ḥasidim*, however, records an additional reason for the death of the *ḥakham*'s children: others within the community claimed that his children died precisely because he had restored the missing stones to his father's grave.[120] Since the *ḥakham*'s personal misfortunes are perceived as being a direct result of his having tampered with a grave, this claim stems from a belief in the vengeance of the dead.

This ghost tale, like the one cited before it, departs in some of its features from the stories of vengeance in Icelandic and north European sources. The encounter with the dead occurs only indirectly, through the medium of a dream, and the dead person has no corporeal substance. Yet fear of the vengeful dead is noticeably present: the local townspeople express it vociferously. Despite the fact that the son, in wishing to replace the missing stones and earth, is acting in accordance with his dead father's will and seeks to benefit him by making improvements to his gravesite, his acquaintances warn him not to tamper with the grave. For some members of the community, the death of the *ḥakham*'s children proves they were right.

Violation of gravesites was widely seen by ancient people as a crime that aroused the ire of the dead. Several Icelandic sagas describe the violent retribution meted out to grave robbers and others who violate tombs.[121] When Grettir, for example, enters the tomb of Kar the Ancient in order to despoil it, he becomes locked in a vicious hand-to-hand struggle with the

[118] According to the rabbis, Judah was guilty of not having fully saved Joseph when he had the opportunity to influence his brothers (Gen. 37: 26–7). The rabbis attribute the death of his sons Er and Onan soon after (Gen. 38: 7 and 38: 10) to Divine punishment for his failure. See BT *Sot.* 13*b* and *Midrash bereshit rabah* 85 (ed. Theodore and Albeck, ii. 1034).

[119] This rabbinic principle is enunciated in BT *Sot.* 13*b* and *Midrash bereshit rabah* 85 (ed. Theodor and Albeck, ii. 1034).

[120] See Gross, 'The Bond between the Living and the Dead' (Heb.), 35 n. 199. I wish to thank Dalia Gross for sharing her thesis with me.

[121] Lecouteux, *Fantômes et revenants*, 72–4.

dead buried there.[122] Early medieval Christianity appropriated this belief and Christianized it by relegating it to the domain of the holy dead. The saints use supernatural power to defend their territory and guard their rights.[123] Gregory of Tours tells the story of the bishop martyr Helius, who rises from his tomb to seize a grave robber, releasing him only when he repents.[124] By the time of the high medieval exemplum, the belief had moved to the domain of ordinary people.[125] A thirteenth-century Latin manuscript recounts how a widow's son, who has desecrated several graves, is summoned by the dead in that cemetery. Despite the presence of his mother and a priest, he is carried away by the dead, who appear in the form of evil spirits.[126] A fourteenth-century Latin manuscript relates how a certain dead knight appears to his fellow knight begging for aid as he is suffering in Purgatory for having violated a cemetery.[127] In this ghost tale, the vengeance of the dead in this world has been replaced with purgatorial torment in the next, and the notion of the violation of graves has been extended from one particular gravesite to the burial ground as a whole.

Whereas the restoration of the gravesite demanded of the son in the Pietist story above may reflect pagan notions, the second request of the deceased, repayment of debts, does not. Jean-Claude Schmitt argues that, while the belief in the returning dead may have had ancient roots, the social situations documented in this narrative attest to contemporary structures and ideas. To whom the dead appear and what is demanded of them to ensure that they get their proper rest is specific to the time period in which the tale circulated.[128] Repayment of the deceased father's outstanding debts

[122] *La Saga de Grettir*, ch. 18, quoted in Lecouteux, *Fantômes et revenants*, 73.

[123] Gurevich, *Medieval Popular Culture*, 46–7, 50. One of the earlier types of miracle is that of the saint taking revenge on anyone who attacks his or her shrine. See Ward, *Miracles and the Medieval Mind*, 69.

[124] Gregory of Tours, *Liber in gloria confessorum*, 62, quoted in Schmitt, *Ghosts in the Middle Ages*, 30.

[125] A notable exception to this is a tale in which the holy dead take their revenge on the living. Saints Crispin and Crispinian appear at night to a bishop who has damaged the basilica at Soissons, under which they are buried. For his having violated their 'burial ground', the two saints cut off the bishop's right arm and leg, which ultimately leads to his ignominious death (*Catalogue of Romances*, iii. 588 no. 84). Although this tale is found in a fourteenth-century manuscript, it perhaps emanates from an earlier source, as violent, vengeful action on the part of saints is more common in early medieval tales.

[126] MS BL Add. 27909B (*Catalogue of Romances*, iii. 464 no. 9).

[127] MS BL Add. 15833 fo. 132 (*Catalogue of Romances*, iii. 588 no. 82). The same story also appears in MS BL Add. 11284 fo. 30*b* (*Catalogue of Romances*, iii. 386 no. 222) and MS BL Harley 3244 fo. 85*b* (*Catalogue of Romances*, iii. 463 no. 119). The knight is guilty of the double offence of having robbed a holy man (a priest) on hallowed ground (the cemetery).

[128] See Schmitt, *Ghosts in the Middle Ages*, 3–4.

accords well with the high medieval emphasis on a son's charitable obligations on behalf of his father's soul.[129]

Alongside the manifest threat posed by the dangerous dead that *Sefer ḥasidim* records, there exists a minor narrative strand which reflects a more contemporary, thirteenth-century view of the dead. In one ghost tale,[130] a man loses his way in the forest and encounters a rather pitiful but placid ghost who wanders the forests in expiation of a crime he committed during his lifetime. When the man realizes that the other is actually dead, he tries to flee, but the ghost cries out to him not to run away for he intends no harm. He then proceeds to tell him the reason for his posthumous peregrinations. This interchange between man and ghost, which is otherwise extraneous to the moral message of the tale, is here a mere literary vestige of the ancient fear of the dangerous dead, whose violent physical assaults are a source of dread in the Icelandic sagas. With constant repetition during the high medieval period, a certain standard or schematic ghost tale had emerged.[131] The encounter with a ghost was no longer a terrifying event, yet the element of fear that had once existed was retained in the telling over and recording of these tales—a phenomenon that has been described as the 'domestication of ghosts'.[132] The words of the ghost, 'Fear nothing. I have not come to harm you', became a standard feature of the ghost tales recorded in the exempla collections.[133] The ghost in *Sefer ḥasidim* who utters just such a reassurance is an instance of a literary form found in the exempla collections of the mendicants.[134] Some degree of corporeality, however, is maintained in this tale as man and ghost meet in a face-to-face encounter.[135]

Despite this mention of a 'domesticated ghost', literary sources emanating from outside the Pietist circle attest to a continued belief in the

129 Ibid. 66–7. Regarding the return of the dead on account of the failure of the living to pay back a debt incurred by the deceased, see ibid. 69–70.

130 *SḤ* 35.

131 Schmitt, *Ghosts in the Middle Ages*, 136.

132 A term used by Schmitt, ibid. 140. In describing this phenomenon earlier, he writes, 'The apparition of a dead person, which so many writings present as a stupefying and frightening phenomenon, was no longer anything but a scenography in which each role was known in advance and whose unfolding led back, most of the time, to the same schema' (ibid. 136).

133 Ibid. 136.

134 The very next ghost tale recounted in *Sefer ḥasidim* (no. 36) contains an identical dialogue between man and ghost. A certain servant, apparently also out wandering, encounters his former non-Jewish master, who has already died. The first words that the ghost utters are: 'Don't flee; I will not harm you.'

135 In *SḤ* 36, proof is offered of the bodily return of the dead master. He appears in a tree to the townspeople the next morning, and his grave, when opened, is found empty.

corporeal, harmful dead. A later addition[136] to the early twelfth-century *Maḥzor vitry* records the following:

I copied from the responsa of Rashi: The prayer of 'Magen avot', as explained in [tractate] *Shabat*, was instituted because of danger [*mishum sakanah*], for [at that time] permission is granted to the harmful ones [*lamazikin*], as it is taught in a *beraita* in [the chapter] 'Arvei pesaḥim', 'A man should not go out alone on Tuesday and Friday nights because Igeret bat Mahlat goes out [then] and 180,000 angels of destruction accompany her, and each one has permission to destroy.'[137] And even though in later generations Abaye decreed that she must not pass through settled areas ever again, [still] there is life-threatening danger from the dead, who find respite at night. And it is their nature to come to the synagogue [on a Friday] night within twelve months [of their death]. And the rabbis feared lest, perhaps, after the congregation have left [the synagogue], there would be one who does not pray along with the congregation and he would pray alone and place himself in danger. [The rabbis] stood up and instituted for the leader of the prayer services the 'one blessing that contains seven' [*berakhah aḥat me'ein sheva*].[138]

According to the Talmud (*Shab.* 24*b* and *Pes.* 112*b*), it was the rabbis' fear of harmful demons that led them to institute a special additional prayer on Friday nights. It was to be recited by the leader of the service in order to protect any latecomer who might be left alone in the synagogue after the others have gone. For the author of this passage in the *Maḥzor vitry*, however, the reason for the institution of the additional prayer was fear of harm from the wicked dead. It is they who frequent synagogues on Friday nights, the only time when they are allowed respite from the tortures of Gehenna in the first year after their passing.[139] What was once, for the talmudic rabbis, the threat of destructive angels has become a fear of the dangerous dead, specifically in the form of the 'bad dead', for the author of this addition to the *Maḥzor vitry*.[140] Once again, the dead have filled the role for-

[136] According to Stahl, 'The Prayer of Dead Souls in the Synagogue' (Heb.), 184, this passage is a later addition by a scribe or student since it is not found in any parallel text of the *sifrut devei rashi* or in Rashi's commentary on the relevant passage in BT *Shab.* 24*b*, s.v. *mishum*.

[137] Little is known about Igeret bat Mahlat apart from this brief mention in the Talmud and in *Bemidbar rabah* 12, where she is feared for her journeys through the night with her host and other harmful demons. For the role of demons in rabbinic literature, see Bohak, 'Conceptualizing Demons'.

[138] Simhah b. Samuel of Vitry, *Maḥzor vitry*, i. 172–3, and notes there.

[139] Mishnah *Edu.* 2: 10 allots twelve months from the moment of death to the judgement of the wicked in Gehenna. See the extensive discussion of this topic in Ch. 6 below.

[140] It must be noted that it is possible that the author of this addendum was a Pietist. In fact, several other Ashkenazi halakhists who cite this passage retain the original *mazikin* as the source of the danger. See Stahl, 'The Prayer of Dead Souls in the Synagogue' (Heb.), 184 n. 33.

merly occupied by demons.[141] This author's fear recalls the dread palpable in previously mentioned passages of *Sefer ḥasidim*.

The Summoning Power of the Dead

Corollary to belief in the return of the violent or vengeful dead is the notion that an apparition of the dead can itself cause death. As mentioned earlier, according to Germanic beliefs, disease is caused by the dead.[142] Failure to burn the bedding of the dead leads to a chain of deaths in the *Saga de Snorri le Godi*. An apparition of a *draugr* precedes many of these deaths. Thorir, for example, manages to escape a violent encounter with the *draugr* of a shepherd only to fall ill soon afterwards and die. After Thorir's *draugr* then appears together with the shepherd's, a domestic of Thorodd dies three nights later. Six other deaths on the farm follow in close succession.[143] The role of the dead in summoning others to die is more explicit in the *Saga des Gens du Flói*. During an epidemic, deaths are presaged by the appearance of former victims of the plague to those who are about to die, and their *draugar*, in turn, appear to the next victims. Thorgils finally puts an end to this cycle of events when he burns all the victims' corpses.[144] The appearances of the *draugar*, in this case, are so attached to the deaths that follow in their wake that they are themselves viewed as the cause of the deaths. These apparitions are feared more than the disease, so that the prime means of controlling the spread of the epidemic is to prevent the return of the dead.

Presaging death was also a common function of ghosts in early medieval literature. As early as Augustine's letter to Evodius (414 CE), ghosts appear to the living to announce their approaching death. In such cases the two parties are either related—a dead son appears to his father, asking him to join him—or share a bond of some kind, for example a dead student returns in a dream to get his friend.[145] In contrast to similar situations in the sagas, these apparitions are not met with dread or horror. Instead, the tone is positive as the visitor from the other world wishes to share the joys

However, there are many other addenda to the *Maḥzor vitry* whose authors' ideals bear no necessary affinity with those of the Pietists. See also Trachtenberg, *Jewish Magic and Superstition*, 67.

141 See pp. 21–2 above.

142 Disease is caught either by being wounded by elves and dwarfs (the Christianized forms of the pagan demons who represent the 'bad dead') or by failure to burn the bedding of the dead. See Lecouteux, *Fantômes et revenants*, 109–10.

143 *Eyrbyggja Saga*, chs. 51–55; Lecouteux, *Fantômes et revenants*, 107–8.

144 *La Saga des Gens du Flói*, ch. 22, cited in Lecouteux, *Fantômes et revenants*, 91–2.

145 Schmitt, *Ghosts in the Middle Ages*, 19.

of his blessed fate with his relative or friend. Knowledge that they will participate in the eternal state that the dead person is currently enjoying serves to comfort the living and grant them peace of mind. In a similar fashion, in stories recorded in the eighth century, monks and recluses appear after death to those with whom they shared a religious bond, informing them of their coming demise and offering them advice.[146] Such advance knowledge is useful to the living and enables them to prepare for death.

The high medieval exemplum maintained the constructive goal of the dead in summoning the living. Caesarius of Heisterbach, in his *Dialogus miraculorum*, recounts several ghost tales in which the dead aid the living by revealing to them the time of their death or by calling on them to join them in death.[147] At times, merely seeing the living standing beside the dead in a vision or dream is a sufficient indicator of approaching death. In these tales, the dead reassure the living of their blessed posthumous fate, and those summoned embrace death as a means of reunion with deceased loved ones. Penitents and the wayward are especially grateful for advance notice of their death as it confirms to them their future spiritual status.[148]

[146] These stories originate in Bede, *Historia ecclesiastica*, 4: 8, 9 (a. 664), 5: 9 (a. 690), quoted in Schmitt, *Ghosts in the Middle Ages*, 33.

[147] In one tale, a senior priest who has died appears to his successor, a certain Conrad, and gives him his own tunic to wear. Conrad dons the tunic. He immediately falls ill, and dies several days later. The passage of the tunic from the dead priest to his live successor serves as a symbolic summoning of the latter to join the former. Conrad's death is foretold in his vision, and he accepts his fate both peaceably and willingly. In a second tale, a priest named Gregory becomes deathly ill. He comforts his weeping sister by telling her about a vision he has just seen. Their dead mother, who was a holy and devout woman, has appeared to him and has beckoned him to come to her. He dies soon after. In a third tale, a young Cistercian named Gunther weeps daily at the grave of his dear friend Theodoric, who has recently died, wishing to be together with him in heaven. His tears are effective. Theodoric calls to him from the grave, saying, 'Be comforted, be comforted, brother, for thou shalt soon come to me.' Gunther joins him a few days later. The tale is told by a third friend, Siger, the only one of the group who remains behind (the three had joined the order together). See Caesarius of Heisterbach, *Dialogue*, 11: 32, 11: 34, 12: 52.

[148] *Dialogue*, 11: 14 tells the story of three dead monks who appear in a vision to a penitent monk named Rudinger. Having led a sinful life, Rudinger, whose body is racked by sickness, turns, in the end, to prayer and repentance. As a reward for this change of heart, three dead monks, among them a saintly one known as David, appear to him, informing him that today he will die. He is also told that the blessed David will beseech 'the whole host of heaven' for him in an effort to secure his salvation. Rudinger dies at precisely the hour foretold in the vision, his entry into Heaven secure.

Another story in *Dialogue* (7: 38) tells how the Virgin Mary summons Dom Walter, a knight who has repented of his secular lifestyle and joined the Cistercian order, to death. A certain monk, asleep in Villers, has a vision of Mary 'accompanied by personages of different ranks . . . in a marvellous blaze of light'. At first the monk is saddened because Mary does not call him;

Other ghost stories found in the *Dialogus miraculorum*, however, depart from this positive attitude to death and reveal voices of reluctance and a wish to avoid the summons. In one such story, a monk named Lambert, who has a vision while asleep during choir, refuses the summons to death presented to him by a dead cellarer named Richwin. Richwin then turns to another, older monk named Conrad, who sits opposite Lambert in the choir, and summons him instead. In the vision, Conrad places his cowl over his head and follows Richwin. When Lambert awakes, he immediately reports his vision to Conrad, who responds: 'I care not. I should like to be dead.' Needless to say, Conrad falls ill the next day and dies soon after; he is buried in that very cowl.[149] In a second tale, a canon of Bonn named Winric, who has recently died, appears in a dream to a certain Erwin, canon of Cologne, summoning him to join him. When Erwin refuses, Winric summons instead the second dean of Cologne, a man by the name of Hermann. When Hermann dies, Erwin, fearing his own death is imminent, takes preventative measures to ensure that he remains among the living.[150] In both these tales, something compels the dead to fulfil their mission to summon the living; if the initial invitation is rebuffed, a substitute must be found.

Sefer ḥasidim contains many examples of tales in which the dead summon the living, and several passages affirm the reliability of dreams which foretell a person's death.[151] In other ghost tales the apparition of the dead heralds a coming death. In one such tale, a man who has fallen asleep at night in a synagogue awakes to see the dead standing in prayer. Among them he sees two men whom he recognizes and knows to be alive. The tale

but then, taking pity on him, she sends another monk, who is standing very close to her, to call him; he reacts with great joy. The monk standing close to Mary turns out to be Dom Walter, who soon falls ill; he prepares for death with confession and contrition, and dies. The monk of Villers follows soon afterwards. Foreknowledge of Dom Walter's death enables him to prepare himself and thus die in a state of purity and sanctity. A summons to death from the Virgin herself is viewed as an honour: the penitent knight is privileged to receive it, and it is welcomed by the monk of Villers.

149 *Dialogue*, 11: 33. On the importance of burial in a cowl, see Ch. 4 below.

150 *Dialogue*, 11: 45.

151 *SḤ* 1521, 1522, 1523, 1524, 1563. Sections 1523 and 1563 speak of dreams which include symbolic summonses to death. Section 1523 tells of a non-Jew who sees himself mounted on a red horse that stands next to an unclean animal. His friend informs him that this means he will soon die and will be carried on a bier, just as he was carried on the horse's back. The dream comes true in the end. According to section 1563, a dream in which one sees a Torah scroll placed inside an ark is a portent of death. *SḤ* 1522 and 1524 assert only in general terms that if one dreams that a living person is dead, one should take the dream very seriously and act accordingly, because 'it is impossible that it will not be fulfilled'.

concludes with the report that these two men died shortly thereafter.[152] This tale bears a striking similarity to one that is recorded in the earliest surviving ghost tale collection of the Middle Ages, embedded within the eleventh-century Saxon *Chronicon*. There, Thietmar of Merseburg tells of the dead who reinhabit their former church in the Eastern Marches of the Ottonian empire and hold services there. A living priest, who encounters them in his church, is informed by a member of the congregation (whom he recognizes as having recently died) that he, too, will die soon. And so he does.[153]

As Nancy Caciola has argued, Thietmar's tale reflects notions of the dangerous dead; the dead who assemble in their local church are the former townspeople of Walsleben, who were all brutally massacred.[154] Their 'bad death' causes their unrest and their repopulation of former living spaces. The priest who encounters them perceives them as dangerous; he approaches them only after invoking the sign of the holy cross.[155] In the *Chronicon*, Thietmar's tale is one of a series of tales involving a 'dead congregation',[156] and the motif repeats itself throughout the Middle Ages.[157]

Another tale in *Sefer ḥasidim* tells of a non-Jewish noblewoman who is thought to have died, but when she is placed on a bier, she recovers consciousness and tells all those present what she has witnessed in the other world.[158] Among other matters, she speaks of having seen people who are yet living, together with others who have already died, and she is able to predict their time of death.[159] This tale, with its manifest Christian provenance, is a borrowed one. Elisheva Baumgarten has identified the recipient

[152] *SḤ* 271. Slight variations exist between the various manuscripts and printed editions. MS Parma H 3280 reads *shenei benei adam omedim veḥayim* and *lo ḥayu yamim muatin umetu*; MS JTS Boesky 45 no. 118 reads *shenei benei adam she'adayin ḥayim omedim* and *lo hayu yamim muatin umetu*. Bologna print edn., no. 711 reads *shenei benei adam omedim baḥayim* and *lo hayu yamim muatin umetu*. However, the essential meaning of the passage is retained.

[153] Caciola, *Afterlives*, 118.

[154] Ibid. 117. [155] Ibid. 118. [156] Ibid. [157] Ibid. 153–6.

[158] Tales of returning to life immediately after dying are common in the exempla collections. Most often the return to life occurs in order that the dead may confess their sins; see *Catalogue of Romances*, iii. 380 nos. 122, 127; 386 no. 215; 482 no. 47; 567 no. 108; 581 no. 1; 603 no. 72; 676 no. 9; and Banks (ed.), *Alphabet of Tales*, 229–30 no. 331. Occasionally, the living report having seen the torments of the dead in the other world. In one such tale, a dead man who refused to confess a mortal sin rises up at his funeral to announce that he is damned (*Catalogue of Romances*, iii. 680 no. 58). In another, the brother of a knight uses magic to transport himself to the other world. There he sees the soul of the landgrave Ludwig of Thuringia, among others, undergoing torment in Hell. See Banks (ed.), *Alphabet of Tales*, 469–70 no. 701; *Catalogue of Romances*, iii. 350 no. 5.

[159] *SḤ* 272. Although the tale is not explicit in this regard, the implication is that the noblewoman witnesses the living people undergoing torments in Hell among the dead ones who are

of the vision as Christina Mirabilis (1150–1224), 'a well-known figure in the Rhineland', who apparently returned to life during her funeral and reported having seen the dead and some of the living in the afterlife, foretelling that these would soon die.[160] Just as in the dreams and visions recorded by Caesarius of Heisterbach and Thietmar of Merseburg, seeing or experiencing the living standing in the company of the dead is enough to indicate that they will soon join their ranks.

The conflicting attitude towards a summons to death expressed in Caesarius's tales manifests itself in *Sefer ḥasidim* as well. In two passages, foreknowledge of death is welcomed as it allows the hasid to prepare for the event. These passages state that when the 'spirit of death' (*ruaḥ shel mavet*) appears in a dream to a living person, beckoning him to join it, either that person or one of his children or a close friend will die. What prompts the dead to do this? The text offers a clear answer: either the dead person himself or the living person's guardian angel (*hamemuneh*) wants to aid the living one by giving him the opportunity to repent and put his affairs in order[161] before he leaves this world.[162] What holds true for the monks of Caesarius's tales applies equally to the everyman of *Sefer ḥasidim*; forewarning allows for a proper death.

already actually there. This vision of the living among the dead signifies their imminent death and posthumous fate.

160 See Baumgarten, 'A Tale of a Christian Matron', 94.

161 It is interesting to note that, while the tales of Caesarius of Heisterbach highlight solely the religious avenues of preparation for death (i.e. confession and Communion), the tales in *Sefer ḥasidim* include, beyond repentance, the material dimension of these preparations as well. The promulgation of a testament is a significant event in the Pietist work and it is mentioned on six separate occasions (*SḤ* 242, 307, 309, 310, 1456, 1515). That this testament is an oral testimony made on one's deathbed is clear from the author's repeated insistence on the presence of trustworthy and righteous individuals as witnesses to the event (even family members cannot always be trusted; see especially *SḤ* 307, 309). *SḤ* 1515 suggests an oral testimony but it is not explicitly stated. *SḤ* 242, 309, and 1456 describe the content of the testimony as pertaining to the posthumous disbursement of funds to heirs and/or to charity. It is stressed that one should not delay in doing this; pious behaviour dictates finalizing or even executing one's will as early as possible so as to ensure faithful adherence to its stipulations. (*SḤ* 310 praises those who give their possessions to charity before they die. See also *SḤ* 309.) This pietistic concern for proper preparation before death should be seen in light of the growing importance attributed by the wider society to the time immediately prior to death. Le Goff, *The Birth of Purgatory*, 292, argues that this new approach was linked to the birth of Purgatory as a distinct locus in the hereafter: since retribution and reward would be meted out immediately after death, fear of dying in a state of sin or dying intestate (without having provided for the distribution of alms or the offering of masses for one's soul) is greatly magnified.

162 *SḤ* 1550 and the last five lines of no. 329. The two passages are identical, with one slight exception. *SḤ* 1550 contains the smoother reading of *lehakhin takanato* ('to prepare his testament') instead of the awkward *lehashiv takanato* ('to reverse his testament') found in *SḤ* 329.

The stories of R. Judah reflect another reason for a positive outlook on the summons to death. In one tale, a dead Torah scholar appears in a dream to his disciple, who ministered to all his needs when he was alive. The scholar beckons to his disciple to join him in the world of the dead. On waking, the student consults a *ḥakham*, who advises him to accept his master's request as long as he is assured that he will enter into the scholar's private quarter in Paradise. Although the text of the manuscript is corrupted, according to the best reading of the passage the disciple dies within the year, having apparently been assured of his high station in the afterlife.[163] As in the tales recounted by Caesarius, assurance to the living of their blessed fate after death and the desire to be reunited with deceased loved ones are valid motives for the acceptance of a summons to death.

In another of R. Judah's stories, however, the outcome is different. A seriously ill disciple steadfastly rejects his dead master's summons to death. Having consulted a *ḥakham*, the student is able to call up a second apparition of his master in order to refuse his offer, despite repeated requests, saying that 'for the sake of the Creator, he should desist from me, for I do not want to come with him'. After making his master swear that he will leave him alone, he recovers.[164] It is perhaps for this reason that the author of 'Testament of R. Judah the Pious' appears to advise readers to accept nothing from the dead who appear to the living in a dream, nor to promise them anything.[165]

Sefer ḥasidim also reflects a negative attitude to foreknowledge of death; R. Judah asserts that one must mount a strong resistance to death and actively defy its summons. Several consecutive passages urge one who has dreamt of a forthcoming death to engage in fasting and prayer as a means to prevent the fulfilment of that dream.[166] One passage reports how a certain individual is able to thwart repeated dreams foretelling his death through fasting, recital of psalms, and tearful confessions.[167] Another individual successfully evades a death omen by inordinate fasting and by distributing copious amounts of money to the poor.[168] Two cases are cited, one of which involves someone selling a dream that contains a death omen.[169] In these cases, death forewarned may be death forestalled.

When a summons to death does occur, one must actively try to escape it—at least according to this source. *Sefer ḥasidim* outlines the following

[163] This story is based on the manuscript text of MS Bodl. 1567 as cited in Dan, 'Demonological Stories from the Writings of R. Judah' (Heb.), 286, no. 24 and n. 73.

[164] Ibid. 286, no. 25.

[165] 'The Testament of R. Judah the Pious' (Heb.), no. 13, p. 14.

[166] *SḤ* 1521, 1522, 1523, 1524.

[167] *SḤ* 1524.

[168] *SḤ* 1544.

[169] *SḤ* 1523.

very precise procedure, to be implemented in the case of such an eventuality: If a dead person appears in a dream, to a Jew or non-Jew,[170] requesting that they follow him, they must go to the cemetery, and there make him swear to desist, shouting the following words at the dead one's grave three times in a voice loud enough to be heard at a distance of four cubits:

> And I, so-and-so (male or female) [son or] daughter of so-and-so, do not want to come after you, nor after anyone (male or female) who is called by your name, nor after any other dead person (male or female); and regarding this I make you swear and I request of you, because I want to live many more years, and you (male or female), who are called by the name of the one who comes after me, should go and say to that dead soul so-and-so (male or female) son or daughter of so-and-so (male or female) that he [or she] should not come after me, nor do I want to come after [him or] her and also [he or] she should not come to me.[171]

As in the ghost tales found in Caesarius's work, only a refusal to follow after the dead saves one from death. Therefore, an integral part of the oath, aside from preventing the dead from returning and summoning the living, is the loudly proclaimed declaration by the living of their refusal to accept the call.

The fact that *Sefer ḥasidim* takes this graveside oath very seriously is evident in the provisions it makes for all possible eventualities.[172] If one who receives the summons to death is unable to go to the cemetery because it is too far away, or is not permitted to go there because the dead person is not Jewish, and one would therefore have to enter a Christian burial ground,[173] one must find a surrogate person or grave. In the former case, another Jew with the same name as the dead summoner must be found. If this Jew is unable to go, then a surrogate grave must be found, and the person buried in it—Jew or Gentile[174]—must have the same name as the dead summoner in the dream. In the latter case, one must find a surrogate Jewish grave of someone with the same name as the dead summoner.[175] The oath is

170 See MS JTS Boesky 45 no. 146.

171 *SḤ* 329. The parallel passage in MS JTS Boesky 45 no. 146 reads the same. See also 'The Testament of R. Judah the Pious' (Heb.), no. 9, 12–13.

172 *SḤ* 328, which is incomplete, is to be connected with the subsequent paragraph and is to be understood in this context.

173 Different language is employed in the two cases: in the former, R. Judah writes 'and he cannot go there', whereas in the latter he writes 'he should not go there'.

174 It is unclear why, in this case, going to a Christian grave is allowed. Perhaps the earlier case refers to burial in or around a church, while this one refers only to burial in a non-Jewish cemetery, outside the environs of a church.

175 It was common for thirteenth-century Ashkenazi men, and even more so for women

constructed in such a way as to include all these permutations; it admonishes not only the dead person who appears in the dream but also any dead person who is called by that name against summoning the living.

A similar oath appears in the fourteenth-century Ashkenazi legal compendium of R. Shalom of Neustadt, mentioned earlier. The individual at risk pronounces the following formula: 'I conjure you, in the name of God, not to kill any person, [or take with you] neither man nor woman, neither minor nor adult, neither relative nor stranger.'[176]

The permission to substitute one individual for another with the same name appears in another situation of incipient death recounted in *Sefer ḥasidim*. A certain individual, coming to visit a deathly ill person who shares his name, takes the other's sickness on himself and dies. The sick person, now recovered, fasts for the soul of the dead man annually on the day of his visitation.[177] Because this belief was current, it was considered a sin to send a child or pupil to the home of an ill person with the same name, and it was permissible for that child or pupil to disobey the commands of his superior and not enter, since it was a matter of life and death.[178] Similarly, someone bearing the same name as one who has been decreed from above to die was considered certain to die as well.[179]

Substitution other than by name occurs in a different tale in *Sefer ḥasidim*. The angel of death, bidden by God to kill a newly married man, snatches the wrong person; instead of a teacher, he takes his student, who got married on the same day as his master. The young man then appears in a dream to his mother and explains the circumstances leading up to his wrongful death. The teacher, living on in place of the student, is given the remaining years that the other would have lived.[180] In this tale, a shared situation (the men get married on the same day) rather than a common name allows the substitution of one individual for the other, both in death and in life: the young man dies instead of his teacher, and the teacher receives the remaining lifespan of his student.

(who often were not given sacred Hebrew names), to have the same vernacular names as those used by the local Christian population. This tendency increased as the Middle Ages progressed. See Assaf, 'The Language of Names', 151–3, 157.

[176] *Hilkhot uminhagei rabenu shalom minoyshtat*, 159–60 no. 544, quoted in Schur, 'When the Grave Was Searched', 183.

[177] The reason offered by R. Judah for this meritorious practice is that, since the living person died in place of the dying man, it is only right for the now living man to provide atonement on behalf of the dead person's soul. *SḤ* 1552.

[178] *SḤ* 1551. R. Judah reports that such a case indeed occurred and the ruling favoured the child.

[179] *SḤ* 1871.

[180] *SḤ* 375.

While name determinism plays a role in *Sefer ḥasidim*,[181] it is also possible to view these substitutions as having an affinity with those in the Christian exempla discussed above. What makes the substitutions recounted in *Sefer ḥasidim* possible is the fact that a relationship exists between the two parties—either a common name or a shared identity. Relationships tie the substitutes in Caesarius's ghost stories together as well: Conrad, who replaces Lambert, sits opposite him in the choir, and Hermann, the second dean of Cologne, dies instead of Erwin, who is its canon. Underlying both sets of substitution is the shared premise that when death calls, someone must answer.

Not only must the living resist a call to death; they are also forbidden to cause the dead to summon them. *Sefer ḥasidim* recounts how one woman wished to rid herself of her many children in order to marry a certain man. After bringing them into the proximity of the dead, she placed her children's hands upon the hands of several of the bodies, whereupon the dead called after them and they died.[182] Another passage describes this act of hand-holding between the living and the dead as a suicidal gesture and one which is strictly forbidden by the Torah.[183] Those who are devastated by the death of a loved one are admonished not to instigate a summons to death. *Sefer ḥasidim* instructs: 'one may not say to the dead person that he should draw him after him'.[184] Even one who performs an act that suggests death can bring death upon himself: someone who extinguishes a candle shortens his own life.[185]

Kissing the dead is another example of bodily contact between the living and the dead that has the power to initiate a summons on the part of the dead. Parents whose child has died are sternly warned not to kiss the body, for this will shorten the lifespan of one's remaining children.[186] Similarly,

181 According to *Sefer ḥasidim*, the name of a person determines his fate—how long he will live, whether he will sire offspring, his personality traits, even how successful he will be in Torah learning, the performance of good deeds, and his level of fear of God. See *SḤ* 363, 364. One can avert a bad fate by changing one's name (*SḤ* 365, 368) or place of residence (*SḤ* 366, 367, 368), since place is as determinant of one's fate as name is. On the confluence of a person's name and fate, see Trachtenberg, *Jewish Magic and Superstition*, 78–9.

182 *SḤ* 173. It is interesting to note that the laying of hands upon hands, which here leads to death, is an inversion of the vivifying miracles of the prophets—Elijah in 1 Kgs 17: 21–2 and Elisha in 2 Kgs 4: 32–5.

183 *SḤ* 327, p. 103, quoting Gen. 9: 5.

184 Ibid.

185 The soul of man is compared to the flame of a candle in Prov. 20: 27 (*SḤ* 1781). A similar belief existed among Germanic peoples: a lone lamp extinguished in a house served as a death omen. See Lecouteux, *Fantômes et revenants*, 161. See also *SḤ* 1549, where R. Judah forbids the dissemination of the method of determining the time of one's own death.

186 *SḤ* 327, p. 103.

the 'Testament of R. Judah the Pious' says that 'A person must not kiss one of his sons when he dies, because not even one [of his sons] will survive.'[187] R. Yeruham b. Meshulam records this teaching in the name of R. Judah himself.[188] And R. Eleazar of Worms forbids his readers to kiss the dead as such a practice places the remaining family in danger.[189] Similarly, one who sees a dead person kiss him in a dream is being notified that a close friend or loved one will soon die.[190]

In *Sefer ḥasidim*, attitudes towards kissing the dead, like those to live encounters with them, diverge significantly from those found in rabbinic sources. On the basis of the biblical model of Joseph kissing his dead father Jacob,[191] rabbinic opinion in the Midrash and Talmud validates the practice,[192] and even mandates it at times.[193] Additionally, geonic opinion, as well as southern French and Spanish exegetical and Italian halakhic sources ranging from the eleventh to the fifteenth centuries, reinforce the positive attitude displayed by the rabbis towards kissing the dead.[194] By contrast, there exists in twelfth- to thirteenth-century Ashkenaz a 'widespread prohibition' against kissing the dead, as evident from sources within the Pietist circle.[195] R. Judah the Pious warns against such an act and Eleazar of Worms offers a reinterpretation of the biblical passage in order to exonerate Joseph from any culpability for kissing his dead father.[196]

What could have caused this change in custom, particularly in the milieu of medieval Ashkenaz? When one places the Pietists' warnings against kissing the dead in the context of the Germano-Christian belief in the dangerous dead, many aspects of the strictures they formulate become clear. While it is certainly true that both R. Judah and Eleazar of Worms conceive of the kiss as a transfer from the spirit of one individual to that of another, so that by kissing the dead the individual incorporates the spirit of death within himself,[197] it is also possible that fear of initiating a summons

[187] 'The Testament of R. Judah the Pious' (Heb.), no. 4, p. 11.

[188] Yeruham b. Meshulam, *Sefer adam veḥavah, ḥelek ḥavah*, sec. 28, cited in Kosman, 'Kissing the Dead' (Heb.), 491–2.

[189] Ibid.

[190] See Eleazar of Worms, *Sefer ḥokhmat hanefesh*, 13*a*.

[191] Gen. 50: 1.

[192] See *Midrash bereshit rabah* 65 (ed. Theodor and Albeck, ii. 740) for Joseph's kiss. JT *Shab.* 2: 7, 5*b* and *Pesikta derav kahana, Divrei yirmiyahu*, 9 cite other examples of holy personages kissing the dead without incurring rabbinic disapproval. For the full range of rabbinic sources on the matter, see Kosman, 'Kissing the Dead' (Heb.), 483–6; see also Horowitz, 'Regarding Kissing the Dead' (Heb.).

[193] According to *Midrash bereshit rabati* (ed. Albeck, 257), Joseph's example teaches that one is obligated to kiss one's loved ones on their departure from this world.

[194] Kosman, 'Kissing the Dead' (Heb.), 485–9.

[195] Ibid. 492.

[196] Ibid. 491–4. R. Eleazar's reinterpretation is based on the talmudic statement in *Ta'an.* 5*b*, 'Our patriarch Jacob did not die.'

[197] Kosman, 'Kissing the Dead' (Heb.), 498–9.

to death, an act that *Sefer ḥasidim* prohibits, may be a prime factor in the strictures against kissing the dead. The prohibition on parents kissing a dead child appears together with the prohibition to ask the deceased to summon the mourner after him and the even stronger stricture against holding hands with the dead.[198] In another reinterpretation of the biblical passage, R. Eleazar confirms the link between kissing the dead and the fear of summoning. He writes in *Sefer ḥokhmat hanefesh* that Joseph kissed his father after his passing because he wished to join him in death.[199] The connection between the two is made explicit in the following statement, cited in the name of R. Eleazar of Worms: 'It is a danger to kiss the dead, for when he kisses him, the dead loves him and brings him to his world . . . and anyone who kisses his son after he dies, it is certain that all his sons will die during his lifetime.'[200] This somewhat puzzling consequence of kissing the dead becomes comprehensible only when one views it against the backdrop of the summoning power of the dead.[201] The Icelandic sagas repeatedly report how the appearance of a dead person in a dream puts the entire family at risk, not merely the one to whom the deceased appears. Kissing the dead, therefore, may lead to the summoning of not necessarily the one who kissed, but of anyone in his intimate family circle. Additionally, as evidenced in both the exempla literature and *Sefer ḥasidim*, individuals who have some aspect of their identity in common often substitute for each other in death; thus it is logical that a parent kissing a dead child, thereby initiating a summons to death, could endanger the lives of his or her other children.

Belief in the summoning power of the dead as part of an ancient Germanic belief in the dangerous dead might also explain why exegetes and halakhists from other milieus, where such pre-Christian beliefs were not as strongly maintained, might have retained the rabbis' more positive stance towards kissing the dead, while those reared in medieval Germany did

198 *SḤ* 327, p. 103. 'And how much more so' (*vekol sheken*) is the language used regarding holding hands with the dead according to several of the manuscripts in the Princeton database.

199 Kosman, 'Kissing the Dead' (Heb.), 494.

200 *Perush rabenu efrayim b"r shimshon ugedolei ashkenaz hakadmonim al hatorah*, 168, s.v. *vayipol*, quoted in Kosman, 'Kissing the Dead' (Heb.), 493. R. Eleazar's explanation that kissing the dead arouses their love and awakens a desire in them to have the living join them is highly original; it stands in opposition to a talmudic account in which Samuel's father, hearing of his son's imminent death, is saddened by the news. See BT *Ber.* 18*b*.

201 Kosman describes how the seventeenth-century Italian author of a Jewish funerary manual, R. Aaron Berakhyah of Modena, struggles to explain the phenomenon in his *Ma'avar yabok*. See 'Kissing the Dead' (Heb.), 500–1.

not. Having absorbed strongly rooted local notions, the Pietists spoke out against what, to them, was a potentially murderous action.

Beyond prohibiting the active initiation of a summons to death, the Pietists also wanted to prevent acts that might unintentionally lead to such a summons. The author of the 'Testament of R. Judah the Pious' states that one ought not to dig a grave and leave it open, unless someone is to be buried in it on the same day. Ignoring this stricture means that 'in a few days [up until sixteen days later],[202] one resident of the city will die'.[203] The author is clear about the link between cause and effect: an open grave is an open invitation to death. As with one who kisses the dead, the open grave is not necessarily a summons to the person who performs the act or fails to prevent it; anyone in the city could be at risk. Possibly as a result of the same belief, *Sefer ḥasidim* reports that a man who wished to be buried in the cemetery away from the rest of the dead suffered the loss of his children in quick succession soon after.[204] The empty space surrounding his grave became an open invitation to summon his family members to join him in death. Their new graves filled the gap in the cemetery.[205]

According to the 'Testament', walking in front of a body as it is being carried out of the house is also a life-threatening action.[206] A similar rationale may be at work here. The act of preceding the dead body as it leaves the domain of the living is a form of initiating a summons to death; one who leads the dead person joins him. By contrast, in the rabbinic period walking in front of the deceased was confirmed practice: the Talmud records an opinion that women always walked in front of the bier.[207] Other sources mention a divergence of custom: in the north of the Land of Israel, the men walked in front of the bier and the women walked behind it, while in the south the custom was for the women to walk in front and the men behind.[208] The only cautionary words found in the Talmud warn one not to stand in front of women when they return from having been in the presence of a dead body.[209]

[202] The parenthetical addition is supplied by Reuven Margaliot and is based on the Munich manuscript. See 'The Testament of R. Judah the Pious' (Heb.), 11 n. 4.

[203] Ibid., no. 2, pp. 10–11. Evidence of this concern is found in the early modern period, as seen in the words of the author of *Ma'avar yabok*: 'A man ought not to open the mouth of the earth, unless he immediately stops it up with a stone.' See Bar-Levav, 'A Separate Place' (Heb.), 12.

[204] *SḤ* 1538.

[205] Bar-Levav interprets the event in this fashion; see 'A Separate Place' (Heb.), 12–13.

[206] 'The Testament of R. Judah the Pious' (Heb.), no. 8, p. 12.

[207] BT *San.* 20*a*.

[208] N. Rubin, *The End of Life* (Heb.), 132.

[209] BT *Ber.* 51*a*.

As documented by the Pietists, unintentional acts pose as much danger as intentional ones. The author of the 'Testament' warns those who ritually prepare the body for burial not to overturn the board upon which it was prepared,[210] 'for there is danger in this matter lest someone die within three days'.[211] A variant precept in another manuscript adds that in those communities that do not have their own cemeteries, care should be taken not to overturn the board within three days of its use for ritual preparation, 'for if, God forbid, they overturn the board within three days, a great man in the city will die that year'.[212] Overturning the board could intimate that it is ready to receive another corpse—the unintentional provocation of a summons to death.[213] The precise time periods set (three days, within the year), along with the specification of distinct individuals (a great man of the city), suggest the certainty with which the Pietists spoke in this regard. Such exactitude also reveals the popular nature of the belief in the inherent danger of these actions. Since no laws or guidelines regulating this conduct exist anywhere in halakhic or midrashic sources of the time, one can assume that these 'rules', relating highly specific consequences to individuals, were popularly held.[214]

Not only is an untimely summons to death an undesirable phenomenon, involvement in death in general is portrayed as something to be greatly feared. Several repeated passages in *Sefer ḥasidim* describe the popular practice of avoiding involvement with anything death-related. The sewing of shrouds for the dead and of garments of mourning is described as an occupation that no one wishes to engage in. The book relates the following poignant story. A father of many daughters apprentices them in the art of weaving. All but one engage in the manufacture of garments or tapestries for the living to don or use at times of celebration, while to one daughter the task of producing shrouds for the dead and garments of mourning is relegated. All except that daughter find husbands. The unmarried girl complains to her father that the reason for her predicament is directly related to the task he had assigned to her; since she is involved in an occupation 'from which all distance themselves', no one wishes to marry her.

210 On the use of planks in actual cases of ritual preparation for burial, see Schur, 'The Care for the Dead', 41–2.

211 'The Testament of R. Judah the Pious' (Heb.), no. 6, p. 12.

212 Ibid., n. 11, based on the Munich manuscript.

213 Trachtenberg, *Jewish Magic and Superstition*, 175–6, interprets the warning not to overturn the board in a different light: such an act would 'incite the ire of the deceased'. If he is correct then this stricture is a manifestation of belief in the vengeance of the dead.

214 See ibid. 176.

Her father comforts her, saying that he will extol her virtues to all so that she can find a husband.[215]

Similarly, *Sefer ḥasidim* reports that the study of those tractates of talmudic law that contain death-related material, such as *Mo'ed katan*, is so neglected as to be categorized as a *met mitsvah*; like an abandoned body, no one wishes to be involved with it.[216] This was a relatively new phenomenon, even in Ashkenaz; in the early Ashkenazi period, the tenth to eleventh centuries, there was seemingly no aversion to such study.[217] Danger is the reason cited in *Sefer ḥasidim* for abandonment of the study of these areas of law: people are afraid of the sickness and death that may result from it. The following passage illustrates this:

> And now why do they say that it [study of *Mo'ed katan*] is a danger? Because it is written, 'And do not scorn his rebuke' [Prov. 3: 11]. And he rushes and is not scrupulous [to study it] as in the case of other tractates. And also because every matter that [is related to it] is a danger.
>
> And I also heard [that] regarding two matters the Angel of Death is close by to listen: [regarding] one who expounds [the topic of] the Heavenly Chariot and [one who expounds] *Mo'ed katan*. For [upon hearing] this, the Angel of Death responds, 'Yes. Yes.' [We see this regarding the topic of the] Heavenly Chariot, as [in] the story of Rabban Yohanan ben Zakai and R. Eleazar ben Arakh—that if he does not have proper intent, [he is liable] to be punished by him [the Angel of Death]. So, too, with regard to tractate *Mo'ed katan*, since it is appointed over [the topic of] death. Therefore, he should toil over it [the tractate] with all his heart to exert [himself], devoid of any levity.[218]

R. Judah cites two reasons for the danger involved in studying the tractate: first, those who do study it 'rush' through it, and 'unscrupulous' study of certain topics provokes death. Second, 'every matter' relating to it is 'a danger'. He offers talmudic support for his first contention by comparing the study of *Mo'ed katan* to study of the Heavenly Chariot as described in a

[215] *SḤ* 1 and 588. On the role of women in sewing shrouds, see Toch, 'The Economic Activities of German Jews', 49 n. 107.

[216] *SḤ* 1 and 588. See also nos. 586, 587. Apart from tractate *Mo'ed katan*, *Sefer ḥasidim* labels the neglected *seder Kedoshim* as a *met mitsvah*. Unlike *Mo'ed katan*, study of which is avoided out of fear, *Kedoshim* is neglected because the laws it treats are not applicable in the post-Temple era (see *SḤ* 1, p. 2). According to Kanarfogel, 'The Scope of Talmudic Commentary in Europe', 43–52, *seder Kedoshim* was studied by tosafists in northern France. The neglect may have been an exclusively German phenomenon.

[217] See Schremer, 'Regarding the Commentaries on Tractate *Mo'ed Katan* Attributed to Rashi' (Heb.). Schremer argues that *perush* Rashi on tractate *Mo'ed katan* is really *perush* Magentsa. Although his implication is that Rashi did not author a commentary on that tractate, it is still an early Ashkenazi *perush*.

[218] *SḤ* 1 and 588.

passage about the *tana'im* R. Yohanan ben Zakai and R. Eleazar ben Arakh found in *Ḥagigah* 14*b*.[219] He interprets this proof text in a novel way, revealing the strong link that he perceives between the dead and danger. The text is an enthusiastic description of the joy felt in heaven on hearing two spiritual giants engage in study of the Heavenly Chariot. The Divine Presence itself descends in the form of a fire that surrounds all the trees in the field, and the trees simultaneously burst forth in a song of praise to God. In response, an 'angel from the fire' joins in, saying 'Yes. Yes.' The *Tosafot* records the variant reading which R. Judah must have had—'Angel of Death'—but states that the correct reading is 'angel from the fire'.[220] Even if R. Judah did possess the variant reading, the context of the passage suggests a mood of exultation, not of retribution; neither the angel nor the fire harms anyone or anything. His interpretation thus defies the plain meaning of the talmudic text. For him, the mere presence of the Angel of Death in the midst of a learned discussion of a sensitive topic—one which involves unravelling the mysteries of the godhead—automatically signals danger of death, regardless of the fact that the text indicates the contrary, that God is clearly pleased with the rabbis' discussion.

R. Judah's forced reading of the passage in *Ḥagigah* indicates that he strongly identifies with the idea he feels the text espouses. In any discussion of the interpretation of traditional literature, there is always the question of which elements from that literature are rote and which are seriously embraced by an author. The fact that R. Judah reinterprets the talmudic passage attests to the fact that he is aware that the sacred literature conflicts with his view. His instinctive association of death with danger overrides any and all legitimate interpretations of the text, even by Pietist standards.

R. Judah then applies his reinterpretation of the events in *Ḥagigah* to the study of *Mo'ed katan*: if death results from study of the Heavenly Chariot conducted improperly (without proper intent) then it will also result from improper study of a death-related tractate such as *Mo'ed katan*. This logical extension from study of one tractate to another, however, lacks any rabbinic support. Whereas the study of *Ḥagigah* is known to be a guarded topic, reserved only for those spiritually worthy and emotionally fit,[221] study of *Mo'ed katan* is not. Why do people 'rush' irreverently through this

219 A parallel passage exists in JT *Ḥag.* 9*a*.

220 See *Tosafot*, *Ḥag.* 14*b*, s.v. *ne'eneh*.

221 On that very same page of the Talmud, on both *Ḥag.* 14*b* and JT *Ḥag.* 9*a*, a *tosefta* is cited which recounts a fateful incident: four great rabbis entered *pardes* (here an acronym and metaphor for immersion in the study of the mysteries of the Godhead that led to an actual mystical ascent), and of the four, only R. Akiva emerged unscathed. One died, a second became mad, and a third became an apostate.

tractate? R. Judah's second reason suggests the answer: 'every matter that [is related to it] is a danger'. Since it is believed that voluntarily involving oneself in death-related matters suggests a willingness to die, those who study the tractate voluntarily avoid doing so intensively. It is an instinct for danger, once again, rather than any textual basis, that underlies R. Judah's contention, and his instinct resonated within a culture in which the summoning power of the dead was strongly rooted and vigorously maintained.

Beliefs about the dead circulating in Germany in medieval times differed vastly from those held by the rabbis of the Talmud. In rabbinic times, women were hired as professional wailers and mourners, thereby elongating the time spent in proximity of the dead.[222] The Mishnah and Talmud mention the practice several times, without recording any trace of hesitancy on the part of women to engage in it.[223] Furthermore, it is self-evident that the rabbis did not neglect the study of any tractate which they themselves had helped develop.

By contrast, Germanic Jewry of the late twelfth and early thirteenth centuries absorbed an instinctive fear of the dangerous powers of the dead from the Germano-Christian environment in which they lived, and extended it to all matters related to death. Women of this culture avoided exposure to the accoutrements of the dead, while its scholars purposefully neglected study of the subject. By recording his beliefs as well as popular customs relating to death in *Sefer ḥasidim*, R. Judah disseminated these ideas more widely and strengthened their hold on the Germanic Jewry of his time at all levels of society, in both popular and elite circles. Medieval Jews had indeed travelled far since rabbinic times.

Conclusion

In the Talmud the holy dead appear bodily to the living. Elijah the prophet returns to instruct, converse with, and protect the rabbis and other pious men, and appears to his subjects in any place, without prompting. R. Judah the Prince visits his family weekly after he dies. The ordinary dead, however, do not appear to the living of their own accord; the living must seek them out, either in the cemetery or in the 'courtyard of death'. With regard to both the holy and the ordinary dead, neither their voice nor their bodily presence in the midst of the living elicits any fear.

In *Sefer ḥasidim*, by contrast, the holy dead make no appearance at all.

222 N. Rubin, *The End of Life* (Heb.), 194.

223 Mishnah *Ket.* 4: 4; JT *Ber.* 3: 1, 5*d*; BT *San.* 47*a*, *MK* 28*b*.

Despite the fact that the exempla literature is replete with visions of Mary, Jesus, and the saints, who appear to individual members of the Christian faithful for a variety of purposes,[224] *Sefer ḥasidim* does not contain any visions or dreams of the holy dead, such as the patriarchs, matriarchs, or Moses, for any purpose whatsoever. Haym Soloveitchik has documented the noticeable absence of these archetypal figures in the work.[225] Rather, it is the ordinary dead who seek out the living and appear to them in any place. Fear is the dominant emotion expressed by the living, who anticipate a violent encounter with the dead.

The tremendous disparity between the Talmud and Pietist accounts in terms of the emotional response elicited by the returning dead can be understood only in the light of the latter's reflection of a firmly rooted and strongly held belief in pre-Christian notions of the dangerous dead. *Sefer ḥasidim* and other Pietist sources reveal evidence of German Jewish belief in the violence, vengeance, and summoning power of the dead. These sources prescribe methods of protection against harm from ghosts, exhumation of bodies in order to stop the spread of disease, and various apotropaic funeral practices which parallel other, similar methods and practices extant in the Germano-Christian environment.

Rather than being only at the 'heart of pietistic traditions',[226] notions of the corporeal return of the harmful dead were held beyond the small circle of Pietists, among both elite and popular groups. As we have seen, stories in *Sefer ḥasidim* express fear of the violent dead and warn against tampering with graves and even with the remnants of coffins. Customs involving quick burial, opening graves during times of epidemic, and stuffing up the mouths of dangerous cadavers all testify to the widespread nature of the belief. Both the learned author of the addition to the Ashkenazi legal customary, the *Maḥzor vitry*, and a popular tale recounted in *Sefer ḥasidim* describe the same phenomenon—a mass assemblage of the dead in synagogues at night, an event that portends death in both cases. Moreover, there is testimony in fourteenth-century Austrian and German Jewish legal sources of oaths administered by the rabbinic elite to the dead at funerals, with grave sanctions attached. The dead are adjured not to make bodily reappearances until the time of the resurrection, nor to return and inflict

224 Although examples are too numerous to cite, see e.g. Caesarius of Heisterbach, *Dialogue*, book 7, 'On the Blessed Virgin Mary'.

225 Soloveitchik, 'The Midrash, *Sefer Ḥasidim* and the Changing Face of God', 167. A possible explanation for this absence is bound up with a discussion of the role that prayer for the dead plays in *Sefer ḥasidim*—a topic I discuss in Chapters 7 and 8 below.

226 Schur, 'The Care for the Dead in Medieval Ashkenaz', 102.

harm upon the living. So powerful is the fear of the dead that Pietist sources attest to a deliberate avoidance of anything death-related within contemporary Ashkenaz.

Scholars argue that by the thirteenth century belief in the 'real' dangerous dead existed only on the peripheries of western Europe.[227] In tales originating in Yorkshire and Brittany, one still finds ghosts who emerge from their graves, violently assault the living, and terrify the local townspeople. In the Ariège region, the invisible yet corporeal dead of Montaillou are everywhere: 'one risked running into them if, while walking, one stuck one's arms or legs out too quickly'.[228] It is true that the violence of the dead and the corporeal nature of the ghosts in *Sefer ḥasidim*, seen at times in indirect accounts and indirect assaults in dreams rather than in waking visions, are greatly reduced versions of the original model of the Icelandic *draugar*, and the language of certain ghost tales in the work is similar to that found in the most standardized tale characteristic of the mendicants. Yet alongside these domesticated ghosts there exist ghosts of a different order: ones that are endowed with a body, who leave the grave to have a face-to-face encounter with the living, and who inspire real terror in the hearts of men. Let us recall one fourteenth-century Ashkenazi source that records R. Judah's belief in a 'double-body' phenomenon that is strikingly similar to that of the Germanic corporeal ghost and makes bodily reanimation of the corpse possible. In light of this, *Sefer ḥasidim* testifies that within a peripheral subculture of thirteenth-century Germany a genuine fear of the pre-Christian *draugar* lived on. Such a trenchant fear of the harmful powers of the dead is absent from rabbinic literature; it is very much alive, however, in *Sefer ḥasidim*.

227 Schmitt, *Ghosts in the Middle Ages*, 140–8.

228 Ibid. 141.

CHAPTER TWO

THE SINFUL DEAD

IN THE ELEVENTH CHAPTER of tractate *Sanhedrin*, the Talmud cites a tannaitic teaching that lists various groups of sinners who are denied resurrection and/or who have forfeited their portion in the World to Come. One such group is the assembly of Korah.[1] Concerning their posthumous punishment, the Talmud writes:

Rava gave the following exposition: What is meant by the verse, 'But if the Lord make a new thing, and the Earth open her mouth?'[2] Moses said to the Holy One, blessed be He, 'If Gehenna has already been created, it is good; if not, let the Lord create it.' Now, in respect to what? If actually to create it, doesn't Scripture say 'there is no new thing under the sun'?[3] Rather, [he prayed] that its mouth should be brought up [to the spot where Korah and his followers were standing]. [But what about] 'The children of Korah did not die'?[4] A *tana* taught: It has been said on the authority of our Master: A place was set apart for them in Gehenna where they sat and sang praises [to God].

Rabah b. Bar Hanah said: I was proceeding on my travels when an Arab merchant said to me, 'Come and I will show you where the men who were swallowed up of [the assembly of] Korah are.' I went and saw two cracks from which smoke came out. Thereupon he took a piece of clipped wool, soaked it in water, attached it to the point of his spear, and passed it over there, and it was singed. He said to me, 'Listen to what you are about to hear.' And I heard them saying thus: 'Moses and his Torah are true, but they [the men of Korah's assembly] are liars.' The Arab then said to me, 'Every thirty days, Gehenna causes them to turn back [here] like meat in a pot, and they say thus: 'Moses and his Torah are true, but they are liars.'[5]

Sefer ḥasidim also records an account of the posthumous punishment of a group of sinners. It tells the following narrative:

It once happened that a man was riding alone at night, and the moon was shining that night. He was riding in the desert and behold there was a great army of

[1] The rebellion of Korah and his assembly is recounted in Num. 16.

[2] Num. 16: 30.

[3] Eccles. 1: 9.

[4] Num. 26: 11.

[5] BT *San.* 110*a*–*b*. A parallel text exists in *BB* 74*a*.

wagons and more wagons. On the wagons, people were sitting and those pulling the wagons were people. And he wondered what they were doing. When he approached them, he recognized some of them [and these were people] that had already died. He said to them, 'What is this [that you are doing], that you are pulling the wagons all night and some of you are on the wagons?' They said to him, 'Because of our sins; when we were alive in that world, we were wont to sport with women and virgins/young girls,[6] and now we must pull the wagon until we are [so] tired and weary that we are unable to pull it any longer. [Then] those who are on top of the wagon descend and we ascend and rest, and we ride until they are weary. And afterwards these [ascend and ride].'[7]

According to the exposition in the Talmud, Gehenna is the locus of punishment for the men of Korah's assembly. Both the manner of their death as well as the eyewitness account of Rabah b. Bar Hanah testify that it is a subterranean place: the earth swallows up the rebels, and the rabbi sees smoke and hears voices emanating from cracks in the ground. Even the sons of Korah, who, Scripture says, did not die, are positioned in a subterranean chamber of Gehenna, albeit above its incendiary fire.[8]

Rather than burning in the everlasting fire of the subterranean Gehenna, the dead sinners of the Pietist account continuously ride upon and pull wagons on Earth. The living man on horseback encounters 'the great army of wagons' of the dead riding on the same plain where he is—a wasteland (*midbar*). Instead of merely hearing the voices of the dead as Rabah b. Bar Hanah does, the anonymous man of the Pietist narrative is able to see the physical bodies of the dead riding, pulling, ascending, and descending. More than a passive listener, he conducts an engaging conversation with the dead; he asks, they answer. Whereas fire consumes the sinners of Korah's assembly, the sinners in *Sefer ḥasidim* are subject to a different form of posthumous punishment—they must exert themselves physically by pulling heavily loaded wagons in a Sisyphean manner.

Where, in midrashic and talmudic sources, do we find dead sinners wandering and toiling on Earth as punishment for a life of sin? Clearly, we have strayed far from the rabbinic model of a subterranean Gehenna of fire. In *Sefer ḥasidim*, we encounter a Hebrew version of Hellequin's Hunt—a well-known medieval ghost tale that is predicated upon an ancient Ger-

[6] Whereas some manuscripts (MS Parma H 3280 and MS JTS Boesky 45 no. 51) and printed editions (Bologna, no. 169) record Wistinetzky's reading of 'women and virgins/young girls' (*nashim uvetulot*), others (MS JTS 2499 no. 56 and MS Vatican ebr. 285 no. 56) have the variant 'virgin women' (*nashim betulot*).

[7] *SḤ* 63.

[8] See Rashi on BT *Meg.* 14*a*, s.v. *nitbatser lahem*. According to BT *Sot.* 10*b*, Gehenna is composed of seven levels.

manic belief in the dangerous dead, appropriated by Christianity to refer to the sinful dead.

Loci of Punishment of the Dead in Rabbinic and Post-Rabbinic Sources

Apart from the narrative about the assembly of Korah, numerous other talmudic statements confirm the subterranean location of Gehenna. A passage in tractate *Nedarim* speaks of Gehenna's mouth, while *Eruvin* enumerates three openings of Gehenna on Earth—in the desert, on the sea floor, and in the valley of Gei ben Hinom in Jerusalem.[9] In another passage, the rabbis assert that the intense heat and smoke emanating from the underground hot springs of Tiberias make it a suitable opening to Gehenna.[10] Several of the various scriptural names attributed to Gehenna reflect its underground position—*she'ol* (grave), *be'er shaḥat* (well of destruction), and *bor sha'on* (pit of raging waters).[11] According to rabbinic terminology, one descends (*yored*) or falls into (*nofel be-*) Gehenna.[12]

There is a lone source in the Babylonian Talmud, *Tamid* 32*b*, which posits that Gehenna is above the firmament or beyond the mountains of darkness. Two sources in the Jerusalem Talmud do not confirm Gehenna as being under the ground.[13] However, the weight of the talmudic evidence clearly points to a subterranean locus. One passage, which highlights the enormity of Gehenna, uses an analogy that substantiates its subterranean position: 'The entire world is like the cover of a pot for Gehenna.'[14]

While fire is not the only feature of Gehenna,[15] it is its prime characteristic according to the rabbis. Distinct from ordinary fire, which was created upon the conclusion of the first sabbath, the inextinguishable fire of Gehenna came into existence on the second day of Creation.[16] The name itself reflects an association with fire: Gei ben Hinom in Jerusalem is

9 BT *Ned.* 39*b* and *Eruv.* 19*a*; see also *Suk.* 32*b*.

10 *Shab.* 39*a*.

11 *Eruv.* 19*a*.

12 See *Eruv.* 19*a*, *RH* 17*a*, *BM* 58*b*, and *Shab.* 149*b* for examples of 'descending to' Gehenna. *Ber.* 19*a*, *Sot.* 41*b*, and *BM* 59*a* among other sources refer to a sinner 'falling into' Gehenna. *Shab.* 33*a* speaks of the 'deepening of' (*ma'amikin lo*) Gehenna for a sinner, as does *Eruv.* 19*a*.

13 JT *Ḥag.* 2: 2, 77*d*, and *San.* 10: 3, 29*b*. See Lieberman, 'Some Aspects of After Life in Early Rabbinic Literature', 236–8.

14 BT *Pes.* 94*a*. Similarly, according to *Ta'an.* 10*a*, Gehenna has no dimensions.

15 Other features of Gehenna include cold (alternating with heat) and darkness. The former appears in JT *San.* 10: 3 and *Midrash tanḥuma*, 'Re'eh', 13 (ed. Buber, p. 23), while the latter appears only in the Midrash—*Shemot rabah* 14: 2 (ed. Shinan, pp. 262–3) and *Vayikra rabah* 27 (ed. Margaliot, iii. 615).

16 BT *Pes.* 54*a*. See also Tosefta *Ber.* 6 (ed. Zuckermandel, p. 14).

infamous in the Bible as the site where child immolation took place.[17] The fire of Gehenna (*or shel gehinom*) is identified as the posthumous punishment of the wicked in several places in rabbinic literature.[18] The smoke seen rising from the grave of the apostate Elisha ben Avuyah indicates to the rabbis that that sinner now suffers in Gehenna.[19]

Gehenna is not the only locus of posthumous punishment for the wicked. Contrasting the tranquillity of the righteous after death with the disturbance of the wicked, the rabbis speak of the 'zooming and roaming' (*zomemot veholekhot*) of the souls of the wicked.[20] They cite as proof the scriptural verse, 'May my lord's soul be bound up in the bond of life with the Lord, God, and the soul of your enemies He should sling out as from the hollow of a sling',[21] and conclude that the souls of the righteous peacefully rest under the heavenly throne of God, while those of the wicked are hurled ceaselessly through the air.[22] The Talmud in *Gitin* reports that the wicked Titus, the Roman emperor responsible for the destruction of the Second Temple in Jerusalem, is punished after death by having his ashes strewn over the seven seas every day.[23] Despite the rabbis' designation of forms of posthumous punishment outside the realm of Gehenna, the loci of punishment are still not terrestrial ones.

In post-rabbinic literature, the punishment of the sinful dead takes place in a sphere wholly removed from the world of the living. Its discussion of post-mortem punishment assumes the form of tours of Hell; the apocalyptic works of this period (late antiquity until the fifth century) depict various visionary figures who travel with a guide from Earth to both Paradise and Hell.[24] Although the precise location of Gehenna is unclear in these accounts, the details of the narrative used to describe both Gehenna

[17] 2 Kgs 23: 10; Jer. 7: 31, 32: 35.

[18] BT *Ḥag.* 27*a* (parallel passage in *Eruv.* 19*a*), *Ta'an.* 5*a*, JT *San.* 10: 3, and *Midrash bereshit rabah* 6 (ed. Theodor and Albeck, i. 46–7). BT *BM* 85*a* records one rabbi's meritorious act that spared him the fire of Gehenna. BT *Ber.* 15*b* speaks of the cooling down of Gehenna for one who is scrupulous in his pronunciation of the Shema prayer. BT *Eruv.* 19*a*, *Shab.* 33*b*, and *Ḥag.* 15*a*, for example, describe Gehenna as the locus of punishment for the wicked.

[19] BT *Ḥag.* 15*b*.

[20] BT *Shab.* 152*b*. The translation is Lieberman's based on a parallel text in *Avot derabi natan*, 12 (ed. Schechter, p. 50). See Lieberman, 'Some Aspects of After Life in Early Rabbinic Literature', 240 and n. 29. For a full discussion of the meaning of the terms, see pp. 239–40.

[21] 1 Sam. 25: 29.

[22] BT *Shab.* 152*b*. See also *Sifrei* on Num. 139 (*Sifrei devei rav*, ed. Horowitz, p. 185) and *Midrash tanḥuma*, 'Zot haberakhah', 5 (ed. Buber, p. 56).

[23] BT *Git.* 56*b*–57*a*.

[24] For a full description of the literature on tours of Hell in Jewish and Christian apocalyptic sources, see Himmelfarb, *Tours of Hell*.

and Paradise suggest that they are otherworldly habitations. In several accounts, the visionaries travel to Heaven on a chariot—as does Elijah.[25] There they witness God's heavenly throne and the mysteries of Creation from their places on high.[26] Eschatology is woven into these narratives as the heavens reveal the messiah's exalted dwelling.[27]

With parallels in Christian and Muslim apocalyptic writings,[28] the Jewish tours of Hell describe the different levels or compartments of Hell or Gehenna and the fate of the souls therein. The *Book of Enoch*, for example, identifies Gehenna as the locus of punishment of the wicked, but only in the period following the resurrection of the dead. In the meantime, Enoch is privy to a vision of the compartments—described as hollow abodes—in which the sinful dead lie waiting.[29] The *Apocalypse of Joshua b. Levi*, on the other hand, is rich in its description of posthumous punishment. In this text, various groups of the dead occupy different compartments of the seven levels of Gehenna on the basis of the severity of their sins. Hanging is the predominant form of punishment in this and several other apocalyptic tours of Hell, with the sinner hanged by the body part with which he committed the sinful act.[30]

In contrast to rabbinic and post-rabbinic sources, there exist in *Sefer ḥasidim* accounts of sinners who receive their punishment not in Gehenna but on Earth. Instead of the living being escorted to the various domains of the dead, as occurs in the Jewish apocalyptic literature, in Pietist accounts the dead return to the land of the living; they perambulate on Earth in places where the living catch sight of them and engage them in conversation. Neither an everlasting fire nor a punishment by hanging appears in these narratives of dead sinners in *Sefer ḥasidim*.[31] Instead, the dead roam the Earth pulling wagons and carrying heavy loads. What is the origin of such imagery, which is unlike anything recorded in earlier sources?

[25] 2 Kgs 2: 11.

[26] Kohler, *Heaven and Hell in Comparative Religion*, 65, 127.

[27] Ibid. 125.

[28] See Himmelfarb, *Tours of Hell*; Lieberman, 'On Sins and Their Punishment'.

[29] Kohler, *Heaven and Hell in Comparative Religion*, 65–6.

[30] Ibid. 125–6, and Himmelfarb, *Tours of Hell*, 82–91, esp. 87. Himmelfarb notes that hanging as a punishment in Hell figures more in early Jewish and Christian apocalyptic texts than in later ones (*Tours of Hell*, 115).

[31] R. Eleazar of Worms, in *Sefer ḥokhmat hanefesh*, 7*a*, does quote a *midrash* which describes women being hung by their breasts after death as punishment for sin. Such a *midrash* is merely a residue of old material and not representative of the distinctive view of the Pietists.

Terrestrial Post-Mortem Purgation: Pre-Christian Origin and Christian Appropriation

The idea that the dead return to Earth in order to expiate sin originated in the pre-Christian notion of the dangerous dead. Ancient pagan beliefs associated the return of the dead with those who have suffered an abnormal death. Unable to rest in peace, they wander on Earth and reappear among the living. Those individuals who have seen a violent end return to haunt the place where their murder was committed or their suicide took place. The Icelandic sagas repeatedly tell of the 'bad dead'—men who were disagreeable when alive and who become violent and vengeful after their death. They return bodily to harm their families and to terrorize their neighbours. The violence is stopped only by decapitation, cremation, or dismemberment of their corpses.

These beliefs regarding the physical return of the dead and the distinction between bad and good deaths were common property of northern European pagan cultures. Despite the Christianization of the Slavs in the region, pagan beliefs persisted either in protest against or in tandem with Christian beliefs and practices.[32] Western European literature of the high medieval period preserved vestiges of this phenomenon; like the sagas, it supplies records of live, physical encounter with the violent dead. Archaeological evidence gathered from excavations of ancient north German cemeteries as well as Icelandic and Germanic funerary rites confirm the literary documentation; medieval people feared the dangerous dead and took all sorts of preventative measures against their corporeal return.

Christianity appropriated these ancient beliefs by Christianizing their basic elements. The dangerous dead of pagan belief, who were marred by an abnormal death, became, in Christian thought, the dead who were stained with sin. These dead, like their pagan counterparts, were forced to return to Earth, to remain among the living, unable to find peaceful rest in the other world.[33] Instead of seeking violent revenge for their ignominious end, the Christian dead received punishment for their sin. In both cases, the interventions of the living allowed the dead to rest in peace.

[32] See most recently the detailed study of this topic by Caciola, *Afterlives*, 121–6.

[33] This phenomenon is apparent in the Old Irish 'Vision of Adamnán', dating from the eleventh century. Sinful souls, which cannot proceed immediately to the heavenly Jerusalem, 'find a restless and unstable habitation until the coming of the Judgement, on heights and hill-tops, and in marshy places': *Book of the Dun Cow: An Irish Precursor of Dante*, 34–5, quoted in Edwards, 'The Idea of Post Mortem Purgation', 141.

These Christianized beliefs passed into patristic writings and were used to promote the Church's own agenda with regard to its cult of the dead. Gregory the Great's tales of the dead in the Roman baths are symptomatic of just such a transformation.[34] In his *Dialogues*, Gregory recounts two instances of the dead returning to suffer for their sins on Earth.[35] In the first, a deacon named Paschasius appears in the bathhouse to the bishop of Capua and explains that he must remain in this 'place of punishment' and serve as a humble attendant at the baths because of his sin of supporting the 'false' pope, Laurentius. In the second, a former bathhouse administrator continues after his death to prepare baths for the living due to the (unspecified) sins he had committed during his lifetime. Both ghosts obtain the aid of the living; the bishop prays fervently over the next few days on behalf of Paschasius, and a priest who regularly attends the baths offers masses for an entire week on behalf of the bathhouse administrator. The intercession of the living is successful; the two ghosts never appear there again.

In both of Gregory's tales, the dead return bodily to Earth, functioning in the same capacity as the living, yet they are still dead men.[36] They return in order to achieve posthumous purgation, whose specific locus—the Roman bath—has partly to do with its hellish qualities and partly with its purgative dimension: hot and cold treatments alternate and steamy vapours are used,[37] while water acts as a purifying agent.[38] Further, the bath is a place that the characters used to frequent in their life; this is especially true in the case of the second ghost tale. A one-time administrator of the baths, the dead man has been sent back to his former place of work on account of his sins.[39] The suffrages of the Church—prayers for the deceased and the performance of masses on his behalf—of which Gregory the Great was a strong proponent, bring an end to the physical presence of the ghost on Earth. It is the intervention of the Church that ensures the peaceful repose of the sinful dead, in much the same way that the decapitation and dismemberment of corpses puts an end to the violent marauding of the dangerous dead.

34 Lecouteux, *Fantômes et revenants*, 56.

35 Gregory the Great, *Dialogi*, 4: 55, 4: 57, 1–7, quoted in Le Goff, *The Birth of Purgatory*, 92 n. 48.

36 This is in contrast to both the 'false dead' of the high medieval exempla, who revive immediately after death in order to obtain posthumous absolution, make confession, cry out about their fate, or petition the living for aid, and those who are restored to life by God or the Virgin Mary for longer periods in order to do penance, confess their sins, repay a debt, or return stolen goods.

37 Le Goff, *The Birth of Purgatory*, 93.

38 Lecouteux, *Fantômes et revenants*, 55–6.

39 Le Goff, *The Birth of Purgatory*, 92.

As late as the end of the twelfth century, in the writings of the English Augustinian William of Newburgh, one can witness the transformation from pagan belief in the dangerous dead to the Christian notion of terrestrial post-mortem purgation. In his *Historia rerum Anglicorum*, William records a ghost tale in which a man from the county of Buckinghamshire returns bodily from the dead and terrorizes the inhabitants of his village. He also documents the response of various people to the events; the terrified local villagers petition their archdeacon for help, and he, in turn, summons the aid of Bishop Hugh of Lincoln. While some companions of the bishop say that 'such things had happened before in England, and cited frequent examples to make clear that peace could not be restored to the people unless the body of this most miserable man was dug up and burned', the bishop himself disagrees. Instead, he orders that the man's grave be opened, his body inspected, a letter of absolution from sin (which he himself writes) be placed on his chest, and then his grave should be closed once again. After this was done, the body of the dead man was no longer seen to wander, nor was he permitted to inflict trouble or terror on anyone.[40]

The tale contains all the important elements of the pagan belief—a miserable dead man, the trouble and terror he inflicts on familiar people in a familiar locale, the intervention of the living, and the cessation of the violence in the end. The reaction of the churchmen surrounding the bishop (they call for cremation of the corpse) clearly mirrors the ancient precedent for treatment of the dangerous dead. The tale illustrates the Christianization of the pagan belief at an interim stage of development. On the one hand, the bishop sees sin as the cause of the dead man's wanderings on Earth rather than a desire for vengeance, and so absolution from sin, not cremation, will put him to rest. At the same time, his commands to reopen the man's grave, to examine his corpse, and to have a letter of absolution placed on his chest parallel elements associated with pre-Christian beliefs.

As we have seen in the previous chapter, it was common pre-Christian practice to exhume the bodies of the dangerous dead and mutilate their corpses, fix them with stakes, or rebury them far away from the community in order to put an end to their violent excursions. Oftentimes, their bodies were found to be either intact or missing from their graves—both indicated that the deceased had not passed on to the world of the dead but was still physically present on Earth among the living. The placement of the letter of absolution upon the man's chest suggests that it functioned as a token of

[40] William of Newburgh, *Historia rerum Anglicorum*, v. 22, quoted in Watkins, 'Sin, Penance, and Purgatory', 23.

admission to the hereafter, operating in a similar manner to ancient Germanic customs of placing footwear and hoods upon the dead as means of a swift passage to the world of the dead—a topic I discuss in a later chapter. In contrast to the English tale, the dead sinners who return to Earth in Gregory's stories, although physically present in the baths, are non-violent and their graves do not feature in their stories.[41]

Two centuries after the composition of the *Historia rerum Anglicorum*, a monk from Byland abbey, a monastery only a few miles away from Newburgh, described a similar encounter with a corporeal dead person. In this story, all the discrepancies regarding the nature and treatment of the dead have fallen away; all present instinctively assume that the dead person is a repentant sinner who has returned to Earth in order to solicit suffrages from the living.[42]

During the medieval period, the notion that sinners return from the dead in order to expiate their sin on Earth expressed itself in a number of different ways. One of them, a direct outgrowth of Gregory's tales, was to assign to dead sinners an exact locus for their penance—they had to return to the place where they had committed their sin. Here, the connection between the dangerous dead and returning sinners is close: just as he who has suffered a violent end haunts the place of his killing, so too, the sinner returns to the site of his (spiritual) misfortune; the sinner's attempts at atonement in situ replace the victim's desire for vengeance. Although nowhere is the sin of the former bathhouse administrator specified in Gregory's second tale, Jacobus de Voragine in *The Golden Legend* cites just this tale as proof that souls are sometimes punished in the place where they had sinned.[43]

This notion of atonement in the locus of sin forms the central motif of

[41] It is possible to argue that William of Newburgh's tale, which dates from the end of the twelfth century, reflects an earlier stage of development than Gregory the Great's stories written at the close of the sixth century, because of the high degree of Anglo-Saxon influence in northern England (and specifically that of the tradition of the *draugar* of the Icelandic sagas) and its rather late Christianization in the medieval period. See Davidson, 'The Restless Dead', 170–2. Most recently, Carl Watkins has documented the change manifest in ghost tales of the restless dead in this period as part of 'an intensifying desire to reinterpret the returning dead as souls in need of aid' (*History and the Supernatural in Medieval England*, 185).

[42] See Simpson, 'Repentant Soul or Walking Corpse?', 389.

[43] Jacobus de Voragine, *The Golden Legend*, ii. 284. The belief that the dead wander the Earth in order to atone for their sins persisted into the modern era. As late as the seventeenth century, the poor people of Herefordshire in England were employed as 'sinne eaters'; by consuming bread and beer over the corpse, they took upon themselves the sins of the deceased so that he did not need to walk the Earth. See Davis, 'Ghosts, Kin and Progeny', 95.

a ghost tale found in more than one exempla collection. A young girl, a nun named Gertrude, dies at the tender age of 9. Three years later, she is seen by another young nun named Margaret—a girl of about the same age—entering the choir during the service, bowing profoundly before the altar, and resuming her place where she used to stand in the choir. When questioned by sister Margaret as to why she has returned here, sister Gertrude replies that since she sinned by whispering with her during choir, uttering only half-words of prayer, she has been ordered to make atonement in the same place where she sinned. She also warns sister Margaret that 'unless you beware of the same fault, when you die you will suffer the same punishment'. The dead girl is seen repeating her penance four times, after which she is never seen again.[44] As in Gregory's tale and in literary accounts of the dangerous dead, the dead who return to Earth to dwell among the living eventually return to the world of the dead, whence they came.

Hellequin's Hunt: Christian and Pre-Christian Roots

Another form which the notion of terrestrial post-mortem purgation often assumes in the medieval mind is to deny the dead that eventual return.[45] Many different sources refer to sightings of a troop of dead who wander the Earth seemingly endlessly as punishment for sins. Acquiring the name Hellequin's Hunt only at the end of the twelfth century, this army of the dead is first mentioned in the eleventh century by Raoul Glaber in his *Historiae*. Spotted by the priest Frotterius, who is terrified by the spectacle, the assembly of dead men mounted on horseback and outfitted for battle forms an army of the damned, whose members refuse to communicate at all with the living.[46] Similarly, in the first half of the twelfth century, in the province of Worms, the German chronicler Ekkehard reports sighting a troop of knights recently killed in battle who inspire fear within the hearts of the local townspeople. After adjuring the dead in the name of God and crossing himself for protection, one individual speaks to a member of the troop, who reveals the reason for their peregrination—posthumous punishment for sin. The tools of their class—weapons, armour, and horses—with which

[44] Caesarius of Heisterbach, *Dialogue*, 12: 36; Arnold of Liège, *Alphabetum narrationum*, no. 363.

[45] Most recently, Swanson, 'Ghosts and Ghostbusters', has labelled this phenomenon 'individual purgatory' as distinct from 'general purgatory'. While the latter refers to the Purgatory of Christian doctrine, where the majority of Christian souls go after death, the former refers to a place of terrestrial purgation where some souls go to expiate their sins until Judgement Day.

[46] *Rodulfi Glabri, historiarum libri quinque*, quoted in Schmitt, *Ghosts in the Middle Ages*, 102.

they sinned are now the instruments of their torture and are all aflame on their bodies.[47]

At around the same time, the *Liber miraculorum sancta Fidis* tells of the apparition of two different troops of the dead seen by a knight named Walter. The first troop, whose members are dressed as pilgrims and entirely in white, consists of those who completed their penance while alive; not damned and yet not blessed, they must wander on Earth without rest until they reach the state of perfect happiness sometime in the far-off future. The second troop, mounted on horseback and dressed entirely in red as a sign of sinfulness, consists of those who died without having done penance for their sins; they are marching towards eternal damnation in the 'mountain of Hell'—a site located on Earth.[48]

The most extensive contemporaneous account of the troop of the dead is to be found in the writings of the Anglo-Norman monk Orderic Vitalis. In his *Ecclesiastical History*, Orderic documents the sighting of the troop by a young priest named Walkelin, who sees several waves of numerous people passing by and marching on endlessly. First, ordinary men on foot march, then women on horseback, followed by clergy and monks, until finally soldiers pass by. The dead of the various orders are heard lamenting greatly, 'bewailing the excruciating sufferings with which they were tormented for their evil deeds'. Walkelin describes in painful detail these hellish punishments, involving intense heat and cold, an intolerable stench, and burning, which are meted out on an individual basis—many of them tailor-made to fit the crime. A knight who had retained the mill of a poor man as security for a usurious loan is tormented by having to hold a hot iron bar of unbearable weight from the mill in his mouth. Another knight, having used sharp and bright spurs when hurrying to shed blood, is made to wear spurs of fire which weigh him down 'more than if [he] had Mount St Michael on his heels'. While the overwhelming majority of the dead are swept along furiously by the horde, some individuals are able to pull themselves away from the crowd momentarily to speak to Walkelin (one is his own brother Robert), tell their tale of woe, and petition him for aid, until they too are swept away.[49]

The theme of torture meted out to the dead by the tools of their own profession, as seen in Walkelin's tale, also appears in the early twelfth-century *Chronicle of Ekkehard*. At the end of the twelfth century, the

47 Ekkehardus Uraugiensis, *Chronicon Uraugiensis*, quoted in Caciola, *Afterlives*, 157.

48 *Liber miraculorum sancta Fidis*, 269–75, quoted in Schmitt, *Ghosts in the Middle Ages*, 104–6.

49 Orderic Vitalis, *The Ecclesiastical History of England*, ii. 511–20.

Cistercian Herbert of Clairvaux describes in his *Book of Miracles* how a peasant heard an unbearable noise only to behold a troop of dead artisans, each one being tormented by the tools of his trade.[50]

Contemporaries such as Walter Map already noted the pre-Christian roots of the theme of the wandering troop of the dead. It had originated, Map claimed, in a pact enacted between the Celtic King Herla of the Britons and a king of the pygmies (the dead), as a result of which King Herla forever had to bear the 'gift' of the pygmy king. Subject to lamentable unrest, he was condemned to wander eternally on horseback, without stop or stay, along with his band.[51] The term Hellequin and its cognates Herlequin or Helething can be traced back to the ancient Germanic words for army (*Heer*) and the class of arms-bearing free men (*thing*).[52] As a mythical figure, King Herla became known as king of the dead.[53]

The motif of the wild and motley group of dead, oftentimes following a leader, also bears a resemblance to beliefs associated with ancient Germanic gods and goddesses. The god Wodan was known for his wanderings through the sky in his wagon, while the goddesses Holda and Bertha were known to drive about in wagons with the souls of infant children in their host. These goddesses, once gracious, beneficent, and adored, were transformed, with the retreat of paganism, into malignant beings who became the heads of furious hosts or of witches' nightly expeditions.[54] The horde of warriors originated in Wodan's *einherjar*, an army of the dead that incessantly fights, dies, and revives to fight yet again.[55]

Hellequin's Hunt has been directly linked to the activities of the dangerous dead as documented in the Icelandic sagas and in ancient Germanic tales. Those who suffer a violent end return to haunt their former domain, accompanied by a horde of other dead individuals, whose deaths they themselves have caused.[56] One high medieval English ghost tale associates a

[50] *Libri de miraculis cisterciensium monachorum*, quoted in Schmitt, *Ghosts in the Middle Ages*, 115.

[51] Map, *De nugis curialium*, 31. See also Schmitt, *Ghosts in the Middle Ages*, 111–12. Lecouteux, *Fantômes et revenants*, 98–101, connects the Herla myth recounted by Map with ancient Germanic beliefs regarding the dead. The myth centres around a hound dog given as a gift to King Herla by the pygmy king, who orders that neither he nor his men may dismount until the dog that Herla is carrying descends on its own from the horse. When some of Herla's men do dismount, they immediately turn into dust, while Herla is condemned to remain forever on his horse, as the dog never descends. Lecouteux points out that both dogs and horses were commonly found buried in the ancient German burial grounds along with their masters.

[52] Schmitt, *Ghosts in the Middle Ages*, 100.

[53] Ibid. 203.

[54] See Grimm, *Teutonic Mythology*, i. 150–1, 282–3, 288; iii. 932.

[55] Caciola, *Afterlives*, 158.

[56] Lecouteux, *Fantômes et revenants*, 98–101; Caciola, *Afterlives*, 159.

troop of the dead with infants who have died prematurely and without baptism—another group of individuals who have met a disagreeable end. These infants are part of a wild and motley group of dead people mounted on horseback, sinners who have returned to wander the Earth in search of atonement.[57]

In some accounts of Hellequin's Hunt, certain pagan elements associated with the dangerous dead still remain. The individual who sees the horde is violently assaulted or threatened by the dead, or falls deathly ill soon after their appearance. In the account of Orderic Vitalis, for example, all three elements are present: the priest Walkelin, who sees the troop, is attacked by a certain dead knight named William of Glos, who separates himself from the troop. Filled with rage, William seizes him by the throat and drags him on the ground, uttering terrible imprecations. Walkelin is violently threatened by the leader of the troop, who is a man of enormous stature armed with a massive club, and by three dead knights who attempt to seize him. Finally, he becomes seriously ill after the encounter.[58] The giant leader of the troop is a standard mythical character; beings of unusual size, whether oversized or dwarfed, are common in pagan lore and represent deceased ancestors.[59] The weapon of choice, the armed club, is reminiscent of the ancient Briton king Arthur, a pre-Christian figure who assumed the role of leader of the dead.[60]

The motif of danger apparent in Orderic's narrative is also found in a thirteenth-century tale of the Hunt recorded by the Cistercian Helinand of Froidmont. Helinand's uncle dies within fifteen days of having seen in a vision a troop of dead souls and demons carrying heavy weapons and riding on horseback through the forest, and his soul is taken away by evil spirits.[61] Like the dangerous dead, those in the Hunt narratives are corporeal and violent, and the Divine name is often invoked to neutralize their harmful actions.[62]

57 James, 'Twelve Medieval Ghost Stories', 421. See also Lecouteux, *Fantômes et revenants*, 116–17, and Schmitt, *Ghosts in the Middle Ages*, 143–4.

58 See Orderic Vitalis, *The Ecclesiastical History of England*, ii. 517, 512, 516, 519. Another pagan element in the account is the appearance of the army of the dead on 1 January, a day associated with appearances and hauntings of the dead in the Icelandic sagas and among ancient Germanic peoples. See Lecouteux, *Fantômes et revenants*, 143; Grimm, *Teutonic Mythology*, iii. 933.

59 Caciola, *Afterlives*, 170–2.

60 Ibid. 177–8.

61 See Helinand of Froidmont, *De cognitione sua*, chs. 10–13, quoted in Schmitt, *Ghosts in the Middle Ages*, 114. Here again, the association of demons with the dangerous dead appears. See pp. 21–2 and 40–1 above.

62 The chronicles of the bishops of Mans record the appearance of a spirit who haunts the house of a provost, asking his relatives to help him perform suffrages, which will detach him

The effects of Christianization are everywhere apparent in the accounts as the horde of dangerous returning dead is transformed into an army of sinners sentenced to march endlessly on Earth as punishment for their sins. The violence which once accompanied encounters with the troop of the dead becomes muted and is transformed into a feeling of terror which the troop's appearance evokes. The element of corporeality once present in these encounters is transposed onto the various penances which the sinners must assume; they are described as carrying material objects of great weight on their heads, shoulders, and backs, crying and wailing, being poked and prodded, and bleeding from all different parts of their bodies. The pagan belief in the dangerous dead has become a Christianized attestation to the presence of the sinful dead on Earth.

Hellequin's Hunt in *Sefer Ḥasidim*

The idea of terrestrial post-mortem purgation forms the background to several ghost tales found in *Sefer ḥasidim*. The first tale, cited in full above, is a Hebrew version of Hellequin's Hunt. To recall, it tells of a man who beholds multiple groups of the dead pulling other dead people on wagons as punishment for their sins. The motifs mentioned in the tale are all central elements of the Hunt—the lone horseman who sees the vision, the army of the dead passing by, the need to accept punishment for sin on Earth, and a description of the torments that the dead suffer. Even the setting—night-time, with the marked presence of the moon and the deserted area in which the dead appear—is one which is common to accounts of the Hunt.[63] The type of punishment assigned to the dead in this tale—carrying a heavy load on their backs—also predominates in Orderic's account of the Hunt. There, each peasant in the group carries on his head and shoulders some bulky item, such as sheep, clothing, or pieces of furniture, and specific individuals of the knightly class are described as carrying items of

from the 'evil troops' that he is bound to and who wish to harm the members of the household. See Schmitt, *Ghosts in the Middle Ages*, 109–10. Regarding use of the Divine name to neutralize the dead in a Hunt narrative, see Orderic Vitalis, *The Ecclesiastical History of England*, ii. 517.

[63] In Orderic's account the vision occurs at night with the 'moon being in her eighth day in the constellation of the Ram, shed[ding] a clear light'; see *The Ecclesiastical History of England*, ii. 511–12. In Caesarius's tale, too, which is a diabolized version of the Hunt, a certain knight and his servant see the apparition at night, 'while the moon was shining' (*Dialogue*, 12: 20). As far as the location is concerned, Orderic's account records that the army appeared in a spot 'far from any habitation of man' (*Ecclesiastical History of England*, ii. 511). According to Walter Map (*De nugis curialium*, 371), the last sighting of the troop was in the 'march of Wales and Hereford'. More often the scene is an uninhabited forest.

enormous and abnormal weight. The overwhelming fatigue mentioned in the Pietist vision is present in other accounts of the Hunt as well.[64]

Apart from individual motifs, the tale has an entire scene which appears in Orderic's description of the Hunt: the image of the dead pulling a wagonload of dead people in the Pietist account parallels Walkelin's sighting of a troop of corpse-bearers, who carry as many as fifty biers with large groups of people seated upon them, and who march along with a procession of other dead people.[65] The use of wagons in the Pietist tale in place of biers recalls a scene common in medieval life for both the living and the dead: the bodies of Jewish martyrs were carted away in wagons, as *Sefer ḥasidim* testifies.[66] The dead men who pull each other in wagons in the Pietist story replace the horse, a prominent feature of the Hunt, whose presence among the dead is only suggested in this vision.

The encounter of the living with wagonloads of damned souls being pulled by horses forms the central motif of two German legends. In one legend, which takes place in Speyer, a certain messenger comes across a rattling carriage, covered all in black, in which dead monks ride. The messenger stands aghast as the carriage, surrounded by roaring flames, disappears into the air and emits a tumultuous roar which sounds like 'the clanging noise of swords, as though an army were going into battle'. According to the second legend, a man is terror-stricken when he encounters at midnight two fiery carriages that make a terrifying clatter. It is not only the carriages that are aflame but also the people riding in them, as are the horses which pull them.[67] These legends contain elements which clearly link them to Hunt narratives. The Pietist tale may, indeed, be the product of a melding of the German wagon legends with that of the sinners of Hellequin.

Two other tales recorded in *Sefer ḥasidim* speak of individuals who return to Earth as a punishment for their sins. The stories are told in the context of an evaluation of the effectiveness of acts of the living on behalf of the dead.[68] In the first one, a man, walking alone, loses his way in the forest. At night, by the light of the moon, he encounters a man who, he realizes, is dead. His first reaction is to flee. The ghost asks him not to, assuring him that he means no harm. When the ghost reveals his identity, the man recognizes him. Puzzled, he asks the ghost, 'But didn't you die several years

64 For example Walter Map describes the visions of the Hunt as 'lamentable . . . unrest': *De nugis curialium*, 31.

65 Orderic Vitalis, *The Ecclesiastical History of England*, ii. 513.

66 *SḤ* 1530. See Schur, 'The Care for the Dead in Medieval Ashkenaz', 196.

67 See Grimm and Grimm, *The German Legends*, vol. i, nos. 276 and 278.

68 This topic is the focus of Chs. 7 and 8 below. For the stories see *SḤ* 35.

ago?' The ghost responds, 'Yes, but because of a certain field that I had stolen, I have no rest and they tire me out in the forests because of a certain object that I had stolen from it/him.'[69]

This tale displays features common to accounts of the Hunt. A lone man, travelling at night, by the light of the moon, encounters a dead man who must perpetually wander on Earth as a punishment for sin. While no specific torment is mentioned here—although there is an allusion to carrying a heavy object—the ceaseless wandering, which takes place once again in the uninhabited region of the forest, is the key element in most accounts of the Hunt. The appearance of only one dead individual rather than an entire troop suggests that perhaps he has succeeded in separating himself from the others, as in Walkelin's vision. Additionally, it is not uncommon in accounts of the Hunt for the living to encounter, and interact with, a single dead individual without having seen the entire troop. In the chronicles of the bishops of Mans, a single dead person appeals for aid, which he says will help to free him from the troop of the dead to which he is attached.[70] A similar phenomenon occurs in a tale recounted by Helinand of Froidmont. A dead man, Noel, appears to John, his former companion, and appeals for aid. John first asks him whether he is a member of Hellequin's army. While John never sees or hears the army, he still associates the single person with the entire troop.[71]

The second tale of the pair likewise speaks of the appearance of a single dead individual—this time it is the ghost of a non-Jew. A certain master dies, and his servant, who goes out at night a few days later, encounters him. The ghost encourages the servant not to flee, assuring him that he means no harm. The servant asks him, 'But aren't you dead?' The master responds, 'Yes, but they tire me out, because I took a certain individual's patrimony [*naḥalah*] against his will. Now go and tell my wife to return it to him.'[72] The servant responds, 'But they won't believe me.' The master then offers a sign of proof (*signum*) to him: 'Tell them to go to a certain place tomorrow and they will see me there', he says. The servant goes and tells everyone in the town. When the people ask for a sign, the servant informs them that the ghost will appear to them on the following day in a tree, as

[69] The Bologna print edn., no. 170, p. 177, and MS JTS Boesky 45 no. 31 reiterate here that the man had stolen a field rather than an object.

[70] Schmitt, *Ghosts in the Middle Ages*, 109–10.

[71] Helinand of Froidmont, *De cognitione sua*, chs. 10–13, cited in Schmitt, *Ghosts in the Middle Ages*, 113–14.

[72] MS JTS 2499 records a variant reading: the dead master requests that the servant tell his forefathers (*avotai*) to return the stolen patrimony.

specified by his master.[73] The next day, the entire town goes to that tree and sees the ghost of the master, whereupon they dig up his grave and find that his corpse is missing. The servant explains to them that they must return the stolen property; only then will the man be able to rest. So the tale ends.

This tale is similar in many respects to the previous one. The lone encounter with the ghost by night, the initial fear of the ghost and its subsequent assuagement, the weariness of the dead man, which serves as his punishment, and the sin of theft of land are all shared elements. The central element of this tale, which aligns it with accounts of the Hunt, also parallels that of the first one—the ceaseless wandering of the dead as punishment for sin. The phrase 'they tire me out' is a further parallel.

The second tale, however, introduces a new element—the scepticism of the townspeople. The servant anticipates that no one, the master's wife included, will believe him. His fears are justified: the entire town demands a visible sign to verify his claim.[74] In a similar way, in Orderic's account of the Hunt, Walkelin, who suspects that he has just beheld a vision of the famed 'Harlequin's people', endeavours to grab one of the horses which parade past him in an attempt to offer some tangible proof of what he has just witnessed. Otherwise, he reasons, 'no one will believe me when I tell the tale'.[75] Although Walkelin is unable to ride the horse as it both burns and freezes him at the same time, he still manages to come away with a proof: a mark on his face made by the dead knight William of Glos, who, at one point during the apparition, attacks him. Orderic writes that he himself has seen the mark and was convinced by it of the truth of the vision.[76]

The pre-Christian roots of the Pietist tale are here manifest. The fact that the dead master offers to appear in person as proof of the truth of the

[73] The precise place is not specified in two manuscripts that contain parallel passages (MS Vatican ebr. 285 no. 67 and MS JTS 2499).

[74] The motif of the *signum*—the 'proof of the truth of the vision'—appears not only in Hunt narratives but also in numerous ghost stories of the exempla literature. Thus, for example, in a tale recounted by Otloh of St Emmeram in the eleventh century, a dead knight offers the visionaries a burning lance as the *signum*. See Schmitt, *Ghosts in the Middle Ages*, 46. In the thirteenth century, in the hands of the mendicants, the motif of the *signum* became part of the standardized type of ghost tale (ibid. 136). It appeared also in early medieval journey narratives as proof of the visionary's trip to the other world. In the eighth century Bede recounted how, in the 'Vision of Fursey', Fursey returns to the Earth with burns on his shoulder and chin as a result of his visit to the world of the dead. See Seymour, *Irish Visions of the Other World*, 19–20, and Le Goff, *The Birth of Purgatory*, 112–13. The peasant Gottschalk, in a twelfth-century story, similarly acquires bodily wounds and burns on his journey to the other world which continue to pain him for the rest of his life. See Gurevich, 'Oral and Written Culture of the Middle Ages, 60–1.

[75] Orderic Vitalis, *The Ecclesiastical History of England*, ii. 515.

[76] Ibid. 519.

vision, rather than present an identifying object or a brand upon the visionary, highlights the corporeal nature of the ghost. He appears bodily in a tree for the whole town to see. Moreover, the actions of the townspeople, who, after the encounter with the restless dead master, reopen his grave and check the status of his body, become intelligible only when associated with the pre-Christian belief in the return of the dangerous dead. The physical presence of the dead person on Earth, combined with the simultaneous disappearance of the corpse from the grave, is the hallmark of the corporeal Germanic ghost, as seen in the Icelandic sagas.

A similar tale, in which the *signum* is the body of the deceased, or a part thereof, takes place in the archbishopric of Mainz. In a diabolized narrative of the Infernal Hunt, Caesarius of Heisterbach tells how the hair of a dead woman, who is wrested away by the Devil mounted on horseback, remains in the hands of a certain knight, the visionary who witnesses this scene. The townspeople refuse to believe the knight's story despite the *signum* he displays to them; they reopen the woman's grave and discover that the corpse is missing its hair.[77]

Another difference between the pair of Pietist tales is that, whereas in the first one the man who encounters the dead person is lost and wandering in the forest, in the second tale the servant encounters his master on what appears to be his former domain, just outside his property. In the first tale, the dead man, whom the visionary does not recognize at first, died several years prior to his appearance. In the second one, the servant immediately recognizes his former master, who only died a few days before.[78] Has the master been sentenced to return to suffer punishment for his sin in the familiar places of his past, like the bath attendant in Gregory's tales? Is he sentenced to wander restlessly on the very field which he illegitimately wrested from another—the locus of his sin?

The two tales recorded in *Sefer ḥasidim* resemble very closely a story of German origin that is found in several medieval sources. Caesarius of Heisterbach tells of Erkinbert, a citizen of Andernach, who, while travelling alone at night, encounters a dead knight riding on a black war horse whose

[77] Caesarius of Heisterbach, *Dialogue*, 12: 20.

[78] In the Bologna edition of *Sefer ḥasidim*, the passage contradicts itself regarding the length of time that has passed since the death of the master. At first, it states that the servant encounters his master after 'a few days'. Later on, it refers to the master as having been dead for 'several years' (no. 170, p. 177). In another manuscript (MS Vatican ebr. 285 no. 67), the terms 'days' and 'years' appear side by side. Given the internal contradiction in both manuscripts and the confusion that could easily have occurred between the two tales, it is reasonable to assume that 'days' is the correct reading, while 'years' was mistakenly borrowed from the previous tale.

nostrils shoot smoke and fire. Originally riding on the road, the mounted knight turns off and is seen galloping over the fields. Erkinbert, seeing the knight riding towards him, is immediately seized with terror and, unsure if the rider is a demon or a man,[79] proceeds to sign himself with the cross and brandish a sword to fight against him. When the knight approaches, Erkinbert recognizes him; he is the lord Frederic of the manor of Kelle, who has recently died. The dead lord appears clothed in sheepskins and carries a heavy load of earth on his shoulders. He explains to Erkinbert that he is in great pain because of the sins he has committed. Having unjustly taken those sheepskins from a widow, he is now forced to wear them burning hot; and having stolen a portion of land, he is now crushed under its weight. He then informs Erkinbert that if his sons restore this property, they will greatly lighten his punishment. With that he disappears. Although Erkinbert relays the message to the sons, they refuse to relinquish their inheritance, preferring to abandon their father and condemn him to perpetual suffering.[80]

Caesarius's tale begins in the manner characteristic of the Hunt narratives—the lone encounter takes place at night, in an uninhabited area, and the dead figure is mounted on horseback. The story parallels the two Pietist ones in terms of the nature of the sin—the dead in all three narratives must suffer punishment for acquiring things by unfair means. Caesarius's tale resembles more closely the first Pietist story, in which both an object and land have been usurped, while it shares a different detail with the second Pietist tale: both speak of a non-Jewish lord who has recently died. Evidence of belief in the dangerous dead is likewise present in Caesarius's tale. The terror that grips Erkinbert upon his encounter with the dead knight and the act of crossing himself, as well as his readiness for physical violence in order to stave off the other's perceived corporeal assault, are all elements associated with the dangerous dead.

Additionally, in both Caesarius's story and the second Pietist tale, the

79 On the confusion of demons and ghosts, see pp. 21–2, 40–1, and 71 above.

80 Caesarius of Heisterbach, *Dialogue*, 12: 14. The tale also appears in Banks (ed.), *Alphabet of Tales*, 352 no. 522, and in a fourteenth-century Latin manuscript, Addit 18364 fo. 55, found in *Catalogue of Romances*, iii. 615 no. 131. Otloh of St Emmeram tells a similar tale involving a dead knight who separates himself from the troop of the dead, seen flying in the air. The knight petitions two brothers to restore land that their father had stolen from a monastery in order to save him and themselves from damnation. In this tale, the brothers acquiesce and return the land. Whereas this eleventh-century story sets out to protect monastic holdings from being usurped and to ensure their eventual return to monasteries, the tale recounted by Caesarius aims to rebuke the 'rapacious lifestyle' of the knightly class in general. See Schmitt, *Ghosts in the Middle Ages*, 46, 99–100.

dead seek the aid of close relatives and beseech them to restore the stolen property in order to lessen or abrogate their torment. While perpetual wandering is not made explicit in Caesarius's tale, it is implied; the knight's punishment requires him to don the sheepskins and continuously carry a heavy load of earth. The motif of the sheepskins burning his body,[81] as well as the great weight of the earth that he must bear, recall other knights' sufferings depicted in Orderic's account of the Hunt: one of them must do penance by carrying in his mouth a hot iron bar of enormous weight from the mill of a poor man, which he kept as security for a usurious loan.[82] The addition of these two elements—the donning of the red-hot sheepskins and the carrying of the heavy load of earth—could possibly explain the meaning of the cryptic repetition that appears in the first Pietist tale. The dead man complains to the living one whom he encounters that 'because of a certain field that I had stolen, I have no rest and they tire me out in the forests because of a certain object that I had stolen from it/him'. The double expressions of 'I have no rest' and 'they tire me out', on the one hand, and of the field and the object on the other, complement the double crime and punishment meted out to the lord in Caesarius's tale. Moreover, the extreme weariness described in both Pietist tales can now be accounted for: Caesarius's knight, Frederic, is crushed under the weight of the load he must perpetually carry.

In all four tales—Orderic's, Caesarius's, and the Pietist ones—the objects that are the focus of sin become the instruments of torture of the dead. We may recall Orderic's account, in which the knight carries a burning iron bar, and the punishment of Walkelin's brother, Robert, is to wear fiery spurs of enormous weight because he would use his spurs to hurry to shed blood. Caesarius's knight, the lord Frederic, wears the burning hot skin of the animal he stole and carries a heavy load of earth from the land he usurped. The two Pietist tales, as we have seen, parallel Caesarius's story in terms of both crime and punishment. In the Christianized form of what was once an account of an encounter with the dangerous dead, these tales deflect the violent physical assault against the living onto the dead themselves. Rather than harming the living, they are being harmed; their sins

[81] One version of the tale attributes the same burning characteristic to the load of earth; see Banks (ed.), *Alphabet of Tales*, 352 no. 522.

[82] The commonality between the punishment of Walkelin's knight and of the one in Caesarius's story suggests that the object and patrimony, which are evidently stolen in the German tale, may have, in fact, not been stolen so much as having been items kept by the knight as securities for usurious loans.

turn against them and become the instruments of their punishment and suffering.

Pietist Identification with Terrestrial Post-Mortem Punishment

Beyond mere citation of Hebrew versions of Hellequin's Hunt in the pages of *Sefer ḥasidim*, R. Judah the Pious accepts the validity of the notion of terrestrial post-mortem punishment for Jews as much as for Christians. Following the account of the dead pulling wagons filled with other dead people, he attaches his own comments, which substantiate the message of the vision. He cites a string of biblical verses which associate harsh punishment with the loading of heavy wagons (Amos 2: 13), compare the acquisition of sin to the pulling of the ropes of a wagon (Isa. 5: 18), or compare man to animals (Ps. 49: 13). These verses indicate that Scripture itself foretells that people who sin will be punished by literally being forced to serve as animals and draw heavy wagons when they die.

R. Judah then cites Psalm 49, verses 13 and 15, to explain more fully the punishment described in the vision. According to these verses, the righteous will overpower at daybreak the large group of dead, who, 'like sheep, are destined for the pit [*she'ol*]'. He applies the verses to the punishment as follows: 'The upright beat the wagon-drawers in the same way that the wagon drivers beat the animals.' R. Judah makes it clear that he understands the analogy in the verses literally: just as the wagon driver beats the horses that pull the wagon, so, too, the upright dead beat the sinners, who serve as animals and must perpetually pull the wagons.

After citing this string of biblical verses, R. Judah lists various groups of Jewish sinners who suffer the posthumous fate witnessed in the vision. They include those who have behaved like animals by involving themselves in sexual sin, those who enslaved other men or put undue fear upon them, and even those who have mistreated their animals.[83] He then explains the appropriateness of this punishment for these sinners. For the first group, who acted like animals while alive, it is fitting that they work like animals after death. The second group, who enslaved others, will, in turn, be enslaved: they are harnessed to the wagons which they must pull. The third group of sinners, who mistreated their animals, will suffer like animals after death. While the punishments of all three groups reflect the rabbinic

[83] For an identical statement regarding these groups of sinners and their posthumous punishments, see *SḤ* 144. For a similar statement which denounces those who mistreat their animals, see *SḤ* 138.

principle of *midah keneged midah* (measure for measure), which permeates R. Judah's way of thinking with regard to Divine retribution and fills the pages of *Sefer ḥasidim*, one cannot avoid noticing the commonality they share with the punishments found in Orderic's and Caesarius's accounts of the Hunt—the sinful dead are punished in a manner related to the objects of their sin. This phenomenon is most noticeable in the punishment of the third group of sinners; they become the object of their sin.

Whatever hesitancy R. Judah may have displayed towards the existence of post-mortem punishment on Earth in his comments on the above-cited tale about the dead pulling the dead in wagons, he exhibits no such hesitancy in his remarks concerning the other pair of Hunt tales he cites. After presenting the stories, with the second one involving a dead non-Jew, he writes:

> This is so regarding the Gentiles; it may be truth or falsehood. However, regarding Jews there is such a law[84] . . . But if he [has both] merits and sins, and on account of his sins they chase him out of Paradise or they punish him in Gehenna or they tire him out along a thorny path[85] . . . then it benefits . . . if he stole and [his] heirs return [the stolen object].[86]

Whereas R. Judah doubts whether or not the restitution of ill-gotten goods will succeed in redeeming a non-Jew from his posthumous torment (as is suggested in the second of the pair of tales), he is convinced that, as far as Jews are concerned, given certain criteria,[87] such restitution by living relatives can help put to rest those who are being tormented for their sins by being forced to tire themselves out along a thorny path—an oblique reference to the torments depicted in the Pietist stories.[88] By accepting the message of the tales, he also accepts as valid the punishment meted out in them—being forced to continually wander on Earth—and its application to Jews.

The fact that R. Judah refers to the torment of having to walk along a thorny path immediately after relating the two tales (both of which employ the same verb, *meyagim*) suggests an association between the tales and this

84 In a parallel passage in the Bologna print edition (no. 170, p. 178), the word 'certainly' is inserted here: 'regarding Jews, there is certainly such a law'.

85 In a parallel passage in MS JTS 2499, the phrase reads, 'or they pain him along a thorny path'.

86 *SḤ* 35.

87 The exact nature of R. Judah's position regarding the efficacy of suffrages for the Jewish dead is examined in Chapter 7 below. For this reason, I have deliberately omitted parts of his comments in the above quotation.

88 The peasant Gottschalk, for example, recalls crossing a 'field strewn with terrible thorns' in his vision. See Gurevich, 'Oral and Written Culture', 61.

particular form of torment, thereby confirming its terrestrial locus. Additionally, it appears in the midst of a list of various types of posthumous punishment experienced by sinners. The juxtaposition of those who are being punished in Gehenna with those whom 'they tire out along a thorny path' suggests that the latter torment occurs outside Gehenna—that is, on Earth.

Eleazar of Worms echoes the belief in the existence of terrestrial post-mortem punishment espoused by R. Judah. In the section of the laws pertaining to Yom Kippur in his halakhic work *Sefer haroke'aḥ*, R. Eleazar states:

> Measure for measure [is the way that] they punish man for his sins. If they are few, they punish him in this world or after his death without Gehenna; they tire him out or they make him stumble over thorns and thistles or [they hurl him from] a sling from one end of the world to the other.[89]

In his list of posthumous punishments for some Jews, R. Eleazar clearly delineates three specific forms that exist outside the realm of Gehenna. The first two are the type of continuous roaming discussed by R. Judah in his tales—a tiresome wandering on even ground or over rough terrain. In either case, the punishment is a terrestrial one. The use of identical language—'they tire me [him] out' and 'path of thorns' (*meyagin oti* and *derekh kotsim*)—by both R. Eleazar and R. Judah makes the transmission of this teaching from master to pupil evident. R. Eleazar adds to this another punishment that exists outside Gehenna, the slinging of a sinner's soul from a slingshot, which originates in the Talmud.[90] The inclusion in his halakhic work of forms of terrestrial post-mortem punishment common to the Hunt narratives alongside one that was recognized by the rabbis demonstrates R. Eleazar's acceptance of the notion.

Moreover, in his *Sefer ḥokhmat hanefesh*, R. Eleazar adds two novel points that highlight his identification with the idea:

> There is one who does not enter Gehenna but they decree upon him to be a wanderer [*lihyot na venad*], sometimes by himself, but if there is one who did as he did and this one has already died and performed his deeds, [even if he is] in a faraway land, when he dies they walk together.[91]

Like the biblical Cain, this sinner must perpetually wander the Earth as a punishment for his sin, albeit in this case the sinner has already died. R. Eleazar adds that if there is another individual who has committed the same sin as the first, then after the death of the latter the two roam the

89 *Sefer haroke'aḥ hagadol*, ed. Shneerson, 104.

90 BT *Shab.* 152*b*.

91 *Sefer ḥokhmat hanefesh*, 24*b*.

Earth together. The notion that sinners of the same category walk together is reminiscent of several of the Hunt narratives, in which separate groups of knights, artisans, and others march as a troop.

After pairing up similar sinners, R. Eleazar cites a string of six scriptural phrases,[92] all of which speak of travel and destinations far away. This leads to his next novel assertion—that dead sinners are forced to wander only six days a week. The reason for this he explains as follows:

> And if he observed the sabbath according to its laws, even though the dead are free from the commandments, they will not pass him over the *teḥum shabat* and they will not afflict him on the sabbath. 'Every day I stretch out my hands to you' [Ps. 88: 10]—this applies to six days [of the week].[93]

Despite the fact that the dead individual is a sinner and sentenced to wander the Earth, if, while alive, he observed the sabbath appropriately, he will not be afflicted on that holy day. Here R. Eleazar is transferring a well-known belief in the sabbath rest of souls in Gehenna[94] to the context of posthumous punishment on Earth. However, unlike the dead in Gehenna, who enjoy complete respite from punishment on the sabbath, those that R. Eleazar speaks of continue to wander on Earth on that day, although the distance they walk is curtailed or the pace is more relaxed so as to grant them some relief from suffering. In order to uphold such a position, R. Eleazar must qualify the verse from Psalms, which seemingly reflects the tormented dead sinner's daily cries of desperation to God, to refer only to six days of the week.

Even more innovative is his belief that the dead still maintain a connection to the commandments, a talmudic statement regarding their freedom from them notwithstanding.[95] He asserts that those who were careful in their sabbath observance during their lifetime and who are wandering the Earth after death are not made to violate the sabbath by walking more than 2,000 cubits outside a populated area on the day of rest (law of *teḥum shabat*) even though in saying this he contradicts the halakhah, according to which the dead are not bound by *mitsvot*. Elsewhere, R. Judah the Pious is cited as maintaining that demons (*shedim*) observe the sabbath.[96] As I observed earlier, demons and the dead were often confused in medieval minds as

[92] These phrases originate in Ps. 139: 2–9.

[93] *Sefer ḥokhmat hanefesh*, 24*b*.

[94] The origin and acceptance of this belief, as well as the role it plays in *Sefer ḥasidim*, are discussed below, in Ch. 6.

[95] See BT *Shab*. 30*a*.

[96] 'And my master, R. Judah, may the memory of the righteous serve as a blessing, would say that demons believe in the Torah and observe all that the rabbis said' (*Or zarua*, vol. ii, 'Hilkhot shabat', 147).

they shared certain characteristics and were warded off in similar fashion.[97] This instinctive replacement of the demons with the dead, coupled with R. Eleazar's seeming unawareness of the halakhic contradiction, indicates all the more clearly that his beliefs regarding the dangerous dead are deeply ingrained and that he maintains a firm, instinctive belief in the post-mortem peregrinations of the Jewish dead as punishment for sin.

In substantiating Pietistic belief in terrestrial post-mortem punishment—a belief not found anywhere in the rabbinic and post-rabbinic literature—*Sefer ḥasidim*, as well as other Pietist writings, marks a turning point in the constitution of elements which penetrated contemporary Jewish views regarding the afterlife. Germanic notions of the dead have infiltrated not merely the ideas that relate to the nature of the returning dead, but also those about the place assigned to them for punishment. The biblical *she'ol* and Gei ben Hinom and the rabbinic Gehenna have now been integrated with the medieval Germanic 'Earth' as the site of the torment of the sinful dead.

Conclusion

Accounts of Hellequin's Hunt, which espouse the concept of terrestrial post-mortem punishment, are present in the ghost tales recounted in *Sefer ḥasidim*. The notion that the dead return to Earth in order to suffer punishment for sin is rooted in pre-Christian beliefs surrounding the return of the dangerous dead. That such notions appear in high medieval sources testifies to the tenacity of pagan ideas regarding the dead; these beliefs survived for centuries under the veneer of Christianization, especially in the Germanic environment which formed the background to *Sefer ḥasidim*. The pre-Christian belief in the return of the corporeal dead to Earth, as well as an unabashed belief in the corporeal nature of the post-mortem punishments assigned to sinners (which, as we have seen, is a Christianized version of the pagan idea), were ones that R. Judah the Pious absorbed from his environment and shared with his contemporary Caesarius of Heisterbach, among other Christian writers. The presence of the same beliefs regarding the dead in the writings of the German Cistercian and the German Pietist reveals a commonality between them. Ancient imaginings of the dead here cross religious boundaries and reflect a world-view that was shared by medieval Jew and Christian alike.

In the previous chapter we witnessed the absorption of the pagan

97 With regard to demons, see above, pp. 21–2 and nn. 28 and 29 there.

notion of the dangerous dead in *Sefer ḥasidim* as well as in the medieval Ashkenazi community at large. It is not surprising that in a premodern society, where belief in the power of unseen forces was widespread and where there was a need to provide some rational explanation for the spread of disease and sudden death, notions of the dead causing harm and illness to the living would be shared and cross-culturally accepted. In this chapter, we have uncovered the adoption of more than just religiously neutral cultural ideas. The acceptance by R. Judah the Pious of a form of posthumous punishment of sinners that lies outside the dictates of rabbinic and post-rabbinic teaching testifies to a validation of specifically Christian notions of sin and punishment. What motivated R. Judah to look beyond the received canon of Jewish belief in such matters? What propelled him to adopt a religious outlook that was alien to his tradition? The answer to these questions lies in an in-depth understanding of R. Judah's ideology of sin and punishment—an examination that awaits in a later part of this study.[98]

[98] See Chs. 6 and 9 below.

CHAPTER THREE

THE HOLY DEAD

IN TRACTATE *Sanhedrin*, the rabbis of the Talmud discuss the reason for the Mishnah's ruling that the bodies of convicted criminals to whom capital punishment by the Jewish high court has been administered are not to be buried in their family burial plot, but rather in cemeteries specifically designated for criminals executed by the court. The rabbis question this ruling:

And why such an extreme [position]? Because [of the principle] that 'They are not to bury a wicked person [*rasha*] beside a righteous one [*tsadik*].' As R. Aha bar Hanina said, 'From where do we learn that they are not to bury a wicked person beside a righteous one? As it says, "And they were burying a man and, behold, they saw the troop [of Moabite soldiers coming], and they cast the man into the grave of Elisha [the prophet]. And [the body of] the dead man came into contact with the bones of Elisha and he [the man] came back to life and he stood on his feet" [2 Kgs 13: 21] . . . And just as [there is a principle] that they are not to bury a wicked person beside a righteous one, so [is there a principle] that they are not to bury a severely wicked person [*rasha ḥamur*] beside a moderately wicked person [*rasha kal*].' And should they not therefore establish four cemeteries [one for each of the four types of execution]? They [the rabbis of the Mishnah] received a tradition regarding two cemeteries [one for those executed by stoning and burning and another for those executed by the sword and by strangulation].[1]

Sefer ḥasidim also records a situation of improper burial of the wicked beside the righteous:

One wicked person was buried among the martyrs. The martyrs[2] came in a

1 BT *San.* 47*a*. A parallel text appears in *Ḥul.* 7*b*. There, however, the Talmud speaks only of the incident in 2 Kings where the man is resuscitated, and makes no mention of the burial of criminals executed by the court. Also, in their analysis of the passage from Kings in *Ḥul.* 7*b*, the rabbis draw no conclusions regarding inappropriate burial. Instead, they glean a different lesson: the righteous are even greater when they die than when they were alive; that is, they perform more exalted miracles than they did in their lifetime.

2 The plural 'martyrs' is based on MS Parma H 3280 no. 265 and MS JTS Boesky 45 no. 115; the print editions (Wistinetzky and Margaliot) as well as MS CUL Add. 379 no. 224 record a single subject ('he came in a dream').

dream to an important living man [and said] that they should remove him from their midst, for it was very difficult [painful] for them.[3]

In their discussion of the Mishnah's ruling, the rabbis of the Talmud identify three different scenarios of improper burial of the wicked beside the righteous. The first is that of which the Mishnah speaks regarding all executed criminals: they must not be buried alongside their ancestors.[4] The second refers to the biblical source for the principle the rabbis enunciate regarding the illegitimacy of burial of the wicked beside the righteous: a man's body, inadvertently thrown into the grave of the prophet Elisha, is restored to life upon contact with the prophet's bones, and is then buried elsewhere.[5] In another place,[6] the rabbis identify this anonymous dead man as the false prophet Tsidkiyah b. Kena'anah, a wicked man who had caused the death of a true prophet of God.[7] The rabbis understand this miraculous event as proof of the impropriety of the wicked resting alongside the righteous.

The third instance of improper burial of the wicked that the Talmud records is the burial of criminals of different degrees of wickedness side by side. This principle is based on the teaching of the Mishnah which establishes two separate cemeteries for those executed by the Jewish high court. Those who have committed a more grievous sin and are executed by harsher means, such as stoning and burning, are to be buried in one cemetery, whereas those whose crime is less grievous and who are executed by a lighter method, such as the sword and strangulation, are to be buried in another one.

Common to all three instances cited in the Talmud is the need to remove the corpse of a wicked person who has been buried in the company of the righteous. In all three situations, the wicked are objectively defined: they are either executed criminals or murderous false prophets. The righteous, however, comprise a wider spectrum of individuals. On the basis of the scriptural incident, the righteous man is no less holy a personage than the prophet Elisha, pupil of Elijah, whose prophetic and miraculous powers surpass twofold those of his master.[8] In the incidents recorded in

[3] *SḤ* 265.

[4] The relevant section of this *mishnah* appears at BT *San.* 46*a*.

[5] According to the passage in *Sanhedrin*, the dead man is only resuscitated for a short while; he dies soon after and is reburied.

[6] *Kohelet rabah* 8: 13. See also Rashi on BT *San.* 47*a*, s.v. *vayehi vayakom al raglav*.

[7] See 1 Kgs 13.

[8] Elisha's reception of twice as much prophetic capacity as Elijah had is recounted in 2 Kgs 2: 8–13. The rabbis, in their discussion surrounding 2 Kgs 13: 21, further assume that his miracle-working ability had also doubled; see BT *San.* 47*a*.

the Mishnah and repeated in the Talmud regarding the burial of executed criminals in specially designated cemeteries, the righteous are described as the sinners' dead relatives. Since the rabbis do not supply any information on the relatives' sanctity or superior moral conduct, the category of the righteous here includes any Jewish person not convicted of a capital crime.[9]

In sum, the rabbinic models set up here for burial of the wicked at a distance from the righteous apply to objectively defined wicked people, who are to be kept apart either from any dead Jew or from the holy dead, specifically the great biblical prophets. A scriptural miracle provides the source for the Mishnah's halakhic ruling regarding the burial of executed criminals apart from both other Jews and other, less heinous, criminals at a time when the high court functioned in Judaea and the power of capital punishment resided in Jewish hands.

In contrast to this model, the paradigm *Sefer ḥasidim* establishes for separate burial of the wicked involves a man labelled wicked by the Pietists, and who is buried in a mass grave of martyrs.[10] While it is certainly possible to accept at face value this categorization of the man, one cannot exclude the possibility that the usage reflects the fact that the Pietists often cast a starkly negative light on their opponents—who were, at times, men of great erudition and moral worth—by using a term such as *rasha* to describe them.[11]

More revealing than the designation of individuals as wicked in *Sefer ḥasidim* is the identification of Ashkenazi martyrs as the righteous dead. Rabbinic literature speaks of at least a dozen Jews, mostly holy and pious scholars, who were martyred by the Roman government,[12] yet no mention is made of, or significance attached to, their burial arrangements.[13]

9 On the basis of a tannaitic teaching recorded at the beginning of chapter 11 of *Sanhedrin*, all Jews are considered righteous unless heinous, sinful behaviour on their part demonstrates otherwise.

10 Several passages in *Sefer ḥasidim* mention a mass grave of martyrs. See *SḤ* 1530, 1531, 1532.

11 See Soloveitchik, 'Three Themes in *Sefer Ḥasidim*', 330–3. For purposes of contrast, compare the generalized term *rasha eḥad* in the above-cited passage (*SḤ* 265) with the very specific one that appears only a few short paragraphs later (*SḤ* 268), where the wicked person, whose grave is separated from those of the others, is described as having died while under the sanctions of communal excommunication.

12 The martyrdom of the two brothers of Lod is recorded in BT *Ta'an.* 18*b*. The stories of the Ten Martyrs of the (Roman) Empire and their various tortures are depicted in BT *AZ* 17*b*–18*a*, *Midrash eikhah rabah* 2, *Sifrei al sefer devarim*, 'Ha'azinu', 307 (ed. Finkelstein and Horovitz, 346), *Midrash tehilim* 9 (ed. Buber, pp. 88–9), and 'Asarah harugei malkhut' in Eisenstein (ed.), *Otsar midrashim*, 439–49.

13 The one exception to this rule may be the burial of R. Akiva, which is recorded to have taken place in Caesarea. However, this has more to do with the fact that the Christian martyrs

Additionally, in the Pietist tale it is not one martyr who complains of the burial of a wicked man beside him; rather, it is the group as a whole that proves intolerant of such a character in its midst.

Living in a post-prophetic age, the Pietists may certainly have expanded the talmudic principle of 'they are not to bury a wicked person beside a righteous one' to include a more contemporary example of the righteous dead—the martyrs of the Rhineland massacres, who were killed during the Crusade of 1096. However, it is also possible to suggest that another, outside, model influenced their thinking. The literary medium selected by the Pietists to convey the injunction of not burying the wicked alongside the righteous—the ghost tale—differs from the miraculous episodes recounted in the Talmud and from the legal rulings of the rabbis. It does bear an affinity, however, to a large body of ghost tales present in the medieval exempla literature. This body of tales speaks of the intolerance of the Christian holy dead of burial of the unworthy in their midst. Have the Pietists appropriated Christian notions of the holy dead—saints and martyrs—and adapted them for Jewish use? Do Pietist attitudes towards the burial sites of the Rhineland martyrs in any way approximate Christian ideas of holy space?

Burial of the Wicked and the Righteous in Rabbinic Literature

Apart from the source in *Sanhedrin*, two passages in tractate *Mo'ed katan* speak of the application of the principle of not burying the wicked alongside the righteous. In one passage, the rabbis of the Land of Israel debate where to inter the body of the Babylonian scholar Rav Huna. They select the burial cave of Rav Hiya, since they consider him to be of equal calibre to Rav Huna; regarding each of them, the rabbis proclaim, '[He] disseminated Torah among the Jewish people.'[14]

Whereas the rabbis, in this passage, correctly estimate the moral stature of the deceased scholar in question, they are not as successful in a second passage in *Mo'ed katan*, which describes the case of the burial of a certain unnamed young rabbinic student. Despite his scholarly prowess, the young scholar's bad reputation earns him the excommunication of the rabbis. Although he later repents of his misdeed, he dies while still under

were buried in that city than that other Jewish martyrs may have been interred there as well. See Goldin, *The Ways of Jewish Martyrdom*, 63.

[14] BT *MK* 25*a*.

the ban. At first the rabbis take his body to the burial cave of the pious, but 'they did not accept it'; a snake encircles the mouth of the cave, barring entry to the corpse.[15] Then the rabbis take the body to the burial cave of the judges, and 'they accepted it'; nothing prevents entry of his corpse into the cave, so the rabbis inter him there. Although the moral standing of the judges, who head the rabbinic courts of law, is lower in comparison to that of the pious, the rabbis question the scholar's acceptance into the cave of the judges. They conclude that his sin, committed without public desecration of God's name, complied with the ruling of Rav Ilai, who taught that if someone feels the urge to sin overtake him, he should go to a place where he is not known, put on black clothes, don a black cloak, and do as his heart desires so as not to profane the name of Heaven openly. For this reason, the scholar merits burial in the company of the judges.[16]

The two passages from *Mo'ed katan* extend the application of the talmudic principle enunciated in *Sanhedrin*, 'They are not to bury a wicked person beside a righteous one.' It now includes prevention of the inappropriate burial of a high-ranking righteous person together with one of lower rank—the concern of the rabbis in the first passage—or of a low-ranking righteous person together with those of higher rank—the outcome of the situation in the second passage.[17] It is not only the wicked who have legally recognized status differences on the basis of the principle of 'they are not to bury a severely wicked person beside a moderately wicked person', but also the righteous, on the basis of *Mo'ed katan*. As in the case of the inappropriate burial of the false prophet in the grave of Elisha, in this latter source, too, a miraculous occurrence (the snake encircling the mouth of the cave) prevents an inappropriate burial. However, it is an impropriety in the matter of gradations of righteousness that the miracle seeks to correct, rather than burial of the wicked beside the righteous as recounted in 2 Kings 13: 21.

Whereas the story involving the attempted burial of the excommunicated scholar speaks of designated burial caves for various groups of the righteous—such the pious and the judges—rabbinic literature makes no mention of any such burial caves for martyrs. Although the Talmud extols

15 Rashi on BT *MK* 17*a*, s.v. *velo kibeluhu*.

16 BT *MK* 17*a*.

17 Nahmanides, in his halakhic compendium on the laws of death and mourning entitled *Torat ha'adam*, cites these two passages as sources for his novel ruling that, 'Just as "they do not bury a wicked person beside a righteous one", so too "they do not bury a severely wicked person beside a moderately wicked person", and so an average righteous person [*tsadik beinoni*] is not buried beside an exceptional, wholly pious individual [*ḥasid gamur umuflag*].' See *Torat ha'adam*, in *Kitvei ramban*, ed. Chavel, ii. 118.

the martyrs of Lod as deserving a uniquely exalted status in the hereafter —'No one can stand in their company'—their place of burial on Earth is not discussed.[18] The same holds true for the Ten Martyrs of the Roman Empire, ten distinguished Jewish leaders murdered by the Romans in different periods of time, and whom midrashic sources meld into a single group of martyrs.[19] Admittedly, it is possible to argue that their corpses were not handed over by the empire for burial, and at first glance the incident involving the corpses of the martyrs of Betar, all of whom were slaughtered by the Romans,[20] strengthens such an argument. As recorded in the Talmud and Midrash, the rabbis established a special blessing to give thanks for the twofold kindness that God granted the Jews with regard to the corpses of the Betar martyrs. The blessing declares God 'good' on account of the miracle he had performed, namely, that the martyrs' bodies did not rot although they remained unburied for a long period of time. It also describes God as 'beneficent' because he ensured that the Romans eventually permitted the corpses to be buried.[21] While the initial prohibition of the burial of the Betar martyrs might indicate that such was the case with all Jewish martyrs of Rome, the fact that the Midrash calls it a decree, which was subsequently annulled by a later emperor, implies that this was an extraordinary case.[22]

Veneration of Jewish martyrs is present in the Talmud. In the very same passage that extols the martyrs of Lod, according them a uniquely exalted status in the hereafter, the Ten Martyrs of the Empire are similarly praised. The rabbis expand upon and rework various biblical models of martyrdom,[23] while also highlighting the martyrdom of figures who suffered during the periods of Greek and Roman persecution.[24] However, even though

[18] BT *Pes.* 50*a*. Regarding the story of the martyrs of Lod, see n. 12 above.

[19] Goldin, *The Ways of Jewish Martyrdom*, 78–9. Regarding the story of the Ten Martyrs of the Empire, see n. 12 above.

[20] Betar was a fortress held by the Jews during the Bar-Kokhba revolt of 135 CE. On the massacre there, see JT *Ta'an.* 4: 5, 24*a–b*; BT *Git.* 57*a–b*; and *Midrash eikhah rabah* 2: 5.

[21] BT *Ber.* 48*b*, *Ta'an.* 31*a*; *Petiḥta de'eikhah rabati*, 33; and *Midrash eikhah rabah* 2: 5.

[22] *Midrash eikhah rabah* 2: 5.

[23] These models include Abraham and Isaac, Esther and Mordecai, and Daniel and his companions. See Reich, 'Sacrifice for Mitsvah Observance' (Heb.), 25–51. I wish to thank Haym Soloveitchik for this reference.

[24] These figures include the woman and her seven sons who feature in BT *Git.* 57*b*, the children who jump into the sea (BT *Ta'an.* 29*a* and JT *Shek.* 6: 2), and the *kohanim* who hurl themselves into the flames of the burning Temple (BT *Git.* 57*b*). We may also add the death of R. Hanina ben Tradyon (BT *AZ* 18*a*), the death of R. Akiva (BT *Ber.* 61*b* and JT *Ber.* 9: 5), and the martyrdom of Lulyanus and Papus (JT *San.* 3: 5 and JT *Shevi.* 4: 2). See Reich, 'Sacrifice for Mitsvah Observance' (Heb.), 65–84, 85–8, 89–94, 95–104, 105–13, and 114–18 respectively.

by the third and fourth centuries a specific 'discourse of martyrdom' appeared among the rabbis,[25] who conceived of martyrdom as proof of Jews' special relationship with God,[26] such an attitude is not universal in rabbinic literature. Several key accounts in the Midrash lack the notion that the martyrs died as an expression of their love of God.[27] Palestinian sources, primarily tannaitic literature and the Jerusalem Talmud, are far more likely to portray martyrs in a positive light than the Babylonian Talmud.[28] Two narratives in the latter source record the martyrdom of R. Hanina b. Tradyon and criticize him for his active role in the event as well as for his concomitant insufficient regard for the sanctity of life.[29] Furthermore, even in Palestinian sources there is no uniformity of opinion; rather than portraying the Ten Martyrs as perfect and blameless, the early rabbis of the tannaitic period sought to attach personal sins to them which would have occasioned their persecution.[30]

Martyrs as the Holy Dead in Ashkenaz

In contrast to the more tempered attitude displayed towards martyrs in rabbinic literature, martyrdom in medieval Ashkenaz assumed a heightened measure of sanctity and venerability. Rabbinic sources on the theme took on greater significance in this period and the notions they used were refashioned in novel ways. Entirely new elements were added as well. Whereas the biblical prophets and outstanding Torah scholars served as the holy dead in rabbinic sources, medieval Ashkenazi sources elevated their own indigenous martyrs to that status in ways that correlated with contemporary Christian accounts of martyr-saints.[31]

Scholars have demonstrated that the language and motifs used by the twelfth-century Hebrew chroniclers of the Crusades are suffused with the notion of martyrdom as the supreme act of consummate love of God.[32]

25 Boyarin, *Dying for God*, 94–5 and 107.

26 Goldin, *The Ways of Jewish Martyrdom*, 63.

27 Shepkaru, *Jewish Martyrs*, 185–6.

28 Reich, 'Sacrifice for Mitsvah Observance' (Heb.), 69–73, 82–4, 85–7, 89–90, 100–4, and 105–10.

29 BT *AZ* 17*b*–18*a* and BT *AZ* 18*a*. See the discussion in Reich, 'Sacrifice for Mitsvah Observance' (Heb.), 97–100.

30 Urbach, *The Sages*, 521.

31 Shepkaru, 'To Die for God', 312.

32 The Hebrew chronicles of the Crusades are printed, in the original Hebrew, in E. Haverkamp, *Hebräische Berichte über die Judenverfolgungen*, and in Habermann, *Persecutions in Medieval France and Germany* (Heb.). They are available in English translation in Eidelberg, *The Jews and the Crusaders*, and two of the three (the Mainz Anonymous and the Solomon bar Shimshon Chronicle) appear in Chazan, *European Jewry and the First Crusade*.

Although these chroniclers drew upon rabbinic martyrological texts and early medieval Italian Jewish sources,[33] they extended the parameters of earlier models beyond their original context to include cases of self-sacrifice, voluntary death, and child sacrifice, all of which were performed as the ultimate expression of love of God.[34] Additionally, identical language and motifs to those used by the Hebrew chroniclers permeate Christian crusading literature. Latin chroniclers depict love of God as the dominant emotion motivating the Crusaders, who also express a willingness to volunteer for martyrdom.[35]

Talmudic accounts of martyrdom, including those of the Ten Martyrs of the Empire, either contain generalized mention of the post-resurrection life or lack reference to any reward altogether.[36] In contrast to the vagueness or absence of celestial reward allotted to martyrs in rabbinic literature, the Hebrew chroniclers of the twelfth century are both elaborate and specific regarding the rewards awaiting the Rhineland martyrs—ones that closely resemble those delineated in Christian sources.[37] Golden thrones in Paradise and a supernal light are part of their portion, just as Latin sources promise Crusaders who undertake their perilous journey.[38] Similarly, the Hebrew chronicles describe the martyrs as basking in the direct presence of the Divine, much the same way that Latin sources apportion the *visio Dei* to the Crusaders as their ultimate reward.[39]

Most importantly, both the Rhineland martyrs and the Crusaders merit an exclusive status as martyrs in the hereafter. Both sets of sources declare that the souls of martyrs and Crusaders reside in the 'bosom of Abraham',[40] in the company of other ancient martyrs:[41] the souls of Crusaders are purported to reside alongside earlier Christian martyr-saints in Paradise, while the Rhineland martyrs are said to rest in the company of the Ten Martyrs of the Empire in Gan Eden.[42] Unlike any previous Jewish text on martyrdom, the twelfth-century Hebrew chronicles laud the Rhineland martyrs as 'the pious of the Most High' (*ḥasidei elyon*).[43] Other scholars have pointed to a

[33] On the influence of *Sefer yosipon* and other Italian Jewish sources upon the chronicles of 1096, see Reich, 'Sacrifice for Mitsvah Observance' (Heb.), 129–70.

[34] Shepkaru, *Jewish Martyrs*, 186–7.

[35] Ibid. 187–8.

[36] Talmudic accounts of martyrdom apart from that of the Ten Martyrs include BT *Git.* 57*b*, *Ḥul.* 142*a*, *Kid.* 39*b*, and JT *Ḥag.* 2: 1. See Shepkaru, 'From After Death to Afterlife', 21–6.

[37] Shepkaru, 'From After Death to Afterlife', 31–6.

[38] Shepkaru, *Jewish Martyrs*, 200.

[39] Ibid. 199 and 202–4.

[40] Ibid. 201–2.

[41] On Christians' view of their own dead as martyrs, see J. Cohen, *Sanctifying the Name of God*, 89.

[42] Shepkaru, *Jewish Martyrs*, 199, 201, and 203.

[43] Shepkaru, 'From After Death to Afterlife', 31.

difference in the tombstones of the Rhineland martyrs as compared with non-martyrs of the same period.[44] Whereas the tombs of ordinary Jews of the twelfth and thirteenth centuries in Ashkenaz bore blessings for the safe reception of the interred in Gan Eden, those of the Rhineland martyrs were devoid of any such blessings. Not in need of the prayers of the living, the martyrs were held in such high esteem by their co-religionists that their entry into Paradise was considered both immediate and assured. For this same reason, one thirteenth-century Ashkenazi rabbi recorded a ruling in the name of a certain Rav Shemaryah that martyrs were not to be mourned.[45]

The exalted status that martyrs had in Ashkenaz registered in halakhic texts as well. From a legal perspective, the voluntary martyrdom, suicide, and child-killing undertaken by Jews in order to prevent their own or their children's conversion to Christianity, as reported of the events of 1096 in the Hebrew chronicles,[46] extended far beyond acceptable parameters.[47] Yet these acts, which are deemed murder by the standards of Jewish law, were reinterpreted by Ashkenazi scholars as permissible.[48] What motivated such uncharacteristic conduct on the part of these rabbis? It was an unquestioned and instinctive belief that the martyrs of 1096 had acted legitimately—that they were correct in intuiting that martyrdom, in all its forms, is the ultimate sacrifice desired by God. Legal and logical considerations aside, the martyrs had acted out of deep religious conviction, a conviction that few in their community would question, whether laymen or scholars.[49]

44 See Reiner, 'The Dead as Living History', 209–10.

45 The author of this responsum, R. Isaac ben Hayim, was a grandson of R. Isaac of Vienna. See Reiner, 'The Dead as Living History', 210–11. Regarding R. Shemaryah (son of R. Hayim), see Kohen, *Otsar hagedolim, alufei ya'akov*, ix. 54.

46 A vigorous debate over the historicity of the information found in the chronicles occupies scholars. While Ivan Marcus questions the historical truth of the narratives, Robert Chazan defends it. See Marcus, 'From Politics to Martyrdom', 42, and Chazan, *European Jewry and the First Crusade*. Whether or not the chronicles record the events as they happened, their authors clearly extol the martyrs' voluntary acts.

47 While martyrdom is mandatory if one is presented with the choice between idolatry and death (medieval Jews viewed conversion to Christianity as idolatry), it is forbidden to suffer voluntary martyrdom, i.e. to kill oneself and others for the sake of preventing idol worship, baptism, or falling into Christian hands. See Maimonides, *Mishneh torah*, 'Hilkhot yesodei hatorah', 5: 1–5. See also Soloveitchik, 'Halakhah, Hermeneutics, and Martyrdom: Part I', 80–1.

48 Soloveitchik, 'Religious Law and Change', 210–11. The act of killing family members to prevent them from falling into Christian hands, although not permitted, was granted a weak ex post facto halakhic justification in a responsum of R. Meir of Rothenburg. See Soloveitchik, 'Halakhah, Hermeneutics, and Martyrdom: Part I', 98–101.

49 Soloveitchik, 'Religious Law and Change', 209, 211; id., 'Halakhah, Hermeneutics, and Martyrdom: Part I', 101.

The Rhineland martyrs' appellation *kedoshim* (holy ones) testifies to the community's approbation of their actions.[50]

The variety and often novel character of methods of commemoration of the Rhineland martyrs further testifies to the centrality of their position in the Ashkenazi community. With the exception of a few model figures—great rabbis such as R. Akiva, Judah b. Bava, and Hanina b. Tradyon—the martyrs of the rabbinic period were not commemorated at all.[51] By contrast, the Rhineland martyrs were remembered in prayers, prose, and poetry, and in specially designed memorial books.[52] These books, from which the names of individual martyrs were publicly read out in the synagogue, represented a specifically medieval mode of commemoration,[53] whose intent was as much to remember and immortalize the dead as to educate the Ashkenazi communities towards the ideal of martyrdom.[54]

Scholars have shown that the German Pietists had no special teaching with regard to martyrdom, and they warned others not to actively seek it out.[55] They did, however, view it as an axiomatic act when forced upon a person: '[Just as,] if [at a time of religious persecution] they were trying to kill you or torture you so that you are forced to choose death over life, you would suffer, how much more so regarding this matter, which [i.e. the cost] is not so great, [you should suffer].'[56] Martyrdom was the expected, natural mode of conduct when one found oneself in such a situation.[57] Also, despite their admonitions regarding future conduct, the Pietists showed no disregard for the acts of voluntary martyrdom performed by their ancestors, the Rhineland martyrs. On the contrary, through the medium of the ghost tale, they elevated their status to that of the holy dead.

Inappropriate Burial in *Sefer Ḥasidim*

R. Judah the Pious is forthright in his ruling regarding the impermissibility of burying the wicked alongside the righteous. In one passage, he reiterates

[50] Soloveitchik, 'Religious Law and Change', 209; id., 'Halakhah, Hermeneutics, and Martyrdom: Part I', 79.

[51] Goldin, *The Ways of Jewish Martyrdom*, 129.

[52] Ibid. 123–50. See also Wachtel, 'The Ritual and Liturgical Commemoration of Two Medieval Persecutions', 3–6. I wish to thank Haym Soloveitchik for providing me with this source.

[53] Goldin, *The Ways of Jewish Martyrdom*, 129.

[54] Ibid. 91–2 and 133.

[55] Soloveitchik, 'Halakhah, Hermeneutics, and Martyrdom: Part II', 291. Joseph Dan also argues that martyrdom is not central to Pietist ideology. However, he feels that it informs the Pietists' pessimistic outlook on life, while at the same time serving as the culmination of their ascetic practices. See Dan, 'The Problem of *Kidush Hashem*' (Heb.).

[56] *SḤ* 2, pp. 4–5.

[57] For similar thinking in other Ashkenazi texts, see MS Paris hebr. 363, 'Hilkhot teshuvah', and MS Vatican ebr. 183, 'Iskei teshuvah', 162*a*, cited in Kozma, 'The Practice of *Teshuvah*', Appendix 2, pp. 6 and 63 respectively.

the talmudic statement in *Sanhedrin* and says, 'It is forbidden to bury the wicked beside the righteous . . . rather, we bury the wicked beside the wicked and the righteous beside the righteous.'[58] He cites the passage from Scripture in which the remains of the prophet Elisha resurrect the wicked man's bones as proof that 'he should not have been buried beside him'. In a related passage, R. Judah points out that in his day the talmudic dictum has practical application: the Jewish communities bury any individual who dies excommunicate on the outskirts of the Jewish cemetery. His grave must be more than eight *amot* away from the nearest grave, 'so that the area of any grave, which is four *amot*, should not touch his grave'.[59] As in the passage in *Sanhedrin*, the wicked person's grave is to be at a distance from those of the rest of the Jewish community, who are deemed righteous. With the power of capital punishment removed from Jewish hands, and with excommunication serving as the most potent means of internal discipline in force in the medieval Ashkenazi communities, it is small wonder that the excommunicate replaced the executed criminal of the Talmud.[60]

In addition to his reference to the statement in *Sanhedrin*, R. Judah also accepts the message conveyed in tractate *Mo'ed katan* that the righteous have recognized differences in status when it comes to burial, as do the wicked. He exhorts one to bury only righteous individuals who possess the same degree of piety side by side. Here, however, his wishes are not in consonance with the accepted practice in his community. He phrases the above-mentioned exhortation in the conditional: 'If the Good [*hatovim*, i.e. the Pietists or their supporters] have the upper hand, they should bury only righteous individuals, who are similar to each other, together alone [in a separate area].'[61] Eleazar of Worms echoes this view in his *Sefer ḥokhmat hanefesh*, a work whose target audience was Pietist or quasi-Pietist, but not in his *Sefer haroke'aḥ*, written for a general audience. In *Sefer ḥokhmat hanefesh*, he forbids one to bury an average righteous person (*tsadik she'eino hagun*) beside a fully righteous one (*tsadik gamur*).[62] R. Isaac of Vienna, student of R. Judah, makes the following further distinction:

58 *SḤ* 267.

59 *SḤ* 268; see also *SḤ* 1540.

60 The minor tractate *Semaḥot* lists three types of sinner who are to be buried outside the Jewish cemetery: the suicide, one who separates himself from the community, and the criminal executed by a court. The excommunicate is not mentioned. See *The Tractate Mourning*, ed. Zlotnick, 2: 1–6, 8. Interestingly, in medieval times the Christian excommunicate was buried outside the churchyard. See Schur, 'The Care for the Dead in Medieval Ashkenaz', 144 n. 70.

61 *SḤ* 1535 (last two lines).

62 See *Sefer ḥokhmat hanefesh*, 22*a*. A responsum issued by R. Shalom of Neustadt indicates that in his day (late thirteenth- to early fourteenth-century Vienna) there were operative

We should be mindful about not burying a righteous man by a pious man. The righteous man is one who abides by the letter of the law and lives up to the manifested legal standards, allows what is allowed and forbids what is forbidden; but a pious man is one who segregates and sanctifies himself even with that which is permissible.[63]

R. Judah further extends the application of the talmudic dictum regarding proximate burial when he stipulates that only a *tsadik* should bury a *tsadik*, and a *rasha* should not be seated next to a *tsadik* even while alive.[64]

R. Judah's admonitions concerning proximate burial are not mere theorizing, and they may perhaps have been prompted by the following story. *Sefer ḥasidim* recounts how once a righteous scholar (*talmid ḥakham tsadik*) was buried beside a person of improper conduct (*mi she'eino hagun*). The dead scholar appears afterwards in a dream to all the members of the community, complaining that they have harmed him by burying him next to a 'stinking cesspool'. In addition to the intolerable smell, the smoke is also bothering him. The townspeople come to his aid by erecting a stone wall as a partition between his and his unworthy neighbour's graves. The scholar never appears to them again.[65]

Comparison of this story with the scenario depicted in *Mo'ed katan* and cited previously highlights the contrast between the treatment of the principle in rabbinic times and in the Middle Ages. Whereas both stories demonstrate the inadmissibility of the improper burial of a low-ranking individual next to a righteous person of higher rank, the elements of the narratives differ sharply. In the talmudic story, the miraculous appearance of the snake, witnessed by those attempting to bury the repentant excommunicated scholar, prevents the inappropriate burial from taking place, while in the Pietist narrative nothing out of the ordinary suggests itself to those who wrongfully bury the righteous scholar beside the person of improper conduct. It is only the oral testimony of the dead person himself, transmitted via a dream, that proclaims the action to have been inappropriate. Additionally, the unworthiness of the person in the Pietist story expresses itself in the form of an intolerable smell and bothersome smoke,

distinctions regarding status among the righteous in the burial grounds. The responsum speaks of a separate area of the cemetery assigned to the 'great ones' (*hagedolim*) and an area at the entrance assigned to 'people of proper conduct' (*hagunim*). R. Shalom rules that the distinctions must be maintained. Schur, 'The Care for the Dead in Medieval Ashkenaz', 135. The Pietist definition of the terms in question may have particular, sectarian meanings that are absent from R. Shalom's ruling.

[63] Isaac b. Moses, *Or zarua*, vol. ii, no. 422: 4, cited in Shoham-Steiner, 'Burial *ad sanctos* for a Jewish Murderer?', 139.

[64] See *SḤ* 1563 and *SḤ* 60 respectively.

[65] *SḤ* 266.

which are elements perceived solely by the dead person—unlike the snake, which is visible to everyone. The smell and smoke are indicative of the dead man's status in the hereafter—a topic wholly absent from the talmudic narrative. Finally, instead of an immediate proper burial effected by the same individuals who engaged in the first, mistaken, burial attempt, as in the talmudic narrative, a different set of people (all the townspeople, to whom the deceased appears in the dream) comes to the aid of the righteous scholar and rectifies the situation in the Pietist account.

The new elements of the Pietist story as compared to the talmudic account are not simply a reflection of necessary adjustments to reality made by an astute storyteller in a different society. Instead, they reflect the conscious adoption of well-known motifs of the exempla literature. It is through the medium of the high medieval ghost tale, with its roots in pre-Christian notions, that the principle of not burying the righteous alongside the wicked is illustrated in *Sefer ḥasidim*.

The Motif of Improper Burial: Pre-Christian Roots and Christian Origins

It is an ancient belief that a prime cause of the restlessness of the dead is the failure to bury and/or remember them in an appropriate manner. Germanic funerary rites describe in detail the procedure of preparing, washing, and wrapping the body of the deceased prior to burial.[66] The Icelandic sagas stress the importance of the burial of a loved one in close proximity to the community of the living.[67] Both Roman and Germanic custom obligate the living to honour the dead with banquets and festivities and to perpetuate their memory in specific rituals.[68] According to ancient Germanic law, a person is considered dead only when his living relatives have satisfied the requirements of customary funerary rites. Those heirs who fail to honour the deceased in this fashion disquiet him and expose themselves to his wrath and vengeance.[69]

[66] Lecouteux reconstructs these rites on the basis of elements found in the Icelandic sagas. Their basic features included the following: all the orifices of the dead were obstructed, the body was washed, the head was wrapped in linen, and boots were placed on the feet. Later on, under the influence of Christian custom, the body was clothed in a pinned shroud. The dead were buried in tombs called tartars, although sometimes burial on a boat is recorded. See Lecouteux, *Fantômes et revenants*, 38–43.

[67] Ibid. 65, 145, 198, 230.

[68] Ibid. 58. Among the Germanic peoples, ceremonies celebrating the memory of the deceased were held on the third, seventh, and thirtieth day after a person's death. See ibid. 47.

[69] Lecouteux, *Fantômes et revenants*, 47, 58.

The Icelandic sagas tell of the dead, referred to as 'false ghosts', who return to life immediately after death to specify their last wishes and burial requests.[70] Others, known as the 'recalcitrant dead', express their reluctance to die or their wish to be buried in a specific spot by making their body unnaturally heavy so that they cannot be moved or dragged further.[71] Still others appear to the living to complain of an improper burial, which does not allow them to rest in peace. These are the 'true ghosts', who populate the ghost tales recorded in the sagas.[72]

The *Livre de la colonisation de l'Islande* records one such ghost tale. The dead hermit Asolf appears in a dream to one of the monks of Baer. He orders the monk to send a servant to Holm and have him buy the 'tuft of grass' in the spot where Asolf is buried for a certain amount of silver. The monk obeys Asolf's command. Having acquired the piece of land, the servant begins to dig up the earth at Holm, where he uncovers the bones of Asolf. He collects them and brings them to Asolf's house. That night, Asolf appears in a dream to Halldor, the new owner of his former domain at Holm, threatening that 'his two eyes will leave his skull' if he does not buy his bones. Fearing his words, the owner buys the bones, fashions a wooden reliquary for them, and places them above the altar of the local church.[73]

In this tale, in which Christian and pagan elements are mixed together, Asolf returns to demand a proper burial. Whereas in ancient society burial took place outside the city, in the medieval period the burial ground was moved increasingly inwards, into the very heart of Christian settlements—the church and its immediate vicinity. Similarly, whereas in Carolingian times funerary space had no cultic significance, by the end of the eleventh century this space was considered sanctified.[74] Following a ritual of consecration and dedication, in which holy water was sprinkled on the walls of the church, the burial places in and around the church also became hallowed ground.[75] As a Christian, and perhaps even more so as a hermit, Asolf feels he has to be buried in consecrated ground; he therefore appears

[70] Lecouteux refers to these dead as *faux revenants* since they appear to live on after death rather than return from the grave as the *vrais revenants* do. See *Fantômes et revenants*, 65, 83.

[71] Ibid. 65–7.

[72] These ghost tales record 'dysfunctions of the rite of passage of the dead'; Schmitt, 'Les Images des revenants', 288.

[73] *Le Livre de la colonisation de l'Islande*, 13, cited in Lecouteux, *Fantômes et revenants*, 87.

[74] Lauwers, *Naissance du cimetière*, 136.

[75] Ibid. 137. Lauwers states that the inclusion of the area surrounding the church (which included the burial ground) within the rite of benediction, thus sanctifying it, coincided with the period in history when the burial ground became termed a 'cemetery'. See *Naissance du cimetière*, 139.

to a monk and asks for his bones to be exhumed and reburied in the church.[76]

Still very much a pagan in his mentality, however, Asolf requires that his bones be purchased by the current owner of his former home so that they stay connected to the ground where he lived and died, acting like a guardian spirit of the land according to the Nordic belief system of the time.[77] The threat of real danger posed by the dead looms large in this tale (Halldor's two eyes will be gouged out), recalling at once the violence of the *draugar*. Seemingly, this threat motivates the new owner to exceed Asolf's own demands; instead of burying him in the sanctified ground of the church, he places the man's bones in a reliquary above the altar—a treatment usually reserved for the most holy, the saints themselves.[78]

A similar tale is recounted in *La Saga des habitants du Val au Saumon*. In this story, a dead woman, draped in a woollen cloak, her head covered with a rag, and looking altogether unappealing, appears in a dream to a young girl named Herdis. She complains that the girl's grandmother, who kneels and prays nightly in church, weeps over the exact spot where she is buried, and her tears are so hot that they burn her entire body. Upon awakening, Herdis shares her dream with her friend Gudrun. The next day, Gudrun enters the church, removes the floor planks in the specified place, and digs up the underlying soil. The bones of the dead woman, 'black and disquieting', are uncovered, along with a magic wand. The blackness of her bones symbolizes her sinful nature,[79] and the wand indicates that she was a

[76] Although Asolf does not say so explicitly to the monk, his intentions are clear from the events which occur at the end of the tale.

[77] Lecouteux, *Fantômes et revenants*, 88.

[78] See Lauwers, *Naissance du cimetière*, 57.

[79] The colour black is indissolubly associated with the dead in the Icelandic sagas. Night-time and wintertime—as nights are longest then—are the domain of the dead; most of their appearances in the sagas occur at this time, with the prime haunting season being during the twelve-day period around Christmas. The Germanic rituals that involve commemoration of the dead, such as family feasts, sacrifices, and games, also take place in darkest winter. See Lecouteux, *Fantômes et revenants*, 142–3. It is unclear, however, whether, in the belief system of the Germanic peoples, there existed a definitive link between the colour black and sin, although the evidence does seem to point in that direction. According to the testimony of Tacitus, the ancient Germans would portray the corpse as black. In medieval romance, black is the colour of the other world, whether magical or evil (see Lecouteux, p. ii). In the *Saga de Snorri le Godi*, an association is made between the 'bad dead', the transmission of disease, and the colour black; the various places that the evil ghost of a shepherd occupies are described as being 'black like coal' in that story. See Lecouteux, 107–10.

When one looks at the high medieval Christian ghost tales, the link between blackness and sinfulness is explicit. A common motif in Cistercian and mendicant tales is the successive appearance of a dead sinner to a living relative who is offering him posthumous aid. At first, the sinner appears with either his body or his clothing entirely black. A short while later, he

magician. The bones are then exhumed and reburied in a 'place less frequented by people'.[80]

As in the previous tale, the dead person is disquieted by some impropriety in her place of burial. That impropriety, however, is reversed in this story. Whereas in the preceding tale Asolf, a Christian hermit, is buried inappropriately in unconsecrated ground, here a sinful magician is buried undeservedly in too holy a spot; the pure tears of a devout Christian woman sear her bones. Not being able to sustain those tears, the magician's body must be reburied in a more profane spot, perhaps outside the church. This tale, which reflects a high degree of Christianization,[81] lacks the violent intensity that marks the previous tale; instead of verbally threatening to attack the living as Asolf does, the magician appears to the girl in a dream, which frightens her and urges her to satisfy the demands of the dead woman. The threat of actual harm has been reduced to a mere display of the power to harm. The moral of the story, however, remains the same; the Christian faithful (and only the truly faithful) are to be buried in the hallowed ground of the church—and all other Christian dead, both deserving and undeserving, will return to ensure that the living abide by that rule.

As in the Icelandic sagas, the dead of the high medieval ghost tale have much to say about their last wishes, burial, and subsequent commemora-

reappears with his body or clothing partly black and partly white, reflecting a moderate improvement in his spiritual status. In the final appearance, the ghost's body or garment is entirely white, a sign of his release from sin and of his salvation. See Caesarius of Heisterbach, *Dialogue*, 2: 2 and 12: 24, and Banks (ed.), *Alphabet of Tales*, 351 no. 519. This tale enjoyed wide popularity as the *Catalogue of Romances* lists several versions: MS BL Sloane 3102, fo. 51 (iii. 96 no. 37); MS BL Add. 11284, fos. 23*b* and 24 (iii. 383 no. 170, 384 no. 173 (*Speculum laicorum*)); MS BL Harley 268, fo. 153*b* and 2851 fo. 111*b* (iii. 436 no. 67 and 505 no. 33 respectively). Two exempla illustrate the phenomenon that the corpses of sinful men turn black immediately upon dying. Versions of the first of these tales are contained in *Catalogue of Romances*, iii. 502 no. 303 and 635 no. 108, while variants of the second are present in Caesarius of Heisterbach, *Dialogue*, 10: 41, as well as in *Catalogue of Romances*, iii. 365 no. 166 and 368 no. 56. Finally, the anonymous author of an early fifteenth-century manuscript declares that sin for a monk is like a stain on a white garment. See MS BL Add. 27336 fo. 24*b* (*Catalogue of Romances*, iii. 654 no. 103). See also Schmitt, *Ghosts in the Middle Ages*, 204 and n. 44; Le Goff, *Your Money or Your Life*, 85.

Since the tale from *La Saga des habitants du Val au Saumon* reflects a high degree of Christianization, although it is found in the Icelandic sagas, one can be sure that, in this case, the blackness of the dead magician's bones bespeaks her sinful nature. On the symbolism behind colour in medieval art, see Gage, *Color and Meaning*, 70–6.

80 Mossé, *La Laxdoela Saga*, ch. 76, cited in Lecouteux, *Fantômes et revenants*, 88.

81 Lecouteux, *Fantômes et revenants*, 88. The didactic aim of this story, its setting inside a church, the lack of any direct violence on the part of the ghost, the role of both women (the sinful magician and the devout grandmother), as well as the power attributed to sincere prayer and weeping are elements which together suggest a high degree of Christianization.

tion. Both the categories of the false ghost and of the recalcitrant dead appear in the story, albeit with substantial changes due to Christianization. While the false ghosts of the sagas seem to live on in order to specify their last wishes and burial requests, the false dead of the high medieval exempla return for the purpose of obtaining absolution,[82] making confession,[83] crying out about their posthumous fate,[84] and petitioning the living for aid.[85]

The unusual heaviness characteristic of the corpses of the recalcitrant dead is an element found in one ghost tale of Jacques de Vitry.[86] Whereas in the sagas this heaviness is an expression of unwillingness to be put to eternal rest on the part of the *draugr*, who wishes to cause unrest among the living,[87] in de Vitry's tale it symbolizes the sinfulness of a dead usurer (the 'bad dead' of thirteenth-century France[88]). In another of de Vitry's tales, a further change may be perceived in the role assumed by the recalcitrant dead; in place of the resistance of the bodies in the sagas, de Vitry tells of a soul's unwillingness to leave the body.[89] Caesarius of Heisterbach recounts the unnatural attachment to life one condemned criminal's body manifests until a sacrament for the salvation of his soul is performed.[90]

[82] See e.g. *Catalogue of Romances*, iii. 476 no. 65.

[83] This motif of rising up for posthumous confession enjoyed wide popularity and appeared in a large number of manuscripts of the period.

[84] *Catalogue of Romances*, iii. 588 no. 84 and 704 no. 30.

[85] Caesarius of Heisterbach, *Dialogue*, 7: 16.

[86] A certain usurer's body is so heavy it cannot be carried to the grave by his neighbours. A wise old man informs them that the custom of the town is for members of the same profession as the deceased to bring the body to burial. The body is then easily lifted by other usurers. Jacques de Vitry, *Exempla*, no. 178.

[87] When Thorolf l'Estropié's body resists burial, those present perceive this as a bad sign. Fearing that he will return to cause harm, they bury him on the spot under a pile of stones. *Eyrbyggja Saga*, ch. 33, cited in Lecouteux, *Fantômes et revenants*, 67.

[88] Lecouteux, *Fantômes et revenants*, 139, argues that the dead whose return is most feared are those who 'remain on the margins of social life'. From the point of view of a French ecclesiastic of the thirteenth century, usurers are most definitely on the margin of a holy Christian society. They are among the most depraved men in de Vitry's tales, all of whom deservedly meet a horrible, ignoble end: toads and serpents cover their rotting corpses, their designated place of burial is on the dungheap, and their souls are consigned to hellfire. See Jacques de Vitry, *Exempla*, nos. 168, 170, 175–7, and 179. In this tale (no. 178), the sinfulness of the profession is doubly manifest when the unnaturally heavy body of the usurer (indicative of his sinful state) becomes light and easy for the other usurers to carry, stressing that they too are in an unnatural, sinful state.

[89] A pilgrim's soul must be consoled by the music of King David in order for it to leave the body. See Jacques de Vitry, *Exempla*, no. 132.

[90] A knight is hanged by Barbarossa but his body stays alive to receive the Host (Caesarius of Heisterbach, *Dialogue*, 9: 49). This story also appears in Banks (ed.), *An Alphabet of Tales*, 456 no. 681, and in *Catalogue of Romances*, iii. 363 no. 147, 368 no. 47, 605 no. 9, and 614 no. 119.

The dead of the high medieval exempla, like those of the Icelandic sagas, return to complain of an improper burial. In the Middle Ages, burial in a church or other holy place was perceived as an aid to the salvation of one's soul since it enlisted the intercessory powers of the saint or other holy person in whose proximity one was buried.[91] In the thirteenth century, laymen were increasingly seeking to secure for themselves such a burial, a privilege which had until then usually been reserved for monks and clerics.[92] Improper burial, which disquiets the dead of the exempla, is linked with this wish to be buried in Christian holy space.

As early as the eleventh century, in the *Liber Visionum* of Otloh of St Emmeram, a tale is told of a monk from Fulda who drowns in a body of water. Presuming he has committed suicide, the cellarer buries him outside the cemetery.[93] The dead monk appears to the cellarer and warns him that only God can judge the actions of man.[94] In the twelfth century, the English chronicler Walter Map recounts the tale of a corpse that wanders for more than a month, until it is determined that it needs proper burial. The corpse finally remains in its grave when the townspeople affix a cross to mark the site.[95] The collection of tales entitled *Alphabetum Narrationum*, which dates from the late thirteenth or early fourteenth century,[96] records a tale in the name of St Gregory of a bishop who allows a renegade sinner named Valerius to be buried inside the church. St Faustinius, the patron saint of the church, appears at night to the keeper of the church, bidding him to go and warn the bishop to remove the body of the sinner within thirty days or else he will die. The bishop ignores the saint's warning, as a result of which he is found dead in his bed on the morning of the thirtieth day.[97]

This latter tale mirrors closely the role played by the dead in the above-cited Icelandic tales. Like Asolf and the magician, St Faustinius cannot rest

[91] Iogna-Prat, *Order and Exclusion*, 223.

[92] Le Goff, *The Birth of Purgatory*, 276.

[93] Suicides, as well as Jews and unbaptized infants, were denied burial in the 'holy space' of the Christian cemetery, which, in this period, was a walled-in piece of land marked by a large cross. See Schmitt, *Ghosts in the Middle Ages*, 183.

[94] Migne, *Patrologia Latina*, vol. cxlvi, vision no. 16, cited in Schmitt, *Ghosts in the Middle Ages*, 47.

[95] Map, *De nugis curialium*, 204, quoted in Caciola, 'Wraiths, Revenants and Ritual', 20.

[96] The author of this treatise, designed for use by preachers, has traditionally been held to be Etienne de Besançon, a Dominican who died in 1294. J. A. Herbert, the editor of vol. iii of the *Catalogue of Romances*, disputes this point, arguing that the author is Arnold of Liège, who compiled it in 1308. See *Catalogue of Romances*, iii. 423–7.

[97] Banks (ed.), *An Alphabet of Tales*, 470–1 no. 702. Two fourteenth-century manuscripts also contain this tale: see MS BL Add. 15833 fo. 169*b* and MS BL 18347 fo. 78*b*, col. 2 (*Catalogue of Romances*, iii. 594 no. 137 and 598 no. 6 respectively). According to the account in the manuscript, the bishop was bribed to allow the sinner to be buried in the cathedral.

in peace because an impropriety in the place of burial has occurred. As in the case of the magician buried under the floor planks in the place of prayer of the devout grandmother, the body of the sinner Valerius has also been unjustly granted too holy a tomb. The dead must once again remind the living that only the Christian faithful can be buried near the saintly ones, inside the church.[98] Here, however, it is the patron saint of the church rather than the sinner who returns from the dead to correct the injustice. The threat of real violence rings forth here as well: like Asolf, who threatens to gouge out the eyes of the new owner of his domain for failure to bury his bones in consecrated ground, St Faustinius demands that the bishop remove the body from the church or he will cause his death—which, in fact, is what happens.

The living are responsible for the correction of improprieties in the burial of the dead in several other tales drawn from the exempla literature. The above-mentioned passage from the *Alphabetum Narrationum* continues and cites another tale of a sinner buried undeservedly in a church. This time strange voices and cries, 'as though there had been men drawn out against their will', are heard emanating from the church at midnight, the time of day most suited to the appearance of ghosts.[99] The body of the sinner—most likely along with those of others like him—is seen being removed from the grave, thrown out of the church, and cast into a foul dike. In a fourteenth-century manuscript, a tale cited in the name of Nicholas de Flavigny, archbishop of Besançon, tells of a usurer who is buried in a cloister. He arises at night, disturbs the monks, and demands that they remove his body, or else his marauding will continue.[100] In a variant version, the usurer rises up to announce that he is damned, and his body is seen being carried off by devils.[101] It is not surprising, then, to find that Rudolf von Schlettstadt, in his 'Vita Remigii', chronicles accounts of saints who would not allow themselves to be buried next to the unworthy.[102] Here the righteous dead, rather than the wicked, demand the removal of the one who does not belong.

98 See Le Goff, *The Birth of Purgatory*, 276.

99 See n. 79 above.

100 MS BL Add. 28682 (*Catalogue of Romances*, iii. 83 no. 6). A very similar tale is found in an early fourteenth-century manuscript. It tells of a usurer who is buried by monks (whom he has bribed) in front of the altar of a church. Having been sent to eternal damnation instead of the promised salvation, he begins to attack them. His corpse is then removed and reburied outside. MS BL Arundel 506 fo. 27, col. 2 (*Catalogue of Romances*, iii. 551 no. 143).

101 MS BL Egerton 1117 fo. 188, col. 2 (*Catalogue of Romances*, iii. 474 no. 50).

102 'Vita Remigii', 17 and 25, quoted in Gurevich, *Medieval Popular Culture*, 47.

The moral of all these stories is one: when the living blur the boundary between the holy and the profane, it is the dead who restore the balance.

The Motif of Improper Burial in *Sefer Ḥasidim*

While no evidence of the recalcitrant dead appears in *Sefer ḥasidim*, one ghost tale in the work contains a parallel to the role played by the false ghost in the medieval exempla literature. In the tale, a certain non-Jewish noblewoman rises up soon after dying. While still on her bier, she stands up and announces what she has seen in the other world.[103] Like other Christianized false ghosts of the medieval exempla, this noblewoman appears to live on after death in order to tell of the posthumous fate of others.

A much larger group of narratives in *Sefer ḥasidim* speaks of the dead who return to complain to the living of improprieties in the place of their burial. This group of tales forms the bulk of the material included under the heading 'Inyan metim' ('Matters Relating to the Dead').[104] One such tale is that mentioned above regarding the burial of a righteous scholar beside a man of improper conduct. The dead scholar appears in a dream to all the members of the town, complaining that they have harmed him by burying him next to a 'stinking cesspool'. In this regard, the hasidic tale follows the pattern set by the Icelandic story of Asolf, Otloh of St Emmeram's tale of the drowned monk, and the *Alphabetum Narrationum*'s tale of the patron saint, St Faustinius—all righteous, or at least faithful, individuals who appear to the living and complain of a wrongful burial.[105] Like St Faustinius, the righteous scholar of the Pietist story cannot rest in peace so long as the unworthy person is buried in his vicinity. The appellation assigned to the man of improper conduct (stinking cesspool) is reminiscent of the other tale recorded in the *Alphabetum Narrationum*: the sinner who has been undeservedly buried inside a church is seen being cast out and thrown into a foul dike.

The Pietist narrative reflects other elements of the ghost tales mentioned above. Both the sagas and the Pietist story recount incidents in which the dead appear to individuals who were not involved in their initial improper burial. Most similar to the Pietist tale in this regard is the account of Walter Map, in which all the townspeople participate in the burial of the wandering corpse. Several other tales drawn from the exempla literature

[103] *SḤ* 272.

[104] *SḤ* 1530–67, pp. 375–84.

[105] St Faustinius differs from the dead of the other tales in that he complains of the improper burial of another individual, not his own.

underscore the responsibility of the living to correct the improprieties that occur in the burial of the dead—an important component of the Pietist tale. Additionally, the stench of the dead sinner described in the Pietist tale, along with the smoke that surrounds him, is a common indicator in medieval literature of the sinner's fate in the afterlife. A putrid smell and an ever-burning fire are characteristic of both Hell and Purgatory.[106] In the exempla, other elements associated with Hell and Purgatory, such as the presence of toads and snakes around the corpse and the feeding of burning hot coals or gold coins into the mouth of the cadaver, are found, and they too are indicative of the posthumous fate of the sinner.[107] The marks on the corpse are reflective of the tortures being experienced simultaneously by the person's soul in Hell or in Purgatory.[108]

The Pietist tale, however, differs in two important respects from the saga narratives and the Christian exempla. Firstly, it is devoid of any threat of violence on the part of the dead. Secondly, it lacks the extreme designations of righteousness and irreverence commonly found in the exempla literature. In that literature, it is only the renegade sinner, typically a usurer, whose proximity cannot be tolerated by the extremely holy—a saint, the

106 While the fires of Hell and Purgatory are well known, their stench is less so. In visionary literature, for example the *Apocalypse of Paul*, stench is one of the many tortures in the region known as upper Hell, which, according to Le Goff, is the precursor of Purgatory. In the voyage of Thurkill (told over in 1206 by the monk Roger of Wendover in his *Flores historiarum*), Thurkill smells the 'fetid odour' of Hell. In Guibert of Nogent's account of his mother's vision, a horrid smell is described among the tortures of Purgatory. See Le Goff, *The Birth of Purgatory*, 36, 296–7, 182–5 respectively. Apart from visionary accounts, Honorius of Autun's *Elucidarium*—a work of enormous popularity in the high medieval period—lists as the fourth torture of lower Hell 'an unbearable stench'. In rabbinic literature, smoke surrounds the grave of a person who has been sentenced to Gehenna, but there is no mention of stench. See BT *Ḥag.* 15*b*.

107 See the following examples of sinners whose graves are opened in the *Catalogue of Romances*: a toad is found in the mouth of an oppressive bailiff (iii. 564 no. 68, 640 no. 16); a woman who has murdered her children is found with two serpents at her breasts (iii. 545 no. 51); snakes coil around the neck and waist of a vain woman (iii. 542 no. 7, 615 no. 121, 643 no. 12); money is seen pouring into the mouth of a greedy nun (iii. 597 no. 2, 600 no. 16). See also Caesarius of Heisterbach, *Dialogue*, 11: 39, where toads are feeding money into the mouth of a usurer in his grave, and Jacques de Vitry, *Exempla*, no. 168, in which demons fill a usurer's mouth with red-hot coins.

108 Cynthia Ho examines Jacques de Vitry's conception of the human body as reflected in his exempla. She argues that de Vitry 'conceives of the dead individual in two simultaneous existences: the buried body and its soul, clothed in a quasi-disembodied remembrance mirroring the person's earthly form, suffering in atonement for the sins of the soma, or (much less often) enjoying the rewards of good action'. While Ho refers only to Jacques de Vitry's belief, this conception of the dead underlies all the aforementioned tales regarding punishment in the grave. See Ho, '*Corpus Delicti*', 209.

patron saint of the church, or monks buried near the altar. In the Pietist tale, however, it is the rather mild designation of *eino hagun* that is used for the man whose presence so disturbs the *talmid ḥakham tsadik*. This could possibly explain why a partition of stone suffices here to satisfy the deceased, while exhumation is always the demand issued in the typical tale. The dead of *Sefer ḥasidim* appear to be far more sensitive to the degree of religiosity of their neighbours in the grave than those who regularly feature in the exempla. Pietistic elitism here extends beyond the realm of the living and into that of the dead.[109]

Martyrs as Holy Dead in *Sefer Ḥasidim*

The motif of improper burial found in the sagas and the exempla literature surfaces several times in *Sefer ḥasidim*, in connection with the burial of martyrs in particular. Interestingly, the Christian concept of burial *ad sanctos* (next to the saints) originally referred exclusively to burial beside martyrs.[110] As the Christians martyred by the Romans were considered saints 'in the highest degree', their bodies were sought for proximate burial as early as the third century and were coveted for this purpose for centuries afterwards.[111] A desire to share in their exceptional merits, useful for Judgement Day, prompted the faithful in this early period to act thus.[112] As powerful intercessors and sources of miraculous healing, martyrs became the holy dead, a category that was later extended to include all Christian saints.[113]

With regard to the martyrs' tales in *Sefer ḥasidim*, Pietist terminology here closely adheres to the more extreme designations of sinner/wicked and faithful/righteous which regularly appear in ghost tales of the exempla literature. A case in point is the story of the Jewish *rasha* who is buried among martyrs, mentioned at the outset of the chapter.[114] The martyrs appear in a dream to an 'important living man', urging him to have the body removed from among them as it is 'very difficult for them'.[115] The

[109] Regarding the Pietists' elitist ideal of settlement, in which they encouraged their followers to separate themselves physically from the rest of the Jewish community, see Marcus, *Piety and Society*, 87–106.

[110] Bartlett, *Why Can the Dead Do Such Great Things?*, 14–15.

[111] Ibid. 15. During the first centuries of Christianity's existence, the term 'saints' referred to all Christians. However, as the desire to be buried near the graves of martyrs became widespread, the designation gradually acquired the more narrow meaning of 'perfect or heroic Christians' (see ibid. 14–16).

[112] Ibid. 15, 625.

[113] Ibid. 16.

[114] Several passages in *Sefer ḥasidim* mention a mass grave of martyrs. See *SḤ* 1530, 1531 and 1532.

[115] *SḤ* 265.

elements of the hasidic tale here parallel those of the Icelandic saga and the exempla cited earlier. Like the dead magician of the saga and the sinner Valerius or the usurer of the exempla collections, the *rasha* of the hasidic tale is inappropriately buried by the living in too holy a spot.[116] The 'important living man' to whom the dead person appears parallels the cellarer and the keeper of the church in the exempla—living men who are in a position to effect a change in burial. Any trace or threat of violence by the dead has vanished here, however.

Most importantly, as we have seen in the second tale from the *Alphabetum Narrationum*, in which the body of the sinner is thrown out of the church at night, the tale recorded in *Sefer ḥasidim* describes how the martyrs are disturbed by the presence of the sinner's body among them. The mass grave of martyrs here replaces the consecrated ground of the church and serves as the *terra sancta* of the Jewish community. The role played by the martyrs resembles that of the saints in Rudolf von Schlettstadt's 'Vita Remigii'; their sanctity precludes the toleration of the unworthy in their midst. The Pietists have appropriated Christian notions of the holy dead and adapted them for Jewish use. Even more strikingly, Pietist attitudes towards the burial sites of the Rhineland martyrs here approximate Christian ideas of holy space.

From the early eleventh century, medieval Jews possessed their own communal cemeteries.[117] In Judaism, the cemetery is not in itself a sacred

116 According to the variant reading of the Pietist tale mentioned above in n. 2 (in which a singular subject appears, 'He came in a dream'), it could potentially be the *rasha* of the hasidic tale who appears to the living, demanding to be removed from the midst of the martyrs. If this were to be the case then the hasidic tale echoes more closely the stories of the magician and the usurer—tales in which the sinful person herself or himself appears to the living to protest against the improper burial.

117 The first Jewish cemetery was nearly coeval with Jewish settlement in Germany. As early as 1012, Mar Solomon and his wife Rachel bequeathed land for a cemetery in Mainz (see Aronius, *Regesten zur Geschichte der Juden*, 62 no. 145). The Jewish cemetery at Worms contains tombstones that date from the last quarter of the eleventh century (the earliest one from 1076/1077). In 1084, the charter of residence granted to the Jews of Speyer, which served as a model for other medieval German Jewish settlements, specified their right to a separate cemetery (Aronius, 70 no. 168). See also Toch, 'The Jews in Europe: 500–1050', 554.

One historian of late medieval Jewish burial practices, Sylvie-Anne Goldberg, argues that the notion of an exclusively Jewish burial ground was linked to the exclusion of the Jewish dead from Christian sacred burial ground. She writes: 'The idea of a funerary space shared by Jews and Christians later became unthinkable, due in part to Christians' increasing sense of the sacred, which extended to the bodies of the dead, and in part to irreconcilable differences regarding the conduct of the living at the cemetery.' The Jewish cemetery as an entity continued to exist 'in this spatially identical way' until the end of the eighteenth century; Goldberg here alludes to the fact that Jewish cemetery space was conceived of in a parallel fashion to its space;[118] any land is fit for the purpose so long as it is outside the area of settlement, at a distance of at least 50 cubits (approximately 23 metres).[119] The various prohibitions enacted during the tannaitic period regulated conduct at the cemetery and reinforced its distance from the community of the living.[120] The rabbis of the Mishnah and the Talmud viewed the cemetery as a place devoid of sanctity, and the living were forbidden from observing the commandments in the presence of the dead buried there. Since the dead can no longer observe the commandments, to do so 'in front of them' would be to mock them.[121] Such action was considered reprehensible as it clearly demonstrated a flagrant disrespect for the dead.

Despite this fact, the ghost tales recorded in *Sefer ḥasidim* portray Jewish burial sites in a way that reflects the notion of the cemetery as a holy space. Apart from the Pietist tale just mentioned, another passage in *Sefer ḥasidim* describes a similar occurrence, in which sinners' bodies are buried inappropriately among those of the martyrs. Citing a passage from Ecclesiastes, R. Judah the Pious states that the ground in which the martyrs are buried is comparable to a full stomach, wide at the bottom and narrow at the top, into which bones are cast all jumbled up. This causes the martyrs undue pain and anguish: 'It causes them pain when the bones of the righteous are thrown, [and] also the bones of the wicked, and a person cannot recognize one from the other.'[122] Unlike the biblical case of the bones of the wicked false prophet being cast upon those of the righteous Elisha, here there is no miracle to resolve the problem. Instead, the dead must speak up for themselves.

In yet another ghost tale in *Sefer ḥasidim* involving inappropriate burial

Christian counterpart—Jews, too, would reject the interment of the unholy dead in their midst. See Goldberg, *Crossing the Jabbok*, 24–6.

118 Goldberg says this explicitly; *Crossing the Jabbok*, 25.

119 N. Rubin, *The End of Life* (Heb.), 143.

120 Rubin (ibid. 143–4) separates these prohibitions according to their function: (*a*) performing everyday labour in the cemetery, such as pasturing of animals or passage of water for irrigation; (*b*) leisure activities, such as leisurely walks or pulling grass; (*c*) mystical endeavours (sleeping overnight); and (*d*) religious activity, such as performance of certain *mitsvot*. This ban on so many varied forms of activity within the cemetery, along with the absence of any stipulation to visit the dead buried there, leads Rubin to conclude that, in the eyes of the rabbis, the Jewish cemetery was a *lo makom* ('no-place'), meant to remain apart from the community of the living.

121 Tractate *Semaḥot* forbids the performance of certain commandments (such as the donning of *tefilin*, recitation of the Shema, or even the carrying of a Torah scroll) in the cemetery for this reason. See *The Tractate Mourning*, ed. Zlotnick, 13: 3–4. The Talmud echoes this sentiment: see *Ber.* 11*a* and 18*a*. A comprehensive treatment of this topic can be found in Lichtenstein, 'From the Impurity of the Dead to Their Sanctification' (Heb.), 1–137.

122 *SḤ* 1531.

and a mass grave of martyrs, the dead do precisely that. Following an instance of mass martyrdom, the bodies of all those who are killed in defiance of baptism are carted off in wagons for burial.[123] During the course of the rather lengthy journey to the burial site, the body of one martyred woman falls off the wagon unnoticed. After the remaining bodies are interred, the dead woman appears in a dream to a certain (unnamed) individual. Angry, she asks why, having died in sanctification of God's name like the other martyrs, she has been denied burial among them.[124] After investigating the matter, the unnamed person pledges money as a reward to anyone who finds her body. A shepherd steps forth and identifies the place where the body is located, and the woman is laid to rest in the martyrs' mass grave.[125] On that very night, she reappears to the same individual and thanks him for his actions. In exchange for his pledging money on her behalf, she reveals to him the exact whereabouts of a small amount of gold which she had stashed away while she was alive. Indeed, the hidden wealth is uncovered.[126]

In this tale of the female martyr, as in the others previously cited, the dead yet again come to correct the injustice committed by the living. What is novel here is the second appearance of the martyr. While it is common in the exempla literature for ghosts to return to the living people who have aided them to show the efficaciousness of their actions and to thank them,[127] it is mentioned in only this one tale in the Pietist work. The reappearance of the martyr, with her voluntary offering of hidden treasure, amplifies the edifying component of the tale: if one helps the dead, the dead will pay one back.

This is an inversion of the earlier tale; there an unworthy individual is buried inappropriately in the *terra sancta* of the martyrs' grave, whereas

[123] Wagons were used to transport the remains of martyrs, as attested by Ephraim of Bonn. In his *Sefer zekhirah*, he writes the following regarding the martyrs of the Second Crusade: 'The bishop ordered that all the slaughtered martyrs should be collected in carts, including all substantial remains . . . and all that could be found of their bodies and limbs, and he gave instructions to bury them in his garden' (*Sefer zekhirah*, quoted in Reiner, 'The Dead as Living History', 200).

[124] See MS JTS Boesky 45 no. 640.

[125] That it is a mass grave is evident from the following description: 'And they buried the corpses in large and wide ditches.'

[126] *SḤ* 1530 (this is the first of two ghost tales in the passage).

[127] A prime example is the oft-repeated tale of the usurer of Liège, who is saved by his wife's prayers. Appearing first in black clothes, he informs her that her prayers have saved him from Hell, but begs her to continue her prayers in order to relieve him from the torments he still faces. After some time, he appears again, dressed all in white, and informs her that, on account of her prayers, he is now free of torment. Caesarius of Heisterbach, *Dialogue*, 12: 24. See also Le Goff, *La Bourse et la vie*, 92–3.

here a righteous martyr is excluded from such burial. More than seeking mere interment, she wishes to be buried among the martyrs, which underscores the connection between holiness and the martyrs' grave. Has exclusion from their company in the grave prevented her from joining their ranks in Paradise above? Another ghost tale in *Sefer ḥasidim* suggests that, indeed, the martyrs have a specially designated area in Paradise which is exclusive to them and which is coveted by others. R. Judah the Pious prefaces that story with the real-life account that many devout Jews, at the time of persecution, desired martyrdom and prepared themselves for it, but were eventually saved from death. The tale is told as a means to reassure these would-be martyrs. A martyr named R. Shabetai appears to someone in a dream, proclaiming, 'All those who consciously and fully committed themselves to dying a martyr's death have a portion in Paradise with us.' The last word, *imanu* (with us), suggests the exclusive place in Paradise allotted to the martyrs that is so desired by those who have committed themselves to sharing their lot.[128] The evidence from the Hebrew Crusade chronicles cited above demonstrates that other Ashkenazi Jews also held this belief.[129] But there could be another reason for the woman's insistence on being buried in the mass grave. The soil in which the martyrs' corpses lie has become hallowed by their sanctity, and she, having been abandoned on profane soil, yearns to be moved to that holy space. Most likely, it is an intertwining of both notions, as is manifest in the Christian desire for burial *ad sanctos*—a longing both to be interred in the company of the saints and to rest in hallowed ground.

The inscription on the headstone of a wealthy Jew from Frankfurt, Alexander Wimpfen, who was buried beside R. Meir of Rothenburg in the early years of the fourteenth century, testifies to a similar belief regarding a righteous non-martyr. Having paid an enormous sum of money for the transfer of the body of R. Meir, who had died in a non-Jewish prison, to the burial ground in Worms, Alexander was able to secure the privilege of having his remains interred beside those of R. Meir. The inscription on Alexander's tombstone expresses the desire of the deceased to merit a place beside the great rabbi in Paradise, just as he is privileged to be next to him in the cemetery.[130]

[128] *SḤ* 264. See also no. 263, in which those individuals who would have chosen martyrdom had the situation presented itself are considered in Heaven to be actual martyrs (even though they died comfortably in their beds), to the extent that their reward is calculated as such and then adjusted accordingly: a deduction is made for the years they lived and the pleasures they enjoyed in place of having been martyred.

[129] See above, p. 92.

[130] Raspe, 'Sacred Space, Local History, and Diasporic Identity', 159. I wish to express my

We have seen that the concept of martyrs as holy dead was not exclusively Pietistic—it was part of the world-view of medieval Ashkenazi Jews at large. The same appears to be true with regard to the notion of the martyrs' burial site as holy space. The following incident, which Ephraim of Bonn chronicles, supports this point. In 1186 a mentally ill Jew murdered a Christian girl in Neuss, a town in Germany. The Christian residents of the town buried the murderer alive, killed several other Jews, and forcibly converted yet others. The bodies of the murdered were tied to the wheels of wagons and left outside on public display for forty days. When the Jews of Neuss were finally allowed access to the bodies, they ferried them up the Rhine to Xanten (a distance of 100 kilometres) in order to bury them 'by the graves of the righteous who were buried there during the events of 1096',[131] and, perhaps not coincidentally, in a town revered for its graves of early Christian martyrs and whose name means *ad sanctos*.[132] Although the victims of Neuss were never given the choice of conversion or death, as were the martyrs of 1096, their horrific murder by Christians on account of their Jewish identity earned them the prestige of martyrs. Having merited such status, they received the privilege of interment in the *terra sancta* of the Rhineland martyrs' burial site.[133]

As late as the second half of the seventeenth century and the early years of the eighteenth, the Rhineland martyrs' grave continued to attract those yearning for burial near the holy dead. Between 1670 and 1703 R. Shimshon Bachrach, his son, and his wife were all buried in close proximity to what is traditionally held to be the site of the mass grave. The area became known as Rabbis' Valley, and the Jewish community of Worms attached

gratitude to Ephraim Shoham-Steiner for this reference. Most recently, Shoham-Steiner has argued that Alexander was a murderer who had defied a ruling of R. Meir and sought atonement for the deed through his extraordinary expenditure of money to ensure appropriate burial of the rabbi's remains, as well as through arranging to be buried in proximity of the great sage. See Shoham-Steiner, 'Burial *ad sanctos* for a Jewish Murderer?'

131 These are the words of Ephraim of Bonn. See Goldin, *The Ways of Jewish Martyrdom*, 123 and 209.

132 The town of Xanten was founded on a burial site of Christian martyrs that was situated outside the ancient Roman city Colonia Ulpia Traiana in the Northern Rhine region of Germany. See Bartlett, *Why Can the Dead Do Such Great Things?*, 10.

133 The earliest evidence of the 'hierarchy of sacred space emerging in the cemetery' with regard to righteous non-martyrs dates from the early fourteenth century. In addition to the example of Alexander Wimpfen, evidence of the same phenomenon appeared much later in the Mainz cemetery. Beginning in 1644, prominent rabbis were laid to rest there near the tomb of the eleventh-century Ashkenazi liturgical poet, R. Shimon b. Isaac. See Raspe, 'Sacred Space, Local History, and Diasporic Identity', 158–9 and 156–7 respectively.

prestige to the martyrs' grave through communal processions conducted there on fast days.[134]

Given the aura surrounding the burial site of the Rhineland martyrs, it is not surprising to find that the notion of the cemetery as a holy place (*makom kadosh*) is first documented in the halakhic writings of a German scholar. In the fifteenth century, the *Sefer maharil* records an explanation in the name of R. Jacob b. Moses Moelin as to why the custom of visiting the cemetery on fast days ought to be continued, in addition to the reasons already cited in the Talmud:[135] 'For the cemetery is the resting place of the righteous. Therefore, it is a holy and pure place, and prayer is most acceptable on holy ground [*admat kodesh*].'[136] With his choice of the words *admat kodesh*, R. Jacob associates the Jewish cemetery with the place in which God first revealed himself to Moses.[137] Just as God sanctified that desert spot, so too the righteous dead sanctify the Jewish cemetery. Unquestionably these righteous dead included the martyrs of Ashkenaz. In fact, there is evidence from the late thirteenth century that Ashkenazi Jews observed the practice of praying at the gravesites of the martyrs.[138]

The rabbis of the Mishnah and the Talmud saw the cemetery as a place devoid of holiness. The rabbis of Ashkenaz characterized it as hallowed ground. Herein lay a turning point in Jewish notions of the dead and their burial which reflected the appropriation of the twin Christian concepts of holy dead and holy space. Undoubtedly, in the tense religious climate of medieval western Europe, Jews would venerate their holy dead no less than the Christians venerated theirs. If Christian saints' bodies rested in *terra sancta* then surely, medieval Jews would reason, Jewish martyrs did too. This innovation in Jewish thinking about the righteous dead led directly to

[134] Ibid. 160. The custom of visiting cemeteries on fast days is an ancient one; see n. 135 below.

[135] BT *Ta'an.* 16*a*. The Talmud offers two possible reasons for the custom; one is that the living demonstrate that they are 'like the dead' before God, while the second is to implore the dead to pray on their behalf. The *Tosafot* there (s.v. *yotsin*) mentions the contemporaneous practice of praying at the cemetery on the fast of the Ninth of Av as an outgrowth of the talmudic custom.

[136] *Sefer maharil*, 'Hilkhot ta'anit', no. 18, quoted in Shoham-Steiner, '"For a Prayer in that Place would be Most Welcome"', 379.

[137] See Exod. 3: 5. According to Lucia Raspe, the term is a reference to the Holy Land. The use of the phrase by the Ashkenazi rabbi in reference to local Jewish cemeteries suggests that Askenaz was 'revalu[ed] . . . as an alternative Holy Land'. See Raspe, 'Sacred Space, Local History, and Diasporic Identity', 162–3.

[138] The practice is mentioned in a responsum of R. Hayim Paltiel of Magdeburg, which appears in the Lemberg edition of the responsa collection of R. Meir of Rothenburg, no. 164. See Shoham-Steiner, '"For a Prayer in that Place would be Most Welcome"', 376 n. 23.

a novel attitude towards burial and, by extension, transformed Jews' relationship to the cemetery.[139]

Conclusion

Changes in the rabbinic principle of not burying the wicked beside the righteous reflected a significant shift in attitude that had transpired between the rabbinic period and the Middle Ages. The holy dead of talmudic times comprised a wide spectrum of groups ranging from biblical prophets to ordinary Jews and including 'the pious', scholars, and great leaders. Martyrs were considered individuals of great integrity, but they were not granted the exclusive status, the pride of place, that they were in people's psyches in medieval Ashkenaz. There, consciousness of the martyrs' acts lingered; they were commemorated in ways that they never had been in rabbinic times. The ghost tales of *Sefer ḥasidim* reflect the martyrs' exalted position as the holy dead of Ashkenaz.

The use of the medium of the ghost tale in *Sefer ḥasidim* in order to illustrate the impropriety of burying the wicked beside the righteous attests to the influence that outside forces had in shaping the Pietist conception of the martyrs as the holy dead. Instead of miraculous interventions that prevented situations of improper burial in the talmudic narratives, in the Pietist stories the dead themselves seek out the living in order to correct existing situations of improper burial. Shared motifs between the relevant ghost tales of *Sefer ḥasidim* and those found in the Icelandic sagas and exempla literature reveal the affinity between pre-Christian, Christian, and Pietist notions regarding the burial of the wicked amidst the righteous. These shared motifs testify to the appropriation by the Ashkenazi community of the Christian notion of the martyr-saints as the holy dead, and its adaptation to the Rhineland martyrs.

The Pietist tales likewise affirm that the Christian concept of burial in holy ground, sanctified by the presence of the holy dead, has been appropriated and adapted for Jewish use. The Rhineland martyrs' bodies have hallowed the ground of their mass graves and, as such, are intolerant of any profanation which burial of the unworthy in their midst might precipitate. Conversely, martyrs bereft of such burial yearn to lie beside other martyrs' bodies in the holy ground of their burial site. These borrowed notions of holy dead and holy space transformed Jewish attitudes towards the cemetery and relations to the dead buried therein.

139 On Jews' relation to the cemetery in late medieval times and the associated literature, see Goldberg, *Crossing the Jabbok*, and the sources cited above in the Introduction, n. 35.

In the previous chapter we saw that the holy dead of the rabbinic era, prophets such as Elijah and scholars of the calibre of R. Judah the Prince, do not appear in the ghost tales of *Sefer ḥasidim*. In this chapter, we have found that the holy dead who do appear are Ashkenazi martyrs. They return not to educate, visit, or protect the living as the holy dead do in the rabbinic era, but to complain of an improper burial, like their Christian counterparts in circulating exempla of the period. The conception of the holy dead in *Sefer ḥasidim* is clearly a medieval phenomenon.

CHAPTER FOUR

THE NEUTRAL DEAD AND THE PIETIST DEAD

IN TRACTATE *Berakhot*, the rabbis of the Talmud discuss whether the dead have knowledge of events in the world of the living. As part of this discussion, the following story is told in order to validate the opinion that the dead do know:

It is related that a certain pious man gave a dinar to a poor man on the eve of the New Year in a year of drought, and his wife scolded him, and he went and passed the night in the cemetery, and he heard two spirits conversing with one another. Said one to her companion, 'My dear, come and let us wander about the world and let us hear from behind the curtain [which shields the Divine Presence] what suffering is coming to the world.' And her companion said to her, 'I am not able to, because I am buried [clothed] in a matting of reeds. But you go, and what you hear, tell me.' So the other one went and wandered about and returned. Said her companion to her, 'My dear, what did you hear from behind the curtain?' She replied, 'I heard that whoever sows seed at the time of the first rainfall will have his crop smitten by hail.' So the man went and did not sow until the time of the second rainfall, with the result that everyone else's crop was smitten [by hail] and his was not smitten.

The next year he again went and passed the night in the cemetery, and heard the same two spirits conversing with one another. Said one to her companion, 'Come and let us wander about the world and let us hear from behind the curtain what punishment is coming upon the world.' The other said to her, 'My dear, did I not tell you that I am not able to, for I am buried [clothed] in a matting of reeds? But you go, and whatever you hear, come and tell me.' So the other one went and wandered about the world and returned. And she [her companion] said to her, 'My friend, what did you hear from behind the curtain?' She replied, 'I heard that whoever sows at the time of the second rain will have his crop smitten by blight.' So the man went and sowed at the time of the first rain, with the result that everyone else's crop was blighted and his was not blighted.

His wife said to him, 'How is it that last year everyone else's crop was smitten and yours was not smitten, and this year everyone else's crop is blighted and yours is not blighted?' So he related to her all his experiences. The story goes that shortly afterwards a quarrel broke out between the wife of that pious man and the mother of the child [whose spirit was conversing in the cemetery], and the former said to the latter, 'Come and I will show you your daughter, who is buried in a matting of reeds.'

The next year, the man again went and spent the night in the cemetery and heard those same [spirits] conversing together. One said [to her companion], 'My dear, come and let us wander about the world and hear from behind the curtain what suffering is coming to the world.' She [the other] said to her, 'My dear, leave me alone! Our conversation has already been heard among the living.'[1]

The author of *Sefer ḥasidim* recounts this story from the Talmud; however, he alters some significant details. These modifications shed light on his perspective on the neutral dead and their function vis-à-vis the living. The passage appears as follows:

There is a night when the souls leave their graves, such as the night of Hoshana Rabah. They exit [their graves] when the moon appears. They go out and pray. And two [of the living] went out and hid themselves in one place in the cemetery. And they heard that one [soul] was saying to her companion, 'Let us go out and pray together.' And all the souls went out and prayed and requested mercy that death not be decreed on the living; also that those who are to die should return in repentance from their evil ways, and regarding [punishments consisting of] moderate illnesses, and about every matter relating to the living and the dead, and, regarding themselves, that punishment be removed quickly from upon them and other [dead ones]. And they [the two living men] told their community [what they had witnessed].

The following year, on the night of Hoshana Rabah, two others [from among the living] went [and slept in the cemetery]. And only one young girl, who had died before the sabbath, emerged from the graves. They [the other dead in the cemetery] said [to her], 'Go out [and pray].' She said, 'I am not able to, because my father was rich and he lost his wealth', and [so] he had buried her without any clothes. And they [the two living men] heard that some of the souls said, 'We will not gather together [for prayer], because two [from among the living] have already revealed [things] about us to the public. Instead, let each one pray separately in his grave, so that the living shall not hear.'

And they [the two living men] told the community. And they [the members of the community] got angry at the father, and they took clothing, and dressed that young girl.[2]

The main motifs of the talmudic story are present in the Pietist one. A man spends the night in a cemetery and overhears the conversation of the dead.

1 BT *Ber.* 18*b*. 2 *SḤ* 1543.

A dead girl is unable to leave her grave upon the bidding of the other due to her improper attire. In the end, the dead refrain from any further conversation when they find out that the living have overheard their words.

Despite this basic similarity, the two stories are radically different. Many aspects of the talmudic story have been changed in *Sefer ḥasidim*, such that the focus of the one is the antithesis of the other. Although the talmudic story recounts a conversation between two dead girls in a cemetery, at its centre is the world of the living. The story is prefaced by a scenario involving two living people—the pious man and his wife—which provides the motive for the man's stay in the cemetery: to escape the wrath of his wife. The story concludes with another scenario involving two living people, the wife and the mother of the dead girl. The incident takes place repeatedly on the eve of the New Year—the annual day of judgement of the living. The dead discuss matters relating to the living, and the living benefit greatly from their conversations: as a result of his newly gained knowledge, the pious man is able to avoid the misfortunes that plague the fields. In fact, the upshot of the talmudic story is that the pious are rewarded in *this* world; having sacrificed much-needed funds (a dinar in a year of drought) for the sake of the poor, the man is abundantly blessed with material prosperity—the event occurs two years in a row—to the exclusion of everyone else.

Not so in the Pietist version of the story. By substituting key words and choice events, R. Judah the Pious has shifted the focus. The narrative now centres on the dead rather than on the living; absent are the two scenes involving the living that frame the talmudic story. Additionally, in the Pietist version, a day which has become associated with the prayer of the dead, Hoshana Rabah,[3] replaces the day set aside for judgement of the living (Rosh Hashanah), and R. Judah highlights the fact that the events take place at night, specifically a moonlit night—an image commonly associated with the dead.[4] The term 'souls' (*neshamot*), with its more concrete death referent, substitutes for the rather vague 'spirits' (*ruḥot*) used in the talmudic story. The dead proliferate in the Pietist version: the text claims that all the dead come out and participate in what seems to be a communal prayer event, as opposed to only two dead individuals being cited in the talmudic source. Although the dead in *Sefer ḥasidim* discuss matters relating to the living, request mercy on their behalf, and pray for their repentance,

[3] On the significance of Hoshana Rabah as a day of prayer among the dead, see Ch. 7, n. 3 below.

[4] See Lecouteux, *Fantômes et revenants*, 143.

they also pray for themselves and the other dead.[5] Furthermore, unlike in the talmudic account, the awareness of the dead that the living have been privy to their conversations does not bring a complete end to their activity; they continue to pray, albeit in a more private fashion.

Apart from a shift of focus from the living to the dead, the Pietist story registers a marked change from the talmudic one in terms of the role assigned to the clothing of the dead. In the talmudic story, the meagre clothing of the girl serves as an indication of her low economic status. A sense of embarrassment prevents her from wandering along with her companion. Despite the fact that her shame is made known to the living (and to her own mother!), no one rectifies the situation. If, in fact, it is rectified, the matter is considered unimportant and is omitted from the narrative. Furthermore, her improper attire is only tangential to the story; it creates an opportunity for the pious man to overhear the reports brought back by the girl's companion.

The clothing of the dead, by contrast, assumes a central role in the Pietist story. Rather than being shabbily clad, the girl is lacking any attire; she has been buried without a shroud. Although her situation is also a result of lack of funds, her sense of embarrassment is muted. Instead, her inability to participate in the public prayer due to her naked state takes centre stage. Furthermore, her lack of attire arouses the anger of the living and spurs them to action. The two men who overhear the conversation of the dead report it to the entire town. They, in turn, denounce the actions of the girl's father and demand that she be properly attired in the grave. The townspeople take it upon themselves to clothe the young girl in place of her father. Unlike in the talmudic story, clothing the dead is seen as a responsibility of the entire community.

The centrality of the clothing of the dead in the Pietist story is highlighted in yet another way. Immediately after relating the story, R. Judah adds the following caveat: 'And if the shroud has disintegrated, this does not impede the soul.'[6] He adds this because the story raises a problem in his mind regarding the causal connection between lack of clothing and the movement of the soul after death. The upshot of the tale, as it is recounted in *Sefer ḥasidim*, is that the girl's soul is unable to leave her grave and join the other souls in public prayer in the cemetery because she is buried without a shroud. At the same time, this appears to contradict what R. Judah also knows to be true—that the dead do exit their graves and some do so

[5] The appropriation of this story as a medium for conveying R. Judah's views on prayer of the dead is discussed below, pp. 269–71.

[6] *SḤ* 1543.

long after they were buried. If so, their shrouds have surely withered away. How, then, can they leave their graves? His response is illuminating; the disintegration of the shroud does not prevent posthumous movement of the soul, in the same way that the disintegration of the body does not impede it.[7] It is only having been buried without a shroud in the first place (or its later removal from the body in the grave, as we shall soon see), rather than its disintegration, that impedes the movement of the dead.

The particular redaction of the talmudic story in *Sefer ḥasidim* and its subsequent commentary reveal that, while a belief in the movement of souls after death may not be alien to the early rabbis, for the Pietists it is axiomatic. The dead are known to exit their graves and they must be buried in a shroud in order to be able to do so.[8] Lack of burial in a shroud is not just a form of dishonour, but it also debilitates the dead, depriving them of the crucial ability to perambulate. The living, therefore, are obligated to meet these burial needs; if not, the dead will return and demand that they do. These notions are characteristically medieval.[9]

The dead described in this Pietist story are neither sinful nor dangerous. They are not prophets, scholars, or martyrs. Instead, the category encompasses all the dead buried in the Jewish cemetery. They actively inhabit the cemetery, gathering together annually to form a public prayer group or praying privately in their graves. These are the neutral dead of *Sefer ḥasidim*.

*

Proper attire for the dead is the theme of several ghost tales in *Sefer ḥasidim*. R. Judah records the fact that many righteous people (*harbeh tsadikim*) have

7 See ibid. R. Eleazar of Worms, *Sefer ḥokhmat hanefesh*, 5*b*–6*a*, confirms this notion when he states that the dead who are stripped of their shroud before it disintegrates appear to themselves as if they are naked and will not perambulate. If, however, the shroud disintegrates naturally or is burned together with the body, the dead can 'clothe' themselves and perambulate.

8 On the obligation to bury Jews in a shroud see *The Tractate Mourning*, ed. Zlotnick, 2: 12, no. 10.

9 A possible parallel to this story appears in a fifteenth-century Islamic source. In that tale, a widowed man beholds in his sleep a group of dead women, with his wife noticeably absent from it. He is told that she is embarrassed to join the others on account of having been buried in insufficient clothing. Her husband rectifies the situation by 'sending' her a saffron robe, which he buries alongside the body of a newly deceased person. In his sleep, he sees her again. This time, enrobed, she stands proudly in the company of the other dead women. See Jane Smith, 'Concourse between the Living and the Dead'.

This story, with its emphasis on the embarrassment of the improperly attired dead woman, resembles more closely the talmudic version than the Pietist one. However, the facts that the dead person appears in a dream and that action is demanded of the living relative to clothe the deceased reveal the medieval roots of the Islamic story.

had their garments stripped from them posthumously. Complaining that they are naked and asking to be dressed, these figures appear in dreams to their local townsmen. When, after opening their graves and examining their corpses, the claims are verified, the townsmen clothe them.[10] Similarly, in a story told about a man who dies from food poisoning, the dead man appears in a dream to his sons, requesting that they open his grave and see what is disquieting him. The sons' immediate thought is that the father's body has been stripped and he is in need of a new shroud.[11]

R. Eleazar of Worms, in his *Sefer ḥokhmat hanefesh*, states that the dead who return and appear to the living do so either in their shroud or in any other garment they used to wear while alive.[12] Two ghost tales in *Sefer ḥasidim* prove that, indeed, this is the case. In the first, a dead Jew appears to the gravedigger who buried him. As proof of his identity, the ghost shows the gravedigger the torn sleeve of his shroud, which the gravedigger himself ripped while burying him. A new element, a vestment from the afterlife, is also added here. The ghost appears wearing a fragrant herbal wreath from Paradise on his head in order to combat the stench omnipresent in the world of the living.[13] In the other ghost tale, several dead people appear to the living at night in the synagogue wearing *talitot*,[14] as appropriate in that setting.

The notion that the dead appear to the living in garments that they used to wear while alive is a common theme in the ghost tales of the exempla literature. Caesarius of Heisterbach writes in his *Dialogue on Miracles* that when monks return after their death and appear to the living, they do so dressed in their own familiar habit.[15] Two sequential tales recorded in the *Dialogue* tell how apostate monks, who die in sin and are buried in secular garb, appear later in monastic garb, owing to the power of contrition and posthumous prayer. In the first of these tales, the apostate appears in a vision wearing the habit of a monk, while in the second, the body is exhumed and found dressed in such fashion in the grave.[16]

[10] *SḤ* 335.

[11] *SḤ* 321. In the end, the sons' initial thoughts are proven wrong. It is not insufficient clothing that disturbs their father but the intactness of his corpse. (The problem inherent in the intactness of a corpse is discussed below, pp. 231–2.) Yet the fact that this was the sons' initial thought demonstrates that it was a familiar occurrence—something they expected could happen.

[12] See *Sefer ḥokhmat hanefesh*, 6*a*. See also *Sefer ḥasidim*, ed. Margaliot, no. 1129, where it is stated that 'the soul is in death as it is in life'.

[13] This tale is an addition written on the margins of MS Parma H 3280; it is found in Wistinetzky's edition of *Sefer ḥasidim*, 126–7

[14] *SḤ* 271.

[15] See e.g. *Dialogue*, 12: 25.

[16] Ibid., 2: 2 and 2: 3.

The exempla literature also demonstrates that, as in the case of an improper place of burial, a failure on the part of the living to properly attire the dead will cause their return. The following tale, transcribed in the *Dialogue*, illustrates this point well. In the Cistercian house of Szere in France, a monk lies dying of some painful illness. Suffering from fever, he begs his caretaker to remove his habit and cowl. The caretaker takes pity on him and agrees to dress him in a lighter garment. While he is momentarily gone, the monk dies. The following night, as his fellow monks recite psalms beside his body, the monk revives and calls for the abbot. In the presence of all assembled, he tells how, as he was being led by the angels to Paradise, he was stopped at the entrance by St Benedict. The founding father of Western monasticism did not recognize him and questioned his identity. When he answered that he was a monk of the Cistercian order, St Benedict responded, 'Certainly you are not. If you are a monk, where is your habit?' and barred his entry into Paradise. Upon heavenly intercession, he was allowed to 'return to the body' in order to don the appropriate vestments. The abbot of Szere then changes the monk's clothing and, with habit and cowl on, the man dies again.[17]

As the monks of Szere, so the dead of *Sefer ḥasidim*; they require clothing not only when they appear on Earth, but also in Paradise. Several passages in *Sefer ḥasidim* indicate that the dead actually wear clothes in the afterlife. One such passage records a dispute between two people, seemingly over the reason why some are found naked in the grave after having been buried in proper attire:

Two individuals were arguing. One said that they strip the wicked who are wrapped in finery, and [with] those very clothes they dress the righteous. For, in fact, one person saw in a dream that they strip those individuals who are disrespected for their impropriety of conduct [*et she'eino hagun*] and they dress [in those very clothes] the righteous, who are not wrapped in finery because of their [economic] distress. His companion said that many righteous people had [indeed] been stripped of their garments and they came naked in a dream to the people of the town and said that they had to dress them. They inspected [the graves] and found that they had been stripped [of their garments].[18]

One disputant claims that the reason these righteous people are naked in the grave is that they have merited the removal of their shabby, poor-looking shrouds. These are stripped from them in Paradise and replaced with the more sumptuous ones taken from the wicked. Such a position

[17] Ibid., 11: 36. See also Banks (ed.), *Alphabet of Tales*, 341–2 no. 501, and MS BL Add. 21147 fo. 111*b* (*Catalogue of Romances*, iii. 704 no. 37).

[18] *SḤ* 335.

assumes that the dead don clothing in the hereafter and that those garments must befit the true religious station of their bearers. The other disputant rejects such a notion. The righteous dead have had their shrouds stripped from them not in Paradise but in the grave, perhaps by even poorer living people, who lack shrouds altogether for the burial of their own dead.

A second reference to the fact that the dead are clothed in the afterlife is found in a different passage in *Sefer ḥasidim*. A deceased Jewish woman appears to the living in a dream and complains that the sleeve of her garment is filled with animal fat. She suffers this indignity on account of a sin she committed with the substance while alive.[19] In yet another place, R. Judah states that, since in the afterlife *haneshamot beto'ar hagufot* (the souls appear as the bodies do in life), one must take great care to wash the body of the deceased well and remove all dirt, especially from the face. If not, R. Judah warns that 'his soul experiences shame there'—that is, in the afterlife.[20] This statement assumes that the appearance of the soul in Paradise is similar to that of the body in the grave.

Although R. Eleazar of Worms, in his work *Sefer ḥokhmat hanefesh*, disagrees with the claim that the dead require clothing before the Divine Presence, he does affirm the need for garments when they stand 'behind the curtain' listening in to the heavenly proceedings. The dead who are unclothed are ashamed when standing there.[21] In another place in the same work,[22] when discussing the various punishments meted out to sinners in Gehenna, R. Eleazar describes the punishment of adulterous men and women: they are hung naked from the organ involved in the sin. His description emphasizes the role that clothing plays for the souls in the afterlife; exposure itself is considered a punishment. The concern for the physical appearance of the dead in the afterlife displayed by both R. Judah the Pious and R. Eleazar of Worms demonstrates the belief of these Pietists that the souls of the dead have a corporeal dimension.

Corporeality in the Afterlife: Clothing and the Dead

The earliest source that depicts the returning dead as wearing clothes is a biblical one. The prophet Samuel, raised from the dead by the necromancer of Ein Dor, appears as 'an old man . . . garbed in a cloak'.[23] Presumably he is clad in a cloak he was wont to wear while alive, for it serves as his identifying feature: 'And Saul knew that it was Samuel.'[24]

19 *SḤ* 272. 20 *SḤ* 331. 21 *Sefer ḥokhmat hanefesh*, 14*a*.
22 Ibid. 7*a*. 23 1 Sam. 28: 14.
24 Ibid. See also the commentaries of R. David Kimhi (Radak) and Rashi ad loc.

The talmudic passages recounting Elijah's or R. Judah the Prince's appearances to the living do not describe their clothing.[25] However, their easy identification by the living implies that they appeared with a familiar visage and garb. In one passage, which contains variant readings, Elijah appears 'disguised as an Arab merchant'.[26] Clothing here suits the role Elijah is to perform on Earth, rather than reflecting his previous, familiar appearance.

All this pertains to the clothing that the dead wear when they appear to the living, which is not necessarily an indication of what they wear, if anything at all, in the afterlife. Apart from the *talit* with *tsitsit* (which is treated below as a topic in its own right) and the custom of burial in a shroud,[27] the rabbis of the Mishnah and Talmud do not discuss the question of clothing worn by the dead in the afterlife. One passage in the Talmud indirectly speaks of cosmetics in relation to the dead. A certain dead landlady, to whom R. Ze'iri had gone to speak in the cemetery, requests him to send her comb and tube of eye-paint to her via a specific person who is about to die.[28] It is unclear from the passage what use she will make of the objects. One scholar understands the scene as a 'remnant of the ancient belief that the dead in the grave use their earthly possessions'.[29] However, Rashi, in commenting on the passage, connects the woman's request to another rabbinic source, which speaks of the burial of personal items of the deceased along with the body—a source that does provide a reason.[30] The Mishnah in *Semaḥot* states in the name of Shemuel Hakatan that at times items such as the deceased person's key and notebook are placed in the coffin alongside the body 'on account of anguish', and that Shemuel Hakatan himself was buried in this manner, 'because he did not have a son'.[31] Rashi attributes the request of the above-mentioned woman to the same reason: 'because she died as a young girl, she said so on account of anguish'. Scholars have proposed that personal items were sometimes buried with their owners in order to intensify the gravity of the loss and arouse the anguish of the living. This may have been especially true in the case of those who died young and childless.[32] If this explanation is correct then the burial of personal items was directed at the living—not the dead.

25 While it is logical to assume that the dead would appear clothed to the living, this is not necessarily so. They could appear naked or as skeletons (as they are often depicted in late medieval macabre art), or simply as incorporeal spirits in a glowing body of sorts. For a description of the dead in late medieval art, see Huizinga, *The Waning of the Middle Ages*.

26 BT *Ber.* 6*b*.

27 See BT *Ket.* 8*b*, *MK* 27*b*.

28 BT *Ber.* 18*b*.

29 See Hirsch, *Psychology in Our Ancient Literature* (Heb.), 181.

30 See Rashi ad loc., s.v. *guvta*.

31 *The Tractate Mourning*, ed. Zlotnick, 8: 7.

32 This is the opinion of G. Alon and Y. Herskovitz, cited in N. Rubin, *The End of Life*

The separation of body and soul upon death is a complex topic in rabbinic literature. One opinion in the Babylonian Talmud states that for the first twelve months, when the body has not yet disintegrated, 'the soul rises up and goes down'. After the initial twelve months, when the decomposition of the body is complete, 'the soul rises up and never again returns'.[33] An alternative view is espoused in the Jerusalem Talmud, according to which the soul hovers over the body for only three days after death. Upon seeing the beginnings of decomposition, it realizes it can no longer inhabit the body and departs.[34] The rabbis of the Mishnah speak of a 'treasure house of souls' into which the souls of the righteous ascend after death; it is located 'under the Throne of Glory'. The souls of the wicked first ascend on high and then are 'cast to the ground' or are 'slung from the hollow of a sling'.[35] The souls of average people reside with an angel called Dumah.[36] Jewish apocalyptic literature likewise speaks of the separation of body and soul after death and makes mention of the storehouse of souls.[37] While some scholars maintain that contradictory opinions on the matter exist in rabbinic and post-rabbinic sources,[38] others have noted an increasing tendency among the rabbis to favour separation of the soul from the body from the time of the Hadrianic persecutions.[39]

In *Sefer ḥasidim*, R. Judah the Pious describes in detail the decomposition of the corpse.[40] He wholeheartedly accepts the division of souls formulated in the Mishnah, wherein the souls of the righteous ascend and those of the wicked descend (although at times he uses different terminology for their abodes).[41] While he believes that some sinners are punished posthumously on Earth, he designates Paradise and Gehenna as the prime loci of reward and punishment in the afterlife—two distinct areas in the world of souls.

(Heb.), 138. Rubin notes that archaeological excavations of burial caves and cemeteries in Israel dating from the rabbinic period reveal that it was customary to bury the female dead with their jewellery and other personal items. He offers an alternative reason: these items had sociological significance in that, by being buried with them, a woman could lay 'claim' to them as her possessions in an age when ownership was mostly restricted to men (ibid. 139–40).

33 BT *Shab.* 152*b.*

34 JT *MK* 3: 5, 82*b.*

35 *Sifrei*, Num. 139, ed. Horowitz, 185; *Sifrei*, Deut. 344, ed. Finkelstein, 401; *Kohelet rabah* 3, and BT *Shab.* 152*b*. For a fuller discussion of this topic see Urbach, *The Sages*, 238–40.

36 BT *Shab.* 152*b.*

37 Early apocalyptic literature conceives of a storehouse of souls on Earth, while later works place it in Heaven. See Hirsch, *Psychology in Our Ancient Literature* (Heb.), 183–5.

38 Ibid. 189.

39 N. Rubin, *The End of Life* (Heb.), 69.

40 *SḤ* 305, pp. 96–7.

41 In one passage, he places the souls of the righteous under the 'wings' of the Divine Presence (*taḥat kanfei hashekhinah*), and those of the wicked in Gehenna. Both terms are of rabbinic origin, as is evident from BT *Ber.* 17*a* and *RH* 16*b*. See *SḤ* 1474.

Yet the beliefs hitherto expressed in *Sefer ḥasidim*—that the dead demand to be properly attired in the grave and that they wear clothes even in Paradise—raise the question of the soul's corporeality. Why do the dead need garments if they are only souls? R. Judah appears relatively untroubled by the degree of corporeality assigned to the souls and ghosts in *Sefer ḥasidim*. In one passage, however, he does seem aware of the difficulty and makes an attempt to resolve it. In describing how it is possible for a dead person to reappear to the living in a wakeful state, he explains that the deceased requests from his appointed angel, who directs all his affairs, to clothe him in *demut malbush*.[42] This 'semblance of clothes' removes some of the corporeality associated with the image of a ghost who appears in 'real' clothes. R. Judah makes no such statement regarding the clothed souls in Paradise, however.

R. Eleazar of Worms, too, in his *Sefer ḥokhmat hanefesh*, represents an ambivalent stance regarding the degree of corporeality accorded to dead souls and to ghosts that appear on Earth. The main points regarding the soul that R. Eleazar maintains throughout his treatise are its Divine origin,[43] its immortality,[44] and its antithetical nature to the body.[45] He clearly and repeatedly states that, at the moment of death, the soul separates from the physical body and that the souls of the righteous return to their heavenly source and attach to the repository of souls situated underneath the throne of God.[46] At the same time, other pronouncements in the work point to a soul with a more corporeal nature to it. While in one passage R. Eleazar states that the souls of the dead lack the ability to express ordinary human emotion,[47] in another passage he highlights the embarrassment that the souls of the righteous feel when they stand naked 'behind the curtain' in Paradise.[48] When describing the punishment of wicked souls, he stresses that one form of suffering they endure is viewing from a distance the reward of the righteous: souls dressed in fine clothing enjoying many delights.[49] When delineating the bodily punishment of sinners' souls in Gehenna, he even goes so far as to state outright that the soul does have some sort of body, and that body dons some type of garment; the more ephemeral *ruaḥ* (spirit) is clothed in the less ephemeral *re'aḥ haguf* (lit. the scent of the body), which is, in turn, dressed in *re'aḥ malbushav* (lit. the

42 *SḤ* 324. 43 *Sefer ḥokhmat hanefesh*, 1*a*, 1*b*, 5*a*, and 5*b*. 44 Ibid. 1*b*, 3*b*, 5*b*, 32*a*.
45 Ibid. 1*b*, 5*b*, 12*a*, 15*b*, 32*a*.
46 Ibid. 3*b*, 4*b*, 5*b*, 6*b*, 7*b*, 13*b*, 14*b*, 19*b*, 24*a*, 28*b*. This belief is so firm that R. Eleazar takes great pains to explain how it is possible that Elijah's body could have ascended heavenward in the chariot of fire (2 Kgs 2); see ibid. 24*a*. See also Soloveitchik, 'Topics in the *Ḥokhmat ha-Nefesh*', 73. 47 *Sefer ḥokhmat hanefesh*, 15*b*. 48 Ibid. 14*a*. 49 Ibid. 6*a*.

scent of its clothes).[50] Perhaps he, like R. Judah, attempts here to mitigate somewhat the measure of corporeality that his pronouncements seem to affirm.

The role attributed to the clothing of the dead in both *Sefer ḥasidim* and *Sefer ḥokhmat hanefesh* reflects belief in a certain degree of corporeality of the soul. Both authors show some sign of discomfort with this notion, yet continue, for the most part, to espouse a corporeal-like view of the soul of the dead in the various ghost tales and in the ethical and philosophical statements that they record.

Scholars have argued that the Pietists adopted the concept of corporeality from the rabbis' elaborate physical descriptions of reward and punishment for the righteous and the wicked after death. These rabbinic descriptions, however, concern the period after the resurrection of the dead—the era referred to as *olam haba* (the World to Come). The Pietists keep these physical descriptions but apply them instead to the world of the souls—the afterlife.[51]

While undoubtedly these physical descriptions influenced the Pietists' view, they were not the only shaping force. Let us recall the ghost tales from the Cistercian collection of exempla, the *Dialogue of Miracles* cited above, where the clothing of the dead fulfils a similar function to that in *Sefer ḥasidim*. The monk of Szere, for example, cannot enter Paradise unless outfitted in his habit and cowl. Similarly, the two apostate monks gain entry to Paradise only after their clothing changes from secular dress to monastic garb. The fact that the garments of the body buried on Earth parallel the attire of the soul in Heaven reflects the belief in the existence of a physical aspect of the soul. Additionally, the transformation of the monks' apparel represents the achievement of a long-awaited posthumous absolution and the attainment of entry into Heaven.

Medieval art, especially the monumental art of churches and monasteries, reinforced the role assigned to clothing in the hereafter. In the Last Judgement scenes sculpted on the tympanums of cathedrals and abbeys of western Europe throughout the twelfth and thirteenth centuries, groups of the elect and the damned are often dressed according to order, class, or rank. Kings, bishops, monks, pilgrims, knights, merchants, and Jews, who are all identifiable by their distinctive dress and accompanying symbols, are visualized as entering Heaven or Hell in these artistic representations. Groups of the elect, such as apostles, prophets, virgins, confessors, and

50 *Sefer ḥokhmat hanefesh*, 5*b*.

51 Dan, *The Esoteric Theology of Ashkenazi Hasidism* (Heb.), 246–7.

martyrs, depicted in Heaven alongside Christ, are also dressed according to their status.[52] Although these artistic representations show the eschatological age after the resurrection of the dead, when body and soul are reunited, rather than the period following the death of the individual, seeing these scenes often led to a conflation of the two events in the mind of the common faithful.[53] Thus, while gazing at these monumental sculptures, one could possibly imagine the dead entering Paradise or Purgatory immediately after dying, dressed in the same manner as they are depicted entering Heaven or Hell in a Last Judgement scene.

Similarly, the image of reclothing the elect in Paradise was a common motif in the art of the high Middle Ages. On the tympanums of churches at Reims, Chartres, Bourges, Le Mans, and Rouen, the elect ascend to Heaven clothed in the garments they wore in this world, but at the gate of Heaven angels clothe them in garments of royalty and adorn them with crowns.[54] In these elevation scenes, the clothing of the just (saints and martyrs) by the angels highlights their righteousness and signifies the heavenly glory that awaits them.[55] These visual images complement the claim of the disputant, recorded in *Sefer ḥasidim* and cited earlier,[56] that the reason the righteous are naked in the grave is that they have merited the removal of their shabby, poor-looking shroud in Paradise and its replacement with the more sumptuous garments taken from the wicked dead.

The ghost tales recorded by Caesarius of Heisterbach which refer to clothing in the afterlife accord a measure of corporeality to the soul after death, which is in opposition to the official theological position of the Church. Whereas Christian teaching states that an immaterial, incorporeal soul survives after death and awaits unification with the body at the time of the resurrection, in Caesarius's tale the monk's soul must 'wear' certain vestments in order to enter Paradise.[57] In a recent comprehensive study of

[52] See Mâle, *Religious Art in France*, 415, 418–19, as well as his other work, *The Gothic Image*, 378–83. See also Katzenellenbogen, *The Sculptural Programs of Chartres Cathedral*, 86–9. In particular, on the portal of the abbey at Conques, St Benedict, in his role as 'father of monks' and dressed in the habit of a monk, leads one of the saved into Heaven; Mâle, *Religious Art in France*, 413. Similarly, in the carved artwork of the churches at Bourges and Le Mans, St Francis, attired in his mendicant robe with a distinctive three-knotted girdle, leads the procession of the elect; Mâle, *The Gothic Image*, 382. Mâle argues that medieval artists, in their representations of the elect 'wear[ing] long robes or even the dress of their rank or earthly calling', acted 'contrary to the doctrine of Honorius, who endeavours to show that the just will be clothed in their innocence and the splendour of their beauty alone'; *The Gothic Image*, 381.

[53] See Gurevich, *Medieval Popular Culture*, 144–6.

[54] Mâle, *The Gothic Image*, 382–3 and n. 1. [55] Baschet, *Corps et âmes*, 136–7. [56] *SḤ* 335.

[57] That it is the monk's soul and not his body that is being referred to is evident from the fact that when he revives in order to don his habit he needs to re-enter his body. He then dies again.

the body and soul in Christian thought, Jérôme Baschet has demonstrated that the twelfth and thirteenth centuries saw a marked increase in the positive evaluation of the body, which had been set in motion by Augustine in the fourth century. The 'anti-dualistic' notion that body and soul are related in a type of mutualism, in which the soul bestows its gifts upon the body in exchange for protection by it, and that the two reside together in a harmonious relationship within the person, is advanced by Christian scholastics of the period.[58] This anti-dualism coexisted with the dualistic conception of the body as bad and the soul as good, which was proposed in the early centuries of Christianity and which continued to be fostered by monastic thought. The two contrary formulations resulted in the expression of paradoxical notions regarding body and soul throughout the medieval period.[59] These were reflected in theology in the idea of the 'spiritual body' of the resurrected,[60] and, in Christian art, in the representation of the soul as body.[61] Additionally, in art, the soul was not only embodied, it was also clothed. Whereas souls are depicted as naked bodies in images of the moment of death,[62] in elevation scenes, as we saw above, the souls of the just are being clothed in Heaven by angelic or saintly figures.[63] Thus, although the body was always suspect in medieval theology, thinkers continued to identify the self with the body much more than with the soul.[64]

Jean-Claude Schmitt and Nancy Caciola have argued that this contradictory stance, which was maintained throughout the entire medieval period, manifested in the ambiguity of the Church's definition of the word 'spirit' (*spiritus*). Positioned between the soul (*anima*) and the body (*corpus*), the spirit had aspects of both without being identical to either.[65] According to this argument, a dead person, as soul separated from the body, would be closest to the word 'spirit'; hence the latter's part-soul, part-corporeal nature. A possible reason for this ambiguity may have been 'the necessity to

[58] Baschet, *Corps et âmes*, 28–30, 32.

[59] Baschet refers to them as 'oxymoronic', ibid. 59; see also ibid. 29.

[60] Ibid. 52, 59.

[61] Ibid. 123–4.

[62] Ibid. 123, 126–31.

[63] That these clothes are often indicative of the former earthly status of the deceased (as clergy) testifies to the correlation between self-identity and body, and to a favourable characterization of the latter. At other times, the supreme sanctity of the soul is highlighted by the lavish garments the just are given in Heaven. Ibid. 136–7.

[64] Bynum, *The Resurrection of the Body*, esp. 202–15.

[65] See Schmitt, *Ghosts in the Middle Ages*, 196–7, and Caciola, 'Wraiths, Revenants and Ritual', 7–9, which documents the unique role that *spiritus* played in medieval medical theory as well. Whereas in medical terminology it is associated with the vital force of life that regulates the physiological systems of the body, in theology it corresponds to the soul, the spiritual force of life. In the twelfth and thirteenth centuries these two concepts merged.

imagine the invisible and thus to situate it in space and time, to conceive of the places, the forms, the volumes, and the bodies in the very place where they should have been excluded'.[66] The need to imagine the soul caused even scholarly Christians to describe it in corporeal terms, thereby aligning it more with *spiritus* than with *anima*.

It is very likely that ancient Germanic notions of the dead, of a much more corporeal kind than those of medieval Christianity, shaped the images of the dead in the medieval mind. Alan Bernstein argues that this is certainly true for early medieval visionary literature—a genre with much the same audience as the ghost tale. In the visions, the souls in the other world appear as bodies even before the physical resurrection, and as such undergo bodily torment there in part or in their entirety. According to Bernstein, official theology, which would deny corporeality to the soul after death, was irrelevant here, since the primary function of the visions was to express the 'psychological history of individuals'.[67] The thought world of those who experienced and/or reported visions of souls as bodies was the product of a Christian environment influenced by 'residual, indeed resistant, Germanic and Roman paganisms'.[68] In a similar vein, the belief that the dead needed clothing in the various stages of their posthumous existence—while in the grave, during their stay in Paradise, and when walking on Earth—went back, in some measure, to ancient Germanic conceptions and customs perpetuated over the centuries through circulating ghost tales and oral testimonies. Caesarius of Heisterbach, like R. Judah, was untroubled by the degree of corporeality assigned to the clothed souls and ghosts in the tales of his *Dialogue on Miracles*. The fact that elements of these beliefs are present in the writings of both the German Cistercian and the German Pietists bespeaks a common source. Ancient imaginings here cross religious boundaries and reflect a world-view common to medieval Jew and Christian alike.

The issue of burial in a *talit* with *tsitsit* in *Sefer ḥasidim* provides an illustration of this phenomenon.[69] It demonstrates how ancient Germanic customs of clothing the dead, with all their attendant corporeality, influenced the beliefs of Pietists, Cistercians, and others in high medieval Germany.

[66] Schmitt, *Ghosts in the Middle Ages*, 197.

[67] Bernstein, *Hell and Its Rivals*, 200.

[68] Ibid. 201.

[69] *Talit* is a four-cornered garment, similar to a shawl, which is customarily worn by Jewish men for prayer, while *tsitsit* (pl. *tsitsiyot*) refers to the specially knotted tassel-like ritual strings that hang from the corners of the *talit* in fulfilment of the biblical command of Num. 15: 38 and Deut. 22: 12.

The Pietist Dead: Burial in a *Talit* with *Tsitsit*

Certain passages in *Sefer ḥasidim* indicate that, in addition to the shroud, the *talit* with *tsitsit* was seen as suitable, even desirable, for the burial of Jewish men. In one passage, R. Judah proclaims the importance of burial in a *talit*:

He who is wont to wrap himself in *tsitsit* and not in a cloak [*me'il*], when he dies they should bury him only in the *talit* in which he was accustomed to [*shehayah ragil be-*] wrapping himself, the one of wool, as it says, 'His garment was as white as snow'; therefore [they should bury him] in white [garments].[70]

Although he may possess other cloaks,[71] the man who is accustomed to wearing a *talit* in his lifetime should be buried in that white woollen shawl. The Pietist is one who is regular in his performance of the *mitsvah* of wearing *tsitsit*; he wears it daily and, ideally, all day long.

In the matter of wearing a *talit*, the Pietist stood apart from his contemporaries. Most male Jews of thirteenth-century Ashkenaz were negligent in the performance of this commandment and did not regularly don the *talit*, if they did so at all. R. Judah's contemporaries, the tosafist scholars of medieval France and Germany, attest to the widespread nature of this negligence.[72] They explain that in the time of the Talmud, when it was com-

[70] *SḤ* 332. [71] *SḤ* 1612 makes mention of several other garments of the Pietist.

[72] The tosafists report in the name of R. Isaac of Dampierre (Ri) that some of their contemporaries do not wear *talit* at all (see BT *Nid.* 61*b*, s.v. *aval*). In their commentary on tractate *Avodah zarah*, they state that, while in earlier times, Jews were careful to wear *tsitsit* every day, this is no longer the case (see *AZ* 65*b*, s.v. *aval*). Furthermore, in their commentary on *Berakhot*, the tosafists seemingly include themselves among those who do not follow the practice (*Ber.* 18*a*, s.v. *lemaḥar*). At best, even the tosafists wore a *talit* only occasionally.

Similar reports are found in the halakhic writings of individual scholars. See *Tosefot rabenu yehudah sirleon al masekhet berakhot*, ed. Zaks, 18*a*, s.v. *deleih*, 214; *Tosefot harashba al masekhet pesaḥim*, ed. Fromm, 105; *Tosefot rabenu perets lemasekhet berakhot*, ed. Hershler, 31; *Or zarua*, vol. i, 'Hilkhot avelut', no. 421; R. Meir of Rothenburg, *Teshuvot, pesakim uminhagim*, ed. Kahana, vol. iii, 'Hilkhot semaḥot', no. 7; *Tosefot harosh: masekhet berakhot*, ed. Edwin, 34; R. Asher, *Piskei harosh al masekhet mo'ed katan*, no. 80, and 'Hilkhot tsitsit', no. 9; and Mordecai b. Hillel, *Mordekhai*, 'Halakhot ketanot', no. 945. R. Moses of Coucy, in his *Sefer mitsvot gadol* (*aseh* 26), exhorts his readers to wear *tsitsit* in the marketplace and the street and not just in synagogue. An itinerant preacher in Spain in the year 1236, R. Moses chastises the Spanish Jewish community for its laxity in the performance of certain *mitsvot*, among them that of *tsitsit*. He writes how tens of thousands of Jews have heeded his words and accepted upon themselves that *mitsvah* among others. See Urbach, *The Tosafists* (Heb.), i. 467. By the mid-fourteenth century, the practice had been re-established in Spain: R. Yom Tov al-Sevilli (Ritva) reports that, 'praise be to God, most people are now scrupulous in the performance of *mitsvat tsitsit* during their lifetime'. See *Ḥidushei haritva*, *Pes.* 40*b*, s.v. *aval*.

mon to wear a four-cornered garment, people were careful in the fulfilment of the commandment of *tsitsit*,[73] whereas there was now great laxity in this matter since such four-cornered garments were highly uncommon. Additionally, these scholars neutralize the talmudic statement of *Menaḥot* 41*a*, which threatens Divine punishment at a time of wrath for failure to don the *talit*, by asserting that the law no longer applied in an age when four-cornered garments were not regularly worn. Acquiring such a garment solely in order to perform the commandment is commended as praiseworthy but is not deemed obligatory.[74]

The same statement in *Menaḥot*, however, is accepted by scholars with direct ties to the Pietists. According to R. Eleazar of Worms and R. Isaac of Vienna (also a student of R. Judah the Pious), God's punishment at a time of wrath still awaits those who do not don the garment.[75] R. Eleazar, therefore, mandates that every Jewish man must acquire for himself a *talit*. His ruling is in keeping with the Pietists' steadfast commitment to the practice. R. Eliezer ben Joel Halevi (Ravyah), a German authority without known ties to the Pietists, alludes to the fact that, despite the widespread negligence in performing this *mitsvah*, there were some exceptions to the rule. A *gavra raba*—person of importance—who was accustomed to wearing a *talit* should be buried in it.[76] Pietist and non-Pietist conceptions of regularity in the performance of this *mitsvah* differed, however: in *Sefer ḥasidim*, R. Judah makes it clear that regularity refers to donning the *talit* daily, not weekly, as others were wont to do.[77]

[73] Regarding the practice of wearing *tsitsit* during the rabbinic period, both in Babylonia and in the Land of Israel, see S. Glick, *Light has Dawned* (Heb.), 147–50. For a treatment of the topic beginning with the rabbinic period and continuing up until the early modern period, see Lichtenstein, 'From the Impurity of the Dead to Their Sanctification' (Heb.), 93–137. See also Kanarfogel, 'Rabbinic Attitudes toward Non-Observance', 7–14.

[74] The first scholar to neutralize this talmudic statement was R. Judah Sirleon, in his tosafist commentary on BT *Ber.* 18*a*. See *Tosefot rabenu yehudah sirleon al masekhet berakhot*, ed. Zaks, 18*a*, s.v. *deleih*, 214–15. R. Meir of Rothenburg, in his 'Hilkhot semaḥot', Rabenu Asher (Rosh) in his *tosafot* on tractate *Berakhot*, as well as R. Mordecai ben Hillel in his 'Halakhot ketanot' all accept R. Judah Sirleon's position.

[75] See *Sefer haroke'aḥ hagadol*, ed. Shneerson, no. 361. Although R. Isaac of Vienna does not state his opinion as forcefully as R. Eleazar does, he rejects R. Judah Sirleon's neutralization of the statement in *Men.* 41*a*. After quoting the latter's position verbatim, R. Isaac writes: 'But this reason is not clear to me since in the synagogue, and even all day long, [he] is under [i.e. wrapped in] the garment, [therefore] [he] is not an anomaly.' Apparently the fact that some people in R. Isaac's day (first half of the thirteenth century) wore a *talit* in the synagogue or even all day long (i.e. the Pietists) invalidates R. Judah Sirleon's protest that 'nowadays anyone who wears a four-cornered garment is considered an anomaly'. See *Or zarua*, vol. i, 'Hilkhot avelut', no. 421.

[76] This is Ravyah's position, cited in *Or zarua*, vol. i, 'Hilkhot avelut', no. 421.

[77] *SḤ*, ed. Margaliot, 57.

In addition to his stringency in the wearing of the garment, by prescribing burial in a *talit* with *tsitsit*, the Pietist once again deviates from common practice. It was customary in thirteenth-century Ashkenaz to bury Jewish men in a *talit* with the *tsitsit* cut off. R. Isaac of Vienna, who, apart from his Pietist ties, was also a tosafist, author of numerous responsa, and composer of a major halakhic compendium entitled *Or zarua*, states: 'We have the custom of removing the *tsitsit* from the *talit* of the dead',[78] and cites the opinions of other major tosafists (such as Rabbenu Tam, Ri, as well as his own teacher R. Judah Sirleon) in support of this practice.[79] Admittedly, one of their contemporaries, Ravyah, permitted burial in a *talit* with the *tsitsit* attached, but, as stated above, only for men of great importance, such as Ravyah himself, who wore it regularly during their lifetime. Nevertheless, the regnant practice in Germany at the time was not to bury men in a *talit* that had *tsitsit*.[80] The custom was rooted in the oldest traditions of Germany; it appears to have had antecedents that went back to the early days of Jewish settlement there. A report regarding the burial of Rabbenu Gershom in the first quarter of the eleventh century states that he requested to have his *tsitsit* 'left out' (either removed from the *talit* or left out of the coffin altogether),[81] and Rabbenu Tam is said to have received a tradition from the mid-eleventh century in the name of the elders of Lotharingia not to bury men in *tsitsit*.[82]

[78] *Or zarua*, vol. i, 'Hilkhot avelut', no. 421.

[79] R. Isaac quotes Rabbenu Tam as stating, 'we do not put *tsitsit* on the garment of the deceased'; Ri as asserting, 'one can rely upon that passage in tractate *Semaḥot*'; and his own teacher, R. Judah Sirleon, who wrote, 'certainly one is to remove the *tsitsit* from a *talit* in which the deceased is buried'. This practice is corroborated by the printed *Tosafot*: see *Pes.* 40*b*, s.v. *aval* (which provides the textual support for the custom); *AZ* 65*b*, s.v. *aval*; *Nid.* 61*b*, s.v. *aval*; *Ber.* 18*a*, s.v. *lemaḥar*; and *BB* 74*a*, s.v. *piskei*.

[80] *Or zarua*, vol. i, 'Hilkhot avelut', no. 421.

[81] R. Meir of Rothenburg records this in *Teshuvot, pesakim uminhagim*, ed. Kahana, vol. iii, 'Hilkhot semaḥot', no. 7. Rosh also mentions the request of Rabbenu Gershom, as does the *Mordekhai* and Rabbenu Perets. See *Piskei rabenu asher*, *MK* 3: 80; *Mordekhai* on *Mo'ed katan*, 'Hilkhot avelut', no. 863; and the gloss on the *Semak* in *Sefer hasemak mitsurikh*, ed. Har-Shoshanim-Rozenberg, i. 108, no. 33.

[82] According to A. Grossman, the *ḥakhmei lotir* or *ziknei lotir* (sometimes also known as *ḥakhmei reinus*) were among the earliest scholars of Ashkenaz, who settled in an area known as Lotharingia on the west bank of the Rhine, more specifically in the communities of Mainz and Worms. The reference made here by Rabbenu Tam to the elders of Lotharingia might specifically indicate the masters of Rashi, R. Isaac Halevi and R. Isaac ben R. Judah, who are referred to as *raboteinu benei lotir* by subsequent generations. See Grossman, *The Early Sages of Ashkenaz* (Heb.), 1 n. 1 and 267, 271. In the *Tosefot harashba* of R. Shimshon of Sens, the report is issued in the name of *benei alemayna*. See *Tosefot harashba, Pesaḥim*, ed. Fromm, 40*b*, s.v. *aval*.

The report in the name of Rabbenu Tam first appeared in *Tosefot rabenu yehudah sirleon al masekhet berakhot*, ed. Zaks, 18*a*, s.v. *deleih*, 213, and was then repeated by almost all subsequent

Even the French position, which penetrated into Germany around 1220, late in the life of R. Eleazar of Worms, supported the practice of burial without *tsitsit*. The tosafists, over the course of two centuries, uncovered textual evidence from the Talmud and Midrash which appeared to be at odds with the custom.[83] Using legal casuistry, they tried to put the practice of removing the *tsitsit* on solid halakhic grounds.[84] Individual tosafists, particularly of the French school, feared that their arguments supporting the contemporary custom were weak; they therefore proposed a compromise position, in which the *tsitsit* was to be retained on the *talit* but was to be concealed.[85] The mainstream opinion, however, still required that the *tsitsit*

tosafists of France and Germany in their discussions of the topic, as well as in the printed *Tosafot* on *Ber.* 18*a*. The teaching from *Tana devei eliyahu*, which is cited to substantiate this ruling, is based on a play on the word *ledorotam* mentioned in regard to *tsitsit*—*ledor shekulo tam*—'[referring to] a generation that is entirely pure'. See *Sefer tana devei eliyahu*, ed. Weinfeld, 26: 19.

According to Grossman, Rabbenu Gershom originated from Lotharingia (see *The Early Sages of Ashkenaz* (Heb.), 114–15). If so, the two reports (one regarding Rabbenu Gershom and the other regarding the *ziknei lotir*) would complement each other.

83 This evidence includes the following: (1) a passage in *Men.* 41*a*, which states that at the time of burial *tsitsit* is certainly put on; (2) a passage in *BB* 74*a*, which describes the generation of the wilderness going into their graves wearing a *talit* with *tsitsit*; and (3) a *midrash* from *Sifrei zuta* on Num. 15: 38, in which the juxtaposition of the *mitsvah* of *tsitsit* with the stoning of the wood gatherer teaches that the dead are bound by the *mitsvah* of *tsitsit*. See *Sifrei zuta*, 36.

84 After citing the counter-evidence, the *Tosafot* states: 'And one may wonder regarding our custom, in which they remove the *tsitsit* from the *talitot* of the dead.' The following rationales and proof texts are then offered to justify the current practice: (1) the testimony of *ziknei lotir* (as reported by Rabbenu Tam) that this generation is not worthy of burial in *tsitsit*; (2) the opinion of Ri that nowadays no one wears *tsitsit*, so burial in *talit* with *tsitsit* would be another form of *lo'eg larash* (mocking those who are poor in *mitsvot*, i.e. the dead), which is described in *Men.* 41*a*; (3) the authoritative ruling of R. Yohanan that the dead are free from *mitsvot*, as stated in *Shab.* 30*a*, *Shab.* 151*b*, *Nid.* 61*b*, and inferred from *AZ* 65*b* and *Pes.* 40*b*; (4) a *mishnah* in *Semaḥot* 12, in which Abba Shaul commands his sons to remove the *tekhelet* (strands of the *tsitsit* dyed with a special sky-blue dye) from his cloak prior to burial.

Ri allows one to rely on the authority of the Mishnah in this minor tractate, despite talmudic evidence which points to the contrary, since on other occasions we also follow the customs cited in *sefarim ḥitsoniyim* (extra-canonical works) against the ruling of the Talmud. Furthermore, his student, Rabbi Judah Sirleon, employs dialectic to reconcile the discordant conclusions of various talmudic and midrashic passages regarding burial in *tsitsit* by differentiating between them and aligning each of them with one of the opposing sides of a dispute between two scholars, cited elsewhere in the Talmud, as to whether or not the dead are required to perform *mitsvot*. See *Tosefot rabenu yehudah sirleon al masekhet berakhot*, ed. Zaks, 18*a*, s.v. *deleih*, pp. 213–21.

85 After detailing at length the halakhic legitimacy of the contemporary practice of removing the *tsitsit* from the garments of the dead, R. Judah Sirleon advocates as a better practice (*minhag kasher yoter*) retaining the *tsitsit*, in case the opposing position of Samuel (i.e. that the dead are bound by *mitsvot*) is really the correct one. R. Judah, however, does not specifically mention concealing the *tsitsit*. See *Tosefot rabenu yehudah sirleon al masekhet berakhot*, ed. Zaks,

be removed for burial. This position was accepted as authoritative and was cited and relied upon by numerous tosafists afterwards.[86]

It is in the context of this halakhic discussion that the insistence of Hasidei Ashkenaz on burial in a *talit* with *tsitsit* rendered their position so unusual. R. Eleazar of Worms, in his halakhic work entitled *Sefer haroke'aḥ*, argues strongly that one is required to bury men in *tsitsit*.[87] In clear defiance of the accepted contemporary practice, he writes: 'And no one should

18*a*, s.v. *deleih*, pp. 220–1. The full compromise position is cited in the name of Ritsba (R. Isaac ben Abraham), a student of Ri. See *Tosefot rabenu perets, Berakhot*, ed. Hershler, 31. R. Isaac ben Joseph of Corbeil, in his *Sefer mitsvot katan*, records the divergent customs regarding this matter and advocates retaining the *tsitsit* but covering it. See *Sefer amudei golah*, ed. Harfenis, 25, no. 31. R. Moses of Zurich cites Mordecai b. Hillel, who writes that in his day this compromise position has become accepted practice. See *Sefer hasemak mitsurikh*, ed. Har-Shoshanim-Rozenberg, i. 108, *mitsvah* no. 32, n. 164. Elsewhere, the *Mordekhai* notes that Ri (more likely a reference to the Ritsba, R. Isaac ben Abraham of Dampierre, than to R. Isaac of Dampierre) requested of his sons to tie *tsitsiyot* onto the corners of his garment when he was buried. See *Mordekhai*, 'Hilkhot tsitsit', no. 946. See also the printed *Tosafot* on *Ber*. 18*a*, s.v. *lemaḥar* (last two lines), which cites the custom in the name of Ritsba.

At the conclusion of a rather lengthy passage recorded in the *Maḥzor vitry* (ed. Goldschmidt, p. 246), the compromise position of burial with the *tsitsit* concealed within the *talit* is quoted in the name of R. Elijah, who, according to the report, had instructed his sons to bury him in such fashion. This passage is an addition to the original *Maḥzor vitry*, as it is absent from Sassoon 535 and contains dialectic of a type not common to the *sifrut devei rashi* (eleventh-century literature that emanated from the school of Rashi). The identity of this R. Elijah is uncertain; perhaps he is the son of R. Judah of Paris, a contemporary of R. Tam, who is known to have disagreed with him; or possibly R. Elijah, the father of R. Perets of Corbeil, although no mention is made of this practice by R. Perets's master, R. Isaac of Corbeil, in his work *Sefer mitsvot katan*. The origin of the passage is equally difficult to ascertain. The author claims that the report he has heard regarding R. Elijah came from a R. Yedidyah. The most well-known figure by that name was R. Yedidyah son of R. Israel of Nuremberg, a contemporary of R. Meir of Rothenburg. He presents a strong case against those who are accustomed to removing the *tsitsit* (much akin to the German position, as will soon be seen), but concludes with the aforementioned compromise, similar to the later French position.

A different compromise position is cited in the last line of the printed *Tosafot* on *BB* 74*a*, s.v. *piskei*. Here the custom, recorded as one that is currently practised in Germany, is to place the *tsitsit* on the *talit* of the dead but then to immediately remove it. This same custom is also recorded, albeit for a different reason, by R. Meir of Rothenburg, who discovered it in the *Sefer hama'or* of R. Zerahyah Halevi. It is cited in the name of R. Isaac ben Malki Tsedek from Siponti, and is also found in an anonymous statement in the *Tosefot harosh*, 'and there are those who explain'. See R. Meir of Rothenburg, *Teshuvot, pesakim uminhagim*, ed. Kahana, 'Hilkhot semaḥot', iii. 37, and *Tosefot harosh: masekhet berakhot*, ed. Edwin, 33.

[86] See *Tosefot harashba al masekhet pesaḥim*, ed. Fromm, 40*b*, s.v. *aval* (p. 105); *Tosefot rabenu perets lemasekhet berakhot*, ed. Hershler, 18*a*, s.v. *lemaḥar* (p. 33); R. Meir of Rothenburg, *Teshuvot, pesakim uminhagim*, ed. Kahana, 'Hilkhot semaḥot', iii. 33–4; and *Tosefot harosh: masekhet berakhot*, ed. Edwin, 18*a*, s.v. *deleih* (p. 34). See also the printed *Tosafot* on *Ber*. 18*a*, s.v. *lemaḥar*; *BB* 74*a*, s.v. *piskei*; *AZ* 65*b*, s.v. *aval*, and *Nid*. 61*b*, s.v. *aval*.

[87] See *Sefer haroke'aḥ hagadol*, ed. Shneerson, 'Hilkhot tsitsit', no. 361.

remove the *tsitsiyot* from the *talit* of the dead.' In a passage which is uncharacteristically dialectic in tone, he disputes the halakhic evidence marshalled by those tosafists who are in favour of removing the *tsitsit*, even though this means adopting a minority position,[88] advocating a view which is clearly against an accepted ruling of the Talmud,[89] and maintaining an internal inconsistency within his own position.[90] Additionally, he cites an earlier authority who mandates burial in a *talit* that has *tsitsit*[91] and stipulates that the *talit* should be one that the deceased owned and used during his lifetime, and it should be wrapped around him in his grave.[92]

It is certainly possible to argue that, basing himself on the ruling of this earlier authority, R. Eleazar simply maintained an opposing halakhic tradition that existed in Germany when he insisted on burial in a *talit* with *tsitsit*. However, given the weight of the opposing evidence and the uncharacteristic nature of his argument, one can suggest that he had a strong disposition towards burial in *tsitsit*, and this disposition probably originated from his Pietism.

The ostensible reason why it is beneficial for the hasid to be buried in his *talit* with *tsitsit* is based on the talmudic supposition that when the righteous are resurrected, they will be brought back to life in the very clothing in which they were buried.[93] Therefore, the tosafists argue, the passage in

88 Roke'ah follows the opinion of R. Yanai against that of the rabbis in *Nid.* 61*b*.

89 He argues that one must follow the opinion of R. Yanai (who holds, like Samuel, that the commandments are not nullified) against the opinion of R. Yohanan (who holds that the commandments are nullified), despite the fact that the Talmud rules elsewhere (*Eruv.* 47*b*) that, whenever there is a dispute between Samuel and R. Yohanan, we follow the opinion of R. Yohanan.

90 In the process of discounting (and reinterpreting in his favour) the main proof text of those tosafists who argue for removing the *tsitsit*—Mishnah *Sem.* 12 regarding Abba Shaul—Roke'ah states that *tsitsit ḥovat talit hi velav ḥovat gavra* (*tsitsit* is a requirement for the *talit*, not for the individual), whereas later on in his halakhic discussion, when he speaks about how the four *tsitsiyot me'akevot zu et zu* (each one of the four *tsitsiyot* is necessary, such that, if even one is missing, it nullifies all of them), he states that it is *ḥovat gavra* (an obligation upon the individual). Additionally, he clearly argues against the position of the tosafists who advocate removal of the *tsitsit* when he states unequivocally, 'We do not accept a legal ruling from a *mishnah*', thereby disqualifying the proof text of Abba Shaul in tractate *Semaḥot*—a major support for his contenders.

91 *Sefer haroke'aḥ* records this authority as R. Judah ben Kalonymus of Mainz (Rivak). N. Zaks, the editor of *Tosefot rabenu yehudah sirleon*, however, comments that, in the manuscript of *Sefer haroke'aḥ*, the name that appears is that of R. Isaac ben Asher Halevi of Speyer, who lived in the beginning of the twelfth century and was the first tosafist in Germany. See Urbach, *The Tosafists* (Heb.), i. 165. See *Tosefot rabenu yehudah sirleon al masekhet berakhot*, ed. Zaks, 18*a*, s.v. *deleih*, 221 n. 132.

92 See *Sefer haroke'aḥ hagadol*, ed. Shneerson, 'Hilkhot tsitsit', no. 361.

93 BT *Ket.* 111*b*; the *Tosafot* there, s.v. *bilvusheihem*, interprets 'clothing' as the shroud.

the Talmud which requires burial in *talit* with *tsitsit* does so in order that, at the time of resurrection, the deceased will be found wearing the appropriate garment.[94] By burying the dead in this fashion, the living prevent them from violating the prohibition on wearing a *talit* without *tsitsit* at the time of their resurrection.[95]

However, it is also possible to suggest that, according to *Sefer ḥasidim*, an additional benefit accrues to the hasid from burial in his *talit*. While the Talmud and the tosafists view the *talit* with *tsitsit* as necessary for the time of resurrection, R. Judah finds the garment beneficial for the period immediately after death. In one passage he explains that the righteous wrap themselves in their *talitot* as a form of respect and reverence when in the presence of the awesome God:

> When a man comes before a king of flesh and blood, he should not come as a man who comes from the marketplace; rather, he should wrap himself to be in his presence with dread and with fear and with honour. We who go to stand in the presence of the Master of the entire Earth, blessed be His name, how much more so must we wrap ourselves to be in His presence with dread and fear. Woe to those who wait to wrap themselves from one sabbath to the next sabbath so that men should not laugh at them. And they do not consider that maybe they will die and they will not be able to give honour to Him who put on His own cloak, as it is written, 'His garment was as white as snow' [Dan. 7: 9], and regarding them and those like them it says, 'He may prepare, but a righteous man will wear it' [Job 27: 17].[96]

R. Judah wails about the posthumous fate ('Woe to them') of those individuals whose inability to withstand public shame prevents them from wearing the garment on a daily basis.[97] These foolish people do not realize what they have voluntarily surrendered. Their loss will be twofold. Not only will they be unable to render proper honour to God, who himself is attired in a white *talit*-like garment (on the basis of the verse in Dan. 7: 9), but also the

[94] *Men.* 41*a*. Rashi explains the passage to mean that, whereas Samuel states that a garment that is kept in a box and is not currently being used requires *tsitsit*, he admits that a shroud set aside for burial is exempt from the obligation. However, the passage continues and Samuel stipulates that, at the time of burial, 'we definitely put it [i.e. the *tsitsit*] on'. See Rashi ad loc.

[95] See *Tosefot rabenu yehudah sirleon al masekhet berakhot*, ed. Zaks, 18*a*, s.v. *deleih*, pp. 217–19. This passage follows the opinion of Samuel, cited elsewhere in the Talmud (*Shab.* 151*b*), that the commandments will not be nullified in the World to Come. Therefore, when the dead arise to their renewed existence they will be required to attach *tsitsit* to their garments. R. Judah's position is accepted and cited in full by R. Meir of Rothenburg as well as Rabbenu Asher (Rosh). See R. Meir of Rothenburg, *Teshuvot, pesakim uminhagim*, ed. Kahana, 'Hilkhot semaḥot', iii. 36, and Rosh on *MK*, no. 80.

[96] *Sefer ḥasidim*, ed. Margaliot, 57.

[97] See the discussion below, p. 199, regarding the shame involved in wearing a *talit*.

righteous will wear their *talit* instead of them (on the basis of the concluding verse in Job 27: 17). The connection between the actions of those who fail to wear the *talit* daily and their posthumous fate is only understandable in light of the ruling of Ravyah, as well as the exhortation of R. Judah, only to bury in a *talit* an individual who is *ragil bo*—that is, wears it regularly. As mentioned previously, for R. Judah, regularity means a daily, not weekly, practice. Therefore, only an individual who wears the *talit* daily will be able to be buried in it and thereby greet the presence of God while adorned in dignity.

The passage in *Sefer ḥasidim* speaks of the time immediately after death. The language 'we who go to stand in the presence of the Master of the entire Earth' befits more the posthumous encounter of the soul with God than the period of the World to Come, which will follow the resurrection of the dead. The verse from Job also suggests that the meeting with God will take place immediately after death, in the hereafter. In the context of describing the futility of the actions of the wicked, that verse states that the garments that the wicked one prepares for himself will, in the end, be worn by the righteous. A different passage in *Sefer ḥasidim*, cited earlier, records the view that in the afterlife the wicked are stripped of the rich garments that they are wrapped in and the righteous are dressed in them instead.[98] A dream corroborates this view: a certain individual sees the wicked dead being stripped of their lavish shrouds and the righteous dead being dressed in them in place of their own poor ones. This is offered as an explanation for actual incidents in which the dead were found, upon examination of their graves, to have been stripped of their shrouds.[99] Thus, while naked in the grave, these righteous ones are richly attired in Paradise.[100]

R. Eleazar of Worms, too, states that immediately after death the righteous stand in the presence of the Holy One, wrapped in a *talit* with *tsitsit*. After a detailed exposition on the precise number of strings that the *tsitsit* possesses, R. Eleazar states the following:

> Therefore, whoever wraps himself in *tsitsit*, it is as if the Divine Presence is upon him: 'And you shall see it' [Num. 15: 39]. And all that is before the Kavod for glory, its opposite is in Gehenna for punishment. In Gehenna, [there is] a putrid odour and sulphur for the wicked, while up above, 'the cloud of incense shall

[98] *SḤ* 335.

[99] Ibid.

[100] This story bears strong affinities to two sequential tales of Caesarius of Heisterbach mentioned above, in which monks who are buried in secular clothing appear later in monastic garb. In these narratives, as well as in the Pietist one, changing one's clothing in Paradise becomes the measure of true righteousness.

cover the Ark cover' [Lev. 16: 13]. 'His garment was as white as snow' [Dan. 7: 9], and for the wicked, 'in it shall those in shadowy darkness whiten' [Ps. 68: 15].[101]

R. Eleazar's assertion that whoever wraps himself in *tsitsit*, it is as if the Divine Presence is upon him, has a talmudic basis. In *Menaḥot* 43*b*, in a discussion of *tsitsit*, the Talmud states, 'whoever is eager to do this commandment merits to greet the Divine Presence'. R. Eleazar understands the talmudic statement in a novel way: the souls of the righteous who have observed the commandment during their lifetime merit to stand before the Divine Presence in Paradise, clothed in the white *talit*-like garment which God himself is described as wearing in the verse from Daniel. This is evident from the juxtaposition of R. Eleazar's two statements—one referring to the man who wraps himself in *tsitsit* and the other to the fate of the righteous and wicked souls in the afterlife.[102] He cites Daniel 7: 9, clearly reading it as a reference to the afterlife and to the souls of the righteous dead who inhabit Paradise.

Another passage in *Sefer ḥasidim* further suggests that benefit accrues to the Pietist who is buried in a *talit* with *tsitsit*:

A certain old man was sick. There was a righteous poor person who possessed nothing; even bread was scarce for him. The old man said that when he dies they should give that *talit* of his to that righteous poor person. They said to him [that it was] better that they should lay him [i.e. the old man] to rest in it. He said, 'Since he has nothing with which to buy himself a *talit*, it is better that I give him my *talit*, for I will not pronounce the benediction over it in the grave, while he will pronounce the benediction over it every day.'[103]

It is a meritorious act on the part of the old, dying Pietist[104] to give away his *talit* to a righteous poor man (*ani tsadik*, the prime beneficiary according to the elitist doctrine of Pietist charity),[105] who can use it for the performance

101 *Sefer ḥokhmat hanefesh*, 20*b*.

102 The argument regarding the juxtaposition of statements in *Sefer ḥokhmat hanefesh* is valid, since many of the discussions and digressions in the work are associative in nature.

103 *SḤ* 333.

104 One can assume that the old man is a Pietist as he conforms to the pietistic ideal of charitable giving.

105 In *SḤ* 879, the assumption of the author is that the string of quotations from the sages regarding charity refers to the righteous poor. In *SḤ* 1679 and 1680, it is once again the assumption of the author that the recipients of charity are the *aniyim tovim* (good poor). In *SḤ* 884, charity to an *ani tsadik* is called *tsedakah me'uleh* (an elevated form of charity). In *SḤ* 1684, giving charity to *aniyim tovim* even replaces the commandment of redeeming captives, which is seen by the sages as the classic *mitsvah rabah* (important commandment). In *SḤ* 912, the author advocates forcing the hand of the rich to give charity to the righteous poor. See also *SḤ* 917, 925, and 1696. In *SḤ* 1706 the common practice of giving charity to the non-righteous poor,

of a commandment. At the same time, it is also a sacrificial act that he performs: despite the fact that others advise him to the contrary, he forfeits the benefit of being buried in his *talit* for the sake of another. The subsequent passage in *Sefer ḥasidim* records the same act being carried out by another dying man, who offers his *talit* to a man in need so that he can accrue merit through it.[106] Thus, while Pietist practice dictates burial in one's own *talit*, *Sefer ḥasidim* encourages one to forgo that benefit for the sake of fulfilment of the Pietistic ideal of charity.

It is now possible to suggest that an added benefit of being buried in a *talit* is that one is then properly attired not only in the grave but also for one's sojourn in the hereafter. This understanding of the need to bury the dead clothed was characteristically medieval. The early rabbis viewed clothing for the dead as necessary primarily for the World to Come—the period after the resurrection of the dead.[107] Let us recall the passage in the Talmud which mentions burial in *talit* with *tsitsit* so that the righteous could rise to life wearing the appropriate garment.[108] An additional passage corroborates this view. The Jerusalem Talmud recounts an episode involving the burial request of the scholar R. Jeremiah. A Babylonian sage who immigrated to Palestine in the third century CE, R. Jeremiah asked to be buried near a public road with his cane in hand and sandals on his feet, so that when the messiah came, he would be ready to greet him. R. Jeremiah's focus is solely on the time of the resurrection; he does not express any need for attire in the afterlife.[109] The Pietists, however, view burial in one's own *talit* with the *tsitsit* attached as necessary in order to present oneself respectfully when standing awe-struck before God in Paradise.

Passage to the Hereafter

Being buried in one's *talit* with *tsitsit* may, in fact, benefit the deceased not only in his stay in, but also in his passage to, Paradise. It is an ancient Germanic belief mentioned in the sagas that clothing is necessary for the swift

rather than to the righteous poor, is cited as an illustration of the problem of theodicy, i.e. why the righteous suffer and the wicked prosper in this world. On the elitism of the Pietists, see Marcus, *Piety and Society*, 101–2.

106 *SH* 334.

107 See Schur, 'The Care for the Dead in Medieval Ashkenaz', 48.

108 JT *Kil.* 4: 4, 32*b*. See also Lieberman, 'Some Aspects of After Life in Early Rabbinic Literature', 250 and nn. 25–7; Schur, 'The Care for the Dead in Medieval Ashkenaz', 57. Another passage, in JT *Ned.* 3: 8, suggests that the righteous sit in Paradise wrapped in *talitot*. However, the repeated use of the term 'in the future to come' (*le'atid lavo*), and the fact that the wicked Esau will attempt to enter their company 'in the future', make it clear that the passage refers to *olam haba*—the World to Come.

109 BT *Ket.* 111*b*.

passage of the dead. In the saga of *Gisli Sursson*, Thorgrim speaks of an 'old custom' of placing footwear on the feet of the dead and burying them in such a manner.[110] The footwear, known as *Helskór* (boots of Hel), is meant to aid the deceased in his walk and entry to Valhöll, the paradise of warriors.[111] Caesarius of Heisterbach, in his *Dialogue*, mentions this ancient Germanic custom.[112] In a rather long and elaborate tale regarding the ghost of a sinful priest's mistress, who is seen being hunted by the devil, Caesarius writes that the woman requests 'new shoes of the best sort' to be made for her before she dies. She asks to be buried in them as 'they are very necessary to me'[113]—they allow an easy passage to the hereafter.

This ancient Germanic belief regarding footwear for the dead appears in *Sefer ḥasidim* in one brief reference. After stating the general principle that one should not perform charity with a dangerous object, R. Judah cites the following anecdote. A certain individual is given the shoes of a dead person. Wishing to be charitable, he intends to give them to the poor. His contemporaries, however, caution him not to do so by citing Leviticus 19: 18, which enjoins one to love one's fellow Jew as oneself, and they exhort him to sell the shoes to a non-Jew and give the money to the poor instead.[114] A Jew may not offer his fellow Jew shoes of the dead because to do so would surely be an invitation to a swift death. Instead of a charitable act, it would be a highly dangerous and irreverent one—a violation of the biblical command of brotherly love. This otherwise enigmatic anecdote is comprehensible only when one is cognizant of the belief in the power of *Helskór*, which is still prevalent today in parts of Germany and England.[115]

Shoes were not the only articles of clothing that were deemed desirable for the hereafter. The hood, called *Tarnkappe* (or *Tarnhut* or *Hüttlin*), was believed to possess magical powers of movement in ancient Germanic folk-

110 *Gísla Saga Surssonar*, ch. 14, cited in Lecouteux, *Fantômes et revenants*, 39.

111 Lecouteux, *Fantômes et revenants*, 38, 156–7.

112 Lecouteux writes (ibid. 40) that, since it is not possible for Caesarius to have known the Icelandic saga, there must have been an oral tradition regarding the custom still alive in his day. This passage of his work, therefore, exists as independent testimony, besides the saga, both to the authenticity of the custom as well as to its ancient Germanic provenance.

113 *Dialogue*, 12: 20.

114 *SḤ* 1544.

115 In Germany, in the district of Henneberg, the last rites rendered to the dead are called *Totenschuch* (shoe of the dead). In Yorkshire, England there exists a belief that it is proper to donate one's shoes to the poor while alive, so that, after one's death, those same shoes will be returned in order to help one pass through the thorny, rocky path of the hereafter. Presumably, the merit of having given the shoes to the poor will stand one in good stead after death and benefit one in the passage to the other world. See Lecouteux, *Fantômes et revenants*, 119. There is also a widespread tradition among eastern European Jews not to 'inherit' or offer as a gift shoes of the dead.

lore.[116] It was linked with the notion of swift passage to the hereafter. A specific hood, known as *Hellekeppelin*, served as the 'crown' of Hellequin, king of the dead.[117] During the incipient Christianization of Germany, Anglo-Saxon missionaries appropriated the motifs of the magical, charismatic power of the pagan warriors and kings and assigned them to Christian holy figures. They deliberately translated the Latin word *sanctus* as *hailig*—a word rich in meaning for the pagan Germans with its supernatural association with *heil*.[118] A portion of this supernatural power was transferred to the monk's habit, known as *cuculla*, a garment composed of a cape with a hood. In one of Caesarius of Heisterbach's tales, the *cuculla* is used as a weapon to successfully fight off demons in Purgatory.[119] It wields the same power to counteract otherworldly evil as the name of Jesus and the cross do.[120] Perhaps this is one reason why a monk is buried in his *cuculla*; it ensures for him a swift and safe passage to the hereafter. Let us remind ourselves yet again of Caesarius's tale in which St Benedict bars a monk from entering Paradise because he has failed to wear his monastic habit.

Given that many of the ideas regarding death were drawn from the surrounding culture, it is not implausible that an added advantage of burial in a *talit* was derived from the notion of *Hellekeppelin*. The Pietist distinguished himself from his contemporaries by the type of *talit* he wore. Resembling the medieval cloak called *capuchon*, the hooded *talit* of the Pietists was distinctive in its appearance.[121] Possibly for this reason, R. Judah encouraged his fellow Pietists to have themselves buried only in the *talit* that they were accustomed to wearing every day, because burial in the Pietist *talit* might offer them a swift and safe passage to Paradise.[122] A lingering belief in the

116 Schmitt, *Ghosts in the Middle Ages*, 203.

117 Ibid.

118 See Russell, *The Germanization of Early Medieval Christianity*, 206.

119 A certain Cistercian monk, while alive, voluntarily enters St Patrick's Purgatory, one of the legendary earthly openings to Purgatory in Ireland. He is immediately apprehended by devils, 'who, as it were, bubbled up from the abyss' and who order him to lay down his 'cross' —what they are really referring to is his hood, which forms the shape of a cross. The monk refuses to disrobe, insisting that he is ready to fight, but not without the 'garb of my profession'. He miraculously survives the night. Caesarius of Heisterbach, *Dialogue*, 11: 39.

120 In the dialogue which immediately precedes the above-mentioned tale, Caesarius instructs his novice on the horrors of Purgatory and informs him that those who enter St Patrick's Purgatory can endure the night there and combat the 'assaults of demons' only if they continually invoke the name of Jesus. If at any time they cease to do so, they will surely perish. *Dialogue*, 11: 38.

121 See *She'elot uteshuvot maharam*, ed. Bloch, no. 287, in the name of R. Shimshon of Sens.

122 According to common wisdom, the implication of the word *mutav* in the phrase *mutav sheyashkivu bo et atsmo* ('it is advantageous for him to be laid to rest in it') suggests such an interpretation.

ancient Germanic legend could easily attach itself to the practice of burial in a hooded cloak and add to it a high degree of potency. It is not implausible, moreover, that this very same belief in the magical powers of the *Hellekeppelin* could serve as a contributing factor to the Pietists' unusually strong attachment to the practice of wearing their distinctive hooded *talit* in life—every single day, and ideally all day—as much as in death. They maintained both these idiosyncratic customs against the majority practice of their Ashkenazi contemporaries.

Furthermore, it is not insignificant that the Pietists selected a distinctive, hooded *talit*, with all its attendant supernatural powers, as one of the hallmarks of their movement. With its similarity to monastic garb on the one hand and its ritual fringes or *tsitsit* on the other, the Pietist *talit* must have identified its wearer as belonging to a distinct group with its own particular ideology in much the same way that members of various monastic orders donned garments of specific colour, texture, and design. These visual symbols of identity did not go unnoticed by medieval Jews.[123] The affinity between Pietist aspirations and monastic ideology, however, awaits more detailed analysis in a later chapter.[124]

Although the Pietist practice of wearing the *talit* and *tsitsit* in both life and death remains an anomaly, the outlook from which it may have stemmed was one that their Ashkenazi contemporaries did share. A belief in the magical powers of clothing to aid the swift passage of the dead to the afterlife can be detected in the writings of Ashkenazi halakhists. Rashi, in his commentary on tractate *Yevamot*, speaks of shoes as part of the attire prepared by an old man for his burial.[125] Similarly, the *Sefer haroke'aḥ* states: 'And they dress him [i.e. the deceased] in pants and a shirt and shoes [*ve'anfala*].'[126]

A combination of two ancient Germanic beliefs—that of *Helskór* alongside a belief in the summoning power of the dead—may explain the origin of a peculiar practice cited in Ashkenazi sources. The *Sefer ma'aseh hage'onim* relates that the son of the eleventh-century scholar of Mainz, R. Isaac b. Judah, was instructed by his father to walk barefoot to the cemetery when his mother was buried.[127] A later, thirteenth-century, source questions this practice, since the customary procedure was for the bereaved to remove their shoes only after the burial, when they assumed the halakhic

[123] Baumgarten, *Practicing Piety in Medieval Ashkenaz*, 174.

[124] See below, Ch. 9.

[125] BT *Yev.* 104*a*, s.v. *veshel zaken he'asui likhvodo.*

[126] *Sefer haroke'aḥ hagadol*, ed. Shneerson, no. 194. See also Schur, 'The Care for the Dead in Medieval Ashkenaz', 57–8.

[127] *Sefer ma'aseh hage'onim*, ed. Epstein, 50.

status of a mourner.[128] While R. Isaac b. Judah's instruction may have been a reflection of the exceptional status of his wife,[129] in light of the notion that shoes provide a swift passage to the hereafter, it is not implausible that he saw his son's walking to his mother's grave with shoes on as a summons to death. This is certainly the case in a passage in the 'Testament of R. Judah the Pious'. Here, in describing the graveside oath to be taken by someone who has had dreams of the dead summoning him to join them, the author writes that the procedure should be performed three times, 'without shoes on'.[130] Wearing shoes at a time when one is trying to stave off a summons to depart to the other world may be viewed as counterproductive, and is therefore discouraged.

In addition to the supernatural power of footwear, Ashkenazi sources outside the Pietist circle speak of burial in *tsitsit* in a way that suggests that they regard it as a 'key' to Paradise. R. Eleazar of Worms testifies regarding an earlier Ashkenazi figure[131] that he had asked to be buried wrapped in his *talit*, with his *tsitsit* in his hand.[132] A similar practice is mentioned in the *Hilkhot avel* of R. Jacob ben Judah Hazan of London. Here the practice was to wrap the deceased in a *talit* and remove the *tsitsiyot* (because the dead are not bound by *mitsvot*), but to place them on the heart of the deceased.[133] The image of *tsitsit* which emerges from these requests is that of a key being held in the hand or placed on the heart of the deceased, allowing him immediate and guaranteed entry into Paradise. This image is very different from the Talmud's description of the burial of an actual key in the graves of certain people, whose purpose was to arouse the anguish of the living.[134]

Additionally, a tradition whose origins went back to early Ashkenaz equated the *tsitsit* with the entire gamut of 613 *mitsvot*, so that it testified on behalf of its wearer that he had fulfilled all of his Torah obligations.[135] This

128 *Shibolei haleket*, ed. Buber, 'Hilkhot semaḥot', no. 15, p. 346.

129 This is the opinion of Avraham Grossman in his *Pious and Rebellious*, 223. On this see Schur, 'The Care for the Dead in Medieval Ashkenaz', 130–1.

130 'The Testament of R. Judah the Pious' (Heb.), no. 9, p. 13. While this work was not written by R. Judah, it seems to reflect much, if not all, of the world-view of *Sefer ḥasidim*.

131 According to the printed text of the *Sefer haroke'aḥ*, this figure was R. Judah ben Kalonymus of Mainz, while according to the manuscript of the work as cited by N. Zaks (editor of *Tosefot rabenu yehudah sirleon al masekhet berakhot*), it was R. Isaac ben Asher (Halevi) of Speyer. See n. 91 above.

132 See *Sefer haroke'aḥ hagadol*, ed. Shneerson, 'Hilkhot tsitsit', no. 361.

133 See Hazan, *Ets ḥayim*, 390.

134 *The Tractate Mourning*, ed. Zlotnick, 8: 7.

135 BT *Men.* 43*b* equates *tsitsit* with the *mitsvot*, while Rashi, in his commentary there, adds that the numerical value of the word *tsitsit*, together with the number of its strings and knots, equals 613. See *Tosefot rabenu yehudah sirleon al masekhet berakhot*, ed. Zaks, 18*a*, s.v. *deleih*, pp. 211–13.

testimony was understood to apply specifically in the grave and in a most literal fashion. According to the elders of Lotharingia, who were among the earliest scholars of Ashkenaz,[136] one was no longer permitted to bury the dead in *tsitsit* because the present generation was not worthy. By doing so one would be guilty of rendering false testimony regarding the deceased, who was not in complete observance of Torah law while alive.[137] The implication of this stricture is twofold. Firstly, in an earlier period, when the generation was worthy, burial in *tsitsit* offered tangible testimony regarding the deceased and his righteous conduct—he was one who had fulfilled all of his Torah obligations. Secondly, although failure to fulfil the entirety of Torah law did not preclude the living from wearing *tsitsit*, its testimony was quite real and literal for the dead, the unworthy ones among whom were prohibited from wearing it. The tosafists themselves were aware of this contradiction. Regarding the position of the elders of Lotharingia, they wrote, 'And, additionally, Rabbenu Tam said that he had heard from the men of Lotharingia[138] that they remove the *tsitsit* [for burial], because *tsitsit* adds up in numerical value to 613 with [its] eight strings and five knots. And if one would wear *tsitsit* [in the grave] it would appear as if he had fulfilled the entire Torah, and that would be a lie.' The *Tosafot* then asks the following question: 'And this is not clear, for even the living, why do they now wear it? They have not fulfilled the Torah in its entirety.'[139] The tosafists are puzzled by the curious fact that it is somehow acceptable in medieval Ashkenaz to render false testimony about oneself in this world, but to do so after passage to the hereafter is blatantly not. This contradiction notwithstanding, the tosafists clearly view the *tsitsit* as a tangible and literal testimony to the righteous character of the deceased. Such an outlook is much akin to the one that sees it as a key to Paradise.

Following this pattern of thinking, it is possible to suggest that ritual objects were buried with their martyred owners in the belief that these material items, through which highly honourable religious acts had been performed, would ensure the swift and certain passage of the deceased to Paradise.[140] *Sefer ḥasidim* relates that martyrs were buried with the very

[136] Their group can be dated back to the pre-Crusade period; it originated in Mainz and Worms, the cradle of Ashkenaz.

[137] See *Tosefot rabenu yehudah sirleon al masekhet berakhot*, ed. Zaks, 18*a*, s.v. *deleih*, p. 213.

[138] R. Tam did not hear this ruling directly from the elders of Lotharingia; see n. 82 above.

[139] See *Tosafot* on *Ber*. 18*a*, s.v. *lemaḥar*.

[140] This practice can be linked to the ancient custom of burying the dead with 'material objects, such as clothing, food, arms, and tools', in order to ensure for them 'a safe journey and favourable reception' in the world of the dead, as documented by the French ethnographer and folklorist Arnold van Gennep, *The Rites of Passage*, 154.

knives they had used to slay themselves.[141] In the Crusade chronicles, these knives were given ritualistic status as they were checked for imperfections, just like knives used for ritual slaughter.[142] A knife that was used to perform the consummate act of sanctification of God's name would undoubtedly attest to the righteous character of the deceased, in the same way that burial in *tsitsit* would, and it should therefore allow the martyr immediate entry into Paradise.

The same may be true for a later period. The Spanish biblical exegete Bahya ben Asher (1255–1340) reports that contemporary custom among the pious of France (*ḥasidei tsarfat*) was to 'fashion a coffin for burial out of their dining table'. The reason given is that a person who has died 'can carry nothing in his hand . . . except for the charity he performed in his lifetime and the goodness he dispensed at his table'.[143] The upshot of this explanation is that, in order to merit entry into Paradise, one needs to literally 'carry' one's good deeds in one's hand.

Similarly, a late fourteenth-century text penned by the northern French R. Jacob ben Solomon records the request of an Ashkenazi woman named Esther to be buried with her headscarf and wedding ring as testimony to her dutiful fulfilment of her role as a Jewish wife.[144] The *Leket yosher*, a fifteenth-century halakhic collection of Ashkenazi origin, tells of an important Jewish woman who returns after death to demand that her last wishes, specified in her will, be implemented. She requests that her hair, which she had kept covered all her life (a sign of piety in fulfilling the commandment pertaining to married women), be buried with her. Her casket is then opened and the hair placed inside.[145] The fifteenth-century R. Israel Bruna of Regensburg relates that a certain Jewish woman was buried, at her request, in a girdle that she had worn during her lifetime. A token of her husband's love, the girdle could also attest to her fidelity as a married woman and serve as a key to Paradise.[146]

Evidence that belief in the supernatural powers of the *Helskór* and the *Hellekeppelin* persisted into the thirteenth century can be found in two Germanic collections of radically different orientation—a Cistercian exempla collection and the ethical treatise of a Jewish Pietist. This demonstrates that ancient imaginings of the dead traversed religious boundaries and

141 *SḤ* 1532.

142 Barak, 'Time of Rage' (Heb.), 59–60.

143 Bahya ben Asher, *Rabenu beḥaye al hatorah*, ed. Chavel, ii. 279–80.

144 Although R. Jacob wrote his work *Evel rabati* in Avignon, he was of northern French origin and all the names he mentions are known from Ashkenazi sources. See Barak, 'The Early Ashkenazi Practice of Burial with Religious Paraphernalia', 189.

145 Ibid. 191.

146 Ibid. 192–3.

reflected a shared outlook. Moreover, the fact that requests to be buried with certain material objects were made by both men and women in Ashkenazi sources both within and outside the Pietist orbit offers tangible testimony to the tenacity of these beliefs and their widespread diffusion among the German Jewish populace.

Conclusion

The neutral dead of *Sefer ḥasidim* are more reflective of the medieval Germano-Christian environment in which they appeared than of their counterparts in rabbinic literature. Discussion of the neutral dead in the Talmud centres on the world of the living. Similar discussion in *Sefer ḥasidim* is steeped in the world of the dead. Additionally, the role assigned to the clothing of the dead in the Talmud is peripheral in comparison to that in the Pietist work. The dead of *Sefer ḥasidim* insist on being wrapped in a shroud in order to perambulate, and if it is absent they will return to the world of the living to demand it.

The dead of *Sefer ḥasidim* have much in common with the dead of the exempla literature. Both groups require proper garments in each stage of their posthumous existence—when they are buried, while they are in Paradise, and during the times that they return to the world of the living. The Cistercian author of an exempla collection and certain key Pietists maintain this position regarding the clothed souls of the dead despite the theological difficulties involved and the received traditions that it contradicts. The corporeal imaginings associated with the ancient Germanic dead may be responsible for these deviations.

The Pietists were set apart from other Ashkenazi Jews in their steadfast commitment to the practice of wearing a *talit*, which gave them the opportunity to be draped in it after their death. They were among the very few in their era to bury their dead in that garment, whose distinctive hood created a semblance between the Pietists and the monks in their *cuculla*. For the Pietist, the advantage of being buried in his distinctive *talit* with *tsitsit* may very well have lain in the supernatural power of the hood to offer a swift and safe passage to the hereafter. Evidence of a belief in the ancient Germanic *Helskór* and *Hellekeppelin* in both the *Dialogue on Miracles* and *Sefer ḥasidim* testifies to the strong influence that these notions had and to their ability to straddle cultural and religious divides. These beliefs concerning clothing for the dead may go a long way in explaining the Cistercian and Pietist positions with regard to issues of corporeality and the nature of the soul after death.

Between the eleventh and fifteenth centuries, requests by both men and women to be buried with religious or ritual articles testified to the existence of beliefs predicated on the same world-view that underlay the ideas of *Helskór* and *Hellekeppelin*. The belief that physical objects possessed the power to propel their bearers to Paradise was present in Ashkenazi sources both within and outside the Pietist circle. In this light, various Ashkenazi halakhists viewed specific garments of the dead, such as the *tsitsit*, as aids in the passage of the soul to the hereafter. These garments were not solely intended, as the talmudic rabbis would profess, for the time of the resurrection. The focus on the period immediately after death, rather than a concern with the World to Come (a point which I elaborate in the next chapter), was a hallmark of the medieval period and one which separated yet again the world of the Pietists from the world of the rabbis of the Talmud.

PART II

THE AFTERLIFE IN *SEFER ḤASIDIM*

CHAPTER FIVE

STATUS IN THE HEREAFTER

IN TRACTATE *Mo'ed katan*, which contains a considerable amount of rabbinic discussion on matters of death and mourning, the rabbis tell the following pair of stories:

R. Se'orim, Rava's brother, while sitting at Rava's bedside, saw him going to sleep [i.e. dying], when he [the invalid] said to his brother, 'Do tell him [the Angel of Death], Sir, not to torment me.' R. Se'orim replied, 'Are you, Sir, not his intimate friend?' Said Rava, 'Since my *mazal* [fate] has been delivered [to him], he takes no heed of me.' R. Se'orim then said to the dying man, 'Do, Sir, show yourself to me [in a dream after you die].' He did show himself, and when asked, 'Did you, Sir, suffer pain?', he replied, 'As from the prick of the cupping instrument.'

Rava, while seated at the bedside of R. Nahman, saw him sinking into slumber [i.e. dying]. Said he to Rava, 'Tell him [the Angel of Death] not to torment me.' Said Rava, 'Are you, Sir, not a man esteemed?' Said R. Nahman to him, 'Who is esteemed, who is regarded, who is distinguished [before the Angel of Death]?' Said Rava to him, 'Do, Sir, show yourself to me [in a dream after you die].' He did show himself. [Rava] asked him, 'Did you suffer pain, Sir?' He replied, 'As [little as] the taking of a hair from milk; but were the Holy One, blessed be He, to say to me, "Go back to that world in which you were", I wish it not, for the dread of it [i.e. death] is great.'[1]

In *Sefer ḥasidim*, R. Judah the Pious records a similar event involving a promise to return after death:

If two people who were friendly during their lifetime swore or pledged loyalty one to the other that, if one of them were to die [before the other], he would inform his friend how it is in that world, either by means of a dream or [by means of a vision] in a wakeful state: if by means of a dream, the spirit [of the dead] will whisper in the ears of the living person or near his brain, just like the master of dreams [i.e. the angel in charge of dreams] [does]. And if they swore that he [i.e.

[1] BT *MK* 28*a*.

the deceased] would speak to him while awake, the dead person will request the angel appointed over him to dress him in the semblance of clothes, and the scattered spirit [will act in such a way as] to make it cling together until [it is possible] for him [the deceased] to speak with his friend, the one with whom he contracted a pact.[2]

The primary focus in the talmudic stories is fear of death. In each case, the dying rabbi requests his living friend, who will be present at the moment of his death, to instruct the Angel of Death not to torment him as he takes his soul. Although the rabbis accept the decree of death, they fear its pain. The living rabbis share the same fear: each of them requests his friend to return to him after death, and when he does, he questions him regarding the pain he experienced. Even when the pain of death is found out to have been minimal, there remains an almost irrational fear of death; after having experienced the taking of his soul to be as painless a process as the removal of a hair from milk, Rav Nahman still does not wish to return to the world of the living because the fear of death is so great.

Noteworthy also is the fact that the rabbis of the Talmud cite these stories for an altogether different purpose. They serve to bolster support for a pronouncement made by Rava immediately beforehand, namely, that three things in life are dependent upon *mazal* (fate) and not merit, one of which is one's lifespan. Both stories illustrate this point; in each case, the living rabbi expresses surprise that the dying rabbi has no control over the Angel of Death, regardless of his great merits, and the dying rabbi in turn responds that he lacks the power to postpone death once it has been decreed.[3]

R. Judah the Pious's remarks about similar situations, in which a promise is made to appear after death, reveal an entirely different focus to that of the rabbinic stories. Here, the intent of the promise is for the dead to inform the living, not of the experience they had at the moment of death, but of their state in the hereafter—'how it is in that world'. Unlike the two isolated incidents of the Talmud, R. Judah's words suggest that it is not uncommon for two friends to swear or make a pact with each other that whoever dies first will appear to the other. His rather detailed description of the mechanisms by which each encounter transpires, whether by means of a

[2] *SḤ* 324.

[3] Such an interpretation explains the sequence of the stories, which are deliberately arranged in a non-chronological order (Rava dies in the first story and is still alive in the second). The rabbis offer first the one in which Rava dies because the incident surrounding his own death substantiates more powerfully the pronouncement which he makes in the discussion earlier.

dream or a wakeful vision, suggests this possibility; he explains that if the dead person is to appear in a dream, the message is whispered into the ear of the living friend,[4] whereas if he is to appear in a wakeful state, he is dressed in a 'semblance of clothes' and speaks directly to his partner. R. Judah is familiar with each mechanism and how it functions; the deceased appears to his or her living partner in the precise medium (dream or wakeful vision) previously agreed upon by the two.

Additionally, unlike in the pair of rabbinic stories, in R. Judah's description the promise to appear after death is not incidental or secondary. His primary intention is to speak about the return of the dead via a dream or vision. His remarks are prefaced by a number of stories involving the appearance of the dead in dreams to the living, and are succeeded by various statements and stories that educate the reader as to how one should distinguish between a dead person who appears to the living in a wakeful state and a demon in the guise of the deceased.[5] These various cases testify to the increased frequency of, or at the very least heightened interest in, appearances of the dead in R. Judah's world as compared to the rabbinic one.

The text in *Sefer ḥasidim* demonstrates that people's fears about death have noticeably shifted since rabbinic times. No longer does the Angel of Death predominate in their discussions. The act of dying, no matter how painful, is but a moment in eternity. It is, rather, the eternal fate of their soul in the afterlife that preoccupies them. This heightened concern with the posthumous state of the soul is a uniquely medieval phenomenon.

Fears Surrounding Death and the Role of the World to Come in Rabbinic Sources

The pain experienced at the moment of death is one major concern voiced in rabbinic sources. The sages in *Berakhot* declare that there are 903 types of death, identifying the 'hardest' of them as croup and the 'easiest' as death by 'Divine kiss'.[6] They offer concrete examples as to the nature of the pain associated with these two types. Death by croup feels like 'a thorn in a ball of wool pulled backwards' or, according to others, like '[pulling] a rope through the loopholes [of a ship]', whereas death by Divine kiss is comparable to 'pulling a hair out of milk'. In the *Mo'ed katan* passage cited above,

4 For the exact mechanics of dreams according to Pietist ideology, see *SḤ* 382. On dreams, see Harris, 'Dreams in *Sefer Ḥasidim*', and more recently Idel, 'On *She'elat Ḥalom* in Ḥasidei Ashkenaz', and Alexander, 'A Ḥasid Came in a Dream' (Heb.).

5 See *SḤ* 321, 322, 323, 324, 325, 326, and 327. On the affinity between demons and the dead, see above, pp. 21–2, 40–1, 71, and 77.

6 BT *Ber.* 8*a*. All 903 types of death are not itemized by the rabbis.

the rabbis classify the varying periods of suffering associated with illness according to gradations and assign each one a name.[7] The fact that elsewhere they refer to mankind as 'decay' indicates that they see life as a gradual process of dying.[8]

Concern over the pain experienced by the body after dying also occupies the rabbis. R. Isaac states, 'the worm is as painful to the dead as a needle in the flesh of the living'.[9] The Talmud teaches that the soul mourns over the loss of the body and over its putrid state during the first seven days following death, and is in need of comfort.[10] In fact, a story is told of a man who returns from the dead in a dream to thank one of the rabbis for having comforted his soul during those initial seven days by assembling a quorum of men to observe mourning customs in his house.[11] The man makes no mention of the fate of his soul in the hereafter, and the comfort he receives from the living is restricted to the pain his soul endures while it mourns over the body, which is not due to any punishment of the soul.[12]

Since the rotting of the flesh is considered painful to the body, there is discussion among the rabbis as to whether the bodies of the righteous rot. A story regarding the cadaver of R. Ahai b. R. Yoshiyah—whose body in the grave is found to still have flesh on it—teaches that the bones of those who are free from envy do not rot.[13] The incorruptible nature of the dead scholar's corpse, however, has seemingly no impact on the judgement of his soul in the afterlife; he is spared only the pain suffered upon the rotting of his flesh.[14]

While the Talmud contains several stories of rabbinic scholars who return from the dead and speak of the afterlife, these do not describe the state of the soul there. In one story, Rav Joseph, son of R. Joshua b. Levi, who falls into a death-like trance and then recovers, reports having seen 'an upside-down world', in which those who are at the top (that is, highly

[7] *MK* 28*a*. [8] *Tem.* 31*a*. [9] *Ber.* 18*b* and *Shab.* 152*a*. [10] *Shab.* 152*b*. [11] Ibid.

[12] Interestingly, when R. Judah the Pious cites the rabbis' dictum about the soul mourning over the body, he assumes that the soul returns to the house in which the deceased lived and mourns there; *Sefer gematriyot*, i. 328–9, no. 308. His assumption confirms the instinctive nature of his belief in the return of the neutral dead to the familiar places of their past on Earth. We may recall, for instance, the dead who inhabit the synagogue, discussed in Ch. 4 above.

[13] BT *Shab.* 152*b*.

[14] As characteristic of the rabbinic period, there is no seeming connection between the intactness of the body of the deceased and his ability to perambulate on Earth either. When the living sage R. Nahman invites him to his house, he refuses, stating that only God can release the dead from their graves, at the time of the resurrection. This statement stands in sharp contrast to the ancient Germanic belief of the wandering corporeal dead, whose ability to walk on Earth is directly related to the amount of flesh still left on their body (see above, Ch. 1, n. 87).

esteemed) on Earth are at the bottom (of low esteem) in Heaven.[15] Rav Joseph refers here to a correction of social inequality, not retributive justice, which takes place in the afterlife. A second incident involves the near-death of R. Huna bereih derav Yehoshua. After recovering from his illness, Rav Huna reports having heard God instruct the angels not to be particular with him, since he had overlooked the misdeeds of others towards him. His testimony serves to verify the statement made by Rav, 'He who forgoes his right [to exact punishment] is forgiven all his iniquities', which he derives from a scriptural verse.[16] Rav Huna's account not only confirms Rav's statement but qualifies it as well, on the basis of an additional point he learned in Heaven: God's beneficence applies only to a portion of the Jewish people, not to all of them. In this episode the rabbis are less concerned with Rav Huna's status in the afterlife than with the validation and clarification of Rav's dictum.

The Jerusalem Talmud in one place describes Paradise as replete with gardens, orchards, and water fountains. It talks about a pious individual who enjoys these benefits after death, and contrasts this with the punishments of two sinners: one has his tongue hanging out but cannot ever drink, and another hangs from her breasts, or, according to a different opinion, has her ear attached to the pivot of the doorpost of Gehenna.[17] While the Talmud here provides a detailed account of reward and punishment in the hereafter, its goal is not to highlight the post-mortem fate of individuals but rather to justify God's ways in this world. By revealing the ultimate fate of these people, it rectifies an impropriety that had occurred during the simultaneous burial processions of two unrelated individuals. Due to circumstances peculiar to the situation, the pious person was buried with indignity—no one attended his funeral procession and burial—while the wicked one was buried with great fanfare and honour. The description of their respective reward and punishment in the afterlife teaches that both of them have received their rightful due in the end, and it serves as a corrective to their seemingly unjust fate on Earth. It is also made known that the indignity suffered by the pious man was in fact just, as he had committed a lone 'sin' while alive: he once donned the phylactery of the head before that of the hand, and has now been punished for it.

A third tale, in the Babylonian Talmud, involves R. Joshua b. Levi's request to the Angel of Death to show him his place in Paradise. While his wish is granted, it soon becomes clear that the request was merely a

15 BT *Pes.* 50*a*.
16 BT *RH* 17*a*. Rav's statement is based on Micah 7: 18.
17 JT *Ḥag.* 2: 2, 11*a*.

subterfuge on his part, for as soon as he is taken there, he jumps over the wall into Paradise and swears that he will never leave. The rabbi's scrupulousness in the matter of oaths forces the Angel of Death to uphold the oath, and he is allowed to remain.[18] R. Joshua b. Levi's request does not stem from a desire to know his future status in the afterlife; rather, it serves as a means for him to enter Paradise without having to suffer the pain of death. Also, while the story contains a short description of his stay in Paradise, the discussion centres on whether or not R. Joshua b. Levi satisfies the criteria for admission to that elite abode; R. Shimon b. Yohai asks him whether a rainbow ever appeared during his lifetime. R. Joshua's greatness is highlighted when he intentionally offers a false answer to the question out of extreme humility.

It is clear from the context of the story that anxiety, or even curiosity, about one's state in the afterlife does not preoccupy the rabbis. Immediately after this anecdote, a very similar story regarding R. Hanina b. Papa appears.[19] Here, too, a rabbi uses a request to see his place in Paradise as a subterfuge, has the power to manipulate the Angel of Death, and must prove his righteousness. This story, which lacks any description of Paradise, emphasizes the two main points of the previous one—a rabbi's desire to escape or control the Angel of Death and a testimony to the rabbi's righteousness.

In contrast to this, in the high medieval period, the R. Joshua b. Levi story was embellished in such a way as to add a new theme to it. With several elements of the original talmudic version excised and elaborate descriptions of Paradise and Gehenna inserted, the medieval version focuses on the various abodes of the afterlife and the inhabitants thereof. The detailed description of the seven levels of Gehenna forms the central part of the narrative. One manuscript version concludes with a short prayer asking God to rescue Israel from the pit of Gehenna.[20]

The only rabbinic story which describes anxiety over one's status in the afterlife appears in *Berakhot* 28*b*. Rabbi Yohanan b. Zakai, lying on his deathbed, weeps in front of his students. He explains that he fears the judgement of God—a Judge who cannot be bribed with money or persuaded with words; whose anger is everlasting and whose punishment is

[18] BT *Ket.* 77*b*.

[19] Ibid.

[20] R. Kushelevsky, 'R. Joshua b. Levi and the Angel of Death' (Heb.), 263–4, and ead., *Penalty and Temptation* (Heb.), 29. See also Micha Perry, *Tradition and Change* (Heb.), 197–254. On the early twelfth-century version of this tale, see Perry's most recent study, 'Jewish Heaven and Christian Hell'; I wish to thank Micha Perry for sharing his essay with me.

interminable—and he is unsure of his fate: 'There are two paths before me—one [leading to] Paradise and one to Gehenna, and I do not know towards which one they will take me.' It is possible that R. Yohanan's concern stems from a momentous decision he was forced to make earlier in his life: in his negotiations with the Roman general Vespasian he asked for the safety of the sages of Yavneh at the cost of the destruction of the Temple and the sack of Jerusalem—a decision which would weigh heavily on anyone's soul.[21] But this story is *sui generis*; of the nineteen deathbed scenes that appear in talmudic literature, it is the only one where this fear is mentioned.[22] When R. Hiya, for instance, enters the bedchamber of the dying R. Judah the Prince and witnesses him weeping, the latter informs him that he cries because of his sorrow over his impending separation from the Torah and its commandments.[23] A further feature that distinguishes R. Yohanan's case from R. Judah's is that the latter is found to have been crying even before R. Hiya's entrance, whereas, in the case of the former, the dying rabbi begins to cry only when he sees his students before him. R. Yohanan's delayed weeping might reinforce its didactic aim: he wishes to arouse within his students the fear of God's judgement and its consequences—a quality they might otherwise lack.[24]

The rabbis equally fear lack of burial,[25] and at times the 'after death', referring to the posthumous fate of the body, scares them even more than death itself—a characteristic feature of the ancient mindset.[26] The consumption of the corpse by worms and maggots, as well as its exposure to the elements, disgrace the human body in a way that is intolerable to the rabbis. The following *midrash* illustrates this point well:

There were once two wicked men who were partners with each other. One of them predeceased the other and repented before his death, while he was alive, and the other did not repent before his death. The one who repented while he was alive stood in the company of the righteous, while the other one stood in the

21 See BT *Git.* 56*b*.

22 Saldarini, 'Last Words and Deathbed Scenes'. More than fifty years ago, George Foot Moore, in his study of Judaism, noted this phenomenon: 'There is no indication that pious Jews were afflicted with an inordinate preoccupation about their individual hereafter. The anxiety of a few eminently godly men in the hour of death is recorded because exceptional; it was never cultivated as a mark of superior piety.' *Judaism in the First Centuries of the Christian Era*, iii. 321.

23 BT *Ket.* 103*b*. See Saldarini, 'Last Words and Deathbed Scenes', 40–1.

24 This might support Moore's conclusion that the case of R. Yohanan ben Zakai is unique and indicative of an individual who possesses a 'peculiarly sensitive conscience' (*Judaism in the First Centuries of the Christian Era*, iii. 321 n. 4).

25 Lieberman, 'Some Aspects of After Life in Early Rabbinic Literature', 257.

26 The term 'after death' originates with Seneca as quoted by Lieberman (ibid. 257 and 261).

company of the wicked. The latter, upon seeing the condition of the former, said, 'Perhaps there is bribery in this world! Woe to man! This one [i.e. I] and he, we were together in the world as one—we stole together, we robbed together, and we committed all evil acts possible in the world together. Why is this one among the company of the righteous and that man is [I am] in the company of the wicked?' And he said to him, 'Fool, you were disgraced after your death for three days, your body was not put into a coffin, and you were dragged to the grave with ropes, [as it says], "the maggot is spread under you and the worms over you" [Isa. 14: 11]. Your partner saw your disgrace and swore to turn away from his evil path and repented like the righteous. His repentance caused him to receive here life, honour, and a portion with the righteous.'[27]

The authorities execute one of a pair of robbers and, as part of the punishment, deny him a proper burial. His partner in crime, who witnesses the event, is so horrified by this that he repents and abandons his evil ways. His sincere repentance earns him a place among the righteous when he dies.

In this allegorical story, the rabbis exploit a fear they share with their audience. It is not the execution of the robber which horrifies the living partner, but the disgraceful treatment of his corpse. Details of the execution are omitted, while specifics of the corpse's disgrace abound—the lack of a coffin, the dragging of the corpse with ropes, and the worms and maggots. It is this factor that sparks the other criminal's repentance and which, the rabbis hope, will inspire others as well.

So important is burial in the mindset of the sages that a high priest—who, Scripture states, must not defile himself even with the dead body of his closest relative—is obligated in the Mishnah to contaminate himself by burying an abandoned corpse.[28] Similarly, the rabbis went to great lengths and expense to redeem the bodies of the unburied.[29] It was not only burial that mattered to them, but all of its circumstances as well. The tale from the Jerusalem Talmud mentioned earlier is demonstrative in this regard. The indignity of the righteous man's funeral and the elaborate procession of the wicked man are central elements in that narrative.

When it came to matters of reward and punishment, more predominant among the rabbis than a concern about people's fate in the afterlife was their preoccupation with resurrection and the World to Come. A simple comparison of the space devoted to each topic in the rabbinic corpus attests to this: scattered pronouncements and dicta related to Paradise and Gehenna and their inhabitants pale in comparison to an entire

[27] *Kohelet rabah* 1: 15.
[28] *Nazir* 7: 1.
[29] Lieberman, 'Some Aspects of After Life in Early Rabbinic Literature', 260.

mishnaic chapter[30] and long sections of the Talmud[31] that systematically discuss those who merit and those who are denied a portion in the World to Come. Belief in resurrection is intimately tied to rabbinic discussion of the World to Come, in that he who denies the former is excluded from the latter.[32] In some cases, anxiety over resurrection is at the root of the fear of not having a burial. The Talmud in *Gitin* relates that 400 Jewish children, captives of the Romans, wished to commit suicide by jumping into the sea. They hesitated on account of an express fear that not being granted an earthly burial would deny them bodily resurrection.[33]

The World to Come occupies so large a place in rabbinic thought that it encompasses, in many instances, even the period immediately following death.[34] Rabbinic terms such as *olam haba* and *le'atid lavo* fluctuate in meaning between the far distant post-messianic world and the immediate posthumous existence of the soul in various tannaitic and amoraic passages.[35] Several important thematic elements overlap in the two.[36] This mixture of meanings and conflation of elements on the part of the rabbis signifies their lack of emphasis on the individual hereafter as the primary locus of posthumous reward and punishment. Instead, eternal life in the World to Come, the corporate destiny of the People of Israel, is the focus of rabbinic attention.[37]

The Individual Afterlife: Christian Background

Whereas in the earliest centuries of Christianity some thinkers believed that all members of the Church would be saved, by the fourth century the late Church Fathers clearly distinguished between the good and the bad, the elect and the reprobate. Similarly, the original expectation of the first Christians that Christ's return to Earth to judge the living and the dead was imminent soon gave way to the image of a Last Judgement, to take place only at the End of Time. Then bodily resurrection would follow and the elect would receive eternal reward in the presence of God, while the reprobate would endure eternal damnation as punishment. Until that time, Christians believed, the souls of the dead would 'sleep' or 'rest'. Yet even in this 'waiting period' the saved and the damned would be separated, with

30 *San.* 10.
31 See e.g. *San.* 90*a*–92*b*.
32 Mishnah *San.* 10: 1.
33 BT *Git.* 57*b*.
34 Segal, 'Judaism', 21.
35 See Costa, *L'Au-delà et la resurrection*, 28, 37–57, and 62–71.
36 Ibid. 110–32.
37 See Avery-Peck, 'Death and Afterlife in the Early Rabbinic Sources', 265.

the former group occupying a place of refreshment and the latter one of discomfort. Both states, however, were vaguely defined.[38]

Early Christians shared the widespread fear of lack of proper burial. The Church Fathers wrote several treatises on resurrection in order to assuage the fears surrounding martyrdom in this regard. The early martyrs embraced their execution but feared the disgrace to their bodies: after having been mutilated by torture or, worse yet, consumed by beasts in the arenas, they would have few physical remains left from which they could be resurrected in the future.[39] The tie between fear of lack of proper burial and a strong belief in bodily resurrection is demonstrated once again.

Although resurrection and the Last Judgement were still the central foci of Christian thought regarding the after-death experience in this early period, the seeds of a belief in Purgatory had already been planted.[40] In the writings of Augustine one can detect the origins of the doctrine of post-mortem purgation. He is the first to speak, albeit vaguely and tentatively, about a purgatorial fire (based on 1 Cor. 3: 11–15) which purifies the souls of the *non valde mali* (sinners who are not truly bad) for a certain period of time in anticipation of the Last Judgement. Purgation allows these souls to escape the fate of the *mali*, the truly bad sinners, who are condemned to Hell for all eternity.[41] The *non valde mali* merit purgation because they have performed some good works during their lifetime. Augustine's originality lies in his introduction of the concept of temporality into post-mortem existence—specifically the interim period between death and resurrection.[42] He thus emphasizes an individual eschatology that unfolds sometime before the collective resurrection ensues.[43]

In the writings of Gregory the Great one finds stronger affirmation of the concept of posthumous purgation; he displays a certainty about it which Augustine lacks.[44] Additionally, Gregory assigns an increased role to the supernatural and the dead: miracles and saintly and demonic interven-

[38] McLaughlin, *Consorting with Saints*, 186–8. The place of refreshment is often termed the 'bosom of Abraham'. The liturgy of the Carolingian era retained the notions of sleep and a waiting period between death and resurrection, as did funerary art, in which the dead were sculpted as sleeping happily on top of their tombs, with hands clasped in prayer. See Ariès, 'Une Conception ancienne de l'au-delá'.

[39] Bynum, *The Resurrection of the Body*, 43–6.

[40] On the dramatic shift from a focus on resurrection to the individual fate of the soul after death in Christian thought, see Brown, *The Ransom of the Soul*, esp. 14–16.

[41] See Carozzi, *Le Voyage de l'âme dans l'au-delà*, 20–34; Brown, 'Vers la naissance du purgatoire', 1247–8, and Atwell, 'From Augustine to Gregory the Great', 173–7.

[42] Carozzi, *Le Voyage de l'âme dans l'au-delà*, 32–3.

[43] McLaughlin, *Consorting with Saints*, 189.

[44] Atwell, 'From Augustine to Gregory the Great', 173 and 177.

tions become prominent motifs, as does the appearance of the dead in visions and the potency of relics of the saints.[45] This interpenetration between the world of the living and the world of the dead in Gregory's writings may have had its roots in pre-Christian beliefs.[46] It is his clear and unequivocal articulation of these concepts that proved to be critical for the emergence of the idea of posthumous purgation as a doctrine in mainstream Christian thought. His use of exempla, in Book IV of the *Dialogues*, to illustrate that doctrine later led to the popularization of Purgatory in the high medieval ghost tale.[47]

Individual accountability in the afterlife is vividly described in early medieval visionary literature. Emerging out of palaeo-Christian apocalyptic texts, accounts of voyages to the hereafter began to multiply at this time.[48] The 'Vision of Fursey', which relates the journey of an Irish monk and preacher to the other world, was the first to reflect this development.[49] In the vision, Fursey witnesses, while still alive, the purgatorial fires that burn the souls of the dead. He is informed that the fires burn only to the degree to which the souls still harbour sin. This cleansing of souls takes place long before Judgement Day. The proportionality between the amount of sin and the length of purgation, to ensue immediately after death, is a new notion and serves to replace older ideas, according to which the souls wait until Judgement Day to be cleansed by fire right before that ultimate event.[50] However, in Fursey's vision, the geography of Purgatory is indistinct. The self-same fire encompasses both Hell and Purgatory;

45 Ibid. 185.

46 According to Atwell, Augustine's more rationalistic world-view caused him to downplay the existence of supernatural events, while his fight against paganism precluded his acceptance of the existence of any real contact between the dead and the living. Most Christians, however, with Gregory among them, were influenced by pagan beliefs regarding the living and the dead, which were now entering into Christian thought via a large influx of pagan converts. See ibid. 185–6.

47 Le Goff, *The Birth of Purgatory*, 88–9.

48 Early medieval visionary literature was narrowly tied to hagiography until the twelfth century. Over time, the visionary accounts began to deviate significantly from earlier models of saints' lives and emerged as an independent genre. Losing their 'fairy tale-like quality', these later accounts became more rooted in reality, spoke more about Hell than about Paradise, and switched from Latin to the vernacular. See Braet, 'Les Visions de l'invisible', 399–401, 405–7, 409.

49 The story appears in the 'Life of Fursey', written down in the 650s in northern Francia. See Dunn, 'Gregory the Great, the Vision of Fursey and the Origins of Purgatory', 248–9. Le Goff disagrees with this early dating of the vision and attributes its first full account to Bede in his *Historia ecclesiastica gentis Anglorum* in 731. See Le Goff, 'The Learned and Popular Dimensions of Journeys in the Otherworld', 22.

50 Dunn, 'Gregory the Great, the Vision of Fursey and the Origins of Purgatory', 240, 247–50.

sinners condemned to Hell burn at its core, while purgation for minor sins occurs at the fringes.[51]

Prayer for the dead received new potency in the 'Vision of Drythelm'. Recorded by the English monk Bede in the eighth century, the account tells of Drythelm's voyage to Heaven, Hell, and a Hell-like valley in which souls undergo purifying punishments for having delayed penance until their dying hour. Drythelm is told that prayers, alms, fasting, and the offering of a mass by the living benefit these souls. A somewhat vague correlation between prayer and masses for the dead and the notion of posthumous purgation is here replaced by a concrete connection: the soul can complete its posthumous penance 'ahead of time' and end its purgation with the aid of a specified number of masses or set periods of intercessory prayer.[52]

During the Carolingian period, visionary accounts acquired a political role. The souls of specific figures of high renown were seen by voyagers to the afterlife to be populating the other world. The narratives of the other world, which now often served to legitimize dynastic claims, became less fantastic and more realistic in nature. Individualized tortures were ascribed to various historical personages who were known for having committed certain crimes. These visionary accounts often assumed a hellish cast, as descriptions of the tortures of Hell were favoured over depictions of the delights of Paradise.[53] In some of these politicized visions, it was the power of the saints alone that could release Carolingian rulers from places of expiation and punishment,[54] while in others the efficacy of suffrages (prayers and masses for the dead) was stressed.[55]

Changes in monastic liturgy for the dead during the Carolingian

[51] The idea of a single fire with a dual function was articulated as a doctrine by Caesarius of Arles in the sixth century and by Julian of Toledo in the seventh. See Bernstein, *Hell and Its Rivals*, 206.

[52] Ibid. 252. McLaughlin, while agreeing with this assertion regarding Bede's account, highlights the *Dialogue on the Nature of the Soul* of the early sixth-century grammarian Julian Pomerius (as recorded by Julian of Toledo) as the first text in the Christian West to establish an explicit link between prayer for the dead and posthumous purgation. See *Consorting with Saints*, 192–4. The nature of the purgation which the souls in Drythelm's account undergo, however, remains unclear and imprecise. See Foot, 'Anglo-Saxon "Purgatory"', 90–2.

[53] Braet, 'Les Visions de l'invisible', 408–9. See also Edwards, 'The Idea of Post Mortem Purgation', 125–6, 130.

[54] See e.g. the 'Vision of Charles the Fat' in Edwards, 'The Idea of Post Mortem Purgation', 129, and Le Goff, *The Birth of Purgatory*, 120–1.

[55] See e.g. the 'Vision of Wettin'; the 'Vision of a Certain Poor Woman', which took place sometime between 818 and 840 in the Lodi region of northern Italy; the 'Vision of Bernoldus'; and the 'Vision of Rotcharius' in Edwards, 'The Idea of Post Mortem Purgation', 127, 128, 130, 131.

period, especially the establishment of All Souls' Day by the abbot Odilo of Cluny, led to an increase in the number of tales of the returning dead. These tales, which circulated in and were collected by monastic houses, emphasized the special role of the Cluniac monks in praying for and aiding the dead. The need for intercessors—a holy individual, such as Odilo himself, or a religious community, such as the house of Cluny, whose prayers and offerings of masses would be especially favourable before God—was keenly felt by the laity of this period. A growing fear of judgement, coupled with the need to do complete penance for sin during one's lifetime, led to a system of lay donation to and support of Cluniac institutions. By connecting with these specialists of prayer, people hoped to secure for themselves a release from the punishment and purgation that awaited them after death.[56]

The vast and varied changes in Western Christian society that ushered in the twelfth century brought with them major developments in the arena of the afterlife as well. The crystallization of medieval feudal society into three orders—those who prayed, those who fought, and those who worked[57]—was paralleled by a shift in the understanding of the afterlife. Such a shift made possible the rise of Purgatory at this time as a distinct realm in the hereafter. Purgatory occupied a middle position between Heaven and Hell; it was a corrective of middling-type sins, and was situated midway between earthly time and eternity.[58] Such a tripartite division, in which the souls of the dead pass on to one of three fixed locations, now replaced, or was superimposed on, earlier divisions of souls into two or four categories: the elect and reprobate, on the one hand, and Augustine's *mali, boni, non valde mali*, and *non valde boni* on the other.[59] While purgatorial fire and places of purgation had been described up until now in various texts and narrative accounts, it was only in the second half of the twelfth century

[56] McLaughlin, *Consorting with Saints*, 207–14.

[57] Duby, *The Three Orders*.

[58] Le Goff, *The Birth of Purgatory*, 130–1, 133–5, and 154–76.

[59] According to Le Goff, this shift paralleled the change from the early medieval orders of *oratores*, *bellatores*, and *labores*, based on an agricultural society, to the high medieval orders of the great (both laypeople and clerics), the small (rural and urban workers), and the new, emerging bourgeoisie—products of a commercial society. The earlier medieval orders did not truly represent a tripartite division of society; since they were so grossly unequal, they primarily divided between the two opposing extremes of rich and poor or ecclesiastical and lay. The high medieval orders, on the other hand, were more balanced and hence reflective of a true tripartite division of society. Ibid. 220.

According to one critic of Le Goff, the ternary model never fully replaced the binary one; it was merely superimposed upon it. See Bernstein, Review of *La Naissance du purgatoire*, 181. Edwards, 'Purgatory', 639, disputes the notion that there ever was a bipartite division of souls, and, citing excerpts from the *Enchiridion*, he argues that Augustine speaks of only three categories of soul—the *valde boni*, the *valde mali*, and the *non valde mali*—not four.

that the term Purgatory appeared in the literature of the scholastics and the Cistercians as a substantive noun (*purgatorium*).[60]

The thirteenth century saw the broad dissemination of the doctrine of Purgatory and its message of hope through the agency of exempla, preached by the mendicants in the thousands and recorded in dozens of written collections. A standard form of ghost tale emerged, in which the dead appeared to the living and described their suffering in Purgatory either in order to warn the living to repent or to petition for aid. Oftentimes there was a second appearance, in which the ghost acknowledged the assistance of the living person in mitigating or entirely abrogating his suffering and informed him of his release from Purgatory.[61] While reflecting the profound sense of anxiety among medieval people concerning their fate after death, the pious legacies included in medieval testaments, which prescribed the distribution of money for the benefit of the soul of the deceased, also indicate a firm belief that one could save oneself from the terrors of the afterlife.[62] The notion of an individual afterlife had earned itself a new-found primacy in the high medieval period.

The Individual Afterlife in *Sefer Ḥasidim*

A product of the thirteenth century, *Sefer ḥasidim* bears the influence of the popularization of the doctrine of Purgatory which occurred at that time.

[60] Le Goff, *The Birth of Purgatory*, 229. Some historians have criticized Le Goff for his dogmatic insistence on the correlation between the birth of a complex theological doctrine and the appearance of a single linguistic term in the writings of *literati*. Others wish to soften his approach by speaking of the evolution of the doctrine and its rise to prominence at this time, rather than of its birth. Yet others highlight different aspects of change (such as changes in penance, the concepts of Hell and Paradise, and the belief in the communion of saints, or the increase in plenary indulgences) that arguably played a more seminal role in the rise to prominence of Purgatory at this time than Le Goff's criteria. Historical anthropologists have pointed to Le Goff's over-reliance on theological discussions of the doctrine of Purgatory to the detriment of popular conceptions of the notion. Despite these criticisms, I feel that the general, overall conclusions that Le Goff draws regarding the belief in Purgatory and its relationship to high medieval society are still valid. Furthermore, none of these historians would deny his premise that the notion of Purgatory received new emphasis at this point in time. For reviews of Le Goff's work and of the aforementioned arguments against his thesis, see Bernstein, Review of *La Naissance du purgatoire*, 179–83; Edwards, 'Purgatory: "Birth" or "Evolution"?', 634–46; Brown, 'Vers la naissance du purgatoire'; McGuire, 'Purgatory, the Communion of Saints, and Medieval Change'; Gurevich, 'Popular and Scholarly Medieval Cultural Traditions'; and Davis's review of *The Birth of Purgatory*, 31.

[61] Le Goff, *The Birth of Purgatory*, 177, 294, 298. See also Bowyer, 'The Role of the Ghost-Story in Medieval Christianity', 188–9.

[62] Deregnaucourt, 'Autour de la mort à Douai', i. 34, 36, and 38. I wish to thank John Moryl of the Yeshiva University library for obtaining the microfiche of this dissertation.

The work contains several ghost tales, as well as the vestiges of a visionary account, that depict the punishments and rewards of dead individuals in the afterlife. According to R. Judah the Pious, a prime reason for the return of the dead is to inform the living of their state in the hereafter. In some cases the return is prearranged: two friends make a pact with each other that whoever dies first will inform the other of his or her fate. This topos, which forms the central plot of the above-mentioned story entitled 'The Promise of Two Friends', enjoyed tremendous popularity in the high medieval period.[63] In the early twelfth century the monk Guibert of Nogent noted in his autobiography that his mother had made such a pact with a close friend of hers.[64] The Cistercians made wide use of the tale: Helinand of Froidmont mentions it once in his autobiography,[65] while Caesarius of Heisterbach records the tale four times in his *Dialogue on Miracles*. Each time he tells of a different pair of friends from a different social class (two clerics, two monks, two nuns, and a knight and his daughter) who make the pact with each other.[66] 'The Promise of Two Friends' received standardized form in the hands of the mendicants, who disseminated it widely to the masses; it appeared in numerous exempla collections from the thirteenth century on.[67] In one such exemplum, preserved in a fourteenth-century manuscript, a drunkard and a miser agree that whoever dies first will appear to the other and inform him about his posthumous condition. It is the drunkard who dies first, reports on his suffering, and warns the miser that his fate will be even worse.[68] R. Judah, in his generalized account of the tale, uses a standardized form in which no details are supplied about who the friends are or what their status is in the hereafter.[69]

63 See Schmitt, *Ghosts in the Middle Ages*, 137, and most recently Rider, 'Agreements to Return from the Afterlife', 174–83. See also Tubach, *Index Exemplorum*, no. 3976.

64 See *A Monk's Confession*, 51–3, quoted in Schmitt, *Ghosts in the Middle Ages*, 50.

65 *De cognitione sua*, chs. X–XIII, quoted in Schmitt, *Ghosts in the Middle Ages*, 113.

66 *Dialogus miraculorum*, 1: 33, 12: 31, 12: 41, and 12: 44, quoted in Schmitt, *Ghosts in the Middle Ages*, 137. See also Caesarius of Heisterbach, *Dialogue*, 2: 6, an example which Schmitt does not mention. In most of these cases, the promise made between the pairs is mentioned as an aside within the context of another tale being told. This confirms the impression that the motif was a popular one, and that it was familiar enough to Caesarius's audience so as not to have to be told separately.

67 See e.g. MS BL Add. 11284 fos. 38, 46, and MS BL Harley 2316 fo. 54*b* (*Catalogue of Romances*, iii. 391 no. 295; 393 no. 342; 578 no. 43 respectively). Schmitt, *Ghosts in the Middle Ages*, 193, argues that the motif of the promise of two friends is related to the bonds of kinship which lay at the heart of the confraternities of the time. On the appearance of the motif in late medieval exempla, see Rider, 'Agreements to Return from the Afterlife'.

68 This tale is told by Simon de Henton, a Dominican who flourished around 1360. See MS BL Harley 2316 fo. 58 (*Catalogue of Romances*, iii. 579 no. 62).

69 On the lack of specificity in the stories of *Sefer ḥasidim* in general, see n. 75 below.

The motif of the promise of two friends was known in medieval Ashkenaz beyond the confines of the Pietist work. The twelfth-century French tosafist and pupil of Rabbenu Tam, R. Eliezer of Metz, was clearly aware of it as he discussed the permissibility of such a pact according to the dictates of Jewish law. In his *Sefer yere'im*, R. Eleazar rules that it does not violate the biblical prohibition on 'enquiring of the dead' (Deut. 18: 11), which applies only to enquiries initiated after the other's death. He states that it is permissible to put a living person under oath that he return after death in order to answer any questions the living may ask of him.[70] Not only is this tosafist aware of the trope (which he treats as generally accepted practice), but he endorses belief in it.

Apart from prearranged visits, the dead also appear to the living unexpectedly to inform them about their status in the hereafter. In one passage in *Sefer ḥasidim*, R. Judah explains why they do so: either on their own initiative or on that of the angel appointed to direct them, they return in order to urge their living friend or relative to repent.[71] The report of the deceased describing his punishment frightens the listener into repentance, as he states elsewhere:

If so, why does it say, 'God is good to all' [Ps. 145: 9]? This is the good that He does: If there was to be from every single nation one whom He raises up and returns his soul to his body after death [so that he can appear] to some of the faithful from every nation in order that they make known to their nation how they were judged after death, [then] they would repent from their evil deeds out of fear. And the World to Come is for those who perform His will out of love, not for the sake of reward, and with the understanding that he is not concerned about misfortunes, because he will not cease [to serve God] regardless [of knowledge of] punishments [that are to come after death], and, regarding the wicked, he sees that they have it good [in this world] and, regarding the good [righteous], he sees that they have it bad [in this world], and even so he does not forsake service of the Holy One, blessed be He, with all his heart.[72]

What R. Judah presents here is a medieval version of an age-old answer to the problem of theodicy. God cannot punish the wicked and reward the

[70] *Sefer yere'im*, no. 335. See Horowitz, 'Speaking to the Dead', 312–13, which discusses the opinion of the *Yere'im* in the context of the controversy among medieval rabbinic authorities regarding the permissibility of visiting gravesites in order to pray there.

[71] *SḤ* 329.

[72] *SḤ* 1517. Although there is a segment of this passage that differs in the parallel text recorded in MS JTS Boesky 45, the reading in the Parma manuscript is more logical. Boesky 45: 'Regarding the wicked, he sees that they are suffering, nevertheless he should not depart from serving the Holy One with a full heart.' 'Regarding the wicked, he sees that they are suffering' does not substantiate the 'nevertheless' of the second half of the statement.

righteous in this world, for if he did, people would serve God solely out of fear or for the sake of reward and not out of love. R. Judah utilizes the ghost tale as an example because in his mind, and in that of his audience, it best illustrates this argument. Those who worship out of fear are the faithful, who are filled with the dread of punishment inspired by the reports of the dead. If God were to allow the dead to return so pervasively, his ability to reward his followers with life in the World to Come (post-resurrection) would be inhibited, as such a reward is reserved solely for those who serve God out of love, not because of any fear of punishment.

By entertaining the possibility that God allows the dead in every single nation to return, R. Judah legitimates reports of judgement in the hereafter from rival religions. Even if a religion makes exclusive demands regarding worship and morality that are at odds with the dictates of his own faith, R. Judah does not discredit otherworldly accounts of sin and punishment by members of the rival religion.

Furthermore, the passage substantiates the effectiveness of the ghost tale in compelling adherence among its listeners. It is, in fact, so persuasive that it automatically leads people to repent. This repentance, however, is imperfect—it is motivated by fear of punishment—and prevents the righteous from receiving the reward they deserve in the World to Come. R. Judah's argument about theodicy here emphasizes the potency of the fear of the living regarding their individual fate; the message of the ghost tale serves as the best contemporary example of improperly motivated service of God. Perhaps this is the reason for Eleazar of Worms's statement that the dead do not have permission to return to the living, for 'were he [the dead person] allowed to, he would come in a dream to his loved ones and warn him [them]'.[73] The underlying assumption is that, given the opportunity, any dead person would return and warn his family members of what transpires in the other world so that they can repent before it is too late.

Let us compare this medieval fear of individual suffering in the afterlife with the fear of bodily disgrace and lack of burial operative in rabbinic times. In both cases, people feared an after-death experience to the extent that obvious demonstration of it motivated an immediate and drastic transformation of lifestyle, indicative of repentance; yet their fears differed. Undoubtedly, people living during the rabbinic period were not unconcerned with their fate after death. They could not possibly walk by the

[73] *Sefer ḥokhmat hanefesh*, Safed edn., 14*b*. See there also R. Eleazar's account of the man who lies in a semi-conscious state, 'like one who faints', for three consecutive days and nights, and who sees 'the living and the dead in Gehenna or in Paradise'.

opening to Gehenna at the hot springs of Tiberias and fail to wonder what happens there, just as they could not possibly ignore the many scattered references to Gehenna in rabbinic literature. Even so, in rabbinic times fear of the afterlife was one of several death-related fears, whereas in medieval times it dwarfed all others. Concern about one's state in the hereafter was at the forefront of the medieval mind—Christian and Jewish alike.

Ghost Tales: Punishment in the Hereafter

In *Sefer ḥasidim*, R. Judah the Pious presents several ghost tales meant to frighten the listener into repentance. In doing so, he uses motifs as well as language that parallel those found in the exempla collections. In one such tale, an elderly woman who regularly attends synagogue and performs good deeds dies. She returns in a dream to several people, who ask her about her circumstances in the hereafter. She informs them that she is in great torment and is chased out of the company of the righteous, while they experience a state of joy and contentment. The reason for her predicament, she explains, is that while she was alive she used to leave synagogue early, in the middle of the recitation of the Kedushah prayer, before the rest of the congregation.[74]

It appears that this woman is undergoing torment in Paradise.[75] Although she is in proximity with the righteous, she is not allowed to share their full reward. In another context, R. Judah lists various punishments that can be meted out to a person after death; one of these is that of 'a righteous man who, on account of sin, is not admitted into the quarters of the righteous'.[76] The woman in our story clearly falls into that category. Yet is

[74] *SḤ* 464. A possible motive for her behaviour is supplied in the subsequent tale, in which a woman leaves synagogue early, returns home, and sends her maid to retrieve some keys from her husband as he exits the synagogue. She does so in order to return items held as a collateral, safeguarded in their home, to Christian women who need them for their own church service. See *SḤ* 465.

[75] The anonymity of the woman, and of all other characters in the ghost tales of *Sefer ḥasidim*, stands in marked contrast to the attention to detail regarding names and places apparent in much of the exempla literature. This is due to the Pietists' total lack of interest in time and place, and to their lack of specificity in general. The stories of *Sefer ḥasidim*, in this regard, are more parables than stories. The anonymity and lack of detail also contrasts with the stories of the rabbis in the Midrash. One can reconstruct material life in Palestine to some extent from the Midrash, while attempting to do so for medieval German life from the stories of *Sefer ḥasidim* would be near-impossible.

Eli Yassif offers an alternative explanation, attributing the anonymity of the stories of *Sefer ḥasidim* to the Pietist penchant for humility. In general, as well, Yassif notes that the tales in *Sefer ḥasidim* appear in a very truncated form as compared to their parallels among the exempla. See Yassif, 'The Exemplum Tale in *Sefer ḥasidim*' (Heb.), 222, 227–8.

[76] *SḤ* 35.

her torment limited to being excluded from the joy and contentment of the righteous? Caesarius of Heisterbach believes that 'for some, purgatory is nothing else than the loss of God's presence'.[77] He proves his point with a tale of the monk William, who appears after death to a fellow monk and informs him that he is in pain. The source of his pain, he explains, is being deprived of the sight of God.[78]

Another, more probable, interpretation is that the dead woman receives corporeal punishment in addition to being deprived of the reward of the righteous. Hence the use of the conjunction 'and' in the phrase 'they punish me with great punishments, and while other righteous men and women are in a state of happiness and rest, they chase me out from amongst them'. In one version of *Sefer ḥasidim*, the verb *makin* replaces *danin* ('they beat me with great punishments'), thus substantiating the use of corporeal punishment.[79] Caesarius, once again, is illustrative here. A certain lay brother named Mengoz returns to life for a brief communication with his superior. He describes having been in Paradise and having seen there the sacristan of their monastery, who was 'in great glory, but on his foot appeared a spot, because when he was with us, he went out to work unwillingly'.[80] Punishment in Paradise exists, even of a corporeal nature.

In another tale, a very zealous monk returns from the dead, his countenance all aglow—an indication that he is from Paradise. He says he has been 'quite well' in the hereafter, yet he still suffers 'many very great torments'.[81] This last phrase, much repeated in the exempla literature and often recorded without specifying the nature of the torment,[82] recalls the old woman's words in R. Judah's tale:[83] describing her condition in the afterlife, she says that 'they punish me with great punishments', without ever specifying the exact nature of these torments.

That the dead woman's words refer to a specific corporeal punishment becomes evident on comparison of R. Judah's tale with an exemplum recorded by an anonymous English Franciscan in his work *Liber exemplorum*. A dead widow appears to her sister and informs her of her fate in the hereafter. She is 'horribly burned because on feast days she used to leave church before Communion'.[84] This tale provides a possible clue to the

77 *Dialogue*, 12: 36. 78 Ibid., 12: 37. 79 Bologna print edn., no. 782.

80 Caesarius of Heisterbach, *Dialogue*, 11: 11. 81 Ibid., 12: 29.

82 The phrase is a standard feature of ghost tales and appears several times (sometimes with slight variations, such as 'in great pain' or 'in the bitterest pains') in the *Dialogue on Miracles*. See e.g. 12: 25 and 12: 26. See also Schmitt, *Ghosts in the Middle Ages*, 136.

83 MS Parma H 3280 no. 464 and MS JTS Boesky 45 no. 196.

84 *Liber exemplorum*, 2: 62, quoted in Schmitt, *Ghosts in the Middle Ages*, 134.

torment of the old woman in the Jewish story, as the 'great punishments'—*dinim gedolim*—she mentions may well refer to 'horrible burning'.[85] At the same time, the exemplum also sheds light on why the Kedushah is specified in R. Judah's version: that prayer may be considered as central a point in the Jewish service as Communion is in the Christian one. Indeed, the choice of subject in *Sefer ḥasidim*, as well as the nature of the sin involved, reflect the borrowed character of the story. Although medieval Jewish women were praised at times for their piety in prayer,[86] failure to attend synagogue was not typically included among women's sins. Additionally, the Kedushah does not share an essential characteristic of Christian Communion: the latter is effective for only those participants, male or female, who are present in the sanctuary at the time of its offering. For this reason, one would expect the Christian woman's absence from the mass to be viewed more negatively than the Jewish woman's absence from the Kedushah.[87]

Furthermore, this tale, in which a pious woman commits a lone act of 'sin' and is punished for it in Paradise, can be contrasted with the narrative in the Jerusalem Talmud mentioned earlier. There a pious man, who also commits a sole misdeed when he dons the phylactery of the head before that of the hand, is similarly punished after death—no one attends his funeral procession and burial. Once he has suffered this disgrace, however, the man moves on to the afterlife, where his reward is unadulterated—he strolls among the gardens and fountains of Paradise. The difference between the arenas of posthumous punishment (this world immediately after death in the talmudic tale versus Paradise in the Pietist one) highlights yet again how the focus of medieval people had shifted from fear of bodily disgrace to the individual soul's suffering in the afterlife.

In addition to this shift, comparison of the tales demonstrates the novelty of the concept of punishment in Paradise. While corporeal punishment exists in the Paradise depicted in the exempla literature, this notion is

[85] Burning may not contradict the beating cited earlier as a possible corporeal punishment for this woman, as visionary literature and Pietist manuals of penance speak of demons beating sinners with rods of fire in the afterlife.

[86] Baumgarten, *Practicing Piety in Medieval Ashkenaz*, 49–50.

[87] It seems likely that the Pietist tale was modelled on the story in the *Liber exemplorum*, although R. Judah had no doubt heard it from a different source. The version in the *Liber exemplorum* is much longer and includes a second appearance of the dead widow.

Another exemplum also tells of the sin of leaving church before communion: a man tries to leave the Church of the Holy Trinity in Oxford prior to the Mass of the Virgin, and is prevented by a sharp pain in his heart. Unlike in R. Judah's tale and in the *Liber exemplorum*, the punishment here is meted out in this world, not posthumously. See MS BL Cotton Cleopatra D VIII fo. 116*b* (*Catalogue of Romances*, iii. 641 no. 30).

foreign to traditional Jewish thought. According to rabbinic teaching, Gehenna is reserved for the wicked and serves as the place of punishment for sinners, whereas Paradise awaits the righteous as a place devoted to pleasure.[88] While differences in the degree of reward exist there,[89] the concept of corporeal punishment in Paradise has no known source in rabbinic literature.[90]

The Gravity of Sin in the Afterlife

Apart from punishment in Paradise, another element that R. Judah's tale shares with the exempla literature is the disproportion between sin and punishment.[91] Despite the fact that the elderly woman in the tale above is described as having good deeds to her credit and as regularly coming early to synagogue, she suffers great torments after death. In addition, one could hardly describe her actions as sinful—a woman is not obligated to attend synagogue at all. By contrast, the pious man of the Jerusalem Talmud

[88] On the diametrical opposition of the two domains and their respective occupants, see BT *Eruv.* 19*a*. Sinners, while being tormented in Gehenna, proclaim: 'Master of the Universe, You judged well, You exonerated well, You incriminated well, You prepared well Gehenna for the wicked and Gan Eden for the righteous.' For a similar idea see *Ḥag.* 15*a*. On the punishment of sinners in Gehenna, see *RH* 16*b*–17*a*. In *Shemot rabah* 7, the inability of sinners to gain admission to Paradise is made evident in the following pronouncement of the sages: 'In the future Gan Eden will cry out and say, "Give me the righteous; I have no dealings with the wicked."' In *Vayikra rabah* 27: 1 (ed. Margulies, iii. 616), the Midrash describes the righteous leaving their abode in Paradise and watching the wicked being punished in Gehenna. They are happy and thankful to their Creator for having made them suffer already during their lifetime. On the pleasures of Paradise, see BT *Ta'an.* 31*a*, *Vayikra rabah* 25 and 27 (ed. Margulies, iii. 570 and 613–18), *Shir hashirim rabah* 6, and *Shokher tov al tehilim* 149. See also the later sources of *Yalkut bereshit* 20 and *Yalkut yeshayahu* 429.

R. Eleazar of Worms (*Sefer ḥokhmat hanefesh*, 6*a*) states emphatically that 'In Paradise, there is no pain, only pleasure.' Even emotional pain is absent; although the righteous may freely view the punishment of sinners in Gehenna, if seeing relatives suffer might cause any emotional pain, they will not be shown their suffering. Such a position conflicts with that presented in the aforementioned tale of R. Judah the Pious.

[89] On the varying portions allotted to the righteous in Paradise, see *Sifrei al sefer devarim* 1 (ed. Finkelstein, 18) and *Vayikra rabah* 27 (ed. Margulies, iii. 613–18).

[90] The Talmud does speak of shame felt by the righteous in Paradise. BT *Ta'an.* 25*a* tells the story of the wife of R. Hanina ben Dosa, who was so poor that she prayed to acquire some wealth. She was shown in a dream that the wealth she would obtain now would be subtracted from her reward in the afterlife. The only suffering she would endure in Paradise would be the possible pain of embarrassment over the fact that her reward would be less than that of others—but no punishment, corporeal or otherwise, for any misdeed is mentioned.

[91] According to Pietism, Jews are obligated to observe every one of its myriad injunctions. The smallest infraction labels one as 'wicked' and makes the perpetrator 'subject to the most dire punishment in this world and in the next'. See Soloveitchik, 'Three Themes in *Sefer Ḥasidim*', 326–7.

suffers much less for a misdeed regarding a commandment he is obligated to perform.[92] Examples of individuals of noble character who receive harsh, disproportionate punishments in the hereafter are found in several ghost tales recounted by Caesarius of Heisterbach. In one such case, the abbot of a Cistercian house 'who was quite perfect in the discipline of the Order' appears after death with his legs 'ulcered and black as coals', having suffered torments that 'no tongue could express'.[93] An unwillingness to do manual labour with his monks caused this terrible fate. In another case, a 'quite pious' sacristan at Villers begs his abbot to pray for him to be released from Purgatory, where he suffers on account of having been 'a trifler in words and signs'.[94]

What these two exempla share with the Pietist tale is the unexpected gravity of the punishment meted out in the afterlife to individuals who would otherwise be regarded as pious. This points to a severity in God's justice: he scrutinizes every individual misdeed, however minor, and does not judge humans by the majority of their actions.[95] Moreover, God punishes these particular misdeeds in a fashion that is beyond the expected measure. What differentiates Caesarius's tales from that of R. Judah is the inherent sinfulness of the actions. Manual labour was an essential part of the monastic rule, especially in Cistercian houses (Caesarius was the abbot of one such house), hence the unwillingness of an abbot to perform that task could be viewed as a not insignificant breach of monastic conduct.[96] Similarly, although the rule does not require absolute silence on the part of the brothers, it does forbid idle words and chatter that provoke laughter.[97] The posthumous suffering of the sacristan may thus not be totally undeserved. In contrast to these cases of obvious misbehaviour on the part of monks, the elderly woman of the Pietist story commits no violation of Jewish law. The disproportionate harshness of the punishment she receives in Gehenna is therefore all the more glaring. Additionally, this ghost tale sets the standard for normative Pietist behaviour. In one version, it is preceded by the injunction that 'One should not leave synagogue early, before the conclusion of the prayer service, unless one must attend to one's bodily needs or has to vomit.'[98] Pietist standards were evidently higher than those set by Jewish law. While the monastic rule, too, was stricter than general

[92] The obligation of males to don phylacteries stems from Deut. 6: 8.

[93] Caesarius of Heisterbach, *Dialogue*, 12: 31.

[94] Ibid., 12: 30.

[95] This theme will be developed more fully in Ch. 8 below.

[96] On the role of manual labour in Cistercian houses, see Lekai, *The White Monks*, 147 and 229.

[97] See Butler, *Benedictine Monachism*, 289.

[98] MS JTS Boesky 45 no. 196.

Christian law, the monks did not expect the average Christian to adhere to their *regula*. From this woman's punishment, however, it is evident that the Pietists demanded such heightened obedience from their common folk.

The severity of justice in the afterlife is manifest in another tale in *Sefer ḥasidim*. It tells of a certain city where it is customary for the women on Friday afternoon to concern themselves solely with preparations for the sabbath. One woman, however, occupies herself with spinning on that day. After she dies, she appears in a dream to a man. He sees that her hands and eyes are being burned with husks of flax. It is explained to him that this punishment is due to her having worked with flax on Fridays instead of preparing for the holy day.[99] Here, too, a woman has committed a misdeed which cannot be classified as sinful since no actual violation of the sabbath has occurred. At worst, she has deviated from local custom by failing to properly honour the sabbath before its arrival, and yet she has to undergo great torment.

Like the dead widow in the exemplum above, the woman who spins on Friday receives corporeal punishment by fire. Here, however, it is clear that the principle of measure for measure has governed the choice of her punishment:[100] only those parts of the body that were involved in the 'sin' are being burned. Although the rabbis assume that 'all God's ways are directly proportionate', and Ephraim Urbach calls the rabbinic principle of *midah keneged midah* (measure for measure) 'the prevailing rule' among the sages 'both in personal and in collective retribution',[101] this holds true predominantly for this-worldly punishment. Surprisingly, the principle of retaliation is not, of necessity, part of posthumous punishment in the talmudic literature. Out of the three cases cited above from the Jerusalem Talmud, in which a man has his tongue hanging out but cannot ever drink and a

99 *SḤ* 591. In two manuscripts, MS Vatican ebr. 285 no. 44 and MS JTS 2499 no. 44, there is an additional line to the tale, making it explicit that, due to her improper occupation with flax on that day, she is punished through the medium of flax specifically.

100 Retributive justice as part of God's punishment in general is a major theme of *Sefer ḥasidim*. Under the banner of *midah bemidah lo batlah* (*SḤ* 238, 240, and 242), this principle is operative, R. Judah claims, in all spheres of this-worldly punishment and reward, as well as in biblical narratives. Examples of it permeate the work. R. Judah identifies the ability to discern God's use of retributive justice in the world as a gateway to Pietism itself in the following passage: 'A gateway to Pietism requires that one search in the actions of men . . . one must take it to heart when he sees them sin; he should realize that in the measure in which they committed [the sin], so they punish them. From this [knowledge], one ought to search one's deeds and distance oneself from sin' (*SḤ* 993).

101 BT *San.* 90*a*. See also BT *Shab.* 105*b* and *Ned.* 32*a*, Tosefta *Sot.* 2 and BT *Sot.* 8*b*, and *Midrash bereshit rabah* 9. See Urbach, *The Sages*, 438–9.

woman hangs from her breasts or has her ear attached to the pivot of the doorpost of Gehenna, only the first one is based on the principle of *midah keneged midah*.[102] The direct correspondence between sin and punishment in the afterlife appears regularly only in late midrashic apocalyptic literature, where the dominant type of retributive punishment described in the tours of Hell is hanging by means of the organ involved in sin.[103] This material, however, could not be the influence for the retributive punishment found in *Sefer ḥasidim*, as hanging does not appear in its ghost tales.[104] Additionally, the *heikhalot* literature, a body of late antique mystical texts which suffused the world of the Pietists, contains no evidence of measure-for-measure punishment in its descriptions of Gehenna.[105] Instead, fire, hail, glowing coals, and derivatives thereof (fiery swords, rivers of fire, rods of coal) are the mediums of punishment of the wicked in Gehenna, regardless of the nature of their sins.

If it is not the antecedent Jewish sources that imparted the notion of measure-for-measure punishment in the afterlife to *Sefer ḥasidim*, then what did? The principle of *talio* (retaliation) is a common motif in the exempla literature.[106] Eli Yassif has argued that retributive justice in *Sefer ḥasidim* is used in a way that conforms more closely to its popular use in non-Jewish society, as seen in the exempla tales, than to the legalistic understanding of rabbinic literature. Free of logical abstractions, it has a simplicity that appeals to the masses, and its use in narrative is a 'prime

[102] The man's thirst results from overindulgence in food and drink. The woman is being punished for either arrogance or deception involved in fasting, neither of which is directly related to the type of suffering she is undergoing. See Lieberman, 'On Sins and Their Punishment', 35–6.

[103] Martha Himmelfarb, in her study of early Jewish and Christian tours of Hell, points to the significant role played by measure-for-measure punishments in this literature: see *Tours of Hell*, 82–7.

[104] It is present in a passage in *Sefer ḥokhmat hanefesh*, *7a*, and in the addendum to *She'elot uteshuvot maharam* entitled *Darkhei teshuvah*. See *She'elot uteshuvot maharam*, ed. Bloch, iv. 162. These passages, however, are simply literary ballast of older material rather than an organic part of Pietist penitential doctrine, as the text there sounds midrashic.

[105] The influence of the *heikhalot* literature upon the mystical teachings of the Pietists was first recognized by Gershom Scholem: see his *Major Trends in Jewish Mysticism*, 84–110. For a full bibliography on the subject, see Kanarfogel, *Peering through the Lattices*, 28 n. 25. These punishments appear in the *heikhalot* texts; for the Hebrew original, see Schäfer, *Synopse zur Hekhalot-Literatur*; 3 Enoch MS V228, nos. 49, 62, and M40 nos. 915, 928; *Seder rabah debereshit*, no. 755, cited in Wertheimer (ed.), *Houses of Study* (Heb.), 35. For the texts in English see Davila, *Hekhalot Literature in Translation*, 74, 392, and 403.

[106] Although *lex talionis* originated well before the medieval period, it enjoyed much wider popularity at that time; see Lieberman, 'On Sins and Their Punishment', 36 and n. 56.

characteristic of popular religion'.[107] We have already encountered the sacristan in Paradise on whose leg a spot appeared because of his unwillingness to go to work.[108] Another tale tells of Godfrey, canon of St Andrews, and his posthumous punishment. An avaricious man and former master of the mint, he is seen placed on an anvil and beaten with a mallet until he is 'as thin as a penny'.[109] Similarly, a knight has so taken to drinking that 'he frequented consecrations at various manors only for the good wine'. After he dies, he appears to his daughter as previously agreed, and carries the very same cup he used to drink from when alive. He reports that he must endlessly drink from this cup a loathsome mixture of pitch and brimstone.[110] In yet another tale, a priest neglects to pray for the soul of a pilgrim who had bequeathed a cloak to him, and as a result he is transported to Hell in a dream. There some demons dip the same cloak into 'stinking, boiling lava' and strike his face and neck with it. The priest awakens screaming, 'Help! Help! Behold I die, I burn.' Indeed, upon inspection, his fellow monks find that his head is so badly burned that he is only 'half alive'.[111] In all these tales, the otherworldly punishment conforms to the principle of *talio* and is corporeal in nature. In the last tale, the corporeality of the punishment is unmistakably real. While the priest only witnesses the future fate of his soul in a dream, he awakens to find that his body is burned now, in this world.

The paradoxical nature of the corporeal punishment of the souls of the dead is particularly evident in the case of William, count of Julich. Murderer, enemy of the Church, lustful, and incestuous, William is a knight so wholly corrupt that his posthumous punishment is for his entire body to burn in flames of sulphur. When he appears in a vision to a certain canon of Aix, who enquires about his state in the hereafter, William replies, 'I am all on fire.' After this, as he 'lifted up the miserable dress in which he seemed to be clad, at once flames burst out, and so with a shriek he vanished'.[112] Under his garment, the 'body' of William's soul burns in Hell. In the same vein, the woman who weaves on Friday in the Pietist tale has the 'eyes' and 'hands' of her soul burn in the afterlife.

This tale from *Sefer ḥasidim* does not merely contain parallel elements with other, similar, narratives in the exempla literature; it is most likely also a borrowed tale. Like the story of the woman who leaves the synagogue

[107] In fact, Yassif states that its wide use throughout the work is 'overwhelming proof of the centrality of popular religion in *Sefer ḥasidim*'; see 'The Exemplum Tale in *Sefer ḥasidim*' (Heb.), 234 and n. 37. [108] Caesarius of Heisterbach, *Dialogue*, 11: 11. [109] Ibid., 11: 44.

[110] Ibid., 12: 41. See also the previous tale (12: 40), which specifies the punishment that awaits drunkards in Hell; the devil himself makes them drink 'a sulphurous draught from a fiery cup'. [111] Ibid., 12: 42. [112] Ibid., 12: 5.

service early, it shares a distinct motif with a widely circulated tale of the time, found among collections of miracles of the Virgin Mary.[113] In that story, the Virgin punishes a woman who works on her holy day, Saturday.[114] The association of the Virgin Mary's holy day with Saturday, in turn, reveals the borrowed nature of the Christian tale. In ancient Germanic belief, a deity named Holda or Holle, originally a goddess of the wild host and water springs, assumed the role of a spinning-wife, under whose dominion the cultivation of flax lay. In her position as 'superintenden[t]', in control of 'strict order in the household', Holle rewarded industrious housewives with bountiful spindles full of thread, while she punished lazy ones by burning their distaff. Out of reverence, popular Germanic tradition assigned to her some holy days of her own, including Saturday, and on these days no spinning or farm work could be done. Upon the Christianization of Germanic society, Mary, especially in her role as Mother of Heaven, assumed the qualities as well as the role of Holle.[115] In the Marian tale, all the elements associated with Holle—supernatural woman, matron of spinning, who burns the distaff of slothful spinners and is vengeful towards those who violate her holy day, Saturday—combine to form the tale of punishment associated with the Virgin.[116]

Not only was the pagan tale appropriated by Christian tradition, it was further appropriated by R. Judah for his readers and enriched with a basic

[113] Originating in Jerusalem and its immediate environs and circulating in Syria and Egypt at the end of the fourth century, stories and legends of the life and miracles of the Virgin Mary were copied and collected in the monasteries of Europe. By the end of the eleventh century, and increasingly throughout the next three centuries, wherever a church was built in her honour or was dedicated to her, a copy of the book of her miracles was kept. Local miracles which took place at her shrines were also added to the collection. These stories enjoyed enormous popularity, and were told and retold so often that they too, like the exempla of the same period, took on a standardized form, often losing particulars of time and place and 'follow[ing] the same pattern of vengeance, protection, and cures'. By the end of the period, the stories of the Virgin's miracles outnumbered those of all other saints. See Ward, *Miracles and the Medieval Mind*, 132–5, 145.

[114] Entitled 'Compline' or 'Saturday', this tale appears in collections devoted to miracles of the Virgin which took place at her shrines in Laon, Soissons, and Rocamadour. The books were read on the Virgin's feast days and on Saturdays. See Ward, *Miracles and the Medieval Mind*, 157.

[115] See Grimm, *Teutonic Mythology*, i. 266–70. Grimm adds that the main occupation of German housewives was spinning: the Anglo-Saxon word for housewife, *fridowebban*, means 'peace-weaver'. On the influence of Holle on Ashkenazi family ritual, see Baumgarten, *Mothers and Children*, 92–9.

[116] The violation of Christian holy days was a sin quite commonly listed in medieval penitentials and one that could carry a severe penalty: one twelfth-century manual warns that whoever violates the Sabbath (Sunday) 'will burn in Hell'. See Baschet, *Les Justices de l'au-delà*, 105 and n. 79.

Pietist notion: whereas in the original the woman sinned by violating the sanctity of the holy day itself, the protagonist of the Pietist tale violated only a custom relating to the day of preparation for the holy day.[117] This degree of accountability is typical of the Pietist work, which demands supererogatory behaviour in all spheres of religious activity and ethics.[118]

Another ghost tale recorded in *Sefer ḥasidim* speaks of the punishment of the righteous. A righteous dead man appears to a certain anonymous individual. His green and pallid face reflects the painful state he is in.[119] When questioned as to his looks, he explains that, when he was alive, some forbidden fat (tallow) used to get trapped underneath his long nails and he would eat hot food without cleaning them.[120] He continues, and states that he is also being punished because he used to speak in synagogue between the congregation's recital of 'Vayekhulu' and 'Magen avot' during the Friday night service, as well as in the middle of Kaddish.[121] While some trace of sin is present in the first action,[122] it does not belong in the category of outright sinfulness. The second action is considered sinful by Pietist standards alone,[123] yet the righteous individual suffers for it in the afterlife. This tale reinforces the message of the two earlier Pietist tales—God's judgement in the hereafter is harsh and exacting. Whereas the strictness of God's judgement of the righteous in this world is commonplace in traditional Jewish thought,[124] that he punishes them harshly in the afterlife reflects a unique way of thinking on the part of R. Judah the Pious.

117 In the Christian manual of penance, too, the violator worked on the day of rest itself. See the preceding note.

118 Soloveitchik, 'Three Themes in *Sefer Ḥasidim*', 313–20, esp. 319–20.

119 The words *ufanav yerukot* would seem to suggest that his face is pale and sickly, as the similar expression *paneiha morikot* (mentioned in *Sot.* 3: 4) refers to the sickly appearance of the adulterous woman after she has drunk the water by means of which she is to be judged. Similarly, Queen Esther's pallid complexion is referred to as *yerakroket* in BT *Meg.* 13*a*. In the *heikhalot* literature *keyerakot* is the description given of the pallid faces of the middling group of sinners, who suffer purgation in the fires of Gehenna. See Schäfer, *Synopse zur Hekhalot-Literatur*, 291 (Enoch 3 MS M40, no. 928 and its parallel MS V228, no. 62).

120 This ghost tale is placed among passages which discuss eating in purity and avoiding the consumption of forbidden fat. See *SḤ* 1068–71 and 1074–6.

121 *SḤ* 1073.

122 In *SḤ* 1071, R. Judah warns that a hasid should always trim his fingernails so that fat does not get trapped under them.

123 The *Tur*, the earliest halakhic source to document this prohibition, cites this very ghost tale from *Sefer ḥasidim* in its laws of the Friday night prayer service. The *Shulḥan arukh* codifies the prohibition on speaking during the congregation's recital of 'Vayekhulu' and 'Magen avot' and in the middle of Kaddish on the basis of the ghost tale recorded in the *Tur*. See *Tur*, 'Oraḥ ḥayim', 268: 12, and *Shulḥan arukh*, 'Oraḥ ḥayim', 268: 12.

124 'The Holy One, blessed be He, is exacting with the righteous even in matters as small as the thread of a hair' (BT *BK* 50*a* and *Yev.* 121*b*).

The 'sin' of speaking during the prayer service is also the subject of a ghost tale we have seen earlier; it is recorded in Caesarius's *Dialogus Miraculorum* and repeated in the exempla collection entitled *Alphabetum Narrationum*. In this tale, a young nun, a child of about 9, appears to her cousin, a nun of the same order, after dying. She explains that she must do penance now for having 'whisper[ed] with you in choir at will, uttering half-words', and warns her cousin to do penance now lest she suffer the same fate when she dies.[125]

Apart from the ghost tales in which the dead share with the living their otherworldly experiences, *Sefer ḥasidim* contains one visionary account of a woman who returns from the other world and reports her findings. In this story, whose Christian origin R. Judah acknowledges outright, a certain non-Jewish noblewoman is thought to have died, but at her funeral she recovers consciousness and tells of her otherworldly visit. First, she witnessed the punishment of the damned in Hell, where she saw bishops, some of whom were not yet dead.[126] Then she was privy to a view of Paradise. She saw Jews there, one of whom she recognized. Noticing something unusual about her—the woman's glove was soiled with tallow—she asked: 'Why are you different from your companions?' The woman responded, 'Once I lit a lamp[127] for the sabbath,[128] and my glove was soiled with tallow; that is why I suffer this embarrassment.'[129]

This tale, as I have mentioned, has a manifest Christian provenance; Elisheva Baumgarten has identified the protagonist as Christina Mirabilis. R. Judah adds to the existing story the anecdote regarding the Jewess in

[125] Caesarius of Heisterbach, *Dialogue*, 12: 36, and Banks (ed.), *Alphabet of Tales*, 249–50 no. 363. Punishment for speaking in church is first mentioned in the third-century *Apocalypse of Paul*. In this early Christian tour of Hell, people who are guilty of that sin are seen submerged up to their knees in a stream of sulphur and pitch. See *Visio Sancti Pauli*, sec. 31, cited in Lieberman, 'On Sins and Their Punishment', 41 and n. 73. Similarly, in the appendix to the responsa of R. Meir of Rothenburg, the scribe, copying from an unknown *midrash* (with ties to the *Apocalypse of Paul*), describes hot coals of juniper being fed to those who talked during the prayer service in the synagogue. See Lieberman, 'On Sins and Their Punishment', 39 and n. 68.

[126] In the 'Vision of Bernoldus', recorded by Archbishop Hincmar of Reims sometime between 877 and 882, Bernoldus, on his visit to the other world, witnesses the torment of forty-one bishops.

[127] See Baumgarten, 'A Tale of a Christian Matron', 86 n. 15.

[128] While the Parma manuscript and several parallels describe her act as lighting *beshabat*, 'on the sabbath', one manuscript, MS Bodl. Opp. Add. 34 no. 105, which is a parallel to *Sefer ḥasidim* Parma no. 619, has *leshabat*, 'for the sabbath'. See Baumgarten, 'A Tale of a Christian Matron', 86 n. 16. Although outnumbered, this manuscript reading is more logical given the nature of the other types of 'sin' that R. Judah records in his ghost tales. Lighting on the sabbath would be a clear desecration of the day, whereas lighting with tallow for the sabbath would not (see fuller discussion below in text).

[129] *SḤ* 272 and 619.

Paradise who is punished for lighting sabbath lights with tallow. Given that Christina was a well-known woman in her time, by appropriating her story R. Judah added authenticity and credibility to his own.

The story confirms the lesson conveyed by several of the previously cited ghost tales in *Sefer ḥasidim*—there is punishment in Paradise. As in the case of the woman who spun on Friday, this woman's posthumous punishment is also based on the principle of *talio*; she must suffer indignity by means of the object that she used to dishonour the sabbath. Corporeality is evident here as her hands are the object of torment and tallow is the agent of torment in an abode reserved exclusively for souls. There is further similarity in the nature of the transgression: the action for which the deceased must suffer could not be labelled as an obvious sin, at least not by medieval standards. Although the rabbis disallow the use of tallow for the purpose of sabbath lights, circumstances peculiar to the times led medieval Jews to use lamps made of or containing that substance, with the full knowledge of the legal experts.[130] Since lighting sabbath lamps made of tallow was common practice at the time, it is only in light of the stricter observance and higher standard of piety demanded by R. Judah that this woman's act becomes a sin.

The exacting nature of judgement in the afterlife is highlighted yet again as a single misdeed results in prolonged shame.[131] Moreover, the punishment is disproportionate to the sin not only in duration, but also in intensity. In medieval times, when lepers were known to wear tallow gloves, the indignity this woman suffered would have been magnified.[132] The leper's physical deformity was believed to reflect a serious spiritual malaise.[133] By associating the Jewish woman's posthumous punishment

130 See Baumgarten's discussion in 'A Tale of a Christian Matron', 87–9.

131 A similar disproportion between sin and punishment is found in another ghost tale in *Sefer ḥasidim*. R. Judah tells how once the body of a righteous individual was extracted from the grave, stripped of garments, and assaulted. Afterwards, the dead man appeared to someone in a dream and explained the reason for this harsh treatment of his corpse: while alive, he saw Jewish holy books that were torn in places and did not properly secure their pages by tying them upon tablets (see *SḤ* 647). Whereas the punishment is enacted upon the man's body here on Earth rather than in the hereafter, the principle remains the same—a righteous dead man suffers great indignity and pain for a seemingly minor transgression.

132 Baumgarten, 'A Tale of a Christian Matron', 91, and *SḤ* 566 and 567.

133 Richards, *The Medieval Leper and His Northern Heirs*, 5–6. Even though R. Judah cautioned Jews not to spit upon lepers (*SḤ* 99), this does not mean he did not share the belief that was common at the time, or that he would refrain from making use of a belief that his audience would have related to. On the attitude towards lepers within the medieval Jewish community, see Shoham-Steiner, 'An Ultimate Pariah?'. For a broader treatment, see id., *On the Margins of a Minority*.

with the condition of a leper, R. Judah would be sending a powerful message to his co-religionists, all of whom either lit or allowed their wives to light in this manner: 'The true nature of your spiritual condition—interpreted as a "severe spiritual smear"[134]—will be evident to everyone in Paradise.'

Until now, we have seen ample evidence that the Pietist ghost tales involving individual punishment in the afterlife have a high rate of literary borrowing. Specific terms, motifs, literary elements, and even entire narratives were lifted from circulating exempla and miracle tales and adopted by R. Judah the Pious. In the case of the sole visionary account in the work, R. Judah openly admits its Christian provenance. Nor is his borrowing limited to words and sources; as we have seen regarding the notion of punishment in Paradise, it extends to the conceptual arena as well. Turning now to the motifs of demonic agents and corporeal punishments inflicted on souls in the afterlife, we find once again that *Sefer ḥasidim* reflects notions circulating in the contemporary Christian environment.

Demonic Agents

The presence of demons as executors of Divine punishment in the afterlife is suggested in two of R. Judah's tales. In the story involving the woman who spun on Friday, the man who witnesses it sees that 'they burn her hands and eyes with husks of flax'. He then converses with the anonymous 'they', the agents of her punishment. He asks them why they are doing this to her and they respond that it is because she was spinning flax instead of busying herself with the needs of the sabbath. The anonymous 'they' is also mentioned in another previously cited Pietist tale—that of the woman who left synagogue early: 'They punish me with great punishments', she laments. Although unnamed, these appear to be some type of angels of torment.

According to traditional Jewish sources, the role assigned to angels of torment is limited. The Talmud speaks of two angels who fling the souls of the wicked back and forth in a slingshot. That punishment is meted out to the worst category of sinners (*resha'im* as opposed to *tsadikim* and *beinonim*), whose torment is eternal.[135] As far as the punishment of the middling group of souls is concerned, the Talmud mentions a single angel named Dumah who is appointed over them. In one midrashic source, Dumah serves as the caretaker of souls in Gehenna, announcing the commence-

[134] Baumgarten, 'A Tale of a Christian Matron', 91.

[135] BT *Shab.* 152*b*.

ment and cessation of their weekly respite from suffering on the sabbath.[136] In another, Dumah conveys the souls to the *ḥatser mavet etsel haruḥot* (the courtyard of death adjacent to the spirits).[137] In neither forum is the angel described as carrying out any act of torment. While the Talmud, in one place, does speak of torment, it assigns the angels the sole function of pronouncing curses aloud to the wicked upon their death, never any type of corporeal torture.[138] Overall, the emphasis in rabbinic sources is on God's dominance over and containment of the actions of the angels of torment.[139]

Early Jewish extra-rabbinic sources speak of the presence of angels of torment, albeit descriptions of their duties are flat and unimaginative. Absent from the Bible, they appear for the first time in Judaeo-Christian apocalyptic works, probably as a result of Greek influence.[140] 1 Enoch mentions the punishment of the wicked by angels of torment, but that punishment is due to occur only after the resurrection of the dead.[141] Another source speaks of heavenly angels made of fire, such as the *keruvim*, *ofanim*, and *ḥayot hakodesh*—not *malakhei ḥabalah* (angels of destruction)—burning the wicked in Gehenna.[142] Part of the *heikhalot* literature, 3 Enoch describes a tour of Hell in which two different groups of angels of torment officiate over two different groups of sinners—the middling group and the completely wicked.[143] At the head of the former group a supporting and encouraging angel named Simki'el is placed; he is an agent of mercy whose task is to purify the soul. Over the latter group, the angel Za'afi'el presides. Although his name means 'wrath of God', the torment perpetrated by Za'afi'el is limited to the following: 'to cast them [the spirits of the wicked] down from the presence of the Holy One, blessed be He, and from the splendour of the Shekhinah to She'ol, to be punished in the fire of Gehenna with staves of burning coal'. The faces of the middling group are 'green-like', while those of the wicked are as black as a 'pot bottom'—a description found in the Talmud itself.[144] No further, more explicit, tortures enacted by any group of subordinate angels are mentioned. In fact, the most frightening visionary description in the work is not of demons but of God himself, who, at the time of the Final Judgement, shoots forth at every moment fire

136 *Pesikta rabati* 23. 137 *Midrash tehilim* 11: 6 (ed. Buber, p. 52). 138 BT *Ket.* 104*a*.
139 Urbach, *The Sages*, 162. 140 See Himmelfarb, *Tours of Hell*, 121.
141 See Hirsch, *Psychology in Our Ancient Literature* (Heb.), 78–9.
142 *Pirkei heikhalot rabati* 8: 2.
143 Odeberg (ed.), *3 Enoch*, 136–7, and Schäfer, *Synopse zur Hekhalot-Literatur*, V228 no. 62; M40 no. 928. In English, see Davila, *Hekhalot Literature in Translation*, 403.
144 *RH* 17*a*. On the cooking pot of talmudic times and its blackness, see Weingarten, 'The *Quederah*'.

and flame, and brandishes a sword of supernatural size that spews sparks of limitless number with which to punish the wicked.[145]

The medieval Jewish tours of Hell, by contrast, reflect the more detailed accounts prevalent in early medieval visionary literature. The tenth-century composition of Muslim provenance, *Ḥibur yafeh min ha-yeshuah*, records two Jewish tours of Hell. In both cases, the angel of death guides R. Joshua b. Levi on his tour of Paradise and Hell.[146] In the high medieval Ashkenazi version of the tale, which we saw above,[147] the description of Gehenna and its tortures is greatly elaborated upon, more so than in the Muslim version with its focus on Paradise, and angels of destruction figure prominently.[148] While in Hell, R. Joshua witnesses several different angels beating the dead with rods of fire, then tossing them into the flames. The sinners, however, resume their original form, as if they had never been burned, and they are subjected to repeated beatings and burnings 'seven times a day, three times a night' every day.[149] The early twelfth-century version of the tale speaks of the angel Kushi'el, who occupies the 'second abode' of Gehenna. Striking with a flaming lash, he hurls sinners into the fire, where they are reduced to ashes. The tale, which was widely circulated in the medieval period and had specifically medieval motifs pertaining to the afterlife grafted onto its story line, has been referred to by scholars as 'Joshua's Vision of Heaven and Hell'.[150]

A vivid account of the tortures of Gehenna is also present in the *Seder rabah debereshit*. This text delineates seven levels of Gehenna, each successively lower than the previous one. The lowest one, named Arka, is where the souls of the worst category of sinners suffer for all eternity, never to ascend. Angels of destruction are appointed to oversee the punishment of these souls. At each level, 40,000 such angels bathe the souls of the wicked in alternating rivers of fire, hail, and snow repeatedly, as the souls are resuscitated and incinerated in an endless cycle of suffering.[151] This text also highlights the fact that the angels direct their punishments at the organ

[145] See Schäfer, *Synopse zur Hekhalot-Literatur*, V228 no. 49; M40 no. 915.

[146] See *Sefer ma'asiyot*, no. 761, pp. 500–1.

[147] See n. 20 above.

[148] MS Parma 2295 (de Rossi 563), cited in Kushelevsky, *Penalty and Temptation* (Heb.), 26–8.

[149] Kushelevsky, *Penalty and Temptation* (Heb.), 27.

[150] Micha Perry, 'Jewish Heaven and Christian Hell', 5.

[151] See Wertheimer (ed.), *Houses of Study* (Heb.), i. 32–8. Mention is made of Arka and the angels of destruction in the *heikhalot* literature; see Schäfer, *Synopse zur Hekhalot Lieratur*, O1531 nos. 447, 754, and 756. On the *heikhalot* literature, see n. 105 above. Nahmanides, in his *Sefer sha'ar hagemul*, cites this text from a *midrash* called *Orko shel olam*. See Nahmanides, *Torat ha'adam*, 284.

which was involved in the sin.[152] According to scholars, the principle of *talio* here is an addition to the original text of the *Seder rabah debereshit*,[153] and is a prominent feature of sources that emanate from Pietist circles.[154]

Similarly, while not a visionary account per se, the *Perek gehinom*, which appears in medieval Jewish texts and is possibly a creation of medieval Ashkenaz,[155] contains all the elements of Hell and the hyperbolical description evident in early medieval visionary literature. Rivers of fire, pitch, and boiling sulphur and alternating torments of heat and cold are pictured in a landscape of fantastic dimensions. Here the angels of destruction number in the thousands, with nine of them pushing each wicked person into a gaping Hell-mouth.[156]

Early medieval Christian accounts of the other world are replete with descriptions of demons inflicting all types of corporeal torture upon sinful souls. In the 'Vision of Fursey', recounted by Bede the Venerable, demons stoke a huge fire. Into this fire the souls of the damned and those who require purgation are thrown. The former burn there forever; the latter burn only until the evil desires which provoked their sins are extinguished. Additionally, the fire 'tests each person according to his deserts', so that 'that which you did not kindle will not burn you'.[157] The fire purges only those parts of the body guilty of sin, and, as in the Pietist tale, the purgation is specific to the nature of the sin committed. Fursey is confronted with the physical reality of the fire when he is struck by a burning soul flung at him by a demon. His jaw remains forever burned afterwards.[158] In four of the six extant Carolingian visions, demons figure as executors of otherworldly punishment.[159]

[152] Wertheimer (ed.), *Houses of Study* (Heb.), i. 38.

[153] See Geulah, 'Lost Aggadic *Midrashim*' (Heb.), 94 n. 52.

[154] It is present in a story in *Darkhei teshuvah* (see Rotman, 'The Marvelous in the Medieval Hebrew Narrative' (Heb.), 371) and in *Perush haroke'aḥ al hatorah*, where the author ascribes the idea—'with whichever organ he sins he is punished'—to *Midrash asufah*. While there the punishment is administered to a sinner during his lifetime, nevertheless the application of the principle to otherworldly, posthumous punishment is not to be discounted. See Geulah, 'Lost Aggadic *Midrashim*' (Heb.), 94.

[155] Kushelevsky, *Penalty and Temptation* (Heb.), 33, 37.

[156] Ibid. 33–4. See also 'Masekhet gehinom', 147–9. For a quick overview of the various elements of Hell in early medieval visionary literature, see the summaries in E. Gardner's *Visions of Heaven and Hell*. On the motif of Hell-mouth in medieval art and literature, see Schmidt, *The Iconography of the Mouth of Hell*. An extensive psychoanalysis of Hell-mouth is put forth by Baschet, *Les Justices de l'au-delà*, 506–14.

[157] Bede, *Historia ecclesiastica*, 3: 19, quoted in Edwards, 'The Idea of Post Mortem Purgation', 123.

[158] Ibid.

[159] The first is the vision of an anonymous woman from northern Italy in the first half of the ninth century. The others (all from the second half of the ninth century) include the 'Vision of

This phenomenon becomes more specific and elaborate in the high medieval period.[160] In two mid-twelfth-century visions, demons are the agents of purgation rather than of damnation only.[161] The blurring of distinctions between Hell and Purgatory is evident here as they occupy both domains. In one mid-twelfth-century narrative, the 'Vision of Tundale', the corporeal nature of the torments is described in vivid detail as 'demons skin and chop up the souls with sharp instruments', while 'demon smiths', as they are referred to, 'melt down, hammer, and toss [souls] from anvil to anvil'.[162] This highly popular vision circulated in the vernacular in southern Germany in the late twelfth century.[163] Composed at the same time, the legend of St Patrick's Purgatory tells of multifarious types of corporeal torture—one of which involves passing burning nails through various organs—inflicted by demons upon souls in Purgatory according to the nature of the sin committed.[164] The image of demons purging the dead of their sins in this way reflects the influence of popular notions, as the more scholarly works on the afterlife denied demons entry into Purgatory.[165]

These visionary accounts were accessible to high medieval readers through a variety of popular sources. Firstly, the corporeal tortures perpetrated by demonic agents figure prominently in the descriptions of Hell found in the twelfth-century *Elucidarium*. Written by Honorius of Autun as a manual for the lower clergy with the express purpose of teaching theology to the masses in a digestible fashion, the *Elucidarium* enjoyed enormous popularity in the Middle Ages. In the third book of his work, Honorius details how 'terrifying and grimacing demons' snatch the souls of the damned at the time of death and subject them to nine different types of torment. Despite the fact that these souls in Hell have separated from their bodies, the tortures of Honorius's Hell include burning of the sinners' limbs, exposure to unbearable cold, and beatings with whips 'which demons

Charles the Fat', the 'Vision of Bernoldus', and the 'Vision of Rotcharius'. See Edwards, 'The Idea of Post Mortem Purgation', 128–31.

160 For a full discussion of the high degree of corporeality and the complex and intricate nature of the tortures evident in the visionary literature of the twelfth and thirteenth centuries, see Baschet, *Les Justices de l'au-delà*, 99–134.

161 One is a vision told by a monk of Liège. See 'Visio status animarum post mortem', 4, quoted in Edwards, 'The Idea of Post Mortem Purgation', 139. The other is the 'Vision of Tundale' ('Visio Tnugdali').

162 'Visio Tnugdali', 19–32, quoted in Edwards, 'The Idea of Post Mortem Purgation', 230.

163 For a fuller discussion of this vision and its relationship to the southern German city of Regensburg, see p. 247 below.

164 See Le Goff, *The Birth of Purgatory*, 195.

165 The works of the scholastics such as Albertus Magnus and St Thomas Aquinas are examples of these. See Le Goff, *The Birth of Purgatory*, 262 and 273.

handle as blacksmiths use hammers'.[166] Perhaps it is not insignificant that at the end of his life, Honorius settled in the Irish monastery at Regensburg, which was located in very close proximity to the Jewish area. Less than a century later, R. Judah the Pious would reside in that city.[167]

Apart from the *Elucidarium*, the theme also appears in the exempla literature, especially in the tales of Jacques de Vitry. In several stories, the souls of usurers who failed to make restitution for their ill-gotten gains before they died are commended to demons, who carry them off to Hell.[168] In one of these tales, the specific torment that awaits usurers is exposed for all to see: upon opening his grave, the usurer's family members see demons filling his mouth with red hot coins.[169] The otherworldly punishment is doubled as the corpse in the grave suffers the self-same torment as the soul does in Hell.

Finally, medieval monumental art of the twelfth and thirteenth centuries confirms the popularity of the idea of otherworldly torture in the hands of demonic agents. In scenes sculpted on church tympanums depicting the Last Judgement, an artistic rendering of Christ seated as Judge overseeing the separation of the elect and the damned at the End of Time,[170] demons take possession of the damned and carry them off to Hell.[171] The representation of Hell on the mid-twelfth-century tympanum of the cathedral of St Foi at Conques is most explicit in this regard; close to sixty figures are depicted being tortured corporeally in a variety of ways. Demons armed with clubs or forks beat, pull, and push the damned, hang them upside down, and roast them on a spit.[172] Nourished by popular imagina-

166 Gurevich, *Medieval Popular Culture*, 159–60.

167 See below, pp. 247-8 and 260-2, regarding the connection between R. Judah and the Irish monastery in Regensburg.

168 See Jacques de Vitry, *Exempla*, nos. 106, 168, 170.

169 Ibid., no. 168. This tale also reflects the principle of retributive justice in otherworldly punishment, as the usurer, who lusts after money, asks to be buried with a bag of coins hung around his neck. It is these very coins, made fiery hot in hell, which the demons feed into his mouth.

170 Baschet distinguishes between earlier artistic renderings of Christ, known as the theophany, in which a triumphant Judge is depicted as returning at the End of Time and whose theme is Divine glory and exultation, and that of the Last Judgement scene, a later image which highlights the separation of the elect and the damned at the End of Time, emphasizing justice and recompense. See Baschet, *Les Justices de l'au-delà*, 139.

171 Such depictions appear on the portal of the Gothic church at St Denis (1133–40), on the tympanum of Autun (*c.*1130), as well as on the portal of Chartres Cathedral (1220–35). See Mâle, *Religious Art in France*, 181 and 419, and Katzenellenbogen, *The Sculptural Programs of Chartres Cathedral*, 87. For a more recent study of Last Judgement iconography, see Baschet, *Les Justices de l'au-delà*, 135–73.

172 See Denny, 'The Date of the Conques Last Judgment', 8.

tion, demonic, otherworldly torture became a widespread motif, reappearing in different forms on churches in the thirteenth century.[173] At Bourges, for example, demons poke and prod their victims with various tools and boil them in a huge cauldron over an open fire.[174]

While all these monumental representations depict the collective fate of the damned condemned to Hell at the End of Time, people also perceived in them the individual judgement of souls sentenced to either Purgatory or Hell. This phenomenon occurred because the two stages of collective judgement of all of humanity at the End of Time and the judgement of individuals immediately after death became conflated in their minds.[175] Aron Gurevich has argued that medieval people 'read this "Bible of Stone" in a synchronous rather than diachronous arrangement of time', and that 'angst of the anticipated repayment [final judgement and reward or punishment] transposed the future into the present'.[176] Along the same lines, Anca Bratu has proposed that the Last Judgement is not to be understood as '"an act" at the End of Time' but rather as 'a judgment "to come"', so that it incorporated within it all future judgements in both the near and the distant future. Furthermore, the depiction of Christ sitting in judgement, as it appears in monumental church art, rendered the image forever in the *present* in the mind of the spectator, which served to conflate the different time periods of Christ's judgement into one unified whole.[177]

173 Mâle, *The Gothic Image*, 378. Mâle, commenting on the variety of corporeal tortures enacted by demons in Hell, writes that 'hardly a trace of dogmatic teaching is here to be found . . . all were the outcome of popular fancy'. Similarly he writes regarding the torments of the damned that 'the artists did not accept the doctrine of Aquinas and of the greater number of theologians, where the torments of hell are taken in a symbolic sense . . . The artist remained faithful to the letter' (p. 381). Barbara Palmer, in her study of the iconography of demons in medieval English art, echoes this notion; see 'The Inhabitants of Hell: Devils', 24. See also Gurevich, 'Die Darstellung von Persönlichkeit und Zeit', 31. I would like to thank H. Regensteiner for his translation of this essay. See also Gurevich, *Medieval Popular Culture*, 161, and Baschet, *Les Justices de l'au-delà*, 522–6.

174 Mâle, *The Gothic Image*, 381. B. Palmer points out that the tools used by the demons to push the damned into Hell or to torment them were not weapons of war or torture but ordinary domestic tools. This reinforces the popular dimension of the notion. See 'The Inhabitants of Hell: Devils', 25. In the twelfth-century Vision of Tundale, J. Baschet notes that nearly half of the methods of torture described employ tools of human industry. See Baschet, *Les Justices de l'au-delà*, 112.

175 This conflation of time periods was extended to include two additional permutations—a collective judgement immediately after death and an individual one at the End of Time. The former is discussed in the thirteenth-century 'Vision of Thurkill', while the latter is depicted on a Florentine fresco from around the year 1335. These and isolated others are exceptions to the rule. See Baschet, *Corps et âmes*, 208–18.

176 Gurevich, 'Die Darstellung von Persönlichkeit und Zeit', 43, 37.

177 Bratu, 'Fin des temps', 70–1, and Brown, 'The Decline of the Empire of God', 45.

Thus, while contemplating the Last Judgement scenes sculpted on church tympanums, people often perceived the terrors of the Final Day as awaiting them personally, immediately after their death.[178] The corporeal horrors of Hell imposed upon bodies after resurrection became the pain of souls undergoing posthumous torment in Hell and Purgatory.[179] This visual image, which was a direct outgrowth of written texts and oral stories, reinforced the corporeal nature of the punishments recorded in visionary literature, in contemporary popular manuals such as the *Elucidarium*, and in circulating ghost tales.[180] It is perhaps such visual representations that R. Judah had in mind when, in delineating various types of posthumous punishment for individuals, he included the one in which 'angels of destruction play with him'.[181] To become the plaything of demons—poked and prodded, beaten and boiled, and, of course, burnt and roasted—could only be imagined corporeally. R. Judah's tales reflect this corporeality.

Sefer ḥokhmat hanefesh, too, speaks in vivid detail of demons inflicting corporeal torments on dead souls. R. Eleazar of Worms mentions 'cruel angels filled with anger', who are assigned to 'torment and beat' the souls of the wicked using varying types of torture throughout the seven levels of Gehenna.[182] Even the faces of the wicked dead resemble the 'angels of torment, with faces of anger and smoke'.[183] In another passage in *Sefer ḥokhmat hanefesh*, R. Eleazar embellishes a talmudic account that describes the nature and activities of the foetus inside the womb.[184] The Talmud asserts that the foetus 'sees from one end of the universe to the other', and immediately before birth it is sworn to live as a righteous individual and not as a wicked one. R. Eleazar expands on this account by narrating how the foetus, guided by an angel, is taken on an otherworldly journey. After a tour of Paradise, it is shown the torment of the wicked in Gehenna. They are beaten mercilessly by demons with rods of fire until they shout, 'Woe! Woe!' and then they are burned.[185] R. Eleazar seemingly draws here upon a text known as *Seder yetsirat havalad*, which, like the *Perek gehinom*,

[178] Gurevich, 'Die Darstellung von Persönlichkeit und Zeit', 37–43.

[179] Once again, conflation of the two phenomena led to doctrinal inaccuracy. Purgatory, which was to disappear at the End of Time according to official teaching, was first depicted as a part of Last Judgement scenes in the third quarter of the thirteenth century in Castile. Such depictions became common during the fifteenth century in other places too. See Baschet, *Corps et âmes*, 218–21, and Bratu, 'Fin des temps', 72.

[180] Jérôme Baschet highlights the internal unity between visionary literature, exempla tales, and iconography in portraying the tortures of the afterlife. He goes so far as to proclaim that 'there is scarcely an iconographic motif for which one cannot find, here or there, a textual equivalent'; see *Les Justices de l'au-delà*, 503.

[181] *SḤ* 35.

[182] *Sefer ḥokhmat hanefesh*, 28*a*.

[183] Ibid. 7*a*.

[184] BT *Nid.* 30*b*.

[185] *Sefer ḥḥokhmat hanefesh*, 7*b*.

circulated at this time.[186] From that long narrative, which describes the various worlds the soul must pass through from the moment of conception until the moment of birth, he extracts the section that tells of the soul's visit to Paradise and Gehenna. With its detailed description of tortures inflicted by demonic agents, this section bears the influence of early medieval visionary literature. Thus, in presenting R. Eleazar's own version of a Jewish tour of Hell, his account is more in consonance with contemporary Christian narratives and visual images than with the apocalyptic tradition of his own religion.

The Problem of Corporeality

We are presented here with the problem of how non-corporeal souls can suffer physical torments carried out on body parts or organs in the afterlife. There are few descriptions within rabbinic and post-rabbinic literature of corporeal punishment of souls in Gehenna. Apart from the one passage in the Jerusalem Talmud (*Ḥag.* 2: 2) mentioned above, the bulk of the evidence comes from Judaeo-Christian apocalyptic texts.[187] In contrast to the punishment of individual body parts described in these sources, the rabbinic text of *Seder olam* speaks of the burning of the entire body alongside the destruction of the soul.[188] This total annihilation, however, is set to take place in the eschatological period rather than in the afterlife.[189]

In *Sefer ḥasidim*, R. Judah appears untroubled by the problem of corporeality in the punishments of the afterlife. As we have seen, he presents without any explanatory remarks images of a woman whose hands and eyes burn, and of another whose arm and glove are soiled with fat.[190] R. Eleazar, however, is more attentive to the problem. He is emphatic about the bodily torture experienced by the wicked in Gehenna and clearly states, 'Just as there is a body to a person in this world, so is there after death.' In reference to posthumous punishment, he declares that 'there is, after death, in

[186] See Jellinek (ed.), *Beit hamidrash*, i. 153–8.

[187] Milikowsky argues that the punishment of individual body parts described in these sources stemmed from the inability of authors to detail punishments of the soul in any other fashion than by using physical language. It in no way necessitates the presence of the body in the hereafter. See Milikowsky, 'Gehenna and Jewish Sinners' (Heb.), 324.

[188] See also its parallel in Tosefta, *San.* 13: 4–5 (ed. Zuckermandel, p. 434), and the commentary of *Tosefot rishonim* on line 13 there.

[189] Milikowsky, 'Gehenna and Jewish Sinners' (Heb.), 324.

[190] Interestingly, there is a relatively high proportion of women in the tales of both R. Judah the Pious and Caesarius of Heisterbach. Schmitt, *Ghosts in the Middle Ages*, 130, notes this phenomenon regarding Caesarius and offers a possible explanation.

Gehenna [a body], just as there is in life'.[191] Writing about the punishment of the wicked, idolatrous Israelite king Menasseh, R. Eleazar asserts that he descended body and soul to Gehenna.[192] However, he softens these statements by speaking of a more substantive *re'aḥ haguf* (scent of the body), which encapsulates the more ephemeral *ru'aḥ* (spirit),[193] and similarly the *re'aḥ hamalbush* (scent of the garment) clothes the *re'aḥ haguf*.[194] By adopting this terminology, R. Eleazar accomplishes a twofold objective. Not only does he mitigate somewhat the paradox of non-corporeal souls undergoing corporeal torments, but he also explains how bodies can eternally burn (or be eaten, beaten, cooked, and so on) without ever being destroyed. Since the body in the afterlife is composed of *ruaḥ* and *re'aḥ*—spirit and scent—and these are indestructible substances, the bodies of sinners in Gehenna can sustain everlasting corporeal torment.[195] Furthermore, in R. Eleazar's other esoteric writings the human soul assumes corporeal features and a quasi-corporeal form in Heaven called the *demut*.[196]

Many Christian thinkers make similar accommodations in order to resolve the problem raised by the corporeality of punishment in the afterlife. Honorius Augustodunensis argues that the dead who burn in purgatorial fire do so 'in the form of the bodies they wore in this world', and yet, paradoxically, he understands that purgation in a metaphorical sense.[197] The thirteenth-century scholastic William of Auvergne explains that the damned in Hell burn for eternity not because of the special nature of their body but because of the special quality of hellfire; it burns without ever consuming.[198] According to some historians, William speaks of two types of fire: to intellectuals he presents a pseudo-fire, while to the masses he describes a material one.[199] Caesarius of Heisterbach, however, like R. Judah the Pious, remains untroubled by the paradox.[200] His exempla unabashedly portray bodies burning in the afterlife, some doing so eternally.

191 *Sefer ḥokhmat hanefesh*, 5*b*. 192 Ibid. 24*a*. 193 Ibid. 5*b*, 7*a*.

194 Ibid. 5*b*. For an understanding of R. Eleazar's term *re'aḥ haguf* in the light of the Christian doctrine of 'spiritual bodies', see Soloveitchik, 'Topics in the *Ḥokhmat ha-Nefesh*', 75. On the sense of smell as the mediator between the physical and spiritual senses, see Dan, *The Esoteric Theology of Ashkenazi Hasidism* (Heb.), 248. 195 *Sefer ḥokhmat hanefesh*, 5*b*, 7*a*.

196 See Shyovitz, '"He Has Created a Remembrance of His Wonders"', 184–91.

197 See Le Goff, *The Birth of Purgatory*, 136–7. 198 See ibid. 245.

199 Gurevich cites Le Goff as advancing this claim and then concurs with it after clarifying it somewhat. See *Medieval Popular Culture*, 175.

200 Gurevich argues that one should not be surprised by the fact that medieval men and women, even theologians and clerics, held paradoxical views on this matter. Rather, the paradox of corporeal punishment of the non-corporeal soul, along with that of two types of judgement (the collective one at the end of time and the individual one after death), is an 'integral

Posthumous Punishment in *Sefer Ḥasidim*: Monastic Affinity

The aforementioned ghost tales recorded by R. Judah the Pious all describe ghosts who return from the afterlife to tell people about the harsh nature of their punishment in Gehenna. The 'sins' recounted in these tales, however, do not reflect precepts that are in any way particular to Pietist ideology, such as their unique doctrine of penance, their particular method of prayer, and the like. Instead, these misdeeds are deviations from standard practices in Jewish law and life. For this reason, the ghost tales of posthumous punishment do not appear in the section of the book labelled 'Matters Relating to the Dead';[201] rather, they are scattered throughout *Sefer ḥasidim*, episodically attached to the paragraph that discusses a particular area of conduct. The ghosts of *Sefer ḥasidim* had stumbled in the areas of sabbath observance, Jewish dietary laws, and public prayer in the synagogue: one woman lit a candle made of tallow for the sabbath, while another spun thread on the eve of the sabbath; a man ate hot food with forbidden fat under his nails; and yet another woman left the synagogue service early. These three spheres of life encompass the typical medieval Ashkenazi orbit—R. Judah's tales thus enter into the everyday life of medieval Jews.

Yet the stumbling of these people is measured by Pietist standards. Accepting upon themselves a larger corpus of law than that which was traditionally received, and demanding supererogatory behaviour in every aspect of that law,[202] the Pietists reckon even the smallest misdeed a grave offence. Moreover, it is specifically in the afterlife that the minor trappings of daily life are exposed for what they really are—serious sins which carry with them a harsh and enduring sentence.

R. Judah thus appropriates medieval exempla and visionary material that deal with punishments in the hereafter to serve his own Pietist agenda, in much the same way that some monastic writers do. Whereas more generalized exempla collections highlight the worst sins and sinners in general society, the monastic tales scrutinize the misconduct of monks and illustrate the exceedingly harsh nature of the punishments that await them.

A cursory reading of the high medieval exempla literature reveals

feature of medieval consciousness'. Generated by a 'clash between a theological conception and a notion rooted in popular culture and religiosity', both paradoxes were part of the 'fundamental paradoxicality of medieval mentality'. See ibid.

[201] Although the arrangement of sections in the work follows a pattern of free association, there are some thematically organized sections with their own titles. 'Inyanei metim' is one such section title; see *SḤ* 375.

[202] See Soloveitchik, 'Three Themes in *Sefer Ḥasidim*', 311–17.

that the subjects of this type of tale are most often adulterers, fornicators (including members of the clergy), murderers and thieves, usurers, magicians, and scholastics, who are consigned to Hell or Purgatory for having indulged in a life of sin.[203] In short, this list comprises the arch-criminals of medieval society, as perceived through the eyes of the Church.

Monastic tales of the dead, on the other hand, often serve the purpose of maintaining discipline and obedience within the abbey or order.[204] One way they accomplish this task is by focusing on an infraction committed, sometimes infrequently, by a less than zealous monk or lay brother who is pious in every other way, and describing the strict punishment he receives in the hereafter. Let us recall the vision of the lay brother Mengoz, who notices that the sacristan of his monastery has a spot on his foot in Paradise because he 'went out to work unwillingly', or the Cistercian abbot who endures a more severe posthumous punishment for a similar violation; with black, ulcerated legs, he suffers a torment that 'no tongue can express'. We may also remember the 'quite pious' sacristan of Villers, who appears to the abbot Ulrich and begs for his prayers in order to escape the torments of his purgatory. His downfall was being a 'trifler in words and signs'.

R. Judah's tales share a commonality of style and purpose with the monastic tales that record punishments in the afterlife. More akin to these monastic tales than to the generalized exempla, his stories require exemplary conduct in the service of God, not in the arena of morality. As horrific as it will be, R. Judah does not describe the murderer's or the adulterer's torment. Instead, he warns his readers that one who fails to honour the sabbath properly or is negligent in handling forbidden food substances will suffer greatly in the afterlife. One should not conclude from this observation that there were no murderers or adulterers in the Jewish society of R. Judah's day, or that he was unconcerned with their penance.[205] Rather, as

203 See e.g. Jacques de Vitry, *Exempla*; *Le Speculum laicorum*, ed. Welter; *Liber exemplorum ad usum praedicantum*, ed. Little; *Catalogue of Romances*, vols. i and ii; and Banks (ed.), *Alphabet of Tales*.

204 Farmer, 'Personal Perceptions, Collective Behavior', 231–9. Another purpose of this type of tale is to inhibit the deleterious actions of any detractors of the monastery and its holdings—e.g. knights and nobles are damned for appropriating monastic land. The tales in Caesarius's *Dialogue* serve both these purposes when they speak of damned nobles and knights as well as of negligent monks who suffer in the afterlife. See Schmitt, *Ghosts in the Middle Ages*, 131.

205 *Sefer ḥasidim* itself speaks of the penance to be assigned for them. Regarding a murderer, see e.g. *SḤ* 175 and 176, and regarding an adulterer, see e.g. *SḤ* 19, 40, and 41. A perfunctory glance at the Pietist penitential manuals reveals the prominence of these two types of sinner. On the Pietist manuals of penance, see Marcus, 'Hasidei Ashkenaz Private Penitentials', and

a religious reformer with a particular mission, he consciously selected tales that promoted his agenda.

Marcus Bull has revealed that the *miracula* tales, which record extraordinary events as evidence of the hand of God through the functioning of the saints in the world, and which were collected by monasteries such as the one at Rocamadour, were also 'exercises in selectivity'. Rather than portraying the different societal groups that visited the monastery, these tales speak of only a specific target group, and its redactors chose only those tales which best suited the message they wished to impart.[206] Although not speaking solely to a group of initiates as the monastic writers do, R. Judah wishes to frighten his audience into obeying the demanding dictates of Pietism in the context of everyday Jewish observance. He, like others of his time, chooses the medium of the ghost tale to accomplish his goal.

Upon analysis of R. Judah's selection of ghost tales depicting posthumous punishment, one could say that he would essentially agree with the following testimonial of a deceased Cistercian monk, recorded by Caesarius of Heisterbach. When the living ask him about his state in the afterlife, the monk responds: 'I should never have thought that the Lord was so severe. For He notices the very smallest faults which have not been blotted out by atonement.'[207]

Ghost Tales on Posthumous Reward: Validation of the Pietists' Values

It is especially in the realm of reward in the afterlife that the unique doctrines of Pietist ideology reveal themselves. Here, tales that glorify adherence to the particular method of Pietist prayer, the donning of their distinctive *talit*, and the Pietist doctrine of penance appear. Visions of those who embraced these specifically Pietist practices enjoying the delights of Paradise validate these customs in the eyes of readers. Once again, the Pietist tales of posthumous reward that R. Judah compiles are most akin to parallel stories that appear in monastic sources.

One such tale is found as an addendum on the margins of the Parma manuscript of *Sefer ḥasidim* added by R. Isaac of Vienna, a thirteenth-century tosafist with ties to the Pietists.[208] R. Isaac tells the following ghost

id., 'The Penitentials of the German Jewish Pietists' (Heb.). For a comprehensive collection of medieval Ashkenazi penitential manuals, see Kozma, 'The Practice of *Teshuvah*'.

206 Bull, *The Miracles of Our Lady of Rocamadour*, 76.

207 Caesarius of Heisterbach, *Dialogue*, 12: 28.

208 In the Parma manuscript, the tale appears adjacent to no. 427; in the printed edition of

tale in the name of his teacher, R. Judah the Pious, who had heard it from an elderly gravedigger named Binom. Early one morning, outside the synagogue, Binom encounters a ghost who wears a wreath of greenery, possibly of vine, on his head.[209] As mentioned previously, after a brief interchange in which the ghost reassures the frightened gravedigger that he is not a demon, Binom approaches the ghost and recognizes him as someone whom he himself had buried. He asks the apparition, 'How do you fare in that world?' The ghost responds, 'Very well!' The gravedigger, apparently surprised by this response, asks, 'What merit do you have? Weren't you just an ordinary man?' The ghost replies that his sole merit was to have recited the blessings in the synagogue in a pleasant voice. On the basis of this merit, 'they brought me into Paradise and they honour me there'. He then offers as proof of his identity the ripped sleeve on his shroud, which testifies that he is the very man whom the gravedigger had buried, as the gravedigger himself tore the sleeve while burying him. Before the ghost disappears, Binom questions him regarding the wreath he wears on his head. The ghost explains that it is made of herbs or vines from Paradise, and he has put it on his head to offset the foul odour of this world.[210]

Sefer ḥasidim, ed. Wistinetzky, it appears on p. 126. See also Isaac ben Moses, *Or zarua*, vol. ii, 'Hilkhot shabat', 42: 7, which contains a shortened version of this tale.

209 The Hebrew text reads: *uverosho keter shel asabim shekorin bilshon ashkenaz tsafilu uvilshon kena'an vinits kabitani*. The word *tsafilu* has a possible cognate in the Middle High German *zafel/zavel*, which means decoration or adornment. The use of the vernacular here serves to identify the type of crown (*keter*) the ghost wears: one made of grasses, i.e. a wreath. Another possible cognate is the Middle High German word *zepfe*, meaning grape. (Also suggestive in this regard is the Greek *staphyle*, meaning 'bunch of grapes'.) The use of the second vernacular term would reinforce this meaning, as *vinits* could be a cognate of the Latin word for wine, *vinum*. *Kabitani* could then suggest the Capitanata in the northern part of Puglia, a red wine-exporting region in the Middle Ages. The vernacular serves to specify the type of wreath: one made of grapevine. I wish to acknowledge the invaluable help of Graeme Dunphy, Jim Marchand, and John Dillon, who helped me with these cognates and their translations. D. Rotman offers different cognates and translations that relate to head coverings, such as the French *chaperon* or Italian *cappucio*; see 'The Marvellous in the Medieval Hebrew Narrative' (Heb.), 403 nn. 191, 192. Kushelevsky sees in the wreath a proto-Christian 'crown of thorns'; see *Penalty and Temptation* (Heb.), 265–8.

210 The medieval midrashic collection entitled *Yalkut shimoni* contains a lengthy description of the pleasures awaiting the righteous in Paradise ('Bereshit' 20). Among the long list of delights and riches are included two crowns (one made of precious gems and pearls, the other of gold) as well as eight myrtle branches. Angels place the crowns on the heads of the righteous and the myrtles in their hands. The crown or wreath of fragrant herbs which the dead man in our story wears may be a fusion of the two elements.

Another possible source lies in the *Sefer gematriyot lerabenu yehudah heḥasid*. Basing himself in part on *Midrash seder gan eden*, R. Judah describes how the archangel Michael burns the souls of the righteous upon the supernal altar along with the fragrant spices of Paradise, in a parallel

The tale is recorded on the margins of *Sefer ḥasidim*, beside passages which discuss the necessity of saying the blessings and praises of the morning prayer service out loud.[211] In another passage, R. Judah speaks of the importance of singing these psalms and blessings in a sweet melody before God. Like King David on his lyre and the Levite choir in the Temple, the Pietist must sing aloud the praises of God.[212] Additionally, the psalms must be recited in a protracted fashion—*ein na'im ela bemeshekh*[213]—in order to allow sufficient time for the Pietist to mystically calculate the numerical value and hidden symbolism of each letter in the text of the prayers.[214] These three elements—recital of the psalm sections of the prayer, out loud,

fashion to the burning of the incense on the terrestrial golden altar of the Temple. Accompanied by the fragrance of all types of spice made from grasses, trees, and herbs, the souls of the righteous then ascend to their place under the Throne of Glory (*Sefer gematriyot*, ed. Stahl, vol. i, no. 114). In another passage of the same work, R. Judah makes mention of a prevalent custom in which people would burn spices and herbs (similar in composition to the fragrant incense of the Temple) in order to release a person from the grip of a demon; the fragrance emitted from the burning spices would cause the evil demon to depart (ibid., no. 226). This custom is reiterated by Eleazar of Worms in his commentary on Num. 17: 12. See also *Sefer gematriyot*, 236 n. 94. A combination of these two notions could bring one to associate the return of a righteous dead person from Paradise with the use of fragrant herbs in order to dispel the evil odour of this world, as outlined in the ghost tale recorded above.

Y. Y. Stahl, the editor of the print edition of *Sefer gematriyot*, notes that, while the earlier part of the description of the practice of the archangel, in which the righteous souls are burned upon the supernal altar, has its source in the *Midrash seder gan eden*, the latter part, in which the ascending souls are surrounded by the fragrance of spices and herbs of Paradise, is not traceable to any known *midrash* (see *Sefer gematriyot*, 125 nn. 9, 13).

The fragrant aroma of Paradise and the foul odour of this world also appear in the *heikhalot* literature (see Schäfer, *Synopse zur Hekhalot-Literatur*, M40 no. 902, V278 no. 36, and D 1531 no. 811), and are well attested in medieval visionary accounts of the other world. The pleasing aroma which emanates from the dead bodies of saints is documented in medieval hagiographical accounts. An exemplum of Caesarius of Heisterbach attests to the presence of the fragrant aroma of Paradise on the corpse of a seemingly ordinary man: 'so great and so very sweet a perfume breathed from' the grave of a pious precentor at Paris (*Dialogue*, 12: 48). *Sefer ḥasidim*, Bologna print edn., no. 528, and MS CUL Add. 379 no. 472 also make mention of the 'good smell' of Paradise.

211 *SḤ* 427, 428, and 429.

212 *SḤ* 839.

213 Ibid.

214 *SḤ* 1575. In this passage, a hasid describes the nature of the Pietists' mystical intent of prayer as follows: 'When I prolong the recitation of psalms, I count on my fingers the number of times *alef* and then *bet* [and each of the letters in turn] appear in the text of the prayers and then give a reason for each figure.' See also *SḤ* 441 and 445, in which improper intent disqualifies the prayer. Both R. Judah the Pious and R. Eleazar of Worms wrote extensive commentaries on the prayer book. For a fuller discussion of the specific techniques of the Pietists' mystical prayer (including gematria, *notarikon*, and *temurah*), see Scholem, *Major Trends in Jewish Mysticism*, 100–3. See also Soloveitchik, 'Three Themes in *Sefer Ḥasidim*', 333. Most recently, see Fishman, *Becoming the People of the Talmud*, 203–10, who thoroughly explains the praxis and function of Pietist prayer calculations.

and in a protracted fashion—form the cornerstone of the unique Pietist prayer ritual as outlined in *Sefer ḥasidim*.[215]

The emphasis on protracted prayer—which could last until midday for a hasid[216]—was a cause, at times, of confrontation between Pietists and non-Pietists.[217] Two such incidents are recorded in *Sefer ḥasidim*. In one passage, R. Judah speaks of 'a learned man who is an expert in Torah', a composer of liturgical poems, who rushes the recital of the psalms during the synagogue service while prolonging the recital of his own compositions. R. Judah exhorts his readership to cease recital of this man's poems.[218] In the second case, which precedes the aforementioned ghost tale, a 'great and publicly acclaimed rabbi', who wishes to leave the synagogue as early as possible in order to hasten to his studies, screams aloud in protest at the protracted Pietist prayer. R. Judah is quick to mention that such a person is punished for his misconduct already in his lifetime.[219]

In both cases, men of scholarship and renown publicly oppose Pietist demands for lengthy recitation of psalms in the synagogue. While in the second case R. Judah sees Pietist practice vindicated, in the first he does not. He therefore urges his readers to impose their own sanctions upon such an individual. Undoubtedly this was not the only time that the Pietists did not succeed in imposing their unique, and potentially burdensome, ritual of prayer upon the community. An otherworldly revelation, which confirms the sublime sanctity of one who nevertheless adheres to the demands of that prayer ritual, thus serves the Pietists well in validating their practice. It is solely thanks to his singing aloud the blessings in the synagogue in a melodious voice that the common man of R. Judah's tale merits entry into Paradise and a place of honour therein.

215 Regarding the requirement to sing out loud in prayer, see *SḤ* 11, 427, 428, 429. *SḤ* 1604 equates the loud blast of the shofar with the loud praise of God. Three incidents described in *Sefer ḥasidim* testify to the vocal nature of the Pietists' prayer: see *SḤ* 419, 472, and 1368. On the primacy of the 'blessings and praises' (*pesukei dezimrah*), known as 'the psalms' in Pietist prayer, see *SḤ* 427, 1484, and 1620. See also nos. 418, 419, additions adjacent to 428–432, 472, 479, 839, and 1575. For evidence of the centrality of protracted prayer see *SḤ* 11, 418, 479, 837, 1578, 1589, 1603, 1618, 1620, and 1952. Additionally, the three elements often cluster together in the same passage or in nearby passages in the work. See also Grossman, 'Prayer in the Teachings of the German Pietists' (Heb.), 52–4.

216 Pietist prayer must be kept short on the sabbath and the festivals so that the Pietist does not violate the prohibition of fasting past midday on these days. See the additions to the Parma manuscript and in the printed edition of *Sefer ḥasidim* adjacent to no. 432.

217 According to Avraham Grossman, the slow pace of Pietist prayer was the 'main cause of friction in the synagogue between Pietists and non-Pietists'; see 'Prayer in the Teachings of the German Pietists' (Heb.), 43.

218 *SḤ* 1620.

219 See the additions to the Parma manuscript and the printed edition of *Sefer ḥasidim* adjacent to no. 427.

In another passage in *Sefer ḥasidim*, R. Judah again uses reward in the afterlife as an affirmation of the unique Pietist prayer ritual. Here he offers a lengthy discourse on the various groupings that form the landscape of reward and punishment; for every merit and sin there is a designated section in Paradise and Gehenna.[220] In the context of this exposition, R. Judah refers to one who 'praises the Holy One, blessed be He, with intentions of the heart during the Praises, or involves himself with the Praises to glorify them [Him], and they are not a burden upon him'. With his emphasis on proper attention to, and intention during, the Praises section of the service, which could be a burden to the less devout, he is clearly referring to the Pietist mode of prayer. Even though such a person may lack any other merit, on this basis alone he will be deemed worthy to enter Paradise and sit among the righteous as they offer praises before God. In this way, the unique Pietist prayer ritual is elevated to the status of a Divine commandment, on a par with the commands of almsgiving and Torah study.[221] Conversely, disregard for Pietist-style prayer is deemed a sin. One who rushes through the praises of God or prevents the enactment of the Pietist ritual in the synagogue will not only be deprived of reward but will be punished in Gehenna for that sin in the company of like sinners, despite the fact that he may possess many merits.[222]

The use of otherworldly reward to justify practices unique to a religious movement was not solely the province of the Pietists. Many stories in the *miracula* of the monastic houses of both the Cluniacs and the Cistercians served as 'propaganda for the Order'.[223] These miracle stories stamped a Divine seal of approval upon certain distinctive customs and dogmas of the movement. A form of internal control, they provided encouragement to the monks in the performance of their worship, while at the same time threatening with dire punishment those who disobeyed or were lax in their practice.[224] One of these practices was the communal prayer service of the

[220] *SḤ* 1952.

[221] R. Judah's description of the reward of one who adheres to the Pietist norms of prayer follows immediately after mention of the reward of those who give charity and study Torah.

[222] Thus R. Judah writes: 'And a man who rushes through them, for they are a burden upon him to draw out, or he prevents others from drawing [them] out and he impedes their intention and their tune, even though he has in his possession many merits, he will not enter with the righteous when they are praising, and he will be punished at that time.'

[223] Ward, *Miracles and the Medieval Mind*, 195.

[224] Ibid. 195. At times, monastic propaganda was aimed at critics and rivals. Those stories, for example, which highlight the greatness of Citeaux in Conrad of Eberbach's *Exordium Magnum Cisterciense* were meant to silence accusations raised by Benedictines in Germany. See McGuire, 'The Cistercians and the Rise of the *Exemplum*', 239.

monks, which had originated with the Desert Fathers, was incorporated into St Benedict's Rule, and was expanded into its full form in the Benedictine houses of Cluny. The number of psalms monks would recite had increased markedly by the twelfth century.[225] With its loud choral singing, Cluniac prayer occupied monks for almost an entire day, and its curtailment became one of the major areas of Cistercian reform.[226] Maintaining religious fervour in the face of such a demanding ritual must have been a daunting challenge for any monk. It is small wonder then that visions of Heaven were granted to those who sang aloud in the choir with great fervour.[227] Pietist prayer and monastic prayer went hand in hand here, with clear parallels in their ideals of devotion—lengthy and loud singing of praises to God—and its heavenly approbation via a ghost tale.[228]

It is especially the controversial practices of the order that were the subject of stories of miraculous intervention. The vows of silence and extreme poverty, the rigours of the monastic diet—all subject to criticism from without and difficult to enforce within—were substantiated by means of supernatural revelations, miraculous rewards, or Divine aid.[229] Furthermore, a great number of stories in Cistercian collections were devoted to visions of pious monks sitting among the elect of Paradise and enjoying bountiful rewards; this abundance of heavenly reward was meant to 'balance the austerities of Cistercian observance'.[230] At times, the monks themselves needed to see proof of the benefits of their practice.

The exempla, too, convey this message; it is through the lens of the other world that the pious practices of this world are to be evaluated. Beginning with the 'Life of St Odilo', the founder of All Souls' Day, many Cluniac tales tell of the dead who return to announce that they can only be delivered from their torment in the hereafter by means of the prayers of the monks of Cluny.[231] These tales offer clear testimony to the power of the

225 According to the Rule, the entire book of Psalms, consisting of 150 chapters, was to be completed over the course of the week. In the late eleventh century, Cluniac custom had set the number at 170 per day. See Little, 'Romanesque Christianity in Germanic Europe', 460.

226 Duby, *The Age of the Cathedrals*, 71. See also Van Engen, 'The "Crisis of Cenobitism" Reconsidered', 293; Lekai, *The Cistercians*, 248–9; Hunt, *Cluny Under St. Hugh*, 99–108; ead., *Cluniac Monasticism in the Central Middle Ages*, 44–5; and Evans, *Monastic Life at Cluny*, 81–3.

227 Ward, *Miracles and the Medieval Mind*, 197.

228 I develop this point further in Ch. 9 below.

229 Ward, *Miracles and the Medieval Mind*, 197.

230 Ibid.

231 Peter Damian, in his eleventh-century biography of St Odilo, reports that such an apparition of the dead Pope Benedict occurred shortly after the abbot established the Feast Day of the Dead, or All Souls' Day. See Peter Damian, 'Vie de saint Odilon', cited in Schmitt, *Ghosts in the Middle Ages*, 68. Peter the Venerable, in his twelfth-century work *De miraculis*,

Cluniac liturgy of the dead and promote its 'economy of salvation': positive reinforcement of the efficacy of Cluniac prayer for the dead served to increase pious endowments made to the monastery in wills and testaments, thus enriching the order.[232] Similar proof exists for the aggrandizement of the Cistercian order. Caesarius of Heisterbach tells of a dead lay brother, a former member of the Benedictine order, who appears to two Benedictine monks. The monks question him about the status of several deceased brothers from their order as well as about some Cistercian monks. The lay brother responds that, while some of their brethren are faring quite well, it is the grey monks (the Cistercians) rather than the black monks (the Benedictines) that enjoy the greatest glory in Heaven; 'Their reward is greatest', he says, 'and they shine like the sun in the realm of the sky.'[233]

One ghost tale in *Sefer ḥasidim* documents heavenly approval of another distinctive and controversial practice of the Pietists—that of wearing *tefilin* and *talit* all day. The opening words of the passage record the following incident: 'It once happened regarding a certain hasid who would wear his *tefilin* and *tsitsit* all day, that when he died, they heard that elevated beings [in Heaven] eulogized him.'[234] This incident appears to be a truncated version of an actual ghost tale, in which a dead individual returns in a dream to several (or all, as is sometimes the case in such ghost tales[235]) of a deceased Pietist's former friends and neighbours. The ghost informs them of the exalted nature of the Pietist's practice of wearing *tefilin* and *talit* all day, which is highly regarded in Heaven—elevated beings eulogize him. In another passage, R. Judah laments over those who only don the *talit* once a week, on the sabbath, and labels them wicked (*resha'im*);[236] true Pietists wear it daily.[237] In a different passage, a Pietist is praised for not waiting until the sabbath to don the *talit* but wearing it on a weekday due to the importance of the commandment. The implication is that he will continue to don it on all subsequent weekdays in addition to the sabbath.[238]

continues the tradition and recounts numerous tales of this nature. See Schmitt, *Ghosts in the Middle Ages*, 75–7.

232 Schmitt, *Ghosts in the Middle Ages*, 77. See also McLaughlin, 'Consorting with Saints', 233. On the Cluniac economy of salvation see Iogna-Prat and Picard, 'Les Morts dans la comptabilité céleste des Clunisiens', 68–9.

233 Caesarius of Heisterbach, *Dialogue*, 12: 53.

234 *SḤ* 1036.

235 See *SḤ* 335 for an example where the ghost appears to the entire town.

236 *Sefer ḥasidim*, ed. Margaliot, no. 57.

237 This is evident from *SḤ* 986, in which *talit* and *tefilin* are listed as two examples of challenging practices of *ḥasidut* which apply daily but are difficult to adhere to unless one is trained in them from early youth.

238 *SḤ* 439. The Bologna print edn., no. 838, records two contemporary practices regarding wearing a *talit*—one is to don it on the sabbath only, the other is to don it daily in the synagogue.

As I have discussed in the previous chapter, the Pietists stood apart from their contemporaries in this practice. Wearing the distinctive, hooded Pietist *talit* was seen as one of the hallmarks of the movement—'a matter of *ḥasidut* that is practised every day'.[239] The Pietist *talit* served as a constant source of mockery of the hasidim, who were exhorted to wear it publicly in order to inspire others to imitate this practice.[240] In the Pietist doctrine the endurance of shame was the very essence of being a hasid.[241] *Sefer ḥasidim* condemns the actions of a certain wicked non-Pietist who once took the *talit* of a righteous Pietist and gave it to a scoffer, who then publicly paraded around in it in an attempt to mock the Pietist to his face.[242] In another passage, R. Judah exhorts the Pietist follower to wear his *talit* publicly 'even though they will mock him', since his reward will be commensurate with his shame.[243] He admits that even *tovim* (good ones) find the *talit* difficult to wear because of the shame involved.[244] Yet, despite the stigma, the most praiseworthy Pietist wears his *talit* all day every day. The above-mentioned ghost tale, which lauds such exemplary behaviour, thus serves a dual purpose. Aside from encouraging other Pietists to emulate this individual, it vindicates Pietist practice in the face of any detractors.

While the ghost tales of *Sefer ḥasidim* do not have a missionary agenda in the same way as the Cistercian ones do,[245] they share a similar function—to convince sceptics and self-doubters that their distinctive way of life is most favourable before God.[246] The following tale is instructive in this regard. A certain hasid is accustomed to afflicting himself with various tortures. In the summer he lies on the ground among vermin; in the winter he

[239] *SḤ* 986. See also no. 976.

[240] See *SḤ* 1589 for the assertion that a hasid ought to wear his *talit* publicly, despite the general Pietist principle that 'he ought to perform whatever commandment he can privately'.

[241] See *SḤ* 975, where the term *ḥasid* is shown to derive from the word *ḥasidah*, which translates as *ḥavarita* in Aramaic, and in English means 'the pale or blanched one'. The hasid is called thus because of the continual blanching of his face due to public mockery and derision of his practices and ideals.

[242] See *SḤ* 1344.

[243] *SḤ* 1589.

[244] *SḤ* 986.

[245] The entire first chapter of the *Dialogue* (entitled 'On Conversion') is devoted to tales involving men and women who convert to the Cistercian Order from lay life or from another monastic order. One reason Caesarius begins his work with this collection of stories is to inspire imitation on the part of others.

[246] An exception to this statement can be found in *SḤ* 634. A scholar sees in a dream that a certain *zaken* (elder) is being ushered into the next world—the world of reward. Upon enquiry, he learns that the merits of this man included being trustworthy, poor, exceedingly honest in his speech, careful to avoid even listening to lies, and frugal in his weekday spending in order to purchase good wine for the sabbath. None of these qualities, which acquire for him otherworldly reward, are associated with uniquely Pietistic doctrines. This is not surprising, since *Sefer ḥasidim* was also intended for a general audience.

places his feet in buckets of ice, and at times he casts fire on his body. His friend, who deems these dangerous practices to be life-threatening, questions him as to their permissibility on the basis of Genesis 9: 5, which prohibits suicide. The hasid responds that, while it is true that he has not committed sins of such magnitude as to warrant this suffering, it is impossible that he has not committed any sins—even small ones—and he does not want others, more righteous than he, to suffer for his sins. Equating himself with the 'messiah, who bears iniquities', he quotes Isaiah 53: 5, 'He was pained because of our rebellious sins.' Furthermore, he adds that when the righteous suffer, many benefit—as in the case of R. Eleazar b. Shimon and R. Judah the Prince.[247] His students are unconvinced; they still fear that he will be punished for his actions. At the very least, they argue, his self-inflicted tortures take him away from Torah study, which itself is a sin. The hasid then dies. One of his students fears that he may have died on account of his ascetic regime. Wishing to know if his master is being punished or rewarded, the student stretches himself out upon the grave of the hasid and requests that he return to him in a dream and inform him of his status in the hereafter. The hasid heeds his request; he appears to him in a dream and says, 'Come with me and I will show you.' When he takes his student into Paradise, the student asks him, 'Where is my place?' 'In that place', the master responds and shows it to him. 'And if you increase your merits, you will have a higher place', he adds. The student then turns to the hasid and asks, 'Where is your place?' The hasid responds, 'In that high-up place.'[248] The student then asks to see the place of his master in Paradise. The master responds that the student, at this point in time, cannot see it; he has insufficient merit to do so. The tale concludes with a jubilant student, who is 'so happy about the great light that was there and that he did not have the merit to see his master's place [because it was so high up], and [happy because] now he knew that he [i.e. his master] was not being punished'.[249]

[247] The Talmud in *BM* 84*b* tells of the self-imposed suffering of R. Eleazar b. Shimon, who procures a blessing for himself as well as for his city: his body does not decay after he dies, and the entire time his body remains unburied, in the attic of his home, no wild beast enters the city. R. Judah the Prince, seeing the benefits of suffering, exclaims, 'Beloved is suffering!' On the next page (*BM* 85*a*), the Talmud tells of the illnesses which R. Judah the Prince accepts as punishment for a sin he once committed. In the merit of his suffering, the land never lacks rain.

[248] On the hierarchical seating arrangement of the righteous in front of the Kavod in Pietist thought, see Dan, *The Esoteric Theology of Ashkenazi Hasidism* (Heb.), 248. According to Dan, the hierarchical structure of feudal society influenced R. Eleazar's formulation of the seating order.

[249] *SḤ* 1556. The great light mentioned in the tale may draw upon the motif used to describe Paradise in the Crusade chronicles. On the motif of light in the martyrs' Heaven, see

Suffering, especially voluntary suffering, occupies a prominent place in Pietist ideology. Leading to much-needed atonement,[250] corporeal suffering forms an integral part of the Pietists' distinctive doctrine of repentance. Its innovative nature is apparent to the Pietists themselves.[251] As part of the prescription of *teshuvat hakatuv* (self-administered atonement based on the punishment prescribed in the Bible for a sin), a Jew guilty of a sin which is punishable in a Jewish court by public flogging should take upon himself that punishment as penance.[252] He may even enlist someone else to strike him 'until blood spills forth', as long as the other person does not kill him.[253] Similarly, a murderer is to be beaten until the point of death.[254] Serious crimes that are punishable in Jewish law by *karet* (a 'cutting off' of the soul of the sinner from those of the Jewish people) are to be atoned for by means of various corporeal tortures. The penance prescribed for adultery is immersing oneself in icy waters up to one's nose regularly in winter, or to sit on an anthill or among bees during the summer months.[255] Prolonged periods of fasting are mandated for other sexual sins as well as to atone for stealing.[256]

Moreover, voluntary suffering, beyond the prescribed penances, is extolled many times throughout *Sefer ḥasidim*.[257] One reason for undertaking voluntary suffering is that by doing so the hasid becomes *naki*

Shepkaru, 'To Die for God', 326. The only variation of significance in some parallel texts of this passage is the mention of a 'good smell' in Paradise alongside the 'great light'; regarding the former, see n. 210 above. Regarding the notion of sitting higher up in Heaven, see also the story of Akiva and the faithful woman recorded in MS Parma 2295 and cited by Kushelevsky (*Penalty and Temptation* (Heb.), 159), in which a student is three steps above his master in Paradise.

250 The Pietists need atonement more than the average Jew because of the notion of unwitting sin incorporated within their doctrine of *retson haboré*. The Pietist is held fully responsible for sin, which is both omnipresent and, many times, unknown to him—a product of the larger will of God, which extends beyond both the Written and Oral Laws. See Soloveitchik, 'Three Themes in *Sefer Ḥasidim*', 311–17.

251 See *SḤ* 22.

252 *SḤ* 37.

253 *SḤ* 18.

254 *SḤ* 630.

255 *SḤ* 19.

256 *SḤ* 19 and 22.

257 In *SḤ* 43, R. Judah states unequivocally, 'Regarding all pains that he accepts upon himself, behold, they are like suffering, which atones', and in *SḤ* 278 he declares, 'in every pain there is gain'. For these reasons, never does a righteous person suffer in vain. Even if he is unaware of it, his suffering serves to ease the burden of another righteous individual who is suffering (*SḤ* 399). Similarly, the righteous among Israel suffer for the sins of the wicked in order to remove punishment from them (*SḤ* 115). In keeping with the ideal of voluntary suffering and its salvific benefits, the biblical Job, according to R. Judah's conception, beseeches God to afflict him with the suffering that befalls him (*SḤ* 32, p. 31). Similarly, Mefiboshet, mentioned in 2 Sam. 4: 4, and who was rendered lame in early childhood due to a fall, apparently became a cripple, according to R. Judah, due to self-flagellation; he mortified his flesh for the sake of King David in an effort to aid him in the expiation of his sins (*SḤ* 496).

mehakadosh barukh hu ('clean [i.e. free from the punishment] of the Holy One, blessed be He'); he hopes that his self-imposed penance in this world will mitigate the fearsome judgement which may await him after death.[258]

In light of the positive evaluation of suffering within Pietism, *Sefer ḥasidim* explores further the parameters of this value. How far can one take voluntary suffering as atonement for sin without it being deemed sinful? The ghost tale cited above grapples with the dilemma created by the confrontation between the unique Pietist doctrine of repentance, with its accent on self-imposed corporeal suffering as atonement for sin, and the biblical prohibition of suicide. While suicide is the prohibition specifically enunciated in this tale, the larger issue is the permissibility of inflicting harm upon oneself. Deliberately injuring oneself is prohibited in Jewish law.[259] Yet self-flagellation, a common medieval penitential practice, especially in monastic circles, and one which is in line with the Pietists' own doctrine of penance, is permitted according to the dictates of *Sefer ḥasidim*. In the paragraph immediately preceding the above-mentioned ghost tale regarding the hasidic master,[260] R. Judah matter-of-factly rules that a public figure (for example a teacher or an emissary to the king, to the nobility, or to courts of law) is not permitted to flagellate himself. This is due, he argues, to the fact that his injuries will incapacitate him in his role as public agent, causing a loss of services to the public—and it is unrelated to any prohibition of self-harm (*isur ḥabalah*). The clear implication of this passage is that a private person is allowed to engage in such acts. Additionally, although the hasidic master, who is a public figure and nevertheless practises mortification of the flesh, violates the ruling of R. Judah, he emerges as one who has acted in a most righteous manner. Through the medium of the ghost tale, the Pietists are able to extol a practice which is otherwise halakhically forbidden. Any controversy that might surround their veneration of self-mortification is mitigated in light of the unequivocal Divine approval granted to the master after his death.[261]

In this tale, the Pietist doctrine of penance is taken to its extreme limits. The master himself admits that he has not committed crimes of such mag-

[258] *SḤ* 22. [259] See Mishnah *BK* 8: 6 and BT *BK* 91*b*. [260] *SḤ* 1555.

[261] A similar glorification of a pious individual who mortifies his flesh appears in the *Dialogus miraculorum*: despite the fact that his regular routine of beatings with the scourge hastens his death, Godfrey, monk of Villers, is praised posthumously by his fellow monks, who 'all marvel greatly' when they uncover his back and see it 'so bruised with the blows of the rod'. The monk assumes the position of a quasi-saint on account of his ascetic regime, and his bones are preserved in the monastery as relics. See Caesarius of Heisterbach, *Dialogue*, 1: 35.

nitude as to warrant the harsh nature of his self-torture—the types of penance he inflicts upon himself are usually reserved for those guilty of more heinous crimes, such as adultery. Instead, equating himself with the messiah in Isaiah's allegory of the suffering servant—a well-known Christological passage[262]—he wishes to voluntarily accept this severe suffering upon himself in order to accrue merit for mankind. The master, whom his student initially suspects of having committed suicide and whom he thus regards as a likely sinner, emerges from the tale as a hero of supernal proportions. He is to be properly judged only by God himself, who perceives and validates his good intentions. As a result, the master is eternally glorified in the world of truth. This ghost tale serves, then, to vindicate in the eyes of any detractors, including within their own camp, the Pietists' severe forms of penance and their penchant for voluntary suffering. In doing so, it glorifies the Pietist movement itself. Their distinctive doctrines are greatly valued by God; the master's seat in Paradise is substantially higher than that of his doubting student—it is in a realm that he cannot even see.[263] Like the exempla extolling the houses of Cluny and Cîteaux, this ghost tale pronounces that it is the Pietists who enjoy the greatest glory in Heaven.

The above tale complements other complex narratives found in *Sefer ḥasidim* which explore the conflict between inappropriate action and good intention. Although neither ghost tales nor exempla, the 'Tale of the Herdsman', 'The Pious Sinner', and the 'Tale of the Three Confessors' all involve 'pious sinners', whose external conduct, like that of the hasidic master, at

Kushelevsky, *Penalty and Temptation* (Heb.), 140, points out the liminality of the Pietists' doctrine of repentance. Transporting penitents from life to death (their extreme form of penance often brought them to the verge of death) and then to rebirth, it functioned as a rite of passage.

262 An entire literature surrounds the interpretation of this passage in Isaiah, as its Christological interpretation made it the focus of an intense polemic between Jews and Christians in the medieval period. See Neubauer and Driver, *The 'Suffering Servant' of Isaiah*.

263 The motif of seeing a more exalted place prepared in Heaven for a person of exceptional merit has parallels in the exempla literature. In one tale, the abbot Pontius gives up the place reserved for him in Heaven for a knight who had become a monk and who is tempted to leave the order. After all of Pontius's merits have been transferred to him, the former knight remains in the order. When he dies, he is taken to Pontius's originally allotted place, but then he is shown 'a still more exalted place' reserved for the abbot as a reward for his pious act. See MS BL Royal 7 D I fo. 86*b* (*Catalogue of Romances*, iii. 487 no. 95). A similar tale is told of St Bernard, in which he transfers all of his merits to a dying priest in order to persuade him to confess. After the priest's death, St Bernard sees him in a vision, sitting on a throne in Heaven, while 'a more exalted throne' is reserved for Bernard himself. See MS BL Add. 33956 fo. 68 (*Catalogue of Romances*, iii. 632 no. 75). Yet another tale involves the positions in Heaven of St Francis and St Mark: see MS BL Add. 33956 fo. 30*b* (*Catalogue of Romances*, iii. 629 no. 50).

first appears reprehensible but in the end is revealed to be praiseworthy.[264] In all three tales, the conflict surrounds issues which are important elements of Pietistic thought or practice.[265] Otherworldly reward is a key factor in justifying and extolling the otherwise seemingly sinful behaviour.[266]

Our ghost tale, too, uses otherworldly reward to praise the apparently sinful action of its protagonist. The ghost tale as a genre is best suited for this role: by allowing the visionary to see while alive, in this world, the glory that awaits the pious sinner in the afterlife, it not only provides the necessary celestial affirmation for the questionable Pietistic doctrine, as some of the other, non-ghost, tales do,[267] but it also takes that affirmation one step further. It concretizes the reward that awaits the pious sinner and provides a scale of value for measuring that reward: the Pietist resides at the highest echelon in Paradise. The protagonist of the ghost tale is more than just pious; his brand of piety is the best.[268]

[264] Alexander-Frizer, *The Pious Sinner*, chs. 3, 4, and 5 respectively. The tales appear in *SḤ* 5–6, 80, and 52–3 respectively.

[265] Both 'The Pious Sinner' and 'The Tale of the Three Confessors' probe the limits of merit gained from self-imposed trial. The positive value inherent in overcoming trial was a central feature of Pietist ethics, and the concept of self-imposed trial was specifically advocated by R. Judah. See Alexander-Frizer, *The Pious Sinner*, 111 and 135.

The conflict in the 'Tale of the Herdsman' revolves around the issue of formalized, standard prayer with a fixed text, an important element in the Pietist doctrine of prayer. The tale, however, minimizes the importance of that element when measured against spontaneous prayer motivated by a genuine love of God. R. Judah neutralizes the effect of the tale by placing it within an opposing context, thereby restoring value to the unique Pietist mode of prayer. See ibid. 74–7 and 78–82.

[266] In the 'Tale of the Herdsman', God appears in a dream revelation and declares that the herdsman—who is at first castigated as a fool—is destined for Paradise. In the 'Pious Sinner', a pious man is informed in a dream enquiry that a pious sinner is his future neighbour in Paradise. In 'The Tale of the Three Confessors', the talmudic sage who prescribes punishment to the confessors also informs them that they will receive reward which only God can measure. According to Tamar Alexander, the conflict in the story is resolved by relegating punishment for sinful actions to this world and reward for good intentions to the next. See *The Pious Sinner*, 145.

[267] This is true only for the 'Tale of the Pious Sinner' and the 'Tale of the Three Confessors'. In the case of the 'Tale of the Herdsman', celestial affirmation of the individualized, spontaneous prayer of the herdsman goes against the idea of formalized, fixed prayer which forms the basis of the Pietist prayer practice.

[268] A similar ghost tale, which tells of a man whose desire for atonement leads him to commit suicide, is recorded in the *Hilkhot semaḥot hashalem* of R. Meir of Rothenburg. A certain very rich and erudite talmudic student in England, named R. Yom Tov, is found dead on the eve of Shavuot, having hanged himself by his belt. (Urbach, *The Tosafists* (Heb.), ii. 498–9, identifies this R. Yom Tov as the son of R. Moses, a tosafist from one of the wealthiest families of England and a contemporary of the students of Ri. He also postulates that he may possibly be the Cresse or Deulecresse (d.1269) spoken of in glowing terms by the English king.) Following the

Conclusion

With its emphasis on the fate of the individual in the hereafter, *Sefer ḥasidim* moves far from the rabbinic orbit. No longer does fear of death, or of the fate of the corpse, or of lack of burial animate the medieval Jew. Instead, he worries over the fate of his soul. The primacy of eschatology—the resurrection and the World to Come—in rabbinic thought is supplanted by a fascination with the afterlife. It is primarily there that medieval Jews and Christians anticipate their future reward and punishment.

dictates of Jewish law regarding suicides, his father abstains from mourning. His body receives undignified treatment when community members well below his station in life—mere servants and ignorant people—prepare it for burial, and only a few learned men accompany his casket. While his casket is en route to London for burial there, R. Yom Tov appears to R. Meir, among others, in a dream. He is resplendent in death, even more so than when alive, and is surrounded by a great light—a clear sign that he has been ensured immediate entry into Paradise. It later becomes known to R. Meir that the student had once been tempted to worship in some way before a cross and that he killed himself as an act of penance for that crime. (While he may have killed himself as a preventative measure, R. Meir does not interpret his action as such.) The student is then recognized as a righteous individual and he merits a funeral service befitting his true station. Although a cautionary note is inserted, stating that one who is not motivated by pure love of God when killing himself as an act of penance is considered guilty of having improperly forfeited his life, the passage concludes with an unequivocal pronouncement in favour of self-inflicted corporeal penances: 'It is better if a person accepts upon himself penance involving mutilation, torture, and flagellation in this world, so that afterwards he can serve God with all his heart and all his soul, and bear children who will be of pure and wondrous lineage, and his days shall be renewed like Job's.' A halakhic proof for the permissibility of suicide as an act of penance is cited from *Midrash rabah*, 'Toledot' 25: the nephew of R. Yosi ben Yo'ezer perpetrates upon himself, as penance for his sins, all four forms of execution that may be rendered by the Jewish court in cases of capital punishment, and he is subsequently assured by a heavenly voice that he will inherit the World to Come. See R. Meir of Rothenburg, *Hilkhot semaḥot hashalem*, no. 89, and Kupfer, 'The History of the Family of R. Moses b. Yom Tov' (Heb.), 385–7. This same proof from rabbinic literature is found in *SḤ* 18, p. 23. Although the Pietists consciously draw upon early examples of extreme penance found in the rabbinic literature, these are not the main influence for their ascetic practices. Regarding their use of these sources, see Fishman, 'The Penitential System of *Ḥasidei Ashkenaz*', 201–5.

While no actual dialogue is reported to have transpired between the ghost and R. Meir, the luminous appearance of the deceased makes it obvious that he is enjoying heavenly reward. As in the tale of the Pietist master, a negative action (suicide) is pitted against a positive intention—the desire for repentance motivated by true love of God—with the latter once again predominating. Likewise, it is the controversial Pietist doctrine of penance which forms the focus of the tale. Also parallel is the otherworldly reward, which plays a pivotal role in both stories: it is solely in light of the appearance of the ghost, whose elevated status in the afterlife now becomes apparent, that the earthly status of the dead man is transformed from renegade to righteous.

The story of R. Yom Tov would indicate that the distinctly Pietistic doctrine of penance resonated in other sections of the Jewish community. This finding is confirmed by Elbaum, *Repentance and Self-Flagellation* (Heb.), 11–44. Since this literature is highly normative, however, it is indeed an accident of history that the London tale has come down to us.

In both language and content, the Pietist tales of *Sefer ḥasidim* that describe the state of the individual in the hereafter contain elements that parallel those found in the early medieval visionary literature, as well as in the high medieval exempla collections. Popular motifs, such as vivid descriptions of corporeal torture by demonic agents, figure prominently in both *Sefer ḥasidim* and contemporary literary sources and artistic representations. Other shared characteristics include the principle of *talio* and the disproportion between sin and punishment. The problem of corporeality—already apparent in the areas of the dangerous dead and the attire of the dead—surfaces yet again both in *Sefer ḥasidim* and in the Christian exempla collections.

The exemplum as a literary medium was uniquely suited to convey R. Judah's message. Despite the individuality of each particular tale, that genre succeeded as a mode of preaching to the masses precisely because of its universal nature. As a 'cultural object that was to be shared regardless of any differences in status, nationality, or language', the exemplum held a lesson for everyone.[269] Moreover, it could reach more people as it illustrated an idea rather than verbally formulating it; it was a 'visual' medium, not an ideational one. With the standardization of the ghost tale in the thirteenth century, the exempla conveyed narratives that were familiar and expected.[270] Persistent repetition of the same motifs and elements reduced the individuality of the stories, making them the common property of all, Pietist Jew and Christian monk alike. Each tale was then remoulded to conform to the specific requirements of a given group or movement.

R. Judah adapted the tales he selected regarding punishment and reward in the afterlife to his Pietist agenda, but his stories shared certain characteristics with monastic tales. He set exacting standards in the performance of commandments that represented the basic building blocks of life for the medieval Jew—public prayer in the synagogue, sabbath observance, and adherence to Jewish dietary laws. Ghost stories that showcase otherworldly punishment for laxity in the service of God are a distinctive feature of the monastic collections of tales.

In the realm of otherworldly reward, R. Judah highlights the unique Pietist practices of protracted prayer in praise of God, daily donning of the Pietist *talit*, and voluntary acts of mortification of the flesh. All three were characteristic features of monasticism: as we have seen, Pietist prayer resembled the Cluniac model of loud choral singing of psalms; the Pietist *capuchon* recalled the monk's *cuculla*; and mortification of the flesh was

[269] Schmitt, *Ghosts in the Middle Ages*, 129. [270] Ibid. 136.

common to several monastic orders. It was not only the practices that were parallel, however, but also the praise of them. Pietist ghost tales, like their Cluniac and Cistercian counterparts, served to validate the movement's own particular set of doctrines and practices by offering celestial affirmation. The Pietist narratives, in tandem with their monastic equivalents, aimed to convince sceptics and self-doubters that their distinctive way of life was favourable before God. All these parallels suggest a common mode of thought regarding the afterlife which straddled religious and cultural boundaries.

In this chapter we have witnessed the shifting of interest and emotion regarding death and the afterlife that transpired between the rabbinic and medieval periods. It has become clear that the ghost tales of *Sefer ḥasidim* owe a huge literary debt to the early medieval visionary literature and the high medieval exempla collections. This cultural borrowing also extended to the conceptual arena and included ideas such as punishment in Paradise and corporeal torture inflicted by demonic agents in Gehenna. Finally, there was a noticeable affinity between the Pietist agenda and the monastic one. In the next chapter, as we explore Pietist notions of sin, penance, and purgation, I bind all four of these strands together.

CHAPTER SIX

ON SIN, PENANCE, AND PURGATION

ALTHOUGH no authoritative dogma on details of eschatology and the afterlife exists in Jewish tradition,[1] there is an opinion, cited by R. Akiva in the Mishnah and repeated in the Talmud in several places,[2] that the sentence of the average wicked person in Gehenna is no longer than twelve months. As part of a list of five punishments of twelve months' duration, the Mishnah in tractate *Eduyot* states, rather laconically: 'The sentence of the wicked in Gehenna is twelve months.'[3]

In *Sefer ḥasidim*, R. Judah records the following ghost tale, which addresses R. Akiva's position on the matter:

It happened once that an individual saw someone who had died several years before. He said to him, 'Why is your face black?' He said to him, 'Because they punish me in Gehenna.' He asked him, 'Regarding what [sin]?' He said, 'Regarding [the fact that] I was not scrupulous in reciting the blessing of *hamotsi* [over bread], the blessing on fruits, and grace after meals with proper intent. They said to me,[4] "You had in mind only your own benefit, but for your Creator you did not wish to pronounce the blessing with proper intent!"' He said to him, 'And I was certain that the sentence of the wicked in Gehenna is twelve months, and [yet] you have been dead for several years already and they still punish you?' He said to him, 'They do not punish me with harsh punishments [now] as [they did] in the first twelve months.'[5]

[1] See Lévi, 'Le Repos sabbatique des âmes damnées', 4. Lévi comments that the Talmud is in a state of veritable chaos when it comes to these matters. For a full list of relevant tannaitic and amoraic sources on the afterlife, see Costa, *L'Au-delà et la resurrection*, 311–17 and 359–91.

[2] BT *Shab.* 33*b*; *RH* 17*a*; and JT *San.* 10: 3, 53*a*.

[3] *Edu.* 2: 10. R. Akiva's opinion appears in the tannaitic work *Seder olam* as well, though without mention of his name. See Milikowsky, 'Gehenna and Jewish Sinners' (Heb.), 311. (Milikowsky's excerpts from the text of *Seder olam* are based on MS St Petersburg Evr. Antonin B 891.)

[4] The anonymous plural subject here refers to the angels of destruction who are tormenting him in Gehenna.

[5] *SḤ* 555.

The question posed by the living individual in this tale makes it evident that R. Akiva's opinion was widely known and accepted.[6] A contemporary Ashkenazi text that describes a vision of Gehenna also confirm this,[7] and it is further corroborated by the tosafist commentary on the Talmud.[8] The fact that the dead man has been punished for several years thus challenges the authoritative rabbinic opinion,[9] and the ghost resolves this apparent contradiction by saying that the truly severe punishment in Gehenna lasts for only the first twelve months.[10]

In this tale, a confrontation between rabbinic tradition on the afterlife and notions about the hereafter portrayed in *Sefer ḥasidim* comes to the fore. Far more audacious than R. Judah's assertion elsewhere in the book that punishment exists for the righteous in Paradise, or that corporeal punishments are inflicted on non-corporeal souls by demonic agents,[11] this statement is an outright negation of an accepted and authoritative rabbinic teaching, found in no less authoritative a source than a *mishnah* in tractate *Eduyot*.[12] As we shall see, the Pietists had their own understanding of the nature of posthumous punishment, which differed radically from the rabbinic one. In this matter, they had completely shed the world-view of the rabbis and adopted an early medieval, pre-purgatorial one in its stead.

The Rabbinic View of Posthumous Punishment

The rabbinic term Gehenna originated as a designation for an actual location in Jerusalem—Gei Ben Hinom, infamous in the Bible as the site where child immolation took place.[13] The prophet Jeremiah refers to this valley as

[6] R. Eleazar of Worms clearly accepts this teaching as authoritative when he states, 'The heavenly judgement before the Holy One, blessed be He, lasts for three days. The judgement of the grave lasts for seven days. The judgement of Gehenna lasts for twelve months' (*Sefer ḥokhmat hanefesh*, 8*a*).

[7] See MS Bodl. 1466, no. 330*a*, cited in Rotman, 'The Marvellous in the Medieval Hebrew Narrative' (Heb.), 368.

[8] See *Tosafot Ḥag.* 27*a*, s.v. *poshei yisra'el*, where the *Tosafot* says unequivocally, 'and even those who are judged [to descend to Gehenna], they ascend after twelve months, and there is no sentencing for longer than one complete year'; and *Tosafot BM* 58*b*, s.v. *ḥuts*: 'The sentence of the wicked of Israel in Gehenna is twelve months.'

[9] This challenge is given added emphasis in the Bologna print edn., no. 46, and MS Moscow 103 no. 46; it serves to introduce the story told there.

[10] This answer, which presents a resolution by distinguishing between two apparently contradictory statements of authority, has a distinctly tosafist tone.

[11] See above, pp. 168–71 and 180–9 respectively.

[12] *Eduyot* is called *beḥirta* (selected) because all of its statements are accepted as halakhah. See BT *Ber.* 27*a*.

[13] 2 Kgs 23: 10; Jer. 7: 31, 32: 35.

the place of punishment of the wicked at the End of Time, after the resurrection of the dead, when the Final Judgement takes place: 'Therefore, behold, days are coming', he warns the people, 'when this place will no longer be called . . . the Valley of ben-Hinom, but the Valley of Killing'.[14] Whereas the scriptural verse speaks of the destruction of the sinners there at the End of Days, in rabbinic literature the concept of Gehenna is detached from its original meaning as a particular geographical location and describes instead the more generalized punishment of the wicked.[15] Additionally, the rabbis extend the future punishment beyond that originally stated in the verse: Gehenna serves as the locus of punishment both at the End of Days and immediately after the death of the individual. Although the term takes on both meanings in tannaitic and amoraic sources, references to Gehenna as a place of eschatological punishment occur more frequently in the tannaitic literature, whereas Gehenna as the site of individual punishment in the afterlife is more common in amoraic writings.[16] However, in the overwhelming majority of cases, the two meanings coexist, or it is impossible to determine with certainty which meaning is indicated.[17]

In addition to the ambiguity within rabbinic literature in reference to the time period within which Gehenna operates, there also exists an ambiguity of function—is it purgatorial or is it punitive? The rabbis, once again, recognize both possibilities.[18] Several sources attribute a cleansing function to Gehenna:[19] its fire purifies sinners 'as one purifies silver', and refines them 'as one refines gold'.[20] In light of this, one can understand the

[14] Jer. 19: 6.

[15] See Milikowsky, 'Gehenna and Jewish Sinners' (Heb.), 315.

[16] Ibid. 320. For examples of the use of Gehenna to refer to the eschatological period, see the following tannaitic sources cited by Milikowsky: Mekhilta, 'Beshalaḥ', 4 and 5 and Tosefta *San.* 13: 3 (ed. Zuckermandel, p. 434). For tannaitic evidence of the use of the term to refer to the afterlife, see *Sifrei al sefer devarim* 305 (ed. Finkelstein, pp. 326–7); *Avot derabi natan* 1: 25; *Kohelet rabah* 3: 21; and BT *Ber.* 28*b*. See Milikowsky, 'Gehenna and Jewish Sinners' (Heb.), 318–19. For amoraic material that Milikowsky cites in reference to Gehenna, see BT *San.* 110*b*, *Shab.* 149*b*, *Sot.* 10*b*, and *BB* 74*a* among others. See also JT *San.* 10: 1, 49*a* and 10: 3, 53*a*.

[17] Milikowsky, 'Gehenna and Jewish Sinners' (Heb.), 320 and 322. Milikowsky notes that in only one out of the five citations of Gehenna found in the Mishnah is it clear which meaning is being referred to.

[18] Whether purgative or punitive in nature, Gehenna is perceived by the rabbis as serving a retributive, rather than utilitarian, function. See Ehrlich, 'The Theory of Retributive Punishment' (Heb.). On the definitions of retributivism and utilitarianism, see pp. 2–3 there.

[19] See BT *RH* 17*a*, *Eruv.* 19*a*, and *BM* 58*b*, as well as JT *San.* 10: 3, 53*a*. J. Costa argues that *BM* 58*b* proves that the rabbis view Gehenna primarily as Purgatory, not as Hell. See Costa, *L'Au-delà et la resurrection*, 379.

[20] Zech. 13: 9. The rabbis cite this verse in reference to Gehenna in *RH* 17*a*.

above-mentioned statement of R. Akiva to mean that, after twelve months in Gehenna, having been cleansed of sin, the wicked are transferred to a place of reward. The scriptural verse quoted in a parallel tannaitic source supports such an interpretation:[21] after the requisite twelve-month sentence,[22] 'all flesh will come to bow down before Me, says God' (Isa. 66: 23). When that purification takes place, however, remains indistinct. According to one talmudic statement, it begins immediately after death,[23] whereas in another rabbinic source it is said to occur at the End of Days.[24] According to this latter interpretation, the *mishnah* in *Eduyot* which records R. Akiva's position is in line with the *mishnah* in *Sanhedrin* 10: 1, which assigns a portion in the World to Come to every Jew—even the wicked among them, after having completed their twelve-month atonement in Gehenna. The only exception to this general rule is a group of truly wicked individuals and sinners of the most grievous sort, whom the Mishnah proceeds to list in detail.

Apart from its purgative role, Gehenna also functions as a place where the wicked receive the appropriate recompense for their actions—punishment without any atoning effects. Two categories of wicked people suffer this fate: one for the duration of twelve months, in keeping with R. Akiva's

21 Milikowsky, 'Gehenna and Jewish Sinners' (Heb.), concluding section (*Seder olam*, ch. 3). See also *Midrash tanḥuma* on Gen. 33 (ed. Buber, p. 23), *Yalkut shimoni* on Isa. 66, and JT *San.* 10: 3, where Gehenna takes on a clearly purgative function at the End of Time. In the context of a discussion of who is deprived of resurrection and a portion in the World to Come, the Jerusalem Talmud records the following opinion regarding the generation of the Flood: 'And the Holy One, blessed be He, punishes the wicked in Gehenna for twelve months . . . and they will receive their punishment and they will have a portion in the World to Come.'

22 From the beginning of the verse 'It shall be that at every New Moon and on every sabbath' (Isa. 66: 23), the rabbis learn: 'From that month to that [same] month, behold, it is twelve months.'

23 In *Kid.* 31*b* the rabbis assert that a son should use the following phrase in reference to his deceased father within the first twelve months after his passing: 'Behold, I am the atonement of his bed [i.e. his soul]', which means that he can secure atonement for his father's soul. After the initial twelve months, he is to say, 'His memory should be a blessing for life in the World to Come', i.e. he can no longer achieve atonement for his father's soul. See Rashi ad loc., s.v. *mikan va'elakh*.

24 At the End of Days, the righteous will request God to have mercy on the wicked, whom he will then 'set upright from the dust, onto their feet' (*Seder eliyahu rabah* 3). The origin of the composition is a matter of scholarly debate; some assume a third-century core redaction, others a much later, tenth-century one. The author of the scholarly edition (M. Friedmann) is of the former opinion. See Stemberger, *Introduction to the Talmud and Midrash*, 340–1. See also *Midrash mishlei*, 17, which clearly refers to Gehenna in the eschatological period as it says, 'In the future to come, Gehenna is destined to cry out and say before the Holy One, blessed be He, "Give me the wicked." Our rabbis have taught, "The sentence of the wicked is twelve months."'

position, and another for all eternity. Thus, in *Rosh Hashanah* 17*a*, a salient text on the matter, the rabbis declare that the *poshei yisra'el begufan* (Jews who never in their life donned *tefilin*[25]) and the *poshei umot ha'olam begufan* (non-Jews who had committed sexual sins[26]) descend to Gehenna and are punished there for twelve months.[27] After that, their bodies perish, their souls are burned, and a wind scatters them under the soles of the feet of the righteous.[28] Other, more heinous, sinners such as 'the heretics, the informers, the apostates who denied the Torah and who denied the resurrection of the dead, those who separated themselves from the ways of the public, those who placed their dread over the living, and those who sinned and caused the public to sin, like Jeroboam son of Nevat and his companions', descend to Gehenna and are punished there for all eternity—so much so that 'Gehenna perishes and [still] they do not perish'.[29] It is only the truly wicked—individuals with grave ideological deviations or sinners of the worst calibre—whom the rabbis sentence to an interminable punishment in Gehenna. For all other sinners, the maximum duration of punishment or purgation can be no longer than twelve months.[30]

[25] Rav offers this interpretation on the same page of the Talmud (BT *RH* 17*a*). The tosafists neutralize Rav's interpretation in several ways: (1) One who learns Torah is equivalent to one who dons *tefilin*, and he is therefore exempt from this commandment. (2) To be considered a sinner in this regard, one has to reject the commandment out of revulsion and not because one is afraid that one lacks the appropriate degree of physical purity (R. Tam). (3) If someone repents of the sin, his repentance along with his death atones for his sin (so he does not suffer the punishment in Gehenna prescribed for those who never donned *tefilin*). See *Tosafot* ad loc., s.v. *karkafta delo manaḥ tefilin*. The tosafists feel a need to neutralize the meaning of the text here due to the blatant and widespread laxity in medieval Ashkenaz regarding the wearing of *tefilin*. On this phenomenon see Kanarfogel, 'Rabbinic Attitudes toward Non-Observance', 7–9.

[26] Again, this is Rav's interpretation; see *Tosafot RH* 17*a*, s.v. *amar rav be'averah*.

[27] This is a tannaitic teaching that originally appears in Tosefta *San.* 13: 1 (ed. Zuckermandel, p. 434) and is cited by the Talmud here.

[28] BT *RH* 17*a*. See also Milikowsky, 'Gehenna and Jewish Sinners' (Heb.), 311, in which this punishment applies only to the *poshei yisra'el*, with a slightly different formulation. See also *Yalkut shimoni*, Zech. 13.

[29] BT *RH* 17*a*. See also Milikowsky, 'Gehenna and Jewish Sinners' (Heb.), 311–12, and Tosefta *San.* 13: 4–5 (ed. Zuckermandel, p. 434), which have slightly different formulations regarding both the sinners and their punishment.

[30] There is one exception, however, in which the rabbis do assign eternal punishment to sinners who are not of the worst calibre. The Talmud in *BM* 58*b* and 59*a* allots eternal punishment for one who publicly embarrasses another person; he is listed as one of three types of sinner who descend to Gehenna and do not ascend (58*b*), and who are denied a portion in the World to Come (59*a*). Similarly, the same treatment awaits one who refers to his friend by a derogatory nickname. These statements reflect a novel teaching meant to underline the heinous nature of such acts (which one might not otherwise have anticipated); these people share the same punishment as the worst category of sinners. The statements may, in fact, be only for

And yet in R. Judah's tale a Jewish sinner testifies that he has suffered in Gehenna for several years. In deference to the accepted position, he distinguishes between his torment in the first year and that in subsequent years. What is the source for R. Judah's position—one that clearly opposes that of the rabbis?

Christian Notions of Posthumous Penance and Purgation

Although Augustine is the first to speak of a purgatorial fire which purifies the souls of the *non valde mali* (sinners who are not truly bad) for a certain period of time before the Last Judgement, his notion of post-mortem purgation is quite limited.[31] He is unclear about the nature of the fire,[32] and he speaks about the interim period after death as one of passive anticipation rather than active purification.[33] He denies the possibility of direct contact between the living and the dead,[34] and he does not connect purgation with prayer for the dead.[35]

In the writings of Gregory the Great one finds stronger affirmation of the concept of posthumous purgation; Gregory displays a certainty about it which Augustine lacks.[36] At the same time, he empowers the living to affect the world of the dead by combining the doctrine of ecclesiastical prayer for the dead with that of posthumous purgation,[37] and by stressing the importance of the role of the Eucharist in aiding the dead in the hereafter.[38] Saints, too, can intervene for the dead when invoked.[39] Gregory's clear and unequivocal articulation of these concepts proved to be critical for the emergence of the idea of posthumous purgation as doctrine in mainstream Christian thought.

Penance, that is, an attempt to placate God for post-baptismal sin, was

rhetorical effect, as is, in part, another talmudic statement pertaining to one who embarrasses his friend in public—'Better to throw oneself into a fiery furnace than embarrass one's friend in public.' See *Sot.* 10*b* and *BM* 59*a*. Dror Ehrlich also raises this possibility, arguing that these types of rabbinic statements, which earmark specific lower-level sins for punishment in Gehenna, were not necessarily meant to be taken literally. See Ehrlich, 'The Theory of Retibutive Punishment' (Heb.), 9 n. 32.

31 According to M. McLaughlin, Augustine himself is very tentative about the existence of post-mortem purgation, such that he treats it as 'a mere hypothesis'. See McLaughlin, *Consorting with Saints*, 189. For more on Augustine's position, see above, p. 160.

32 Atwell, 'From Augustine to Gregory the Great', 176, and Carozzi, *Le Voyage de l'âme dans l'au-delà*, 33.

33 Carozzi, *Le Voyage de l'âme dans l'au-delà*, 33.

34 Ibid.

35 Atwell, 'From Augustine to Gregory the Great', 185.

36 Ibid. 173, 177.

37 Ibid. 185. See also Ntedika, *L'Évocation de l'au-delá*, 105, 135.

38 Atwell, 'From Augustine to Gregory the Great', 179–80.

39 Ibid. 178–9.

another factor that played a key role in this process. In the Christian West of antiquity, individuals did not necessarily feel the need to do penance for their sins, whether in this life or the next. The power of mercy of the late Roman emperors was a model relying on which a sinner could hope for God's forgiveness. Angels and saints, patrons of the court of God, could plead on one's behalf.[40] It was only with the weakening of monarchical institutions of absolute power in the West, or in certain outlying areas such as Ireland, which had never submitted to such modes of government, that the notion of individual responsibility for sin and the attendant need to appease God arose.[41] A society characterized by horizontal bonds of control rather than vertical ones, and operating by means of a system of payments of honour and exchanges of pledges, where each debt had to be fully satisfied, was one in which the ideas of penance and purgation could take root.[42] By the turn of the eighth century, attitudes to God, sin, and forgiveness had decisively and irrevocably shifted in Western Christendom.[43] God was no longer envisioned as the all-powerful emperor but as the abbot of a great monastery. Notions of sin had become more internalized and individualized, and forgiveness no longer consisted in grand acts of pardon but was modelled after the extremely rigorous views of the Celtic penitential system regarding personal accountability.

In early medieval visionary literature, these new attitudes towards sin and penance became manifest in conceptions of the afterlife. The 'Vision of Fursey', an account of the Irish monk and preacher St Fursey's journey to the other world, was the first to draw on these new ideas. In it, the system of 'tariffed penances', developed in seventh-century Ireland by the monk Columbanus and disseminated on the Continent by monks and clerics,[44] was extended to the afterlife. In the vision, Fursey witnesses the purgatorial fires that burn the souls of the dead, yet only to the degree to which they still harbour sin. Since, according to the mechanics of the system, every sin is accounted for and its debt must be fully satisfied, an incomplete penance in this world may be completed in the next. Old notions of posthumous purgation, in which souls waited until Judgement Day to be cleansed by fire right before that ultimate event,[45] began now to be replaced with the

[40] Brown, 'Vers la naissance du purgatoire', 1252.

[41] Ibid. 1253–5. [42] Ibid. 1255. [43] Ibid. 1257, 1260–1.

[44] On the Celtic penitential system and its acceptance on the Continent, see McNeill and Gamer, *Medieval Handbooks of Penance*, 28–9.

[45] This is evident in the 'Vision of Adamnán', dated as early as the eighth century. See Seymour, *Irish Visions of the Other World*, 153.

newer notion of a fixed and gradated period of purgation, to ensue immediately after death and in accordance with the penalty still owed.[46]

The novel concept of immediate judgement of souls after death in the 'Vision of Fursey' and in the late seventh-century 'Life of Columba' had originated in early Christian Egyptian ascetic circles, which produced a seminal apocalyptic text, the 'Visio Pauli'. It was this concept of the afterlife that influenced Gregory's thought and enjoyed a resurgence in seventh-century Irish thought with the rise of monasticism there.[47] Irish monks, filled with missionary zeal, established monasteries in the Frankish kingdom and in England, where they circulated their ideas of posthumous penance and purgation.[48] Medieval handbooks of penance, available on the Continent, were born out of the desire of Irish missionaries to impose their own rigorous system of discipline upon the laity.[49]

The high medieval period witnessed a dramatic reworking of the doctrine of penance. The early medieval notion of total expiation of sin, to be performed through rigorous and ascetic external penances, slowly began to

46 Dunn, 'Gregory the Great', 240, 247–50. Dunn argues that the Irish system of tariffed penances was pivotal to the development of this new notion of posthumous purgation, and that the novel ideas found in Book IV of Gregory's *Dialogues* can only have emerged from such an environment. Following F. Clark's lead, Dunn denies the authenticity of the *Dialogues*. She claims that, instead of being penned in the 590s as an original Gregorian text, it was a composite work redacted by English monks around 670. These monks were well versed in 'a theology of purgatory which had developed from the system of private confession and tariffed penance known in Ireland, England and the Hiberno-Frankish monasteries of the continent' (p. 253).

M. Smyth validates the novelty inherent in the 'Vision of Fursey', while still maintaining the authenticity of Gregory's *Dialogues*. Although it is true that none of Gregory's successors make reference to the novel elements of his doctrine on posthumous purgation (an argument advanced by Clark and Dunn), this silence is due to the slow or even delayed acceptance of his original ideas on the matter. Even in seventh-century Ireland, the traditional view on the fate of souls after death (i.e. that, except in the case of saints, the decision regarding Christian souls would be made only in the fire of the Last Judgement) is reflected in a wide range of texts. This view persisted in Ireland as late as the twelfth century. The new concept of immediate judgement stands in marked contrast to these more standard and well-accepted texts. See Smyth, 'The Origins of Purgatory', 91–132.

Le Goff also maintains that Gregory's work is authentic, yet he explains the novel approach to posthumous purgation in the *Dialogues* in another way. The early medieval Church embarked on a conscious campaign to quash any records of otherworldly journeys because of the popular elements they contained. Gregory's writings on purgation and the afterlife appear novel only because they are the only extant fragments of what otherwise would have been a much larger and richer corpus of material on the subject that had not survived. See Le Goff, 'The Learned and Popular Dimensions of Journeys in the Otherworld', 34. According to Le Goff, the genre of early medieval visionary literature was an outgrowth of a composite and varied source group, only one segment of which was of Celtic-Irish provenance (ibid. 23–4).

47 Smyth, 'The Origins of Purgatory', 91.

48 Dunn, 'Gregory the Great', 253.

49 McNeill and Gamer, *Medieval Handbooks of Penance*, 24–9.

yield to the belief in the power of the inner contrition and sorrowful confession of the penitent to remove some parts of the sin.[50] Beginning with Anselm of Canterbury in the eleventh century and maturing in the *Sentences* of the scholastic Peter Lombard in the mid-twelfth century, penitential theory was cast in a new light. Due to the sinfulness of man, St Anselm postulated, no amount of earthly penance could ever render full satisfaction for sin before God. Anselm's interpretation emerged precisely at a time when laypeople were finding it increasingly difficult to perform fully the rigorous penances then in practice.[51] Changing notions of the concept of justice in canon, feudal, and civil law of the twelfth century provided the backdrop to a new understanding of the nature of sin and penance. The doctrine of intentionality, which emerged from these legal systems, entered into the realm of theology. That doctrine enabled Peter Lombard to distinguish between the *culpa*, or guilt, of sin and its *poena*, or punishment. Since intentional sin was a product of will and consent, reasoned Lombard, its guilt (which should necessitate damnation) could be mitigated through contrition and sincere confession. Its punishment, however, remained as a debt that had to be satisfied by means of penance.

Such a separation between the two dimensions of sin created an opening that Purgatory would fill. If a sincere penitent managed only to remove the *culpa* of sin during his lifetime, a post-mortem penance in Purgatory could substitute for a Church-imposed one that was left unfulfilled.[52] Both Hugh of St Victor in the twelfth century and William of Auvergne in the thirteenth formulated a conception of Purgatory based entirely on this notion: purgatorial penance was but a continuation of earthly penance.[53] The same period saw the development of the concept of venial sin—a lighter sin which stemmed from one's weakness in flesh, was not damnable, and therefore could be atoned for through penance in Purgatory. It was to be distinguished from cardinal sin, which stemmed from knowledge and intent, was damnable, and could only be expunged by means of unremitting punishment in Hell.[54]

[50] Mansfield, *The Humiliation of Sinners*, 2. Although Mansfield argues against too rigid a demarcation between the terms 'public' versus 'private' and 'external' versus 'internal' when it comes to a shift in the system of penance over the course of the twelfth and thirteenth centuries, she still acknowledges the new 'stress on private confession and the necessity of contrition' for the individual sinner. On the appearance of emotion and tears in penitence, see Payen, *Le Motif de repentir*, and Nagy and Boureau, *Le Don des larmes au Moyen Age*.

[51] Watkins, 'Sin, Penance and Purgatory', 3–4.

[52] Le Goff, *The Birth of Purgatory*, 213–14. See also Mansfield, *The Humiliation of Sinners*, 48–9.

[53] Le Goff, *The Birth of Purgatory*, 140, 243.

[54] Ibid. 216–17.

Despite the great advances in the theological conceptualization of Purgatory in the twelfth century and its popularization in the thirteenth, there is significant evidence that it was not uniformly assimilated into the medieval consciousness. Few, at best, grasped the scholastic definition of Purgatory in its pure form.[55] Visionary literature, exempla collections, and even the liturgy testify to a blurring of distinctions between Hell and Purgatory in the minds of many—clerics and peasants alike—in the twelfth, thirteenth, and even fourteenth centuries. Furthermore, older notions of posthumous penance, firmly rooted in popular consciousness, persisted at this time alongside the more novel developments taking place in the realm of sin and punishment. The need for total expiation of sin in this world—a vestige of the Irish system of tariffed penance—the concept of death as a waiting period, the lack of an assigned place for purgation, the idea that only a select few would be saved while most souls would be eternally damned, the belief that little could be done to aid the dead, and a general feeling of doom and helplessness—all these elements remained evident in visionary literature, ghost stories, and exempla of the period in which Purgatory emerged and was popularized.[56]

55 The *Liber de anima corpore exuta sive de regressu animarum ab inferia* of the Parisian theologian Hugh of Pisa testifies that, even in the writings of the scholastics, which were the 'birthplace' of the doctrine of Purgatory according to Le Goff, there exists confusion regarding the meaning of the term. Hugh speaks of at least two hells, each of which has several divisions. One of these is home to both souls in need of purgation and less sinful souls. These souls suffer hellish tortures, such as extremes of heat and cold and fire, and receive aid from the living through suffrages on their behalf. See Edwards, 'The Idea of Post Mortem Purgation', 140–1. Edwards presents strong evidence to support the claim that the purely scholarly definition of Purgatory in the period of its dissemination was far from widely accepted. He writes, 'We have cause to wonder whether the Augustino-Gregorian system of post-mortem purgation taught by such men as Aelfric was either universally preached or popularly accepted' (ibid. 141).

56 C. S. Watkins, through careful and highly nuanced analysis of twelfth- and thirteenth-century visions, as well as of several ghost tales from varying twelfth-century sources, has demonstrated that older notions of penance and purgation still dominated the minds of parishioners in the Anglo-Norman realm, despite the dissemination of newer ideas. A gap is shown to have existed between the knowledge and acceptance of these newer notions by the parishioners and lower clergy on the one hand and by the higher clergy on the other. In a representative sample, evidence from the exempla shows that several members of the religious orders embraced the novel ideas, as opposed to one from a secular order who clung to older notions of sin, penance, and purgation. The thirteenth century saw greater progress in the dissemination of the newer ideas. See Watkins, 'Sin, Penance, and Purgatory', 3–33. The twelfth-century 'Vision of Tundale', despite its purgatorial content, is devoid of any mention of the efficacy of masses, prayers, or alms for the dead. Instead, the dead await purgation at the time of the Last Judgement. See Seymour, *Irish Visions*, 153. Edwards, 'The Idea of Post Mortem Purgation', 228–47, documents the existence of older notions of penance and purgation among varying classes of the medieval population of western Europe, and extends the evidence to the fourteenth and fifteenth centuries.

Pre-Purgatorial Notions in *Sefer Ḥasidim*

Despite the affinity of the Pietist tales with thirteenth-century Christian notions about the afterlife popularized in the exempla of the time, there is much evidence in *Sefer ḥasidim* that points to the existence and persistence of older notions of posthumous penance which did not conform to the scholastic doctrine of Purgatory. These notions were firmly rooted in popular consciousness and were, in part, nourished by pre-Christian beliefs.

Pietist penitential ideas emanated directly from early medieval notions of sin and penance, and bore the imprint of the Celtic system of tariffed penances.[57] Aside from very few instances of inner contrition that appear in *Sefer ḥasidim*,[58] the Pietists' notion of repentance proceeded in an entirely different direction. It was based on acts of external penance assigned by a *ḥakham* or *moreh*, much as a doctor prescribes a cure, to sinners who had made a verbal confession.[59] These acts of penance, whose relation to the sin was at times arbitrary and which were unconnected to the penitent's state of mind, reflected the early medieval understanding of penance as satisfaction rendered for a debt owed to God.[60] Private, individualized confession of sin before an ascetic monk or nun who assigned acts of penance or commuted them is one of the main features of the early Irish penitential system. It departed from earlier forms of penance in the Church, which were pri-

[57] For a full discussion of the scholarly debate regarding Christian influence on the Pietist doctrine of penance, see above, Introduction, n. 13.

[58] See the following brief lines regarding the penitent: 'He should pray with a broken heart about his sins', 'he should pray about it with all his heart', and 'he should pray and subdue his heart until he does repentance', in *SḤ* 41, 44, and 1238 respectively. One instance of a penitent's prayer which displays some elements of interiority can be found in *SḤ* 41.

[59] Repentance is synonymous with penance in the mind of the Pietists. For this reason, they employ the same term, *teshuvah*, to refer to both concepts, in the same way as the German term *Busse* refers to both. See A. Rubin, 'The Concept of Repentance among the *Hasidey 'Ashkenaz*', 169–70. On the requirement of confession before a sage, see *SḤ* 38, p. 40. In the 'Tale of Three Confessors' (*SḤ* 52–3), each sinner fulfils this requirement and confesses his sin before the *ḥakham*. On the role of the *ḥakham* and the assignment of penance, see *SḤ* 38, 17, and 43. The analogy between the *ḥakham* and a doctor is made explicit in *SḤ* 17.

Rubin notes that the Latin word for 'confessor' in the Christian penitentials includes the meanings of both 'teacher' and 'doctor' (both terms are mentioned in *Sefer ḥasidim*), because 'the offices of teacher and confessor were often combined in Celtic Christianity'; 'The Concept of Repentance among the *Hasidey 'Ashkenaz*', 173. Examples of the commutation of penance are found in *SḤ* 19, p. 24, where the milder option of fasting for three sets of three days and nights within one year is offered instead of the original penance involving repeated cycles of fasting for sets of three days and three nights for a period of three years, and in *SḤ* 109, where giving charity is offered in place of fasting as penance for a sin.

[60] A. Rubin, 'The Concept of Repentance among the *Hasidey 'Ashkenaz*', 164–5, 168–9.

marily public and ceremonial in nature.[61] *Sefer ḥasidim* advocates this newer method of individual confession. Additionally, the Pietists' proclivity for ascetic behaviour and self-mortification and the rigorous nature of their penances had parallels in early Irish monastic traditions. These traditions, having been incorporated in the eleventh century into the penitential tract of a mainstream canonical text penned by Bishop Burchard of Worms, became available in the Rhineland before the emergence of the Pietist movement.[62]

Ascetic acts, sometimes assuming 'extreme and fantastic forms', were a novel dimension of the Old Irish penitentials and distinguished them from the earlier monastic discipline and the more traditional 'prayers and outcries to God' described therein.[63] Many of these acts—extended periods and repeated cycles of fasting, lying in water for long periods of time, flagellation, voluntary exile for murder—existed in both Irish and Pietist penitential systems.[64] Rigorous as they were, these penances were to be doled out in small increments; both *Sefer ḥasidim* and Irish penitential manuals caution the authority figure assigning the penance to reveal it in a stepwise and calculated fashion. Exposure to the penance in its entirety could overwhelm the penitent so that he or she may never come to perform it.[65] The Pietists announce the primacy of suffering as an integral and even indispensable component of their atonement doctrine in multiple declaratory statements found within *Sefer ḥasidim*.[66]

Furthermore, fundamental elements of each of the four categories of

[61] The Lateran decree of 1215, requiring confession of all Christians at least once a year, was a direct outgrowth of the acceptance, with modifications, into mainstream Christianity of this feature of the early Irish penitential system. See Fratzen, *The Literature of Penance in Anglo-Saxon England*, 5–6, and McNeill and Gamer, *Medieval Handbooks of Penance*, 28–9.

[62] Fishman, 'The Penitential System of *Ḥasidei Ashkenaz*', 215–17. On the novel dimensions of Burchard's *Decretum*, see Austin, *Shaping Church Law Around the Year 1000*. On its diffusion, see Gilchrist, 'The Perception of Jews in the Canon Law', 11–12. On the role it played in Gratian's *Decretum*, see Larson, *Master of Penance*.

[63] See McNeill and Gamer, *Medieval Handbooks of Penance*, 30.

[64] Ibid. 30–5. See *SḤ* 19, p. 24, and *SḤ* 50 on fasting and lying in water; *SḤ* 1555 and 1556 on self-flagellation; and *SḤ* 175 on voluntary exile. It is not unlikely that the Pietists' emphasis on the protracted recitation of psalms is linked to the penitential singing of the psalmody so common in Irish monasteries. See McNeill and Gamer, 30–1, and the discussion of the Pietists' doctrine of prayer above, pp. 194–6.

[65] See Fishman, 'The Penitential System of *Ḥasidei Ashkenaz*', 209–10 and nn. 32 and 33 there.

[66] These statements include the following among others: 'Behold, suffering redeems him, as it says, "In every pain there will be gain" [Prov. 14: 23]' (*SḤ* 278, 385, and 1133), and 'No sin is removed without harm, as it says, "Behold, this has touched your lips; your iniquity has gone away and your sin shall be atoned for" [Isa. 6: 7]' (*SḤ* 43, p. 41).

repentance outlined in *Sefer ḥasidim* mirror those found in these same early Irish traditions.[67] *Teshuvah haba'ah*, the first such Pietist category, prepares the sinner for successfully overcoming trial, should the sin present itself again.[68] This act of self-imposed trial finds its parallel in an act of penance of Irish origin practised by Christian penitents on the Continent, in which temptation was deliberately aroused and then vanquished.[69] The Pietists' second category, *teshuvat hakatuv*, premises itself upon the voluntary acceptance of suffering as a means of atonement. Pietists are to accept suffering upon themselves in equal measure to, or even in excess of, the punishment mandated by the Bible for a specific sin.[70] Asceticism, often in its extreme form, was a key element in the Irish penitential system. Thirdly, the extensive network of prohibitions of even permitted activities set up around a possible area of temptation formed the basis of the Pietist category of *teshuvat hagader*. Here, repentance was achieved by guarding off and refraining from anything, including the permissible, that might lead to a repetition of the sin committed in the past.[71] We find a similar notion in the prologue to the penitential of Cummean—a work attributed to a mid-seventh-century Irish abbot and well known on the Continent in the ninth century. The author offers the following advice: 'Contraries are cured by contraries; for he who freely commits that which is forbidden ought freely to restrain himself from that which is otherwise permissible.'[72] Lastly, *teshuvat hamishkal*, which demands proportionality in terms of both intensity and duration between the ascetic act of penance and the pleasure involved in perpetrating the sin, is closely associated with the early medieval notion of penance as 'payment of amends, a form of compensation to God for having sinned'.[73] An example of penance that is similar to the Pietist principle of proportional compensation appears in an Old Irish table of commutations from the eighth century:

> Now every penance, for both the severity and the length of time in which one is at it, depends on the greatness of the sin and on the space of time one perseveres in it, and on the reason for which it is done, and on the zeal with which one departs from it afterwards.[74]

[67] The four categories of repentance are outlined in *SḤ* 37.

[68] Ibid.

[69] See Fishman, 'The Penitential System of *Ḥasidei Ashkenaz*', 208–9. See also McNeill and Gamer, *Medieval Handbooks of Penance*, 143.

[70] See *SḤ* 19, p. 23.

[71] *SḤ* 37.

[72] McNeill and Gamer, *Medieval Handbooks of Penance*, 101. See also A. Rubin, 'The Concept of Repentance among the *Hasidey 'Ashkenaz*', 167–8.

[73] See A. Rubin, 'The Concept of Repentance among the *Hasidey 'Ashkenaz*', 169.

[74] McNeill and Gamer, *Medieval Handbooks of Penance*, 143.

Pietist doctrine drew upon early medieval notions not only in the mechanics of penance but also in other aspects. The need for the total expiation of sin in this world, an important underlying element of the penitential landscape of the time, is a prominent theme in *Sefer ḥasidim*. It appears in an ideal form in the persona of the hasidic master, who voluntarily takes upon himself severe forms of external penance in total disproportion to the sins he commits. Likening himself to the messiah as represented by Isaiah's suffering servant (Isa. 52–3),[75] he wishes to fully atone in this world not only for his own sins but for those of others as well. Additionally, R. Judah repeatedly asserts that one should take voluntary suffering upon oneself in this world whenever possible in order to reduce punishment after death.[76] Even the smallest amount of self-imposed suffering will be deducted from the total amount of suffering that awaits one in Gehenna as punishment for one's sins.[77] To be totally cleansed of sin (*lihyot naki mehakadosh barukh hu*) in this world, so that one is not called to judgement before God (*shelo yikare ladin*) in the next, is the ostensible goal of both *teshuvat hakatuv* and *teshuvat hamishkal*.[78] A similar function of penance is found in the early Irish monastic tradition. The above-cited Old Irish table of commutations lists various harsh and extensive bodily torments to be practised by the penitent in order to 'sav[e] a soul out of Hell'—as a means of redeeming the soul from future punishment.[79] In fact, a 'primary purpose' of the Pietist doctrine of voluntary suffering was 'to save the sinner from future divine retribution by forcing him to anticipate it in the present'.[80]

It is precisely in this manner that we ought to understand one of the main goals of the Pietist movement and a prime reason for the redaction of *Sefer ḥasidim* itself. Like the Irish monastic penitentials, *Sefer ḥasidim* strives to 'save souls from death and Gehenna'[81] through the revelation of the dictates of Pietism to the uninitiated—which the *ḥasid ḥakham* alone is privy to. In his programmatic statement at the very beginning of the book,

[75] This passage in Isaiah became the focus of an intense polemic between Jews and Christians in the medieval period; see Neubauer and Driver, *The 'Suffering Servant' of Isaiah*.

[76] 'Everything [all forms of pain and suffering] is calculated against the suffering of Gehenna' (*SḤ* 15, pp. 15–16). See also *SḤ* 22, 630, and 632.

[77] *SḤ* 15, p. 15.

[78] *SḤ* 22, 630, and 632. In *SḤ* 632, R. Judah cites as proof an incident which occurred in the days of R. Hai Gaon. Here the penitent was so desirous of total expiation that he doubted whether his near-fatal flogging, which was repeated on three separate occasions, was sufficient to completely atone for his crime of murder. R. Judah assures his readers that this self-imposed penance had achieved its purpose (*ki nitkaper lo*) because the penitent embraced it with joy.

[79] See McNeill and Gamer, *Medieval Handbooks of Penance*, 142–3, no. 7, nos. 1, 2, 3, and 4.

[80] A. Rubin, 'The Concept of Repentance among the *Hasidey 'Ashkenaz*', 169.

[81] *SḤ* 1474.

Samuel the Pious, father of R. Judah and reputed author of the first thirteen paragraphs of the work,[82] asserts that his aim is to make known the *retson haboré*, the larger, hidden Will of God, for breaches of which people are being punished whether they are aware of that Will or not.[83] A main pillar of Pietism is to 'act for the common good', and failure to do so is a lethal sin that carries grave punishment.[84] More than this, Samuel the Pious advocates compulsion and force to correct the behaviour of others and to make it conform to Pietist teaching and practice. He interprets the Israelites' unanimous declaration accepting the Torah as a mission in the compulsion of others rather than as mere acceptance of the Law.[85]

Although not as extreme in his formulation, R. Judah reveals a similar pedagogical drive to correct others in his opening statements to a section on the study of Torah. He interprets Psalm 19: 8, 'God's Torah is perfect, restoring the soul', in the following manner:

> Which is a Torah that is 'perfect'? One that 'restores the soul'. Whoever helps the soul obtain merit and returns it from Gehenna [so that it rests] under the wings of the Divine Presence, as it says, 'And many he turned away from iniquity' [Mal. 2: 6] . . . For this reason, one should involve oneself in helping the public perform meritorious acts, so that they should not sin through him. When is the Torah 'perfect'? When one does good deeds that cause [another's] soul to be restored from death and from Gehenna.[86]

R. Judah then proceeds to list examples of Torah scholars whom the Talmud records as having resuscitated someone or rescued someone from Gehenna.[87] Is this not what the Pietists endeavour to do in revealing the 'dual revelation' inherent in the *retson haboré*, along with and including the unique dictates of Pietist penance? Do they not do so in order to save the public from unknown sin, so that they do not face punishment in this

[82] A. Epstein attributes possible authorship of these paragraphs to R. Samuel on the basis of a gematria by R. Margeshet. See the final note on p. 490 of Wistinetzky's edn. of *Sefer ḥasidim*. Ivan Marcus has named the first twenty-six paragraphs of *Sefer ḥasidim Sefer hayirah*; see Marcus, *Piety and Society*, 27.

[83] *SḤ* 1, top of p. 2. See Soloveitchik, 'Three Themes in *Sefer Ḥasidim*', 325–6.

[84] Soloveitchik, 'Three Themes in *Sefer Ḥasidim*', 325–6.

[85] In Exod. 24: 3, the People of Israel declare, 'All the words which the Lord has spoken we will do [*na'aseh*].' R. Samuel reads the last word differently: instead of *na'aseh* (we will do), he reads *ne'aseh* (we will compel). See Soloveitchik, 'Three Themes in *Sefer Ḥasidim*', 327.

[86] *SḤ* 1474.

[87] R. Judah mentions R. Hanina bar Hama resuscitating a dead servant (*AZ* 10*b*), Rabah reviving R. Zeira (*Meg.* 7*b*), and R. Yohanan bringing Rav Kahana back from the dead (*BK* 117*b*). In reference to rescue from Gehenna, he cites the case of R. Yohanan, who rescued his master Elisha ben Avuyah (*Ḥag.* 15*b*).

world by premature death,[88] or, even worse, through the dreaded Divine judgement in Gehenna?

Eternality of Punishment in *Sefer Ḥasidim*: The Hunt Narratives

Prevalent in the early medieval penitential tradition, the desire to avoid post-mortem punishment stemmed from a belief not only in the bitterness of that future punishment but also in its eternal nature. Finian, an Irish monastic founder and teacher of the second quarter of the sixth century, explicitly states this when he writes in his penitential, 'But the medicine of immediate penance in the present time is needful to prevent perpetual pains in the future.'[89] Purgatory had as yet little significance and so perpetual pain awaited the sinner.

Eternality of punishment is evident in *Sefer ḥasidim* in the tales of encounters with groups of dead, known as Hellequin's Hunt. As has been noted, the effects of Christianization are apparent in these narratives as the horde of dangerous returning dead is transformed into an army of sinners sentenced to march endlessly on Earth as punishment for their sins. However, accounts of Hellequin's Hunt do not only reflect the shift from pagan beliefs to Christian ones but also changes in the notion of penance. Older ideas—such as the need to totally expiate a sin during one's lifetime, the harshness and long duration of the assigned penances, their external nature, as well as the overall feeling of doom and utter hopelessness regarding matters of the afterlife—eventually gave way to newer ones that involved inner contrition, the existence of a time limit to purgation, aid from the living, and hope for salvation. The accounts themselves testify to this transition; at times, the elements of different stages are layered within the same narrative.

Stories which reflect older notions of penance tell of a multitude of dead people who are damned to endless suffering and are punished with either specific repetitive tortures or non-specific wandering without ever achieving salvation. The majority of the dead do not solicit aid from the living; the few that do, receive help that serves only to ease their torment,

[88] Most often, the punishment that follows lack of conformity to Pietist teaching is death within a very short period of time; the phrase 'it was not long before he died' is not uncommon in *Sefer ḥasidim*.

[89] See McNeill and Gamer, *Medieval Handbooks of Penance*, 91 no. 22, and A. Rubin, 'The Concept of Repentance among the *Hasidey 'Ashkenaz*', 169.

not to redeem them from it.[90] An example of this latter type is a tale of the Hunt recorded by the Anglo-Norman monk Orderic Vitalis many years after it occurred.[91] Orderic preserves in his version the most extensive account of the troop of the dead, who are sighted by a young priest named Walkelin. Walkelin sees several waves of large numbers of people passing by and marching on endlessly—peasants, then women, followed by clergy and monks, and finally knights. Orderic breaks up the tale with his own comments, which introduce some elements of the newer theological teachings regarding penance. According to these teachings, the dead undergo purgation rather than punishment; their torment is time-bound rather than eternal; and the living can release them from their suffering through the performance of prayers and masses, and by giving alms. Such teachings inject a message of hope into the otherwise gloomy narrative.[92]

Sefer ḥasidim contains an account of Hellequin's Hunt that is similar to that of Orderic. To recall, in this narrative a great army of wagons full of dead people is being pulled by other dead people. These two groups, the wagon riders and the wagon drawers, continually change places. When questioned by the living witness as to why they do this, the dead respond that they are being punished for sins that they committed while alive—they were wont to sport with women and young girls.[93]

As in the vision of Walkelin, the penitential atmosphere here is an early medieval one. A rigorous external penance is assigned to those who have committed some form of sexual sin. This penance, however, while being

[90] See e.g. Raoul Glaber's account of the vision of the Hunt seen by the priest Fratterius (*Rodulfi Glabri historiarum, libri quinque*, quoted in Schmitt, *Ghosts in the Middle Ages*, 102); the vision of the red knights described in the *Book of Miracles of St Foi* (quoted in *Ghosts in the Middle Ages*, 104–6); and Walter Map's report of the last sighting of Hellequin's Hunt in England in *De nugis curialium*, 371. See also *Ghosts in the Middle Ages*, 111–12.

[91] *The Ecclesiastical History of England*, ii. 511–20.

[92] Carl Watkins 'reads' Orderic's description of Hellequin's Hunt in just such a fashion. Using evidence from the text, he demonstrates how Walkelin and his fellow parishioners in early twelfth-century England were quite sceptical about the power of suffrages to aid the dead. For this reason, Walkelin refuses the request of a dead knight named William of Glos, who asks him to petition his wife for aid on his behalf. Only at the end of the lengthy narrative is Walkelin persuaded to believe in the power of suffrages. This time, he accepts the plea for help of his dead brother Robert. This newfound belief is very much a product, according to Watkins, of the novel theological insights that Orderic inserts into the narrative. See Watkins, 'Sin, Penance, and Purgatory', 8–11. In the account of the Hunt recorded in the German chronicle of Ekkehard, a similar picture of the dead emerges. The count Emicho, one of an assembly of damned, torture-ridden knights, detaches himself from the group and tells the living that their prayers and alms can redeem him. See Ekkehardus Uraugiensis, *Chronica*, quoted in Schmitt, *Ghosts in the Middle Ages*, 110.

[93] *SḤ* 63.

performed on Earth, also reflects the severity of punishment meted out to sinners in Hell. The author describes a repetitive punishment that is Sisyphean in nature—a theme encountered not only in Orderic's story but also in early medieval visionary narratives of Hell.[94] The punishment is also of eternal duration, without any hope of salvation or even of mitigation of suffering. Although the masses of the dead are deprived of help in Orderic's account, some individuals do manage to break away and appeal for aid, with one of them even succeeding in obtaining it.[95] In R. Judah's version of the Hunt, however, not one from the horde asks for help. With wagonloads of dead people suffering hopelessly and endlessly, the Pietist vision describes a veritable 'army of the damned'.[96] Both R. Judah's and Walkelin's stories depict a Hell that is 'thickly populated' and where most people suffer eternal punishment without much hope of redemption—a dismal picture indeed.[97]

As Orderic attaches his own theological comments to Walkelin's narration of the vision, so does R. Judah in *Sefer ḥasidim*.[98] After relating the story, he cites a string of biblical verses to substantiate its message: Scripture warns that people who sin will be punished after death by being forced to act literally like animals and draw heavy wagons.[99] R. Judah then uses another verse (Ps. 49: 15) to extend the parameters of the punishment described in the vision, making clear that the sinners are truly beaten like wagon-pulling animals. Additionally, by citing this particular verse, which speaks of a large group of people who 'are destined for the pit', that is, Gehenna, he voices his belief that many are condemned to eternal punishment.

After citing the biblical verses, R. Judah comments: 'Whoever performs during his lifetime an animalistic action, he shall work in that world [i.e. the

94 In Orderic's account, a 'crowd of women who seemed to the priest to be innumerable', and who are guilty of 'the obscene allurements and filthy delights to which they had abandoned themselves when living among men', suffer the following torment: mounted on horseback, they are forced to ride on a saddle from which red-hot nails protrude. As they ride, they are lifted off the saddle by the wind, only to drop down upon the burning nails a few minutes later, until the wind picks up again. They continue riding in this repetitive manner of lift, drop, lift, drop endlessly. See Orderic Vitalis, *The Ecclesiastical History of England*, ii. 513. (It is interesting to note that, whereas Christian sources often detail the punishments of women involved in sexual sin, Pietist sources only detail those of men for such sins.)

On the Sisyphean nature of punishments in Hell narrated in early medieval visionary accounts, see Seymour, *Irish Visions*, 155 (the 'Vision of Drythelm'). See also H. Braet, 'Les Visions de l'invisible', 405–18, and Aubrun, 'Caractères et portée religieuse', 117.

95 Walkelin accepts his dead brother Robert's plea for help; see ibid. 519.

96 The term is Schmitt's: *Ghosts in the Middle Ages*, 102.

97 Watkins, 'Sin, Penance, and Purgatory', 11.

98 *SḤ* 63.

99 See p. 79 above.

afterlife] like an animal. And he who subjugates people, or places his fear upon people, they will make him serve in that world like an animal. And even one who mistreats his animal.'[100] Firstly, he validates the appropriateness of the punishment meted out in the vision by stating that, for one who acted like an animal in his lifetime (involved himself in sexual sin), it is fitting to work like an animal in the hereafter. R. Judah thus offers his approbation for the assignment of eternal punishment for sexual sin. While in consonance with the views reflected in this narrative as well as in others,[101] such punishment for sexual sin is in conflict with rabbinic teaching on the matter.

Having demonstrated how the punishment fits the crime, R. Judah adds on a list of other sinners who can anticipate a similar fate. It is not only those involved in sexual sin who are forced in the hereafter to carry the workload of animals, but also those who have enslaved others or aroused undue fear in them, or even mistreated their animals.[102] By broadening the category of sinners who are sentenced to eternal punishment, he is once again going beyond the dictates of rabbinic tradition. Moreover, he paints an even gloomier picture of the afterlife than that already apparent in the vision: ever more people join the 'army of the damned', for whom there is no hope of redemption.

As mentioned in an earlier chapter, two other ghost stories in *Sefer ḥasidim* share prominent features of Hellequin's Hunt.[103] In the first of a pair of tales, a man meets a ghost who has had to wander ceaselessly in the forests because of his theft of a certain field and an object. In a story recorded by Caesarius of Heisterbach—which parallels this Pietist tale and may possibly have been its source—the wandering dead man is a former knight who has been sentenced to wear a red-hot sheepskin and to carry a great load of earth as a measure-for-measure punishment for his crimes. As his sons refuse to help him atone for his sin, he suffers perpetually.[104] I have already noted the fact that the punishments meted out to the dead in both the Pietist narrative and its German parallel bear a striking similarity to the harsh external penances characteristic of other Hunt narratives, and

[100] *SḤ* 63.

[101] See n. 94 above for women's punishment for sexual sins in Orderic's account.

[102] *SḤ* 63. For an identical statement regarding these additional groups of sinners and their posthumous punishments, see *SḤ* 144. For a similar statement denouncing those who mistreat their animals, see *SḤ* 138.

[103] *SḤ* 35. See above, pp. 73–9.

[104] Caesarius of Heisterbach, *Dialogue*, 12: 14. The tale also appears in Banks (ed.), *Alphabet of Tales*, 352 no. 522, and in a fourteenth-century Latin manuscript, Addit 18364 fo. 55, found in *Catalogue of Romances*, iii. 615 no. 131.

to early medieval penances in general. Beyond this, certain hellish qualities pervade Caesarius's tale. The knight rides a black horse 'whose nostrils shot smoke and fire';[105] his penance involves burning; and the aid he solicits will serve only to lessen his torment, not to release him from it. Furthermore, since the dead do not appeal to the living for help in the Pietist account, and in its German parallel the father's request is callously ignored, the dead are apparently condemned to eternal unrest. This creates an atmosphere of helplessness that is indicative of an early medieval approach to penitence.

The second of the pair of Pietist tales tells of a servant who chances upon the ghost of his former master.[106] Forced to wander on account of having stolen someone's patrimony, the master asks the servant to instruct his wife to return the land in order that he can obtain rest. Whereas in this tale the deceased does beseech the living person for help, it is not the standard type of aid requested by someone who is being tormented in Purgatory, such as prayers, alms, or masses. Rather, it is merely the restitution of ill-gotten gains that is sought. Furthermore, although the dead man here has hope for redemption, we are never informed whether he has received the help he requested; the tale ends without any resolution for him.

This lack of resolution is itself a statement: it highlights the fact that the Pietist version deviates from the common form of this type of tale. Ghost tales that employ a *signum* to substantiate the appearance of the ghost and to testify to the truth of his message usually end with the living accepting that proof and procuring the necessary aid for the deceased. This is true in the case of the Hunt narratives: whenever the *signum* is offered, the living provide help. The same applies in the exempla literature, where the *signum* and the aid offered become permanent features of the standard tales related by the mendicants. Is the omission of a resolution in *Sefer ḥasidim* due to R. Judah's proclivity for brief, laconic storytelling or does it reflect an intentional decision on his part, perhaps to deny a non-Jew successful release from a state of eternal punishment? In any event, the fact that neither Pietist story mentions the redemption of the deceased enhances their hellish dimension.

It is precisely the hellish nature of the Hunt narratives that prompted Orderic to interject his own interpretation of the spectacle. Upon describing Walkelin's testimony of the various groups of sinners who parade before him lamenting their torments, Orderic offers the following instruction:

105 The black steed, as well as 'an immense army' of 'only blackness', appear also in Orderic's account of the Hunt; see *The Ecclesiastical History of England*, ii. 514.

106 *SḤ* 35.

All the dross of carnal desires is therefore consumed in the fires of Purgatory and purified by sufferings of various degrees as the Judge Eternal ordains. So that, as a vessel cleansed from rust and thoroughly polished is laid up in a treasury, so the soul, purified from all taint of sin, is admitted into Paradise, where it enjoys perfect happiness unalloyed by fear or care.[107]

Whereas the spectacle described by Walkelin exudes a Hell-like atmosphere, Orderic, aware of the theological difficulty in the appeals of the damned for aid, and seeing an opportunity to end the torments of those condemned to eternal punishment, explains the scene in light of the doctrine of Purgatory, with which the parish priest is not yet familiar. Orderic asserts that the dead who appear to be undergoing eternal punishment and hellish torture are really only suffering purgatorial torment, which is limited in time and which can be mitigated or abrogated through the suffrages of the living—prayers, masses, and alms.[108]

R. Judah, by contrast, accepts at face value the Hunt tale that he retells; he makes no attempt to correct the narrative in light of a theology of purgation. In both the second Pietist tale and Caesarius's story, the pleas of the dead for aid from the living issue from a place of eternal torment—more Hell-like than purgatorial. The tales of Hellequin's Hunt recounted in *Sefer ḥasidim* are situated in a penitential climate devoid of a belief in Purgatory.

Although R. Judah does not make any attempt to introduce a theology of purgation into the narrative of the second Pietist story, he does attach a commentary of a different sort after presenting the pair of tales:

These occur regarding the Gentiles. They may be true or false. However, regarding Jews, there is such a ruling . . . There is a difference: if a [Jewish] person does not merit, all the charities will not benefit him. But if he merits and sins, and because of his sins they chase him out of Paradise, or they punish him in Gehenna, or they tire him out over a thorny path, or demons 'play' with him . . . then it benefits [him] if he stole and his heirs return it.[109]

Whereas R. Judah doubts whether restitution of ill-gotten goods will succeed in redeeming a Gentile from his eternal torment (as is suggested in the second tale), he is convinced that, as far as Jews are concerned, given certain criteria,[110] such an action performed by living relatives can succeed in

107 *The Ecclesiastical History of England*, ii. 514.

108 See Watkins, 'Sin, Penance, and Purgatory', 8.

109 *SH* 35.

110 The exact nature of R. Judah's position regarding the efficacy among Jews of suffrages for the dead will be examined in the next chapter. For this reason, parts of his comments in the above quotation have deliberately been omitted.

putting to rest those who are being 'tired out along a thorny path'—an oblique reference to the torments depicted in the Pietist tales. He thus accepts the message of the narrative while still doubting its application in the context of the non-Jewish dead.

By adopting the tale, R. Judah tacitly concurs with the punishment meted out in it—eternal torment for obtaining goods or land in an illicit manner.[111] Since, according to rabbinic law, this crime is not punished by eternal damnation, R. Judah here again extends the punishment beyond its traditional halakhic boundaries. Thus, in regard to the category of sinners facing eternal damnation, he espouses a belief more in consonance with that found in circulating Germano-Christian ghost tales than with his own indigenous tradition.

Duration of Punishment in the Exempla Literature

We can now return to the story cited at the beginning of the chapter. In it, a dead Jewish sinner tells of having been tormented in Gehenna for several years, with the first year consisting of very harsh punishments, followed by less severe ones in subsequent years. While such a lengthy sentence is not meted out in the rabbinic literature to anyone but the most grievous of sinners,[112] it is a feature of the exempla literature. Thus the father of Walter, knight of Enthenich in the territory of Bonn, is tormented in Hell for twenty-one years, until he is finally released thanks to the prayers of his widow.[113] A usurer from Liège suffers in the 'pit of Hell' for seven years, and then in a lesser torment for another seven years, until his widow's incessant prayers, fasting, and almsgiving redeem him.[114] This last example lends credence to the dead man's answer in the Pietist tale under discussion. The two-stage punishment of the usurer, with the first set of seven years being more severe than the second, parallels the man's two-tiered torment in our story.

Not only does the Pietist tale affirm the notion of prolonged punishment in the hereafter, but it also shares with the exempla a medieval preoccupation with the afterlife. Whereas in rabbinic literature it is undecided

[111] This can include the crime of acquiring property or land either by outright theft or through usurious lending.

[112] Interestingly, in the *heikhalot* literature a combination of sentences appears. In one text, the wicked who are consigned to Gehenna for all eternity (the nations of the world, who are responsible for the destruction of the Temple in Jerusalem and for the exile of the Jews) suffer successive cycles of punishment of twelve months' duration in each of several levels of Gehenna. See Schäfer, *Synopse zur Hekhalot-Literatur*, O1531 no. 758.

[113] Caesarius of Heisterbach, *Dialogue*, 12: 5.

[114] Ibid. 12: 24.

when the punishment or purgation of sinners in Gehenna will take place, in the Pietist tale, as in the exempla, this question is indisputably resolved; the punishment is everywhere referred to as transpiring in the period immediately after death.

The theme of the Pietist tale echoes one that is extant in the exempla literature as well. The dead man tells the living one that he is being punished for not having recited his blessings over food with proper intent; he had eaten for his own personal pleasure rather than acting for the sake of his Creator. The following tale, recorded in the *Dialogus Miraculorum* regarding a rich official of the duke of Bavaria, imparts a similar message. The official, who had died several years earlier, appears to his wife and informs her that he has been condemned to eternal punishment, one so severe that 'if all the leaves of the trees were turned into tongues, they could not describe my tortures'. Although he lived his entire life in an 'ill' manner, his wife is shocked by the news and asks, 'Have you not given much alms and was not your door open to all pilgrims? Are your good deeds of no avail?' He responds to her, 'They are useless for giving me eternal life, because they were done for vainglory and not out of charity.'[115] In both tales, the sin involved is a lack of pure intention in pious actions; an act must be done solely for the sake of Heaven, with no ulterior motive, otherwise one cannot be spared punishment in Hell.

While the Pietist tale shares some elements with the exemplum, it differs from it in one significant way. In Caesarius's story, the duke was an inveterate sinner. Even his charitable acts cannot save him from eternal damnation because they were carried out without purity of motive.[116] In the Pietist tale, the man's sole sin appears to be his lack of purity of motive in the performance of otherwise pious actions. If so, the incongruity between his sin and his punishment is far greater than that in the exemplum.[117] It is, however, in consonance with monastic tales on the topic.[118] Also akin to the

115 Caesarius of Heisterbach, *Dialogue*, 12: 19.

116 At the end of the previous tale, the novice asks, 'What do you think of those who live but give much alms?' To which the monk responds, 'It is of no advantage to them for eternal life.' See *Dialogue*, 12: 18, p. 305.

117 It is also greater than it would appear to be in rabbinic literature. Although purity of motive in the performance of actions is praiseworthy according to the Mishnah (*Avot* 2: 12), another rabbinic principle legitimates religiously mandated actions that are performed for ulterior motives. This is because, despite their improper motive, such actions may spur similar action in the future which is properly motivated: 'for from [performance driven by] ulterior motives, one comes to [performance driven by] purely heavenly motives'. See e.g. *Sot.* 22*b* and 47*a*, *Arakh.* 16*b*, and *Pes.* 50*b*.

118 Let us recall the disproportionate punishment of the lay brother Mengoz, who was less

narratives of posthumous punishment we have encountered elsewhere in *Sefer ḥasidim*, the story revolves around a deficiency in the man's service of God, not his morality.

The motif of punishment extending beyond the first twelve months after death is found in another tale in *Sefer ḥasidim*. A certain man swallows some poisonous food and dies. He appears to his sons and beseeches them to open up his grave. They heed his request and find that his body is as intact as on the day it was buried, despite the passage of several years. They touch his garments in order to examine how his body was able to be preserved so well, only to have the garment and his body 'fall away' and crumble into dust before their eyes. The father then explains the reason for his return: he was being tormented in the hereafter because his body had remained intact and he was not deserving of this status. He appeared to them so that they should remedy this situation.[119]

In this tale, the prolonged punishment of the father is not due to sin, but rather to the state of his corpse. Like the bodies of the 'bad dead', which remain intact and wander restlessly on Earth, the bodies of the holy dead at the other end of the spectrum are also immune to decay. Saints' bodies defy nature and assume a miraculous state due to their holiness.[120] The dead man in this tale is being punished beyond the usual measure of time because the miraculous preservation of his body accords him saintly status, which does not befit his station. Only the disintegration of his flesh will bring an end to his torment. The ghost petitions the living for aid; although he is being tormented beyond the twelve-month period, his punishments can completely cease if his sons help him. Yet, once again, this intervention does not take the standard form of aid common in the case of ghosts who return from Purgatory.

The link established in this story between the incorrupt state of the body and the perpetuation of torment in the afterlife is a current theme in the ghost tales of the exempla literature. In one fourteenth-century manuscript, a tale is told of a certain gravedigger who finds a woman's incorrupt corpse with two serpents coiled around it—a sign that she is in torment.

than zealous in his work, and of the 'quite pious' sacristan of Villers, the 'trifler in words and signs'.

119 *SḤ* 321.

120 See Schmitt, *Ghosts in the Middle Ages*, 200. On the incorruptibility of the bodies of saints see Vauchez, *Sainthood in the Later Middle Ages*, 427. In *Dialogue*, 12: 48 Caesarius recounts how the right hand of a scribe from a monastery in Arinsburg, who had copied many books with great love and devotion, was found intact in his grave some twenty years after he died as a sign of his sanctity and heavenly reward.

Astonishingly, the woman returns to life and confesses her sins. As a result, her corpse immediately dissolves and the serpents disappear.[121] A similar tale is recorded in the exempla collections of three other manuscripts from the same period. The tomb of an excommunicate is found to be full of boiling water—a sign that he too is in torment. Although nine years have passed since his death, the man's body has not yet decayed. A posthumous absolution is obtained and the body crumbles to dust.[122] Interestingly, while not of saintly character, the deceased in the Pietist tale is not guilty of any heinous sin, unlike the dead of the exempla tales. This is indicated by the fact that he lacks a physical sign of torment that the others possess. Perhaps characteristic of the streak of harshness that runs through other Pietist tales, he suffers nonetheless.

In sum, the aforementioned ghost tales in *Sefer ḥasidim* speak of punishment in the afterlife that extends beyond the maximum twelve-month period allotted by the rabbis. In this they resemble tales in the exempla literature that recount instances of the dead who suffer for prolonged periods of time, ranging from several years to an eternity. The exact duration of punishment in these Pietist narratives, as well as in all the other Pietist tales that deal with posthumous punishment, remains unclear.[123] Let us recall the woman who is in great torment because she used to leave synagogue early, another whose hands and eyes are burning for having worked on Friday, and a third who suffers the shame of wearing a tallow-soiled glove for lighting sabbath lights with tallow. Do these women suffer forever? If not, when does their torment cease? While it is difficult to establish a precise time scale, since no aid is forthcoming and no terminus ad quem is recorded in these tales, it is possible to suggest that some of these dead people do suffer interminably. As we shall soon see, certain Pietist statements, which express a belief in the eternal punishment of even the 'not very bad' (to use Augustine's term), lend credence to such an assertion.

Pietist Pronouncements in *Sefer Ḥasidim*

In a discussion of penance to be performed for sexual sin, R. Judah speaks of eternal punishment. If *teshuvat hagader* fails to keep a man who is lovesick from sinning, then R. Judah exhorts him to beseech God for atone-

[121] MS BL Arundel 506 fo. 11*b*, col. 2 (*Catalogue of Romances*, iii. 545 no. 51).

[122] MSS BL Add. 11284 fo. 36*b*, 18344 fo. 137*b*, and 15833 fo. 104 (*Catalogue of Romances*, iii. 390 no. 281, 511 no. 23, 584 no. 47).

[123] This excludes the Hunt narratives, where the eternal nature of the punishment is more clearly established.

ment with all his heart—'For if regarding suffering of a temporary nature his heart would cry, then regarding sufferings that have no end nor boundary [*yisurin she'ein sof lahem ve'ein ḥeker*], how much more should he pray copiously about them.'[124] He sets up a contrast: the sufferings of this world, as painful as they are, are fleeting in comparison with the infinite torments that await the sinner after death. Furthermore, his use here of the a fortiori principle—*kol sheken*—indicates that his belief in the eternality of punishment is an intuitive one. Again, the sin in question is not punishable in halakhah with eternal torment.

R. Judah speaks of the prolonged suffering of the 'not very bad' also in the context of prayer for the dead. Regarding those sinners who 'did not properly observe the sabbath and Jewish holidays', he instructs the living to pray for them at the onset of every new month and before and after every Jewish holiday—even beyond the initial twelve-month period following their death. These sinners need prayer at these specific junctures because the fire of Gehenna is renewed and intensified at these moments. R. Judah writes:

> Regarding those who have died and the initial twelve months have already passed, one must pray for them every single month and on the Jewish holidays because they overturn the fire of Gehenna [on those days]. As it says, 'And it shall be that at every New Moon and on every sabbath all mankind will come' [Isa. 66: 23], and it is written, 'And their fire will not be extinguished' [Isa. 66: 24]. That is, on every [new] month they renew and overturn it [i.e. the fire of Gehenna] thus, and before every Jewish holiday and after it. Behold, on every [New] Moon, [they overturn] those who did not observe the sabbath and Jewish holidays properly.[125]

R. Judah here employs a non-literal interpretation and, characteristically, understands these prophetic verses, which refer to the collective judgement of mankind following the resurrection of the dead, to refer instead to the individual judgement that takes place immediately after one's death.[126] He consigns these sinners to the eternal, ever-increasing, inextinguishable fire of Gehenna (*ve'isham lo tikhbeh*). Yet people who err in the observance of the sabbath and Jewish holidays are not included in the list of renegade sin-

124 *SḤ* 44.

125 *SḤ* 356. The idea that the fire of Gehenna is renewed every month is also found in *Sefer gematriyot*, ed. Stahl, vol. i, no. 39, p. 38, and vol. ii, 'Toledot', no. 15, pp. 420–1.

126 The interpretation of the two verses is non-literal in that Isa. 66: 23 refers to those who bear allegiance to God and who will, at the End of Time, come periodically to bow down before him. At that time, they will go out and look upon the eternal destruction of those who

ners deserving of eternal punishment outlined by the rabbis.[127] R. Judah's sinners are not even violators of the sabbath and holidays, as his language indicates; they only failed to observe them properly. The vast disproportion between sin and punishment, a common property of the monastic tale, is apparent here once again. Could R. Judah have in mind specifically the woman who spun thread on the eve of the sabbath instead of preparing for the holy day, as was customary in her town? Did she return to the living to report that her hands and eyes not only burned immediately after her death, but did so on every sabbath and New Moon for a seemingly endless period of time?[128] While this woman may not fall into the category, even by Pietist standards, of those who are doomed to eternal punishment, R. Judah is clearly untroubled by the fact that she suffers indefinitely.

Apart from R. Judah's statements, those attributed to his father, Samuel the Pious,[129] reinforce the notion of eternal punishment in Pietist thought.

rebelled against God, as reported in Isa. 66: 24. According to R. Judah's interpretation, however, both verses refer to the eternal destruction of sinners immediately following their death. It is the burning of the flesh of all sinners in Gehenna, rather than the pilgrimage of all loyal people to Jerusalem, that will renew itself periodically. R. Judah's use of Isa. 66: 23 to refer to the period immediately following death has precedents in rabbinic sources. The *Seder olam* cites the verse as proof that the sentence of the wicked in Gehenna is twelve months; see Milikowsky, 'Gehenna and Jewish Sinners' (Heb.), 323.

In *Sefer gematriyot*, the interpretation that the fire of Gehenna is renewed monthly is derived from a different source. Comparing the overturning of the wicked in Gehenna on every Rosh Hodesh to the turning over of the sacrificial meat on the altar, R. Judah explains the meaning behind the following prayer recited on Rosh Hodesh, which reflects on the essence of the day: 'A time of atonement for all generations . . . the salvation of their souls from the hand of the enemy, a new altar in Zion you should prepare'. Weaving together the elements of 'atonement for all generations', 'salvation of souls', and the desire for the erection of 'a new altar in Zion', he asserts that it is specifically on that day that one beseeches God to erect a new altar in Jerusalem, since the burning of the sacrifices (which parallels the overturning of the wicked in the fire of Gehenna) atones for the sins of the wicked and can thereby save their souls from entering the fire of Gehenna. See *Sefer gematriyot*, ed. Stahl, vol. ii, 'Toledot', no. 15, pp. 420–1 and n. 49 there. Stahl points to the passage in *BB* 74*a* as the closest parallel source to this text in *Sefer gematriyot*; the Talmud declares that every thirty days Gehenna overturns the wicked, like meat boiling in a pot (see p. 421 n. 47 there). While the Talmud refers to the renegade Korah and his party, who challenged the leadership of Moses and Aaron, were swallowed up whole by the earth, and were denied a portion in the World to Come, the passage in *Sefer gematriyot* which R. Judah cites refers indiscriminately to all those who suffer in Gehenna.

R. Eleazar, in his *Sefer ḥokhmat hanefesh*, interprets the verses in Isa. 66: 23–4 in a different way. While he, too, believes that they refer to the period immediately following death and not to that after the resurrection of the dead, he interprets them as alluding to regular prayer on every sabbath and Jewish holiday performed by the dead on behalf of the living, rather than vice versa. See *Sefer ḥokhmat hanefesh*, 58.

127 BT *RH* 17*a*.

128 *SḤ* 591.

129 See n. 82 above.

In the midst of a lengthy exposition that appears at the beginning of *Sefer ḥasidim* and which is intended to evoke fear of sin and inspire true worship of God, R. Samuel advances the following argument: If a father is severely distressed over a physical injury to the body of his child—a pain which is passing—how much more should he be concerned and distraught over an injury wrought to the child's soul—a pain which is everlasting? If the child sins, his soul will burn eternally.[130] This is not mere rhetoric. R. Samuel repeats the argument, with slight variation, four times in the very same passage,[131] and buttresses it with citations of biblical verses which speak of the unremitting nature of the future punishment of sinners,[132] as well as of the utter hopelessness of their situation.[133] His discourse culminates in the warning that sinners cause the destruction of their entire being—body and soul.[134] Additionally, he, like R. Judah, promotes the unique Pietistic doctrine of repentance[135] and advocates voluntary physical suffering in this world as the means to exonerate oneself from the eternal punishment which awaits sinners after death. R. Samuel recommends that a father afflict his son with small amounts of physical suffering now in order to prevent 'perpetual pain to his flesh and soul' later, which clearly indicates his belief in the corporeal and eternal nature of the punishments of the afterlife. Furthermore, his way of addressing the father, as well as his lack of specificity as to the type or gravity of the sin in question, lead one to presume that the average sinner is being referred to here. If this is indeed the case, then, just as we have seen in some of the ghost tales of *Sefer ḥasidim*, R. Samuel extends the punishment of the average sinner in Gehenna well beyond the prescribed twelve months.[136]

Eleazar of Worms, too, speaks of eternal punishment for the average sinner. Referring to women who were involved in sexual sins in their lifetime, he writes: 'And they are sentenced to Gehenna, therefore they do

130 See *SḤ* 13, p. 12.

131 All four arguments appear in the Parma manuscript.

132 'And their fire will not be extinguished' (Isa. 66: 24), which, according to R. Samuel, refers to the inextinguishable fire in which those who rebel against God are destined to be burned.

133 He cites Deut. 32: 39—'and there is no rescuer from my hand'—which speaks of the inescapability of ultimate Divine judgement.

134 R. Samuel warns: 'At a time when your heart worries about your son, saying "lest something bad come upon him", your heart should tremble about his soul much more so, lest he sin against the Holy One, blessed be He, so that the result will be destruction of his soul and body.'

135 When a person has sinned, R. Samuel recommends the following: 'He should weigh [*shokel*] which *teshuvah* is equal to it [i.e. his sin] as it is written in *Sefer hateshuvah*.' A careful reading of his words makes it evident that (at the very least) *teshuvat hamishkal* is being referred to here.

136 On *Sefer hayirah*, see n. 82 above.

not perish in Gehenna.'[137] Since their bodies, which are suspended by the organ with which the sin was committed, never deteriorate, their punishment can endure forever. Although sexual sin committed by a Jew is not included in the list of sins enumerated by the talmudic rabbis for which one is sentenced to Gehenna 'for generations upon generations',[138] these women are condemned to eternal punishment.

Pietist versus Tosafist Teaching on Posthumous Punishment

The fact that Pietist teaching on posthumous punishment conflicts with authoritative rabbinic tradition becomes even more salient when the views of the Pietists are juxtaposed with those of their contemporaries, the tosafists, and their understanding of rabbinic tradition on the matter. On three separate occasions, the *Tosafot* subverts the otherwise plain meaning of rabbinic pronouncements referring to the eternal punishment of sinners, so that their sentence is reduced to a twelve-month period or less. Let us examine each passage in turn.

The first instance is in *Rosh Hashanah 16b*, where the Talmud cites a tannaitic teaching from the school of Shammai (Tosefta *San.* 13: 1) outlining the three categories of people that will exist at the time of the Final Judgement (*yom hadin*): the entirely righteous, the entirely wicked, and an intermediate group. In contradistinction to the entirely righteous, who are 'immediately written and sealed for everlasting life', the entirely wicked are described as being 'immediately written and sealed for Gehenna'. The parallel language of the text in reference to the two groups suggests a symmetry in their recompense: just as the former's reward is eternal, so is the latter's punishment. The verse cited next makes the eternality of that punishment explicit: Daniel 12: 2 condemns sinners 'to shame, to everlasting abhorrence'.

The *Tosafot*, however, argues that, even though the verse in Daniel speaks of everlasting punishment for the entirely wicked, it is not to be understood literally, as this would deprive them of any hope of redemption, which is a logical impossibility since it means that the fate of those with a majority of sins is worse than that of an even more wicked group: those with a majority of sins *and* the additional sin of being *poshei yisra'el begufan*, not having donned *tefilin* for their entire life. This group of entirely wicked people is sentenced in the Talmud for only a twelve-month period in Gehenna, after which time its members ascend. The *Tosafot* thus con-

137 *Sefer ḥokhmat hanefesh*, 7*a*.

138 BT *RH* 17*a*.

cludes: 'Even though it is written in the verse, "to everlasting abhorrence", this does not mean that they have no redemption; rather, they are punished for twelve months and [then] they ascend.'[139]

Rabbenu Asher (Rosh) echoes the same sentiment. Accepting the tosafist interpretation of the passage in the Talmud, he reinterprets the words in Daniel, *deira'on olam* (everlasting abhorrence), against the plain sense of the text, as *dai shera'u oto olam* (it is sufficient that they see that world): instead of languishing eternally in Gehenna, it is sufficient that these sinners merely 'see' that world—that is, experience it for a limited duration of twelve months. After that sentence is complete, they are able to enter the World to Come.[140]

In line with the medieval fascination with the afterlife, the *Tosafot* understands the tannaitic statement of *Rosh Hashanah* 16*b* in a way that is contrary to the plain meaning of the text. The beginning of the verse in Daniel—'Many of those who sleep in the dusty earth will awaken'—clearly indicates that the time being spoken about here is that of the resurrection of the dead; the judgement being described is, therefore, the final, collective one at the End of Days. The *Tosafot*, however, understands it as referring to the judgement of individuals after their death.[141] Moreover, the tosafists view the posthumous judgement as the one that is more commonly known, such that they feel a need to explain the necessity and function of the Final Judgement at the End of Days, even though Scripture speaks almost exclusively of the latter.[142] The view of the *Tosafot* is accepted as fact

139 Ibid., *Tosafot*, s.v. *ki leit lehu*.

140 See *Piskei harosh, RH* 1: 5. See also *Tosefot harosh al masekhet rosh hashanah* 17*a*, s.v. *ki leit lehu*, 49, where he repeats these words.

141 This is apparent from the fact that the *Tosafot*, after reducing the sentence of the 'completely wicked' from an eternal one to twelve months, cites two other, apparently conflicting, sources (*BM* 58*b* and *Ḥag.* 27*a*), which speak of the punishment that follows immediately after death; the former seems to imply eternal punishment in Gehenna for three particular sinners, while the latter states an opposite claim, that the sinners among Israel never experience the fire of Gehenna at all. The fact that the tosafists see these two talmudic dictums as making conflicting claims against their own interpretation of the fate of the 'completely wicked' and do not dismiss them as irrelevant (since they speak of a different time period than the tannaitic teaching which the *Tosafot* is interpreting) indicates that the tosafists here understand the tannaitic teaching as relating to the judgement which follows immediately after death.

142 Thus, the tosafists make the following comments on the term Final Judgement (lit. 'Day of Judgement'): 'When the dead are resurrected, as the verse [in Daniel] proves. And even though they have already been judged after their death either [to go to] Paradise or [to go to] Gehenna because of their soul, there will still be a judgement afterwards [to determine] whether they will merit the life of the World to Come, which is eternal. And there are those who have already received their punishment in Gehenna, and on account of this maybe they will merit [life in the World to Come]' (*Tosafot RH* 16*b*, s.v. *leyom hadin*).

by Nahmanides; in his *Torat ha'adam*, and specifically in his comments on the talmudic passage at hand, he inserts a third judgement, beyond those of the living on Rosh Hashanah and of the dead during the Final Judgement at the End of Days (of which the passage explicitly speaks)—that of each individual at the time of his death.[143]

A second occasion on which the tosafists reinterpret the otherwise clear rabbinic pronouncements referring to the eternal punishment of sinners is in *Bava metsia* 58*b*.[144] R. Hanina states in the talmudic text that all who descend to Gehenna ascend, except for three specific types of sinner: one who commits adultery, one who embarrasses another in public, and one who calls another person by a derogatory nickname. These people descend but do not ascend. The *Tosafot* immediately neutralizes the potency of this statement, arguing that one cannot understand it literally, since the Talmud on the very next page allows entry to the World to Come to one of them—the adulterer. Therefore, on the basis of the Talmud's statement elsewhere that 'the fire of Gehenna has no dominance over the sinners of Israel' (*Ḥag.* 27*a* and *Eruv.* 19*a*), the *Tosafot* reinterprets the statement of R. Hanina to mean that all who descend to Gehenna ascend immediately, except for those three, who descend but do not immediately ascend. This is not an obvious reading of the passage, as the *Tosafot* elsewhere interprets the same passage differently.[145]

Additionally, on the basis of a later pronouncement in the Talmud, that one who embarrasses another publicly forfeits his share in the World to Come, the *Tosafot* in *Bava metsia* offers yet another explanation of the passage—that only that sinner may possibly serve an eternal sentence.[146] However, even regarding him, the *Tosafot* offers another alternative: he is punished in Gehenna for twelve months and then, not meriting eternal life nor suffering eternal punishment, he assumes a sort of nebulous state of

[143] Nahmanides, *Torat ha'adam*, 266.

[144] s.v. *ḥuts*. See also *Tosefot rabenu perets* ibid., s.v. *kol hayoredin*, p. 123.

[145] In *Eruv.* 19*a*, s.v. *bar miha*, the *Tosafot* interprets the statement of R. Hanina in *Bava metsia* literally: all who descend to Gehenna ascend, aside from these three specific sinners, who never ascend.

Ritva offers a completely different interpretation of the passage in *Bava metsia* than does the *Tosafot*: all who descend to Gehenna do so for a period of twelve months, and then ascend. The three sinners enumerated are exceptions; they descend for a much longer period of time, yet not for an eternity (like the heretics etc., who are punished 'for generations upon generations'). See *Ḥidushei haritva al bava metsia*, ed. Rafael, 487. This demonstrates, again, that the tosafist interpretation is not a necessary one.

[146] BT *BM* 59*a*. That punishment might also extend to the one who calls his friend by a derogatory nickname, since the Talmud in *BM* 58*b* equates the two.

existence for all eternity: 'Also the one who embarrasses his friend publicly, even though he has no portion in the World to Come, he is not sentenced for more than twelve months. They are not granted life, nor are they punished, rather they exist in a state which is neither good nor bad.'[147] Even though this sinner has no share in the World to Come, he still does not suffer in Gehenna forever. The subsequent words, 'and now it is good', make it clear that this is the preferred interpretation of the tosafists, despite the fact that the first interpretation (that only the one who embarrassed his friend publicly serves an eternal sentence) is exegetically sound and more logical.[148] Why then does the *Tosafot* push this first, seemingly better, option aside in favour of the other, which commutes the sinner's sentence to twelve months?

The tosafists explain the reason for their preference: such a sinner does not belong in the same category as those who deny the fundamentals of the faith, cause the public to sin, and so on, and who suffer eternally, as explained in the *Tosefta* cited in *Rosh Hashanah* 17*a*: 'And now it is good, for [the one who embarrasses his friend] is not considered like the heretics and deniers of the faith, who are sentenced [to Gehenna] for generations upon generations, as it says in the first chapter of *Rosh Hashanah*, "Gehenna is destroyed, but they are not destroyed".' Only the worst types of sinner deserve eternal punishment without end; the one who publicly embarrasses his friend, according to the tosafists' sensibilities, should not be grouped with them. Such an interpretation removes the threat of eternal punishment from all three sinners specified in the statement of R. Hanina.

The third instance in which the *Tosafot* overturns the meaning of rabbinic pronouncements regarding eternal punishment is found in tractate *Ḥagigah*.[149] The Talmud there cites the claim of Reish Lakish, seen above,

147 The text in the *Tosafot* switches from the singular to the plural without explanation. While the one who embarrasses another is clearly being referred to here, it is also possible that the one who calls his friend by a derogatory name also shares this fate, as the sins are almost identical and the passage equates the sinners. This could explain the use of the plural here.

148 The proofs for this are the following: (1) The *Tosafot* cites this interpretation first. (2) Earlier, in the selfsame commentary, the necessary logical link between eternal punishment in Gehenna immediately after death and a person's share in the World to Come after resurrection is revealed. The *Tosafot* argues that it is impossible to understand the statement of R. Hanina literally—that the three sinners he lists descend to Gehenna and never ascend—because one of the three, the adulterer, retains his share in the World to Come, as stated in a subsequent talmudic pronouncement. According to the same line of reasoning, therefore, one who forfeits his share in the World to Come (the one who publicly embarrasses his friend) *should* serve an eternal sentence in Gehenna.

149 *Tosafot Ḥag.* 27*a*, s.v. *poshei yisra'el*. The anonymous speaker in the *Tosafot* (*veli nireh*) is most likely either the tosafist R. Elhanan (upon whose commentary the printed *Tosafot*

that 'the fire of Gehenna has no dominance over the sinners of Israel'. The *Tosafot* cites a parallel passage in *Eruvin* 19*a*, which mentions the same statement and identifies another type of sinner who appears to suffer eternally in Gehenna—a Jew who has relations with a non-Jewish woman. The tosafists ask why such a person is not included in the list of sinners condemned for eternity (according to the plain sense of the text) in *Bava metsia* 58*b*. They answer by reinterpreting that passage yet again, offering a completely new reading. They strip the teaching of any reference to Gehenna altogether: all those who descend, including the three exceptions to the rule, do not descend to Gehenna but to a common place of judgement where their fate is decided, and after this, all but the three exceptions ascend. However, the *Tosafot* continues, 'Even those who are judged [to remain below] ascend after twelve months; never do they remain longer than one complete year.' The upshot of this interpretation is that even those three sinners who are exceptions to the rule do not descend to Gehenna at all. Instead, they remain in this common place of judgement, for no longer than one year.

Although the text which was in front of the tosafists may not have included the word 'Gehenna', Rashi and many tosafists after him felt that it was implied in the plain sense of the passage.[150] The words of the *Tosafot* here—*lav begehinom mayri* ('it does not speak of Gehenna')—clearly indicate that the tosafists are aware of this fact and they are consciously avoiding such an interpretation, choosing a hitherto unknown 'common place of judgement' to replace it. By explaining the teaching of *Bava metsia* in this way, the tosafists deliberately remove any possibility of these three sinners experiencing eternal punishment in Gehenna; on the contrary, they never descend there at all.[151]

In theory, halakhic texts are essentially ahistorical intellectual exercises whose authors are more dedicated to the distillation of halakhic, theological, or some other truths than to presenting personal sensibilities or patterns of thought. In a similar vein, the tosafists were legal commentators whose primary purpose was to resolve contradictions within the text of the Talmud. Nonetheless, as has been demonstrated, in this matter they con-

is primarily based) or his master and father, R. Isaac (Ri). See Urbach, *The Tosafists* (Heb.), ii. 619–20, and Kasher and Mandelbaum, *The Officers of Thousands* (Heb.), i. 214.

[150] In several manuscripts of tractate *Bava metsia*, the word 'Gehenna' is missing, including the manuscript which Rashi had before him, as he corrects the text to include that word. See *Sefer dikdukei soferim*, ix: *Bava kama* and *Bava metsia*, ed. Rabinowitz.

[151] J. Costa points out the optimism exhibited by the *Tosafot* here; see *L'Au-delà et la resurrection*, 379 n. 89.

sciously chose to interpret a passage against the plain sense of the text despite other alternatives, and for reasons other than pure exegesis.

Such reinterpretations of rabbinic pronouncements serve to redefine the categories of accountability, as redemption now becomes possible for a much wider spectrum of sinners. The sinners labelled by the rabbis as 'entirely wicked', and whose fate is to be 'immediately written and sealed for Gehenna', can now achieve redemption. Even one who has sinned so grievously as to forfeit his share in the World to Come is offered respite after having served a finite sentence in Gehenna.[152] Here, too, it is religious sensibility rather than a plain reading of the text which prompts the tosafists to reduce the sentence of a sinner who is otherwise condemned to eternal punishment.

Beyond the reduction of sentences of eternal punishment, the tosafists also adopt positions that soften harsher rabbinic pronouncements regarding other types of post-mortem punishment. They accept unequivocally several rabbinic statements which speak of redemption from Gehenna —one such statement is that of Reish Lakish discussed above.[153] Another one explains that even transgressors who are sentenced to the 'depths of Gehenna, where they weep like the spring [that descends to] the foundations [of the earth]',[154] only descend there 'for that moment', after which time the 'patriarch Abraham comes, pulls them out, and receives them'.[155] The *Tosafot* opens the door of redemption ever wider and expresses an air of optimism when it raises the possibility of repentance; anyone, even one who commits a sin punishable by eternal sentence in Gehenna, can reverse his fate if he repents before dying. The lengthy tosafist discourse on the various punishments awaiting sinners concludes thus: 'And all the aforementioned [applies] in a case where he did not repent, for repentance is effective in every case, as there is an opinion according to which "penitents are greater than those who have always been righteous" [*Ber.* 34*b*].'[156]

In marked contrast to tosafist opinion, R. Judah the Pious offers little or

152 This sinner is the one who publicly embarrasses his friend (BT *BM* 59*a*).

153 See *Ḥag.* 27*a* and *Eruv.* 19*a*.

154 This is the rabbis' homiletical interpretation of a portion of the verse in Ps. 84: 7—'Those who pass through the valley of thorns transform it into a wellspring.' It involves a play on the words *bakha* (thorn) and *bakhah* (weeping).

155 *Eruv.* 19*a*. The *Tosafot* links the two rabbinic statements (that of Reish Lakish with that regarding the patriarch Abraham) in its commentary on *RH* 17*a*, s.v. *ki leit lehu*, and on *Ḥag.* 27*a*, s.v. *poshei yisra'el*. The *Tosafot* on *BM* 58*b*, s.v. *ḥuts*, cites the pronouncement of Reish Lakish as the basis for its reinterpretation of R. Hanina's statement. This reinterpretation overrides the plain sense of the statement, which speaks of eternal punishment for three groups of sinners, and reduces their sentence to twelve months.

156 See *Tosafot BM* 58*b*, s.v. *ḥuts*.

no hope to sinners. Whereas the *Tosafot* neutralizes talmudic pronouncements regarding eternal punishment, R. Judah reads them literally and gives them contemporary relevance. Thus, he understands the statement of *Bava metsia* 58*b* regarding those who 'descend but do not ascend' to mean that they descend to Gehenna never to ascend again. He tells of a particular '*parnas* [a wealthy Jew with political stature in the community] who lorded it over the public' and who intimidated other employers, not allowing them to hire for themselves certain Jewish labourers who had previously been in his employ. In the absence of any other place of employment, the Jewish labourers were forced to work for the *parnas*, who grossly underpaid them. R. Judah states that such an individual is considered one of those 'who visited undue fear upon the living', and 'they descend to Gehenna and do not ascend from Gehenna'.[157] In the Talmud, this group of sinners (those 'who visit undue fear upon the living') is part of the list, enumerated in *Rosh Hashanah* 17*a*, of those who 'descend to Gehenna and are sentenced there for generations upon generations'. R. Judah, however, adopts the language of *Bava metsia* 58*b*, which specifies sinners who 'descend but do not ascend', and associates these sinners with that other group, who 'are sentenced for generations upon generations'. While even the *Tosafot* agreed that the sinners in *Rosh Hashanah* 17*a* must suffer eternally, with regard to the group in *Bava metsia*, the *Tosafot* had removed the literal reading of 'descend but do not ascend', and rendered it 'descend but do not immediately ascend' instead. When R. Judah blends together these rabbinic statements, one of which is understood by the *Tosafot* according to its literal meaning to refer to eternal punishment and the other not, he makes it evident that he understands both pronouncements in a literal manner, as speaking of the eternal punishment of sinners.

Thus, while the tosafists labour to shrink the category of sinners who suffer eternally in Gehenna, three generations of Pietists hold fast to the notion, and even expand the category by condemning those who commit the slightest transgression—for example one who doesn't have proper intent when reciting blessings—to the flames of Gehenna for a prolonged period, beyond the maximum twelve-month sentence set out in the Talmud. While the tosafists avail themselves of rabbinic statements promising a quick release from Gehenna, the Pietists speak of sinners languishing there indefinitely and hopelessly.[158]

157 *SḤ* 1346.

158 This does not mean that the Pietists reject such uncontested rabbinic statements. It only means that these have no salience in their thought.

Moreover, noticeably absent from *Sefer ḥasidim* is the notion of the sabbath rest of souls in Gehenna, a belief of long standing in Jewish traditional sources,[159] and which served as the basis for several customs in medieval Ashkenaz.[160] According to this notion, the souls of sinners sentenced to punishment in Gehenna are afforded relief on that one day of the week. Although it appears in thirteenth-century Ashkenazi sources,[161] and is known in Pietist circles,[162] R. Judah omits any mention of it in his work.

159 The original source for this belief is one of the earliest *midrashim*—*Bereshit rabah* 11 (ed. Theodor and Albeck, i. 92–4). There, it appears in the context of a debate between R. Akiva and the pagan Turnus Rufus over the sanctity of the sabbath. Its sanctity is evident in that even the souls of the dead rest on that day; they are not punished, nor can they be summoned by necromancers. The sabbath rest of souls also appears in a *beraita* cited in BT *San.* 65*b*. Later authorities, such as the *She'iltot* and the *Shibolei haleket*, cite a fuller version of these texts, which includes the role of the angel Dumah. On Friday at dusk, a heavenly voice proclaims to Dumah, who presides over the punishment of the wicked in Gehenna, that he must leave them alone so that they can rest, and on Saturday night at the same time the souls are ordered to return to Gehenna, for the Jews have already concluded their sabbath prayer services. See Lévi, 'Le Repos sabbatique des âmes damnées', 2–3. Additionally, see Rashi on *San.* 65*b*, s.v. *nehar sambatyon yokhiaḥ*, in which he, too, professes a belief in the sabbath rest of the souls of the dead.

160 The thirteenth-century German legal commentator on the Talmud, Mordecai ben Hillel Hakohen, records in the name of R. Meir, Rabbenu Tam's father, that in Lotharingia they would refrain from eating the third meal between the afternoon and evening prayers on the sabbath; instead, they would eat it earlier on in the day. The reason he gives, on the basis of a *midrash* (*Midrash tehilim*, ed. Buber, 102) cited in the *Maḥzor vitry* (ed. Goldschmidt, i. 224, no. 145), is that, since the dead are to return to their judgement in Gehenna soon, they need to drink at this time, and their living relatives are stealing their refreshment. Rabbenu Tam was strict about this matter and rebuked others, such as R. Meshulam of Melun, who were not careful in this regard. R. Meshulam, however, argues that the custom is not to eat between the afternoon and evening prayers on the *eve* of the sabbath, as the souls are weary from their week in Gehenna and are most in need of refreshment then. The *Mordekhai* further reports that, while some wished to limit this practice to only the initial twelve months after the death of a relative, 'everyone is accustomed to being careful [not to eat late in the afternoon on the sabbath] even after the initial twelve months'; see *Mordekhai*, *Pes.* 105*a*. Additional customs, including a prayer in the afternoon service of the sabbath and a prayer recited immediately upon the conclusion of the day, are discussed in n. 162 below.

161 *Tosefot rabenu perets*, BT *Pes.* 105*a*, s.v. *rabanan devei rav ashi* in the Oz Vehadar edn., ed. Y. Leifer (New York, 2006); *Mordekhai*, *Pes.* 105*a* (Vilna edn., p. 37*a*). See also *Piskei harosh*, *Pes.* 10: 13; *Sefer minhagim devei maharam mirotenburg*, ed. Shinhab, 16–17 (the belief that the fire of Gehenna ceases on the sabbath is cited there in the name of Rabbenu Jacob ben Yakar), and *Ets ḥayim*, ed. Brody, 'Hilkhot shabat', 296.

162 In a discussion of the reason for the recital of 'Tsidkatekha tsedek' in the afternoon prayer of the sabbath, the *Or zarua* writes: 'And my master, R. Judah Hehasid, may the mention of the righteous be for a blessing, said to me that the reason why we are accustomed to saying "Tsidkatekha" in the afternoon prayer of the sabbath is that those verses speak of Torah and of angels and of Gehenna. So I heard from his mouth, but he did not explain to me the reason, for I did not ask him.' R. Isaac then proceeds to offer his own explanation of what he thinks R. Judah meant by these words: the third verse in the prayer offers praise to God for allowing

Furthermore, the same verse that describes to one tosafist respite from the flames of Gehenna on Rosh Hodesh signals to R. Judah the Pious the ever-increasing intensity and renewal of fire for sinners on that day. R. Mordecai ben Hillel's commentary on tractate *Pesaḥim* cites a tradition that the fire in Gehenna *ceases* on Rosh Hodesh, on the basis of the following tannaitic statement: 'R. Aptoriki said, the fire of Gehenna rests on the sabbath and on Rosh Hodesh. The rabbis expound it from the verse, "And they went out and they saw the dead bodies of the men", and next to it [it says], "And it shall be that at every New Moon and on every sabbath".' The biblical verse upon which the tannaitic statement rests, Isaiah 66: 23, is the exact verse cited by R. Judah as proof of the fact that the fire of Gehenna *increases* on every Rosh Hodesh.[163] Even R. Eleazar may have parted company here with R. Judah. R. Eleazar interprets the verse from Isaiah in a different way to his master.[164] Not requiring the living to pray for the sinful dead on the days mentioned by Isaiah, R. Eleazar does not negate a belief in the sabbath rest of souls. Could it be that the merciful respite that this belief allowed sinners clashed with R. Judah's view of the intense and ever-increasing fire of Gehenna, and, for this reason, he omitted all mention of it?[165]

In addition to expanding the category of eternal punishment, as mentioned above, R. Judah also condemns the majority of his fellow-Jews to purgation in Gehenna: the average person will spend some period of time there after his death and will not be immediately rescued. By taking this view, R. Judah goes against the talmudic passage which promises immediate rescue to the majority of Jews. This is evident from his statement in ref-

respite to sinners (those who have a majority of sins but observed the sabbath during their lifetime) from the punishment of Gehenna on the sabbath.

Immediately after, R. Isaac cites another contemporary practice that is based on the belief in the sabbath rest of souls. This time the citation is in the name of his other teacher, R. Eleazar of Worms. R. Eleazar explains that the reason the *ḥazan* greatly elongates the recital of the 'Barekhu' prayer during the service at the conclusion of the sabbath is that 'the souls return to Gehenna afterwards, and so long as one elongates, [during that time] they do not return'. See *Or zarua*, vol. ii, 'Hilkhot motsa'ei shabat', no. 89.

In his *sidur*, R. Eleazar reiterates the belief that the souls of those punished in Gehenna rest on the sabbath in his discussion of the reason behind the practice of smelling spices during the Havdalah ceremony at the conclusion of the sabbath: 'in order to dispel the very foul smell of Gehenna, for on the sabbath [its fire] does not burn and, at the conclusion of the sabbath, it returns' (*Perushei sidur hatefilah laroke'aḥ*, ed. Hershler, ii. 590–1, no. 106).

[163] See *Mordekhai* on *Pes.* 105*a* (Vilna edn., p. 37*a*), and *SḤ* 356.

[164] See n. 126 above.

[165] Whereas R. Judah cites Isa. 66: 23 to prove that the fire of Gehenna continually renews itself in ever-increasing intensity on every Rosh Hodesh, he omits mention of the sabbath, even though the verse itself refers to the two days as one unit—'And it shall be that at every New Moon and on every sabbath.'

erence to the biblical command to cover the blood of a slaughtered animal:

When a person slaughters a wild animal or fowl, he should ponder in his heart: 'This one, who did not sin, is slaughtered and they roast him, and man, who is filled with sins, how can he escape being murdered and from Gehenna?' And [so] the Holy One, blessed be He, commanded [us] to cover the blood of a wild animal and fowl lest the angel who is appointed over them say, 'How can the blood of one that did not sin be spilled by a sinner, whose sins are like scarlet wool and crimson?' [And the blood cries out, as it says, 'Land, do not cover my blood.'[166]] And they seal with blood the one who is sentenced to die and the foreheads of men whose sins are like scarlet wool. Therefore, He commanded [us] to cover the blood.[167]

According to R. Judah, God commands a Jew to cover the blood of an animal after ritually slaughtering it because it carries an accusation against him: if the animal, which has incurred no sin, is slaughtered and then roasted, surely the slaughterer, the Jew, who is 'filled with sins', cannot escape his destiny of death and Gehenna. By covering the blood, whose very redness suggests sin,[168] the Jew can, for the moment, silence the accusation and forestall such a sentence.

It is clearly the average person (*adam*) who is being addressed in this passage, as the biblical command to cover blood applies to every Jew. R. Judah highlights the inherent sinfulness of the average Jew by using five different expressions to refer to it over the space of only a few short lines.[169] On account of his sinfulness, a sombre fate awaits every Jew—inescapable torture in the fire of Gehenna. Covering the blood serves only to silence the accusing angel for the moment; it does not remove one's sins. Furthermore, the concrete image of the freshly slaughtered animal roasting and turning on a spit, which signifies to R. Judah that the ultimate fate of the slaughterer will be to burn in the fire of Gehenna, suggests the possibility that a visual representation of Hell in which demons poke and prod the damned as they roast them on a spit[170] may have stirred his mind and produced such an

166 Absent from MS Parma H 3280, this additional phrase appears in MS JTS 2499 no. 39 and MS Vatican ebr. 285 no. 39.

167 *SḤ* 1082.

168 See Isa. 1: 18, where the Jewish people's sins are compared to scarlet dyed wool (*shanim*) and crimson (*tola*). In another work penned by R. Judah, the colour red is equated with both sin and the fire of Gehenna. See Ta-Shma, 'The Notebook *Zekher asah lenifle'otav*' (Heb.), 140–1.

169 The five different expressions are: (1) *ve'adam shehu male avonot* ('and man, who is filled with sin'); (2) *ḥote* ('sinner'); (3) *asher ḥata'av keshanim ukhetola* ('whose sins are like scarlet dyed wool and like crimson'); (4) *hanigzar lamavet* (a reference to Adam's sin, which rendered man mortal and conveyed the death sentence upon him); and (5) *ha'anashim asher ḥateihem kashanim* ('the people whose sins are like scarlet dyed wool').

170 Such a scene is sculpted, for instance, on the cathedral tympanum of St Foi at Conques.

association. One medieval Ashkenazi polemical tract, *Sefer havikuaḥ, teshuvah leminim*, attests to Jewish awareness of Christian monumental art that portrayed scenes of the tortures of Hell,[171] and a halakhic discussion among the tosafists of the permissibility of gazing upon such sculpture confirms this testimony.[172] If so, then such a visual image would serve to augment the already terrifying message of this passage—the average Jew is full of sin and is destined to burn, in a physical sense, in the fire of Gehenna.

Evidence from medieval Ashkenazi penitential texts further supports the assertion that visual representations of Hell on church tympanums, most likely in conjunction with circulating accounts of early medieval visions, informed the way R. Judah viewed posthumous punishment.[173] In one fourteenth-century penitential text attributed to R. Judah, the author describes in rhymed verse the horrors of Gehenna: 40,000 demons beat the sinner mercilessly with rods of fire, bathe him in fire and rivers of molten pitch, boil him in excrement, and cast him down into a deep abyss. There he will encounter 7,000 snakes and stinging scorpions, pass through 600,000 mountains of fire, unprecedented darkness, and an entourage of named demons who will tear him apart limb by limb, reduce him to ashes, and scatter his remains all over the world.[174] Furthermore, the torture is repetitive and unending; in one case, after they have incinerated the soul, the hosts of demons restore it to life so that they can impose on the sinner the ritual of suffering all over again.[175] The exaggerated numbers, the common motifs of torture, and the use of demonic agents are all characteristic features of early medieval visionary accounts and narratives of otherworldly journeys.[176]

One such account was available in the vernacular in southern Germany

For a fuller discussion of this motif in monumental art of the twelfth and thirteenth centuries and its appearance as a literary motif in otherworldly journey narratives, see above, pp. 185–7.

171 See Shyovitz, '"You Have Saved Me From the Judgment of Gehenna"', 70.

172 See *Sefer moshav zekenim al hatorah*, ed. Sassoon, 344–5. For a parallel passage, see MS CUL Add. 3216, cited in Soloveitchik, 'Piety, Pietism and German Pietism', 490.

173 J. Baschet confirms this connection between clerical literature, which preaches on sin and otherworldly punishment, and visual representations of the tortures of Hell. He labels iconographic depictions of Hell as 'discourses on sin'; *Les Justices de l'au-delà*, 497.

174 *Iskei teshuvah*, 162*a*, cited in Kozma, 'The Practice of *Teshuvah*', Appendix 2, pp. 68–70.

175 This is the case of a murderer; see ibid. 69.

176 A further parallel with visionary accounts is the disproportionate number of descriptions of Hell and Purgatory versus those of Heaven and Paradise. In the penitential text, this inequality is taken to extremes as the nearly three-page-long, detailed, fanciful account of the tortures of Gehenna far outweighs the short, flat, and unimaginative two-line statement of the pleasures of Paradise. See ibid. 68–70 (Gehenna) and 71 (Paradise).

in the late twelfth century. Regarded as 'the most popular vision of the Other World',[177] the 'Vision of Tundale' tells the story of the journey to Heaven, Hell, and Purgatory of the Irish knight turned monk Tnugdalus. The story was originally written in Latin and was intended for the Irish Benedictine community in Regensburg, specifically for the monastery of St James.[178] It was translated into German by a priest named Alber, who was well acquainted with the affairs of Regensburg and possibly hailed from there.[179] In the vision, the monk Marcus, a visitor or a member of the monastery,[180] describes the horrors of the tortures of Hell and Purgatory witnessed by Tnugdalus in vivid detail, and even recounts the torments of some souls he sees in Paradise.[181] Tnugdalus's otherworldly vision, which transpired in the year 1148, served, by his own testimony, as the catalyst for his conversion to the cowl.[182] In the German translation of the tale, Alber adds passages which highlight the punishment of the wicked in the afterlife and make clear to the reader the lesson he should glean from the vision: 'Repent and do penance in order to avoid the torments of Hell and to enter the Kingdom of Heaven.'[183]

According to the Pietist penitential text, parts of each of the otherworldly punishments described in visionary literature await sinners not destined to suffer in such fashion by the rabbis: the murderer, the one who is irreverent to his parents, he who eats forbidden food, and anyone who mocks the commandments or the words of the sages. Only extreme forms of Pietistic penance, performed repeatedly over prolonged periods of time, can possibly forestall such a fate.[184]

R. Judah moved to Regensburg from his native Speyer in the late twelfth century, or possibly earlier;[185] it served as his home and the main locus of his activity.[186] Living in the city of origin of the 'Visio Tnugdali', a

177 N. F. Palmer, *'Visio Tnugdali'*, 15. 178 Ibid. 10–11. 179 Ibid. 37. 180 Ibid. 11–12.

181 Punishment in Paradise may be a unique Irish notion, as it is Irish kings who suffer there. See ibid. 15. Regarding the novelty of punishment in Paradise in the ghost tales of *Sefer ḥasidim*, see the discussion above, pp. 168–71. 182 N. F. Palmer, *'Visio Tnugdali'*, 11.

183 Ibid. 39. It is interesting to note that Alber's German translation (as opposed to the Latin original) highlights the *lex talionis* aspect of the punishments of the afterlife. See ibid. 40. This may have been an additional source of influence upon R. Judah's tales apart from, or in tandem with, circulating exempla. 184 Kozma, 'The Practice of *Teshuvah*', Appendix 2, pp. 68–71.

185 In a recent study, Ephraim Shoham-Steiner has argued that R. Judah's father, R. Samuel the Pious, moved from Speyer to Regensburg in the mid-twelfth century, when R. Judah was still a child: see 'From Speyer to Regensburg' (Heb.), esp. 165. Ivan Marcus believes that R. Judah left (or was driven out of) Speyer for Regensburg when he was already an adult; see *Sefer Ḥasidim and the Ashkenazic Book*, 64–7.

186 Shoham-Steiner, 'From Speyer to Regensburg' (Heb.), 163 and n. 46. Lucia Raspe, in a lecture entitled 'Between SHUM and Regensburg: Space and Place in the Early Modern

text which was well known in southern Germany and Austria from the twelfth to the nineteenth centuries, R. Judah and his contemporaries could well have imbibed both Tnugdalus's fear of the other world and Alber's penance-driven moral.

In marked contrast to the Pietist position, the tosafists did not believe that the average Jew was destined for such a dismal fate. In their unqualified acceptance of such talmudic statements as 'the fire of Gehenna has no dominance over the sinners of Israel', or in using the Talmud's description of sinners being pulled out from Gehenna and received by the patriarch Abraham, the tosafists clearly had in mind the average sinner, whom they saw in a favourable light.[187] In the last lines of tractate *Ḥagigah* and elsewhere in the Talmud, the rabbis proclaim: 'The fire [of Gehenna] has no dominance over the sinners of Israel, for they are filled with *mitsvot* [merits] like a pomegranate [is filled with seeds]. As it says, "Your cheeks [*rakatekh*] are like a slice of pomegranate" [S. of S. 4: 3]. Do not read "your cheeks" [*rakatekh*], rather "your empty ones" [*rekanin shebekha*].'[188] The reason why the sinners of Israel are not dominated by the fire of Gehenna, explain the rabbis, is that they are filled with merits, as a pomegranate is filled with seeds. If this is true for the empty ones, all the more so for those who are not empty.

How distant are the assumptions of the tosafists from those of their Pietist contemporaries regarding the average Jew! For one, he is filled with *mitsvot* as a pomegranate is with seeds. For the other, he is filled with sins, stained as red as crimson wool. How diverse is his fate! For the one is spared the fire of Gehenna, pulled out, and immediately rescued, while the other is burned corporeally in that fire, continuously turned and roasted as on a spit.

The assumption of the tosafists that the average Jew is spared the fire of Gehenna may not have been exclusive to them. The tombstones unearthed in medieval German Jewish cemeteries, such as Würzburg, Mainz,

Narrative Tradition about R. Judah the Ḥasid', given at the conference 'Sefer Ḥasidim in Context' (Jerusalem, March 2017), pointed out that all the miracle stories contained in the *Ma'aseh bukh* about R. Judah and his father take place in Regensburg rather than in the Rhineland (except one that is set in Speyer).

[187] These sinners, argues the *Tosafot*, are not the *poshei yisra'el begufan*, as the Talmud in *Rosh hashanah* states that those receive a much longer sentence in Gehenna and then their bodies are destroyed. Rather, they are only light sinners—*poshei ketsat*—all of whom the patriarch Abraham pulls out of Gehenna. The one exception is the Jew who has relations with a non-Jewish woman and has his foreskin pulled back to hide his circumcision, so that Abraham no longer recognizes him as a Jew. See *Tosafot Ḥag.* 27*a*, s.v. *poshei yisra'el*, and *Tosafot Eruv.* 19*a*, s.v. *bar miba*.

[188] *Ḥag.* 27*a* and *Eruv.* 19*a*.

Cologne, Worms, and Regensburg, suggest that such a belief was prevalent among the Jews of the period. The blessings for the dead inscribed on the tombstones reveal a distinct pattern. On those from the eleventh century, some variation of 'May his rest be with the Divine Kavod' (*menuḥato kavod*) predominates. While this blessing continued to be used over the course of the twelfth century, there was a marked rise in the use of a formula which blessed the soul of the deceased so that it would enter into Paradise (*menuḥatah tehe began eden* or *nishmato tehe began eden*). The latter blessing, which had already been used on tombstones earlier, came to predominate in the first half of the twelfth century.[189] Scholars connect the prominence of this blessing of the dead at this particular time to two factors. Firstly, Latin Crusade chronicles and Hebrew accounts of the twelfth century reveal that Paradise served as an important motivator for both the Christian Crusaders and the Jewish martyrs. Secondly, the Hebrew accounts demonstrate that Paradise as a locus for individual reward immediately after one's death penetrated the Ashkenazi consciousness at this time.[190] Additionally, the rise to prominence of the Christian concept of Purgatory in the same period may well have contributed to the noted increase in occurrences of the blessing of Paradise upon Ashkenazi tombstones. Is it merely a reflection, once again, of heightened consciousness of the individual afterlife that medieval Jewry now so keenly experienced? Perhaps. Others feel differently and claim that the prevalence of that blessing was a direct outcome of the popularization of the concept of Purgatory. In the opinion of Avraham (Rami) Reiner, it was part of a conscious attempt to combat the Christian message that the average person was to enter into a purgatorial-type punishment after his death. It was a proclamation that Jewish souls, in contrast to Christian ones, ascended directly to Paradise.[191]

The medieval Jewish tours of Hell—Ashkenazi texts that speak of the detailed tortures of Gehenna—would seemingly support such a proclamation. According to these texts, it is primarily non-Jews who are doomed to punishment there. They suffer *en masse* eternally in all seven levels of Gehenna, where they experience the intense ongoing tortures of each level for a twelve-month period before moving on to the next. By contrast, a small group of the most inveterate Jewish sinners enter only the highest level of Gehenna, where they endure a static, time-bound punishment.[192]

189 Reiner, 'From "Paradise" to "Bound in the Bonds of Life"' (Heb.), 8–14.

190 Ibid. 16–18.

191 Ibid. 19.

192 See Rotman, 'The Marvellous in the Medieval Hebrew Narrative' (Heb.), 383–4, citing *Perek gehinom*.

In one particular text, even the most infamous characters of the Bible and Talmud, such as Jeroboam son of Nebat, Absalom, and Ahab, are able to be released or exempted from suffering there on account of their relationship to the Jewish nation, Davidic descent, or involvement in Torah study.[193] The message that emanates from these tales is: 'Jews inhabit Heaven, while non-Jews are destined for Hell.'[194]

Whereas the Pietists could agree with the latter half of this message, they would not unanimously concur with the former. Pietist authors, as we have seen, condemned many of their co-religionists to Hell for long periods of time. While their line of thinking regarding Jews and their fate in the afterlife departed sharply from both rabbinic and tosafist ideas, it is in harmony with the outlook that was present in the high medieval exempla. Even though the overwhelming majority of the tales in these collections speak of the dead who return from Purgatory, or of notoriously evil sinners who suffer torment in Hell, there are quite a number of tales which assign eternal punishment to the 'not very bad'—vestiges of a pre-purgatorial penitential mentality. In this manner, a nun is damned for her slanderous speech[195] and another for her impure thoughts,[196] while a clerk is damned because improper motives taint his piety.[197] Three dead men appear to two mendicants and reveal their status in the hereafter: one has been damned for vain talk, the other for petty theft, while the third, a slanderer, must forever carry a burning pebble in his mouth as punishment.[198]

In an oft-repeated exemplum that condemns the majority of souls to Hell, a certain hermit has a vision in which he is informed by an angel of the fate of all the men who died on that day. The angel reports that two souls have gone to Heaven (one of a saint, the other of a hermit), a single pilgrim has gone to Purgatory, and all the rest—totalling 5,000—have been

[193] Ibid. 383, citing *Perek gan eden*.

[194] According to Micha Perry, this is the predominant message of the early twelfth-century version of the R. Joshua b. Levi tale cited above in Chapter 5. See 'Jewish Heaven and Christian Hell', 7. Similarly, in the so-called 'Jewish Orpheus legend', a tale composed around 1300, only conversion to Judaism or aiding Jews will save a non-Jew from Hell, whereas Jews are predestined to enter Heaven. See Yassif, 'The Overturned Story' (Heb.), 276–8 and 286–7. I wish to thank Michah Perry and Eli Yassif for sharing their essays with me.

[195] MS BL Add. 27336 fo. 77 (*Catalogue of Romances*, iii. 672 no. 334).

[196] MS BL Egerton 1117 fo. 178, col. 2 (*Catalogue of Romances*, iii. 471 no. 3).

[197] This tale originally appeared in two different collections—the *Liber de dono timoris* and the *Speculum laicorum*—manuscripts of which are gathered in the *Catalogue of Romances*. See MS BL Sloane 3102 fo. 9 and MS BL Add. 11284 (*Catalogue of Romances*, iii. 93 no. 7, 404 no. 562).

[198] MS BL Royal 7 C XV fo. 10*b* (*Catalogue of Romances*, iii. 409 no. ii, originating from *Speculum laicorum*).

sent to Hell.[199] Since, according to this widely circulated exemplum, only the elect can enter Paradise and very few are sent to Purgatory, the average medieval person can expect nothing less than eternal damnation in Hell. Thus, while Purgatory does exist in the exempla, it fails to inspire any hope in listeners as it lies beyond the reach of the ordinary person. The mood of this narrative, as well as of the others mentioned above, is very much in line with Pietist teaching.

In addition to having an affinity with the exempla literature, Pietist teaching presents a notion of the afterlife that has parallels in early medieval visionary literature. In one passage, R. Judah writes: 'And this is the measure for every single sin: he who has in his possession a certain sin, when they punish [in Gehenna] the other sinners who had committed the same sin, he is punished together with them.'[200] According to R. Judah's sketch of the afterlife, every category of sin has its own separate section in Gehenna. Each sinner will be punished alongside all those who sinned in the same manner as he. While unknown in rabbinic literature, the notion that Hell's punishments are divided in this way according to particular sins is present, for example, in an early Irish vision. This fragmented text describes groups who are punished together, with each group receiving a punishment suited to its particular sin: hypocrisy, ignorance, misappropriation of wealth, and dishonest judgement.[201] An appendix to the Irish 'Vision of Adamnán' adds further categories and enumerates varying punishments for murderers, thieves, liars, adulterers, ravagers of the church, and dishonest artisans and traders, among many others.[202]

R. Judah's emphasis on punishment 'for every single sin', great or small, makes it clear that it is not just the very bad who will be sent to Gehenna. What is unique about his schema here is that every sinner is punished, 'even though he has many merits in his possession'. This notion is new. According to rabbinic tradition, the nature and number of one's sins are both important factors in sentencing one to Gehenna. An average sinner (termed a *beinoni*), whose sins and merits are exactly equal, will never enter Gehenna; God, in his great mercy, tips the scales to increase the side of merit for him.

199 MS BL Arundel 506 fo. 57 (*Catalogue of Romances*, iii. 558 no. 238). A similar tale is told of an archdeacon who appears after his death to a bishop, informing him that, of the 1,000 who died that day, only he and Bernard of Clairvaux have entered Paradise, three souls have entered Purgatory, and all the rest have gone to Hell; MS BL Add. 33956 fo. 19 (*Catalogue of Romances*, iii. 626 no. 18). Two other tales make the same point but increase the number of souls who go to Hell to 30,000 in one day. See MS BL Harley 1288 fo. 38*b* and MS BL Add. 21147 fo. 24 (*Catalogue of Romances*, iii. 682 no. 14, 702 no. 16).

200 *SḤ* 1952, p. 475.

201 Seymour, *Irish Visions of the Other World*, 35–7.

202 Ibid. 26–8.

A *beinoni* whose sins include the grave sin of not having donned *tefilin* throughout his life will enter Gehenna, but only for a very brief time: 'They descend to Gehenna and are *metsaftsefin* and ascend.'[203] The one type of sinner who stays in Gehenna for a significant but finite amount of time, up to twelve months, is a *rov avonot*—one who carries a majority of sins.[204] Thus, in the rabbis' view, only a preponderance of sin can sentence someone to Gehenna for an extended period. R. Judah, on the other hand, prescribes this fate to anyone who has committed a single sin—even a small one—and perhaps only once, and despite the fact that he has many merits. The rabbinic understanding of who receives punishment in the hereafter clearly does not bind R. Judah.[205]

Original Sin and Pietist Sin

It is true that the motif of lengthy punishment in Gehenna, beyond a twelve-month period, is a feature of the exempla literature and a prime characteristic of Hunt narratives. However, it is hard to explain the willingness of all three main figures of the Pietist movement—R. Samuel, R. Judah, and R. Eleazar—to negate an authoritative rabbinic teaching on the afterlife, to promote positions which go beyond original rabbinic pronouncements on the matter, and to stand in marked opposition to both Jewish and Christian notions of posthumous punishment as reflected in the *Tosafot* and in the new, purgatorial atmosphere of Christendom, solely on the basis of affinities with these literary sources. A much deeper cause must be at work here, one that serves as the root of the Pietists' radical position on sin, penance, and purgation.

A pervading sense of sin arises from the pages of *Sefer ḥasidim*. The

[203] On the meaning of the verb *ts-f-ts-f*, see Yalon, *Chapters on Language* (Heb.), 36–7.

[204] BT *RH* 16*b*–17*a*. This discussion excludes the very bad, who are sentenced to Gehenna forever, or those sinners who have a majority of sins including the grave sin of never having donned *tefilin*. See *Piskei harosh*, *Rosh hashanah* 1: 5, where Rabbenu Asher (Rosh) summarizes the talmudic discussion and creates six distinct categories to describe the fate of all those mentioned. This categorization reflects R. Asher's own view, as it is absent from his comments in *Tosefot harosh*, which is simply his edition of *Tosefot shants*. See *Tosefot harosh al masekhet rosh hashanah*, ed. Ravits, 48–50.

[205] The statement of the Palestinian *amora*, Reish Lakish, in BT *Sanhedrin* 111*a*, in which he assigns the punishment of Gehenna to one who has committed any one sin, may be an exception to this rabbinic 'rule'. However, his is a minority opinion and has been identified by scholars as 'very radical' and unrepresentative of rabbinic position on this matter. See Ehrlich, 'The Theory of Retributive Punishment' (Heb.), 10 n. 38. Furthermore, the duration of this one-time sinner's stay in Gehenna is not elucidated in the talmudic passage, so that he may descend to Gehenna for only a short period of time.

work is filled with instances, both biblical and contemporary, of unknown sin being revealed. In one such instance, Moses condemns the Israelite soldiers for failing to exterminate the entire Midianite nation—an instruction that was only implicit in God's command.[206] In another, Dinah's rape by Shechem is a result of Jacob's unawareness of her unspoken desire to marry at a young age.[207] Similarly, Joshua is held accountable for his failure to take initiative in eradicating the evil impulse for idolatry amongst the Israelites, as Ezra does during the second commonwealth.[208]

Like Scripture, thirteenth-century Ashkenazi society showcases 'sins' that are particular to Pietist thought. Thus, for example, righteous people die like the wicked do for either not having erected enough fences around a commandment or for having lived together with the wicked.[209] The story is told of a man who cannot obtain the woman he desires in marriage because he has violated the basic Pietist tenet of never glancing at a woman.[210] We have already seen the 'great and publicly acclaimed rabbi' who was punished in his lifetime for screaming in protest against the elongated nature of Pietist prayer.[211] Holy books are burned as a result of their not having been written *lishmah* (with a pure intent)—a highly charged phrase in Pietist ideology.[212] Inaction breeds punishment as much as action does: an entire community can be punished for failure to investigate and prevent suspicious acts of individuals.[213]

The power of sin could not be more real for the Pietists, and its presence is felt everywhere. R. Judah rewrites the Jewish legal categories for culpability when he requires penance for all sins committed by a minor, by an insane person, by someone who is inebriated, and by a non-Jew prior to conversion.[214] The force of evil exceeds that of good: 'If only man's good inclination would overpower him as his evil inclination does in seeking out pleasures for his flesh and his honour', R. Judah writes wistfully, 'then he could be cunning with all intensity to perform the Will of Heaven . . . and he would not have to be so cunning [to outsmart his evil inclination].'[215]

Moreover, the evil inclination continually rearms itself in an attempt

206 Num. 31: 14; *SḤ* 1. 207 Gen. 34; *SḤ* 1107. 208 *SḤ* 1921.

209 *SḤ* 233. Regarding erecting fences around the commandments, see *SḤ* 1006. On the Pietist social ideal of separatism, see Marcus, *Piety and Society*, 91–2.

210 *SḤ* 1137. Not glancing upon a woman is one of the hallmarks of a Pietist. See *Sefer ḥasidim*, ed. Margaliot, no. 10.

211 See the additions adjacent to *SḤ* 427 in the Parma MS and the published edition of *Sefer ḥasidim*, and Ch. 5, p. 195, above.

212 *SḤ* 477. On the intellectual criticism levelled at *talmidei ḥakhamim* and signified by the term *lishmah*, see Soloveitchik, 'Three Themes in *Sefer Ḥasidim*', 343–7.

213 *SḤ* 1886. 214 *SḤ* 216. 215 *SḤ* 2.

to capture its prey—'For the evil inclination of today is not the same as that of yesterday.'[216] The sobering warning never to be content with success is repeated over and over again, as one victory over sin does not ensure another.[217] Precisely because the Pietist is on constant guard against sin, a perpetual accounting of sin is to be his lifetime pursuit. A pillar of Pietism is that 'man should search the deeds of men . . . so that he sees when they sin; that he should know that in the measure that they committed [the sin], they will be punished. And from this [knowledge], he will search his own deeds and distance himself from sin.'[218] In sum, R. Samuel's exegesis of Proverbs 8: 14, 'Happy is the man who is continuously in fear' (of committing a sin),[219] could well serve as an epitaph on the grave of a Pietist.

It is this fear of omnipresent sin which drives the Pietist to increase his obligations towards God in terms of both service to him and atonement before him. Not only does the Pietist refuse to maximize his allowances,[220] but stringency[221] and supererogatory behaviour in all areas[222] characterize his ritual and observance. Ever zealous in the practice of penance, he feels that scriptural punishments for sin (*teshuvat hakatuv*) are wanting; only the innovative *teshuvat hamishkal* can properly expiate a wrongdoing. When asked whether someone who kills himself on account of his sins violates the biblical prohibition on taking one's own life, R. Judah responds, 'It is good for a man to kill himself on account of his sins . . . and [regarding] one apostate it is said that [since] he sinned with water [i.e. underwent baptism], therefore he drowned himself in water to make atonement.'[223]

Beyond atonement for sin, a basic human need, there is the Pietist penchant for voluntary suffering. An all-encompassing fear of posthumous punishment is what drives the Pietist to live a life of ascetic denial and self-affliction—'Such [is the way] for those who do not wish to be called to Judgement.'[224]

Examination of Pietist teaching on the matter of posthumous punishment reveals a conviction of the profound sinfulness of humankind. Let us recall that, whereas the average Jew, according to tosafist and rabbinic conceptions, is meritorious and is spared the fire of Gehenna,[225] R. Judah declares him to be 'filled with sin', stained red 'as scarlet wool', and des-

[216] *SḤ* 13.
[217] *SḤ* 1010. See also *SḤ* 13, 1008, 1011, 1517, and 1520.
[218] *SḤ* 993. See also *SḤ* 1507.
[219] *SḤ* 13.
[220] *SḤ* 1004 and 1011.
[221] *SḤ* 1661, 1664, 1006, and 1939.
[222] *SḤ* 673, 674, and 786.
[223] Spitzer, 'Responsa of R. Judah the Pious' (Heb.), 202. I wish to thank Haym Soloveitchik for this reference.
[224] *SḤ* 198.
[225] The inherent goodness of Jews in rabbinic thought is confirmed in a recent study of the rabbinic understanding of *yetser*. See Rosen-Zvi, *Demonic Desires*, 130.

tined for Gehenna's ever-increasing flames. Despite the manifest hatred of Christianity and the open aversion to its symbols that permeate the pages of *Sefer ḥasidim*,[226] R. Judah has unconsciously imbibed the sense, so keenly felt by early medieval people, of the huge and insurmountable debt that mankind owes to God, a debt that one can never repay. Even the ultimate payment, compensatory penance to the point of loss of life, does not suffice.[227]

Ashkenazi polemical texts testify to Jewish familiarity with the ransom theory of atonement in Christian theology,[228] as well as with the related doctrine of the Harrowing of Hell still prevalent in Europe in the high Middle Ages.[229] The anonymous thirteenth-century *Sefer nitsaḥon yashan* critiques the former,[230] while the anonymous German treatise *Sefer havikuaḥ, teshuvah leminim*, along with the northern French *Milḥamot hashem* and *Sefer yosef hamekane*, questions the veracity of the latter doctrine.[231] It should not be surprising, therefore, that R. Judah was aware of fundamental Christian notions in the areas of sin and atonement.

There is no concept of original sin in Judaism as it exists in Christianity, as the human soul, according to Jewish teaching, has not been indelibly tainted by Adam's sin. R. Judah, however, seems to create in its place an entire realm of unwitting sin: sins that are not specified in the Bible or in rabbinic literature as such, but which God nevertheless expects man to be aware of, and for which he is 'punished because he knows not'.[232] Pietism

226 See e.g. *SḤ* 663 (aversion to the cross), 668 (works of monks labelled 'abominations'), 682 (monk labelled 'uncircumcised one, impure one'), 1348 (Christianity equated with idolatry; aversion to writing, even of Scripture, as well as to liturgical songs, of monks and priests), 1349 (avoidance of business dealings with priests, especially trade in their ritual objects), 1352 (better for a child to die than use a Christian relic for healing), 1353, 1354, 1356, 1358, 1359, 1362, 1363, 1364, and 1370 (aversion to Christian houses of worship), 1361 (aversion to Christian processionals with religious ritual objects), and 1369 (aversion to water used in trial by ordeal). See also Katz, *Exclusiveness and Tolerance*, ch. 8.

227 This notion is perhaps most clearly manifest in R. Judah's comments recorded in a responsum. After prescribing a very harsh penance to someone who has had relations with a non-Jewish woman several times, he writes, 'if he dies from these sufferings, fortunate is he'. See Spitzer, 'Responsa of R. Judah the Pious' (Heb.), 200.

228 Ransom theory, which can be dated back to the early Church, states that the death of Jesus was a payment to Satan in satisfaction of humanity's debt of Original Sin.

229 On the Harrowing of Hell, see below, Ch. 7, n. 72.

230 Berger, *The Jewish–Christian Debate in the High Middle Ages*, 195–7.

231 Shyovitz, '"You Have Saved Me from the Judgment of Gehenna"', 67–8.

232 *SḤ* 1. This statement appears in *Sefer hayirah*, and is thus allegedly uttered by R. Samuel the Pious, not R. Judah. However, given the weight of the evidence—that is, all the other statements and examples that R. Judah cites in *Sefer ḥasidim* and which support such a contention—he would certainly agree with his father here.

has, in effect, substituted sin that is omnipresent and inevitable for that which is embedded in humans and inherited—inescapable sin for original sin. Man, according to R. Judah, is not born with sin; he is fated to sin. It is this concept of humanity's ineluctable sinfulness that is the source of the omnipresent, stubborn, and tenacious sin that is found in *Sefer ḥasidim*.

Furthermore, even though penance does part of the work, this great burden of sin can only be completely lifted off the common person through the atoning sacrifice of a great individual. We may recall the ghost tale in which the Pietist master voluntarily inflicts extreme corporeal suffering upon himself in an effort to do penance not only for his own sins, but for 'the benefit of the public'.[233] He is venerated in *Sefer ḥasidim* as the one who sits highest in Heaven. Thus, although the passage is *sui generis* to this work, it reflects a general Pietist ideal. Equating himself with the 'messiah who bears iniquities', the Pietist master clothes himself in the language and imagery of the Suffering Servant in Isaiah 53, a highly charged Christological passage: he employs two quotations from that biblical chapter and undergoes fatal or near-fatal bodily mutilation. While there is talmudic precedent for the notion that the suffering of the righteous benefits the world, and R. Judah cites such precedent in the figures of R. Eleazar b. Shimon and R. Judah the Prince, the talmudic source he quotes speaks of illness or deprivation allotted to the righteous that brings blessing to the world or finds special favour before God, not of self-inflicted wounds for the sake of mass expiation.[234] With the Pietist master portrayed as an idealized version of Christ, it becomes evident that, despite R. Judah's rejection of Christian doctrine, one of its basic premises—the all-pervasive sinfulness of mankind and its concomitant need to rely upon the vicarious atonement (in this case, corporeal suffering) of the righteous—has seeped into his moral universe.

The notion of the overwhelming burden of sin, having been thoroughly assimilated into the consciousness of the movement's founders, led to their wholesale adoption of the Irish monastic penitential system. Only such a

[233] *SḤ* 1556.

[234] See BT *BM* 85*a*. Could R. Judah possibly be aware of the incongruity between the talmudic examples he cites and the actions of the Pietist master when he adds, in reference to the former, 'and it is as if they did it with their [own] hands'—i.e. the suffering that the rabbis of the Talmud experienced is considered 'as if they did it with their [own] hands' (*SḤ* 1556)? It is one thing to provide meaning to suffering that God brings upon a person; it is quite another to initiate that suffering and expect it to be accepted by God as atonement for others.

In the same vein, Susan Einbinder points out that the twelfth-century poets of the Blois martyrs refer to the 'death of martyrs as expiation for communal sins'. They are depicted as

system of harsh corporeal penances, taking into account every element of sin—its nature, the number of times it is perpetrated, the manner in which it occurred, even the amount of pleasure derived from it—could properly address the profundity of sin which concerned the Pietists. Sin placed the individual in such great debt that only self-inflicted torture could possibly redeem him from the dire punishment awaiting him: 'The suffering [that he takes upon himself] shall be [for him] in place of Gehenna', argues the Pietist.[235] Aware of the novelty of his penitential doctrine, R. Judah writes, 'Even though our rabbis have not mentioned explicitly the depth of this repentance [*teshuvah*], such is the way for those who do not wish to be called to Judgement.'[236]

The Pietists clothe the appropriated categories of penance in whatever traditional garb they can (*teshuvat hakatuv* and *teshuvat hagader* are prime examples[237]), and name talmudic rabbis who suffer on account of their sins. Additionally, they comb Scripture for what simply has to be there—evidence of the notion of unknowing sin and the fierce Divine wrath that follows. They also find biblical characters who seem to purge their soul in accordance with Pietist doctrine.[238]

'sacrificial lambs for each household' (*Beautiful Death*, 31 and 61 respectively). Once again, the poets only paint this image of Jews who were killed forcibly by Christians; the image of the martyrs as expiators does not necessarily invite active emulation. The Pietist master, however, inflicts death upon himself in a deliberate attempt to encourage other Pietists to follow his practices of self-mutilation. See in this regard especially *SḤ* 115, where R. Judah includes within the halakhic mandate of Jewish mutual responsibility (*kol yisra'el arevim zeh bazeh*) the idea that the righteous are commanded to take upon themselves the suffering of the generation and to bear their sins. See also Marcus, *Piety and Society*, 93.

235 *SḤ* 277.

236 *SḤ* 22.

237 Whereas the actual names of these categories are Pietist inventions, they bear an affinity to traditional concepts; *teshuvat hakatuv* reflects the punishments which Scripture (*hakatuv*) mandates for sin, and *teshuvat hagader* incorporates the scriptural command given to the rabbis to erect protective fences (*gedarim*) around the Torah's laws. Additionally, there are specifically four categories of penance in the Pietist canon because '[the word] *teshuvah* appears four times in [the biblical portion of] "Nitsavim"' (*SḤ* 37).

238 King David practises *teshuvat hamishkal* when he risks his life in battle in order to make amends for having caused the death of Uriah the Hittite. He likewise endangers himself on behalf of the women of Israel in atonement for his sin with Bathsheba (*SḤ* 15). Queen Esther and all of Israel fast for three days in expiation of her willingness to consort with Ahashverosh, a non-Jew, in a desperate attempt to save her people (*SḤ* 19). Furthermore, in keeping with the notion of voluntary suffering, Job beseeches God to afflict him with the sufferings that befall him—even though this contradicts the plain sense of the text (*SḤ* 32, 361, and 1512), while Mefiboshet, mentioned in 2 Samuel 4: 4, is crippled as a result of self-flagellation—despite Scripture explicitly offering a different reason. See *SḤ* 496. According to a fourteenth-century penitential text attributed to R. Judah, the evil biblical king Ahab is said to have purged his soul via Pietist doctrine. See Kozma, 'The Practice of *Teshuvah*', Appendix 2, p. 48.

Nor were the Pietists concerned simply with their own sinfulness. Sharing the great missionary zeal of their Irish monastic counterparts, they tried, whenever possible, to coerce their co-religionists (and only them, as Pietists expressed no interest in converting or redeeming the souls of non-Jews) into accepting their concepts of unknowing sin and God's 'unspoken law', known as *retson haboré*, as well as their penitential doctrine. At other times, they would preach to them, or at least hope to make them aware through *Sefer ḥasidim* of these teachings. Like the Irish missionaries, who wished to impose their own rigorous system of discipline upon the laity,[239] the Pietists made reform and correction, acceptance and influence the *raison d'être* of their movement.[240] Indeed, when it came to their doctrine of penance, they were not without success.[241]

Moreover, R. Judah and his colleagues adopted an entire lifestyle of asceticism and voluntary suffering that closely resembled monastic practices. At the low end of the scale, a Pietist was to deliberately withdraw himself from partaking of the pleasant aspects of life. On a daily basis, he was to abstain from playing with his own children, taking recreational excursions, glancing at passing women, and engaging in friendly conversation.[242] Refraining from such acts would atone for sin and accrue reward. At the high end of the scale, a Pietist was encouraged to fast excessively,[243] flagellate himself,[244] expose himself to extreme temperatures, sit among vermin and bees,[245] and immerse himself in icy water.[246] The greatest of all Pietists, the *ḥasid ḥakham*, suffered not only for his own sinfulness, but, vicariously, for that of others as well.[247] This predilection for voluntary punishment, an

[239] This is the opinion of A. J. Frantzen. Whereas other scholars argue that the Irish penitentials arose from a pre-Christian disciplinary tradition based on Indo-European law codes, Frantzen disputes this notion. He claims that the penitentials are an indigenous product of Irish missionary zeal. The handbooks, therefore, are a record of actual cases of assigned penances rather than examples patterned after a literary model. See Frantzen, *The Literature of Penance in Anglo-Saxon England*, 22–3, 25, 30, 32, and 57.

[240] Soloveitchik, 'Three Themes in *Sefer Ḥasidim*', 327.

[241] The Pietists' doctrine of penance (as atonement for sin, not in terms of voluntary suffering) was the only one of their unique doctrines to enjoy a measure of longevity and popularity. See Elbaum, *Teshuvat halev*.

[242] *SḤ* 15. See also *SḤ* 19, 815, 984, and 986.

[243] *SḤ* 67. *Sefer ḥasidim* permits fasting on the sabbath—see *SḤ* 289. According to *SḤ* 22, the performance of acts that cause one added suffering has the power to transform intentional sins into merits. On the heightened role of fasting in medieval Ashkenaz and its correlation to contemporaneous Christian practice, see Baumgarten, *Practicing Piety in Medieval Ashkenaz*, 60–102.

[244] *SḤ* 1555. Here, the act of flagellation is assumed rather than encouraged. See also *SḤ* 66.

[245] Caesarius of Heisterbach, *Dialogue* 2: 32, mentions sitting naked among vermin as a form of penance.

[246] *SḤ* 1556.

[247] See *SḤ* 385 and 1133.

outgrowth of the Pietist theory of omnipresent sin, would aptly characterize the theme of *Sefer ḥasidim* as 'sin in search of punishment'.[248]

Several of the ascetic practices advocated in the work are prominent features of Irish monasticism. Fasting, an age-old Christian practice, increased in importance when fused with the pre-Christian Irish custom of 'fasting against'. Rooted in magical beliefs, this ancient tradition of fasting, sometimes until death, was practised by people of lower status 'against' those of higher status in an attempt to have their claims addressed or rights asserted.[249] Saints' coercive fasting for prolonged periods of time in order to wrest privileges or concessions from God is a 'well-documented feature of Irish hagiography'.[250] One of the heroic acts St Patrick is acclaimed for in his biography is his repeated sessions of prolonged fasting.[251] Excessive fasting is also a feature of Irish penitentials, where it serves as a means of penance for sin. In the Penitential of Finian, for example, it appears as 'a doctrine enforced without reservation'.[252]

Flagellation underwent a similar intensification in Irish monastic practice to fasting. While the Rule of St Benedict lists flagellation as a punishment, it restricts its use to cases when standard means of correction, such as labour, fail. In Celtic monasteries, however, beating was transformed into a common form of penance, prescribed even for the 'most insignificant omissions'.[253] Additionally, the practice of praying and keeping vigil while immersed in icy water was a typical Irish penitential act. Characteristic of early saints, this form of 'humiliating the body' was a common motif in Irish hagiography.[254] The 'Life of St Patrick' attributes the practice to that saint, and immersing oneself in water overnight appears several times as a form of penance in the Old Irish Penitential.[255] One ninth-century Irish monastic text, a collection of memorabilia written in the first person, records actual incidents of monks standing in icy water 'for the purpose of crushing or subduing their desires', or 'simply as an additional labour of

248 The book has been previously characterized as 'guilt in search of sin': Soloveitchik, 'The Midrash, *Sefer Ḥasidim* and the Changing Face of God', 170. Soloveitchik cites it in the name of Judith Baskin. Guilt, however, is an emotional state alien to the Pietist conception of external penance for sin. Moreover, instead of being on the lookout for sin, they found it everywhere; proper punishment and sufficient atonement are what eluded them.

249 Binchy, 'A Pre-Christian Survival in Medieval Irish Hagiography', 168–9.

250 Ibid. 170.

251 Ibid.

252 McNeil, *The Celtic Penitentials and Their Influence*, 133.

253 Ibid. 189.

254 It was thanks to its prominence in that literature, argues Colin Ireland, that this penitential practice spread to the rest of western Europe; 'Penance and Prayer in Water', 52.

255 Ibid. 54–5.

piety'.[256] Other ascetic practices are also documented in the lives of early Irish saints: St Coemgen prayed for so long that birds came to rest in his outstretched hands,[257] St Columba slept on bare earth with a stone for a pillow,[258] and St Finian wore chains that bit into his flesh, producing sores on his body.[259]

These monastic ideals, perpetuated by the Irish Benedictine monks, had a stronghold in southern Germany. In 1080 Irish missionaries founded a colony at Regensburg, and in 1111 a monastery dedicated to St James was established there. In the second half of the century the monastery became the centre of an entire network of affiliated Irish Benedictine houses established over southern Germany and Austria and known as the *Schottenklöster* (Gaelic monasteries). The monastery of St James (St Jakob), in fact, became so powerful at this time that it underwent major renovation by Abbot Gregory sometime between 1155 and 1185 in order to render its stylistic appearance proportionate to its sphere of influence and financial standing.[260] The *Schottenklöster* maintained strong ties in the high medieval period (the twelfth to thirteenth centuries) with their Benedictine counterparts in Cashel, Ireland, and with their Irish noble benefactors through the travels of abbots and monks in both directions.[261]

We have already seen that the most popular medieval visionary account, the 'Visio Tnugdali', originated from the monastery of St James at Regensburg. Its author, a monk named Marcus, was either a member of or visitor to this Benedictine mother house, and the two Irish kings referred to in the account were its founders and benefactors.[262] Marcus records the journey of the Irish knight Tnugdalus through Hell, Purgatory, Paradise, and ultimately Heaven. Owing to the fact that Tnugdalus's vision fills him with such dread of otherworldly punishment that he repents and commits to a monastic life, the account served as a model for others to follow; in this, it resembled a saint's life.[263]

Apart from this vision, which shares features of hagiography, scholars have demonstrated that Irish *vitae* (saints' lives) proper, in circulation on the Continent as early as 1160 through the activity of missionaries, were

256 Ireland, 'Penance and Prayer in Water', 54.

257 Bitel, 'Ascetic Superstars'.

258 O'Hanlon, *Lives of the Irish Saints*, vi. 299.

259 Healy, *Insula Sanctorum et Doctorum*, 200.

260 Ó Riain, '*Schottenklöster*', 42 and 44.

261 Ó Riain-Raedel, 'Cashel and Germany', 176–80, and id., 'Aspects of the Promotion of Irish Saints' Cults in Medieval Germany', 220–34.

262 N. F. Palmer, '*Visio Tnugdali*', 11–12.

263 Ibid. 13.

copied and collected in the scriptorium at Regensburg.[264] The twelfth and thirteenth centuries represented the peak period in the writing and dissemination of early Irish lives, with texts of Irish origin regularly rewritten at Regensburg.[265] The collection of *vitae* that was produced there made its way into a very large collection called the *Magnum Legendarium Austriacum*, most likely compiled in Austria in the late twelfth century.[266]

Irish *vitae* tell of the heroic feats of Irish saints, known for their rigorous ascetic practices, penitential ardour, and missionary zeal, all in the service of God.[267] In particular, the 'Vita Mariani', the life story of Marianus Scotus, founder of the Regensburg *Schottenklöster*, lauds the religious fervour of the earliest Irish saints, who embarked upon voluntary exile, missionized and converted pagans in Germany, and performed miracles along the way.[268] In general, the *Schottenklöster* maintained a high level of devotion to their native Irish saints; calendars with their anniversaries survive from Regensburg.[269] As missionaries, the Irish monks did not isolate themselves from their social environment; on the contrary, they were involved with the surrounding lay communities and cultivated friendly relations with them.[270] Reports from a daughter house in Vienna tell of the active participation of the monks in the life of the city as caregivers to the sick, clergy in the parishes, and hosts to pilgrims and Crusaders.[271]

The monastery of St James was situated about 700 metres from the Jewish area of the city.[272] As stated above, R. Judah arrived there from his native Speyer in the late twelfth century or possibly earlier.[273] He, and presumably other Jews as well, may have acquired knowledge of the stories contained in the *vitae* from Christian neighbours who had heard them read aloud at saints' feast-day celebrations, or from the mouths of the visiting

[264] Ó Riain-Raedel, 'The Travel of Irish Manuscripts', 52. [265] Ibid. 60.

[266] There are different opinions among scholars as to the exact provenance of this work. Whereas Dagmar Ó Riain-Raedel ('Aspects of the Promotion of Irish Saints' Cults', 243) argues for Regensburg as 'the probable source for the southern German collection of Irish Lives', the most recent and comprehensive study of the legendary by Diarmuid Ó Riain posits that a related monastery of Admont in Styria, Austria is the most likely source; 'The *Magnum Legendarium Austriacum*', 129–31. See also Bieler, *Four Latin Lives of St. Patrick*, 233–4.

[267] See Sharpe, *Medieval Irish Saints' Lives*; Carey, Herbert, and Ó Riain (eds.), *Studies in Irish Hagiography*; and Bray, *A List of Motifs in the Lives of Early Irish Saints*.

[268] Bieler, 'An Austrian Fragment of a Life of St. Patrick', 176–81.

[269] Ó Riain-Raedel, 'Ireland and Austria in the Middle Ages', 37. See also id., 'Aspects of the Promotion of Irish Saints' Cults', 229.

[270] Ó Riain-Raedel, 'Ireland and Austria in the Middle Ages', 33. [271] Ibid. 33–5, 282.

[272] I wish to thank Eva Haverkamp for providing me with a map of medieval Regensburg, and for her estimate of the distance of the monastery from the Jewish area.

[273] See the discussion on pp. 247–8 above.

monks themselves.[274] Christian converts to Judaism may also have served as possible conduits for religious and cultural exchange.[275] The voluntary acts of monastic asceticism practised by the early Irish saints and extolled by the natives of Regensburg would thus suggest themselves for imitation by the Pietists. With the doctrines of harsh expiatory penance and asceticism as bedrocks of its faith and with a missionizing agenda, Pietism very likely viewed Irish monastic ideals as a model of sanctity. Why it should have done so is a question that will be explored in Chapter 9.

For now, let us conclude with an example from a manual of penance of R. Eleazar of Worms. On the basis of related talmudic statements in tractate *Ḥagigah*, R. Eleazar regards a man who has relations with a married woman as one who can never achieve atonement for his sin.[276] The passage in *Ḥagigah* refers to such a man as 'something twisted which cannot be straightened'[277] when he sires an illegitimate child (*mamzer*),[278] and as one who is 'cast out of the world' because his adulterous act forbids the woman from ever returning to her husband. With no reference to Gehenna or any form of posthumous punishment, the talmudic passage emphasizes the irreversible nature of the crime committed by the man, suggesting that he cannot undertake repentance for it. However, in *Bava batra* 88*b*, the rabbis state that, with regard to forbidden relations, repentance is possible. The *Tosafot*, in an attempt to reconcile the apparent contradiction, distinguishes between the two cases; the former refers to a relationship that produces a *mamzer*, where repentance is impossible, whereas the latter refers to one which does not, and here the sinner may repent. The *Tosafot* then offers another interpretation, which allows repentance even in the case of a *mamzer*: 'although it [i.e. the *mamzer*] is "something twisted which cannot be straightened", even so, it is possible that he [the sinner] can repent, for God has commanded him so'.[279] Despite the fact that the tragic con-

[274] Bitel, 'Saints and Angry Neighbors', 124. A fourteenth-century manuscript of German origin of a penitential text attributed to R. Judah the Pious speaks of the accessibility of monks and monasteries. Offering penitential advice to a repentant Jewish apostate, R. Judah states that the penitent 'should not sit beside monks and priests, or in a place where they speak of the impurities of idolatry'. He should, likewise, not derive any benefit from the 'shade of the idolatrous abominations', 'from the entrances of their buildings and the courtyards of their abominations'. See Kozma, 'The Practice of *Teshuvah*', Appendix 2, p. 49.

[275] R. Reiner has documented two examples of this phenomenon; see 'The Dead as Living History', 205–8.

[276] BT *Ḥag.* 9*a*–*b*.

[277] Eccles. 1: 15.

[278] A *mamzer* is a child born of an adulterous relationship and who, according to Jewish law, is forbidden to marry a non-*mamzer*. See Deut. 23: 3: 'A *mamzer* shall not enter the congregation of God; even his tenth generation shall not enter the congregation of God.'

[279] *Tosafot BB* 88*b*, s.v. *hatam efshar biteshuvah*. There is an explicit scriptural command for a Jew to do repentance in Deut. 30: 2.

sequences of *mamzerut* are irreversible according to Jewish law, the sinner can repair the breach between him and God through repentance. As in the cases cited above, the *Tosafot* here interprets a rabbinic statement in a way that opens up redemption to sinners.

R. Eleazar also grants redemption to the adulterer, albeit in a radically different manner. He connects the passage in *Ḥagigah* to that in *Bava metsia* 58*b*, thus placing it squarely in the arena of posthumous punishment, whereas the talmudic passage and its tosafist interpreters spoke only of this-worldly consequences. Interpreting the passage in *Bava metsia* literally, R. Eleazar includes the adulterous man in one of the three categories of sinners who descend to Gehenna never to ascend again. Unlike the *Tosafot*, he omits mention of the *mamzer* altogether; it has no salience for him.

In order for the adulterer to avoid such a fate, R. Eleazar suggests, 'if he regrets the evil which he has done, he should suffer a punishment as harsh as death'. The sinner must immerse himself naked in ice and snow once, twice, or even three times daily, except on the sabbath and holidays, throughout the winter, 'as long as he is still alive'. Additionally, he should wear sackcloth that touches his flesh (perhaps a hair shirt commonly worn by monks and penitents) and 'fast all his days', that is, refrain from eating meat and drinking wine on all days except sabbaths and holidays. Furthermore, he must confess his sin twice daily every day, receive lashes, assume a posture of humility, accept rebuke silently, and 'not see happiness all his life . . . [then] maybe He will take pity on him'.[280]

The striking difference in the nature of the corrections offered by the tosafists and R. Eleazar reflects a radical disparity between their perceptions of sin. The tosafists can separate the irreversibility of the sinner's action from his moral standing before God and allow him to restore his connection to the Divine via repentance—traditionally understood as composed of a sinner's mental remorse, inner commitment to desist from sin in the future, and prayerful entreaties to God, at times accompanied by short periods of fasting.[281] Sin can thus be forgiven via a penitential process that is non-corporeal and limited in its scope and duration. For R. Eleazar, on

280 *Darkhei teshuvah* in *Sefer roke'aḥ: hilkhot teshuvah hashalem*, ed. Rosenfeld, 103. The following passages, which describe similarly harsh and elongated penitential procedures for the sin of adultery, appear in other Ashkenazi penitential texts, collected by E. Kozma in 'The Practice of *Teshuvah*': MS Paris hebr. 363, *Teshuvat hakatuv* [Appendix 2, p. 3]; *Darkhei teshuvah* (Prague edn.), 4: 23 [Appendix 2, p. 42]; and MS Vatican ebr. 183, *Iskei teshuvah* no. 162*a* [Appendix 2, pp. 48–9]. On the penitentials of R. Eleazar of Worms, see Marcus, 'The Penitentials of the German Jewish Pietists' (Heb.).

281 See Urbach, *The Sages*, 464.

the other hand, sin must be entirely expunged through a series of harsh acts of corporeal self-torture and the adoption of a penitent posture for the entire duration of the sinner's life. Even then, forgiveness is not assured: 'maybe' God will have mercy upon him. In R. Eleazar's words one senses not only the terror of Divine punishment in the hereafter awaiting man as a consequence of sin, but also the magnitude of the debt that man owes God—a debt he can never fully repay.

Conclusion

In matters of sin, penance, and purgation, we have encountered an outright clash between rabbinic tradition and Pietist teaching. What took place here was more than a mere shift in emotion and outlook; the Pietists had altogether shed the world-view of the sages in the realm of posthumous punishment. Not only did they expand the rabbinic categories of sinners destined to prolonged punishment in the afterlife, they also ignored statements that argued for a quick release of sinners from Gehenna, and contradicted others that restricted lengthy punishment only to those whose sins predominated over their merits. Whereas the rabbis of the Talmud were undecided about when posthumous punishment or purgation was to occur, the Pietists (and other halakhists as well) firmly placed these processes in the period immediately after the death of the individual.

The Pietists did not depart solely from the rabbis' teaching. They also failed to share the new, more optimistic, outlook of the thirteenth century, in which the Christian doctrine of Purgatory, with its concomitant message of hope to sinners, gained prominence. Although an optimism regarding the redemption of sinners is reflected in the writings of their tosafist contemporaries and in some motifs of ghost tales that circulated in their environment, the Pietists adopted instead an early medieval pre-purgatorial penitential tradition that still persisted in the Germano-Christian society of their day.

While absent from rabbinic literature, the notion of the prolonged suffering of sinners appears in the exempla collections and in Hellequin's Hunt accounts. R. Judah's literary borrowing, if it was recognizable to his audience, would only make his tales more familiar, and hence more believable, to them. These tales would be accepted as true because such stories were known to have occurred. The immense cultural borrowing in the conceptual areas of sin, penance, and purgation present in *Sefer ḥasidim*, however, extends far beyond any literary parallelism. New categories of sinners—those guilty of sexual sins, thieves, and even those who mistreat their animals—are destined to prolonged or eternal suffering in the hereafter, some without any hope of redemption.[282] The average person is expected to spend some time in Gehenna, even for a small sin committed only once. The sabbath rest of souls—a belief commonly held by Jews of the time—has no place in R. Judah's vision of Gehenna. Besides increasing the duration of posthumous punishment, the Pietists also heighten its severity. Such punishment is punitive rather than purgative, and is to be avoided as much as possible through the performance of harsh acts of penance in this world. Several important themes of the early medieval penitential literature—the overwhelming sinfulness of man, his profound indebtedness to God for sin, his need to totally expiate all sin in this world, and his reliance upon the atoning sacrifices of the righteous performed vicariously on his behalf—have been transferred onto the pages of *Sefer ḥasidim*. Having substituted the doctrine of Inevitable Sin for Original Sin, and depicted the Pietist master as a Christ-like figure of atonement, R. Judah has unwittingly adopted a thoroughly Christian world-view.

In the areas of sin and penance, the Pietist and monastic agendas once again correspond. The unique Pietist doctrine of penance, in many of its key components, bears the influence of early medieval Irish monastic penitential traditions. In its expansion of the categories of sinners condemned to prolonged punishment in the hereafter, as well as in its description of the severe nature of that punishment, *Sefer ḥasidim* reflects the same disparity between sin and punishment that is characteristic of monastic tales. The dread of posthumous punishment, along with the resultant urge to 'save souls from Hell', is an important factor that underlies both monastic penitentials and *Sefer ḥasidim*. The Pietists displayed no lack of missionary zeal in their preoccupation with the sins of others. Furthermore, R. Judah's advocacy of voluntary corporeal suffering, as well as his definition of the hasid as one who lives in constant daily battle with sin and in ascetic withdrawal from the pleasures of this world, demonstrate the Pietists' identification with several fundamental monastic ideals. With the mother house of the *Schottenklöster* situated in Regensburg and stories of the heroic ascetic acts of Irish saints circulating in the area, these ideals were available for R. Judah to absorb.

282 R. Judah accepts that thieves can be redeemed from Gehenna if their relatives make restitution of the stolen goods; see *SḤ* 37.

In the next chapter we look at the reciprocal bonds between the living and the dead as described in *Sefer ḥasidim*. Could the prayer and alms of the living benefit the dead? Does Pietist teaching on the matter follow traditional Jewish lines, share affinities with contemporary notions prevalent in high medieval Christendom, or isolate itself yet again?

CHAPTER SEVEN

BONDS BETWEEN THE LIVING AND THE DEAD PART I

PRAYER for the dead formed a primary bond between the living and the dead in thirteenth-century Germany in both Jewish and Christian communities. In order to better appreciate the position that it occupies in *Sefer ḥasidim*, as distinct from its role in rabbinic literature, let us return to the narrative I cited in Chapter 4 from tractate *Berakhot*:

It is related that a certain pious man gave a dinar to a poor man on the eve of the New Year in a year of drought, and his wife scolded him, and he went and passed the night in the cemetery, and he heard two spirits conversing with one another. Said one to her companion, 'My dear, come and let us wander about the world and let us hear from behind the curtain [which shields the Divine Presence] what suffering is coming to the world.' And her companion said to her, 'I am not able to, because I am buried [clothed] in a matting of reeds. But you go, and what you hear, tell me.' So the other one went and wandered about and returned. Said her companion to her, 'My dear, what did you hear from behind the curtain?' She replied, 'I heard that whoever sows seed at the time of the first rainfall will have his crop smitten by hail.' So the man went and did not sow until the time of the second rainfall, with the result that everyone else's crop was smitten [by hail] and his was not smitten.

The next year he again went and passed the night in the cemetery, and heard the same two spirits conversing with one another. Said one to her companion, 'Come and let us wander about the world and let us hear from behind the curtain what punishment is coming upon the world.' The other said to her, 'My dear, did I not tell you that I am not able to, for I am buried [clothed] in a matting of reeds? But you go, and whatever you hear, come and tell me.' So the other one went and wandered about the world and returned. And she [her companion] said to her, 'My friend, what did you hear from behind the curtain?' She replied, 'I heard that whoever sows at the time of the second rain will have his crop smitten with blight.' So the man went and sowed at the time of the first rain, with the result that everyone else's crop was blighted and his was not blighted.

His wife said to him, 'How is it that last year everyone else's crop was smitten and yours was not smitten, and this year everyone else's crop is blighted and yours is not blighted?' So he related to her all his experiences. The story goes that shortly afterwards a quarrel broke out between the wife of that pious man and the mother of the child [whose spirit was conversing in the cemetery], and the former said to the latter, 'Come and I will show you your daughter, who is buried in a matting of reeds.'

The next year, the man again went and spent the night in the cemetery and heard those same [spirits] conversing together. One said [to her companion], 'My dear, come and let us wander about the world and hear from behind the curtain what suffering is coming to the world.' She [the other] said to her, 'My dear, leave me alone! Our conversation has already been heard among the living.'[1]

It is worth recalling also the Pietist narrative that retells this story from the Talmud, with significant alteration of its details. This time, let us focus specifically on the motif of prayer of the dead:

There is a night when the souls leave their graves, such as the night of Hoshana Rabah. They exit [their graves] when the moon appears. They go out and pray. And two [of the living] went out and hid themselves in one place in the cemetery. And they heard that one [soul] was saying to her companion, 'Let us go out and pray together.' And all the souls went out and prayed and requested mercy that death not be decreed on the living, also that those who are to die should return in repentance from their evil ways, and regarding [punishments consisting of] moderate illnesses, and about every matter relating to the living and the dead, and, regarding themselves, that punishment be removed quickly from upon them and other [dead ones]. And they [the two living men] told their community [what they had witnessed].

The following year, on the night of Hoshana Rabah, two others [from among the living] went [and slept in the cemetery]. And only one young girl, who had died before the sabbath, emerged from the graves. They [the other dead in the cemetery] said [to her], 'Go out [and pray].' She said, 'I am not able to, because my father was rich and he lost his wealth', and [so] he had buried her without any clothes. And they [the two living men] heard that some of the souls said, 'We will not gather together [for prayer], because two [from among the living] have already revealed [things] about us to the public. Instead, let each one pray separately in his grave, so that the living shall not hear.'

And they [the two living men] told the community. And they [the members of the community] got angry at the father, and they took clothing, and dressed that young girl.[2]

[1] BT *Ber.* 18*b*. [2] *SḤ* 1543.

While the talmudic story speaks of spirits who overhear heavenly decrees issued against the living, R. Judah, in his version of the story, speaks of the dead who leave their graves in order to pray. Additionally, whereas the talmudic account involves only the spirits of two girls, the Pietist version encompasses all the dead in the cemetery, who leave their graves to assemble for group prayer. The date of the occurrence of this annual event also changes: in the Talmud, it always takes place on Rosh Hashanah night; in *Sefer ḥasidim*, it has been switched to the night of Hoshana Rabah and/or one on which the moon is visible—days that were associated in medieval times with the dead.[3] More importantly, while the dead in the talmudic story are aware of the disastrous decrees awaiting the living each year, they do not make any attempt to act upon that knowledge.[4] For R. Judah, however, the annual conversations of the dead regarding the living could have only one purpose—to pray on their behalf. He transforms the appeal of the spirit of one young girl to another to 'traverse the world and hear' into the call of one soul to another to 'go out and pray together'. And pray they do—all of the dead—not merely to cancel evil decrees issued against the living, but for extended life, repentance, easy death, and 'all matters relating to the living'. In R. Judah's mind, the living owe a great debt to the dead, whose prayers, offered regularly, encompass every aspect of their existence.

3 The association between the appearance of the moon and encounters with ghosts has pre-Christian roots, as night-time is the domain of the dead in Germanic culture; see Lecouteux, *Fantômes et revenants*, 143. On the appearance of the moon as an element in accounts of Hellequin's Hunt, see above, Ch. 2, n. 63.

The significance of Hoshana Rabah as a day of prayer for the dead, who assemble in the cemetery, may be due to its calendrical coincidence at times with St Michael's Day on 29 September. The archangel Michael, traditionally regarded as the conveyer of souls to Heaven and slayer of the dragon, i.e. Satan, appears in medieval artistic representations of the Last Judgement as the weigher of souls. His cult, superimposed upon that of various pagan gods before him, had been firmly established in western Europe by the end of the seventh century. The feast of St Michael has occupied a significant place in the customs and rural life of the German people even in modern times. See *Millénaire monastique du Mont Saint-Michel*, iii. 18–22 and 392. In the Middle Ages, on St Michael's Day, Cluniac monks prayed for their dead brothers; see Schmitt, *Ghosts in the Middle Ages*, 173. *SḤ* 193 makes mention of the cultic celebration of St Michael's Day.

The connection of Hoshana Rabah to the resurrection of the dead goes back to geonic times. Its association with the sealing of judgement for the living was first documented in the thirteenth century (see *Sefer ḥasidim*, ed. Margaliot, nos. 452–3, and Nahmanides' commentary on Num. 14: 9). Such an association made it ideal for adaptation as a day of prayer, not for the dead but by the dead, regarding the judgement of the living.

4 Only one man acts upon the information he receives—the one who overhears the conversation of the spirits. However, he does so only for his own advantage.

A similar belief is found in an addendum to *Sefer ḥasidim* cited from the *She'ilta*, whose author espouses the position that the souls of the dead pray daily for the living.[5] The *She'ilta* explains that, although God decrees judgement on the living only once a year, on Rosh Hashanah, he continues to judge them daily. Since he does not decide on Rosh Hashanah which particular day of the year the decree will take effect, he continually 'monitors' people's behaviour in order to determine if any given day will be the day that the decree will be executed. In answer to the question why God troubles himself to judge the living daily rather than once a year (he could decide the day of execution of the decree on Rosh Hashanah), the *She'ilta* responds, 'so as to allow the souls of the dead to hear the decrees [about to be executed] so that they can pray for the living'. Such a position is in line with R. Judah's thinking on the matter and could possibly have emanated from him.[6]

R. Eleazar of Worms, too, espouses the belief that the dead pray for the living in his *Sefer ḥokhmat hanefesh*. However, he accords them not one night but regular times to do so. Reinterpreting a verse from Isaiah, he posits that the dead assemble on every sabbath, holiday, and Rosh Hodesh, essentially to praise their Creator but also, at times, to make requests for the welfare of the Jewish people and on behalf of the living.[7]

It is this great debt owed to the dead that, in turn, obligates the living to aid them—a belief professed by R. Judah in *Sefer ḥasidim*. The reciprocal relationship between the living and the dead that exists in *Sefer ḥasidim* is absent from the rabbinic corpus. While the Talmud does speak of the dead praying for the welfare of the living—let us recall the passage which

[5] The addendum appears in the printed edition of *Sefer ḥasidim* alongside a citation from R. Isaac Alfasi next to no. 33.

[6] Y. Y. Stahl has argued in a recent essay that the aforementioned *she'ilta* is not from Alfasi as was originally thought; rather, it originated with R. Judah the Pious (he speculates that it hails from his *Sefer hakavod*), and it is labelled *she'ilta* because it is presented in the form of a query. See Stahl, 'Repentance in the Matter of Judgement' (Heb.), 39–43. I wish to thank Haym Soloveitchik for this reference.

In addition to daily prayer, the dead appear to be especially effective in their prayer immediately after dying. They can petition God directly with specific requests regarding the living. It is for this reason, R. Judah explains, that the righteous of the Bible offer blessings before they die—so that immediately afterwards they could ascend to Heaven and petition God to accept their blessings and grant them to the living (see *SḤ* 1564). Similarly, in one of the stories of *Sefer ḥasidim*, a man comes before a righteous man who is about to die and beseeches him to petition God regarding his wife's infertility as soon as 'he comes before the Holy One, blessed be He'. The righteous man promises to do so and dies. That very year, the man's wife becomes pregnant. See *SḤ* 1566.

[7] *Sefer ḥokhmat hanefesh*, Jerusalem edn., 58.

proposes that one reason for the custom of visiting cemeteries on fast days is so that the dead buried there will pray on behalf of the Jewish people[8]—the notion of the living praying for the dead in return is a new concept. Also, the most common form that prayer of the dead for the living takes in rabbinic thought is the holy dead—especially the patriarchs and matriarchs—beseeching God on behalf of a sinful Israel;[9] once again, the living do not reciprocate in prayer on their behalf. By contrast, the archetypal figures of the patriarchs and matriarchs, as well as the subject of their prayer—the collective known as *keneset yisra'el*—are absent in *Sefer ḥasidim*.[10] Instead, the average dead assemble to pray on behalf of individuals among the living—that some should not die, that others, who are to die, should repent, and that still others should be cured of 'moderate illnesses'. Furthermore, whereas the ordinary dead of rabbinic times prayed for the welfare of the living when called upon by them (during visits to the cemetery on fast days), their counterparts in medieval times were believed to do so regularly, even daily, and of their own accord.

Eleazar of Worms, too, speaks of the prayer of the average ordinary dead on behalf of the living. He writes that one reason for the contemporary practice of giving alms on behalf of the dead is 'honouring the dead [so] that the righteous [dead] intercede favourably on behalf of their [living] descendants'.[11] The 'righteous dead' here refers to one's immediate ancestors rather than to the forefathers of the Jewish people.[12]

It is not only the nature of prayer of the dead on behalf of the living or its frequency that had undergone radical change since rabbinic times. The notion of the living praying for and aiding the dead also assumed a novel and prominent position in *Sefer ḥasidim*.

8 BT *Ta'an.* 16*a*. It was customary for Jews in the rabbinic period to fast during times of drought. For a further rationale for visiting the cemetery on fast days, see Ch. 3, n. 135 above.

9 See e.g. BT *Shab.* 89*b* (Isaac prays for a sinful Israel) and *Petiḥta de'eikhah rabah* 24 (a very lengthy discourse in which each of the patriarchs and matriarchs petitions God separately on behalf of Israel). J. W. Bowker cites a number of important rabbinic and post-rabbinic sources which highlight the intercessory role played by the holy dead and specifically the patriarchs in his essay 'Intercession in the Qur'an and the Jewish Tradition', 73 n. 2, 76–7.

10 See Soloveitchik, 'The Midrash, *Sefer Ḥasidim* and the Changing Face of God', 167.

11 See *Sefer haroke'aḥ hagadol*, ed. Shneerson, 109.

12 R. Eleazar makes this statement in the context of the contemporary custom of allotting charity on behalf of the dead in the synagogue on Yom Kippur—a practice which involved members of the congregation pledging alms for their deceased relatives.

Prayer and Charity for the Dead in Jewish Legal Tradition and Practice

In rabbinic literature there exist contrary positions on the subject of atonement for the dead. Whereas several tannaitic and amoraic statements indicate that the dead either cannot be atoned for or do not need atonement as death itself is an atonement,[13] some midrashic sources claim that, indeed, 'the dead need atonement'.[14] The sources which negate the concept of atonement for the dead centre around three primary rabbinic teachings. One is the ruling that a sin offering whose owner dies before it is offered is not brought as a sacrifice.[15] Another teaching states that fathers cannot save sons, nor can brothers save brothers from Gehenna, as seen in the cases of Abraham and Ishmael and Jacob and Esau.[16] A third concludes that death itself atones for sin, on the basis of the juxtaposition of the biblical account of the death of Miriam with the laws relating to the purifying sacrifice of the red heifer, although this teaching pertains specifically to the righteous.[17]

On the other hand, as mentioned above, other rabbinic sources point to the need for posthumous atonement. One is the teaching that a son can accrue merit for his dead father;[18] another states, regarding a deceased father, that his son is the 'atonement of his bed';[19] a third proclaims that prayer can release the dead from Gehenna 'like an arrow from a bow',[20] while a fourth source is based on the biblical law of the *eglah arufah*.[21]

[13] *Sifrei*, 'Naso', 4 (ed. Horowitz, p. 7).

[14] *Sifrei*, 'Shofetim', 210 (ed. Finkelstein, p. 244), and *Midrash tanḥuma*, 'Ha'azinu', 1 (ed. Buber, p. 51, and see Buber's note there).

[15] BT *Hor.* 5*b*–6*a*, *Tem.* 15*a*–*b*, and *Yoma* 50*a*, based on Mishnah *Ker.* 6: 7. Z. A. Steinfeld discusses this teaching as it appears in *Horayot* and *Temurah*. He concludes that statements from *Temurah* were transferred to *Horayot*, so one may not infer from the discussion in either passage that such sacrifices achieve atonement for the dead according to the rabbis. 'Atonement for the Dead' (Heb.), 217–28.

[16] *Midrash tehilim* 46: 1 (ed. Buber, p. 272).

[17] *Sifrei*, 'Naso', 4 (ed. Horowitz, p. 7). Regarding all three sources, see the relevant discussion in Glick, *A Light Unto the Mourner* (Heb.), 127–30, and Edrei, 'Atonement for the Dead' (Heb.).

[18] BT *San.* 104*a*.

[19] BT *Kid.* 31*b*.

[20] *Pesikta rabati*, ed. Ish-Shalom, 20, p. 95*b*.

[21] The rabbis in *Horayot 6a* expound on the words recited by the elders of the city as they offer the special sacrifice known as the *eglah arufah*. Deut. 21: 1–9 describes the ceremony, which is to be performed upon the discovery, between two cities, of a dead body whose murderer is unknown, as a means to secure atonement for the residents of the cities involved and to relieve them of any responsibility for the death. As part of the ceremony, the elders of the city proclaim: 'Atone for Your nation, Israel, whom You have redeemed' (Deut. 21: 8). The rabbis note: 'It is fitting that this atonement should apply to those who left Egypt [and are already dead].' See also *Sifrei*, 'Shofetim', 210 (ed. Finkelstein, p. 244), and *Midrash tanḥuma*, 'Ha'azinu', 1 (ed. Buber, p. 51 and note), where a similar interpretation of the verse is offered: '"Atone

Although this last source became an important support for medieval authorities in promoting belief in atonement for the dead, it involves a non-literal interpretation of the talmudic passage at hand and has been shown not to reflect the original intent of the redactors.[22] Additionally, although several examples of prayer for the dead appear in the Talmud, as we shall see below, the sages do not promote such prayer,[23] nor do they make explicit mention of any such contemporaneous practice.[24]

for Your nation"—these are the living; "whom You have redeemed"—these are the dead.' The Midrash concludes, 'This teaches us that the dead require atonement.' This interpretation of the verse as part of a ceremony which revolves around expiatory prayer and sacrifice proves that the living can secure posthumous atonement for the dead.

22 According to Israel Lévi, the passage in *Horayot 6a* speaks of the atonement of the living, not of the dead. The sacrifice of the *eglah arufah* atones for the sins of 'those who left Egypt' only inasmuch as their memory is perpetuated by the living; it does not atone for sins committed by a previously deceased generation. Only later on, in the geonic period, was this talmudic passage cited as the origin of the custom of giving charity for the dead, and then it served to substantiate a practice already in existence. See Lévi, 'La Commémoration des âmes dans le Judaïsme', 52–5, and Urbach, *The Sages*, 510 n. 37. According to Urbach, the talmudic passage itself denies the proposition that the sacrifice atones 'even for a community of dead', yet this does not prevent later authorities from citing this source 'even with reference to individuals' (ibid. 509). In the thirteenth century, R. Tsidkiyah Harofé of Rome, author of *Shibolei haleket*, quotes his contemporary, R. Avigdor Kohen Tsedek, who understands the passage in *Horayot* to refer only to the absolution of that generation, and only from the crime of murder. He rejects the suggestion that it might substantiate the practice of distributing alms on behalf of the dead in order to secure posthumous atonement for them. See *Shibolei haleket hashalem*, ed. Mirsky, 311–12.

23 This is the scholarly opinion of Israel Lévi in 'La Commémoration des âmes dans le Judaïsme'. While he cites some examples of prayer for the dead in the Talmud, he dispels any notion that the rabbis promoted such practice. Urbach would generally concur with Lévi's formulation of the talmudic position on the matter; see *The Sages*, 508–11.

24 Ta-Shma espouses this position when he notes that, apart from asking the basic question 'Is there atonement for the dead?', there is no explicit mention in the Talmud of prayer or other pious practices performed by the living on behalf of the dead. See 'A Remark on the Topic of the Mourner's Kaddish' (Heb.), 561, end of n. 8. A. Edrei, however, disagrees, and argues that the Talmud does speak of the subject in its discussions of how a son can accrue merit for a deceased father. Although it is a matter of debate, some talmudic authorities require a child to assume responsibility for his father's obligations after the latter's death. Such responsibilities include bringing a sacrifice that he intended to bring, paying back his debts, returning items he stole, or performing 'redemption of the firstborn' that he never performed. Failure to fulfil these obligations causes harm to the deceased parent. Edrei argues that later *midrashim* build upon this talmudic basis and add on the notion that any pious action, including prayer, aids the father after he dies. See 'Atonement for the Dead' (Heb.), 1–27. S. Glick feels that, while the issue of whether the living can achieve atonement for the dead through acts of piety was originally surrounded by dispute in rabbinic literature, the notion gained increasing legitimacy in the Talmud and had become widespread by the tenth century: *A Light Unto the Mourner* (Heb.), 127–31.

By the time of the *ge'onim*, even prior to the tenth century, the custom of giving charity on behalf of the dead existed among Jews.[25] At least one geonic authority, the tenth-century R. Sherira Gaon, is known to have been opposed to this practice, either in its entirety or at least in certain cases.[26] In the eleventh century R. Hai Gaon, while accepting the legitimacy of the custom, was unsure about the efficacy of either the distribution of alms or prayer for the dead.[27] Only his contemporary R. Nisim Gaon accepted the validity of these actions and believed in their efficacy. Citing talmudic passages such as *Eruvin* 65*a* and *Ḥagigah* 15*b*, which recount incidents in which prayer succeeds in releasing sinners from their punishment in the afterlife, R. Nisim concluded that 'these are clear proofs that prayerful intercession is beneficial'.[28]

The Geonic Model of Prayer for the Dead

Those geonic authorities who accepted the legitimacy of the regnant practices understood prayer for the dead in a way that resembled ancient systems of patronage. Like the petitionary words of the late Roman *patroni* on behalf of their clients before the emperor at court,[29] it is specifically the prayer of a righteous person (*tsadik*) or a person of great merit (*ba'al zekhut*), says R. Hai Gaon, which, on account of the elevated status and influence of the holy person, can find favour before God and secure a pardon for the dead sinner from the heavenly court.[30] Additionally, the giving of alms to the poor benefits the dead, as long as one among the poor has

[25] According to Lévi, the Jewish custom was unconsciously borrowed from the Christians at this time. See 'La Commémoration des âmes dans le Judaïsme', 47–8.

[26] Lévi and Wistinetzky cite from 'an old collection of responsa' the dissenting opinion of R. Sherira (d.1006), who, they feel, is strongly opposed to the practice. See Lévi, 'La Commémoration des âmes dans le Judaïsme', 53, and *Sefer ḥasidim*, ed. Wistinetzky, p. 29 n. 2. A careful reading of R. Sherira, however, seems to indicate that he opposed it only in a specific situation—that of the advancement of the dead to a place of posthumous reward. A fuller discussion of this topic will be presented later on in this chapter.

[27] R. Hai Gaon expresses his doubts regarding prayer thus: 'it is possible that the Holy One, blessed be He, accepts'; and regarding alms he writes, 'it is possible that it benefits him but it is not certain'. See *Otsar hage'onim*, ed. Levin, 'Ḥagigah', 27–8. See also Glick, *A Light Unto the Mourner* (Heb.), 131–2. The tentativeness of the *ge'onim*, according to Lévi, is due to the Talmud's relative silence on the subject. See 'La Commémoration des âmes dans le Judaïsme', 53.

[28] See *SḤ* 32, p. 30. The entire section of *SḤ* 30–2 is copied by R. Judah from R. Nisim Gaon's *Megilat setarim*. See also Poznansky, 'Megilat setarim' (Heb.), 193, and 'Sefer megilat setarim', ed. Abramson, 335.

[29] On the modelling of intercession before God by holy people after the late Roman system of patronage, see Brown, *The Cult of the Saints*.

[30] *Otsar hage'onim*, ed. Levin, 'Ḥagigah', 28.

sufficient merit with which he can 'find favour' before God and cause him to lighten the posthumous sentence.[31] According to R. Nisim, the success of the intercessor's prayer in mitigating or abrogating the torment of the deceased is directly dependent upon the importance of the intercessor and the severity of the sin involved.[32]

Talmudic accounts corroborate this model; it is only the intercession of righteous, pious, and learned men—such as R. Yohanan, whose prayer releases even the apostate Elisha ben Avuyah from Gehenna, and R. Eleazar ben Azaryah, who boasts that his prayer can exempt the entire world from posthumous punishment—that can be effective. R. Nisim further argues that the punishment that God decrees upon the wicked is dependent upon two conditions: 'if he [the sinner] does not repent, nor does anyone whose intercession is beneficial intercede for him, then he will be punished'.[33] Punishment can only ensue when intercession by a person of high standing (the sinner's patron, as it were) has failed.

The geonic model of prayer for the dead is, to a great extent, rooted in traditional midrashic notions of an enthroned God who consults with his heavenly court before rendering a sentence.[34] These midrashic ideas, in turn, bear a striking similarity to the ancient Roman model of patronage. The Midrash repeatedly draws upon the analogy of earthly patronage when it portrays Moses, a figure of importance in God's court, beseeching the 'King of all Kings' for mercy and forgiveness and requesting amnesty on behalf of a sinful Israel, his guilty client.[35] This midrashic model was still operative in the eleventh century: Rashi made use of it in his Bible commentary,[36] in which Midrash plays a central role in general.[37] It is not hard

[31] R. Hai writes that if the intercession of a righteous person is unsuccessful then 'our practice is to distribute alms to the poor so that they request mercy for the deceased [i.e. pray for him] and they enjoy [i.e. the poor benefit from the alms]. If there is among them one who has merit enough to find favour before Him and to lighten it [i.e. the sentence of posthumous punishment], then it is possible that it will benefit him [the deceased]' (ibid.).

[32] *SḤ* 32, p. 29. See also Poznansky, 'Megilat setarim' (Heb.), 191–3, and 'Sefer megilat setarim', ed. Abramson, 335.

[33] See *SḤ* 32, p. 30, and Poznansky, 'Megilat setarim' (Heb.), 193.

[34] See Urbach, *The Sages*, 177–81.

[35] A prime example appears in *Midrash tanḥuma*, 'Korah', 9 (ed. Buber, p. 88). Here, Moses is analogous to the 'beloved friend' of the king or emperor who intercedes successfully on behalf of the Israelites, gaining for them amnesty from God on three separate occasions (following the sins of the Golden Calf, the complainers, and the spies). Moses despairs of relying on his high standing in court and his favour before God on the fourth occasion—the rebellion fomented by Korah. See also *Midrash tanḥuma*, 'Ha'azinu', 1 (ed. Buber, p. 51).

[36] Rashi on Num. 16: 4 cites *Midrash tanḥuma*, 'Korah', 9, mentioned in the previous note.

[37] On the role played by Midrash in Rashi's biblical commentary, see Zohari, *Aggadic Tales and Rabbinic Halakhah* (Heb.).

to imagine that this model of patronage could easily extend to the arena of the afterlife, so that only figures of immense holiness and righteousness would have the power to successfully intercede in prayer on behalf of the dead.

Although the *ge'onim* resided in a Muslim milieu, their model did not stem from that culture, as Muslim teaching on prayer for the dead did not pattern itself on a patronage model. Whereas the Qur'an, with its emphasis on God's strict justice, seems to deny altogether the efficacy of prayerful intercession, in the later Middle Ages an increasing number of Islamic jurists supported such a belief in an attempt to temper justice with mercy.[38] By the tenth century, the practice of intercessory prayer at the gravesite was firmly established in Islamic lands.[39] However, here it was the prayer of ordinary individuals that served to aid faithful relatives in the period immediately after death, known as *al-barzakh*.[40] From the late eighth century on, prayers emerged which beseeched God to protect the deceased from the 'tortures of the grave'—the punishment meted out in *al-barzakh*.[41] The righteousness of the intercessor was not a requirement for efficacious prayer; on the contrary, it was considered the duty of every son to pray for, and give alms on behalf of, his dead father.[42]

Christian Background: Origins of Medieval Suffrages for the Dead

In contrast to Judaism, prayer for the dead had been an established part of Christian practice from very early on. During the first few centuries of Christian history, the recitation of psalms at the bedside of the dying had the joyful accompaniment of the soul to Heaven as its primary aim.[43] With scant reference to either the notion of penitence or that of Hell, the late antique Roman Christian death rite ensured a positive reception of the soul

[38] Idelman Smith and Yazbeck Haddad, *The Islamic Understanding of Death and Resurrection*, 76–8, 80–2, and Halevi, *Muhammad's Grave*, 227–9.

[39] Shoshan, 'High Culture and Popular Culture in Medieval Islam', 83.

[40] Idelman Smith and Yazbeck Haddad, *The Islamic Understanding of Death and Resurrection*, 59–60. A view did exist, though, that on the Day of Judgement Muhammad was the only suitable intercessor (ibid. 80–1). On the prayers of individuals on behalf of their deceased loved ones, see also Halevi, *Muhammad's Grave*, 228–9.

[41] Halevi, *Muhammad's Grave*, 229.

[42] Idelman Smith and Yazbeck Haddad, *The Islamic Understanding of Death and Resurrection*, 60.

[43] Paxton, *Christianizing Death*, 43. In one sense this original function of the death ritual of the medieval Church is still retained: Holy Communion is also known as the *viaticum*, which literally means 'one for the road'. See Binski, *Medieval Death*, 32.

into the hands of God.[44] The earliest official Roman Christian rite of the dead, the Ordo Defunctorum (Office of the Dead), was a mass which served to identify the death of the individual with the sacrifice of Christ, thus ensuring one's salvation at the time of the Last Judgement.[45] Only with the insecurity of the Barbarian Age did the notion of penitence and the need for purification enter into the now localized rites.[46] It was especially the death rites containing highly developed systems of penance, such as those emanating from Spanish Visigothic and Irish and Anglo-Saxon sources, that became synthesized in Frankish Gaul into the unified medieval rite under the influence of the Carolingian Church.[47]

Augustine's prayer for his mother, with its confident and optimistic tone, expresses well the most ancient functions of prayer for the dead:[48] a positive affirmation of death and thanksgiving to God for the safe passage of the soul and its repose in him.[49] Augustine associates these functions with one specific group of the dead—'the very good'. It is a sign of things to come, however, that he no longer assumes the assured salvation of all the departed faithful. In the same passage that contains his prayer for his mother, he adds a new function—instrumentality. The idea that prayer is efficacious in aiding those who need it and are worthy of it is particularly useful for the group which he labels 'the not very bad'. For this specific group, prayer, along with the offering of the mass and the distribution of alms, is beneficial 'either by [bringing about] a full remission, or, certainly, by making the damnation [*damnatio*] suffered more bearable'. Both the 'very good' and the 'very bad' are excluded, however, from such benefit—the former as they have no need for it, and the latter because they do not deserve it, although prayer here does serve 'as a kind of consolation for the living'.[50] Augustine's pronouncements later became the basis for the understanding of prayer for the dead in the medieval Church.

While Augustine believes that prayer, alms, and the offering of the mass can benefit the souls of the not very bad, he is, at the same time, careful to restrict this benefit. He emphasizes that these actions are efficacious

44 Paxton, *Christianizing Death*, 44.

45 For this reason, the rite includes the reading of the passages describing Christ's Passion at the bedside of the dying. These two elements of this fourth- or fifth-century rite—the offering of the mass and the scriptural readings—eventually separated and developed, between the years 500 and 900, into the medieval rites of the Requiem Mass and the Office of the Dead. See Binski, *Medieval Death*, 32 and 53.

46 Paxton, *Christianizing Death*, 61–9.

47 Ibid. 73–88.

48 Atwell, 'From Augustine to Gregory the Great', 175–6.

49 McLaughlin, *Consorting with Saints*, 191.

50 Augustine, *Enchiridion*, par. 110, quoted in Edwards, 'The Idea of Post Mortem Purgation', 102. See also McLaughlin, *Consorting with Saints*, 191.

only if the deceased 'earned, while living, the privilege of being helped by them afterwards'. So as not to undermine his strong faith in the accountability of individuals for their own actions at the time of judgement, he pronounces, 'Let no one hope to obtain from God after death what he neglected in this world.'[51] Only a person who performs 'good deeds whilst in the body' can hope to be aided in the next world by the pious acts of the living,[52] and even then these cannot provide him 'with new merits, but merely give[s] back to [him] the consequences of [his] old ones'.[53]

In the sixth century, Gregory the Great built upon Augustine's statements regarding the efficacy of suffrages for the dead. He elevated prayer for the dead to the status of dogma,[54] while at the same time illustrating, through the use of exempla, the connection between such prayer and purgation in a way that Augustine never had.[55] Similarly, Gregory accentuated the mass as a 'particularly efficacious form of intercession'. Whereas Augustine speaks of the offering of the mass on behalf of the dead only as a communal, liturgical ceremony of the Church, Gregory conceives of it as a more individualized offering with profound results; it 'consistently aids souls even after death, so that the very souls of the departed seem sometimes to yearn for this'.[56]

Gregory also highlights the beneficial role played by the saints. Drawing upon the model of Roman patronage, he envisions saints as potential patrons of the dead; one can invoke them through prayer to act as one's defenders on Judgement Day.[57] Like Augustine, he is cautious about the utility of suffrages: pious acts of the living cannot mitigate the suffering of the dead or release damned souls from their posthumous punishment. Only those who sinned through ignorance, not malice, or who have

[51] Augustine, *Enchiridion*, par. 110, quoted in Edwards, 'The Idea of Post Mortem Purgation', 101.

[52] Augustine, *De cura gerenda pro mortuis*, 464, quoted in Edwards, 'The Idea of Post Mortem Purgation', 101.

[53] Augustine, *Sermones*, 172, quoted in McLaughlin, *Consorting with Saints*, 190.

[54] Atwell, 'From Augustine to Gregory the Great', 175.

[55] Although Augustine outlines two middling categories of dead who might benefit from posthumous purgation and a middling group of souls who might benefit from prayer, he never links these categories. The first writer to actually forge a connection between the two is the sixth-century grammarian Julian Pomerius. While Gregory suggests the connection through the exempla he records in the *Dialogues*, it is the eighth-century theologian Bede the Venerable who first links the two concepts explicitly. McLaughlin, *Consorting with Saints*, 192–3.

[56] Atwell, 'From Augustine to Gregory the Great', 180. One exemplum that Gregory cites became the source of the medieval practice of offering masses for a soul for thirty consecutive days; it was known by his name as the 'Gregorian trental'.

[57] Ibid. 178–9.

merited the aid of the living through their own good deeds, will be able to benefit from that aid.[58]

Early medieval Irish visionary literature contributed to the dissemination of the new ideas regarding prayer and masses for the dead. Up until the seventh century, Irish views reflected those in various ecclesiastical liturgical texts common to all the main sectors of Western Christendom from late antiquity. The Church prayed for the salvation of the souls of all deceased Christian faithful from the 'clutches of hell' at the time of the Last Judgement.[59] Two seventh-century Irish accounts, the 'Vision of Fursey' and the 'Life of Columba', both bearing the influence of Egyptian early Christian ascetic ideas, introduced a novel function to prayer for the dead in Ireland; the prayer of the faithful, along with the intercession of the saints, could now aid souls immediately after death by freeing them from the struggle of angels and demons over their fate.[60] But even here, in the 'Life of Columba', the dead who benefit from the prayers of the saint and his monks are only those whose behaviour during their lifetime allowed them to merit such assistance.[61]

These seventh-century texts prepared the way for the full acceptance of Gregory's views on the efficacy of suffrages for the dead, not just at the precise moment of death, but in the entire posthumous period of suffering. Eighth-century Irish eschatological texts as well as penitential handbooks promoted short, clearly specified periods of prayer in order to redeem souls from Hell, while small chapels sprang up within Irish monasteries in order to offer additional intercessory masses.[62] In the visionary literature of the period a direct connection was forged between suffrages for the dead and purgation immediately after death.[63]

The utility of suffrages performed by the Church is underlined in several ninth-century Carolingian visions. In a vision of the monk Wettin, those who refuse the requests of the dead to pray for the abatement of their suffering bring upon themselves purgatorial pain.[64] Two other visions tell of famous deceased Carolingian rulers who appeal to their living offspring for aid in the form of masses, oblations, prayers, psalms, vigils, and alms in order to release their soul from posthumous torment.[65] In the 'Vision of

[58] Ibid. 180–1.
[59] Smyth, 'The Origins of Purgatory', 105–6.
[60] Ibid. 116 and 119–20.
[61] Ibid. 118–19.
[62] Ibid. 129–31.
[63] See the English monk Bede the Venerable's account of the vision of Drythelm and the attendant discussion above, p. 162.
[64] Edwards, 'The Idea of Post Mortem Purgation', 127.
[65] In the 'Vision of a Certain Poor Woman' of northern Italy, a message is sent to Louis the Pious to offer seven masses for the soul of his dead father, the emperor Charlemagne. In the

Bernoldus' as well as the 'Vision of Rotcharius', the message that suffrages for the dead work is highlighted: after having fulfilled the requests of the dead, the visionaries return to visit the other world a second time and find those who were in torment to be now 'in good estate' or in a state of glory.[66] The intervention of saints, particularly of the Carolingian patrons, also plays a role in the release of souls from suffering in these visionary accounts.[67]

Prayer for the Damned

In the early medieval period, the notion that one could or even should pray for the damned, either for their release from Hell or for the easing of their torments, was considered by many, including the educated, to be legitimate.[68] This was due to a variety of factors, such as the misinterpretation of Augustine's statement on the matter,[69] confusion regarding purgatorial doctrine,[70] lingering belief in provisional damnation,[71] misrepresentations surrounding the doctrine of the Harrowing of Hell,[72] and 'popular miseri-

'Vision of Charles the Fat', his father, Louis the German, makes a desperate plea to him to undertake on his behalf, along with his bishops, abbots, and the entire ecclesiastical order, all the forms of suffrage specified above in order to free him from his posthumous penance of immersion in boiling water. See Edwards, 'The Idea of Post Mortem Purgation', 128–9.

66 *De visione Bernoldi presbyteri*, cited in Edwards, 'The Idea of Post Mortem Purgation', 130. The Rotcharius text is taken from Wattenbauch, 'Aus Petersburger Handschriften', 72–4, quoted in Edwards, 'The Idea of Post Mortem Purgation', 131.

67 See e.g. the 'Vision of Charles the Fat' in Edwards, 'The Idea of Post Mortem Purgation', 129.

68 McLaughlin, *Consorting with Saints*, 204. See also Baschet, *Les Justices de l'au-delà*, 534–56.

69 Despite his own statements to the contrary, Augustine's use of the word *damnatio* in the passage from the *Enchiridion* quoted above led later theologians and writers to attribute to him a belief in the efficacy of prayer for the damned. Instead of referring to a temporary pain, the term was understood by early medieval authors to mean the state of damnation of the reprobate in Hell. See Edwards, 'The Idea of Post Mortem Purgation', 102–3, 136.

70 On the blurring of the lines between damnation and purgation in the minds of many medieval men and women, see ibid. 133, 139–41, 229–32, 234–5, 241. It is important to emphasize that the doctrine of purgation existed even in the so-called pre-purgatorial period; it was only Purgatory as a distinct place in the hereafter that was a later development.

71 According to this concept, some 'not very bad' sinners would be condemned to eternal punishment were it not for the intervention of the saints or of the living on their behalf. Although this idea is rejected by the great scholars of the early Middle Ages, it still appears in some twelfth-century texts. See McLaughlin, *Consorting with Saints*, 188, 191, and 206.

72 Rooted in 1 Peter 3: 18–20, this doctrine teaches that Christ descended to Hell in order to preach faith in himself to the dead so as to liberate them. While the Church fathers disagreed as to who exactly is freed (merely the 'just' of the Old Testament or all those imprisoned there), there emerged the notion that some souls could be extracted from Hell before the Last Judge-

cordious sentiment', which held that a 'misericordious God would cure and pardon sin as much after as before death'.[73] Church liturgy lent credence to this notion: the above-mentioned ancient Office of the Dead spoke of 'a weeping Church' pleading before a Deus Inferni (God of Hell) to release souls from *locis poenarum* (place of punishment); despite the unrepentant state of the dead souls, the living beseeched God to take pity upon them and save them before they reached Hell, 'in which [there] is no redemption'.[74] Early medieval litanies substantiated the practice; at the turn of the tenth century, the Sacramentary of St Martin of Tours invoked the saints to pray for the departed soul's salvation from 'an infernal place', 'perpetual death', and 'the mouth of Gehenna',[75] while a well-known offertory of a mass of the same century asked Christ to 'free the souls of all the departed faithful from the torments of Hell'.[76] One ninth-century text states that the monks of Fleury pray for the souls of the damned, 'that their pains might at least be eased by the strict Judge'.[77] The contemporaneous Apocalypse of Mary describes how the Virgin, along with the patriarchs, prophets, and saints in Heaven, prays for the damned in Hell and obtains from God an annual respite for them during the days of Pentecost.[78]

Institutionalization under the Carolingians

In the Carolingian period, under the auspices of the great monasteries of Cluny, the function of prayer for the dead was greatly enhanced and expanded. New prayers, designed for the commemoration of the dead, were now inserted into the liturgy of these houses, and recitation of the Office of

ment and that the saintly figures played a dominant role in this. Sometime between the second and fifth centuries, the placid picture of Christ preaching to the damned became 'vulgarized' and was transformed into a hostile scene in which he storms or 'harrows' Hell in order to rescue the righteous of the Old Testament. See Edwards, 'The Idea of Post Mortem Purgation', 64–5. Confusion regarding the doctrine led to various beliefs which circulated during the ninth, tenth, and eleventh centuries—that Christ annually descends to Hell and releases souls from there, that he annually 'empties Hell' of all souls, and that the prayers and masses of the living propel him to make the annual descent to Hell. Such beliefs, in turn, influenced the liturgy; see Edwards, 138, and Baschet, *Les Justices de l'au-delà*, 534–42.

73 Edwards, 'The Idea of Post Mortem Purgation', 135–6.

74 Ibid. 136.

75 Sicard, *La Liturgie de la mort dans l'église*, 52–4, quoted in Edwards, 'The Idea of Post Mortem Purgation', 137.

76 McLaughlin, *Consorting with Saints*, 204.

77 *De miraculis sancti Benedicti*, 21, quoted in Edwards, 'The Idea of Post Mortem Purgation', 136.

78 *The Apocryphal New Testament*, 563, quoted in Edwards, 'The Idea of Post Mortem Purgation', 138.

the Dead became a daily practice in some monastic communities.[79] Clerics of the eighth and ninth centuries described the monastic practice of prayer for the dead as 'orderly intercession through carefully integrated structures'.[80]

Commemoration was also increasingly individualized at this time. Laymen turned more and more to the monks to have their memory perpetuated. In return for the bestowal of land and the granting of privileges, certain royal monasteries prayed for the souls of Carolingian rulers and provided anniversary services for their departed family members. These services included the offering of the mass, the recitation of psalms, and the yearly distribution of alms to the poor.[81] Wishing also to be associated with the 'representatives of salvation', members of aristocratic families donated landed property to monasteries and asked in return for prayers *pro remedio animae*—for the relief of their own souls, as well as of those of their deceased parents and ancestors.[82] These names were inscribed in confraternal books, memorial books, or 'books of life' belonging to the monasteries, and were invoked during the celebration of the mass, so that, in this way, the dead would be present during the ceremony.[83] Whereas all the dead in these books of the ninth and tenth centuries were commemorated every day, by the eleventh century individual names were recorded in necrologies and people were commemorated only on the anniversary of their death.[84]

The establishment of All Souls' Day at Cluny by the abbot Odilo around the year 1000 expanded the sphere of suffrages performed by the Church to include not just the landed laity but all of the Christian faithful. On 2 November every year, Cluniac priests were enjoined to celebrate private masses, undertake to feed a specified number of paupers, and to pray for 'the repose of all souls'.[85] While all members of the *societas Christiana* were now to be memorialized by the Church, by the same token, those who were not members of this community (pagans and heretics) were to be

[79] Lauwers, *La Mémoire des ancêtres*, 95, and Iogna-Prat, *Order and Exclusion*, 222.

[80] McLaughlin, *Consorting with Saints*, 254.

[81] Lauwers, *La Mémoire des ancêtres*, 97.

[82] Iogna-Prat and Picard, 'Les Morts dans la comptabilité céleste des Clunisiens', 58 and 66.

[83] Ibid. 58, and Mclaughlin, *Consorting with Saints*, 99. McLaughlin cites Otto Gerhard Oexle, who states that by invoking the name of a dead person the living invoked the deceased himself.

[84] Iogna-Prat and Picard, 'Les Morts dans la comptabilité céleste des Clunisiens', 64.

[85] *Liber tramitis aeui Odilonis*, 187, cited in Iogna-Prat, 'Les Morts dans la comptabilité céleste des Clunisiens', 63–4.

excluded from this privilege.[86] Prayer for the dead in the early medieval period centred upon notions of 'appropriate' and 'inappropriate', and theologians used a 'language of entitlement' to define the social parameters of inclusion.[87]

Prayer in this period was also 'associative' in nature. Families would establish a tradition of patronage with one particular monastery over the course of several generations. The family members would provide donations of land and money to the monastery, offer themselves as witnesses for the signing of monastic documents, and help out the monastery in times of need. In return, they received from the monks acceptance into their order if they wished to join, hospitality, the prestige of association with a powerful religious house, help in times of need, burial within the monastery, and, of course, inclusion in its prayer services as well as memorialization after death. Despite the wide range of services provided by the monks to their lay patrons, it was especially inclusion in the prayer service that was sought by the laity: 'prayer constituted the power that attracted the patronage'.[88]

With prayer for the dead serving as a 'symbol of identity', those who were prayed for by the House of Cluny were included in its midst and therefore felt more assured of meriting a favourable judgement after death.[89] The precise number of suffrages performed was less important than the existence of the relationship and the formation of close bonds between the lay family (the clients) and the specialists in prayer who interceded on their behalf (their patrons).[90] Prayer also had a wider variety of meanings now; it retained the older functions of prayer for the dead—which included thanksgiving for the joyful reception of the soul and protection on the journey to Heaven, as well as intervention before the heavenly court at the time of the Last Judgement—to which was added the new role of remitting the pains of purgation experienced by the soul immediately after death.[91]

[86] According to McLaughlin, Augustine, in contrast to early medieval theologians, speaks of the Church praying for all the dead, even if they cannot be helped by such intercession. See *Consorting with Saints*, 238.

[87] Ibid. 238–9.

[88] See P. Johnson, *Prayer, Patronage, and Power*, 89–91 and 180. Although speaking of a later period, Joel Rosenthal arrives at a similar conclusion: 'Almost all forms of medieval philanthropy had the purchase of prayers as their ultimate goal' (*The Purchase of Paradise*, 10). See also McLaughlin, *Consorting with Saints*, 237 and 251–2. According to McLaughlin, the fragmentation of society, the trend towards localization, an economy based on plundering and exchange of gifts, widespread illiteracy, and poor communication were all factors which combined to create the social-associative character of early medieval prayer (p. 52).

[89] McLaughlin, *Consorting with Saints*, 248. [90] Ibid. [91] Ibid. 234–5 and 249.

Early Medieval Models

Three models of prayer for the dead emerged during the early medieval period—one particular to saints, another to monks, and a third to clerics. Drawing upon the wide range of meanings which prayer for the dead assumed at this time, authors selected different images and ideas from this repertoire in order to promote their own interests and concerns.

Two of the three models were based upon the Roman system of patronage. The first one, built around saints, demonstrates this connection most clearly. Authors of saints' lives and of vision literature portrayed the dramatic intercession of figures of immense power and holiness in an effort to promote the cult of their community's patron saint. Through their use of miracles, or because of their high standing in the celestial court, saints were able to intercede for the dead in extreme and supernatural ways. For example, they had the power to bring a sinner back to life so that he could confess his sins or do penance for them. Following the model of earthly patronage, saints were described as successfully interceding for their clients in the final moment before posthumous judgement was rendered. In miracle stories, their prayers had the potency to release even the condemned from Hell. It was through donations made to the saints or their churches that the early medieval laity entered into a relationship with them: laypeople expected their patrons to intercede on their behalf and hoped that, owing to the latter's saintliness, their soul would gain entry into Heaven, regardless of their own personal merits.[92]

The influence of the idea of patronage is apparent in the second early medieval model of prayer as well. In various chronicles in the tenth and especially the eleventh centuries, monastic writers praised their own order and, on account of their ascetic holiness and perpetual worship of God, linked its members with the company of the angels. This association with the *vita angelica* invested the Cluniac monks with the power to intercede for the dead; those whose prayers and psalmody mixed in with the heavenly chorus surely merited salvation not only for themselves but also for whomever they included in their prayers.[93] Monastic documents, including that establishing All Souls' Day, depict Cluny's greatness in the realm of prayer for the dead in a way that recalls the model set up by hagiographers.[94] Like the saints in the earlier *vitae*, the monks of Cluny have the power to

[92] Ibid. 215–18.

[93] Ibid. 228–9.

[94] McLaughlin argues that 'the feast of All Souls reflects Cluny's sense of power as much as its sense of charity toward the dead' (ibid. 233).

rescue condemned souls from Hell despite their reprobate status. Peter Damian's 'Life of St Odilo' describes how the prayers and alms of Cluny 'rip the souls of the damned' from the hands of 'innumerable demons',[95] while Raoul Glaber's chronicle proclaims unabashedly the superiority of Cluny on account of the 'frequent offering' of the mass which 'flourish[es] there', for 'scarcely any day passes in which their activity does not snatch souls from the power of evil demons'.[96]

It is only in the third prayer model, that of early medieval clerics, that the influence of the Roman system of patronage is not present. In sermons, theological treatises, commentaries on the liturgy, and penitentials, priests employed the notion of the pious duty of Mother Church to promote the intercession of the secular clergy on behalf of the dead through the traditional medium of the Office of the Dead.[97] Unlike the hagiographic and monastic models, this pastoral model relied not upon the great power or sanctity of its intercessors, but on the regular exercise of their office within the Church.[98] The bishops and priests extended their role as officiators of the sacrament of penance, both public and private, to the domain of the afterlife in order to aid the souls of their flock.[99] They understood prayer for the dead in a novel way, as an extension of the clerical power of absolution on the one hand, and of the practice of vicarious penance on the other.[100] Both of these concepts became associated with posthumous purgation at this time.

The clerical power of absolution was closely linked to the penitential system of the Church, as it was the performance of penance by the sinner that allowed him to be reincorporated within the Church.[101] On the basis

95 Peter Damian, 'Vita Sancti Odilonis', cited in McLaughlin, *Consorting with Saints*, 233.

96 Raoul Glaber, *Historiae*, 125, cited in McLaughlin, *Consorting with Saints*, 233.

97 McLaughlin, *Consorting with Saints*, 218.

98 Ibid. 225.

99 It was the special province of the bishop to perform the sacrament of penance in a situation of public penance. According to the dictates of the ancient penitential system, which was re-established in the early ninth century, the sinner made a public confession before the entire Christian community and was formally excluded from that community until a public, ritualized ceremony of reincorporation was performed. The system of private penance, which originated in the monasteries of seventh-century Ireland, involved the private confession of the penitent and the assigning of a penitential 'tariff'. It was the role of the priest to pray for the absolution of the sinner at the time of the completion of his penance. The two systems of penance coexisted during the medieval period. See McLaughlin, 'Consorting with Saints', 260–1, and ead., *Consorting with Saints*, 219–20. For a more detailed description of the dictates of public penance, the symbolic meaning behind the rituals involved, as well as the history of its transformation from an ancient Romano-Germanic rite to the northern French one of the twelfth and thirteenth centuries, see Mansfield, *The Humiliation of Sinners*, 178–81, 208–9, and 214–19.

100 McLaughlin, *Consorting with Saints*, 221.

101 Ibid. 219–20 and 222.

of the authority vested in them by the apostles, priests had the power to 'bind and loose'—to deny sinners the salvific benefits of the sacraments and then to admit them once again into communion when they had repented of their sins. Importantly, it was not God but the bishop or priest himself who formally loosened the bonds of sin, forgave the sinner, and reincorporated him within the sacramental community.[102] With regard to the afterlife, prayer, fasting, and the offering of the mass by the clergy could bring the period of posthumous purgation to an abrupt end by formally absolving dead individuals of their sins and thereby reincorporating them into the community of the saved.[103] According to this formula, it was the performance of one particular clerical act on behalf of the deceased that brought an immediate end to the suffering of his soul; as soon as the sinner was prayed for or a mass was offered on his behalf, he was freed from his torment.[104]

The second understanding of prayer for the dead among clerics, as mentioned above, was as an aspect of vicarious penance. In the same way that a Christian layperson or a member of the clergy could pray, fast, give alms, or offer a mass on behalf of a living penitent in order to aid him in the completion of his penance, so too, a priest's prayer or offering of the mass (perceived as more effective than the efforts of laypeople), or the distribution of alms on behalf of a departed Christian, could speed up the process of purgation of the soul.[105] According to this formula, it was the accumulation of penitential acts performed vicariously by the living, rather than a single act, as in the case of priestly absolution, that led to the more rapid completion of the penance of the dead person who had failed to complete it during his lifetime, and hence to the liberation of his soul from purgation by God 'ahead of time'.[106]

While promoting the intercessory role of the Church, early medieval clerics were cautious about the dangers inherent in over-reliance on prayer for the dead. Concerned with the moral behaviour of their flock in this world, they emphasized the limited utility of suffrages in the next.[107] Whether by means of vicarious penance or through absolution, the Church

[102] McLaughlin argues that clerical absolution was operative even within the system of private penance. Since most penitents voluntarily abstained from participation in the sacraments of the Church while they were fulfilling their assigned penance, the concept of sin as separation from the Church still applied. See *Consorting with Saints*, 222–3.

[103] Ibid. 223.

[104] Ibid. 224.

[105] It was the concept of vicarious penance as applied to the dead which underlay the formation of all kinds of early medieval prayer associations. See ibid. 221–2.

[106] Ibid. 222, and ead., 'Consorting with Saints', 262–3.

[107] McLaughlin, *Consorting with Saints*, 219.

was aiding only the deserving dead; the souls suffering in the hereafter were merely continuing the penance they had left unfinished during their lifetime. Even without clerical intercession, these souls would complete their penance on their own before Judgement Day.[108] This element accounted for a significant divergence between the function of suffrages according to the pastoral model as against that in the other two models. Whereas the miracle stories of saints or the tales of monastic writers tell of a supernatural turn of events in which the saintly intercessor succeeds in reversing the fate assigned to the soul in question, pastoral texts speak of the regular dispensation of Divine justice to contrite, penitent souls, whose sentence is merely accelerated by the efforts of the Church on their behalf. It is not the release from Hell of condemned souls and the salvation of the unworthy that is achieved by prayer for the dead in these texts, but the faster completion of the posthumous penance of worthy souls undergoing purgation.[109]

Hagiographers and monastic chroniclers were unconcerned with the personal merits of those being prayed for, but not so the clerics, who proclaimed the apostolic teaching that each person will be judged 'according to what he has done while in the body, whether good or evil'.[110] By espousing the notion of personal merit and insisting that prayer for the dead only benefited those who deserved it, early medieval clergy aligned themselves doctrinally with Augustinian teaching on the matter—prayer did not provide the dead with any new merits, but merely gave back to them 'the consequences of their old ones'.[111] Even in the case of those who merited clerical intercession, the priests far preferred good works and repentance in this world to reliance on prayer and other forms of posthumous aid offered by others.[112] Hincmar of Reims expresses this idea when he invokes the words of Gregory the Great that 'it is a safer way for each person to do himself, during his life, the good that he hopes will be done by others after his death. For truly it is more blessed to go forth in freedom than to seek liberty after bondage.'[113] The notions of personal merit and individual responsibility in this world which emanate from such a statement greatly reduce the utility of suffrages for the dead. Described as highly efficacious and urgently needed in hagiographic and monastic texts, in pastoral writings they occupy a far more muted role.[114]

108 McLaughlin, 'Consorting with Saints', 262.

109 McLaughlin, *Consorting with Saints*, 219.

110 Rom. 14: 10 and 2 Cor. 5: 10.

111 Augustine, *Sermones*, 172, quoted in McLaughlin, *Consorting with Saints*, 190.

112 McLaughlin, *Consorting with Saints*, 219.

113 Gregory the Great, *Dialogi*, 4: 60, cited in McLaughlin, *Consorting with Saints*, 219 n. 142.

114 McLaughlin, *Consorting with Saints*, 219.

The Role of Suffrages in the High Medieval Period

The great social and economic transformations of the high medieval period led to changes in the nature of prayer for the dead.[115] Once part of a complex, long-term relationship between laity and clergy, from the twelfth century onward it became increasingly detached from its social context and was reified.[116] No longer bearing a wide range of meanings and functions, it assumed the sole task of liberating souls from posthumous suffering. Whereas earlier the formation of a relationship between the intercessor and the deceased was at the heart of lay requests for inclusion in the suffrages of the Church, in the high medieval period it was a specified number of intercessory acts, to be performed by an ever-widening circle of clerics, that laypeople asked for in charters of donations.[117] Prayer was measured more in terms of its effectiveness than its appropriateness; each performance of a mass, a psalter, or an Office for the Dead was seen as 'a unit of force' which 'push[ed] against the weight of sin' and freed the soul that much sooner from its torment in the next world.[118] The associative early medieval prayer for the dead, with its emphasis on community and social identity, was replaced by prayer that was wholly instrumental and mechanical in nature—it became an object to be purchased and acquired for one's own self-serving interests.[119]

Urbanization and increased economic activity accelerated these changes, while also fostering the growth of the individual. The arithmetic calculations characteristic of commercial life, coupled with the new methods of reasoning employed by the scholastics, combined to create an 'accountancy of the hereafter'.[120] Such an accountancy was evident in late medieval testaments, in which individual testators prescribed precise numbers of masses to be offered, prayers to be chanted, and charitable money to be distributed according to a highly specified programme in order to commute the duration and intensity of their punishment in Purgatory.[121] The time beyond

[115] These transformations included demographic increase, the growth of urban economy, centralization of power on the political, religious, and socio-economic fronts, increased literacy and numeracy, and improved communication. See *Consorting with Saints*, 252–5. For the later medieval period, J. Chiffoleau stresses that the profound social and emotional dislocation caused by urbanization led to changes associated with suffrages for the dead, as evident in wills and testaments of the period. See *La Comptabilité de l'au-delà*, ix and 430.

[116] McLaughlin, *Consorting with Saints*, 235.

[117] Ibid. [118] Ibid. [119] Ibid. 235 and 252.

[120] This forms the subject of Chiffoleau's *La Comptabilité de l'au-delà*. See esp. 209–14.

[121] By the late medieval period, the number of masses requested by lay testators to be offered after their death reached into the tens of thousands. See ibid. viii–ix.

the grave, once measured by God in terms of eternity, became quantifiable according to human reckoning; one's 'sentence' in the hereafter was quantitatively fixed by establishing a proportional relationship between the amount of time spent in sin and the duration of posthumous suffering.[122] Such a reckoning could then be manipulated by human means: a set number of intercessory acts was purported to reduce one's sentence in Purgatory by a specified number of years.[123] These mathematical calculations, which were characteristic of the 'logic of Purgatory', demonstrated how the fear of immediate individual judgement predominated in the minds of laypeople in the thirteenth century.[124]

The role of the saints as intercessors for the dead also changed at this time. In the early medieval period, their power of intercession was predicated upon a long-standing relationship with their lay donors, or clients. Patronage was a localized affair in which laypeople sought to ally themselves with a 'specific liturgical community on Earth' in order to connect to the 'community of saints', who would intercede for their souls.[125] By contrast, in the high medieval period saintly intercession had become universalized.

As devotion to the Virgin Mary's cult intensified in the twelfth and thirteenth centuries, she assumed the role of intercessor par excellence and pleaded for all deceased sinners before Christ the Judge.[126] She intervened

122 Even the application of the term 'sentence' to the Divine punishments of the afterlife was a novel concept; see Le Goff, *The Birth of Purgatory*, 228. See also Chiffoleau, *La Comptabilité de l'au-delà*, 435.

123 Le Goff, 'The Time of Purgatory', 73–4.

124 Ibid. 72. The term 'logic of Purgatory' was coined by Le Goff (*The Birth of Purgatory*, 227). High medieval urbanization, according to Chiffoleau, fostered the growth of the individual in this way. Removed from the physical space of their deceased ancestors and placed outside the binding sphere of ancestral custom, people joined the new family of the 'cult of souls of Purgatory', and found themselves in dire need of masses and prayers. See Chiffoleau, *La Comptabilité de l'au-delà*, ix, 430–3. On the transition between the earlier 'tamed death' (death among family and friends, seen as part of the collective destiny of all men) and the later 'death of the self' or 'one's own death' (the more individualized notion of death in terms of both personal judgement and funerary practice), see Ariès, *Western Attitudes toward Death*.

125 McLaughlin, *Consorting with Saints*, 251. An illustration of this localized form of patronage is the Last Judgement scene sculpted upon the tympanum of Conques. Part of the procession of saints approaching an enthroned Christ, St Foi, the patron saint of the abbey, is depicted interceding for all the departed faithful, and especially for her 'clients'—the patrons of the abbey. See ibid. 250–1.

126 A primary factor that contributed to the centralization of the cult of the Virgin was the following fundamental distinction. Whereas, in the case of other saints, the miracle stories associated with their relics were crucial to promoting their cult, Mary's saintliness, an idea derived from the New Testament, was indisputable and was independent of any relics since her body was believed to have ascended directly to Heaven. See Ward, *Miracles and the Medieval*

to save her devotees, who were no longer bound by regional or familial attachments and often had no prior relationship to her; many of them demonstrated only a one-time loyalty or a nominal form of allegiance towards her, if at all.[127] In miracle stories and exempla surrounding the

Mind, 132–3. The centrality of the high medieval devotion to Mary should not be underestimated. R. Fulton, in her study of the shift in devotion to Christ and Mary as human beings, states that 'by the end of the twelfth century, devotion to Mary—measured in terms of frequency of church dedications, a subject of art, an object of pilgrimage, and a focus of formal liturgy—had surpassed devotion to all other figures of Christian history other than Christ himself' (*From Judgment to Passion*, 201). It was primarily the new orders of the twelfth century, the Premonstratensians and, above all, the Cistercians, which promoted the new-found devotion to the Virgin. Bernard of Clairvaux extolled her in his sermons and writings, and all the monasteries of the Order of Cîteaux were dedicated to her. See Mâle, *Religious Art in France*, 427–8.

Regarding the shift in the devotional image of Mary from regal Queen of Heaven to compassionate Mother of Christ, which began in the late eleventh century and culminated in the twelfth, see R. Fulton's study. By the thirteenth century, the dominant image of Mary was as Mediatrix—one who stands between God and her son, and whom 'God had chosen . . . for the task of pleading the cause of humanity before her Son'. See Pelikan, *Mary through the Centuries*, 133. For a description of a parallel manifestation of this shift in monumental art of the period, see Gold, *The Lady and the Virgin*.

The Virgin's intercessory power was highlighted also by theologians, some of whom considered her even more powerful than Christ. Fulton identifies Eadmer of Canterbury, student of Anselm, as one cleric who placed the 'superiority of her [the Virgin's] intercession over and above the just judgment of Christ'. Eadmer writes that, while Christ 'discerns the merits of the individuals', 'does not answer anyone who invokes him', and renders 'only just judgment', Mary will intercede whenever her name is invoked and will answer all prayers, 'even if the merits of he who invokes her do not deserve it' (cited in Fulton, *From Judgment to Passion*, 246).

Mary's role as intercessor is perhaps most evident in Last Judgement scenes of the twelfth and thirteenth centuries. Prior to this time, sculpted on church tympanums in western Europe, it was Christ who sat enthroned, surrounded only by the apostles. The Virgin Mary was introduced into these scenes for the first time in the twelfth century at Saint-Denis, and was placed on the right side of Christ. At Chartres, the apostles have been eliminated and only the Intercessors, Mary on the right side and St John on the left, surround Christ. Known as diesis and originating in Byzantine art, this motif became common in medieval artistic representations of the Last Judgement. See Katzenellenbogen, *The Sculptural Programs of Chartres Cathedral*, 84.

[127] Caesarius of Heisterbach records, for example, an exemplum which tells of a 'feeble-minded' priest who is deposed by Thomas of Canterbury because he knows only the Mass of the Virgin. For this small act of devotion alone, the Virgin intercedes on his behalf, threatens the archbishop with loss of speech, and has the priest restored to his former position. See *Dialogue*, 7: 4. This well-known Marian tale also appears in MS BL Harley 2385 fo. 67 and MS BL Arundel 506 fo. 3*b* (*Catalogue of Romances*, iii. 526 no. 100, 541 no. 14); see also Jacobus de Voragine, *The Golden Legend*, 528. The story shares many parallel elements with the 'Tale of the Herdsman' in *Sefer ḥasidim*: see *SḤ* 5–6 and its attendant discussion in Alexander-Frizer, *The Pious Sinner*, ch. 3. Another tale tells of an accomplished thief whose sole merit is his devotion to the Virgin, whom he 'saluted . . . with frequent prayers'. The thief is eventually caught and hanged for his crimes. However, due to his reverence for her, the Virgin miraculously saves him from death. See *The Golden Legend*, 527. Similarly, a condemned clerk is restored to life in order to reform his ways thanks to the intercession of the Virgin. She pleads his case on account of

Virgin, it was especially the undeserving nature of her supplicants, upon whom she took pity, that was highlighted.[128] Like the saints and monks described in early medieval hagiographies and monastic chronicles, Mary, too, had the sanctity and power to redeem even the worst sinners; she could wrest them from the clutches of Satan himself.[129] Notions of individual responsibility and personal merit were eclipsed in the face of the supernal grace and overwhelming compassion of the Virgin Mary.

R. Judah's Model of Prayer for the Dead

In the realm of prayer and other forms of aid for the dead, R. Judah's position as expressed in *Sefer ḥasidim* mirrors closely the early medieval pastoral model. He unequivocally states his belief in the utility of prayer, charity, and acts of piety for those who have passed on. He bases this belief on the concept of vicarious penance—an association that was first made by early medieval clerics, as we saw earlier. Like them, R. Judah stresses the importance of personal merit: only those who have accumulated merit during their lifetime will benefit from the actions of the living on their behalf. He clearly prefers the performance of good works and repentance in this world, particularly in the form of voluntary suffering, to reliance on the prayer and aid of others posthumously. For the average sinner who suffers eternally in Gehenna, prayer can help to alleviate somewhat the burden of torment. Yet, in opposition to the messages that emanate from some exempla and miracle stories (particularly those of the Virgin Mary), R. Judah declares that the undeserving can in no way benefit from the posthumous aid offered to them by others. Thus, by restricting the efficacy of these practices to the deserving only, he aligns himself once again with the pastoral model and rejects the two other early medieval models of prayer for the dead.

his 'exceeding love for the Mother of God' and because he had 'recited her holy Hours promptly and devoutly'. See *The Golden Legend*, 528.

128 Ward, *Miracles and the Medieval Mind*, 149. On the development of the Marian miracle stories see Ch. 5, n. 113 above.

129 One of the most famous miracle stories associated with the Virgin tells of a vicar named Theophilus, who makes a pact with Satan, trading his soul for money and power. When he is filled with remorse for his actions, the Virgin takes pity on him, wrests the document of pledge from Satan's hands, and returns it to Theophilus, thus freeing him from his pledge. See Jacobus de Voragine, *The Golden Legend*, 528–9. A similar story is told of an impoverished soldier who, wishing to be restored to his former position of wealth, makes a pact with the Devil; he promises his wife in exchange for the new-found riches. Because of the wife's allegiance to the Virgin, however, the Virgin switches places with her and saves her from falling into the clutches of the Devil. Moreover, she warns the Devil never to plot against those 'who invoke me piously', and casts him down to Hell. See *The Golden Legend*, 458–60.

R. Judah expresses these beliefs in several different passages in *Sefer ḥasidim*. In one place, he writes: 'When they pray in this world it causes good for the dead person.'[130] In another passage, he explains the advantage of burial near the town in which one lived, as proximity to the cemetery enables the bereaved to pray at the grave of the deceased and to 'request benefit for the souls [so that] they benefit them in that world'.[131]

The extent of the benefit that could be gained from the prayer of the living should not be minimized; one ghost tale that R. Judah recounts illustrates this. A certain community wished to relocate. A dead person who was buried in the cemetery nearby appeared to a member of the community in a dream and petitioned him not to leave. 'Don't abandon us', he pleaded, 'for we derive benefit when you visit the cemetery.' The ghost concluded his plea with a warning: if the community members did relocate, they would all be killed.[132] The people, however, did not take the ghost's threat seriously; as a result, the entire community was wiped out.

The fact that the dead rely upon the prayers of the living, and that they will harm or threaten anyone who neglects them, may well be a remnant of the pre-Christian notion of the dangerous dead. Whereas the 'bad dead' return to harm the living according to ancient Germanic belief, in this case the Christian dead return to physically attack or harm only those who neglect to aid them through prayers or through offering a mass for them, or who prevent others from doing so. While the Jewish dead in R. Judah's tale do not kill the community members, they return to forewarn them of impending danger on account of their neglectful behaviour—a well-known motif in the exempla literature.[133]

130 *SḤ* 273.

131 *SḤ* 270 and 1537. R. Judah invokes the statement of Barzilai Hagiladi in 2 Sam. 19: 38, 'Please let your servant remain so that I should die in my city', as scriptural proof for his idea. Yet it is evident that he inflects the meaning of the text to serve his purpose. According to the original meaning, Barzilai asks to remain in his own city until his death on account of his old age, his inability to benefit from the material pleasures the king could offer him, and his unwillingness to become a burden on the king. Ignoring these three explicit reasons, R. Judah infuses new meaning into the passage by inserting his own reason for Barzilai's refusal to join the king and his request to die in his city—because of 'the benefit that the dead gain from the prayers of their loved ones at their gravesites'.

132 *SḤ* 269.

133 One exemplum tells of a certain bishop who suspends a priest for celebrating the mass for the dead every day; the bishop is then threatened by the dead as he passes through a cemetery. This popular tale is found in seven different manuscripts in the *Catalogue of Romances* alone: see iii. 383 no. 158, 456 no. 39, 468 no. 2, 473 no. 22, 519 no. 2, 610 no. 56, and 686 no. 55. It also appears in Jacobus de Voragine's collection about the saints and their feats, *The Golden Legend*, where it is cited in the name of Peter of Cluny (p. 652). In another tale, a priest who regularly passes through a cemetery without praying for the dead buried there has his foot seized by a

Like prayers, alms distributed to the poor by the living also benefit the dead. After presenting several opposing arguments, R. Judah cites three halakhic sources which prove that, indeed, the charitable acts of others achieve posthumous atonement for the dead.[134] By summoning the halakhic evidence as well as the counter-evidence on the issue, R. Judah appears to argue here against the opposing view maintained by R. Shneur Kohen Tsedek, and to dismiss the hesitant position of R. Hai Gaon seen above. Invoking the authority of R. Nisim Gaon, he asserts with confidence the utility of such practices,[135] and elsewhere declares, 'And so it benefits the dead if the living pray on their behalf or give charity for them.'[136]

While R. Judah agrees with R. Nisim Gaon as far as utility is concerned, he rejects the latter's model of prayer for the dead. It is not coincidental that he similarly rejects two of the Christian models, since all three are fashioned after the ancient concept of patronage. Never does R. Judah speak in *Sefer ḥasidim* of the need for a *tsadik*, rabbi, person of exceptional merit, or hasid to pray for, or intercede on behalf of, the dead.[137] Even the *ḥasid ḥakham*, who is privy to the hidden Will of God (*retson haborê*) and

hand thrust out from a grave. See MSS BL Add. 27336 fo. 42 and 11872 fo. 79 (*Catalogue of Romances*, iii. 661 no. 192, 693 no. 10). Yet another story tells of a Cistercian monk (or, in one version, a priest of Limoges) who suffers in Purgatory and who cannot be aided by the prayers and masses of others because he neglected to celebrate masses for the dead when he was alive. See *Catalogue of Romances*, iii. 383 no. 166, 456 no. 40, 464 no. 6, 466 no. 42, 476 no. 61, and 494 no. 199.

134 In *SḤ* 35 and 273, R. Judah cites two of the three sources mentioned at the beginning of this chapter: he presents the biblical passage of the *eglah arufah* and the talmudic statement that a son can accrue merit for his dead father, but does not mention the third source, in which the son refers to himself in relation to his deceased father as 'the atonement of his bed'. Instead, he offers a novel comparison between the rabbinic case of a sin offering that has been dedicated for sacrifice but whose owner dies before it is offered and the laws of charity. In *Kidushin* 13*b*, the Talmud cites the tannaitic teaching that, in the case of a woman who dedicates an animal for a sin offering and then dies, her heirs bring it in her stead. While one opinion in the Talmud asserts that this holds true only in the case when she has set aside a specific animal for this purpose, another maintains that, regardless of that fact, the heirs still offer the sacrifice. R. Judah then compares charity to the offering of sacrifices: 'all that we have found regarding the *olah* [sacrifice] we have found regarding charity', and concludes that just as the child can offer a sacrifice in place of the deceased parent, so too, charity can be performed by the living for the benefit of the dead (even though the parallel is not perfect, since a child cannot offer a sacrifice that the parent had not dedicated before his or her death). See *SḤ* 35.

135 See *SḤ* 32, p. 30.

136 *SḤ* 273; see also *SḤ* 34.

137 While R. Judah refers to the same talmudic stories involving rabbinic prayer for dead sinners as R. Nisim does (*Eruv.* 65*a* and *Ḥag.* 15*b*), he never specifies the character of the intercessor as a factor in the success of such prayer. The average man has the capacity to pray for the dead; only the character of the deceased and his merits (or lack of them) will determine the outcome of that prayer. See *SḤ* 32, p. 30.

who acts as spiritual confessor according to the Pietist doctrine of penitence, is not called upon to intercede on behalf of the dead.[138] It is the common man—the anonymous 'he' or 'they'—who recites prayers or distributes alms for their benefit.[139]

R. Judah's view of the proceedings of the heavenly court also conflicts with that articulated by R. Nisim. Whereas the latter views God as an all-powerful emperor who can be swayed by the pleas of his favourites to forgive sinners, R. Judah describes him as a judge who does not accept bribes in the form of merits,[140] who will never cancel out a sin because of a merit,[141] and who will not pardon even the unintentional sinner.[142] Eleazar of Worms, too, when describing the posthumous activities of souls in Heaven, writes that 'there exists no favouritism or flattery' before God's court, so that even 'a father can sentence his son [to posthumous punishment] if he sinned, because there is no mercy in Judgement'.[143]

Whereas the geonic model of prayer for the dead is akin, as we have seen, to ancient systems of patronage, R. Judah's model hinges on vicarious penance—a notion that forms the basis of the early medieval pastoral model and one that R. Hai Gaon rejects outright. As we may recall, this notion is predicated on the belief that, just as a Christian layperson or a member of clergy could pray, fast, give alms, or offer a mass on behalf of a living penitent in order to aid him in the completion of his penance, so, too, performance of any one of these penitential acts by the living could speed up the process of purgation for the soul of a departed one. Thus, whether performed for the sake of the living or for the dead, vicarious penance

[138] Regarding the Pietists and the doctrine of *retson haboré*, see Soloveitchik, 'Three Themes in *Sefer Ḥasidim*', 311–17. Regarding the *ḥakham* as confessor and his role in the Pietist practice of penance, see above, p. 218.

[139] See e.g. *SḤ* 34 and 35. The one occasion on which R. Judah highlights the supererogatory behaviour of a hasid with regard to charity for the dead is the case of an individual who goes beyond the customary expectation of giving to charity solely for his own dead relatives and instead vows to give for the sake of all who have died. There is no indication in the passage that one needs to be a hasid in order to give to charity on behalf of the dead. See *SḤ* 35.

[140] See *SḤ* 1344. The expression *lisa panim* is used as a synonym for the taking of bribes in Deut. 10: 17.

[141] R. Judah writes in *SḤ* 43, p. 41: 'Never is a sin exchanged for a merit; rather, they calculate the merits alone and the offences alone.' In *SḤ* 1952 he makes the exact same pronouncement with regard to reward and punishment in the afterlife. This topic is treated more extensively later on in the chapter.

[142] See *SḤ* 1 ('Behold, before the Lord, one cannot say, "It is an accident"'), and in more detail *SḤ* 283, where R. Judah argues that, just as it is impossible to consider that a human king would accept the excuse of unintentional error on the part of the accused, or allow this fact to 'bribe' him into exempting him from punishment, so, too, before the King of all Kings one cannot plead that his crime was accidental or unintentional.

[143] *Sefer ḥokhmat hanefesh*, 14*a*.

involved the transfer of merits from one individual to another. Championing the claim for individual moral responsibility, R. Hai, however, explains that neither sins nor merits are transferable.[144] He mentions the case of a person who accustomed himself to fasting every Monday and Thursday and wished to transfer those merits to another, or even 'sell' them to him. Another example he cites is of someone who sought to 'buy with gold' the merit gained by the Torah reading or study of another. In both instances R. Hai asserts that 'these are matters of foolishness, upon which one cannot rely'. In similar fashion, he believes that aid for the dead results from the granting of a special pardon to the sinner, not from the application of any notion of vicarious penance. When asked in a personal enquiry whether charity performed by the living benefits the dead (a clear case of vicarious penance as extended to the hereafter), Rav Hai emphatically states that 'certainly no ordinary human [*enosh*] has the capability to lighten [posthumous suffering] for him'. It is only through the efforts of exceptionally righteous individuals or men of great merit that God may be 'bribed' into reducing the sentence of the guilty dead, but even then they will never be granted posthumous reward.[145]

Unlike his geonic predecessor, R. Judah firmly believes in the validity of vicarious penance and allows the transfer of merits from one individual to another which underlies it. He cites a talmudic passage from *Ḥagigah* 15*a*, which, in an attempt to dispel the notion of predestination, asserts that everyone potentially has a portion in both Paradise and Gehenna.[146]

144 'Would one think', Rav Hai asks rhetorically, 'that the reward for a commandment is something one can carry on his chest and walk around with, so that he can give his reward over to someone else?' With similar mockery, he writes regarding one who seeks to 'buy' merits. Such a person, he exclaims, 'is to be derided and mocked, for all the valuable and desirable wealth [in the world] cannot acquire for a person the merit of his friend'. Citing various scriptural verses and rabbinic statements to prove his point, he concludes that 'each individual receives his reward according to his own toil'. See *Otsar hage'onim*, ed. Levin, 'Ḥagigah', 28–9.

145 R. Hai mentions two possible exceptions to this rule—the return of stolen objects and the repayment of debts by the living on behalf of the dead. Yet these exceptions, too, reinforce his opinion on the issue of vicarious penance. Whereas no ordinary human has the ability to reduce the posthumous suffering of another, in the case of the return of stolen or borrowed objects or the repayment of debts incurred by the dead, the actions of the living do benefit the dead and serve to reduce their suffering in the hereafter. R. Hai explains that the reason for this is that 'the debt is upon him [i.e. the deceased]'. Only because the living are acting as agents of the deceased to help him repair his own misdeeds is their action beneficial, and not because of any transfer of merit. See *Otsar hage'onim*, ed. Levin, 'Ḥagigah', 27–8. Prayer for the dead as a means to achieve posthumous reward is discussed more fully later on in the chapter.

146 In its discussion of a system of opposites which God has placed into Creation, the Talmud remarks that each individual is allotted two portions to inherit after death; initially one of them is in Paradise, the other in Gehenna. If a person is righteous, he receives a double portion

R. Judah reinterprets this statement in a novel way that necessitates belief in the transfer of merits and places responsibility upon the living to perform vicarious penance on behalf of the dead. According to his interpretation, a righteous individual can be punished for having 'usurped' another person's place in Paradise on account of his failure to perform charitable acts for the sake of the other's soul.[147] As part of his reinterpretation, he deliberately changes the supporting scriptural verses which the Talmud cites to ones that reinforce his understanding of the passage and underline the message that the transfer of merits from one individual to another is not only pos-

of Paradise—his own plus that of his wicked fellow. A wicked individual, on the other hand, receives a double portion of Gehenna—his own plus that of his righteous fellow. According to Urbach, the intent of the passage is to dispel the notion of predestination. Another interpretation of this enigmatic passage accentuates the power of the righteous and the wicked: according to the *Iyun ya'akov*, the righteous can, at times, bring blessings to the world from which the wicked benefit. The righteous can then rightfully partake of the portion of the wicked in the Next World. Conversely, the wicked can, at times, bring punishment to the world, which causes the righteous to suffer. Therefore, it is fitting that the wicked receive not only their portion in Gehenna, but that of the righteous as well. See *Iyun ya'akov*, s.v. *notel ḥelko veḥelek ḥavero*, a commentary on Jacob Ibn Haviv's *Ein ya'akov*, vol. iii (Jerusalem: Mesorat Hashas, 2008). See too Urbach, *The Sages*, 262.

147 In the latter part of *SḤ* 33 (p. 36), R. Judah quotes this passage and elaborates on it by providing a detailed description of the process. He explains that two scribes exist in Gehenna and two in Paradise, who inscribe the name of each individual on his 'place' and 'seat him'. Expecting to be seated in his own 'place', the dead individual may be surprised to find that these scribes have led him to his companion's place instead, whether in Paradise or in Gehenna. When questioned by the wicked person, the scribes in Gehenna reply that, since his righteous fellow has lost his portion in Gehenna on his account, 'he must sit in his [i.e. the other's] place and exempt him'. When questioned by the righteous person, the scribes in Paradise reply that he cannot sit in his own seat 'as a punishment for having taken his companion's place in Paradise'. R. Judah explains the accountability of the two on the basis of a pair of verses in Proverbs (11: 4 and 10: 2), both of which contain the phrase 'charity saves from death'. He interprets these verses as referring to alms given while alive in order to escape Gehenna ('death' in the hereafter). Whereas the first verse speaks of one who gives charity for the sake of his own soul, the second refers to one who does not have the means to do so and has others give in his stead. On the basis of this interpretation, the merits accumulated by one individual can transfer to another and succeed in releasing his soul from Gehenna. Immediately afterwards (*SḤ* 34), however, R. Judah limits the application of his interpretation: even though one who gives alms for the sake of another can save that person's soul either in this life or in the hereafter, this applies to the deserving only. It now becomes clear why the righteous individual is punished for having usurped his companion's place in Paradise; he failed to carry out charitable acts for the sake of the other's soul and so prevented him from receiving his allotted portion in Paradise. In like fashion and by implication, the wicked individual exempted his fellow from his allotted portion in Gehenna as the sins of the other were transferred onto him. Instead of voluntarily taking on the penance for the sins of another (as is the case with vicarious penance), here the individual is being saddled against his will with the sins and concomitant punishment of the other.

sible but may even be obligatory; anyone who does not engage in it will be held responsible and punished for his inaction.[148] Moreover, R. Judah embellishes the passage, adding details not found in the original, such as assigned, inscribed 'seats' in Paradise and Gehenna and the notion of occupying someone else's seat there. By contrast, when R. Hai Gaon is confronted with the same talmudic passage, he offers no literary embellishments, supplies no textual substitutions, and rejects outright a conclusion that validates vicarious penance on behalf of the dead.[149]

The details that R. Judah inserts into the talmudic passage are central to well-known tales in the exempla literature that revolve around the transfer of merits and the posthumous aid of the living. Retold many times with variations in characters and setting, the tale recounts how a sinful person (a knight, a harlot, a dying woman, a man who has committed incest and parricide, or a dying priest who has not confessed) is saved from Hell through the transfer of merits from someone holy and pious (a Dominican, Abbot Pontius, the General of the Dominicans, a friar, or St Bernard). The sinful person occupies the holy person's seat or throne in Heaven and reveals that a still holier place—'a seat among the cherubim'—is prepared for the other.[150]

148 The Talmud cites Isa. 61: 7, 'they will inherit a double portion in their land', to refer to the future fate of the righteous, and Jer. 17: 18, 'and devastate them with a double portion of disaster', to refer to the future fate of the wicked. R. Judah omits these and replaces them with two entirely different scriptural verses, even while quoting the remainder of the talmudic teaching verbatim. Regarding the righteous, he paraphrases 1 Sam. 26: 19, 'for they have driven me away this day from attaching myself to the inheritance of God', as 'in order to drive away the wicked one from attaching himself to the inheritance of the righteous'. Regarding the wicked, he loosely quotes Prov. 11: 8, 'The righteous one is released from misfortune, but the wicked one comes in his place', and says, 'And he releases the righteous one from misfortune and the wicked one comes.' While the verses cited by the Talmud speak of the allotment of double portions to both the wicked and the righteous in order to stress the generalized notion of surplus reward and punishment, those used by R. Judah discuss the specific replacement of one individual by his counterpart. This reinforces his interpretation, which highlights the moral responsibility of one Jew towards another. See *SḤ* 33, p. 36.

149 This very passage in *Ḥag.* 15*a* serves as the backdrop to the query mentioned in *SḤ* 34 regarding the possible benefit of giving charity on behalf of the dead. The passage does not form a part of the Gaon's discussion of the topic at all, and his conclusion is the opposite of R. Judah's interpretation.

150 See MSS BL Add. 11284 fo. 13*b*, Royal 7 D I fo. 88*b*, Harley 2316 fo. 1, Royal 8 F VI fo. 17*b*, col. 2, Royal 7 D I fo. 86*b*, and Add. 33956 fo. 68 (*Catalogue of Romances*, iii. 378 no. 87, 487 no. 100, 574 no. 2, 679 no. 38, 487 no. 95, 632 no. 75 respectively). The exempla collections also contain several tales which speak of seats prepared in Hell for sinners. The sinners, while still alive or, most often, while dying, see in visions the specific seat that awaits them in Hell. In one version, the extent of the sinner's wickedness is revealed when he sees who his neighbours in Hell will be—Caiaphas and those who crucified Jesus (see Banks (ed.), *Alphabet of Tales*, 387

Beyond his application of vicarious penance to the hereafter, R. Judah posits that the process operates in both directions. Not only can the living perform vicarious penance for the dead, but so can the dead for the living. A righteous deceased father, upon hearing that evil has been decreed to befall his living descendant, can 'accept [upon himself] his [descendant's] sin while in the grave in order to redeem him'.[151]

R. Eleazar of Worms, too, subscribes to this belief. He is, however, somewhat more reserved in his acceptance of it than his master. In his halakhic work,[152] he argues that the charity of the living benefits the dead only because God, who is able to 'test the hearts of the living and the dead', knows that the dead individual himself would have given such charity—or would have wished to have given if he did not have the means to do so—had he been alive. That is to say, R. Eleazar only accepts vicarious penance in so far as it serves as an extension, by proxy, of the action of the deceased himself; the living, when giving charity, act as surrogates for the dead. R. Eleazar's understanding of *Ḥagigah* 15*a* provides further evidence in this regard. Unlike R. Judah, he accepts the plain-sense interpretation of the passage, which emphasizes the doubling of reward and punishment after death, and cites the original verses offered by the Talmud.[153] He also reduces the overall benefit that the dead can gain from the pious actions of the living: 'Then it will benefit him a little.'

no. 579, and *Catalogue of Romances*, iii. 399, no. 464, 482 no. 36, 410 no. 10). Another tale involves a plan to exchange seats in Hell (*Catalogue of Romances*, iii. 351 no. 14, and Caesarius of Heisterbach, *Dialogue*, 2: 9). A third describes twin brothers, one with a seat prepared for him in Heaven, the other with one in Hell (*Catalogue of Romances*, iii. 588 no. 75).

While some of the exempla cited above illustrate the generous reward that those who transfer all their merits to others can expect, R. Judah speaks of the punishment awaiting those who could transfer part of their merit to others and fail to do so. One tale whose message closely parallels that of R. Judah appears in *The Golden Legend*. There, Jacobus de Voragine tells of a soldier who makes an agreement with one of his relatives: should he die in battle, the relative will sell his horse and give the money to the poor for the sake of the soldier's soul. After his death, however, the kinsman keeps the horse for himself instead. The dead soldier appears to the relative and informs him that, on account of the torment he has had to undergo due to the other's failure to aid him after death, the relative will be punished; a demon will take his soul to Hell the same day, while the soldier's soul will be released to Paradise. See *The Golden Legend*, 657. The harsh punishment of the one who fails to help the deceased, as well as the transfer of the soldier from a locus of posthumous torment to Paradise and his replacement by a more serious sinner, echo the elements in R. Judah's elaboration of the passage at hand. He, too, threatens with punishment those who fail to aid the dead, and speaks of their exclusion from Paradise.

151 See *SḤ* 33, p. 36.

152 *Sefer haroke'aḥ hagadol*, ed. Shneerson, 109.

153 R. Eleazar adds that, in fact, the Bible validates his reading of the talmudic passage. On the basis of a numerological exegesis of Num. 14: 38, the two good spies, Joshua and Caleb, are rewarded posthumously not only with their own individual portions in Paradise but also with the portions originally allotted to the ten renegade spies. See *Sefer ḥokhmat hanefesh*, 5*a*.

R. Judah the Pious on Charity for the Dead

R. Judah believes that, like prayer, charity too can help in alleviating the suffering allotted to souls in the hereafter. He explains the repetition of the above-mentioned phrase in Proverbs, 'and charity saves from death',[154] thus: its first appearance refers to 'salvation from death in this world', while the second refers to 'salvation from death in the afterlife [*mimavet shel atid*]'.[155] As proof for his contention, he cites a story related in the Talmud about how a living rabbi named Samuel intercedes on behalf of a deceased rabbi named Levi, whose sin keeps him excluded from the Heavenly Academy (*metivta derekia*) for a period of time. Samuel is successful and Levi immediately enters the Heavenly Academy.[156] While the story does not speak of punishment in Gehenna, it does illustrate how the prayer of the living can mitigate the suffering experienced by sinners. If prayer for the dead can accomplish this, concludes R. Judah, then 'how much more so' (*kol sheken*) can charity![157]

It is possible that R. Judah's use of the expression 'how much more so' here implies not the superiority of alms over prayer but that a combination of the two actions is a more efficacious force than prayer alone. In a different passage, he indissolubly links the two: 'Those who give [charity] on behalf of the dead to the living must make known [this intention to the beneficiaries] so that they should pray for the dead.'[158] Such a link might be a legacy of the *ge'onim*: R. Hai speaks of charity as an adjunct to prayer, and of prayer as part of charity.[159] The subsequent passage in *Sefer ḥasidim* makes the connection more concrete by specifying the exact formula of the prayer to be recited by those 'who benefit from the money given [as charity] in memory of the souls of the dead within the [first] year of their passing'.[160]

This latter passage explicitly mentions the customary practice of at least some of his audience of procuring alms to the living for the benefit of the dead within a year of their death.[161] Undoubtedly, this practice

154 Prov. 10: 2, 11: 4.

155 *SḤ* 273.

156 BT *Ber.* 18*b*. On the role played by the Heavenly Academy in rabbinic literature, see Costa, *L'Au-delà et la resurrection*, 463–6.

157 *SḤ* 273.

158 *SḤ* 356.

159 First he speaks of the prayer of a righteous person who is supplicating on behalf of the dead. Such prayer may or may not be accompanied by the distribution of alms to the poor (see n. 31 above). He then continues and says that, if this endeavour is not successful, 'we bring the poor near him in order that they pray for mercy on his behalf'. See *Otsar hage'onim*, ed. Levin, 'Ḥagigah', addendum on the left side of p. 28.

160 *SḤ* 357.

161 Further reference to this custom is found in the words of R. Tsidkiyah Harofé, *Shibolei*

coincided with that of prayer on behalf of dead relatives within a year of their passing, mentioned earlier. What is novel here is R. Judah's requirement that the one receiving the alms, too, must pray for the dead person. Additionally, *Sefer ḥasidim* supplies the precise text of that prayer:

> Merciful One, who forgives iniquity, with this benefit from which I am benefiting because of so-and-so son of so-and-so, may his sin be forgiven and may his soul rest in goodness, together with the fortune of the righteous in the goodness that they provide for him for his sake, and may his spirit be tranquil in the portion of the good ones.[162]

Constructed as a commentary on Psalm 78: 38, the prayer requests atonement for the dead person's sin in merit of the charity dispensed, and asks God to grant his soul rest together with the righteous. After the prayer, one is to recite the verse itself: 'He, being merciful, forgives iniquity and does not destroy; He frequently withdraws His anger, and does not arouse His entire anger.'

Drawing upon the scriptural expressions *menuḥah* (rest) and *shalom* (peace),[163] rabbinic literature speaks of the righteous dead who 'rest on their beds'.[164] Yet this prayer, with its regard for the peaceful rest of the soul and the tranquillity of the spirit, also parallels early examples of Christian prayer for the dead, which speak of *pax* (peace), *lux* (light), and *requies* (respite) of the soul and the spirit.[165] Furthermore, in requesting that the soul share in 'the lot of the righteous' and that the spirit dwell 'in the portion of the good', the prayer reflects the principal aim of early medieval Christian prayer for the dead—their inclusion in the society of the saints, of the saved.[166] While it invokes God's mercy and restraint of anger and makes brief mention of forgiveness of sin, its purpose in doing so is not to mitigate punishment; it does not mention Gehenna or express any real fear of Divine retribution.[167]

haleket, ed. Mirsky, 311. In addition to prayer and almsgiving in the first year, fasting on the anniversary of the death of one's father is also mentioned. See *SḤ* 1544.

162 *SḤ* 357.

163 See e.g. Gen. 15: 15, Isa. 57: 2, and Dan. 12: 13.

164 See Costa, *L'Au-delà et la resurrection*, 355–8. Costa argues that the reward allotted to the righteous here may not be restricted solely to peaceful slumber. In talmudic times, the bed or couch was also a place of eating and drinking, and therefore the image of the righteous at repose on their beds might refer to their participation in the pleasure-filled banquet to take place in the afterlife. See ibid. 357.

165 Edwards, 'The Idea of Post Mortem Purgation', 62.

166 McLaughlin, 'Consorting with Saints', 238.

167 Ta-Shma alludes to a connection between the prayer 'Vehu raḥum' and atonement for the dead. He notes that the prayer is a remnant of the earlier liturgical practice of inserting Taḥanun into the 'Birkot yotser', the first blessings of the morning prayer service. It functions

The content of the prayer in *Sefer ḥasidim* may reflect early medieval Christian patterns, but its form resembles high medieval ones. Its insistence on the obligation of the beneficiary to pray for the soul of his benefactor reflects the contractual nature that prayer for the dead assumed in the thirteenth century. The long-term relationship between donor and recipient, the deceased and his intercessor, loses its centrality here. The beneficiary of the alms is obligated to pray for the dead person from whose charity he has benefited,[168] simply because he has benefited from it and not out of any desire to aid the deceased. The prayer forges the link between charitable gift and obligatory prayer precisely at a time when the laity was seeking to 'buy' prayer for the dead as a commodity.[169] In doing so, it reflects the reciprocity of the bond between the living and the dead, so characteristic of the high Middle Ages. Additionally, the fact that the prayer requires the beneficiary to pray for the deceased by name parallels the rise of individualized services, such as solemn anniversaries and special masses, in which the donor was memorialized apart from the collective services of the Church, and which were increasingly being requested by the laity at this time.[170]

Practices of Prayer and Charity for the Dead in Medieval Ashkenaz and R. Judah's Position

R. Judah's certainty with regard to prayer and charity performed by the living on behalf of the dead was not unique in his time. It was customary in thirteenth-century Ashkenaz to pray and pledge to give charity for the dead in the synagogue on the sabbath and Yom Kippur, as R. Tsidkiyah Harofé records. He explains that, after the public recitation of the reading from the prophets, it is customary to 'remember the souls' as part of the communal prayer, and to 'have the living allot, on behalf of the dead, money for charity . . . in order to benefit the dead'.[171] The pledging of charity on their behalf on Yom Kippur was first documented in the *Maḥzor vitry*, which states that, 'in the entire land of Ashkenaz, charity for the dead is allotted only today . . . because it is a day of atonement; it is [one of] forgiveness and pardoning and atonement for them [i.e. the dead]'.[172] R. Eleazar, who also

as a private prayer for the benefit of the dead. See Ta-Shma, 'A Remark on the Topic of the Mourner's Kaddish' (Heb.), 562–3.

168 R. Judah uses the term 'must' (*tsarikh*) twice in this context; see *SḤ* 356.

169 McLaughlin, 'Consorting with Saints', 338.

170 Ibid. 344.

171 *Shibolei haleket*, ed. Mirsky, 311.

172 *Maḥzor vitry*, ed. Goldschmidt, 'Seder yom hakipurim', iii. 784–5. In Ashkenaz, charity

mentions the custom, points to two scriptural verses as its source. The last verse in the biblical portion of 'Tetsaveh' speaks of the atonement ceremony performed on the altar of the Tabernacle on Yom Kippur, while the first verse of the following portion, 'Ki tisa', orders each individual Jew to donate a half-shekel to the Tabernacle as an atonement for his own soul. The appearance of the word 'atonement' (*kaparah*) in both verses forges a connection between the giving of charity as atonement, both for the dead and for the living, and the Jewish Day of Atonement, Yom Kippur.[173]

Ceremonial memorialization of the dead originated in Ashkenaz as part of the formal synagogue liturgy in the twelfth century and became known as Yizkor.[174] The list of names of the martyrs of the Crusades recorded in the communal *memorbukh* (martyrology) was read aloud in the synagogues of Germany on the sabbath before Shavuot, close to the anniversary of the Rhineland massacres.[175] Although the practice of mentioning aloud the names of important people who had passed away had geonic antecedents,[176] striking similarities between the text of the Yizkor ceremony recorded in the *memorbukh*s and that of Christian diptychs have been noted.[177] There is no doubt that Jews' memorialization of their holy dead served a similar role to that played by monastic necrologies of the time. In the second half of the twelfth century, the names of important deceased communal leaders and supporters were read aloud and memorialized on various sabbaths each year. By the late thirteenth century, there existed a practice of mentioning

for the living was allotted publicly in the synagogue on the Jewish holidays, as stated elsewhere in the *Maḥzor vitry* ('Seder pesaḥ' and 'Seder shavuot'), and as alluded to in *Sefer haroke'aḥ* with the words 'regarding the allotment of charity for the dead on Yom Kippur and not on *yom tov*' (see *Sefer haroke'aḥ hagadol*, ed. Shneerson, 109). See also *Sidur rashi*, no. 214. See the relevant discussion in Glick, *A Light Unto the Mourner* (Heb.), 141–2. Interestingly, while R. Judah states that the dead, together with the living, are judged on Yom Kippur, he omits mention of the custom of allocating charity for the dead on that day. See *SḤ* 501.

173 See *Sefer haroke'aḥ hagadol*, ed. Shneerson, 109. See also *Mordekhai* at the end of *Yoma*, no. 727, who writes, 'And regarding the custom of pledging charity on Yom Kippur for the dead, one can cite a proof from the *Sifrei*, that which our rabbis taught [regarding] the topic of *eglah arufah*: "Atone for Your nation"—these are the living, "whom You have redeemed"—these are the dead. It comes to teach us that the dead require atonement.' Regarding this scriptural proof, see n. 21 above.

174 Regarding the discussion surrounding the origin of the Yizkor service, see above, Introduction, n. 30.

175 See Neubauer, 'Le Memorbuch de Mayence', 9. Regarding additional commemorative practices for the martyrs of 1096, see Zimmer, 'The Persecutions of 1096' (Heb.).

176 Rav Natronai Gaon of the ninth century records the custom of mentioning aloud and eulogizing the *nasi* (head) of the academy in the academy within the first twelve months of his passing. See *Sefer sha'arei tsedek*, ed. Safra, 46, and *Otsar hage'onim*, ed. Levin, vol. iv, 'Mashkin (Mo'ed katan)', 48.

177 See Lévi, 'La Commémoration des âmes dans le Judaïsme', 58.

aloud the names of deceased individuals who had donated holy articles to the community in order to be memorialized after their death.[178]

Important communal leaders were not the only ones to be remembered: ordinary individuals were prayed for as well. R. Isaac of Vienna mentions the custom, prevalent in his time in Bohemia and the Rhineland (but not in France), of orphan sons reciting Kaddish in the synagogue after the prayer 'Ein keloheinu' on the sabbath for the welfare of their dead parent's soul.[179] His master, R. Eleazar of Worms, mentions the same practice.[180] An addendum to the text of the *Maḥzor vitry* records orphan sons reciting the 'Barekhu' prayer or Kaddish in the synagogue at the conclusion of the sabbath.[181] Some date the origin of the mourners' Kaddish as a fixed liturgical element in Ashkenaz to the first half of the twelfth century on the basis of documentation in the *Maḥzor vitry*.[182]

Scholars have demonstrated the influence of changing Christian notions of the afterlife, in particular the rise to prominence of the belief in Purgatory and the role played by prayer for the dead, as key factors in the establishment of Kaddish as an intercessory prayer in Ashkenaz—all of which occurred in north-western Europe in the twelfth century.[183] As discussed above, a rabbinic position on the nature of Gehenna as either fundamentally punitive or purgatorial was never authoritatively determined, but with the adoption of Kaddish as a fixed part of the liturgy,[184] the Jews of medieval Ashkenaz clearly shifted the weight of the argument towards the

178 See Glick, *A Light Unto the Mourner* (Heb.), 137–9. See also the relevant discussion regarding the Nuremberg Memorbukh in particular in Baumgarten, *Practicing Piety in Medieval Ashkenaz*, 104–7.

179 See *Or zarua*, vol. ii, 'Hilkhot shabat', no. 50.

180 See *Sefer haroke'aḥ hagadol*, ed. Shneerson, no. 53 end, p. 43.

181 *Maḥzor vitry*, ed. Goldschmidt, 'Hilkhot shabat', i. 224. On the origins and development of the custom of reciting the mourners' Kaddish, see Wieseltier, *Kaddish*. (Although Wieseltier is not a historian by profession and his work contains no footnotes, the book's learned discussions reflect the scholarly training that he received at Harvard under Isadore Twersky.) See also Ta-Shma, 'A Remark on the Topic of the Mourner's Kaddish' (Heb.), and Roth, 'Memorial Prayer' (Heb.). More recently, see Shyovitz, '"You Have Saved Me from the Judgment of Gehenna"', 49–52. Shyovitz distinguishes between commemoration of the dead in the Yizkor and the intercessory nature of the Kaddish. He dates the origin of the latter practice to the late twelfth century (ibid. 53, 67).

182 This is the opinion of Ta-Shma in 'A Remark on the Topic of the Mourner's Kaddish' (Heb.), 566. See also Glick, *A Light Unto the Mourner* (Heb.), 154 and n. 100 there. Whereas Kaddish had existed long before the medieval period, it assumed the role of a mourner's prayer only at this time. For its full history see Glick, 150–2.

183 Shyovitz, '"You Have Saved Me from the Judgment of Gehenna"', 54, 65–7.

184 Ibid. 50–2.

latter. In tandem with their Christian contemporaries, they internalized theological notions of post-mortem punishment, and conceived of it as a purgative, temporary stage in which intercessory prayer served to end suffering.[185]

Implied in R. Judah's statement one can detect the practice, common in Ashkenaz of his day, of praying for one's deceased relatives in the first year following their death:[186] 'And regarding those who have already died, and the twelve-month period [after their death] has already passed, one must [*tsarikh*] pray for them on every Rosh Hodesh and Jewish holiday because [on those days] they overturn the fire of Gehenna.'[187] He mandates this practice for those who have improperly observed the sabbath and festivals, on account of the ever-increasing intensity of the fire of Gehenna on those days. Since these sinners need additional prayer, it is assumed that the general practice was to pray for only the initial twelve months after death. It is evident from R. Judah's statement that he believes in the power of prayer to aid sinners suffering in Gehenna, and that his audience is familiar with the practice of such prayer. What is novel is his advocacy of prayer for the dead on holidays and Rosh Hodesh, instead of on the customary days of sabbath and Yom Kippur, and his extension of the practice beyond the accepted twelve-month period.

It is possible that R. Judah omits mention of the sabbath and Yom Kippur because the prayer on those days is public and communal, and therefore familiar to his audience, whereas the prayer on Rosh Hodesh and the Jewish festivals that he advocates is meant to be of a private nature.[188] While this may be true, it may also be possible that his omission is intentional and relates to his position regarding the sabbath rest of souls. One late *midrash* connects customary prayer for the dead on the sabbath with that notion: referring to the posthumous fate of a sinner, who is lowered 'to

185 Ibid. 67.

186 R. Tsidkiyah Harofé cites BT *Kidushin* 31*b* as the source for the custom. That passage explains that a son can fulfil the duty of honouring his father even after the latter's death by citing the expression 'I serve as the atonement for his death [lit. bed]' after each mention of his name. The talmudic source limits this to the first twelve months after the father's death. See *Shibolei haleket*, ed. Mirsky, 311–12.

187 *SḤ* 356.

188 S. Freehof advances the idea that, in addition to the recorded public liturgical commemorations of the dead, such as on Yom Kippur, there also existed voluntary private individual commemorative acts. He deduces this from the above-mentioned statement, found in *Sidur rashi*, *Maḥzor vitry*, and *Sefer haroke'aḥ hagadol*, that 'there is no allotment of charity on behalf of the dead in all of Germany except on Yom Kippur'. 'There is no allotment of charity on any other day' would thus imply the existence of voluntary ones of a private nature. See Freehof, 'Hazkarath Neshamoth', 188.

the underground pit, the pit and Gehenna', the *midrash* states that if the sinner repents,[189] he is released from Gehenna 'like an arrow from a bow'. This is followed by a comment that appears to be a later interpolation:[190] 'Therefore, it is customary to mention the dead on the sabbath, so that they do not return to Gehenna.'[191] R. Tsidkiyah Harofé offers a different reason for the custom: 'Since the sabbath is a day of rest, a semblance of the World to Come, and also a day on which the dead rest and are not punished, it is fitting to mention them for rest and for blessing and to pray for them.'[192] Both sources connect the custom to the notion of the sabbath rest of souls; the former source promises the release of sinners from Gehenna at the end of that day, while the latter affords them relief once they return there. R. Judah might possibly object to the practice of praying for the dead on the sabbath because of its association with the notion of the sabbath rest of souls—a belief, I have suggested earlier, that he does not subscribe to. Additionally, that prayer practice includes helping the unworthy dead—an idea that, we shall soon see, he vehemently rejects.

Conclusion

In keeping with medieval thinking, R. Judah tightens the bonds between the living and the dead. The living, he believes, owe a great debt to the dead, who continuously pray on their behalf. In rabbinic thought, although the ordinary dead can be petitioned to pray for the living, it is commonly the holy dead—specifically the patriarchs and matriarchs—who pray on behalf of the nation of Israel, and the living are not obligated, nor do they choose, to reciprocate in prayer on behalf of the dead. In *Sefer ḥasidim*, however, the average dead assemble annually to pray on behalf of the living, and the living, in turn, are obligated to pray on their behalf.

A work of the thirteenth century, *Sefer ḥasidim* shares the high medieval belief in the efficacy of suffrages on the part of the living and in the transfer of merits which underlies it. It reflects the new notion of a contract that

189 How can a sinner repent posthumously? The *Ets yosef* records the alternative reading 'after he accepts his sentence' in place of 'if he repents'. See *Midrash tanḥuma*, 'Ha'azinu', 1, and the comment of the *Ets yosef* on the words *ve'im ya'amod bemeryo* there.

190 See Glick, *A Light Unto the Mourner* (Heb.), 140 and n. 44 there.

191 *Midrash tanḥuma*, 'Ha'azinu', 1. A similar *midrash* is found in *Pesikta rabati*, 20 (ed. Ish-Shalom, p. 95*b*). It is cited in the *Maḥzor vitry* on two occasions: in 'Seder shabat', i. 288, and, with slight variation, in 'Seder yom hakipurim', iii. 785 (ed. Goldschmidt).

192 R. Tsidkiyahu cites this explanation in the name of his brother, Benjamin; see *Shibolei haleket*, ed. Mirsky, 311.

binds the prayer of the living to the individual dead, as seen in the contemporary Ashkenazi practices of memorializing the dead in the synagogue on the sabbath and on certain holy days, and in the custom of praying for them individually in the form of the mourner's Kaddish. This latter practice was an outgrowth of a novel twelfth-century theology, shared by Christians and Jews alike in the Ashkenazi orbit, and which embraced belief in the efficacy of prayer to release sinners from a time-bound, purgatorial Gehenna.

R. Judah's views on the prayer of the living for the dead reflect an early medieval Christian pastoral model and differ from the geonic one, which is akin to ancient systems of patronage. Rather than relying on the dramatic intercession of figures of immense holiness, as is common in hagiography and monastic chronicles, the pastoral model extended the penitential system of the Church into the hereafter. In that system, personal merit was stressed, and vicarious penance accelerated the redemptive process set in motion by the deceased while they were alive. Since acquired virtue rather than the prestige of powerful others formed the basis of beneficial prayer, questions such as who can pray for the dead and, alternatively, which dead can be prayed for now rose to the surface. As we shall see in the following chapter, it was particularly R. Judah's passionate claims regarding prayer of the dead for the dead and prayer for the deserving dead that set him apart from talmudic teaching, as well as from contemporary Ashkenazi ideas and practice, and aligned him most closely, once again, with the early medieval pastoral model.

CHAPTER EIGHT

BONDS BETWEEN THE LIVING AND THE DEAD PART II

In the previous chapter I discussed R. Judah's belief that the ordinary dead pray regularly on behalf of the living and that the living should pray on behalf of the dead. What of the dead praying for the dead? In one paragraph of *Sefer ḥasidim*, R. Judah discourages such practice: 'In this world, one can do good for the soul of the dead, but if he was silent in this world and did not seek [benefit], he should also not seek [benefit] in the future.'[1] In this world, one can and should perform pious acts to aid souls; if one fails, however, to pray for a soul while alive, one cannot do so after one has died. R. Judah maintains his position despite talmudic evidence to the contrary.

The Talmud in *Ḥagigah* tells of two rabbis, R. Meir and R. Yohanan, who intercede after their death for the soul of their apostate master, Elisha ben Avuyah; the former brings Elisha's soul down to Gehenna for punishment, so that it can be purified and he can merit life in the World to Come. The latter, hoping to achieve even more for his teacher, pulls his soul up from there.[2] Confronted by the difficulty posed by this talmudic story, R. Judah asks, 'Why couldn't the rabbis accomplish these feats during their lifetime?' He responds by arguing that, since Elisha's sins were so numerous, his soul had to be 'forcibly taken and forcibly removed'—acts that could only be accomplished after the death of the two great men. The case of R. Meir and R. Yohanan is an exception, R. Judah claims, due to the unusual nature of Elisha ben Avuyah's sins. Clearly, the function of prayer

1 *SḤ* 273.

2 BT *Ḥag.* 15*b*. Although the meaning remains unchanged, the actual language of R. Yohanan differs in the varying manuscripts. According to MS Vatican ebr. 285 no. 50 and MS JTS 2499 no. 50, he intends, after his death, to 'extinguish the smoke from his [Elisha's] grave', while, according to MS JTS Boesky 45 no. 119 and MS Parma H 3280 no. 273, he intends to 'take him out of Gehenna'.

for the dead here is to rescue souls from Gehenna, something the living ought to do, not the dead.

R. Judah's argument involves a novel interpretation of the passage; the Talmud finds nothing unusual about the rabbis' conduct, each of whom explicitly states that he will achieve atonement for his master's soul only 'when I die'.[3] Nisim Gaon, too, is untroubled by the actions of R. Meir and R. Yohanan; they reflect normative behaviour and are not seen as exceptional in any way. Not making a distinction between intercession for the dead conducted while the intercessor is alive and intercession after he dies, Rabbenu Nisim cites, in his *Megilat setarim*, the statement of R. Eleazar ben Azaryah that through his prayer he can 'release the entire world from [posthumous] judgement' (*Eruv.* 65*a*) just prior to citing the *Ḥagigah* passage regarding R. Yohanan. Whereas the former example involves a living intercessor and the latter one who is deceased, both equally prove his point: 'they are clear proofs' that the intercession of important people benefits the dead.[4]

The tosafists, in their comments on another talmudic story involving prayer for the dead (BT *Sot.* 10*b*), are also untroubled by the concept of the dead praying for the dead. They explain that the great merits of the patriarchs Abraham and Isaac were insufficient to redeem their wicked children, Ishmael and Esau, from descending into Gehenna in the absence of their prayers on their sons' behalf.[5] King David, however, was successful in rescuing his renegade son, Absalom, from the same posthumous fate on account of his prayer.[6] The implication is that, had the patriarchs acted as King David did, they, too, could have achieved what he did, despite the fact that they would have been praying after their death (they predeceased their sons), while King David prayed while he was still living (Absalom died during his father's lifetime). The *Tosafot* does not distinguish here between prayer of the living and prayer of the dead—both can equally rescue sinners from Gehenna.

Elsewhere in *Sefer ḥasidim*, R. Judah elaborates on his novel position.[7] In an effort to resolve a contradiction between two biblical verses, one indicating that God shows favouritism and the other that he does not, R. Judah concludes that the former passage refers to God's conduct in this world and

[3] *Ḥag.* 15*b*.

[4] See *SḤ* 32, p. 30. As mentioned earlier, *Sefer ḥasidim* contains a portion of R. Nisim's *Megilat setarim*.

[5] While the *Tosafot* here speaks of the prayer of the patriarchs for the living, it does not present them in their archetypal role as Fathers of *keneset yisra'el*, but rather as fathers to their own individual sons.

[6] See *Tosafot*, *Sot.* 10*b*, s.v. *de'aiteih le'alma de'ati*.

[7] *SḤ* 1045.

the latter to his conduct in the afterlife.[8] In this world, God shows favouritism, 'even', he adds, 'from the living towards the dead'—that is, God allows the prayers of the living to change the fate of the dead. He cites two instances in the Talmud in which the living successfully petition God on behalf of the dead and enable them to enter the Heavenly Academy, from which they were formerly excluded.[9] By contrast, he argues that in the hereafter God shows no favouritism; the righteous dead cannot petition God to admit others who are less worthy into Paradise—even a father cannot plead on behalf of his son—nor even to move a soul from one 'enclosure' within Paradise to another, higher, one.[10] Only righteous individuals of equal merit can sit together.

Two talmudic passages, however, conflict with R. Judah's statement regarding the absence of favouritism in the afterlife. Tractate *Ḥagigah*, already mentioned, suggests that R. Yohanan, after his own death, not only secures the release from Gehenna of the apostate Elisha ben Avuyah, but also succeeds in transferring him into his own section of Paradise.[11] This poses a problem for R. Judah, who accepts the suggestion of the Talmud as fact. Since the greatness of the deceased allows a less worthy individual (an

8 Although the two verses, Num. 6: 26 and Deut. 10: 17, both employ the term *yisa panim*, only the context of the second one suggests the meaning 'show favouritism'. The meaning in the first verse, on the basis of its context, seems to be, rather, 'a lifting up of His face'. R. Judah, however, connects the two by giving them identical translations. While R. Judah uses the eschatological terms *olam hazeh* and *olam haba*, from the examples he cites and from the explanation he offers it is evident that he contrasts the world of the living to that of the dead, not this world to the eschatological end of days.

9 The first example (*Ber.* 18*b*) involves the talmudic sage Samuel, who prays on behalf of another sage, Levi. The second (*BK* 92*a*) speaks of Moses' prayer before his death on behalf of the patriarch Jacob's son, Judah. (For the reason why Judah is excluded from the Heavenly Academy, see Rashi ad loc., s.v. *megulgalin be'aron*.)

10 According to R. Judah's conception of Paradise, the righteous have assigned places within specified enclosures (*meḥitsah*) surrounding the Divine Presence, the Kavod, and Elijah directs them to their proper place when they die. One's position is determined on the basis of merit, both in terms of proximity to the Divine Presence (the higher one is seated, the closer one is) and with regard to who sits nearby. Only those of equal merit or those who were partners in a holy endeavour in life can occupy the same enclosure and sit side by side. See *SḤ* 1043, 1044, 1052, 1556. See also no. 80, where a hasid requests to see who will sit beside him in Paradise. Normal distinctions of honour and prestige are not operative here, as a son who is more worthy can sit higher up than his father, and a student is sometimes placed higher than his master, and neither one has to show respect for his superior. There is no 'switching places' in Paradise, declares R. Judah, because 'there is no favouritism in the afterlife'. See *SḤ* 1047.

11 The Talmud in *Ḥag.* 15*b* never states this explicitly. It is hinted at when R. Yohanan says that he will take Elisha by the hand (see Rashi ad loc., s.v. *i nekatei leih beyad*). R. Judah, however, spells out this meaning when commenting on the passage: 'R. Yohanan said, "I will enter Aher [Elisha] into my enclosure"', and states that he did, in fact, succeed in doing so (*SḤ* 1045).

apostate who has not yet completed his sentence in Gehenna) to enjoy the same posthumous reward as he does, it is a clear case of favouritism in the afterlife—a phenomenon that R. Judah denies. Similarly, the Roman executioner mentioned in tractate *Avodah zarah*, who hastens the painful death of the martyr R. Hanina ben Tradyon and then jumps into the flames himself, enters Paradise with him.[12] Once again, a person of much lower spiritual calibre is allowed to share in the same posthumous reward as one much greater simply because of the prestige of the latter in the heavenly court (R. Judah assumes here that the intercession of R. Hanina on behalf of his executioner occurred after both men had died).

R. Judah extricates himself from the problem posed by these two talmudic stories by reinterpreting the passages. He asserts that R. Yohanan mentioned before the heavenly court certain merits of the apostate that rendered him worthy to enter Paradise—a fact that is not recorded in *Ḥagigah*. This is clearly also true for the case of R. Hanina since the executioner performs a meritorious act on his behalf. It is thus on the basis of their own merits, in conjunction with the favourable status of their 'patrons', rather than on the basis of the latter factor alone, that the sinners are admitted into Paradise and are seated beside these two great men. R. Judah insists that one cannot enter Paradise solely through the influence of another, without good deeds of one's own.[13] Yet, interestingly, while he denies the possibility of favouritism serving as the sole cause for admission into Paradise, he does not reject the concept altogether; he acknowledges its validity when coupled with the sinner's merit, and allows it within the confines of this world, even when this world intersects with the other world—that is, when the living pray for the dead. If favouritism itself is not the issue, then why does R. Judah make this distinction? What compels him to reinterpret the talmudic accounts involving prayer of the dead for the dead, while accepting those that speak of the living doing the same?

Could R. Judah be reacting here to the well-known Christian miracle stories of the Virgin and other saints, which, expressive of the religious climate of his age, tell of the power of the holy dead to rescue the souls of the wicked from Hell? Is his assertion that the living, not the dead, must pray for the dead an attempt to neutralize such stories? Certain statements in *Sefer ḥasidim* support this line of reasoning. R. Judah prefaces his assertion that prayer for the dead is to be performed solely by the living with the

[12] BT *AZ* 18*a*. Here again there is no explicit mention of the fact that the executioner will enter into R. Hanina's own enclosure in Paradise; the text merely says that both of them are 'invited to life in the other world'.

[13] *SḤ* 1045.

following qualifying words: 'Specifically if he sinned and merited; but if he did not merit, it will not benefit.'[14] It appears that R. Judah's emphasis on merit is meant to thwart the new mood of intercessionism typified by the Virgin. He seems fearful that another message of these tales—the rescue of the souls of the unworthy—might also seep into the minds of his fellow Jews.

It is the hallmark of the miracle stories and tales of saints that not only do the dead rescue other dead people, but those redeemed are the most grievous of sinners: their sins far outweigh their merits, they died unrepentant, and they are bound for Hell. Thus, Caesarius of Heisterbach tells of a knight whom the Virgin saves from Hell solely because he commends himself to her just before being beheaded.[15] According to another tale, the soul of a nephew of the Dean of Mainz is seen being hurled into a pit by demons. The Virgin rescues him at the last moment by spreading her cloak over the mouth of the pit because he used to recite three Aves and a Salve Regina daily.[16] Could R. Judah have possibly had this tale in mind when he declared that 'no wicked person can use the ineffable name of God in order to enter the other world without good deeds'?[17]

In the highly popular thirteenth-century work *The Golden Legend*, Jacobus de Voragine recounts the story of a sinner who witnesses in a vision his own posthumous judgement. While the Devil vies for his soul (he has made himself a slave to the Devil for thirty years), Truth and Justice try to keep him at bay. They are unsuccessful, however, and the man sees his sins outweigh his merits. Truth and Justice suggest to him that he should petition 'the Mother of Mercy, who sits beside the Lord'. The Virgin rescues the sinner from Hell by placing her hand on the pan of the balance which contains his merits; these now outweigh his sins.[18] In another version of the tale, she throws herself onto the balance.[19] These stories testify to the

[14] *SḤ* 273. Such a statement raises a question about the purpose of the distinction between the dead interceding for the dead and the living doing so, as in both cases the people being prayed for must have merit. Nonetheless, R. Judah makes the distinction.

[15] See *Dialogue*, 7: 57, 58. This popular tale also appears in several high medieval exempla collections. See *Catalogue of Romances*, iii. 367 no. 28, 550 no. 127, 587 no. 64, and 612 no. 82.

[16] See *Catalogue of Romances*, iii. 586 no. 58.

[17] *SḤ* 1452.

[18] See *The Golden Legend*, 460–1. Another, similar miracle story tells of a dissolute monk who is rescued from Hell by the pleas of the Mother of Christ. In a vision of judgement, the monk sees his sins outweighing his merits. The latter outweigh the former, however, when he sees Christ place a drop of blood on the balance following the intercession of the Virgin. See MS BL Add. 19909 fo. 245*b*, col. 2 (*Catalogue of Romances*, ii. 685 no. 50), and MS BL Sloane 278 fo. 46*b* (*Catalogue of Romances*, iii. 519 no. 143).

[19] This tale is recorded in a thirteenth-century Latin manuscript, MS BL Royal 5 A VIII fo. 14*b* (*Catalogue of Romances*, iii. 651 no. 5).

Virgin's salvific power and to the compassion she extends at times towards even the worst sinner. In response to these Marian tales, as well as to those told of other holy dead figures,[20] R. Judah retorts that help must come from the living, not the dead,[21] and that it benefits the deserving only.

Some of the Marian tales involving the balance are visually represented in medieval sacred art.[22] A fourteenth-century English alabaster carving

[20] In the ninth-century 'Vision of Charles the Fat', St Peter and St Remy, the patron saints of the Carolingians, release Lothair and his son, Louis II, from the torments of Hell. See Edwards, 'The Idea of Post Mortem Purgation', 129. Likewise, a mid-twelfth-century vision recorded by a monk of Liège describes how a certain lecherous man is spared a harsh posthumous penance due to the intervention of his patron saint. See ibid. 139. The exempla collections supply additional examples of the intercessory power of the holy dead. The *Alphabetum narrationum* describes how Emperor Henry's sins outweigh his merits until St Lawrence adds a pot of gold onto the merit side of the balance. See Banks (ed.), *Alphabet of Tales*, 297–8 no. 434. The *Dialogus miraculorum* tells of St Benedict interceding on behalf of a deceased nun from the convent in Rindorp: 'Bend[ing] his knees before God' on her behalf, he secures the nun's release from posthumous torment (Caesarius of Heisterbach, *Dialogue*, 12: 35).

[21] There is one exception to this rule. In *SḤ* 1543, in the context of retelling the talmudic story of the young girl who cannot leave her grave because she is improperly attired (*Ber.* 18*b*), R. Judah does not condemn the idea of the dead praying for the dead. On the night of Hoshana Rabah, he claims, all the dead leave their graves and pray. While the majority of their prayers are for the benefit of the living, they also pray for 'matters . . . of the dead, and for themselves, to hasten [God] to remove punishment from upon them and from upon others'. This passage could bear the influence of early medieval visionary literature, in which it is a common feature for the souls seen by the visionary in Hell or Purgatory to cry out for their own salvation. Also, the ordinary dead do not pose the same threat of subversion of justice that the holy dead do in praying for the dead.

[22] The image of the balance used in the Weighing of Souls as an expression of Divine judgement, termed psychostasis, is of ancient origin: it first appears in the Egyptian Book of the Dead, dated around 1400 BCE. In Greek and Roman representations it connotes justice in judgement: the allegorical figure of Justice holds a balance. The psychostasis entered Christian art in representations of the Last Judgement primarily through Byzantine influence. In his role as conductor of souls, St Michael is usually depicted as holding a balance or presiding over the Weighing of Souls. The image became a standard motif in Christian art in the high medieval period, and it appears in Last Judgement scenes sculpted on church tympanums all over western Europe. See Mary P. Perry, 'On the Psychostasis in Christian Art—I', 94–104, and Mâle, *The Gothic Image*, 376–8. Samuel Brandon documents the literary sources which speak of the motif of the balance in pre-Christian and early Christian sources. He notes that the image of the psychostasis was originally used to express individual posthumous judgement, but later it became part of artistic renderings of the Last Judgement of mankind at the End of Time. See Brandon, *The Judgment of the Dead*, 124. While the latter was certainly the intent of medieval sculptors, it is evident from the Marian tales and others like them that people understood the image of the balance to refer also to the individual judgement of souls, taking place immediately after death. *SḤ* 1240 clearly proves that R. Judah understood the idea of the balance literally; describing the scene of personal judgement, he writes, 'God sits on His throne of judgement . . . all sins that a man performs, and their equivalents in merits, are weighed [to see] if they are equal.'

pictures St Michael weighing souls to determine whether they are damned or saved. On the relief, the Virgin casts a rosary into the cup of the balance containing the soul's merits.[23] Other examples in which objects are added onto the merit pan of the balance in an effort to save the soul in question exist within Christian art. On the tympanum of Bourges Cathedral that object is a chalice, while at Amiens it is a lamb. The former symbolizes the sacramental grace of the Church and the latter is a representation of Christ himself.[24] The message which emanates from these judgement scenes is that it is Christian ritual or belief, not personal merit or accomplishment, that has the power to conquer sin—a message R. Judah would find objectionable.

The image of the balance as representative of the posthumous judgement of the soul also appears in a tale in *Sefer ḥasidim*. A certain Jew beholds in a dream the judgement of a fellow Jew who has just died, or is privy to the decision as to what his judgement will be when he dies.[25] In the dream, angels place the dead man's body in one pan of a balance and his sins in the other.[26] His sins preponderate and the man is denied entry into Paradise,[27] whereupon other angels come and place skins and furs of foxes and other animals upon the dead man's body. The additional weight of these causes the cup to outweigh the opposing cup containing his sins. The man now gains entry into Paradise. The angels explicate the meaning of the dream. The man's body represents his merits, as he used his body to perform acts of

23 See Hildburgh, 'Iconographical Peculiarities in English Medieval Alabaster Carvings', 48–9. No fewer than eight late medieval wall paintings in English churches depict this very same image of the Virgin and the rosary. See Mary P. Perry, 'On the Psychostasis in Christian Art—I', 100, and 'On the Psychostasis in Christian Art—II', 215; Hildburgh, 'An English Alabaster Carving', 129.

24 See Mary P. Perry, 'On the Psychostasis in Christian Art—II', 209.

25 The meaning of the text is unclear. It states, 'And the man that he had seen in the dream, he was certain that he was alive, and at the time that he dreamt, the weighed one was dead' (*SḤ* 124). The second suggested reading, that the visionary witnesses the posthumous judgement of someone who is still living, is a common motif in the exempla literature and serves as an exhortation to repentance.

26 It is common in Christian artistic representations of the Weighing of Souls for one or both pans of the balance to contain small human figures. Oftentimes the figure that represents the merits of the individual appears joyful, with hands raised in prayer, while the other, representing the sins, appears miserable, ugly, or devilish. Mary P. Perry attributes this use of the human body to Greek artistic representations of the weighing of the personified destinies, from which medieval artists copied. See 'On the Psychostasis in Christian Art—I', 103. See also Diderot, *Christian Iconography*, 178–9, Mâle, *The Gothic Image*, 377, and Baschet, *Corps et âmes*, 204–5.

27 The exact term that is invoked is *olam haba* (the World to Come). The context makes it clear that Paradise, rather than the post-resurrection World to Come, is being referred to here.

kindness; the skins and furs that are added on are the actual ones he used to pay his allotted portion of the communal tax burden—an act of great merit according to the dictates of *Sefer ḥasidim*.[28]

While the hasidic tale shares many elements with the Marian one (the image of the balance, the sins initially outweighing the merits, the additional weight placed upon the merit side of the balance, the reversal of the judgement, and the entry into Paradise), the two express radically different views on the nature of the posthumous judgement that awaits souls after death. The Marian tale emphasizes the overwhelming compassion of the Mother of God and her growing importance as the greatest intercessor for people in judgement before the throne of Christ. Even more than that, it tells of Mary's ability to subvert the normal judicial process and to override God's sentence; she renders even the damned innocent.[29] By contrast, the hasidic tale stresses the personal merits of the individual alone as the deciding factor in posthumous judgement. It is the man's own actions, accomplished during his lifetime, which give him the extra advantage in judgement and gain him entry into Paradise. R. Judah's tale appears to be a conscious reworking of the well-known Marian tale, with a message all its own. In this light, his emphasis on the good works of the individual as the sole factor in redemption would be an attempt to counteract the supernatural power of the holy dead in manipulating Divine justice, as illustrated by the Marian tale and others like it.[30] R. Judah's reworking of the tale also

[28] *SḤ* 124. Just as R. Judah considers it an act of great merit to faithfully pay one's taxes, so, too, he strongly censures anyone who avoids it. In *SḤ* 1386 he castigates those who do not uphold their share of the communal tax allotment, inform on Jews to the non-Jewish government, and cause monetary loss to innocent Jews. Although they appear to go unpunished in this world, they face an ominous posthumous fate; along with the non-Jews, they will suffer in Hell for all eternity (see *SḤ* 1386). Regarding the medieval tallage and its method of assessment and collection by the Jewish community, see Abrahams, *Jewish Life in the Middle Ages*, 40–2. On the presence of furs and skins in Germany at the time, see Delort, *Le Commerce des fourrures en Occident*, ii. 750–3 and 771–5. Delort documents the highly sophisticated and organized system of urban craftsmen working with furs in the twelfth and thirteenth centuries in western Europe.

[29] Mary's depiction as weighing down the balance in artistic representations of the Last Judgement could possibly have been an outgrowth of earlier such depictions involving St Michael. In Romanesque sculpture, for example on the tympanum of Autun, St Michael not only holds the balance but forcibly restrains it from being tipped by demons to the unfavourable side. Here, his role exceeds that of mere 'weigher of souls'; he intercedes to save man from the clutches of the Devil—another example of the supernatural power of the holy dead to rescue sinners. See Brandon, *The Judgment of the Dead*, 124.

[30] Yet another narrative which demonstrates the Virgin's role in subverting the judicial process by saving those whom justice has already condemned involves an errant English clerk. In a vision of the clerk's posthumous judgement, the Virgin snatches away from the demons the book in which all his sins are listed. She saves the clerk from Hell on account of his one merit—

demonstrates the process of differentiation in *Sefer ḥasidim* between Christian concepts and Jewish ones. By eliminating the intercessory power of the Virgin Mary, he has succeeded in 'Judaizing' the tale.

R. Judah was not the first to protest against the invocation of such power in the face of normative Divine justice; even within the Christian camp, several centuries before him, one early medieval ecclesiast was outspoken against Mary's merciful interventions.[31] Even more so as a Pietist, as one who places himself under intense Divine scrutiny for every action, even for every thought, and firmly believes in moral accountability,[32] R. Judah finds such subversion of justice morally untenable. In his own, unique version of the tale involving the balance, he attempts to dispel any notion of

devotion to her. See MS BL Harley 268 fo. 9 (*Catalogue of Romances*, iii. 562 no. 34). In contrast, R. Judah narrates in *Sefer ḥasidim* a scene in which a dying man sees in a dream a 'cloud in the image of a man' carrying a heavy burden (perhaps a heavy book containing the man's sins, as he is, at first, losing the battle over his soul), and in his hand is gold. Another 'image of a man' wrapped in a *talit* approaches and informs him that the merit of his wearing a *talit*, combined with the merit of once having given some gold to a poor Torah scholar, has redeemed him from death. Immediately he begins to sweat and is cured. See *SḤ* 1524. Although this tale does not involve a balance, the message is the same: only one's own deeds can proclaim one's innocence in the judgement of one's soul.

Several artistic representations of the Weighing of Souls illustrate the theme of the Marian tales; they depict the Virgin standing adjacent to the balance and sheltering souls under her mantle, as in the stone panel of the Church of St Michael in Minehead, Somerset, and in a fifteenth-century English alabaster carving, for example. See Hildburgh, 'An English Alabaster Carving', 129–30. (Once again, artistic representations of the psychostasis of the Virgin Mary parallel those involving St Michael. In the Last Judgement scene at Autun, it is St Michael who shelters two small trembling souls under his mantle. See Mâle, *Religious Art in France*, 418.) S. Brandon sums up the Virgin Mary's role when he writes, 'she became the intercessor *par excellence*, on whom the hopes of sinners were set'. See *The Judgment of the Dead*, 128.

31 The Anglo-Saxon cleric Aelfric spoke out against such a 'heretical' belief, which circulated in anonymous homilies of his day: 'Certain heretics said that the holy Mary, Christ's mother, and certain other saints will pluck the sinful from the devil after the judgement, each [taking] a share. But this heresy originated with those people who wished to remain always in the grip of their corporeal desires and did not wish to earn eternal life with hardships. Let no man have confidence in this lie. Neither the blessed Mary nor any other saint will wish to lead the impure and the wicked and the impious, who always persevered in sins and died in sins, into the pure dwelling of the joy of the kingdom of heaven. But they will be like devils and will suffer eternally in hell-fire with the devils. All the world cannot intercede for one of those to whom Christ will say thus: *Discedite*' (Clayton's translation in *The Cult of the Virgin Mary*, 253 n. 159; see also pp. 253–4 and 260–5 there).

32 'An accountability for thoughts and feelings no less than for actions', as well as a 'heavy sense of God's abiding presence and especially of His ever-watchful eye', are trademarks of pietism in general; see Soloveitchik, 'Piety, Pietism and German Pietism', 464–5. In German Pietism, too, we find the idea of responsibility for one's thoughts as much as for one's actions (see e.g. *SḤ* 15, 38, 199, and 1014). Pietistic law even requires a person to annul his thoughts as he would a vow (see *SḤ* 1197).

supernatural aid for the unworthy that may have penetrated the consciousness of his co-religionists.

The Deserving and Undeserving Dead

R. Judah argues repeatedly, in several different passages of *Sefer ḥasidim*, that acts of piety performed by the living on behalf of the dead only benefit those who are deserving. In one instance, he speaks of other forms of aid, in addition to prayer and charity, which can benefit the dead by mitigating or even abrogating their posthumous suffering. Restitution of stolen goods by the living is one such act.[33] R. Judah records two ghost tales which tell of the dead being forced to wander ceaselessly because of land and goods which they illegally possessed in their lifetime. The stories emphasize that only the restoration of the property by living relatives can put the dead to rest.[34] Although these tales speak of Gentiles enduring eternal torment, and for this reason R. Judah is unsure whether the restitution of ill-gotten goods will succeed in redeeming the souls in question, he is certain that doing so for Jews will, so long as they merit such aid. He writes with conviction: 'it benefits [the soul of a Jew suffering posthumous torment] . . . if he stole and the heirs return it'.[35] Embarrassment and degradation of the corpse also help the dead and reduce their suffering in the hereafter.[36]

[33] This idea is already present in geonic literature; see *Otsar hage'onim*, *Ḥagigah*, 27. In the medieval Jewish world, as in its Christian counterpart, the restitution of stolen goods was viewed as separate from the standard forms of aid for the dead, i.e. prayer and charity. Thus, for example, the eleventh-century Spanish Jewish philosopher Abraham bar Hiya rejected the notion that the prayer and charity of the living could in any way benefit the dead, yet he believed that the restitution of stolen goods by living relatives could achieve atonement for them. See *Sefer hegyon hanefesh ha'atsuvah*, 32.

[34] *SḤ* 35.

[35] Stephen of Bourbon lists the restitution of ill-gotten goods as one form of suffrage that can help the souls in Purgatory, as does the Dominican Thomas of Cantimpré. See Le Goff, *The Birth of Purgatory*, 312, and Schmitt, *Ghosts in the Middle Ages*, 135. This motif also appears as a common element in the exempla collections. In one popular ghost tale, a dead child returns to say that he is in torment on account of an unpaid nursery debt. See *Catalogue of Romances*, iii. 96 no. 38, 436 no. 68. Several ghost tales recount how the dead are restored to their bodies in order to pay back debts they had incurred while alive. See Caesarius of Heisterbach, *Dialogue*, 11: 35, and *Catalogue of Romances*, iii. 702 no. 14.

[36] R. Judah writes, 'Then it benefits . . . if he shames the deceased in order to lessen and diminish his sins' (*SḤ* 35). He cites the biblical example set by the righteous Judaean King Hezekiah, who dragged the bones of his idolatrous father on the ground in order to achieve atonement for his sins; see *SḤ* 34, p. 37, based on BT *Pes.* 56*a*.

The performance of other pious acts can also benefit the dead, albeit in a more vague fashion. Better to learn from a holy book written by a deceased author than from one written by a living man, declares R. Judah, for the merit of the study benefits the soul of the deceased. Such an act will precipitate a reaction from the deceased as well; his spirit will intercede for mercy for

Despite R. Judah's firm belief in the efficacy of the pious actions of the living, he emphasizes their provisional nature; only if the dead are deserving of this aid will it succeed. He writes:

But there is a difference if a person did not merit; [then] all the charities will not benefit him. But if he did merit and he sinned, and because of his sins they chase him out of Paradise or they punish him in Gehenna or they tire him out on a thorny path, or angels of torment play with him, or [in reference to] a righteous man, on account of his sin, they do not allow him to enter into the quarters of the righteous, then it benefits if they pray or give charity for him; or if he stole and [his] relatives return [the stolen item], or if the dead person is shamed in order to decrease and diminish his sins. But the one who did not merit, after his death, all that they do for the deceased will not benefit [his soul], unless he commanded [a pious act] while alive and they carried it out after his death.[37]

Whereas prayer, the giving of alms, the restitution of stolen goods, and the degradation of the corpse, all performed by the living, will benefit the dead, R. Judah emphasizes that this is only true if one merits such aid. If one is undeserving then no amount of aid will be of benefit. The only exception is if the dead person commanded, while he was still alive, that money be distributed to the poor after his death. Only in that case can the deceased benefit, even if he did not merit such aid on the basis of his conduct during his lifetime.[38]

the individual who has benefited him. See *SḤ* 355. (Once again, the idea of the ordinary dead praying for the living does not pose a threat to R. Judah's outlook, unlike the notion of the holy dead doing so.) Similarly, one who wears the *talit* of a deceased person will accrue 'merit and reward' for the soul of the original owner. See *SḤ* 334.

[37] *SḤ* 35.

[38] Ibid. The logic behind this is that, since the dying man commanded the pious acts while still alive, carrying them out after his death is simply an implementation of his own will rather than the voluntary action of others on his behalf (where merit would play a role).

R. Judah takes the fulfilment of pious acts willed in testaments of the dying very seriously. Repeated admonitions are given that one should appoint reliable, God-fearing witnesses and executors, who see to it that the testament is indeed carried out. Especially when it comes to the disbursal of funds to the poor, it is imperative that one relegate this task only to 'faithful, righteous, and well-known men, who will do as commanded'. Experience has proven, says R. Judah, that many a family that has been left with the task has failed to distribute the funds as instructed, despite the presence of witnesses and the taking of oaths. In such cases, one's own soul is put in jeopardy, and such a person must take care that 'his soul should not be chased out from the portion of the living'; see *SḤ* 307 and 309. R. Judah records the praiseworthy act of one individual who gave charity to the poor on behalf of his soul just prior to his death in order not to have to rely on others, as they might fail to keep their promise; see *SḤ* 310. Such acts of disloyalty are not restricted to Jewish executors alone, as the exempla literature testifies. One exemplum tells of a dead peasant who is forced to appear several times in order to demand that his wife and sons execute his testament. See *Catalogue of Romances*, iii. 631 no. 61.

In an earlier passage in *Sefer ḥasidim*, R. Judah explains precisely who the undeserving are. In the context of an approbation of the giving of alms by one person on behalf of another, he writes the following:

And, additionally, someone who gives for his own sake in this world, it will not benefit him in the future—'Wealth will not avail on the day of wrath'—for the one who causes others to sin or who prevents others from giving and doing. And if he did not study [Torah] and did not perform, that is to say, he has not accrued any merit through [the performance of] *mitsvot* and good deeds, [then] if he did not give [the alms] into the hands of a trustworthy person during his lifetime to give [to the poor] after his death, even if others were to give for his sake a house full of gold, it will not benefit the dead person.[39]

R. Judah interprets Proverbs 11: 4, 'Wealth will not avail on the day of wrath', to refer to the act of giving alms on behalf of the sinful dead; such an act will not redeem them, nor relieve them from their posthumous torment (their 'day of wrath'). He argues that the verse refers to specific types of sinners, such as 'one who causes others to sin', 'one who prevents others from giving [alms] and from doing [pious acts]', and 'one who has not studied [Torah]' and 'has not accrued any merit through [the performance of] commandments and good deeds'. These cannot be aided at all when they die, even if others were to give 'a house full of gold' on their behalf. The only exception is, once again, if while they were still alive they instructed others to give charity on their behalf after their death.

Careful examination of these examples reveals that the undeserving dead are not the wholly wicked souls that one might imagine them to be. Whereas the second group appears to comprise Jews who are truly undeserving, as they have neither the merit of *mitsvah* observance nor that of Torah study,[40] the first group may be different. This includes all those who obstruct the will of God either by causing others to sin or by preventing them from performing positive acts. Given the subjective meaning of these character designations within *Sefer ḥasidim*, however, those Jews who 'cause

[39] *SḤ* 34.

[40] It is possible that R. Judah has in mind lack of observance of the more amorphous *mitsvot*, such as charity, acts of kindness, and the like, rather than of all the *mitsvot* that define a Jewish way of life. Given the traditional character of the medieval Jewish community, the thought, for instance, that one of them would not be eating matzah on Passover seems strange. This group, therefore, probably consists of Jews who are devoid of merit—additional merit, that is, of Torah study and acts of kindness—above and beyond the merit accrued from adherence to the everyday dictates of Torah law. However, putting this group in the category of the undeserving, who are to be denied all aid after death, seems logically unsustainable, especially in light of R. Judah's position regarding Jewish apostates.

the public to sin' or 'prevent others from giving and doing' may not only be nefarious sinners in positions of authority. The description may indeed refer to any of the detractors of Pietists mentioned throughout the work, who ridicule them and at times prevent them from practising the dictates of Pietism. We often hear of the constant ridicule aimed at the Pietists and which makes it difficult for them to perform the commandments of *tsitsit*, *talit*, and *tefilin*;[41] of those who 'rush the recital of the blessings and the praises' in the synagogue so that the hasid is forced to pray elsewhere;[42] and of one who 'puts fear upon' the Pietists and 'prevents the righteous [i.e. the Pietists] from performing the commandments'.[43] Eleazar of Worms, too, uses similar terms—such as 'he who causes the public to sin', '[he who] prevents the public from gaining merit', and 'he who mocks and hates the good ones'—to describe those groups of sinners who are punished twice, in this world and the next.[44] They are the Jews who obstruct the will of God as refracted through the lens of Pietism, and whose souls, according to R. Judah, will not benefit in any way from the giving of alms when they die.

Moreover, Jews are not the only ones to whom this distinction applies. R. Judah also groups non-Jews and apostates into categories of deserving and undeserving. In another passage regarding the topic of prayer for the dead, he states: 'if there is a Gentile who does favours for Jews' then one can pray to lighten his posthumous sentence. For evil non-Jews (*goy ra*), however, one may not pray. The same is true for apostates; while 'regular' ones (*meshumad*) can be prayed for in order to lighten their sentence, evil ones (*meshumad ra*) ought not to be.[45] Like his master, R. Eleazar too

41 See *SḤ* 975, 976, 977, 978, and 1589.

42 *SḤ* 1575.

43 This individual also mocks the *talit* of a *tsadik* (clearly a Pietist) and removes it from him, 'is wont to rush the praises in the synagogue', and 'chases out of the synagogue whomever he wishes'. See *SḤ* 1344.

44 *Sefer haroke'aḥ hagadol*, ed. Shneerson, 'Hilkhot yom hakipurim', 105. Although the text here reads *lokeh bezeh la'olam haba*, which, simply rendered, means 'he is punished for this in the next world', the meaning that R. Eleazar ascribes to the word *bezeh* is 'in this world', so that the phrase reads, 'He is punished in this [world and] in the next world.' This reading is corroborated in a later passage on the same topic ('Hilkhot yom hakipurim', 110), where R. Eleazar clearly uses the word *bezeh* to refer to 'this world'. Furthermore, the context makes it evident that such a sinner receives his punishment in both worlds: the same passage (p. 105) states that those individuals who have few sins or merits are recompensed in this world, so that full punishment or full reward is reserved for the period after death. These sinners are contrasted with the detractors of Pietism, who will be made to suffer even more, that is, in both worlds.

The Pietists often used the terms 'wicked' or 'bad' to refer to non-Pietists who opposed their idiosyncratic teachings or behaviour (e.g. in *SḤ* 1375), and the terms 'good' or 'righteous' to refer to themselves and their supporters. See Soloveitchik, 'Three Themes in *Sefer Ḥasidim*', 330–5.

45 *SḤ* 1571.

restricts the utility of charity and excludes the undeserving. Of charity given on behalf of the wicked (*rasha*), he unequivocally states, 'it is of no benefit'.[46]

R. Judah's belief that only the deserving dead can be prayed for forces him to reinterpret a talmudic story that appears to contradict his position. In *Sotah* 10*b* it is related that King David, after the death of his renegade son Absalom, successfully prayed for his redemption from Gehenna.[47] R. Judah explains the permissibility of King David's action by once again highlighting the special circumstances in which it occurred. On the basis of a prophetic statement, he charges the king with full responsibility for his son's rebelliousness.[48] Since, in this exceptional case, David was the sole cause of Absalom's posthumous punishment, R. Judah concludes that it was permissible for him to pray for his son's soul. This is because the sin, in essence, belonged to him, not to his son. King David, therefore, did not pray on behalf of someone undeserving. Rather, he beseeched God for forgiveness of his own sin. R. Judah thus resolves the contradiction posed by the talmudic story by removing it from the context of prayer for the dead altogether.

Whereas the past conduct of the dead serves as the criterion that determines the efficacy of prayer and aid for them according to R. Judah the Pious, it is simply not a factor in geonic discussions of the topic or in contemporary tosafist teaching. Geonic authorities are unconcerned with the spiritual state of the deceased individual; for them, the issue at stake is the aim of that prayer. R. Hai and R. Nisim Gaon argue vehemently that prayer for the dead achieves only the mitigation or abrogation of torment, never the advancement of reward. While the efforts of the living can secure atonement for sin, they can only provide the dead with relief or release from the punishment of Gehenna. It is solely the merits of the deceased himself that can gain entry for his soul into Paradise and determine its proximity to the Divine Presence.[49] When it concerns the dispensation

[46] *Sefer haroke'aḥ hagadol*, ed. Shneerson, 'Hilkhot yom hakipurim', 109.

[47] BT *Sot.* 10*b*–11*a*. The note found on p. 385 of Wistinetzky's edition of *Sefer ḥasidim* (no. 1571, n. 3), where the source is cited as *Sot.* 8*b*, is incorrect.

[48] In 2 Sam. 12: 11, the prophet Nathan informs King David that, as a result of his sin with Batsheva, a renegade will arise within his own household.

[49] Rav Nisim cites two cases of prayer for the dead in the Talmud to support his position: *Ḥag.* 15*b*, regarding R. Yohanan's rescue of Elisha ben Avuyah from Gehenna, and *Eruv.* 65*a*, where R. Eleazar ben Azaryah states that his prayer has the power to release the entire world from posthumous punishment. Rav Nisim points out that both cases involve only the removal of punishment as a result of prayer for the dead, never the acquisition of reward. See *SḤ* 32, pp. 29–30.

of posthumous reward, R. Hai states that, 'Even if all the righteous people of the world were to petition for mercy on his behalf, and all the monies were to be dispensed as charity in order to accrue merit for him, never would these acts benefit him in this regard.'[50]

While R. Hai speaks here about the futility of prayer in granting posthumous reward to a dead person, R. Judah uses a similar exclamatory statement in reference to the futility of charity for the undeserving dead.[51] Unlike the *ge'onim*, he believes in the ability of prayer to ensure posthumous reward. He entertains the possibility that 'one person merits and another benefits' even with regard to the advancement to Paradise. While it is implausible to him that the undeserving dead could 'inherit Paradise through the toil of another', he is prepared to consider that scenario when it comes to the deserving.[52]

In consonance with the geonic authorities cited above, and in contrast to R. Judah, the *Tosafot* teaches that prayer for the dead is beneficial irrespective of merit. The talmudic story recorded in *Sotah* 10*b* is illustrative in this regard.[53] The tosafists, like R. Judah, are troubled by the account of King David's successful prayer for his renegade son, yet for a different reason. The story contradicts the statement in *Sanhedrin* 104*a* that 'Sons can accrue merit for their fathers; fathers cannot accrue merit for their sons, as the verse states, "And there is no rescuer from My hand."[54] Abraham cannot rescue Ishmael, nor can Isaac rescue Esau.' If Abraham cannot redeem his wayward son Ishmael from Gehenna, nor can Isaac do the same for his wicked son Esau, how then, asks the *Tosafot*, can King David rescue Absalom?

The problem facing the tosafists is not the sinfulness of Absalom but the contradiction posed by the text in *Sanhedrin*. One solution which the *Tosafot* offers in order to resolve the contradiction between the two talmudic passages serves as further confirmation that the rebelliousness of Absalom is not the issue at stake. The tosafists argue that the 'fathers cannot rescue sons' principle applies only when prayer is not forthcoming. In the absence of prayer, the honour of the father alone is insufficient to save the son from the posthumous fate of the wicked. However, declares the *Tosafot*, 'prayer is beneficial', and the proof is that 'King David prays for

50 *Otsar hage'onim*, *Ḥagigah*, 28. Wistinetzky cites the same words in the name of R. Sherira Gaon.

51 As mentioned above, with regard to specific types of undeserving dead, R. Judah argues that even if others were to give 'a house full of gold' on their behalf, they cannot be helped (*SḤ* 34).

52 Ibid.

53 See *Tosafot*, *Sot.* 10*b*, s.v. *de'aiteih*.

54 Deut. 32: 39 and Isa. 43: 13.

Absalom'.[55] The plain sense of the passage in *Sotah* leads the tosafists to reinterpret the statement in *Sanhedrin*. They are prepared to accept the plain sense of the *Sotah* text because they believe that prayer for the dead is efficacious, even for the undeserving. Through its merit, King David succeeded where the patriarchs failed; even fathers can save sons. Furthermore, not only did King David succeed in rescuing his son from Gehenna, but he even gained entry for his soul to Paradise.[56]

Further contemporary evidence corroborates the belief espoused by the tosafists. An anonymous thirteenth-century text, *Ketav hapulmus*, records that the righteous Judaean king of the First Temple period, Hezekiah, was reputed to have removed his wicked father, Ahaz, from Gehenna through the power of his prayer.[57] Twelfth-century additions to the text of the *Maḥzor vitry* ascribe the legitimacy of the practice of giving charity in the name of the dead to a teaching recorded in the *Pesikta*. Based on Deuteronomy 21: 8, which describes the law of *eglah arufah* and in which the elders of Israel beseech God to 'grant atonement to the nation of Israel', a *midrash* expounds the following teaching: 'Since they seek mercy on his [the dead person's] behalf, they shoot him from Gehenna to Paradise like an arrow from a bow.'[58] This *midrash*, which attributes immediate and powerful effect to prayer for the dead, makes no qualifications on the basis of merit or anything else. Further, like the *Tosafot* above, it grants prayer for the dead the ability to immediately remove sinners from a place of posthumous torment and to catapult them instantly to one of posthumous reward.

R. Judah argues vehemently against this latter position when he writes, 'If they [the dead] possess no merit, they cannot obtain a portion in Paradise, even if [someone else] exempts them [from punishment].'[59] He neutralizes several talmudic statements in which certain righteous individuals (such as R. Preida, R. Eleazar, and R. Shimon bar Yohai) claim that they can exempt their generation, or even the entire world, from posthumous pun-

[55] *Sot.* 10*b*, s.v. *de'aiteih*.

[56] According to the explanation in *Sotah*, King David's invocation of the words 'my son' eight times during the course of his prayer lamenting Absalom's death (see 2 Sam. 19: 1, 5) accomplished the release of his soul from the 'seven levels of Gehenna' as well as its induction into the World to Come—the eighth level. The comments of the *Tosafot* on the passage, which express the belief that King David's prayer was successful, are appended to the words 'that he brings him into the World to Come'.

[57] While this passage appears in the Roke'ah's commentaries on the *sidur*, Simcha Emanuel has argued that it originated in the *Ketav hapulmus*. See *Perushei sidur hatefilah laroke'aḥ*, ii. 403. I wish to thank Simcha Emanuel for this reference.

[58] See *Maḥzor vitry*, ed. Goldschmidt, 'Seder yom hakipurim', 8, pp. 784–5. See also *Midrash tanḥuma*, 'Ha'azinu' 1 (ed. Buber), 51 and note.

[59] *SḤ* 34.

ishment, or can enable them to enter into a place of reward.[60] He qualifies these statements by explaining that, while these men of great merit may have been able to prevent an entire generation from sinning, and thereby enable them to enter Paradise, 'never did he [R. Preida] say that he could cause *sinners* to enter Paradise'. For sinners to reap such reward solely through the merit of another, even a pious other, would be impossible, argues R. Judah, for 'there exists no favouritism in this matter'.

Since R. Preida, R. Eleazar, and R. Shimon bar Yohai were all living when they uttered these statements, R. Judah's qualification of their applicability signals that he is denying here the power of the holy ones, even among the living, to seek favour before the heavenly court and subvert the normal procedures of justice. His textual reinterpretations are clearly intended to counter the view of those among his audience who would allow such acts and would be untroubled by a simple reading of these talmudic passages. His outspokenness in this matter could have been a response to outside sources that reinforced such a view among his readers. Similarly, his vociferous denial of the power of holy figures who were still living to bring sinners into Paradise could have been prompted, in part, by circulating tales that recorded such actions.

Various exempla of the high medieval period tell stories of the damned, both infamous and ordinary, who are saved from Hell through the prayers, good works, or intercession of the living.[61] The most popular tale of this kind is told by Paul the Deacon in his eighth-century biography of Gregory the Great. Gregory prays for the soul of the Roman emperor Trajan and succeeds in redeeming it from Hell.[62] The tale highlights not only

[60] In *SḤ* 1052 (middle of p. 265), R. Judah refers explicitly to the talmudic statement in *Eruv.* 54*b* in which R. Preida is rewarded by Heaven with the ability to gain entry into the World to Come for himself and his entire generation. In *SḤ* 34, R. Judah refers to the passage in BT *Suk.* 45*b*, in which R. Shimon bar Yohai boasts that he can exempt the entire world, from the time of its creation until his day, from posthumous punishment. A similar statement appears in *Eruv.* 65*a* regarding R. Eleazar ben Azaryah. This last talmudic passage is offered by R. Nisim Gaon as clear proof that the intercession of important people is efficacious. R. Judah here challenges the legitimacy of this proof.

[61] See Edwards, 'The Idea of Post Mortem Purgation', 121. Such tales are recorded in MSS BL Add. 22283 fo. 15*b*; Harley 2391 fo. 222; Add. 11284 fo. 76 and 76*b*; 18351 fo. 29, col. 2; Harley 268 fo. 177; Add. 16589 fo. 91*b*; Royal 12 E I fo. 159; Add. 33956 fo. 35, col. 2; Harley 1022 fo. 4*b* (*Catalogue of Romances*, iii. 325 no. 18, 336 no. 35, 400 no. 494, 401 no. 500, 418 no. 41, 437 no. 82, 469 no. 39, 539 no. 20, 630 no. 58, 638 no. 6 respectively).

[62] Originating in the 'Life of St Gregory' (Migne, *Patrologia Latina*, 80, cols. 56, 104, and 399), it was an oft-repeated exemplum and appeared in many collections throughout the Middle Ages. See e.g. MS BL Add. 22283 fo.15*b* and MS BL Harley 2391 fo. 222 (*Catalogue of Romances*, iii. 325 no. 18 and 336 no. 35).

Gregory's compassion but also the power of his prayer—it has the capacity to pull even a pagan emperor out of Hell. According to Paul, Gregory is told in a dream that his prayers have been successful but is warned not to pray again for the soul of one unbaptized.[63] Few, however, were bothered by the unorthodox nature of Gregory's prayer; the story was repeated many times in the Middle Ages, most often without the additional warning. A version was known to Ashkenazi Jews and was recorded in *Sefer nitsaḥon yashan*, a thirteenth-century polemical work.[64] Monastic writers in particular were eager to write down such tales in an effort to glorify their own order; these stories revealed the power of the monks' prayers, alms, and masses to release dead souls from torment.[65]

In addition to denying the unworthy redemption, R. Judah states that no one can ever 'buy' another's portion of Paradise, whether in whole or in part; only one's own personal merits can grant one a place there. He writes: 'And a person cannot purchase the otherworldly portion of his friend, as it says, "To me belongs the silver and the gold" [Hag. 2: 8], and it is written,

[63] Interestingly enough, in one fourteenth-century Latin manuscript intended for preachers, the story is entitled 'De Traiano imperatore liberato orationibus sancti Gregorii pape de poenis purgatoriis', which states that Trajan was liberated from the punishments of Purgatory thanks to Gregory's prayers. The text, however, tells how the emperor was liberated 'de poenis inferni', that is, from the punishments of Hell. Apparently the scribe felt that a theological emendation was necessary. See MS BL Add. 33956 fo. 35, col. 2 (*Catalogue of Romances*, iii. 630 no. 58). In a variant form of the tale copied in a number of manuscripts, Gregory is actually punished for having prayed for the pagan's soul. He is, however, offered a choice of penalties—either two days in Purgatory or lifelong (or, in other versions, a specified period of) illness. See MSS BL Add. 11284 fos. 76*a*–*b*, Add. 18351 fo. 29, col. 2; Add. 33956 fo. 35, col. 2; and Harley 1022 fo. 4*b* (*Catalogue of Romances*, iii. 400 no. 494, 401 no. 500, 418 no. 41, 630 no. 58, 638 no. 6, respectively).

[64] See Berger (ed.), *The Jewish–Christian Debate in the High Middle Ages*, 175–6. Here the story involves Gregory praying for a dead Muslim prince and God admonishing him never to do that again. I wish to acknowledge my appreciation to David Berger for this reference.

[65] The most famous story of this kind is told by Jotsald, monk of Cluny, in his 'Life of St Odilo'. In the tale, a hermit living near Sicily tells of the tormented souls of the dead, whom he hears wailing in pain and specifically requesting the prayers, vigils, and alms of the monks of Cluny and its abbot, Odilo, to deliver them from their agony. The tale was repeated many times in the medieval period and was popularized primarily through the efforts of Peter Damian in his own 'Life of St Odilo', Jacobus de Voragine in his *Golden Legend* (648), and Vincent of Beauvais in his *Speculum historiale* (25, 105, cols. 102–5). These three writers 'helped to make the efficacy of Cluniac prayers for the dead legendary'. See Iogna-Prat, 'Les Morts dans la comptabilité céleste des clunisiens', 55–6, and Schmitt, *Ghosts in the Middle Ages*, 68 and n. 19.

Similarly, the purpose of the ghost tales recorded and collected in the Cluniac monastery of Martmoutier in the twelfth century was to convince the monks themselves of the efficacy and potency of their fellow monks' prayers on behalf of their deceased brothers. See Farmer, *Communities of Saint Martin*, 135.

"Because the entire Earth is mine" [Lev. 25: 23], and it is written, "Everything under the heavens belongs to me" [Job 41: 3].' The only exception is a case in which the individual does something to earn that purchase. If, for example, someone undertakes to financially support an indigent Torah scholar, he may share in that scholar's portion of posthumous reward.[66] It is not unreasonable to suggest that R. Judah's remark here is intended to negate the legitimacy of the sale of indulgences and the circulating tales which promoted it, whose message his audience might lend credence to. Several tales found in the exempla literature emphasize the great value of indulgences and assert that they are worth more than the money spent on them.[67]

Thus, in arguing his case against both the plain-sense interpretation of internal traditional sources and external tales that his audience would have absorbed unconsciously, R. Judah reasons that the prayer and alms of the living cannot possibly aid the undeserving dead, because 'if so, in what way does the wicked lose out?'[68] He writes, 'This one merits and this [other] one enjoys; it does not benefit . . . behold, he enjoys in this world and, in the future, he inherits Paradise through the toil of the other!'[69] Posthumous aid from the living for the undeserving cannot be efficacious, for that would be unjust; one man would toil to gain merit and the other, undeserving, would benefit. In fact, it would be doubly unfair, as the wicked would receive the best of both worlds; after having lived a pleasure-filled life, free of religious restrictions, they would then advance to delight in the next world.

Sefer ḥasidim presents the corroborating opinion of Rabbenu Nisim on this point: it is illogical (*vadai mevutal hu veraḥok min hada'at*) for one to think that he who 'pursued his fleshly desire to take pleasure in sinning' should share in that 'portion of goodness' allotted to the righteous.[70] Yet,

[66] *SḤ* 1045.

[67] One such tale is that of a poor woman who buys an indulgence at a dedication festival, but has no money for the trip home. A rich man offers to buy her indulgence for its weight in gold. When he weighs the indulgence, he finds that, no matter how many gold coins he places on the scale, they cannot outweigh it. In the end, he leaves her with the indulgence and a sizeable amount of gold coins. See *Catalogue of Romances*, iii. 597 no. 167. Another tale tells of a one-day pardon from Purgatory that is sold for its weight in silver. Although the individual who seeks to buy it offers a large sum of silver, the pardon still outweighs the money. Only when he offers all he has does the money pan of the scale 'immediately' descend (*Catalogue of Romances*, iii. 720 no. 40). Yet another tale tells of the transfer of indulgences and the benefit accrued from it for the dead. A deacon prays that all his earned indulgences be transferred to a dead girl. She appears afterwards to an anchoress with a message of gratitude for the deacon (*Catalogue of Romances*, iii. 393 no. 326 and 479 no. 4).

[68] *SḤ* 34.

[69] Ibid.

[70] Similarly, Rabbenu Nisim writes that 'it is not right to pray for one who dies wicked that

while the *gaon* uses this logic in reference to the granting of posthumous reward as a goal in prayer for all the dead, R. Judah applies it specifically to the case of prayer for the undeserving. In their unqualified acceptance of prayer as a sure means of securing the soul's entry into Paradise, neither the *Tosafot* nor the author of the passage added to the *Maḥzor vitry* would assent to the claims put forth here by Rabbenu Nisim and R. Judah. Thus, in his denial of posthumous reward for the undeserving dead, R. Judah advances a position exclusively his own.

From a Pietist perspective, R. Judah's argument carries more weight. While any person might oppose the advance of the wicked to a place of posthumous reward, a Pietist would find it morally untenable. For the Pietist, the hereafter is the truer, everlasting, and more just world. While a hasid can bear any amount of shame and deprivation in this life, he is greatly disturbed by any loss of his otherworldly reward.[71] The very name *ḥasid* imparts this idea; the constant humiliation of a *ḥasid* in this world will be greatly rewarded in the next. His face, once pale with shame, will radiate with the shining splendour of God's countenance.[72] The only validation of a life lived in suffering and ignominy is, for a Pietist, the recompense vouchsafed him after death. He can lead an austere life because he is assured that poverty and anonymity in this world will lead to honour and prestige in the next,[73] the vanquished will have the upper hand,[74] and a life lived in perpetual discomfort and ascetic withdrawal will be followed by one of intense physical and spiritual joy.[75] In light of this axiom, R. Judah would find it intolerable to share such a highly coveted reward with one who has lived wantonly. Moreover, posthumous reward for the wicked blatantly contradicts a main tenet of Pietist teaching. The Pietists resolve the problem of theodicy by asserting that God allows the righteous to suffer and the wicked to prosper in this world because he wishes to reward the former and punish the latter *fully* in the next.[76] If the wicked were to enter

he should merit [to be] with the righteous, and that prayer accomplishes nothing.' See *SḤ* 31–2 (pp. 29–30).

[71] See *SḤ* 977. There are repeated admonitions in *Sefer ḥasidim* against receiving honour or praise in any form, even in the performance of *mitsvot*, for if one does so, 'then, behold, he has received his reward already in this world'. See *SḤ* 1528 and 996, 997, 1000, 1002, 1045, 1943, 1512, and 1945.

[72] See *SḤ* 975.

[73] See *SḤ* 1086 and 1512.

[74] See *SḤ* 1974 and 1003.

[75] See *SḤ* 1953, 1954, and 1543.

[76] See e.g. *SḤ* 1288, 1291, and 1093. By way of contrast, while Rabbenu Nisim does invoke this argument as a valid method with which God runs the world—i.e. he sometimes allows the wicked to benefit in this world in order to 'use up' the reward for the few merits they possess—he does not restrict his analysis of God's workings of justice to that argument alone. Instead, he proposes an equally valid scenario in which the wicked get punished in this world, but only par-

Paradise then not only would the righteous have suffered here in vain, but God's management of the affairs of this world would become inexplicable and his will capricious. To allow the posthumous reward of the undeserving would not only be unfair; for a Pietist, it would be blasphemous.

Yet despite R. Judah's protests against aiding the undeserving dead, it is evident that his contemporaries did just that. His frequent repetition of the declaration that only the deserving dead can benefit from the pious acts of the living, along with his use of exaggeration in regard to charity given on behalf of the undeserving ('even if one gives a house full of gold, it will not be beneficial'), attest to this phenomenon. Additionally, his novel interpretations of problematic talmudic sources (*Eruv.* 65*a*, *Ḥag.* 15*b*, *Sot.* 10*b*–11*a*) make it clear that he is reacting to a tradition which is not in consonance with his thinking.

The fact that the notion of prayer for the damned was accepted by many Christians of the time[77] would certainly reinforce any traditionally held view on the appropriateness of prayer for the undeserving dead maintained by contemporary Jews. One very popular exemplum related by Caesarius of Heisterbach illustrates the prevalent attitude. A certain usurer of Liège dies unrepentant and is denied burial in the church. Refusing to accept her husband's damnation, the usurer's widow shuts herself up in a house beside his grave and prays, gives alms, and fasts on behalf of his soul relentlessly day and night for seven years. He appears to her in a vision dressed in black and thanks her for rescuing him 'from the pit of Hell and from the greatest pains'. He petitions her to continue her efforts for an additional seven years. After she does so, he reappears, resplendent and dressed all in white, and thanks her for fully releasing him from his torment.[78] Aware of the theological problems associated with prayer for the damned in Hell, Caesarius, after recording the tale, reinterprets the words of the usurer's ghost, and explains that his reference to the 'pit of Hell' is not literal; it is but an allusion to the 'bitterness of Purgatory'.[79]

tially, with the remaining balance of the punishment awaiting them in the next. The wicked (and the righteous) receive the 'interest' (*peri*) as payment for their action while alive, with the bulk of the 'principle' (*keren*) reserved for payment after death. See *SḤ* 30. For a Pietist, full payment is reserved solely for the afterlife.

77 See above, pp. 280–1.

78 Caesarius of Heisterbach, *Dialogue*, 12: 24. See also Le Goff, *Your Money or Your Life*, 85. Caesarius records a similar tale involving the father of William, count of Julich, who is pulled out of Hell after twenty-one years thanks to the incessant prayers of his widow. The Devil refers to her as the 'one-eyed woman' because the 'constant weeping for his soul had lost her the sight of one eye'. See *Dialogue*, 12: 5.

79 Caesarius of Heisterbach, *Dialogue*, 12: 25.

The exempla literature also tells of St Bernard trying to halt futile prayer for the damned: the saint admonishes a priest for praying for his own father's soul.[80] Perhaps R. Judah has a similar case in mind when he states that a convert to Judaism who prays on behalf of his deceased parents will not succeed in lightening their sentence in Gehenna. 'Evil' non-Jews are branded as wicked, and 'the name of the wicked shall rot'.[81] Nevertheless, medieval adherents of both religions refused to accept the notion that their departed loved ones could not be aided, and, despite the instruction of their spiritual leaders, they continued to pray for and perform acts of charity on behalf of the undeserving and the damned.[82]

The Tale of R. Akiva and the Dead Man

A desire to restrain unwarranted prayer for the undeserving dead could possibly be the reason behind R. Judah's startling omission from *Sefer ḥasidim* of a popular ghost tale involving R. Akiva and a dead man.[83] Known from late midrashic and medieval Ashkenazi sources and familiar within Pietist circles,[84] this story shares the most common function of ghost tales

[80] See MS BL Royal 7 D I fo. 89*b* (*Catalogue of Romances*, iii. 488 no. 107).

[81] Prov. 10: 7, cited in *SḤ* 1571.

[82] As late as 1370, William of Nassyngton, a popular ecclesiastical author, tried to convince his audience that prayer for the damned was both futile and wrong. See *The Pricke of Conscience*, 11.2816–51, quoted in Edwards, 'The Idea of Post Mortem Purgation', 235.

[83] The closest reference to this tale in *Sefer ḥasidim* appears in no. 314, which speaks (as part of a very garbled text) about the request made by a dying hasid to another Jew that he teach his son to say Kaddish for him when he dies. Despite the apparent difficulty in teaching the hasid's son, others advise the Jew to do so as it is a *mitsvah*. No mention is made of an encounter with the deceased, of a posthumous punishment meted out to him, or of liberation from that punishment via the prayer of his son—all central elements of the R. Akiva tale.

[84] The tale appears in e.g. *Sefer tana devei eliyahu* 17: 18; *Midrash aseret hadiberot*, cited in Jellinek (ed.), *Beit hamidrash*, 80–1; *Masekhet kalah rabati* 2: 9 (this is a medieval *midrash* according to S. Reinach in 'L'Origine des priers pour les morts', 166), and *Ḥibur yafeh mehayeshuah* in *Ma'aseh hagedolim*, no. 759, p. 498. Scholars dispute the origins of the tale, which is not found in any talmudic or classical rabbinic midrashic source. L. Ginzburg maintains that *Ḥibur yafeh mehayeshuah* is its original source and the basis for all subsequent versions, while M. Lerner points to a Genizah fragment published by J. Mann as the earliest source and the version closest to that which appears in *Seder eliyahu zuta*. See Ginzburg (ed.), *Ginzei shekhter*, i. 237, and Lerner, 'The Story of the *Tana* and the Dead Man' (Heb.), 30. The earliest known Ashkenazi source is the *Maḥzor vitry*, ed. Goldschmidt, 'Hilkhot shabat', i. 223–4, where it is a later addendum to the original eleventh-century text. In Pietist literature, the story can be found in *Sefer ḥokhmat hanefesh*, 8*a* (a source which has eluded scholars who document the tale); *Or zarua*, vol. ii, 'Hilkhot shabat', no. 50; and *Sidur ḥasidei ashkenaz*, ed. Hershler, 75. The tale enjoyed a complex and varied history over time; see Lerner, 'The Story of the *Tana* and the Dead Man' (Heb.), 29–70 for a full chronicling of its history and a suggested line of transmis-

in the exempla literature: the dead return in order to solicit aid from the living.[85] In its high medieval form, it tells of an encounter in a cemetery between the mishnaic sage R. Akiva and a dead man who suffers a difficult and painful punishment: he is to chop and gather wood every day and then is burned upon it.[86] He informs R. Akiva that his only chance of redemption hinges upon the public recitation of a specific prayer by his son, whom R. Akiva must teach to do so.[87] When the son recites the prayer in

sion. For more recent discussions see Kushelevsky, *Penalty and Temptation* (Heb.), 253–71, and Shyovitz, '"You Have Saved Me from the Judgment of Gehenna"', 56–63.

85 The scholar who states this similarity most clearly is B. Heller, when he writes that 'the account of the encounter of R. Akiva with the black dead man from the fires of Hell appears to us as a pastiche from one of the Christian legends of the Middle Ages' ('Notes de Folklore Juif', 311). Heller's point is convincing because (1) the tale, and all similar aggadot which relate to the successful aid offered by the living to the dead (such as *Pesikta rabati* 20), appear only in late midrashic sources of the ninth century; (2) some of the personal and place names in the tale have a non-Jewish, probably Christian, origin; and (3) the story has an affinity, in both theme and detail, to several other Christian legends of the time.

86 In other versions, the encounter takes place 'on the road' (mostly in earlier variants recorded by Lerner), or, according to the *Sidur ḥasidei ashkenaz*, in the forest. See Lerner, 'The Story of the *Tana* and the Dead Man' (Heb.), 31–2. Earlier versions, furthermore, have R. Yohanan ben Zakai as the hero of the tale. These versions include the Genizah fragment published by Mann and found in *Seder eliyahu zuta*. Another difference found in earlier variants is that the dead man has a partner in both crime and punishment. See Lerner, p. 36.

87 In one version, it is R. Akiva who tells the dead man how he can attain redemption. According to Lerner, the nature of the redemption accomplished by the son shifted over time. The earlier sources cite his partaking of the sanctity of the Torah as the merit through which his father is redeemed: he is called up to read from the Torah, he recites out loud the 'Barekhu' blessing, and the congregation responds with further blessings. Later variants, on the other hand, invoke the son's public recital of prayers, such as 'Barekhu' or 'Yehei shemeh raba mevarakh' (i.e. Kaddish), in the evening service at the conclusion of the sabbath as the direct catalyst for the father's redemption. (There is a 'Barekhu' that is recited when someone ascends to read from the Torah and another one that initiates the evening service; prayer for the dead was associated with both of them.) This shift from a general association with the merit of Torah study (the first 'Barekhu', mentioned in earlier sources) to a specific prayer that is directly linked to redemption from posthumous suffering (the second one, mentioned in later sources) coincided with the gradual acceptance that the notion of prayer for the dead gained within the medieval Jewish world. See Lerner, 'The Story of the *Tana* and the Dead Man' (Heb.), 49–52. While A. Roth agrees with this general trajectory, he cites a different reason for it. The shift, he argues, was caused by the emergence of a law in Ashkenaz which excluded minors from being called up to recite the blessings on the Torah. Not having access to the first type of 'Barekhu', orphan minors were granted the opportunity to recite the 'Barekhu' of the evening service and say a mourner's Kaddish specifically at the conclusion of the sabbath.

Israel Ta-Shma, however, argues against viewing Kaddish as a new prayer for the dead that was to replace the 'Barekhu' associated with the Torah reading. Instead, he believes that the two were originally part of one liturgical unit, as they had been since early times (seventh and eighth centuries), and only became separated at the end of the eleventh century. See 'A Remark on the Topic of the Mourner's Kaddish' (Heb.), 563–5.

the synagogue, the man is freed from his torment. In some versions of the tale, he returns a second time to inform R. Akiva of his new, more favourable, status in the afterlife.[88]

Apart from reflecting an important and popular theme within medieval society in general—the significance and efficacy of prayer on behalf of the dead—the tale also occupied a fundamental role within the medieval German Jewish community. Recorded as an addendum to the text of the *Maḥzor vitry*, it formed the basis for the contemporary custom of orphan sons publicly reciting the 'Barekhu' blessing of the evening service or the Kaddish upon the conclusion of the sabbath for the welfare of their parent's soul.[89] Yet despite the fact that the tale was at the heart of the Jewish practice of prayer for the dead and that R. Judah believed in such practice, he omitted the story entirely from *Sefer ḥasidim*. Could it be that, because it was the source for the custom of praying for the dead specifically upon the conclusion of the sabbath—the moment when the souls return for punishment to Gehenna—this association with the sabbath rest of souls, which was problematic for R. Judah, precluded its inclusion in the work?[90] While this may be true, it is also likely that he omitted it because of the undeserving nature of the dead man who was redeemed by the prayer of the living.

Although we cannot be certain which version of the tale R. Judah was familiar with, those that circulated in high medieval Germany and within Pietist circles close to him contained details that pointed to the spiritual and moral degeneracy of the man,[91] his lack of Torah obser-

[88] In some versions of the tale, not only is the dead man released from his torment, but he informs R. Akiva that he has entered into Paradise. For the varying nuances of these versions, see Lerner, 'The Story of the *Tana* and the Dead Man' (Heb.), 54. The second appearance of the ghost, to inform the living individual that his efforts on his behalf have been efficacious and that he is now in Paradise, is a motif that forms part of the standardized form of the ghost tale in the exempla collections of the mendicants. See Schmitt, *Ghosts in the Middle Ages*, 136.

[89] *Maḥzor vitry*, ed. Goldschmidt, 'Hilkhot shabat', i. 223–4. Although uncertain, R. Isaac of Vienna, who mentions the custom, presumes that its source is the tale involving R. Akiva and the dead man, which he then proceeds to recount in full. At the conclusion of the tale, he cites as further proof the corroborating opinion of his master, R. Eleazar of Worms, who proclaims that 'a minor who recites "Yitgadal" saves his father from posthumous punishment'. See *Or zarua*, vol. ii, 'Hilkhot shabat', no. 50. Shyovitz labels the tale a 'myth of origins', as it provides a Jewish source for the custom; see '"You Have Saved Me from the Judgment of Gehenna"', 55.

[90] See the discussion in Ch. 6 above.

[91] According to the *Maḥzor vitry* and *Or zarua* versions of the tale (which contain the fullest accounts), when R. Akiva enquires about the child in his hometown, the townspeople pronounce curses upon his parents ('May the bones of that man be ground up'; 'May her name be erased from the world') upon mere mention of his name. Additionally, they remark that, 'even

vance,[92] as well as the eternal nature of his suffering in the afterlife—a further indicator of his sinfulness.[93] According to these texts, the reason for his posthumous torment was that he lived his life as 'a customs [or tax] collector, who favoured the rich and killed the poor'—a crime that provokes a strong reaction in R. Judah, and whose perpetrator, he foretells, will suffer eternally.[94]

Additionally, the tale contains important motifs which are common to all major accounts of Hellequin's Hunt, along with a number of unusual and specific details that align it most closely with the version narrated by Orderic Vitalis in his *Ecclesiastical History*. In the R. Akiva tale, the dead man's face is described as 'black as coal', while the army of the dead in Orderic's account has 'no colour visible, but only blackness and fiery flames'.[95] The dead man carries an unusually heavy burden, which is described in hyperbolic fashion: both in *Sefer ḥokhmat hanefesh* and in the *Or zarua*, he carries a load whose weight is comparable to that of 'ten loads'. Pulling abnormally heavy loads is a punishment which predominates in Orderic's account. The man appears at first to be alive (that is, physically present in his body), but then he is discovered to be dead, just as the dead in accounts of the Hunt are very much physically present. He runs ceaselessly, so that R. Akiva must 'scream at him and get him to stand still', in the same way that the dead that appear to Walkelin are swept along furiously by the horde. He is described as running 'like a horse', and the dead are mounted

regarding the commandment to circumcise him [i.e. the son], we did not involve ourselves' on account of the father's wickedness; he is known as one 'who has no friend in the world'. A heavenly voice, too, confirms his degeneracy: in response to R. Akiva's fasting and prayer on behalf of the son to help him gain understanding in Torah learning, the voice questions his actions: 'For this one you are fasting?'

92 The description of the dead man as naked (in e.g. the *Maḥzor vitry*, *Sefer ḥokhmat hanefesh*, and *Or zarua* versions of the tale) is an allusion to his gross lack of *mitsvot*, on the basis of the rabbinic dictum at BT *Shab.* 14*a*—'naked, without *mitsvot*'. See Lerner, 'The Story of the *Tana* and the Dead Man' (Heb.), 32.

93 Repetitive punishment that continues in an endless cycle is characteristic of those who suffer eternally in Hell.

94 Both the *Maḥzor vitry* and the *Or zarua* accounts mention this crime, though the truncated *Ḥokhmat hanefesh* version does not. R. Judah cries out against those who wield unjust power over, or place undue fear upon, the public. In *SḤ* 1346, he speaks of one such individual, who lords himself over people and intimidates a certain segment of the Jewish population. R. Judah sentences him to eternal punishment by grouping him with those who 'descend to Gehenna and never ascend' (see above, p. 242). Similarly, in *SḤ* 63, he comments (in the context of a tale that speaks of the dead who suffer eternal punishment) that one who wields undue fear over the public 'will be enslaved in the afterlife like an animal'.

95 See Orderic Vitalis, *The Ecclesiastical History of England*, ii. 514.

on horseback in most accounts of the Hunt. When stopped by R. Akiva, the man pleads to him not to delay him 'lest those who are appointed over me be angry'. A similar pleading occurs in accounts of the Hunt when the dead are stopped and questioned; at times they are subject to physical assault by the leaders of the horde when they do stop.

Beyond parallels in narrative detail, the R. Akiva tale also shares some doctrinal elements of Orderic's account of the Hunt. The version recorded in the *Maḥzor vitry* contains conflicting messages regarding the status of the ghost; at first, the man proclaims himself to be irredeemable—*ein lo takanah*—but then, immediately afterwards, suggests an 'impossible' yet possible redemption (*ela shamati mehem davar she'i efshar lihyot*). If he were to have a son, and if this son could stand up to pray before the congregation and recite 'Barekhu' and 'Yehe shemeh raba mevarakh', then he would be released from his punishment. Such narratives, which present conflicting theological positions on the possibility of redeeming those suffering posthumous torment, are common in accounts of the Hunt such as that of Orderic. Additionally, a single prayer recited even once in the synagogue will 'immediately release him from punishment', just as, with the recital of but a single mass, Walkelin releases his father's soul from Purgatory in Orderic's story.[96] Interestingly, even the dead man's crime, which condemns him to eternal terrestrial punishment, resembles one recorded by Orderic: Landri of Orbec separates himself from the army of the dead and begs Walkelin 'urgently to carry a message to his wife'. Landri, who is 'uttering horrible cries', is described as guilty of 'pervert[ing] judgement for bribes', and, 'while it was in his power [to help]', he was guilty '[of] ha[ving] shut his ears to the cries of the poor'—a very similar description to that of the customs or tax collector who favoured the rich and killed the poor in the Jewish tale.[97]

Such an equation between the story of R. Akiva and accounts of Hellequin's Hunt presents the dead man as one of the army of the damned, who is sentenced to suffer eternal torment on Earth. He could fall within the parameters of R. Judah's category of the undeserving dead, for whom prayer is neither efficacious nor allowed, which would explain why this well-known tale was not included in *Sefer ḥasidim*. Moreover, one of the prevalent versions of the tale involves a model of prayer for the dead that R. Judah rejects—it is the type of dramatic intercession of the holy which secures a supernatural pardon before the heavenly court. In that variant, R. Akiva fasts for forty days and prays to God to open up the mind of the

96 Ibid. 519. 97 Ibid. 515.

child, who is by nature incapable of learning, so that he can teach him to recite the proper blessings in the synagogue in order to help his father's soul. [98] As in the case of the father 'who causes the public to sin',[99] R. Judah may feel that the son in R. Akiva's story should not pray for his father; he must remain where he is—even if this means punishment for all eternity.

R. Eleazar of Worms cites the tale of R. Akiva and the dead man in his *Sefer ḥokhmat hanefesh* (it is the only ghost tale in the entire work[100]) and concludes, 'behold, we see that the prayer of a son helps his father [to be released] from Gehenna'.[101] In doing so, he breaks away from the ideology of his master. Apparently, he is not opposed in principle to the redemption of undeserving sinners from Hell through the agency of prayer. R. Judah, on the other hand, despite recording a whole collection of ghost tales in *Sefer ḥasidim*, fails to mention this one, or any other tale of its type. This last point is significant as it seems to be a statement: while R. Judah clearly considers the redemption of undeserving souls unacceptable, he equally ignores similar stories about more deserving individuals which ought not to pose a theological problem for him. That the most standard type of ghost tale circulating in thirteenth-century Germany is absent from *Sefer ḥasidim* must be more than just an oversight on the part of its author. This silence reverberates loudly.

It has already been suggested that the absence from *Sefer ḥasidim* of the motif of soliciting aid from the living helps to situate the work in a pre-purgatorial penitential climate in which most people are doomed to eternal torment without much recourse to redemption. While this is true, it does not negate the fact that the omission was intentional; R. Judah was certainly aware of this type of tale and believed in the efficacy of prayer and alms for the dead, and yet chose not to include such narratives. This omission reflects his position on the matter; while he permits prayer and charity for the deserving dead, he wishes to limit its use.

Limitations on Prayer and Alms for the Deserving Dead

In seeking to reduce the use of prayer and alms for the dead as avenues of atonement, R. Judah once again aligns himself with the early medieval Christian clerics before him. He too stresses good works and repentance in this world rather than reliance upon the posthumous aid of others. Repeatedly in *Sefer ḥasidim*, he advocates the acceptance of all types of suffering

98 See *Maḥzor vitry*, ed. Goldschmidt, 'Hilkhot shabat', i. 223–4.

99 See *SḤ* 1571.

100 R. Eleazar, however, does not regard the story as a ghost tale but as a *midrash*.

101 *Sefer ḥokhmat hanefesh*, 8*a*.

upon oneself in this life (ranging from the avoidance of daily pleasures to self-inflicted corporeal torture) in order to reduce the suffering of Gehenna. A desire to be *naki mehakadosh barukh hu*—to be clean of sin before God—or *shelo yikere ladin*—not to be called to judgement at all—are primary aims of the Pietist doctrine of penance.[102]

Even when one is forced to rely on the pious acts of others, R. Judah seeks to limit this reliance as much as possible. Instead, he recommends that the living who engage in these acts also impose voluntary suffering upon themselves as a form of vicarious penance in order for their prayer to be efficacious. In speaking about the category of the dead who have sinned but merited posthumous aid, he writes the following:

If he merited and sinned, a living person can fast or pray on his behalf that they reduce his punishment in proportion to what the living person accepts [upon himself] as punishment and as charity in order to reduce his [the dead person's] punishment or to increase his [the living person's] punishment in proportion to the sins [of the deceased]. Even after dying, he can say, 'I accept upon myself certain forms of suffering in order to remove him.' This is only if he merited and sinned; but if he did not merit, it will not benefit [him].[103]

R. Judah states here that, to the extent that one accepts a voluntary 'punishment' upon oneself, the dead person will be relieved from his torment proportionately.[104] Even complete redemption from suffering is possible (*tsa'ar kedei lehotsi'o*), he argues, if the living person has undergone enough voluntary suffering. (Of course, both these releases occur only in the case of a deserving person.) R. Judah here explicitly espouses the doctrine of vicarious penance, and does so in true Pietist form.[105] Voluntary corporeal suffering, in proportion to the amount of time invested in sin and the enjoyment gained from it, is part of the Pietist doctrine of penance.[106] R. Judah

[102] *SḤ* 22.

[103] *SḤ* 34.

[104] In *SḤ* 290, 291, and 295 the book records the practice of fasting on the anniversary of a father's or other important person's death. In these cases, fasting is unconnected to the concept of atonement for the soul. Rather, it appears to be an expression of mourning for the dead.

[105] Earlier, his espousal of the notion was only implicit in his reinterpretation of a talmudic passage; see above, pp. 295–7.

[106] Quoting Jeremiah 3: 13, 'But [you must] know your sin', R. Judah instructs each individual to calculate every day how he sins, how many days he is involved in sin, and how much pleasure he obtains from it, so that he 'accepts punishment in proportion to' those factors; see *SḤ* 1979. In *SḤ* 19, p. 23, he provides a concrete example: an adulterer must sit in a frozen river in the winter, or in an anthill in the summer, up to his mouth or nose, for the precise amount of time that he has engaged in the sin—from the moment he began speaking to the woman until the completion of the act. He should perform this penance repeatedly, in proportion to the number of times he has sinned with her.

extends it to the domain of the hereafter by asserting that voluntary suffering in this life can help in atoning for others even after their death.

He cites talmudic proofs for his assertion but adds his own novel interpretation of the narratives in order to advocate the type of vicarious penance he believes in—an indication of just how alien his notion is to traditional Jewish thought. R. Yohanan, in *Ḥagigah* 15*b*, successfully releases the apostate Elisha ben Avuyah from Gehenna, not solely through his prayer, as the Talmud states, but also 'possibly because R. Yohanan accepts upon himself certain afflictions or righteous acts that are proportionate to the evils' that Elisha had committed. And 'so too' is the case of Samuel, who, in *Berakhot* 18*b*, has Levi admitted into the Heavenly Academy on the basis of his own meritorious acts. For R. Judah, penance is a more powerful tool than prayer in helping the dead.

Similarly, he interprets another talmudic event as the outcome of the self-imposed suffering of the saintly: in *Sukah* 45*b*, R. Shimon bar Yohai releases 'the entire world from posthumous judgement from the day I was created until now'. Although the Talmud never specifies on the basis of what merit R. Shimon is able to accomplish this tremendous feat, R. Judah attributes it to the pain and affliction he has endured during his life, 'in proportion to the tortures which are forthcoming for the wicked on account of their sins'.[107] It is thus specifically as a result of his voluntary suffering—the thirteen years he spends in a cave with his son, 'deprived of the pleasures of his [other] children and wife'—that he is able to benefit his entire generation in the next world.[108] In R. Judah's mind, penance is the most powerful tool of all.

It is noteworthy that R. Judah chooses to give a new slant to the talmudic sources that he adduces as proof rather than turning to the exempla literature, which is replete with tales that illustrate his notion of vicarious penance, without the need to alter any details. While at times, it is true, he aims to counter the message emanating from circulating tales, at other times he articulates the very message that some of those narratives set forth. One such example is a classic tale that involves a penitent who dies before the completion of his penance. Before dying, he asks a friend to complete that penance for him. He then makes successive appearances to his friend, indicating that the penance he has undertaken for him is progressively efficacious. After a year he appears with one-third of his body white; after the second year with two-thirds of his body white; and after the third year

[107] *SḤ* 34. [108] *SḤ* 1052, p. 265.

he is entirely white.[109] Penance left incomplete by a friend is not a matter to be taken lightly. In one story, the friend who is doing a lengthy penance on behalf of a dead monk dies before completing it. He then appears and announces that he suffers great torment not merely for his own sins, but also because of the incomplete penance for his friend.[110]

R. Judah's principle of proportionality between voluntary suffering in this world and benefit for souls in the next was not without parallel in Christian theology. The 'accountancy of the hereafter', so prevalent in high medieval testaments, had clearly impacted on his thought. Just as these testaments establish a relationship between a set number of intercessory acts—such as masses to be offered, prayers to be chanted, and charitable money to be distributed—and the reduction of a soul's sentence in Purgatory by a specified number of years, so too, R. Judah sets up an equation between the amount of voluntary suffering a person undertakes during his lifetime and the amount of posthumous torment that his suffering will abrogate for someone else. The two are proportionately related, so that the more the former is practised, the more relief it brings about. As we have seen, 'a living person can fast or pray on his [i.e. the deceased person's] behalf that they reduce his punishment in proportion to what the living person accepts [upon himself] as punishment and as charity in order to reduce his [the other's] punishment'.[111]

While R. Judah's calculations regarding the hereafter bear the influence of the 'logic of Purgatory'—the rational pattern of thought and quantification of time characteristic of commercial life that underlie the doctrine of Purgatory in the high medieval period[112]—he modifies that logic to suit his

[109] See Banks (ed.), *Alphabet of Tales*, 351 no. 519; *Catalogue of Romances*, iii. 96 no. 37 and 383 no. 170. Other variants of this tale exist: in one it is a dead nun's penance that is completed by the sisterhood of the nunnery (*Catalogue of Romances*, iii. 384 no. 173), and in another a dead monk's penance is completed by the brotherhood of the abbey (Banks (ed.), *Alphabet of Tales*, 386–7 no. 578). Jacobus de Voragine recounts how a certain woman commended herself, while alive, to the Devil for the sake of riches, and committed many serious sins. She died without having confessed them before a priest. Her son, however, confessed the sins for her and did seven years of penance after her death. She appeared to him afterwards in a vision and thanked him for redeeming her from her posthumous torment. See *The Golden Legend*, 655.

[110] See *Catalogue of Romances*, iii. 694 no. 16.

[111] R. Judah's use of the term *keneged mah* sets up this proportionality.

[112] The testators' demand for an increasing number of masses *pro anima* at this time reflected a 'logic of repetition' and a 'logic of accumulation'. Based on quantifiable units familiar to merchants, both these ideas helped the extension of earthly time into the hereafter. The period after one's death was no longer viewed as an infinite and immeasurable eternity; it could now be perceived logically and assessed arithmetically. See Chiffoleau, *La Comptabilité de l'au-delà*, 326.

penitential outlook. It is the acts of self-torment performed by the living, rather than their intercessory acts, that reduce the posthumous punishment of an individual's soul. This unique 'accountancy of the hereafter', as well as the Pietist doctrine of penance more generally, reflect the early medieval penitential system with its rigorous external penances, and not the high medieval penchant for suffrages.

Thus, by denying posthumous aid to the undeserving and by limiting its application even for those who are deserving, R. Judah, like early medieval clerics before him, adopts a position that is very much Augustinian in nature. Although a firm believer in the efficacy of prayer and charity for the dead, he is careful to restrict their benefit only to those who 'sin but merit', much as Augustine limits the efficacy of such acts to those who have 'earned, while living, the privilege of being helped by them afterwards'. In fact, R. Judah's categories of the dead correspond to those set up by Augustine and preserved in the writings of Caesarius of Heisterbach.[113] Those individuals who 'sin and do not merit' in R. Judah's system parallel Augustine's group of the 'very bad' and Caesarius's 'supremely bad', for whom the aid of the living is not at all beneficial. Similarly, R. Judah's category of those who 'sin but merit' corresponds to Augustine's group of the 'not very bad', for whom suffrages performed by the living serve either to bring about 'a full remission' (Caesarius's 'moderately good') or make the 'damnation suffered more bearable' (Caesarius's 'moderately bad'). R. Judah assures his readers that, for Jews, restitution of stolen goods by living relatives will secure a complete annulment of posthumous torment. He also suggests that many others who suffer various post-mortem punishments, and who fall into the category of those who 'sin but merit', will likewise reap the full benefit of the prayer and charity of the living on their behalf (similar to Caesarius's 'moderately good').[114] On the other hand, prayer on behalf of

113 As part of a dialogue between a monk and a novice, Caesarius writes concerning suffrages: 'You ought also to know this, that the supremely good, such as martyrs, do not need these after their death; to the supremely bad, such as unbelievers, they are useless; but they benefit the moderately good and the moderately bad, but in different ways. The former are delivered sooner; the latter receive milder punishment. Yet their punishment knows no end.' Caesarius's fourfold system perfectly parallels R. Judah's; see *Dialogue*, 12: 39, p. 328. In contrast to Caesarius, another contemporary of R. Judah also records Augustine's position on the beneficiaries of suffrages, yet divides them into only three groups. Thus Jacobus de Voragine speaks of the 'very good', who have no need for suffrages; the 'very bad', for whom they have no benefit; and the 'mediocre', for whom they are beneficial. See *The Golden Legend*, 655–6.

114 R. Judah lists the sinner who 'is chased out of Paradise', 'is punished [corporeally] in Gehenna', 'has angels of torment playing with him', and 'is not allowed to enter into the enclosure of the righteous' along with one 'who is tired out along a thorny path', in the very same

'regular' apostates as well as 'non-Jews who do favours to Jews' helps only to lighten their posthumous suffering [115] Regarding Jews who suffer eternally yet still merit some help, he exhorts his readers to pray for their souls on every Rosh Hodesh and Jewish holiday, even if this only results in the alleviation of their torment (as in the case of Caesarius's 'moderately bad').

Thus, while R. Judah is certainly unaware of the finer points of Christian theology, the concepts of efficacious and non-efficacious prayer, of full benefit and amelioration of suffering, and, most importantly, of deserving and undeserving dead seem to have penetrated his thought nonetheless. It is particularly with regard to this last concept, the distinction between the deserving and undeserving dead, that the novelty of his position on prayer for the dead stands out—such a distinction is entirely absent from midrashic, talmudic, geonic, and tosafist discussions of the topic.[116]

Additionally, R. Judah affirms the notions of individual responsibility and personal judgement—a further sign of his affinity with specifically medieval notions of sin and posthumous punishment—and would agree with Augustine's statement that 'no one can hope to obtain from God after death what he neglected in this world'. Despite his strong belief in vicarious penance, he realizes that such a belief conflicts sharply with his Pietist convictions regarding moral accountability. The severe limitations that he places upon the posthumous aid of others are even more pronounced when viewed in light of his position regarding the 'supernatural' aid of the righteous. Denying the privilege and favour showered upon those who are closer to God, he rejects such intercessory acts, which subvert the normal functioning of Divine justice, whether they are performed by the holy living or the holy dead. For this reason, he rejects any and all models of prayer for the dead that are based on a patronage system, whether Jewish (geonic) or Christian (hagiographical and monastic). Instead, he argues that individual

passage which speaks of the benefit accrued to the dead by means of the restitution of stolen goods by living relatives. Such benefit accomplishes the complete annulment of that sinner's punishment. Also, R. Judah uses the term *mo'il* (which suggests full benefit), rather than the phrase *lehakel midinam* (which speaks only of the amelioration of suffering), in regard to the efficacy of the acts of the living on behalf of these souls. See *SḤ* 35.

[115] R. Judah's premise is that most non-Jews are destined for Hell, but he distinguishes between the 'good' (whose suffering can be alleviated) and the 'evil' (whose suffering cannot be alleviated) among them.

[116] Whereas the first two concepts (efficacious versus non-efficacious prayer and full benefit versus amelioration of suffering) are logical categorizations, hence outside influence need not be assumed, the distinction between deserving and undeserving dead, which lacks any parallel in Jewish traditional literature, testifies to outside influence.

merit alone holds the key to posthumous reward. It is through Pietism, not favouritism, that one enters Paradise.

Posthumous Judgement in *Sefer Ḥasidim*

In R. Judah's vision of posthumous judgement, man stands frightfully alone before the heavenly court; he has no one to supplicate for him at the crucial moment. Moreover, the judgement of that court is exacting; no sin is forgotten, no action is overlooked, no intention remains hidden.[117] The individual faces judgement laden with sin, as he is measured by Pietist standards. Beyond revealed sin, that is, the transgression of the traditional Written and Oral Laws, lies an entire panoply of unwitting sin, in which one violates the larger, hidden will of God, the *retson haboré*.[118] Contemporary life and Scripture testify that man is punished as much for unknowing sins as for ones of which he is aware. One is also held accountable for one's failure to perform meritorious acts, even though they fall well beyond the dictates of formal law. Moreover, the heavenly court is stricter than its earthly counterpart,[119] and its proceedings in this world are not the same as those pertaining to the afterlife.[120] After the death of the individual, ever more criteria for punishment are heaped on in judgement—elements such as ingratitude, the pleasure experienced during sinning, and the amount of temptation involved.[121] It is precisely the dread of the posthumous

117 The verse 'For God will judge every deed, even everything hidden, whether good or bad' (Eccles. 12: 14) is repeated several times in *Sefer ḥasidim*: see *SḤ* 54, 886, 1108, 1124, and 1950. According to R. Judah's interpretation in one place (*SḤ* 54), the 'good' mentioned in the verse refers to the 'good' feeling which accompanies sin, and for which man is held accountable. In another case (*SḤ* 1108), he interprets the verse as follows: 'Even if the intention is good but the action turns out bad, one is still held accountable.' Both interpretations point to increased accountability for sin.

118 Concealed within Scripture and nature, this larger, supra-legal will of God awaits decoding by the well-trained eye of the *ḥasid ḥakham* only. See Soloveitchik, 'Three Themes in *Sefer Ḥasidim*', 311–17.

119 See e.g. *SḤ* 1323 and 1725.

120 In *SḤ* 1518, R. Judah writes, 'The entire world is judged measure for measure. And the measure by which they judge in this world is not the measure by which they judge in the future world.'

121 He cites the following case to illustrate the difference between the judgement of the heavenly court and that of an earthly court. If Reuven does Shimon a favour and then Shimon commits adultery with Reuven's wife, in this world Shimon's punishment will be 'only' death by strangulation, while after he dies, his punishment will be much more severe. In the former case, he is punished solely for his act of adultery. In the latter case, he is punished also for his ungratefulness to Reuven, for the pleasure experienced while engaging in sin, and according to the amount of temptation involved in sinning (the less the temptation, the greater his guilt). Similarly, in *SḤ* 1291, R. Judah explains that punishment for the wicked is reserved for the afterlife, for it will be greater according to that reckoning than in this life. This is because

judgement rendered by the heavenly court that propels R. Judah to urge his readers to pre-empt their suffering—to pay now rather than later.[122]

Presiding over this very exacting court sits a strict Judge, before whom no excuses are accepted, nor pardons granted.[123] Unmoved by bribes in the form of merits, God will never use them to cancel out a sin—a statement R. Judah repeats several times in the space of one lengthy passage.[124] Instead, in true Pietist style, he asserts that suffering alone has the power to reduce or completely remove sin, and that is what is being weighed on a balance, in place of merit, opposite sin. Thus, R. Judah writes:

> If a person travels on a ship or in a desert [with others] and they are saved [from danger] and he is not, or if their possessions are found and his are not, or if he is beaten and they are not, [then these experiences] can be used to deduct from his sins. And if the suffering that a person receives [in this world] is weighed and found equivalent to his sins, then his sins are forgiven. But his merits remain untouched, because sin is not exchanged with merit; for this reason, *kaf* and *khaf* are one.[125]

during their lifetime, the wicked can only be punished for their sinful actions, whereas after they die, they can be punished 'for their sins and their pleasure'.

[122] At the end of *SḤ* 277, he writes, 'in direct proportion to the amount of one's suffering in this world, [one's suffering] is reduced in Gehenna'. In regard to one whose entire life is spent in suffering from which he cannot escape (he is married to an evil wife, is mired in poverty, or is afflicted with constant pain), he says, 'his suffering is in place of Gehenna'.

[123] The following text is characteristic: 'For unintentional sins they bring a sacrifice, and if there is no sacrifice they are punished for them, even though that was not his intention. A king who bans the exchange of currency, and one person errs and changes and the king finds out, can such a person say, "I erred"? Will he appease him? Or will he favour him to exonerate him? Also here, it is so with this matter; when it comes to the King of all Kings, the Holy One, blessed be He, a person cannot say before the King that it was unintentional!' See *SḤ* 283. One manuscript (JTS Boesky 45 nos. 121–2) and the Bologna print edn., no. 228, have the variant reading *malakh* (angel) instead of *melekh* (king) in the final phrase: 'A person cannot say before the angel that it is unintentional!' I believe this is a scribal error due to the erroneous insertion of an additional *alef*.

[124] *SḤ* 15, pp. 15–21. He uses the term for favouritism—*lo nasa lo hakadosh barukh hu panim*—to refer to one who has many merits but also commits a 'sin' against Pietists. Despite the fact that this individual may 'wash and dress the dead', 'circumcise boys', 'invite guests', and 'give charity', God does not 'favour him'. Instead, he dies within the year, having mocked a righteous Pietist on account of his *talit*. See *SḤ* 1344.

[125] *SḤ* 15, p. 15. The Hebrew letters *kaf* and *khaf*, which literally mean 'palm of hand', often refer to the cups of a balance, which have the same slightly curved shape. R. Judah explains that the sequence of the two letters, which are almost identical and immediately follow each other in the Hebrew alphabet, reinforces the visual image of a balance with its two cups side by side, equally balanced. For another example in which, in R. Judah's mind, the two letters represent the equally weighted cups of a balance, see *SḤ* 222 and 1856. In these latter examples, however, the balance serves to illustrate a different idea: the equality inherent in retributive justice.

R. Judah maintains this position even though it contradicts a well-known talmudic dictum which states that the world as a whole as well as individuals are judged according to the majority of their actions.[126] The Talmud's teaching rests upon the assumption that man's merits (rather than his suffering) are reckoned against his sins and if they preponderate they can outweigh them. In the rabbinic understanding of justice, merits cancel out sins. Yet R. Judah, who has replaced this conception with his own Pietist one, dismisses the familiar rabbinic idea with the comment, 'The rabbis had something else in mind when they said this.'[127] In his stark vision of posthumous judgement, sin can only be cleansed with pain.

R. Judah's Isolation

R. Judah's harsh vision of posthumous judgement was not shared by his contemporaries, even within his own Pietist circle. Whereas R. Eleazar of Worms appears, in his *Sefer ḥokhmat hanefesh*, to agree with his master's view when he states that 'there exists no favouritism or flattery' in God's court, 'because there is no mercy in judgement',[128] in his halakhic work *Sefer haroke'aḥ*, when discussing the laws of Yom Kippur,[129] he offers a fuller articulation of his position, which deviates from that view. He describes how, after one's death, one's actions 'are placed on a balance'—like that represented in the zodiac sign.[130] One's sins and merits (*demut ha'avonot udemut hazekhuyot*) take on human form;[131] they are then placed on the balance by angels, and are weighed in the presence of God, the Just Judge. Yet the Judge does not always sentence people on the basis of the unbalanced weight of the pans; several different outcomes are possible. If one has 'a majority of sins', each of one's actions is weighed 'according to its measure' (Isa. 27: 8) and 'he is found wanting' (Dan. 5: 27). At other times, God intervenes in the process of justice and tampers with the balance; sometimes, as stated in Isaiah 30: 27,[132] He 'throws [one] of His names onto [the side of] strict justice' and condemns the individual. If he merits, however, and God

126 This tannaitic teaching (*hakol lefi rov hama'aseh*) is found in Mishnah *Avot* 3: 19 and in BT *Kid.* 40*b*.

127 *SḤ* 1952.

128 *Sefer ḥokhmat hanefesh*, 14*a*.

129 *Sefer haroke'aḥ hagadol*, ed. Shneerson, 'Hilkhot yom hakipurim', 105.

130 A correspondence is forged in Jewish tradition between the months of the Hebrew calendar and the twelve signs of the zodiac, one of them being the balance. R. Eleazar uses the term *mazal* in place of *moznayim* at one point.

131 On the use of images of humans in the artistic representations of the Weighing of Souls, see n. 26 above.

132 'Behold, the name of God is coming from afar; His anger is flaring.' R. Eleazar interprets the verse literally: the name of God that represents his anger towards sinners comes from afar onto the scale of judgement to condemn humans.

'wills' to act mercifully towards him, then the reverse occurs; God allows an angel to 'discard his sins',[133] so that 'they cannot be found' (Isa. 41: 12). 'Pardoning the remainder' (Jer. 50: 20) of his sins, God hides them within the 'exaltedness of His throne'. R. Eleazar interprets Proverbs 16: 7 as proof for this: 'When God favours a man's ways, even his foes will make peace with him' refers not only to a person's enemies, he argues, but also to the attribute of strict justice, which seeks to incriminate him and which God subdues in an effort to exonerate him.

Thus, while some traces of R. Judah's harsh vision of posthumous judgement are detectable, a large part of R. Eleazar's portrait is of a different hue. His image of the balance adheres more closely to the rabbinic one, in which merits, rather than suffering, weigh against sin. Additionally, in some cases, God's judgement can be merciful, so merciful, in fact, that it vanquishes the attribute of strict justice and disregards all of one's remaining sins. While Satan is portrayed as a potent accusing force,[134] his power is mitigated by the 'clarion call' (*hakeruz yotse*) that announces, 'He who knows a fault [against this person] should not come [forward]; [he who is able] to proffer a merit should come.' Moreover, while R. Eleazar cites R. Judah's teachings of 'Never do they exchange merits for sins and sins for merits' and *kaf khaf be'alef bet* in the context of posthumous punishment, he never endows them with the particular meanings that his teacher ascribes to them.[135] Instead, he balances the harshness of the former teaching with a rabbinic statement that expresses God's compassion in executing justice,[136] and mitigates the meaning of the latter by interpreting it solely in the framework of retributive justice.[137] Whereas God can intervene to condemn a person, he can equally as often intercede to acquit him; God's justice can be tempered with mercy.[138]

[133] R. Eleazar uses the term *pore'a* here, but the context makes it clear that its meaning is not the usual rabbinic one ('pay back', as in *pore'a ḥov*), but the less frequent biblical one ('discard' or 'reject', as in Prov. 13: 18 and 15: 32). Thus he writes: 'Then the sin will be sought out and it will not be there because the angel discards his sins, therefore "his sins will not be found because I will forgive that which will remain" [Jer. 50: 20]—that is, the [portion of sin] remaining at the time of Judgement, [when on] the high throne.'

[134] R. Eleazar explains that the word *shata* in Ps. 90: 8 ('You have set our iniquities before Yourself') is written as *shat*, meaning 'he has set', because it refers to Satan, who is the accuser and who places man's sins on top of the balance.

[135] See *Sefer haroke'aḥ hagadol*, ed. Shneerson, 'Hilkhot yom hakipurim', 104.

[136] '[God's] good attribute is 500 times greater than His attribute of punishment.'

[137] R. Eleazar writes, '*Kaf khaf* in the Hebrew alphabet represents "measure for measure", [the principle by which] a person is punished for his sins.' Two examples of this interpretation exist in *Sefer ḥasidim*, as mentioned above, in n. 125.

[138] The divide visible here between the ideology of R. Eleazar and that of R. Judah parallels

R. Abraham b. Azriel, a student of R. Eleazar of Worms and whose liturgical commentary bears the influence of the mystical teachings of Hasidei Ashkenaz,[139] also articulates a position which contrasts with that of R. Judah. Invoking the authority of R. Nisim Gaon, who concurs with him in this regard,[140] R. Abraham expresses belief in the exchange of sin and merit in the heavenly court. Although he cites the teaching of R. Judah, 'Never do they exchange merits for sins and sins for merits', he restricts its application to the completely righteous and the completely wicked. The overwhelming majority of people, however, fall into the two remaining categories—those with a majority of merits and those with a majority of sins. Regarding these latter groups, R. Abraham argues that God exchanges sins for merits and merits for sins according to an arithmetical calculation—*maḥlifin lefi haḥeshbon*. Thus, for example, someone who dies with 300 merits and 200 'unpaid' sins (that is, sins for which he has not been punished during his lifetime) will 'receive the reward for 100 merits and will never see the face of Gehenna'.[141] Having had his sins deducted from his merits, this individual escapes posthumous punishment altogether.

A similar calculation involving the deduction of a person's merits from his balance of sins appears in another text with Pietist ties. In a penitential piece attributed to R. Meir of Rothenburg, whether one's soul is sent to Gehenna or Paradise depends on the majority of one's actions. Regarding those who die with a majority of sins, and the very wicked, who 'inherit Gehenna' but have a few good deeds to their name, the reward for those deeds is subtracted from the punishment due to them and serves to reduce their pain 'according to the requisite amount'.[142]

Returning to R. Abraham, in another lengthy section he elaborates further on the process of Divine judgement. Basing his discussion on a talmudic passage in *Rosh Hashanah* 16*b*–17*a*, he outlines six categories of sinners

similar disparities between the men on other issues, such as kabbalistic notions of theurgy and anthropomorphism and sociopolitical questions. See Idel, 'Regarding the Identity of the Authors of Two Ashkenazi Commentaries' (Heb.), esp. 156 n. 352, and Marcus, *Piety and Society*, 55–74, 109–29.

139 See Soloveitchik, 'Piety, Pietism, and German Pietism', 469.

140 Nisim Gaon states that if someone dies with a majority of merits, the few remaining sins he has are left unpunished and their equivalent value is deducted instead from the individual's merits. Although R. Judah disagrees with R. Nisim's position, he cites it nevertheless. See *SḤ* 30.

141 See Abraham b. Azriel, *Sefer arugat habosem*, ii. 101.

142 See *Darkhei teshuvah*, cited in Kozma, 'The Practice of *Teshuvah*', Appendix 2, p. 46. See also *She'elot uteshuvot maharam bar barukh*, 162–3, cited in Rotman, 'The Marvellous in the Medieval Hebrew Narrative' (Heb.), 371.

and their respective judgements in the Divine court.[143] Several of these judgements involve God's compassion and forgiveness of sin. At the conclusion of their delineation, R. Abraham goes one step further and states that even a sinner whose sin predominates and who is sentenced to death (i.e. Gehenna) only suffers this fate if God 'wills [to act according to] the attribute of justice; but if He wills to act with mercy in the midst of justice, then even [in the case of one] with a majority of sins, he is written for life' (that is, he escapes Gehenna).[144]

Furthermore, R. Abraham accepts the position of the school of Hillel, as recorded in *Rosh Hashanah* 17*a*, that God, 'abundant of mercy, tilts [the scales] towards mercy' in the case where a person's sins and merits are evenly balanced. In such a case, God overlooks the first and second sins of that person so that they do not cause his burden of sin to preponderate. The overall tenor of R. Abraham's discussion reflects God's benevolence towards sinners, and he concludes with a detailed analysis of the thirteen Divine attributes of mercy.[145]

R. Abraham's proclivity towards Divine compassion in judgement is to be understood in light of the great weight of the midrashic tradition that Ashkenaz inherited. Invoked as the All-Merciful One,[146] the God of the Midrash makes the attribute of compassion a partner in the creation of humans.[147] Several stories of the aggadah depict the struggle between the attribute of justice, in its attempt to condemn man, and God, who becomes identified with the attribute of mercy and who silences or refutes that accusation.[148] In terms of the individual's judgement, the rabbis identify specific merits, such as charity, that have the power to cancel out sins, even one as heinous as idolatry. The posthumous punishment of the idolater Micah, who is sentenced to be deprived of his portion in the World to Come, is overturned by God in light of Micah's charity to strangers.[149] Thus, while praise of God's attribute of justice is not lacking in the Midrash,[150] rabbinic dicta such as 'The attribute of good exceeds that of retribution five hundred times',[151] and 'He that is abundant of kindness tips [the scales of judgement]

143 For a discussion of the tosafists' understanding of this passage, see above, pp. 236–8.

144 See Abraham b. Azriel, *Sefer arugat habosem*, ii. 97–8.

145 Ibid. 100–5.

146 The epithet *raḥmana*, first coined by the *tana* R. Akiva, appears throughout midrashic literature; see Urbach, *The Sages*, 454.

147 Ibid. 458–9; Urbach's reading is based on *Midrash bereshit rabah* 8 (ed. Theodor and Albeck, i. 60).

148 Urbach, *The Sages*, 460–1.

149 BT *San.* 103*b*.

150 See e.g. *Vayikra rabah* 24: 1, 'R. Shimon b. Yohai said: When is the name of the Holy One, blessed be He, magnified in His world? At the time when He executes justice upon the wicked.'

151 Tosefta *Sot.* 4: 1, 450.

towards kindness',[152] offer a picture of Divine judgement in which justice is greatly tempered by mercy.[153]

It is this midrashic image of the compassionate Judge that nourished contemporary Ashkenazi commentators on *piyut*.[154] R. Abraham b. Azriel and some anonymous commentators cite *midrashim* which describe different forms of Divine manipulation of the scales of judgement. They speak of God 'snatching away one document of sin', 'raising up the pan of sin', or 'placing His hand upon the merit pan of the balance', so that the side of merit preponderates.[155] Thus, for example, in a commentary on Eleazar ben Kalir's *kedushta* for Rosh Hashanah,[156] 'A'apid nezer ayom', an anonymous author describes how God 'snatches away' the sins of Israel and 'throws them to the ground'. In a manuscript of French origin dated 1304, an anonymous liturgical commentator explains the phrase *verav ḥesed mateh kelapei ḥesed* ('Abundant of kindness, He tilts towards kindness') as follows:

152 BT *RH* 17*a*. See also the interpretation of R. Eleazar, who changes the order of the phrases in Ps. 62: 13 in order to expound the following teaching: '"You render to every man according to his work", but in the end "Unto You, O Lord, belongs loving-kindness".' See Urbach, *The Sages*, 459, based on BT *RH* 17*b*.

153 Although Maimonides hailed from a different milieu, he shared the notion of merciful Divine judgement espoused by the Midrash and the rabbis of the Talmud. He too believes that people are judged according to the majority of their actions (see *Mishneh torah*, 'Hilkhot teshuvah', 3: 1), that God overlooks their first and second offences (ibid., 3: 5), and that he readily accepts repentance without demanding payment of outstanding sins (ibid., 2: 1).

154 On the role of *piyut* and its commentary in early Ashkenaz, see Grossman, *The Early Sages of Ashkenaz* (Heb.), 422–3, and for the twelfth and thirteenth centuries see Hollender, *Clavis Commentariorum*, 6–7.

155 R. Abraham b. Azriel, in commenting on the words *gedol ḥesed* from the *piyut* entitled 'Eshḥar el el' (a *yotser* for Shabat Shuvah composed by Menahem b. Makhir), cites a *midrash* which speaks of God snatching away one document of guilt from an evenly balanced scale, so that the merit side outweighs that of sin. See *Sefer arugat habosem*, ii. 96. Regarding another *piyut*, entitled 'Shofet kol ha'arets' (a *pizmon* for the eve of Rosh Hashanah), R. Abraham, in his comments on the words *mateh kelapei ḥesed*, cites this same *midrash* and writes, 'The cups of the scale are sufficiently tilted towards sin, merits on one side and sins on the other, and God snatches the first sin and bears it so that the merits will preponderate.' Immediately afterwards, he offers another interpretation of that same phrase: 'He lifts the pan of sins in order that the merits preponderate, as it says, "He bears iniquity and overlooks rebellious sin."' See *Sefer arugat habosem*, iii. 494–5. In the commentary on Eleazar ben Kalir's *kedushta* (liturgical poem) for Rosh Hashanah, 'Atḥil yom pekuda', the commentator cites the same *midrash*. (See also Rashi's comment on BT *RH* 17*a*, s.v. *nosé*, where he writes, 'He raises the sin pan of the scale'.) I am indebted to Elisabeth Hollender for these manuscript references, as well as for those mentioned in the subsequent two notes.

156 A *kedushta* is a liturgical poem inserted into the Amidah prayer of the morning service. For the anonymous commentary see MS Bodl. Opp. 675 (Neubauer 1210), fo. 17*a*–*b* (no. 113 in Hollender, *Clavis Commentariorum*, 54).

'The Holy One, blessed be He, lifts up the pan of sins, and the pan of kindness outweighs it and [pulls] downward, as it says "He lifts up sin and iniquity" and it does not say "He forgives [sin and iniquity]".'[157] Another anonymous commentator remarks on the words *kovesh kol ke'asim* ('He conquers all anger') in 'A'apid nezer ayom': '[God] places His hand on the balance [in the place where] there are merits, and weighs it downward.'

Although some of the *piyut* commentators refer to the collective judgement of Israel on Rosh Hashanah and not to the posthumous judgement of the individual soul, many of them invoke the verse fragment *mateh kelapei ḥesed* cited in *Rosh Hashanah* 17*a*, which substantiates the position of the school of Hillel regarding individual judgement. These commentators borrow that motif and apply it to the national body of Israel. Whether referring to the individual or to Israel as a people, the message of all these commentaries is the same: Divine compassion and forgiveness outweigh human sinfulness and override justice.

Contemporary Jewish visual representations of the Weighing of Souls are in consonance with the literary ones found in the *piyut* commentaries. In the Dresden illuminated *maḥzor*, dating from around 1290, an artistic rendering of the twelve zodiacal signs includes the image of a balance (which appears on the jacket of the present book).[158] Suspended by a hand,[159] it has a human figure in its left pan, symbolizing the merits of the

[157] The comment is found in the *piyut* entitled 'Atiti leḥaninekha' (a *kedushta* for Rosh Hashanah by Simon b. Isaac). See MS Parma 3006 (de Rossi 654, 1; Richler 1064), fo. 68*a* (no. 9486 in Hollender, *Clavis Commentariorum*, 532). The same comment on the same words appears as an addendum to another Kalirian *kedushta* for Rosh Hashanah, entitled 'Imratekha tserufah'. See MS Parma 3006 (de Rossi 654, 1; Richler 1064), fos. 68*b*–69*a* (no. 6185 in the *Clavis Commentariorum*, 369). A similar note, penned by an anonymous *piyut* commentator from Germany, is found in MS Hamburg 132 (Steinschneider 155), fos. 3*b*–4*b* (no. 9102 in the *Clavis Commentariorum*, 511).

[158] See Sed-Rajna, *Le Maḥzor enluminé*, plate 37, fig. 74, and the attendant discussion on p. 34. I am grateful to Naomi Feuchtwanger-Sarig for this reference. Paralleled early on with the twelve tribes of Israel, and associated with specific biblical figures and episodes, the twelve zodiacal signs became common illustrations which accompanied the liturgical hymns of the Jewish festivals in manuscripts of the medieval period. See Metzger and Metzger, *Jewish Life in the Middle Ages*, 14–16.

[159] Although the balance was not an exclusively Christian symbol, as it originally appeared in ancient Egyptian art (see the discussion above, n. 22) and was well known and used within Jewish tradition, R. Judah's audience would have recognized specifically the hand-held balance as it commonly appeared in Christian representations of the Weighing of Souls. When the balance is not depicted as being held by St Michael, very often it is held by God. See Mary P. Perry, 'Psychostasis in Christian Art—I', 103. One example of this motif is the Weighing of Souls on the tympanum of Autun. See Mâle, *Religious Art in France*, 418.

individual.[160] From the pan on the right, which represents one's sins,[161] a demon hangs in an effort to pull it down, but an angel stands on the left pan, weighing it down decisively. Similarly, in an illuminated manuscript from Germany of the early fourteenth century, a celestial hand holding 'the scale of justice' adorns the word 'King'—the first word of one of the prayers recited on Rosh Hashanah, the annual Day of Judgement. Here, Satan himself hangs from the pan of sins, trying to pull it down, but does so 'in vain, since Divine mercy is watching'; God tips the scales so that the pan of merit preponderates.[162] Such images of Divine judgement, in which a supernatural agent of God, or God himself, intercedes to combat the forces of condemnation and aid the human soul, convey an optimistic message for the medieval Jew—God is compassionate to sinners and actively seeks their redemption.

The midrashic vision of Divine justice tempered by mercy would find resonance and reinforcement in the new religious climate of intercessionism exemplified by the Virgin Mary. Mary's supernatural ability to temper the judgement of Christ and overturn a guilty sentence would not seem foreign to those who were raised on aggadic stories, in which the patriarchs and matriarchs petition the Holy One on behalf of a sinful Israel. Even the undeserving nature of Mary's supplicants could be tolerated by a generation accustomed to the idea of reliance on *zekhut avot* (the merits of the forefathers),[163] and which was familiar with R. Meir's extrapolation of Exodus 33: 19: '"And I will be gracious to whom I will be gracious"—even though he is unworthy; "And I will show mercy on whom I will have mercy"—even though he is unworthy.'[164]

Similarly, the artistic representations of the balance in German illuminated *maḥzorim*, in which Satan hangs on one pan while God tips the other, resemble depictions of the Weighing of Souls on the portals of some twelfth-century churches. Parallel motifs include the Devil (or some other grimacing demon) placing his weight on the scale in an effort to condemn

160 In the Weighing of Souls at the cathedral of Autun, a naked human figure sits in one pan, representing 'what is best in our souls'. See Mâle, *Religious Art in France*, 418. On the use of the human body as a symbol of the soul in Christian art, see above, n. 26.

161 The pan appears empty in the illustration, but from its position (opposite the human figure), and from the fact that a demon hangs from it, it is clear that it represents the sins of the individual.

162 MS Bodl. Reggio 1 fo. 207*v*, cited in Metzger and Metzger, *Jewish Life in the Middle Ages*, 246–7.

163 For the role of *zekhut avot* in rabbinic thought, see Marmorstein, *The Doctrine of Merits in Old Rabbinical Literature*.

164 BT *Ber.* 7*a*.

mankind,[165] and St Michael holding the balance in his hands against the counterweight of the demons, so that it 'obeys justice'.[166] In several other medieval representations, St Michael becomes a 'champion of man against the Devil' in a contest between the two over 'possession of the soul'.[167]

Caesarius of Heisterbach's work keenly reflects the new religious atmosphere and stands in sharp contrast to R. Judah's in this regard. While Caesarius provides ample evidence of God's strict and exacting punishments in the afterlife in his *Dialogus Miraculorum*, he mitigates the harsh judgement of God with the clemency and compassion of Mary.[168] An ardent follower of the Virgin, Caesarius devotes an entire section of his work to her miracles.[169] R. Judah, on the other hand, would never hear of any such attenuation of absolute justice. Let us recall that the patriarchs and matriarchs are nowhere to be found in his book, nor is their merit to be relied upon.[170]

It is this two-headed dragon—the image of God's compassionate judgement in the Midrash and the liturgy versus Mary's merciful petitions of Christ which circulate in the environment—that R. Judah sets out to slay. Nurtured on the former image and having subconsciously imbibed the latter, R. Judah's co-religionists see a Divine justice that is much tempered by mercy, and attribute potency to prayer for the dead, even for the undeserving. R. Judah cannot. Armed with sharp rhetoric and a host of radical

[165] On the portal of the church at Conques, the Devil, with a grimace on his face, puts his thumb on the balance so that the pan of sin outweighs the one of merit. Similarly, sculpted on the cathedral at Autun, howling demons hang from the pan of the scale representing the sins of man and even throw a toad onto it. See Mâle, *Religious Art in France*, 413–14 and 417. On the tympanum of the church at Le Mans, the Devil depresses the sin pan of the balance. See Mary P. Perry, 'Psychostasis in Christian Art—I', 103.

[166] See Mâle, *Religious Art in France*, 418.

[167] See Brandon, *The Judgment of the Dead*, 124. St Michael was venerated in his role as 'defender of souls' in late medieval Ireland; see Ryan, 'Fixing the Eschatological Scales', 189.

[168] See Matsuda, *Death and Purgatory in Middle English Didactic Poetry*, 56, who comes to a similar conclusion.

[169] In the very last section, entitled 'On the Punishment and the Glory of the Dead', Caesarius concludes with a tale which, characteristically, involves the dramatic intercession of Mary on the grandest of all possible scales. In this final tale of the work, Mary intercedes on behalf of all men who 'vex' Christ 'daily with their sins', so that he wishes to utterly destroy all sinners, sparing no one. The Virgin successfully petitions Christ and prevents the sounding of the second trumpet heralding the End of the World: her power of compassion is potent enough to stave off Christ's anger, delay the onset of the Last Judgement, and save mankind on a cosmic level. See Caesarius of Heisterbach, *Dialogue*, 12: 58.

[170] While the concept of *zekhut avot* appears in *Sefer ḥasidim*, it refers only to the merits of one's immediate forebears, whereas traditionally it means those of the patriarchs. See Soloveitchik, 'The Midrash, *Sefer Ḥasidim* and the Changing Face of God', 167.

reinterpretations of sacred texts—all of which illustrate successful models of intercession by figures of great piety and holiness in favour of Divine compassion towards dead sinners—he attempts to disabuse his fellow-Jews of their false notion of Divine judgement. God, he argues, will not be swayed in the dispensation of perfect and true justice; he accepts no bribes, whether in the form of merits or through the influence of favourites.

Furthermore, R. Judah creates his own version of the Weighing of Souls—one that differs noticeably from that portrayed by the *piyut* commentators and the manuscript illuminators of *maḥzorim* mentioned above, as well as from the church tympanum scenes. According to R. Judah, the punishment meted out for the commission of a sin is greater than the reward reaped for abstinence from it, for 'a merit is not of equal weight to the punishment'.[171] The punishment for adultery is greater, for instance, than the reward for one who abstains from the same act, even when all the factors (including desire) are identical. Similarly, the punishment for stealing a certain amount of money is greater than the reward for giving that same amount to charity, just as the sin of murder outweighs the merit of saving a life.

It is not only God's compassion that is absent from R. Judah's depiction, but also Satan's condemning efforts. Consistent with his strong opposition to intercessionism, R. Judah denies the power of the supernatural, whether good or evil, to subvert the normal functioning of justice; only a person's actions can speak for him on Judgement Day. Yet it is only when some exceptional act is included in the performance of the meritorious deed, he argues, that one can place merit on the scale opposite sin and have the two balance each other out.[172] In the case of adultery, this is accomplished when the sinner accepts torture and suffering upon himself in proportion to the punishment prescribed by the Torah; the cumulative weight of that voluntary suffering will allow 'the merit to balance out the sin'. Similarly, the only way the merit of saving a life can balance out the sin of ending one is if the act of saving the life involves putting the rescuer's life at risk as well. The added element of sacrifice allows the two to be measured equally.[173] (It is important to understand that, while the combined merit of the good act and the additional elements of voluntary suffering or self-sacrifice equals the sin so that the two cups are balanced, the good act does not cancel out the sin. Despite the many other merits this person may possess, his sin will still not go unpunished. R. Judah cites King David as an illustration of this: although he risked his life in battle to save the lives of the Israelites such that

171 *SḤ* 15, p. 19. 172 Ibid. 173 Ibid.

this good deed could now equalize his sin of causing the death of Uriah the Hittite, he still received punishment for the latter action.[174])

Thus, despite the fact that Satan is absent from R. Judah's vision of the Weighing of Souls, the sin pan still pulls downward when weighed against the merit pan, even in a situation in which the two should logically counterbalance each other. The difference, however, between the portrayals of the *piyut* commentators, illustrators of the *maḥzorim*, and the church portal scenes, on the one hand, and R. Judah's portrayal on the other, is that the illogical downward pull in his scenario is caused by the natural propensity of sin to outweigh merit, rather than by any supernatural intervention. We see here, once again, the immense power that sin possesses in R. Judah's world-view. Additionally, only two things can weaken that power—acts of voluntary suffering and personal sacrifice. These Pietist ideals replace the mitigating presence of God or St Michael, apparent in the aforementioned scenes, both Jewish and Christian. R. Judah here makes it clear yet again that Pietism, not favouritism, is the key to Paradise.

In R. Judah's vision of posthumous judgement, humanity, bereft of Divine aid, deprived of the intercession of the holy, and heavily encumbered by sin, does not stand much of a chance against the condemning power of sin. Were it not for Pietism and its extraordinary demands, it would not have any chance at all.

*

The uniqueness of R. Judah's position raises some new questions. Both his penitential theory and his general doctrine of prayer reflect significant borrowings from Benedictine monasticism: the former was appropriated from Irish monastic penitential traditions and the latter resembles Cluniac practices.[175] Yet his ideology of prayer for the dead—an arena where the above two spheres intersect—departs sharply from the Benedictine model. One of the prime features of Cluniac monasticism is its 'economy of salvation'—the monks of Cluny are specialists in prayer for the dead and are extolled in the exempla literature for their expertise in this area. Yet despite the Divine approbation accorded the Pietist doctrine of prayer, Pietists are never invoked or idealized in *Sefer ḥasidim* as specialists in praying for the dead. This is doubly surprising in light of the fact that R. Judah fashions the *ḥasid ḥakham* after the abbot in his role as spiritual confessor of the monks. Thus, while there is a clear parallel between the Pietist master and the monastic

[174] *SḤ* 15, p. 20.

[175] On the Pietist doctrine of prayer and its Cluniac affinity, see above, pp. 196–7.

leader in the area of penance, there is no similar correspondence in the field of prayer for the dead. What does R. Judah's conscious rejection of the monastic model in that domain tell us about his fundamental ideas and the relationship of Pietism to monasticism?

A further point, which we also saw earlier, is that R. Judah's strict views on accountability cause him to reject all models of prayer for the dead that are based on a patronage system. It appears that this selfsame notion of accountability propels him to oppose the concept of the exchange of merits for sins. While these assertions are true, they are not the whole truth. Careful examination of R. Abraham ben Azriel's above-mentioned arithmetical calculations regarding posthumous judgement demonstrates that strict accountability alone does not necessitate the adoption of R. Judah's position dismissing the exchange of merits for sins. On the contrary, one can maintain a position of strict accountability, such that every sin and merit is accounted for, precisely by substituting a merit for a sin, as does R. Abraham.

Nor does strict accountability preclude such exchange even in the afterlife. Nahmanides, in his treatise on posthumous reward and punishment, states that, if a person whose sins and merits are equal (a *beinoni*) commits a serious sin 'in proximity' to his death and thereby changes from *beinoni* to one whose sins predominate, he will descend to Gehenna. However, once he is in Gehenna, his merits serve to lighten his sentence. Although Nahmanides maintains that 'everyone merits the World to Come according to his actions', the merits of this person cancel a certain amount of the punishment that his sins have accrued for him.[176]

R. Judah's novel proposition is that people both suffer punishment for their sins *and* experience reward for their merits in the afterlife. Let us recall, he argues that punishment in Paradise exists and that a person is punished and rewarded in the afterlife together with all the others who performed that particular act.[177] What is the source of R. Judah's unusual position? What leads him to replace the midrashic notion of a merciful God with one of absolute, unmitigated justice? Who is the deity that he portrays in his book?

176 He espouses this notion in the context of a long discourse on reward and punishment in the afterlife in his work 'Sha'ar hagemul'. See Nahmanides, *Torat ha'adam*, 264–311.

177 *SḤ* 1952, p. 475.

The God of *Sefer Ḥasidim*

Generally speaking, adherents of monotheistic religions believe that God is an unknowable essence, and so religion in general, and a religious book in particular, can only tell us what humans think of God, not what God is. Humans can only conceive of God in terms that are understandable to them and in images that they can recognize. Thus, both believers and non-believers acknowledge that, if someone imagines God as the Supreme Power of the universe, then he will draw that portrait of God from his own particular experience—from a model of earthly power familiar to him.

Living in an imperial era, the rabbis of the Midrash envisioned God as an enthroned, all-powerful emperor; 'just like a king of flesh and blood' is the oft-repeated introduction to parables offered in the Midrash to describe God. The midrashic portrayal of the *pamalya shel ma'alah* (heavenly retinue), of whom the patriarchs and matriarchs form a dominant component, reflects the imperial court of Roman times with its various contending factions seeking to influence the emperor. Christians of late antiquity also viewed God in emperor-like terms, and conceived of God as granting posthumous pardon for sins much like an emperor would grant amnesty to a criminal.[178] Although all-powerful, this emperor-like God had 'an uncircumscribed reserve of mercy that overshadowed the strict implementation of His justice'.[179] We have already seen how R. Judah rejected the imperial model with its system of patronage in the matter of prayer for the dead. Could he have adopted it to imagine God's judgement after the individual's death? If, for argument's sake, he did, then he would have to deny his God the 'all-important prerogative' of every Roman emperor, a prerogative believed to be an inherent function of his absolute power—the imperial act of pardon.[180] In R. Judah's vision of absolute justice and strict accountability, there is no space for the imperial or Divine grant of forgiveness. If his is not an emperor, then who is R. Judah's God?

Let us, once again, turn to contemporary models. If the rabbis of antiquity could conceive of God's functioning in the world as that of a Roman emperor, then is it surprising that in medieval times the Supreme Power of the world was seen as a feudal suzerain? If Anselm of Canterbury, arguably the greatest philosopher of the Middle Ages and one whose arguments still form the stuff of philosophical debate,[181] could, as we shall see, envision

[178] Brown, 'The Decline of the Empire of God', 46. [179] Ibid. 48. [180] Ibid. 47–8.

[181] For example, the American analytic philosopher Alvin Plantinga employs Anselm's ontological argument in his philosophical discussions. See Plantinga and Tooley, *Knowledge of God*, and Plantinga, *Essays in the Metaphysics of Modality*.

God only in feudal terms, we would do well to ponder whether R. Judah the Pious did the same.

In theory, the Pietists subscribed to a Sa'adyanic deity without form, shape, or emotion,[182] and this notion neutralized to a great extent the midrashic image of an earthly king, with all its all-too-human qualities. However, when the Pietists thought of God and his involvement in human affairs (and *Sefer ḥasidim* reflects their concrete, graphic notions of God's ways in the world), their God took on a medieval visage. Eleventh-century society was characterized by its anarchy and lawlessness. The break-up of the Carolingian empire left the people of western Europe at the mercy of plundering nobles and marauding knights, who seized land and goods from churches and peasants and usurped power from established rulers. In the absence of a strong authority figure, medieval society was rife with the violence of feud, which disrupted the peace and, at the same time, with its own set of unwritten rules, served to regulate it.[183] Through a complicated set of horizontal and vertical relationships, vengeance and feud served a variety of political, economic, religious, and social functions in the medieval period.[184] The peasants, however, suffered greatly from the violence as nobles attacked each other's territories, destroying the locals' goods and lives in the process—by-products of 'indirect vengeance'.[185] Whenever possible, people looked towards their immediate authority figures—the peasant to the master of his land, the knight to the master of his fief—for law and order. Law and order meant, above all, justice, and justice meant punishment. When the peace was broken through an act of violence, the lord had to dispense justice by punishing the violator; the violator was compelled to satisfy not only the aggrieved party but also the lord himself, whose authority he had weakened.[186]

By the end of the eleventh century, the most dominant image of God depicted over a monastery's entrance was that of a judge. Seated on a judge's throne and surrounded by his vassals (the elders of the apocalyptic visions) and dukes (the archangels), God held court like an earthly lord.[187] The notion of God as feudal lord had a profound effect on Anselm's thinking. In formulating his highly influential theory of atonement, Anselm

182 Soloveitchik, 'The Midrash, *Sefer Ḥasidim* and the Changing Face of God', 170–2.

183 W. I. Miller, *Bloodtaking and Peacemaking*, and id., 'Choosing the Avenger', 162.

184 Roche, 'The Way Vengeance Comes'.

185 The term is used to describe tenth-century feuding, but the phenomenon still persisted in the twelfth century as documented by Roche, ibid. 122–3, and Barthélemy, 'Feudal War in Tenth-Century France', 112.

186 Duby, *The Age of the Cathedrals*, 48.

187 Ibid. 47.

employed the analogy of the service that a knight owes his lord and the honour due to him (*servitium debitum*).[188] Humans, he argued, owe a great debt to God, the greatest of all lords, for they have dishonoured him by sinning. Unable to render full satisfaction for the disgrace caused to the 'infinite suzerain', mankind requires the offering of a God-man (Christ).[189] Anselm's theory, as put forth in his *Cur Deus Homo*, is essentially an application of the feudal concepts of obedience, honour, service, penance, satisfaction, and graded personal values to the religious realm.[190]

Anselm's logic may be extended to explain another feature of medieval religious thought and architecture—the harsh punishment of sinners in the afterlife. If sin, according to feudal modes of thinking, is perceived as an affront to the honour of the greatest of all lords, God himself, then punishment requires nothing less than full vengeance to be undertaken against the offender—the sinner. It is this vengeance, in the form of posthumous punishment enacted upon sinful souls, that is visually depicted on medieval tympanums for all to behold—Jews and non-Jews alike. Whereas earlier images of Hell portray fewer figures, which are more simplistic, generalized, and phantasm-like, in mid-twelfth-century western European monumental art there was a marked increase in the number of the damned as well as in the realism and specificity of their punishments.[191] Although not a major theme in the architecture of the Romanesque period, Last Judgement scenes display Christ's punishments, less as the measured justice of a retributive God and more as the zealous acts of vengeance of an aggrieved feudal lord. Two such scenes exemplify a 'radical affirmation of the judiciary principle'.[192] On the portals of Autun and Conques, sculpted in the mid-twelfth century, an oversized Christ presides as Judex 'in full sense of the word' as he gestures to separate the elect and the damned, whose 'anguish is expressed with full force'.[193] The physical tortures of the latter, perpetrated by monstrous demons and illustrated in grotesque detail, provoke the dominant emotions of horror and terror in the mind of the observer.[194] Last Judgement scenes emerged as a dominant theme in

[188] Southern, *Saint Anselm*, 225. This observation was made earlier, in 1923, by J. T. McNeil, in *The Celtic Penitentials and Their Influence*, 197–8. See also Kaeuper, *Holy Warrior*, 118.

[189] McNeil, *The Celtic Penitentials and Their Influence*, 197–8.

[190] Ibid. 197. T. Gorringe champions the same argument; see his *God's Just Vengeance*, 6–7, 11, and 90–8.

[191] See Denny, 'The Date of the Conques Last Judgment', 8–9.

[192] Baschet, *Les Justices de l'au delà*, 147.

[193] Ibid. 147 and 144 respectively. See also Denny, 'The Date of the Conques Last Judgment', 8–9.

[194] Baschet, *Les Justices de l'au delà*, 146. According to Baschet, the Conques Last Judgement

Gothic architecture of the thirteenth century; in some depictions, such as those at Paris and Amiens for example, the Hell scenes are 'exceptionally well developed' and are arranged in such fashion as to 'signify a progression in the horror'.[195]

I would suggest that R. Judah embraced the notion of God as a feudal lord seeking vengeance rather than mere retributive punishment alone. This is not to say that the punishments of the Emperor God envisioned by the rabbis of the Midrash and by late antique Christians were not, at times, exceedingly harsh or severe.[196] The issue is less the intensity of the punishment than its nature. Lords in medieval society operated within a 'society of vengeance',[197] whereas for the rabbis God functioned within a system of 'personal and collective retribution'.[198] Thus, apart from imagining a God of absolute justice who punishes every sin, R. Judah envisioned him as a deity who punishes in a vengeful rather than retributive manner.

Vengeance is distinguished from retribution by several characteristics. Prominent among these is the fact that, while retribution is proportionate to the crime, vengeance can be in excess of it.[199] In rabbinic sources, God's punishment is overwhelmingly viewed as proportionate, with the principle of 'measure for measure' omnipresent.[200] 'With what measure a man metes, it shall be meted out to him again' is an oft-repeated statement of the sages.[201] Only when it concerns the extremely righteous, with whom

scene is a complex representation of the social and political conflicts which the abbey faced and its concomitant vision of the intervention of Divine Justice to resolve them. See ibid. 160–3.

195 Ibid. 163, 169. At the end of a very lengthy discourse on the 'menace of Hell' that presented itself in multifarious ways in medieval art and architecture, Baschet cautions against an over-representation of medieval Christianity as a religion of fear. Instead, he argues that the purpose of these sordid representations of the tortures of Hell was less to evoke emotion as to shock the observer into action—to make confession, do penitence, and lead a life of good works. See ibid. 580.

196 In speaking of the Roman emperor, Peter Brown writes, 'The ruler was as capable of reckless acts of generosity as he was of crushing severity' ('The Decline of the Empire of God', 47).

197 Barthélemy, 'Feudal War in Tenth-Century France', 109. See the volume dedicated to exploring vengeance within feudal society, edited by Throop and Hyams, *Vengeance in the Middle Ages*; Barthélemy, Bougard, and Le Jan (eds.), *La Vengeance, 400–1200*; and Hyams, *Rancor and Reconciliation in Medieval England*.

198 See Urbach, *The Sages*, 436–44, esp. 438, and Lieberman, 'On Sins and Their Punishment', 48–51.

199 Nozick, *Philosophical Explanations*, 366–7.

200 See e.g. BT *Shab.* 105*b*, *Ned.* 32*a*, and *San.* 90*a*.

201 See Tosefta *Sot.* 2, BT *Sot.* 8*a*, and *Midrash bereshit rabah* 9. Urbach, *The Sages*, 438–9, calls the 'measure for measure' principle 'the prevailing rule, both in personal and collective retribution', among the sages. See the discussion on pp. 173–4 above regarding posthumous punishment in rabbinic thought, where the principle occurs surprisingly rarely.

God is exceedingly strict, does he mete out punishment in excess of the sin committed.[202]

Not so with regard to punishment of the average man in *Sefer ḥasidim*. In our discussions, we have clearly witnessed the excessive nature of the punishments awaiting even moderate sinners. The ghost tales recorded in the work are specifically those that highlight the intense suffering of the afterlife as the fate of all those who commit even minor misdeeds, which are reckoned as sins only according to Pietism. Let us recall, for example, the woman whose hands and eyes burn for having failed to properly observe the day of preparation for the sabbath.

In addition to the disproportion between sin and punishment in the afterlife, *Sefer ḥasidim* cites examples of excessive punishment in this world as well. A child's foot is severed because he has stood on a table that is at times used for holy books.[203] A man's sons die because he names them inappropriately.[204] Another man's sons apostatize after having lifted up a cross in an attempt to save their lives during a massacre.[205] R. Judah sees the fury of Divine wrath operative in his own time.

It is not only regarding contemporary life that R. Judah cites numerous examples of disproportionate punishment. Biblical figures are consistently presented in *Sefer ḥasidim* as having provoked the wrath of the Lord. Abraham is cursed with a wicked son, Ishmael, for having mistaken the angels who visited him for Arabs.[206] Sarah dies immediately after the binding of Isaac for having lied to the angel who informed her of his imminent birth.[207] The sons of Ephraim are killed because Joseph failed to contact his father during his sojourn in Egypt.[208] In all these examples, not only does R. Judah highlight the harsh punishments meted out for relatively minor infractions; he also makes novel connections between sin and punishment—connections wholly absent from midrashic and talmudic literature. These examples reflect a heightened sense of causality: one is punished even if the cause is remote, which serves to sensitize an individual to the effects of his actions. At the same time, this supposes a harshness in the nature of God that extends beyond just retribution and into the arena of excessive punishment characteristic of vengeance. Whereas vengeance is but one attribute of a multifaceted God in Scripture, in *Sefer ḥasidim* the image of a vengeful God predominates.[209]

[202] The rabbis state: 'The Holy One, blessed be He, is exacting with the righteous like a thread of hair' (BT *Yev.* 121*b*).

[203] *SḤ* 684. [204] *SḤ* 1527. [205] *SḤ* 1922. [206] Gen. 18: 4; *SḤ* 1976.

[207] Gen. 18: 15; *SḤ* 238. [208] Num. 14: 44–5; *SḤ* 941. [209] *SḤ* 1456.

An important feature of retributive punishment is that the perpetrator has to be aware of the crime for which he is being punished. The purpose of his punishment is to communicate to him how wrong his act was, and so he must be cognizant of that fact.[210] By contrast, the victim of vengeance need not be aware of the reason for his punishment in order for the avenger to derive satisfaction from the act of vengeance.

Although the Bible outlines punishments for crimes committed unintentionally, rabbinic thought interprets this to mean that the sinner had the ability to foresee a possible error or sinful action. In a case where there was no possibility of foreknowledge, the rabbis do not hold the violator culpable.[211] *Sefer ḥasidim*, however, assigns culpability and heinous punishment in situations where no foreknowledge, or even *post facto* knowledge, of the sin exists. Whether in Scripture or in contemporary life, in this world or the next, God inflicts punishment upon 'sinners' who are unaware of their 'sins'. To recall, the author's manifest purpose in composing *Sefer ḥasidim* was that, since man 'is punished regarding that which he knows not', 'therefore I said, I shall write a book for those who fear God, lest they be punished and think that it is for no reason [*she'al ḥinam hu*]'.[212] In the absence of an understanding of the wrongs committed, the punishments visited upon the sinners of *Sefer ḥasidim* leave the domain of retribution and enter the arena of vengeance.

Another fundamental distinction between the two types of punishment is that retribution seeks to redress a moral wrong, while vengeance is a response to an insult or slight.[213] Retributive punishment is felt to be deserved because the violator has transgressed a moral principle or societal law. An objective standard has been broken and justice must be served.[214] In the case of vengeance, however, the transgressor may have harmed the victim by subjective standards only.[215] This means that vengeance can be inflicted on someone who is essentially morally praiseworthy, and whose only crime is to have insulted the victim.[216] The victim seeks punishment in order to elevate his deflated status, apart from, or regardless of, any physical injury caused to him. It is this sense of honour that fuelled blood feuds

210 Nozick, *Philosophical Explanations*, 368–71.

211 Edrei, '"When a Soul Sins Unintentionally"' (Heb.), 38–9.

212 *SḤ* 1, p. 2.

213 Nozick, *Philosophical Explanations*, 366–7. See also Kleinig, *Punishment and Desert*, 39.

214 Murphy, *Getting Even*, 42–3.

215 Orderic Vitalis, for example, describes how 'some slighting remarks' sparked a feud and a vengeful rampage on the part of Countess Helwisse of Evreux against Isabel of Conches in the eleventh century; Roche, 'The Way Vengeance Comes', 125.

216 Kleinig, *Punishment and Desert*, 39.

between kin groups, such that the inability of the aggrieved party to strike back after an attack was perceived as a humiliation to the entire group.[217] In medieval society, with its 'emphasis on symbolic communication, on the defence of honour and face-saving', there was ample breeding ground for vengeance, and the offence against the person was often described in emotional terms.[218]

Related to the honour element is the fact that, while retribution is impersonal, vengeance is personal. When dealing with retribution, so long as the crime is punished, it is of no consequence who metes out the punishment. In the case of vengeance, however, the avenger has a personal tie to the victim (or may be the victim himself) and acts out of a sense of loyalty to him.[219] Such a person feels obliged to take vengeance if the victim himself does not act, and failure to do so is interpreted as an act of betrayal. In fact, the closer the bond between the victim and the potential avenger, the greater the act of betrayal.[220]

Monastic writers relate acts of vengeance committed on Earth in a way that attributes to God and his saints this kind of personal bond. An outgrowth of early hagiographical literature, the *miracula* literature consists of tales that record extraordinary events as evidence of the hand of God, through the functioning of the saints, in the world.[221] While these collections contain various types of miracles, one category, the vengeance-type miracle (most often associated with monasteries), focuses on the miraculous acts of vengeance and violence perpetrated by the monastery's patron saint in order to defeat the monks' enemies.[222] Through the religious prism of the Church, the monastic writers viewed the afflictions that befell the men who caused harm to the monks or the monastery as vivid illustrations of Divine vengeance.[223] Thus, for example, the monks of the abbey of Marchiennes, in their twelfth-century collection of miracles,

[217] W. I. Miller, 'Choosing the Avenger', 166. See also id., *Humiliation and Other Essays*, 120–1.

[218] Roche, 'The Way Vengeance Comes', 125.

[219] Nozick, *Philosophical Explanations*, 367.

[220] W. I. Miller, 'Choosing the Avenger', 164.

[221] Schmitt, *Ghosts in the Middle Ages*, 59.

[222] See Rosenwein, Head, and Farmer, 'Monks and Their Enemies', 766, 769–70, 773, and 777–8, 785. See also Little, 'Anger in Monastic Curses', and Ward, *Miracles and the Medieval Mind*, 47, regarding St Benedict and the abbey at Fleury. Even the Virgin Mary was invoked to miraculously intercede and violently attack the enemies of monasteries. See Bull, *The Miracles of Our Lady of Rocamadour*, 88–9. The medieval practice known as humiliation of the saints, in which they are 'coerced' into miraculously intervening for the sake of their petitioners, is an outgrowth of this function of the saints. See Geary, 'Humiliation of Saints', and Little, *Benedictine Maledictions*, with regard to the related practice of liturgical cursing.

[223] For a discussion of this phenomenon in an earlier period, see Helvétius, 'Le Récit de vengeance des saints'.

interpreted the sickness, horrible suffering, accidental death, and total economic and social ruin of their enemies as direct and indisputable testimony to the supernatural punitive powers of their patron saints.[224] The saints act as God's agents in executing justice against those who dishonour him by violating the rights and property of his men. As the lord must avenge an insult to his vassal,[225] so God punishes those who harm his vassals—the monks.

It is this vengeance-type tale, characteristic of the *miracula* literature, that R. Judah appropriates in the pages of *Sefer ḥasidim*. In the anecdotes he selects, the personal nature of the victim–avenger bond is combined with the importance of defending the victim's honour—God intervenes to defend the honour of his men, the Pietists. Thus someone who fails to accept the rebuke of a *ḥakham* is immediately impoverished,[226] while another person, who changes the customary *piyut* to be recited, dies within thirty days.[227] Similarly, a sick woman who fails to ask a *ḥakham* whether she can drink on Yom Kippur does so anyway and dies—not because she drank on the fast day, but because of her failure to consult with the sage.[228] We saw earlier the story of the 'great and publicly acclaimed rabbi' who, wishing to hasten to his studies and leave the synagogue quickly, screamed aloud in protest against the protracted prayer ritual of the Pietists; he was already punished for this act in his lifetime.[229] Moreover, just as the patron saint of the monastery—or the saint whose relics are buried there—miraculously avenges his own honour against any who blaspheme him, doubt his power, or damage his shrine by striking them down, so too does death await anyone who dishonours the Pietist or obstructs the dissemination of his teachings. Those who drive an extra-zealous Pietist out of town are killed and burned, them and their descendants.[230] Anyone who impedes the work of the Pietists dies soon after,[231] and one who mocks a Pietist dies within the year.[232]

The immediacy of the punishment—'soon after', 'within the year', and elsewhere 'in only a few days'[233]—as well as its this-worldly nature, bespeak the actions of a powerful lord who is quick to take revenge on those who thwart his will and dishonour his retainers. These features are,

224 Platelle, 'Crime et châtiment à Marchiennes', 171.

225 On the obligation of a lord to defend the honour, property, and life of his vassal, see Forquin, *Lordship and Feudalism in the Middle Ages*, 125.

226 *SḤ* 236. 227 *SḤ* 33, p. 34. 228 *SḤ* 239.

229 See the additions to the Parma MS and the printed edition of *Sefer ḥasidim* adjacent to no. 427, and the relevant discussion on p. 195 above and n. 219 there.

230 *SḤ* 1272. 231 *SḤ* 1343. 232 *SḤ* 1344. 233 *SḤ* 1713 and *SḤ* 1004, p. 249.

however, also part of a larger phenomenon within the book: R. Judah interprets accounts of reward and punishment in Scripture and in history according to whether or not individuals have conformed to Pietist norms and doctrines.[234] In a similar vein, he discerns the functioning of the hand of God in the everyday events of his time. 'If you see such and such in the world, know that such and such is the cause' is a fundamental principle expressed in many passages of *Sefer ḥasidim*.[235] At other times, anecdotal events serve as the source for R. Judah's unequivocal explanation of why such and such has occurred to a man or his family.[236] The degree of certainty with which he speaks regarding specifics of causality between crime and punishment in this world is striking.[237]

One may reasonably wonder what is the source of R. Judah's (and the *ḥasid ḥakham*'s[238]) knowledge of the workings of Divine justice in the absence of prophecy, and with no special Pietist claim to Divine inspiration. What engenders his self-assurance in this matter? Admittedly, this question is part of a broader one—how does the Pietist know the unrevealed *retson haborē*?—which cannot be answered on the basis of the findings of this study. Nevertheless, when it comes to the narrower question of how the Pietist in *Sefer ḥasidim* has insight into the nuances of Divine justice, the answer is available. It lies in the adaptation of a function of the *miracula* literature within the book—a function that reveals a personal dimension to God's vengeful punishments.

The medieval author of one miracle tale speaks with the same degree of certainty as R. Judah does about the correlation between human actions and supernatural intervention. Orderic Vitalis tells the story of three brothers who occupy a cathedral tower and incite the anger of its bishop. As a result, they all die a dishonourable and dramatic death. Although each dies independently of the others, Orderic unequivocally connects the brothers'

[234] R. Eleazar also believes in the 'this-worldly' punishment of the detractors of Pietism (see above, n. 44). His statements to this effect, however, are much more muted and generalized. He never cites specific anecdotes or biblical passages in which such punishment is evident, nor does he provide any time frame for that punishment.

[235] See *SḤ* 225, 226, 228, 229, 230, 234, 235, 237, 677, and 948.

[236] See *SḤ* 234, 240, 242, 243, 407, 673, 684, 1004, 1506, 1631, 1713, 1880, 1892, 1893, 1900, 1901, and 1917.

[237] See e.g. *SḤ* 1713: 'only a few days later' such and such happened to so and so, a sinner. See also the last three lines of *SḤ* 1004.

[238] Whereas R. Judah offers the disclaimer 'there is no *ḥakham* who can ever know', he does require that anyone who has any questions about God's management of the affairs of this world should enquire from a *ḥakham*, who is knowledgeable in the *retson haboré* and who can offer him an answer suited to his question. See *SḤ* 1328.

demise with their earlier sacrilegious act in a direct, causal relationship.[239] They had unjustly seized God's property and insulted his retainer, the bishop; their death illustrates 'righteous vengeance' justly served.[240] Furthermore, Orderic notes that all three brothers die 'instantly'.[241] The immediacy of Divine vengeance seen in this monastic tale reverberates loudly in *Sefer ḥasidim*.

The harsh rhetoric that R. Judah uses to describe the enemies of the Pietists—labelling them 'wicked', 'brazen-faced', and 'promiscuous'[242]—and his use of terms that are polar opposites (such as 'wicked' versus 'righteous') to contrast non-Pietists with Pietists in general,[243] suggests further affinity between his work and the *miracula* literature. In the stories recounted by the monastic writers, those who encroach upon the land, dependants, and rights of the monastery are described as enemies by means of a set rhetoric that employs exaggerated negative terminology. Supporters of the monastery's claims are referred to using inverse expressions. This is true even when the enemies and supporters share the same character traits and when both parties have legitimate claims. Enemies of the monastery can also be members of the nobility who had once been its long-time supporters. We have seen that vengeance, as opposed to retribution, can be carried out against someone who is essentially morally praiseworthy. These stories of miraculous intervention, which 'allowed only clear-cut winners and losers' and in which 'friends and enemies . . . were starkly divided', employ the same type of terminology that R. Judah uses to describe the Pietists' supporters and critics.[244] The people who are vilified by the Pietists are often, by the latter's own admission, men of great moral worth: the rabbi who protests aloud against the Pietist method of prayer is venerated by many, and a man who publicly mocks the Pietist *talit* has performed many good deeds.[245]

The detractors of Pietism are clearly the enemy in *Sefer ḥasidim*. In his theoretical orations on the problem of theodicy, R. Judah laments more the

239 Orderic Vitalis, *Gesta Normannorum*, ii. 112–14, quoted in Roche, 'The Way Vengeance Comes', 130.

240 Roche, 'The Way Vengeance Comes', 130.

241 Ibid. One aspect of the immediate death of the Church's enemies in *miracula* tales is invariably lost in the anecdotes of *Sefer ḥasidim*. According to Roche, the implication of Orderic's statement that the brothers died 'instantly' is that they died in an un-Christian fashion, without the salvation accorded by the *viaticum*. R. Judah may have appropriated the immediacy of punishment characteristic of these vengeance-type tales and fashioned it for his own purposes. See Roche, 'The Way Vengeance Comes', 130.

242 See *SḤ* 1512, p. 367, and *SḤ* 449.

243 See e.g. *SḤ* 1334.

244 Rosenwein, Head, and Farmer, 'Monks and their Enemies', 786.

245 *SḤ* 1344.

success of the wicked than the suffering of the righteous.[246] The fact that 'we have no knowledge in our hands regarding the tranquillity of the wicked' is what motivates him to ponder 'the ways of the Holy One, blessed be He'.[247] Surprisingly, it is not leaders of the Church or individual Christians, not Crusaders or Christian marauders, and not bishops or Christian overlords who prosper despite their wickedness in these discussions. Rather, the true wicked of *Sefer ḥasidim* are the rich, arrogant Jewish communal leaders who obstruct the Pietists as they try to achieve their goals.[248] It is in the context of discussion of their fate that the word 'vengeance' is repeatedly invoked to refer to God's punishment. In reference to these wealthy leaders, a man poses the following query to a Pietist master:

Why does God restrain Himself from swiftly avenging [their actions], [and] only against the good ones is he quick to exact vengeance?

The Pietist master responds:

For God exacts vengeance also after man's death on his soul, as it says, 'However, your blood, which belongs to your souls, I will demand' [Gen. 9: 5]. And He punishes the spirit of man with great cruelty and also in Gehenna.[249]

If God does not immediately exact vengeance on the enemies of Pietism, the master explains, he will do so in the afterlife. Here, vengeance perpetrated 'with great cruelty' replaces the retributive punishment commonly found in discussions of theodicy.

There is, however, one important difference between the vengeance-type tales recorded in the monastic collections and those in *Sefer ḥasidim*. Whereas in the former, most often a holy dead person (the Virgin Mary, a patron saint, or a saint whose relics are buried in the monastery) intervenes supernaturally to punish the offenders,[250] in *Sefer ḥasidim* it is God who effects the 'miracles' hidden in daily life, as interpreted by the Pietist master. This denial of the miracle-working capabilities of the dead is very much in line with Pietist thinking and with the God-centred outlook of the book. In its anecdotes, it is God himself who avenges the honour of his men and mercilessly strikes down the offending party.

Knowledge of Irish *vitae* that were prevalent in Regensburg may also have influenced R. Judah's concept of a vengeful God. The most prominent element of Irish hagiography is the miracle-working capacity of the saints,

[246] *SḤ* 72, 948, 989, 1291, 1345, 1512, 1517, 1950 (p. 473).

[247] *SḤ* 1512, p. 368.

[248] See *SḤ* 450 (involving the leader of the prayer service), 1344, 1346, 1347, and 1451.

[249] *SḤ* 1451.

[250] Orderic's miracle story documented earlier is an exception to this rule. Perhaps this is because he is not associated with a monastery.

and noteworthy among the many miracles it documents are those of the punishment-and-vengeance type.[251] Early medieval Irish saints' lives are filled with examples of saints cursing and vilifying their enemies (and even natural objects that obstruct their way), and they catalogue how the recipients of these curses are immediately burned, drowned, and blinded, or simply drop dead.[252] In his twelfth-century account of his journey through Ireland, Gerald of Wales comments, 'The saints of this land . . . are more vindictive than the saints of any other region.'[253] The saints inherited and adapted this power of cursing from the druids—magical holy men of pre-Christian Ireland known for their maledictory 'speech acts'.[254]

Notable in these *vitae* is the fact that the crimes committed against the saints are most often insults to their honour rather than moral wrongs perpetrated against them. The Irish saint is typically moved to strike his opponent with curses or, less frequently, with predictions of death, destruction, and impoverishment when he is ignored and mocked, or when his advice and rebuke fall on deaf ears.[255] In fact, most episodes of Irish cursing occur in response to someone powerful ignoring the rebuke of the saint or dishonouring him by talking back.[256]

In an effort to portray the late sixth- and early seventh-century Irish saint Columbanus as a *vir dei* (holy man), his hagiographer, Jonas of Bobbio, tells of a morally superior individual who rebukes powerful men and women and predicts the punishment of those who seek to harm him or impede his efforts.[257] The acts of miraculous vengeance that the saint performs are a reaction to offences committed against his honour—a derivative of the system of honour-prices and status determinations operative in Irish law.[258] When the great monastic benefactor Brunhild, for example, ignores Columbanus's rebuke and stirs up trouble against him, the saint predicts that her descendants will never rise to power.[259] Similarly, in retaliation for having been expelled, he predicts the death of the Merovingian King Theuderic's entire family. The prediction, of course, comes true.[260]

251 Bray, 'Miracles and Wonders', 136.

252 Davies, 'Anger and the Celtic Saint', 191–2; M. Johnson, 'Vengeance is Mine'; Bray, 'Malediction and Benediction'; and Little, 'Anger in Monastic Curses', 28–9.

253 *The History and Topography of Ireland*, 91, cited in Little, 'Anger in Monastic Curses', 28. See also Julia Smith, 'Oral and Written', 340. On the role of miracles as Divine punishments in Gerald of Wales, see Bartlett, *Gerald of Wales*, 120–2.

254 Bitel, 'Saints and Angry Neighbors', 137; Bray, 'Malediction and Benediction', 48; and Binchy, 'A Pre-Christian Survival in Medieval Irish Hagiography', 167.

255 Bitel, 'Saints and Angry Neighbors', 129.

256 Ibid.

257 Diem, 'Monks, Kings, and the Transformation of Sanctity', 532.

258 Davies, 'Anger and the Celtic Saint', 198–9.

259 Diem, 'Monks, Kings, and the Transformation of Sanctity', 532.

260 Ibid. 533.

In this way, Irish *vitae* speak of the saint as embodying the 'voice of God's will'.[261] As God's representative on Earth, the saint carries the power to effect Divine punishment through his words; having been insulted, he executes Divine vengeance. When St Munnu is insulted by the Irish king Suibne mac Domnaill, he predicts a horrible outcome for him—his kin will murder him and throw his head in the river Berba. The saint's prediction, as his hagiographer recounts, comes true 'within a month'.[262] The immediacy of Divine vengeance evident here recalls yet again the anecdotes of *Sefer ḥasidim*.

As seen above, in *Sefer ḥasidim* actions that provoke vengeance encompass the failure to accept the rebuke of a *ḥakham*,[263] the driving out of extra-zealous Pietists,[264] and the prevention of the performance of Pietist practices—all cases of insult to honour rather than of perpetration of any moral wrong. However, in contrast to the incidents preserved in the monastic *miracula* and the *vitae*, it is God rather than the saint who intervenes miraculously to defend the honour of the Pietist. In only one case in the entire work does the Pietist himself perform the act of vengeance. When a rich Jewish communal leader takes hold of the distinctive Pietist *talit* and openly mocks it—a form of insult that, when perpetrated against a saint, demands payment of the full honour-price, that is, payment with one's own life[265]—the Pietist curses the perpetrator 'that he would not live out the year'. Naturally, the curse is effective: 'And so it was, he did not live out the year and it was only a few days later that he died.'[266] Would that this rich community leader had heeded the words of one hagiographer: 'Obviously, everyone knows it is best to avoid troubles with a *vir dei*.'[267]

Having demonstrated that God's punishments, as recorded in the Pietist work, reflect the characteristics of vengeance more than those of retributive punishment, we can take the argument one step further. If God exacts vengeance upon those who harm his men, then surely he takes revenge on those who dishonour him. If, according to feudal modes of thinking, God is perceived as the greatest of all lords and sin is an affront to his honour, then avenging that honour in any way other than by means of full retribution would be considered the greatest act of betrayal. According to the unwritten laws of feudal conduct, the higher the rank of the victim,

[261] Bitel, 'Saints and Angry Neighbors', 130. [262] Ibid. [263] See *SḤ* 235, 236, and 407.
[264] See *SḤ* 242. [265] M. Johnson, 'Vengeance is Mine', 11. [266] *SḤ* 1344.
[267] The words of Jonas of Bobbio in reference to St Columbanus, as translated in Diem, 'Monks, Kings, and the Transformation of Sanctity', 534. For a further discussion of the Pietist as Holy Man, see below, pp. 390–1.

the higher is the honour-price demanded and the more violent the vengeance.[268] Translated into religious terms, such a premise requires that a harsh external penance mitigate the violent and vengeful wrath of God by having the sinner voluntarily take that wrath upon himself. Following this logic, self-imposed penance and the adoption of voluntary suffering in an attempt to escape the dreaded judgement of God are natural outgrowths of the culture of vengeance. It is no wonder, then, that these doctrines became cornerstones of the Pietist ethic.[269]

As in Pietist penance and voluntary suffering, so too in prayer for the dead: feudal ways of thinking reverberate. R. Judah's unique position regarding accountability for sin and his rejection of the role of intercessors in posthumous judgement now become understandable. Influenced by feudal notions, he cannot allow the substitution of merit in place of sin or the overlooking of sin on account of a 'court favourite', as these acts would constitute the greatest of all dishonours to God. A sin can never be overlooked, regardless of the merit of the intercessor or the number of good deeds in one's possession. Such an act would leave the full honour of the offended, God himself, unavenged. For this same reason, while the Pietist master can be a hero of penance, he can never assume the position of a specialist in intercessory prayer, for the very function of such prayer is to overlook sin, which would mean that God's honour once again remains unavenged. According to the social and moral code of feudalism, such a reality is untenable. Similarly, in the moral universe of Pietism, unexpiated sin is unfathomable.

No longer the merciful emperor who bends to the influence of patrons in his heavenly court, R. Judah's God is a feudal lord writ large. He executes justice without mercy, punishes violators swiftly and violently, and protects

[268] See Kelly, *A Guide to Early Irish Law*, 125 and n. 1 there, and D. A. Miller, *The Epic Hero*, 339–40.

[269] In some circles the twelfth century gave rise to images of a more compassionate, 'human' Jesus; the humanity of Christ occupied a central role in Cistercian spirituality. See Dutton, 'Intimacy and Imitation'. In fact, the famed medievalist R. W. Southern declared, 'The greatest triumph of medieval humanism was to make God seem human. The Ruler of the Universe, who had seemed so terrifying and remote, took on the appearance of a familiar friend' ('Medieval Humanism', 37). Despite this newer, more gentle spiritual impulse, older notions of Christ as a vengeful lord still existed in the high Middle Ages and persisted beyond that time. In late medieval Ireland, it was 'common fare' for Gaelic Irish poets to refer to the murder of Christ as kin-slaying (*fingal*), and to depict him exposing his wounds on Judgement Day in order to indict all of humanity. Mankind would then have to pay the blood price (*éiric*) for having killed him 'illegally'—a vivid scene of bloody retribution described in horrifying detail. See Ryan, 'Fixing the Eschatological Scales', 186–7.

his men in *this* world, even though at other times he only exacts vengeance after a violator's death.[270] God's punishments are in excess of the crime committed and are personal in nature; he directs the full measure of his anger against those whom the Pietists label as his enemies—the individuals who insult his men. Any who dishonour God by sinning can expect a vengeful response, immediately in this world or in the cruel milieu of the next. It is R. Judah's notion of God as the greatest and most vengeful of all lords that determines his vision of posthumous Divine judgement as one of unmitigated, absolute justice and strict accountability. Whereas his co-religionists can sustain a belief in a compassionate, fatherly God—a product of their midrashic inheritance—despite the changed conditions of medieval life, R. Judah cannot. He has imbibed a thoroughly feudal view of God, as refracted through a monastic lens.

Conclusion

While R. Judah shares the high medieval belief in the efficacy of suffrages for the dead, in many other respects he reacts against the religious climate of his day. He rejects the model of intercessory prayer performed by powerful holy figures, both living and dead, as presented in miracle stories of that period; he objects to the subversion of justice that they promote. For this reason, he denounces prayer for the dead by the dead as well as the prayer of the living for the undeserving dead. He does so despite the fact that questions such as who prays for the dead and which dead can be prayed for did not concern the *ge'onim* before him or the tosafists of his day. Furthermore, he maintains his objections regarding prayer for the undeserving dead against the common practice of his contemporaries, both Jewish and Christian.

Thus, while men and women of the thirteenth century were increasingly reliant on the salvific actions of others to rescue even the damned from Hell, and whereas contemporary Ashkenazi Jews maintained a belief in such advocacy in consonance with midrashic notions, talmudic accounts, and a well-known ghost tale involving R. Akiva, R. Judah did not. Armed with a host of textual reinterpretations of talmudic material to the contrary, showcasing his own version of a Marian tale with an emphasis on personal merit, and blatantly omitting from *Sefer ḥasidim* the R. Akiva tale, which

[270] In her study of saintly vengeance in French hagiography of the early medieval period, Anne-Marie Helvétius points to the this-worldly and physical aspects of Divine vengeance recounted there, despite the firmly held belief in posthumous punishment of the soul. See 'Le Récit de vengeance des saints', 423.

told approvingly of the successful intercession of the holy for the undeserving dead, R. Judah protests against popular contemporary notions of prayer for the dead. What he advocates instead is the strict adherence of the individual to the manifold proscriptions of Pietism as the most assured path to escaping posthumous torment and gaining reward. For him, it is personal conduct—regular as well as supererogatory—and conformity to both revealed and hidden law, not the power of others, that aid one's soul after death. Furthermore, R. Judah's definition of the undeserving, who include not only the objectively wicked but the detractors of Pietism as well, and for whom no help at all is possible in the next world, makes it clear that in his mind Pietism is the surest way to Paradise.

Additionally, R. Judah seeks to limit the application of prayer and alms for the dead even when it concerns the deserving. This is evident in the fact that he omits all mention of the most standardized type of ghost tale circulating in thirteenth-century Germany. Although *Sefer ḥasidim* speaks of cases in which the living pray for or give charity on behalf of the dead, the participants do so of their own accord. Of all the tales recorded in the work, not one mentions a dead individual returning to request aid from the living in its most common form of prayer or alms. R. Judah thus preached the same restraint in reliance upon the pious acts of others as did early medieval preachers before him. Like Eligius of Noyon or Jonas of Orléans, popular preachers of that period, he used images of the strict Judge and the threat of eternal damnation to frighten his flock 'into abandoning their sins'.[271]

R. Judah's reluctance to rely on the posthumous aid of others, even for the deserving, aligns his thinking with that of Augustine, who limits the efficacy of pious acts for the dead to those who have 'earned' such help during their lifetime. Additionally, R. Judah's distinctions between those who 'sin and merit' and 'those who sin but do not merit' and between those souls who receive a full redemption, a partial amelioration of their suffering, or no relief at all parallel Augustine's categorization of the 'very bad' and the 'not very bad' and their respective fates, kept alive in the writings of Caesarius of Heisterbach. By way of contrast, R. Judah's rabbinic predecessors and contemporaries allow prayer for all the dead, irrespective of merit. R. Judah's unique position on this question also includes an emphasis on

271 See McLaughlin, *Consorting with Saints*, 207–8 and nn. 108, 109 there. Whereas the fear-provoking sermons of the early medieval preachers led to increasing demand among their followers for intercessors to rescue them from the terrors of the afterlife, R. Judah inspired the same fear of judgement while denying his flock any help from intercessors. See ibid. 209.

voluntary acts of suffering as an integral part of helping the dead. It is the Pietist doctrine of penance, based on the early medieval penitential system, that informs his 'accountancy of the hereafter' and finds its way into his novel interpretations of traditional Jewish descriptions of posthumous aid found in the Talmud.

In opposition to the new religious mood, R. Judah sees justice, not mercy, as the dominant Divine attribute in posthumous judgement. With the individual to stand on trial alone and with the odds more against him than in his favour, R. Judah's view of God's judgement departs sharply from midrashic and contemporary liturgical and artistic images. While Ashkenazi commentators on *piyut* and illuminators of *maḥzorim* depict a compassionate God who throws away one's sins or tilts the scales of judgement in one's favour, R. Judah paints an austere portrait of humankind overwhelmed by the gravity and inescapability of sin in front of an unforgiving and unswayable deity. His rejection of all models of patronage, both Jewish and Christian, his refusal to allow merit to cancel out sin—a view which he holds in opposition to other Jewish thinkers of his day—and his vision of posthumous judgement as absolute justice untempered by mercy serve to isolate him from members of his own Pietist circle, including his student R. Eleazar of Worms, and render his notions of accountability for sin exceptional in Jewish tradition.

Despite R. Judah's resistance to several medieval conceptions and practices, whether Jewish or Christian, reflection upon his unique position regarding prayer for the dead and accountability for sin reveals that he had unconsciously absorbed a thoroughly medieval view of God as feudal suzerain. In place of the emperor-like God of midrashic times who exercises compassion and pardons sinners thanks to the aid of intercessory parties, R. Judah's God is a vengeful lord who metes out punishment swiftly in this world and cruelly in the next, in excess of the sins committed. He pours out his wrath mercilessly against those who dishonour him with acts of sin. Merits can never replace sins, nor can the Pietist master, the *ḥasid ḥakham*, intervene in prayer on behalf of his faithful as that would leave God's honour unavenged. Only the harsh penitential practices and voluntary suffering characteristic of Pietism can fully expunge sin and restore God's honour.

Like his monastic counterparts, R. Judah sees the punishing hand of God in everyday events and, citing appropriated miracle tales, he speaks with certainty about their causal factors. His world, like that of the monastics, is starkly divided between those who support God's holy men and those who thwart them. In symmetry with Irish saints, the Pietist pronounces curses or predictions of death, destruction, and impoverishment when he is mocked or his rebuke is ignored. Ever protective of the Pietists, God, like the saints of the *miracula* literature, avenges the honour of his men and substantiates Pietist predictions; the wicked of *Sefer ḥasidim* are punished with alarming immediacy. While R. Judah's contemporaries still maintain in their mind the midrashic image of a compassionate, fatherly God, he replaces it with the likeness of a vengeful feudal lord.

Indeed, we have journeyed very, very far since rabbinic times.

APPENDIX

A Report Regarding Prayer for the Undeserving Dead in the Name of R. Judah the Pious

In the *Sefer hagan*, a fourteenth-century work attributed to R. Isaac, the son of R. Eleazar of Worms, an incident regarding prayer for the undeserving dead is reported by R. Moses Zaltman (or Zalman), son of R. Judah the Pious, in the name of his father. The author of *Sefer hagan* relates:

When I studied in Speyer before Rabbi Yedidyah of blessed memory, I found in his school the manuscript of Rabbi Zalman [son of R. Judah the Pious]. This is [what it said]: My father and teacher, the Pious, told me that in his time there was an incident involving a wealthy man in Speyer who used scissors to shave his beard. My father and teacher would approach him and protest against [this practice]. The wealthy man did not heed his words, saying, 'A refined person [*istenis*] am I, and I cannot suffer the beard.' My father and teacher told him: 'You should know that you will come to a bitter end, for after your death, demons resembling cows [will] trample your beard. This is the lot of those who cut their beard. And you will know the truth of the verse, "Thou shalt not round the corners of thy head, neither shalt thou mar the corners of thy beard" [Lev. 19: 27], which contains an acrostic for [the Hebrew word for] cows [*parot*].' And when the man of means passed away, all the great men of Speyer sat near [the corpse], and my father and teacher was there. He wrote a name and threw it on that man of means, and he [the dead man] stood up. And all those who had been sitting there fled [in fear]. Then the dead man began to pluck at his head and pull his hair. My father and teacher said to him: 'What [is happening] to you?' He said to him,

'Woe is me that I did not heed you.' My father and teacher said to him, 'Please tell, what is happening to your soul?' He said to him: 'When my soul left [my body], a demon, looking like a great cow, came with a vessel full of pitch, sulphur, and salt, and imprisoned it in it, so that [the soul] could not get out. Then harsh Justice intervened and took the vessel with the spirit [within] from the demon and brought it before the Creator of Souls. A Divine voice [*bat kol*] sounded and said to me, "Have you studied and repeated?" I said to him: "I have studied and repeated." At once, he ordered that a Pentateuch be brought and said to me: "Read it." As soon as I opened the book, I found written, "neither shalt thou mar the corners of thy beard", and I did not know what to answer. Then I heard a voice declaring: "Put this one's soul on the bottommost level." As they were bearing my soul to the bottommost level, a Divine voice sounded: "Wait! My son Judah is more righteous than us [the angels] and he has now asked for mercy. Your soul will not descend to She'ol [the netherworld]."' Up until this point, his own words.[272]

Many elements of this story accurately reflect the character of R. Judah the Hasid as it emerges from the pages of *Sefer ḥasidim*. His audacious nature, his stinging rebuke of others, his contempt for the rich, as well as his great concern for and fear of the harsh punishments of the afterlife are all characteristic of the exhortations made by him or of the incidents he approvingly records in *Sefer ḥasidim*. Yet one element does not fit. R. Judah's invocation of mercy on behalf of the man contradicts his image as portrayed in the work.

As has been demonstrated, R. Judah speaks vociferously against any form of aid for the undeserving dead, whether from the living or from the dead. Such an invocation is inconsistent with his world-view, which limits the efficacy of posthumous help even for the deserving and stands in outright contradiction to his rejection of the intercession of privileged figures on behalf of the dead. While, technically speaking, the man of means who shaves off his beard falls into the category of the not very bad (Augustine's *non valde mali*), for whom, as R. Judah states, prayer could be efficacious, the fact that he had rejected R. Judah's rebuke places him in the category of the very bad (Augustine's *valde mali*), for whom posthumous aid is not at all beneficial. In other similar situations in *Sefer ḥasidim*, in which individuals ignore or violate Pietist advice, they are shown no mercy.

[272] *Sefer hagan*, 9*b*–10*a*, cited in Yassif, *The Hebrew Folktale*, 336–7. According to J. Rochwager, *Sefer hagan* was authored by R. Aaron ben R. Yosi Hakohen, and its title is an allusion to the fifty-three portions of the Torah (*gan* = *gimel* and *nun*, which equals 53 in gematria). See Rothwager, '*Sefer Pa'aneah Raza*' and Biblical Exegesis', 44 n. 193, and Poznanski, *An Introduction to the Commentary of Eliezer Beaugancy* (Heb.), xcviii.

What, then, does one make of this report? Several possibilities exist. One is that *Sefer ḥasidim*, contrary to what I have claimed, is not the product of R. Judah alone, but is a composite work of several Pietist authors, one of whom disagrees with him on this matter. If this were to be true then, on the basis of this tale, we would attribute to R. Judah a belief in the legitimacy of the holy petitioning for mercy on behalf of the very sinful, and would have to search for another author of *Sefer ḥasidim*, who espouses an opposing view. This possibility is difficult to maintain in light of the differences I have noted between the position set forth in *Sefer ḥasidim* and those held by other prominent members of the Pietist group on such matters as post-mortem accountability and Divine judgement. *Sefer ḥasidim* represents a single view: that of strict, even ruthless, judgement, and there is no trace in it of R. Eleazar's or R. Abraham's model of justice tempered with mercy. If the work does not reflect the opinions of R. Judah or R. Eleazar of Worms on this point, then whose opinion does it proclaim? We would have to assume that there is a major voice speaking in *Sefer ḥasidim* on a fundamental issue of human accountability and Divine justice other than that of the two leaders of the movement. This seems too revolutionary an inference to be drawn from a single tale in a mid-fourteenth-century work.

A second possibility is that R. Judah the Pious is, indeed, the author of the relevant section of *Sefer ḥasidim* and the report in *Sefer hagan* is equally true. We then have before us an instance of inconsistency. While R. Judah maintains his unique world-view and imparts the principles of his distinctive Pietism in *Sefer ḥasidim*, the story cited above reveals his (one-time?) compassion when confronted with a real-life situation. Even though his words frequently echo the biblical declaration, 'And the name of the wicked shall rot',[273] and a spirit of extreme harshness pervades his writings, in reality he too has, or at least on one occasion has displayed, a tender side. This all-too-human inconsistency would be perhaps less a failing than a welcome sign of humanity.

A third possibility is that the account is unreliable. The story speaks first of a *bat kol*, then of an angel of the *bet din shel ma'alah* (heavenly court). In brief, it portrays interaction with the celestial world, characteristic of the Midrash but entirely alien to *Sefer ḥasidim* and to the thought of R. Judah the Pious. His world is cut off from any intercourse with heavenly figures, nor are there any celestial beings other than an omnipotent, omniscient Deity. Then there is the characterization of R. Judah as 'my son', *beni*, something that befits the Heavenly Father of Midrash and rabbinic prayer,

[273] Prov. 10: 7; see *SḤ* 1571.

but not the impersonal, vengeful Deity of *Sefer ḥasidim*. The imagination of the teller of this tale still inhabits a midrashic world—as did that of many Jews in R. Judah's time and later—not that of German Pietism.[274] Seeing these major discrepancies, one hesitates to give much credence to the rest of the account. Whether these alterations were conscious and aimed to alter the harsh image of R. Judah the Pious, or unconscious, and whether they can be attributed to R. Judah's son or to a creative transcriber, lies beyond the scope of our discussion.

[274] Soloveitchik, 'The Midrash, *Sefer Ḥasidim* and the Changing Face of God', 163–76.

CHAPTER NINE

CONCLUSION

NEEDLESS TO SAY, any study of the dead reveals more about the world of the living than it does about the world of the dead. What transpires in the world of the dead is very much a product of what the living expect it to be. Questions such as who returns from the dead, where they appear, in what form they return, for what purpose they make their encounter, with what intent, and to offer what type of information are all culturally determined by the living. Few things tell us more about the society of the living than its conceptions and fears regarding the dead and their world.

What this study has revealed is that Jewish attitudes towards the dead and the hereafter in medieval Ashkenaz resembled more those of their Christian neighbours than those of their rabbinic ancestors of talmudic times. The unconscious interiorization, within Ashkenazi society, of Germano-Christian beliefs, customs, and fears about the dead—a result of acculturation—is clearly manifest. Although popular in origin, these practices, beliefs, customs, and fears were found among both elite groups and ordinary people within this small medieval Jewish enclave. Even the literary mediums through which the material was conveyed within the host society—visionary literature and the ghost tale—were adopted in *Sefer ḥasidim* and other, non-Pietist sources. The parallels in language and content between exempla and the tales of *Sefer ḥasidim* are striking. At times one can peel away the various layers of religious and cultural appropriation that a tale has undergone and reveal its pre-Christian root. Beliefs about the dead and post-mortem existence were anchored in long-held popular Germanic notions that had survived for centuries and had been modified by Christianization, only to be adapted, and sometimes even wholly adopted, for Jewish use.

These changed attitudes and practices relating to the dead and the afterlife were so characteristically medieval as to constitute a turning point in the Jewish relationship between the living and the dead. The holy dead, such as Elijah the prophet and R. Judah the Prince, whose appearances are mentioned in rabbinic sources, are absent from *Sefer ḥasidim*; they are replaced by the ordinary dead, who return in visions and dreams. In talmudic sources, if the living wish to initiate an encounter with someone from among the ordinary dead, they must seek him out in the cemetery or in the 'courtyard of death'. By contrast, in medieval Ashkenazi sources, although the ghost can appear anywhere, it is most commonly found in the familiar abodes of the living. Whereas the number of Jewish stories of the ordinary dead is dwarfed by comparison to the many hundreds recorded in the exempla literature, in otherworldly journey narratives, and in collected tales of the Christian majority, I argue that they should be seen as part of the 'invasion of ghosts' that swept across Western society in the medieval period.[1]

Additionally, the rabbis of the Mishnah and Talmud were friendly towards, conversant with, and at times even indebted to their returning dead. Their presence among the living provoked no fear. Medieval Franco-German Jews, on the other hand, were terrified by bodily appearances of the dead, as they feared that they would intentionally perpetrate acts of violence and vengeance against them. A later addition to the *Maḥzor vitry*, in its discussion of Friday night synagogue prayer, testifies to the transition from the malevolent forces feared in the rabbinic period to those of the medieval era. In this passage, the host of harmful demons known in the Talmud as *mazikin*, who sweep through the world on Friday night with permission to destroy, is replaced with the dreaded corporeal wicked dead who inhabit synagogues on the sabbath in order to escape the tortures of Gehenna, and who seek to harm the worshippers gathered there. Adjuration of the dead, hastiness of burial, stuffing up the mouths of cadavers, exhumation of bodies during times of plague, a refusal to kiss or hold hands with the dead, and the general abandonment of anything death-related, whether in practice or in study, were all outgrowths of this fear. The pre-Christian belief in the dangerous dead had infiltrated the minds of medieval Ashkenazi Jews as it did of Christians.

The 'friendly' dead of the rabbinic period were displaced not only by the dangerous dead, reminiscent of the pagan *draugar*, but by the Christian-influenced sinful dead as well. Belief in the latter was superimposed upon the former so that the 'bad' dead, now more religiously errant than ill-tempered, returned to Earth to do penance for their sins. Medieval Jews fashioned tales that were rooted in a popular pre-Christian legend surrounding King Herla, which, in its Christianized form, spoke of a wander-

[1] See Introduction, p. 3, above.

ing army of dead sinners. Several such Hellequin's Hunt-type stories appear in *Sefer ḥasidim*, alongside comments made by R. Judah which substantiate his belief in the terrestrial posthumous punishment of sinners. R. Eleazar of Worms, his student, echoes this belief and adds novel components to it, one of which contradicts rabbinic teaching regarding the dead and their exemption from *mitsvot*. It is therefore surprising to find that a tale about R. Akiva and a dead man, which contains all the main features of the Hunt narratives, appears in R. Eleazar's work but is noticeably absent from R. Judah's. This tale was highly popular in Ashkenaz, and it served as the basis for the newly formed custom of reciting the mourners' Kaddish. The promulgation of such tales testified to the community's unwitting adoption of an alien notion, which deviated from accepted rabbinic opinion regarding the afterlife. Alongside belief in the subterranean Gehenna of fire promoted by the rabbis, medieval Jews had come to believe that some of their dead were tortured corporeally on Earth.

Ancient Germanic imaginings of the dead imprinted themselves upon the minds of Ashkenazi Jews in other ways as well. Matters that are uncertain or are left unstated in the Talmud are axiomatic to the author of *Sefer ḥasidim*, and to his intended audience. The dead have definite knowledge of the actions of the living, are sentient in the grave, take umbrage at their unworthy neighbours in the cemetery, must be clothed in order to exit the grave, occupy synagogues at night and participate in services there, and require proper attire in the afterlife. Similarly, the Pietist work attests to a belief in the power of shoes (an ancient Germanic notion known as *Helskór*) and of the hood (referred to as *Hellekeppelin*) to transport the dead swiftly to the hereafter. Ashkenazi halakhists promoted burial with *tsitsit* in hand, and ordinary German Jews requested various material objects to be placed in their coffin as a means to gain easy admittance into Paradise. In their strongly corporeal imagery, these beliefs had much in common with the Germanic ideas of ghosts and were at odds with traditional Jewish belief in the separation of body and soul after death. Medieval Christianity also harboured this dichotomy of thought, as is evident in the clothed, embodied dead that present themselves in the exempla literature and in Christian monumental art, despite the official theological position of the Church being the post-mortem division of body and soul.

Apart from ancient Germanic beliefs, Christian ideas of the dead also penetrated Ashkenazi Jewish thinking. Whereas martyrs were venerated in rabbinic literature, the attention paid to their commemoration in Ashkenaz and their elevated status in people's consciousness extended far beyond any previous level. The martyrs are over-represented as a group in the ghost tales of *Sefer ḥasidim*. Their complaint of improper burial is characteristically medieval, while their insistence on burial alongside other martyrs, coupled with their rejection of non-martyrs buried in their midst, testifies to an appropriation of Christian notions of the holy dead. Narratives exist in both religions of saints and martyrs who do not tolerate the unworthy buried in their midst. By contrast, the various righteous groups who are granted specially designated burial caves in talmudic literature do not include martyrs. Furthermore, Ashkenazi and Pietist attitudes towards the burial sites of the Rhineland martyrs are far removed from rabbinic ones and, instead, approximate Christian ideas of holy space. Whereas the cemetery in rabbinic sources is not a sacred place, and the performance of commandments therein is prohibited, in Pietist tales the martyrs seek out burial —and even, at times, reburial—specifically in the *terra sancta* of the grave of other martyrs. Actual Ashkenazi practice corroborates such a view of the hallowed nature of the martyrs' grave: in 1186 the Jews of Neuss undertook to ferry the bodies of several martyred local Jews up the Rhine over a distance of 100 kilometres to Xanten in order to bury them beside the martyrs of 1096.

Like attitudes regarding burial and the cemetery, views about the afterlife had undergone a major shift from rabbinic times to the medieval era. A newly found emphasis on the period immediately after death was a seminal feature of the Middle Ages, due, in part, to the popularization of belief in Purgatory among the masses. Among both Jews and Christians, an increasing anxiety over the fate of the individual in the hereafter overshadowed an interest in the collective destiny of the faithful. Whereas rabbinic opinion about when posthumous reward and punishment would ensue was divided between the period immediately after death and the post-resurrection era, with more weight assigned to the latter, for the medieval Jew the former assumed a heightened centrality. Moreover, while rabbinic texts showed a degree of concern for one's welfare in the hereafter, what the Jews of antiquity, as well as their Christian contemporaries, feared most of all was the experience of death and being deprived of burial. In the medieval period, by contrast, anxiety over punishments in the afterlife plagued adherents of both religions. The wish to inform the living of one's status in the hereafter formed a primary reason for the return of the dead in both Jewish and non-Jewish tales of the period. The motif of the 'promise of two friends', which appears in both the Talmud and in *Sefer ḥasidim*, reflects the shift in emphasis from a fear of dying to a terror of the afterlife. The horrific acts performed by demonic agents in Hell or Gehenna were envisaged in the same vivid detail by medieval Jew and Christian. Carved on church tympanums, related in otherworldly journey narratives, recounted in visionary literature, and spread through popular works and exempla, images of the torture of the damned assumed a life-like reality that was wholly absent in rabbinic literature.

The high medieval climate, with its focus on the individual afterlife, supported contradictory notions simultaneously, creating an atmosphere of both fear and hope. On the one hand, people were confronted with realistic images, both conceptual and visual, of the tortures awaiting them immediately after their death. On the other, the popularization of the belief in Purgatory, the promulgation by the Church of an elaborate system of aid for the dead, and the supernatural intervention of the holy dead narrated in highly popular tales, with the Virgin Mary foremost of all saviours, combined to offer people hope and a modicum of comfort. Ashkenazi Jews seem to have imbibed this dual, contradictory emotional stance. The popularity of the R. Akiva tale and the concomitant emergence of the Kaddish prayer in the synagogue at this time bear witness to the absorption within the Jewish psyche of the regnant fear of the harsh corporeal tortures set to ensue immediately after one's death. Anxious about the punishment their loved ones would undergo in the afterlife, Ashkenazi Jews created a parallel practice to the mass, which would serve to release their deceased relatives from that fate. Here, aid for the dead was symptomatic of a culture of fear rather than of hope. On the other hand, tosafist positions on key rabbinic statements relating to the posthumous punishment of sinners, as well as high medieval additions to the *Maḥzor vitry*, reveal a strongly held belief that ordinary Jews, even sinful ones, would be quickly released from Gehenna or would ascend straight to Heaven and be spared these harsh punishments altogether, unlike their Christian counterparts.

This study has shown that the Ashkenazi adoption of all these uniquely medieval notions of the dead and the afterlife occurred amongst both popular and elite groups. Both groups unconsciously absorbed religiously neutral ideas about the dangerous dead, the returning dead, and the corporeal dead as much as they did Christian tenets, such as notions of the holy dead, sacred burial space, post-mortem penance on Earth, tortures in the afterlife, and prayer on behalf of the dead. That is to say, they understood these doctrinal matters, too, to be religiously neutral and a part of the shared intellectual and cultural property of medieval Germany. In this regard, *Sefer ḥasidim* marks a turning point in the nature of elements which infiltrated Jewish beliefs regarding the dead and the afterlife.

What this book has also demonstrated is that foreign elements had penetrated, on an even greater scale, the world-view of R. Judah the Pious himself. These elements are characteristically medieval, some Christian, others feudal, but all of them are pervasive and, at times, radical and isolationist. We have seen that, in matters of the dead and the afterlife, one can at times detect a single voice in *Sefer ḥasidim*. When the author maintains positions that are at odds with the views of R. Eleazar and other members of the Pietist circle, I have identified this voice as R. Judah's. Given the uniformity of thought on matters of death and the afterlife in the book, I have assigned authorship of these topics to R. Judah, even when his views are in consonance with R. Eleazar and despite the fact that I cannot verify the claim that he penned every single passage in it.[2] R. Judah's radical position in regard to sin, punishment, and posthumous judgement widens the gap between him and R. Eleazar on doctrinal matters—differences that were first noted by Haim Hillel Ben-Sasson in questions of social reform, and then later given special emphasis by Ivan Marcus in that arena as well as in the realm of penance. *Sefer ḥasidim* thus contains both the above-mentioned culturally shared ideas and R. Judah's own unique beliefs.

R. Judah's views on sin, penance, punishment, and prayer for the dead demonstrate the high degree of infiltration of foreign elements spoken of above. Remarkably, rather than reflecting dominant contemporaneous beliefs, his notion of sin bears the marked influence of early medieval Christian thinking. Heavily encumbered by sin, humanity owes God a huge debt that can never be repaid. In place of Original Sin, *Sefer ḥasidim* speaks of an entire realm of hidden sin in which one is punished even though God has not revealed his will (*retson haborè*) in that area. Pietism has, in effect, substituted sin that is omnipresent and inevitable for sin that is inherent and inherited—inescapable sin for Original Sin. The Pietist doctrine of penance, with its harsh system of external penances, aims to rid humans of this sinful burden. But, alas, even this appears inadequate as R. Judah constantly exhorts his readers to voluntarily adopt suffering now, in this life, in order to avoid the dreaded judgement of God in the next world. In one ghost tale involving a Pietist master, R. Judah's unwitting adoption of the Christian doctrine of vicarious atonement is revealed. The story culminates in the huge burden of sin, the tremendous debt owed

[2] See Introduction, pp. 5–6, above.

God, being lifted off the common person through the atoning sacrifice of a great man.

Like sin and penance, posthumous punishment as portrayed in *Sefer ḥasidim* also harks back to an earlier period, and reflects early medieval patterns of thought. R. Judah conceives of it in a pre-purgatorial framework: an ever larger group of sinners is condemned to the severe corporeal punishments of an afterlife devoid of any hope for redemption. He expands the rabbinic category of sinners destined to eternal punishment and extends the accepted rabbinic maximum punishment beyond the prescribed twelve-month period for even the average sinner. Additionally, he rejects the widely accepted Ashkenazi belief in the sabbath rest of souls and in the efficacy of prayer for the undeserving dead. He further argues for the limitation of prayer and alms for the deserving dead (a practice his co-religionists engage in), and protests against the commonly held belief in the aid of holy figures, living and dead, to rescue souls from punishment. In tandem with accounts from early medieval visionary literature, he speaks of sinners being punished in the afterlife in homogeneous groups according to the sins they committed.

R. Judah's doctrine of prayer for the dead also shows early medieval influence. It is patterned after a Christian pastoral model, which, in turn, bases itself on the teachings of Augustine. This model extends the penitential system of the Church into the afterlife, allowing the transfer of merit from one individual to another—a notion known as vicarious penance. Even though early medieval preachers espoused the idea, they also emphasized individual responsibility for sin and warned against reliance on the posthumous aid of others. Echoing these sentiments, R. Judah rejects the intercessory model of prayer for the dead presented in rabbinic and geonic sources. That model was based on traditional midrashic notions of an enthroned God, and drew upon ancient systems of patronage that obtained in the rabbinic era. In these earlier sources, it was specifically a righteous person who, on account of his great merit and influence, could find favour before God and secure pardon for the dead sinner from the heavenly court. By contrast, R. Judah decries the subversion of justice performed through the supernatural intervention of the holy. He draws a distinction between the deserving dead, who can be aided by the living, and the undeserving, who must not be given any help. It is for these reasons, I have argued, that he consciously omits the R. Akiva tale from his work, as it champions the supernatural intervention of the saintly on behalf of the undeserving. This merit-based distinction is absent from rabbinic, geonic, and tosafist discussion of the topic, but is very much present in the writings of a Cistercian contemporary of R. Judah's, Caesarius of Heisterbach, who had retained this Augustinian notion.

Although R. Judah's beliefs in these areas are anchored in early medieval thought, he is well aware of high medieval currents. He reworks, for example, a well-known Marian tale that focuses upon the image of the balance as representative of the posthumous judgement of the individual's soul. In his version, he replaces the salvific power of Mary's overwhelming grace with the force of individual merit and suffering. Similarly, his insistence that only the living can redeem the dead and not the dead (a distinction not made by his co-religionists, past or present) is understandable only in light of his awareness of circulating high medieval tales, in which the holy dead do just that. These circulating tales highlight the special privilege of the holy dead, for example the Virgin, to rescue even the most reprobate sinners from Hell. R. Judah rejects such stories because they promote salvation for the undeserving and sanction the subversion of justice—ideas he fundamentally opposes.

Apart from medieval Christian ideas, feudal concepts also permeate R. Judah's mind. He maintains a position of strict accountability: sin can never be cancelled out by merit, and every sin is punished. This position conflicts with well-accepted rabbinic statements that the world as a whole, as well as individuals, are judged on the basis of the majority of their actions. It also clashes with contemporary Jewish opinions—those of Nahmanides and Abraham b. Azriel—on the matter. R. Judah's portrait of God's post-mortem judgement as one of absolute justice unmitigated by mercy departs sharply from both midrashic and contemporary Ashkenazi conceptions, and is not shared even by members of his own Pietist circle, including his student R. Eleazar. Additionally, R. Judah's total rejection of the power of any intercessory figure, living or dead, to plead on behalf of one or aid one after death speaks against both earlier Jewish traditions and the new religious climate of intercessionism exemplified by the Virgin Mary. Finally, his conception of God as a strict judge who is unmoved by pleas for compassion and does not display any himself is in outright contradiction to that of the merciful Father portrayed in the Midrash, which Ashkenaz had inherited and imbibed. This latter image of a God 'abundant in kindness', who overlooks iniquity, forgives sin, and tips the scales of judgement so that merit predominates, was articulated by numerous medieval Ashkenazi commentators of *piyut* and illuminated by artists, yet it was antithetical to R. Judah's concept of the Divine. Only an understanding of feudal notions can explain his startling singularity of thought in these domains.

It is a thoroughly feudal view of God that engendered R. Judah's particular vision of absolute, unmitigated Divine justice. Envisioned as a feudal lord who acts in a 'culture of vengeance', God punishes in excess of the sin committed, in this world and the next. Replacing the Emperor God of the rabbis, who metes out a well-measured dose of retribution to sinners, R. Judah's vengeful God spills his wrath all too copiously against those who dishonour him or his retainers. As the greatest of all lords, God is merciless in his punishment of those who offend him personally by sinning, and he demands full payment in the form of harsh penance and voluntary suffering in exchange. R. Judah cannot allow the substitution of merit in place of sin or the overlooking of sin on account of a 'court favourite', as these acts would constitute the greatest of all dishonours: they would leave the full honour of the offended, God himself, unavenged. According to the social and moral code of feudalism, such an act would be deemed the highest form of betrayal. It is for this reason that, while the Pietist master can be a hero of penance, he can never assume the position of a specialist of intercessory prayer, for the very purpose of such prayer is to persuade God to overlook sin. In the moral teaching of Pietist accountability (and not mere accountability alone),[3] unexpiated sin is unfathomable. It is strictly through Pietism, not favouritism, that one enters Paradise.

Alongside feudal notions, monastic values also deeply inform R. Judah's world. The tales that discuss one's status in the hereafter, and which R. Judah consciously selects and adapts within the pages of *Sefer ḥasidim*, closely resemble those found in monastic collections. In speaking of the severe corporeal punishments meted out in the afterlife to those who commit minor misdeeds, they parallel monastic ones that record a similar disparity between sin and punishment. Both groups of narratives highlight laxity in the service of God as the impetus for the intense Divine punishment suffered in the hereafter rather than commission of a major iniquity, such as murder, adultery, or usury, as was common in non-monastic exempla collections. The Pietist tales that speak of celestial reward in the afterlife also echo monastic ones: both showcase to their own followers the bounty awaiting those who fulfil the challenging dictates of their own particular movement. In this way, the tales function as a form of internal propaganda.

[3] See my discussion on p. 351 above regarding the positions of R. Abraham ben Azriel and Nahmanides on the matter of accountability for sin.

R. Judah, furthermore, possesses a uniquely monastic way of looking at the world at large. Monastic writers perceive in the events of daily life a direct causal link between sin and punishment. In collections of *miracula* tales, they speak with the certainty of swift and decisive Divine punishment of the monks' enemies through the vengeful actions of God's saints. R. Judah appropriates this perspective when he records similar acts of miraculous and punitive intervention, performed directly by God, against the Pietists' detractors. Incidents in the Bible and in contemporary Germany testify to this. Speaking with the same degree of confidence as his monastic counterparts, R. Judah is quick to point out the immediate, this-worldly punishment of those who insult the Pietists or impede their efforts. Enemies of both camps are subjectively evaluated by the dishonour they cause the monks and the Pietists, rather than by any objectively defined moral transgression they have committed, and are spoken of in highly charged, emotional terms. It is this monastic *Weltanschauung* that leads R. Judah to identify the wicked of *Sefer ḥasidim* primarily as the detractors of Pietism rather than as morally unconscionable Jews or even Christians. It is the former group he has in mind, and not his Christian neighbours, monks, or Crusaders, when he asks in his theological orations, 'Why do the wicked prosper in this world?'

Monasticism suffuses the Pietists' unique doctrine of penance. The harsh external punishments of all four categories of Pietist penance have roots in early medieval monastic penitential traditions. The figure of the Pietist sage, who prescribes to the sinner the appropriate penance as atonement following the latter's confession, has long been shown to parallel the priest-confessor, and the need for verbal confession has its roots in monastic practice. R. Judah's advocacy of voluntary corporeal suffering, as well as his definition of the hasid as one who lives in constant daily battle with sin and in ascetic withdrawal from the pleasures of this world, reflect the identification of Pietism with several fundamental monastic ideals. Pietistic penance even plays a role after death; it makes its way into R. Judah's accountancy of the hereafter, where it serves as a more valuable aid to souls than prayer. Additionally, R. Judah's zeal, his preoccupation with the sins of others, and the writing of *Sefer ḥasidim* itself with the explicit aim of 'saving souls from Gehenna'[4] correspond to ideas characteristic of monastic orders with a missionary agenda and a penitential tradition.

The Irish Benedictine monks, just such an order, had a stronghold in southern Germany. In the high medieval period, monasteries in Cologne,

[4] *SḤ* 1474.

Mainz, Würzburg, and Regensburg, originally founded by Irish missionaries, still maintained strong ties with the monasteries and their noble benefactors in Ireland. The monastery of St James at Regensburg served as the mother house for these *Schottenklöster*. Irish *vitae*, in circulation as early as 1160 on the Continent thanks to the actions of missionaries, were copied and collected in the scriptorium at Regensburg. They tell of the heroic feats of Irish saints, known for their rigorous ascetic practices, penitential ardour, and missionary zeal, all in the service of God. Additionally, devotion to these saints was characteristic of the *Schottenklöster*; calendars with their anniversaries survive from the monastery at Regensburg. As agents of missionizing, the Irish monks maintained close relationships with the surrounding lay communities and could easily have shared the saints' stories with them. Given the close proximity of the Jewish area in Regensburg to the monastery, R. Judah, a resident of the town—and, presumably, other Jews—may have heard these stories from their Christian neighbours.

It was more than just familiarity with the ascetic acts of the saints, however, that captured R. Judah's attention. There was something about the ideology of monasticism itself that attracted him. A religious reformer whose spiritual antennae were sharply attuned to the currents of his age, he was deeply troubled by the threat that monasticism posed to his sense of the superiority of Judaism. The monks outshone the Jews of his day in their zeal and devotion to God. That competitive threat was not new to R. Judah; Ashkenazi polemicists were well aware of it.[5] Scholars of medieval Jewish–Christian relations have pointed out how critically important the issue of devotion to God was for medieval Jews' self-image—psychologically speaking, they could not allow themselves to be outdone by their religious competitors.[6] However, whereas polemicists, such as Joseph Kimhi in the twelfth century and the anonymous author of the thirteenth-century polemical work *Sefer nitsaḥon yashan*, deflected the challenges posed by monasticism by discrediting the monks' sincerity or questioning their conduct,[7] R. Judah responded in a novel way. In an effort to rival monastic devotion to God, he fashioned Pietism in such a way that it reflected some of the basic ideals and practices of primarily Irish Benedictine monasticism current in high medieval Christendom and found locally in his city, Regensburg.

[5] See Berger (ed.), *The Jewish–Christian Debate in the High Middle Ages*, 27 and n. 71 there.

[6] Berger, *Cultures in Collision and Conversation*, 94.

[7] Kimhi, *The Book of the Covenant of Joseph Kimḥi*, 35, and Berger, *The Jewish–Christian Debate in the High Middle Ages*, 69, 70, and 223.

Several of the ascetic penitential practices advocated in *Sefer ḥasidim* (both those prescribed as atonement for sin and those voluntarily assumed) were prominent features of Irish Benedictine monasticism. Fasting and flagellation had become more central in Irish practice since their adoption from the Rule of St Benedict, and immersion in icy water was a characteristically Irish form of penance. Additionally, as has been stated, the ideology behind the conversion of souls to monasticism in an attempt to save them from a dreaded fate in the afterlife was strikingly similar to the missionizing agenda of R. Judah, who aimed to force his Ashkenazi contemporaries to conform to the dictates of Pietism. R. Judah's intense fear of the punishments of the afterlife could well have been nourished by the vividly chilling accounts of posthumous torment described in the highly popular Vision of Tundale—an otherworldly journey narrative intended for the Irish Benedictine community in Regensburg and translated into German by a monk with local ties. Furthermore, the supererogatory practices demanded by the Pietists, and which were revealed to them in the form of the *retson haboré*, bore a strong resemblance to the elevated service of God required of the monks, as displayed in the exempla that were collected specifically by monastic houses. With his distinctive hooded *talit*, a *capuchon* similar to the monastic *cuculla* and perhaps sharing in its attendant powers, the Pietist even physically resembled a monk. And when he was insulted and his ire aroused, he, like the Irish saint, would curse or predict doom upon his enemy and have that curse fulfilled almost immediately by God himself. By appropriating some of the key elements of monasticism, R. Judah negotiated and created the identity of Pietism.

Religious Virtuosity and the Tragedy of Pietism

A revealing passage from R. Judah's commentary on the Torah substantiates his feelings towards monasticism:

'Not because you are more numerous than all the nations did God desire you and choose you, for you are the fewest of all the nations. Rather, because of God's love for you and because of His observance of the oath did He swear to your forefathers' [Deut. 7: 7–8].

And is it because of [the fact that] they are numerous and evil that He loves them? And that which it says, 'for you are the fewest of all the nations', is also problematic, for it already says, 'the Lord, your God, has multiplied you' [Deut. 1: 10]. Rather, this is its interpretation: 'Not because you are more numerous in merits than all the nations, [but rather] because you act for the sake of God more than all the nations.' For you are careful [to refrain from] fat and blood and other prohibitions, and from sexual prohibitions. These are equal to what they are doing for their idols. They burn their sons and their daughters in fire, and slaughter men for idol worship. They die from thirst, cut themselves, according to their law, with swords and spears until blood spills forth upon themselves, and many similar such things they do . . . And why does He love you? Because you observe His commandments, even though they are easier than those of the other nations, and because of His observance of the oath.[8]

Although the passage refers to the actions of ancient pagans, its resonance clearly extends to contemporary Christians, and R. Judah is making a statement here about the latter group's level of service to God. In speaking of how the idolaters 'cut themselves, according to their law, with swords and spears until blood spills forth upon them', he makes direct reference to 1 Kings 18: 28. In that biblical verse the prophet Elijah disdainfully mocks the futility of the practices performed by the prophets of Ba'al, whose supplications to their deity go unanswered.[9] Ironically, R. Judah regards these practices as venerable and worthy of emulation—he equates them with the scrupulous observance of the Jews, who are 'careful [to refrain from] fat and blood and other prohibitions, and from sexual prohibitions'—and he has contemporary Christian practices of flagellation and mortification of the flesh in mind when he extols them. While Judaism is incontrovertibly the superior religion for R. Judah, he feels that its system of obligations and prohibitions is grossly inferior when compared to the extreme sacrificial acts voluntarily performed by monks in the service of their false, idolatrous God.[10] R. Judah here fully accepts the validity of the monastic claim to an exalted level of Divine service. He openly and unabashedly admits that the Jewish people are less 'numerous in merits' than the Christian monks, because they observe commandments that are 'easier than those of the

8 *Perushei hatorah lerabenu yehudah heḥasid*, ed. Lange, 202. On the Bible commentary of R. Judah, see most recently Stahl, 'New Passages from the Manuscripts of the Bible Commentary of R. Judah the Pious' (Heb.), 134–51.

9 Child sacrifice and cutting oneself with swords and spears are clear references to pagan practices elsewhere in the Bible as well. See Lev. 18: 3, 21; 20: 1–5; Deut. 12: 31 regarding child sacrifice, and Lev. 19: 28 and Deut. 14: 1 regarding cutting oneself.

10 Identification of Christianity with idolatrous paganism was not uncommon among medieval Jews. The twelfth-century Jewish convert to Christianity, Herman (Judah), in his autobiography, refers to the Cathedral of St Paul in Munster as a 'pagan temple', and to the crucifix there as a 'monstrous idol'. He attributes the association of Christian images with idolatry to his 'Pharisaic' upbringing (the Pharisees were the rabbinic leadership of the Second Temple era). See Schmitt, *Conversion of Herman the Jew*, 115. Jewish polemicists also frequently labelled Christian use and worship of images as idolatry (ibid. 120–4).

other nations'. Instead of questioning the monks' sincerity of devotion, he confronts the threat in another way: he proves the superiority of Judaism by appropriating key elements of that devotion and adapting them to his religion, in the firm belief that these elements of superior service are already contained in Judaism. R. Judah has engaged in an altogether different type of polemic against Christianity.

To be clear, R. Judah is not embracing monasticism as a way of life. He does not advocate the adoption of its major tenets of celibacy, poverty, and total obedience or the undertaking of formal vows to that end. He does not promote claustration as was practised by the Benedictines. Instead, R. Judah's motive is to supplant the claim of monasticism to a monopoly on true service of God and to being the sole avenue towards 'salvation'. When confronted with the tension between the reality of the monastic display of religious devotion and his own axiomatic belief in the objective truth of Judaism, he resolves it by reshaping the ideals and practices of the latter in light of the former.[11] It is important to note that this process of religious appropriation was not a conscious one. In speaking of medieval Ashkenazi Jewish adoption of Christian ideas or practices in general, David Berger has argued that, beyond the formal prohibitions on imitating Gentile practice, Jews felt such a fundamental aversion to Christianity that it 'spoke to elemental instincts'.[12]

Although R. Judah unconsciously appropriates key elements of monasticism in his attempt to resolve the tension he experiences on the theological plane, that tension is not eradicated. In areas where Pietist practice and monastic ritual closely mirror each other and stand in a competitive relationship, one can sense it very keenly. Pietistic prayer is just such an example; it is here that R. Judah explodes in anger against his monastic counterparts. The unique features of Pietist prayer—its communal nature, as well as the loud choral singing of psalms that stands at its centre—have much in common with monastic prayer rituals.[13] The Irish in particular were known for their distinctive prayer and psalmody—'loud' and 'long'.[14]

11 Hiebert, *Transforming Worldviews*, 319.

12 Berger, *Persecution, Polemic, and Dialogue*, 44.

13 R. Judah is aware of the parallel; see *SḤ* 1368, which recounts how a 'good Jew' who was engaged in the Pietist prayer ritual developed a medical condition that prevented him from reciting psalms out loud. When approaching a doctor, he warned the doctor (in Hebrew) not to tell him the cure in the presence of a monk who happened to be nearby (and who understood the vernacular) 'lest he use the cure for [his fellow] monks, who shout [in prayer] in their houses of foolishness' (*beit tiflutam*—a play on the words *beit tefilatam*, their houses of prayer). See also *SḤ* 1589 (end), in which R. Judah expresses competitive jealousy in the realm of prayer.

14 Bitel, 'Saints and Angry Neighbors', 123.

When discussing prayer, R. Judah is astonished ('How is it possible?', he asks) and infuriated by the fact that the monks have gained possession of Psalms, a book which was penned by King David 'for the sake of Heaven', and they recite it to their 'idols'. Undoubtedly, they stole the book from 'incorrigible Jews' who sang them at their feasts.[15]

Additionally, R. Judah's use of vituperative language to refer to monks and their service displays the simultaneous emotions of attraction and repulsion that he feels towards monasticism. He expresses hatred not only towards Christianity and its symbols but also towards monasticism: he refers to monks as 'impure ones',[16] and labels their works as 'abominations'.[17] As stated above, many Ashkenazi Jews shared in this aversion: the polemical *Nitsaḥon yashan* employs similar derogatory terms with regard to Christian religious figures and houses of worship. R. Judah, however, expresses a loathing of Christian symbols which, at least on one occasion, surpasses that of his contemporaries. *Sefer moshav zekenim*, a collection of tosafist commentaries on the Torah, records the opinion of a Rabbi Samuel (possibly Rashbam, R. Samuel ben Meir), who states that, in spite of a rabbinic opinion to the contrary, one is allowed to gaze upon church sculpture and not be in violation of the scriptural prohibition of 'turning unto idols' (Lev. 19: 4). In fact, the commentary notes that it was customary in R. Samuel's city for people 'to gaze upon the figures that were on the churches' (lit. 'abominations'). In defiance of the accepted popular custom and the opinion of a leading talmudic commentator, R. Judah forbids the practice, declaring that it is 'certainly forbidden' and that 'it is proper to be stringent' in this regard.[18] While he does have halakhic precedent for his position, is it not possible to suggest that a visceral revulsion at Christian images as presented in monumental art also plays a role here?

In a set of twelve tightly clustered passages, *Sefer ḥasidim* reflects an exaggerated fear of association with Christian visual symbols and a heightened hatred towards its holy places.[19] In contrast to actual participation in Christian ritual, which would be forbidden by Jewish law as idolatry,[20] these cases involve only visual encounters with the symbols or structures of the

15 *SḤ* 544. 16 *SḤ* 682. 17 *SḤ* 668.

18 See *Sefer moshav zekenim al hatorah*, ed. Sassoon, 344–5. For a parallel passage, see MS CUL Add. 3216, cited by Soloveitchik, 'Piety, Pietism and German Pietism', 490.

19 See *SḤ* 1353–64.

20 See e.g. *SḤ* 1352, in which a Jewess is tempted to use a piece of stone relic from the shrine of Jesus in Jerusalem to cure her ailing son and refuses. Regarding this and other cases of Jewish knowledge and use of medieval shrines and relics, see Shoham-Steiner, 'Jews and Healing at Medieval Saints' Shrines', esp. p. 114.

idolatrous Other. Yet they are regarded with the same contempt and fear of spiritual contamination as the former would provoke. Two passages in the set epitomize this assertion; they speak of Jews who are required to perform a harsh penance of continual fasting for having entered the courtyard of a church or the church itself.[21] Whereas an opinion exists in the Talmud (*AZ* 17*a*) that would prohibit entry into a church on the basis of the scriptural verse 'and do not come near to the entrance of her house' (Prov. 5: 8), R. Judah uncharacteristically makes no mention of this rabbinic passage or its supporting verse, either of which could well have bolstered his claim that such a prohibition extends to the courtyard of the building as well.[22] This noteworthy silence on his part lends further credence to the view that his aversion here is instinctive and not legally driven. Add to this the fact that, independent of any tradition, R. Judah regards entry into the courtyard of a church as a sin that requires penance 'all the days of one's life', and what we witness here is a visceral revulsion at Christianity to an extreme degree.

Christian theology does not attract the Pietist; he rejects the doctrine of the humanity of God by espousing a strongly anti-anthropomorphic position.[23] The Pietist, even though driven by intense emotion, reacts rationally to that which he is opposed to. He reacts viscerally, however, to that which threatens him by its very magnetism. By legitimizing the monastic claim to holiness while retaining a belief in the superiority of Judaism, R. Judah is repulsed by the very forces that attract him. Like fire, whose light beckons even as its heat repels, the monk's zeal and sacrificial devotion to God lure R. Judah even as his competitor's manner of worship revolts him. This dichotomy of attraction and repulsion lay at the very heart of R. Judah's Pietism.

Why did the spirituality of monasticism attract R. Judah so deeply and personally? On the one hand, he saw humans as heavily weighed down by sin—not Original Sin but inevitable, unavoidable sin—and, having absorbed Irish monastic penitential traditions, he required them to pay a steep price in the form of penance and voluntary suffering in order to absolve themselves of the huge debt they owed God. On the other hand, he

[21] *SḤ* 1357 and 1358.

[22] The verse in Proverbs, according to one opinion in the Talmud, refers to a brothel. Given Ashkenazi Jews' identification of Christianity with idolatry, which is often associated in the Bible with harlotry and infidelity, this prohibition ('do not come near') could easily extend to a church ('her house') or churchyard ('the *entrance* of her house').

[23] The Pietists were responsible, for instance, for the burning of the prayer books of Jewish anthropomorphists. See Soloveitchik, 'The Midrash, *Sefer Ḥasidim* and the Changing Face of God', 170–1.

saw the enormous untapped human potential that was not fully channelled to the service of God. He viewed monasticism as a religious way of life that succeeded in harnessing one's full capacity in that endeavour, and shared in its aspiration. The common denominator between these two opposite pulls in the individual—the sense of sin as debt which draws him downward and the 'monastic' drive for perfection and dedication to God which directs him upward—is that they demand unremitting toil to reach the limits of human potential. By embracing both challenges simultaneously, R. Judah made manifest the aspirations of the virtuoso.

The virtuoso temperament is not unique to R. Judah; anyone who leads their life in pursuit of the perfect or the heroic displays this mentality. For one possessed of the virtuoso instinct, mediocrity is a grave sin; far better for one to have not been born, he reasons, than to live a life marked by average accomplishment. In religion, the virtuoso temperament takes the form of the maximum realization of one's spiritual potential, the aspiration to religious rigour and spiritual perfection. R. Judah, through the relentless demands of Pietism, seeks to realize just such a maximalist but ever elusive goal.

He engages the heroic drive for perfection specifically in the arenas of penance and religious and ethical conduct. When sin is present, atonement is required; when sin is omnipresent, the search for atonement is ceaseless. For the aspiring hero, there is no limit to the amount of penance necessary. Let us recall the penance prescribed by R. Eleazar for adultery—a life-long endeavour involving much physical torment with only the hope of forgiveness. Asceticism and withdrawal from the world and its creatures are a necessary corollary of a world filled with sin. *Voluntary* ascetic withdrawal is the hallmark of the religious hero.

The Pietist, although an ascetic, does not escape the world; on the contrary, everyday life becomes the theatre for myriad attempts at self-perfection. With trial and temptation at every corner, the religious hero is continuously challenged to prove his spiritual prowess.[24] This demonstration of spiritual fortitude is always only before the Pietist himself and God, as he is an anonymous hero. By contrast, the saint is glorified in his *vita* for his acts. His biography describes not only his miracle-working ability both in life and after death, but also his religious rigour, his extreme acts of asceticism, and his attempts at self-perfection in the religious domain. While living in Regensburg, R. Judah was undoubtedly exposed to the stories of the Irish saints contained in the *Magnum Legendarium Austriacum*

24 Weber, 'The Social Psychology of the World Religions', 290–1.

and circulating among the locals, and shared in their spiritual aspiration. However, unlike the biographers of the saints, he transcribed the spiritual feats of the Pietists as having been performed by nameless individuals. Never seeking honour and forever shunning pride, the Pietists were models of perfect humility who outshone the saints in this regard.

This compulsory attitude of extreme humility must have been exceedingly difficult for the Pietist to maintain, as one of the natural by-products of the demands of the virtuoso temperament is ego. Knowledge that one has surpassed the limitations of the physical body and achieved unparalleled mastery of a specific area is intoxicating.[25] Yet Pietism demands the suppression of any and all forms of ego and self-aggrandizement.[26] Moreover, dissatisfied with the modest requirements of revealed religion, the Pietist assumed the yoke of the ever greater, more demanding, supra-legal requirements of the *retson haboré*. This larger will of God is not the voluntary province of solitary individuals; it is the obligation of everyone to commit himself to the goal of religious perfection. As evidenced in the ghost tales of *Sefer ḥasidim*, anyone who falls short in the slightest respect of the ideal of service that Pietism demands suffers severe punishment in the hereafter. Conversely, proper fulfilment of the ideals of Pietism ensures that the hasid will 'sit' highest in Heaven.

For these reasons, it does not seem far-fetched to view the Pietist as a *vir dei*. R. Judah, at least, seems to portray him that way. While not meeting all the criteria in Peter Brown's description of the late antique Holy Man,[27]

[25] Halberstam, *The Amateurs*, 61–2, 75–6.

[26] Monks engaged in the difficult struggle for the virtue of humility, too, as documented by Little in 'Pride Goes Before Avarice'.

[27] What the Pietist primarily lacks is the Holy Man's miracle-working capacity (power to heal and save), prophetic insight, and role as specialist in intercessory prayer. While R. Judah deliberately rejects the last function, it is interesting to note that the other two elements are posthumously assigned to him in the cycle of miracle stories perpetuated in his name. See Gaster, *Ma'aseh Book*, and Dan, *R. Judah the Pious* (Heb.), 163–76. Similarly, the stories about R. Judah in Eli Yassif's collection of tales portray him as possessing supernatural powers (nos. 27, 34, 35, 85, 86, 87, 94, and 95), the capacity to heal (nos. 2, 3, and 99) and to save (nos. 29 and 32), and prophetic ability or the power of clairvoyance (nos. 28, 29, 30, 33, 35, 36, and 92). He possesses none of these qualities in *Sefer ḥasidim*. See Yassif, *Ninety-Nine Tales* (Heb.), and the related discussion above, on pp. 4–5, and nn. 16–20 there. The fact that the Pietists lack any miraculous ability to heal or save souls, a common function of saints, reflects the austerity and harshness of their outlook: the Pietist Holy Man uses his power to punish rather than to heal. This may or may not be linked with the relatively small number of healing miracles attributed to early Irish saints as compared with continental ones. See Davies, 'The Place of Healing in Early Irish Society'. Irrespective of R. Judah's portrayal in *Sefer ḥasidim*, Jews at a later time must have instinctively endowed him with those qualities that are to be expected of any true saint; it is *their* saintly assessment of him that is recorded in these miracle stories.

the Pietist does possess several key characteristics, especially as they are adopted and adapted by early medieval hagiographers.[28] With his privileged knowledge of the hidden *retson haboré* and in his role as confessor, the Pietist master serves as mediator between God and mankind.[29] Like the saint in Jonas of Bobbio's description of St Columbanus, he is a strict ascetic who wishes to live outside the existing social order.[30] He has a missionary calling: he exhorts others regarding moral improvement, is not fearful of chastising and advising powerful men, and wills that the social order conform to his dictates. As a 'charismatic public person', he is both 'venerated and despised'.[31] Like Columbanus, he can predict outcomes, has the 'ability to invoke God's punishment', and can rely upon God's intervention to protect his honour and verify his word.[32]

Furthermore, while a hagiographer describes the charisma and holiness of one individual saint, *Sefer ḥasidim* highlights the average Pietist as possessing these traits. (We may recall that one such nameless Pietist curses a detractor who mocks him and his characteristic *talit* with death, and has that curse validated instantly by God.) While this phenomenon may, in part, be rooted in the Pietists' penchant for anonymity, it may also be a reflection of the 'routinization' of charisma evinced in Jonas's treatment of the monks of Bobbio. In the second part of his Vita Columbani, Jonas attaches to the biography of the saint stories of the miracle-working capacities of the monks of Bobbio, the monastery founded by St Columbanus. In so doing, he endows the monks with the holiness and power of the *vir dei* himself.[33] The Pietists, as depicted in *Sefer ḥasidim*, appear to have become, in similar fashion, Holy Men.

What R. Judah seeks to do, then, in the formation of Pietism is to create a class dedicated to religious virtuosity within the framework of Judaism.[34] A similar class of intellectual virtuosi already existed in Ashkenaz—the tosafists. One of their greatest figures, R. Isaac of Dampierre (Ri), mentions in passing the degree of intensity and rigour with which the tosafists study in the academies—they never untie their shoes the entire week, save for the

28 Brown, 'The Rise and Function of the Holy Man'; Diem, 'Monks, Kings, and the Transformation of Sanctity'.

29 Diem, 'Monks, Kings, and the Transformation of Sanctity', 524.

30 On the Pietists' will to withdraw from Jewish society and form 'utopian communities' of their own, as well as their efforts to insulate themselves from non-Pietists when forced to live among them, see Marcus, *Piety and Society*, 87–106.

31 Diem, 'Monks, Kings, and the Transformation of Sanctity', 525.

32 Ibid. 525.

33 Ibid. 526–7, 549–56, esp. 555.

34 Paul Fenton similarly characterizes the leaders of the German Pietists as possessing 'ambitious aspirations to create a community of Jewish saints'; see 'Deux écoles piétistes', 223.

sabbath, for they sleep only briefly every night, with their clothes on.[35] What of those aspiring to achieve excellence in the religious domain? To be sure, there were individuals, both in pre-Crusade Ashkenaz and afterwards, in France as in Germany, who were revered for their ascetic acts and were known to have adopted stringencies in matters of halakhah.[36] However, these acts of self-deprivation (even if performed in a 'quasi-associative manner'[37]) were regarded as voluntary acts of personal piety, never as a mandatory programme of reform aimed at a sinful humanity that had to legitimate its very existence. Similarly, the stringencies these pious individuals adopted pertained to particular areas in halakhah and were not based on the idea of the wholesale inadequacy of the entire system of revealed Law, as is characteristic of the Pietist *retson haboré*.

In contrast to these holy figures, whose pious motives and meritorious actions could not be questioned, Pietism as an ideological movement attempted to transform human nature itself. By advocating the minimalization of relations with one's own children, prohibiting small talk, and encouraging custody over one's eyes and mind, coupled with the adoption of an entire system of supra-legal norms, it did far more than refuse to rely on leniencies in the halakhic system. Instead, by stretching the human capacity to its utmost in every possible situation, it aimed to redefine the very substance of human nature. In essence, the Pietists were fighting for the recognition of a new spirituality—the existence of an entire class of spiritual virtuosi dedicated to the service of God—which echoed the Christian division of religious life into the monastic elite and the lay masses.

Herein lies the tragedy. A religious hero typically represents the values of the entire society in their highest form. The monastic values of strict asceticism, total renunciation of the pleasures of the flesh and all material pursuits, and singular spiritual devotion to the worship of God were ideals of medieval Christendom as a whole. Unable to live out these ideals fully in practice, Christian laypeople venerated the order that did. Ashkenazi Jewry, however, despite its measure of acculturation, did not embrace these values. It is not surprising, then, that R. Judah's radical ideas met with much opposition and antagonism. Whereas Christian society maintained and supported such a class of religious virtuosi in its midst, the Pietists encountered ridicule and shame in their own community. R. Judah was painfully aware of this phenomenon;[38] he mentioned it in his Torah commentary

[35] Moses of Coucy, *Sefer mitsvot gadol*, ed. Shlezinger, 75.

[36] See Kanarfogel, *Peering through the Lattices*, 38–78.

[37] Ibid. 42, 46, 51, 58.

[38] Interestingly, E. Shoham-Steiner argues ('From Speyer to Regensburg' (Heb.), 167–70)

cited above as further proof of the superiority of Judaism. God loves the Jewish nation, he writes, because they 'act for the sake of God more than all the nations'. Pietist dedication to God is greater than that of Christian monks, for only the Pietist acts solely for the sake of God. Only Pietists go unrecognized by all—even by their own co-religionists.

Despite the intensity of his zeal, R. Judah failed to frighten his community into following his example, nor could he inspire its members to strive for religious and spiritual perfection. Within the short span of two generations, Pietism as a movement died out. Why?

While undoubtedly there are many answers to this question, the desire to impose an instinct for perfection upon Ashkenazi society at this time was one reason for the failure of Pietism. One can never force the unmotivated to aspire to perfection. The all too vivid scenes of otherworldly torture and the ever-present circulating ghost tales about the afterlife must have had some effect upon members of medieval Ashkenazi Jewry, so that they sought penances for their sins—perhaps even harsh ones.[39] Yet to volunteer to accede to the rank of religious virtuosity, with all the demanding strictures that it entailed, was quite another matter. Ashkenazi Jewry was not interested in membership in this elect class of virtuosi, as a result of its own strong self-image. Nurtured on the axiom of martyrdom to the point of validating the notion of child sacrifice, Ashkenazi Jews of the high medieval period could feel that they had already amply demonstrated their perfection and zeal in devotion to God. Sufficient Jewish blood had been spilled as testimony to the truth of Judaism, and enough had been voluntarily offered. Additionally, German Pietism arose during the high tide of the tosafist era; the Jewish communities had a sense of living in the heroic age of halakhah. Ashkenazi Jews, proud enough of their religious commitment and intellectual accomplishments, did not feel the need to aspire to the 'perfection' of Pietism.[40]

Additionally, while monasticism provided an avenue to salvation for the laity, Pietism did not. As has been discussed earlier, medieval men and women could establish ties to the local monastery through donations of land, financial support, and confraternity, and burial within the monastery

that the reason for R. Judah's move from his native Speyer to Regensburg was the forceful ejection of his family by the angered Jewish community of Speyer.

39 On the lasting impact of the Pietist doctrine of penance upon later Germanic Jewry, see Elbaum, *Repentance and Self-Flagellation* (Heb.), 11–44.

40 On the collective self-image of Ashkenazi Jewry in reference to its religious practices, see Soloveitchik, *Wine in Ashkenaz* (Heb.), 361–2.

was a means towards gaining inclusion within the community of the saved. Although reified, prayer was performed by an ever-widening circle of intercessors on behalf of the laypeople, and the popularity of this practice increased dramatically in late medieval times. With its outright rejection of the intercession of the saintly (both living and dead), Pietism offered no similar opportunity for the 'laity' to share in the salvation of the Pietists without joining their ranks.

Yet another reason for the swift demise of Pietism had to do with its conception of God and his functioning in the world. Although R. Judah, too, was nurtured on the midrashic tradition that Ashkenaz had inherited, as a Pietist he thought differently. Whereas he had undoubtedly studied Rashi's Bible commentary, which is suffused with the image of the compassionate, fatherly God of the Midrash, R. Judah's working conception of God was one of justice without mercy, and, at times, even of vindictiveness. His model of supreme power in the world was thoroughly medieval, not the imperial one characteristic of the Midrash. There are no advocates for a sinful Israel in his view of Divine judgement as there are in rabbinic literature. Gone are the displays of clemency towards sinners and compassion for the faithful that had characterized an emperor-like Divinity. To R. Judah, God is a feudal lord writ large—a suzerain who is vengeful, vindictive, and excessively punitive both in this world and in the next. His God easily and quickly pours out his wrath upon sinners who insult his honour and upon the wicked who offend his retainers, the Pietists. The Jews of Ashkenaz rejected Pietism because they did not recognize its God.

BIBLIOGRAPHY

Archival Sources

Reference to manuscripts of *Sefer ḥasidim* is to the transcriptions held in the Princeton University Database.

Cambridge, University Library

Add. 379
Add. 3216

Hamburg, Staats- und Universitätsbibliothek

Cod. Hebr. 132

London, British Library

Add. 11284, 11872, 15833, 16589, 18344, 18347, 18351, 19909, 21147, 22283, 27336, 27909 B, 28682, 33956
Arundel 506
Cotton Cleopatra D VIII
Egerton 1117
Harley 268, 1022, 1288, 2316, 2385, 2391, 2851, 3244
Royal 5 A VIII, 7 C XV, 7 D I, 8 F VI, 12 E I
Sloane 278, 3102

Moscow, Russian State Library, Günzburg Collection

103

New York, Jewish Theological Seminary (JTS)

2499
Boesky 45

Oxford, Bodleian Library

Opp. 675
Opp. Add. 34
Reggio 1

Paris, Bibliothèque Nationale

hebr. 363

Parma, Biblioteca Palatina

Cod. Parm. 2295
Cod. Parm. 3006
Cod. Parm. H 3280

St Petersburg, National Library of Russia (Saltykov-Shchedrin State Public Library)
Evr. Antonin B 891

Vatican City, Biblioteca Apostolica
ebr. 183
ebr. 285

Printed Sources

ABRAHAM BEN AZRIEL, *Sefer arugat habosem, kolel perushim lepiyutim*, ed. Ephraim E. Urbach, 4 vols. (Jerusalem: Mekitsei Nirdamim, 1939–63).

ABRAHAMS, ISRAEL, *Jewish Life in the Middle Ages* (New York: Temple, 1981).

ABRAMS, DANIEL, 'The Literary Emergence of Esotericism in German Pietism', *Shofar*, 12 (1994), 67–85.

——'An Unknown Manuscript Source of the Hermeneutic Gates by Rabbi Eleazar of Worms: A Response to the Death of Rabbi Judah heHasid', lecture at the conference '*Sefer Ḥasidim* in Context' (Jerusalem, March 2017).

ALEXANDER, TAMAR, 'A Ḥasid Came in a Dream: Tales of Dreams in *Sefer ḥasidim*' (Heb.), in Avidav Lipsker and Rella Kushelevsky (eds.), *Studies in Jewish Narrative Presented to Yoav Elshtain* [Ma'aseh sipur: meḥkarim besiporet hayehudit mugashim leyo'av elshtain] (Ramat Gan: Bar-Ilan University Press, 2006), 77–97.

——'Neighbour in Paradise in *Sefer ḥasidim*: A Folktale in Its Theoretical Context' (Heb.), *Meḥkerei yerushalayim befolklor yehudi*, 1 (1981), 61–81.

——[ALEXANDER-FRIZER], *The Pious Sinner: Ethics and Aesthetics in the Medieval Hasidic Narrative* (Tübingen: Mohr Siebeck, 1991).

ALEXANDRE-BIDON, DANIÈLE, and CÉCILE TREFFORT (eds.), *À réveiller les morts: La Mort au quotidien dans l'Occident médiéval* (Lyons: Presses Universitaires de Lyon, 1993).

ARIÈS, PHILIPPE, 'Une Conception ancienne de l'au-delà', in Herman Braet and Werner Verbeke (eds.), *Death in the Middle Ages*, Mediaevalia Lovaniensia Series 1 (Leuven: Leuven University Press, 1983), 78–87.

——*Western Attitudes toward Death from the Middle Ages to the Present*, trans. Patricia M. Ranum, Johns Hopkins Symposia in Comparative History (Baltimore: Johns Hopkins University Press, 1974).

ARONIUS, JULIUS, *Regesten zur Geschichte der Juden in fränkischen und deutschen Reiche bis zum Jahre 1273* (Berlin: L. Simion, 1902).

ASSAF, LILACH, 'The Language of Names: Jewish Onomastics in Late Medieval Germany, Identity and Acculturation', in Christof Rolker and Gabriela Signori (eds.), *Konkurrierende Zugehörigkeit(en): Praktiken der Namengebung im europäischen Vergleich* (Konstanz: UVK, 2011), 149–60.

ATWELL, ROBERT R., 'From Augustine to Gregory the Great: An Evaluation of the Emergence of the Doctrine of Purgatory', *Journal of Ecclesiastical History*, 38/2 (1987), 173–86.

AUBRUN, MICHEL, 'Caractères et portée religieuse et sociale des "Visiones" en Occident du VIe au XIe siècle', Cahiers de civilisation médiévale: Xe–XIIe siècles 23 (Université de Poitiers, 1980), 109–30.

AUSTIN, GRETA, *Shaping Church Law around the Year 1000: The Decretum of Burchard of Worms* (Farnham, Surrey: Ashgate, 2009).

AVERY-PECK, ALAN J., 'Death and Afterlife in the Early Rabbinic Sources: The Mishnah, Tosefta, and Early Midrash Compilations', in Alan J. Avery-Peck and Jacob Neusner (eds.), *Death, Life-After-Death, Resurrection and the World-to-Come in the Judaisms of Antiquity*, Judaism in Late Antiquity 4 (Leiden: Brill, 2000), 243–66.

Avot derabi natan, ed. Solomon Schechter (New York: Feldheim, 1945).

BAER, YITSHAK, 'The Social-Religious Programme of *Sefer ḥasidim*' (Heb.), *Zion*, 3 (1937), 1–50.

BAHYA BEN ASHER, *Rabenu beḥaye al hatorah*, 3 vols., ed. C. Chavel (Jerusalem, 1991).

BANKS, MARY M. (ed.), *Alphabet of Tales: An English Fifteenth-Century Translation of the Alphabetum Narrationum of Etienne de Besançon* (London, 1904).

BARAK, NATI, 'The Early Ashkenazi Practice of Burial with Religious Paraphernalia', in Stefan C. Reif, Andreas Lehnardt, and Avriel Bar-Levav (eds.), *Death in Jewish Life: Burial and Mourning Customs among Jews of Europe and Nearby Communities* (Berlin: De Gruyter, 2014), 187–96.

——'Time of Rage: Changing Attitudes towards Death in Ashkenazi Communities from the First Crusade to the Black Death' [Sha'at za'am ve'evrah: temurot bitfisat hamavet uve'itsuvo bikehilot ashkenaz migezerot tatnu ve'ad hamavet hashaḥor] (Ph.D. diss., Tel Aviv University, 2010).

BARBAR, PAUL, *Vampires, Burial, and Death: Folklore and Reality* (New Haven, Conn.: Yale University Press, 1988).

BAR HIYA, ABRAHAM, *Sefer hegyon hanefesh ha'atsuvah*, ed. Jeffrey Wigoder (Jerusalem: Mosad Bialik, 1972).

BAR-LEVAV, AVRIEL, 'Death and Mourning among Oriental Jewry' (Heb.), in Shalom Sabar (ed.), *The Cycle of Life* [Ma'agal haḥayim] (Jerusalem: Yad Ben Zvi, 2006), 281–323.

——'A Separate Place: The Cemetery in Jewish Culture' (Heb.), *Pe'amim*, 98–9 (2004), 5–37.

BARTHÉLEMY, DOMINIQUE, 'Feudal War in Tenth-Century France', in Susanna A. Throop and Paul R. Hyams (eds.), *Vengeance in the Middle Ages: Emotion, Religion and Feud* (Farnham, Surrey: Ashgate, 2010), 105–14.

——FRANÇOIS BOUGARD, and RÉGINE LE JAN (eds.), *La Vengeance, 400–1200* (Rome: École Française de Rome, 2006).

BARTLETT, ROBERT, *Gerald of Wales: 1146–1223*, Oxford Historical Monographs (Oxford: Clarendon Press, 1982).

——*Why Can the Dead Do Such Great Things? Saints and Worshippers from the Martyrs to the Reformation* (Princeton, NJ: Princeton University Press, 2013).

BASCHET, JÉRÔME, *Corps et âmes: Une histoire de la personne au Moyen Âge* (Paris: Flammarion, 2016).

BASCHET, JÉRÔME, *Les Justices de l'au-delà: Les Représentations de l'enfer en France et en Italie (XIIe–XVe siècle)* (Rome: École Française de Rome, 2014).

BASKIN, JUDITH, 'From Separation to Displacement: The Problem of Women in *Sefer Ḥasidim*', *AJS Review* (1994), 1–18.

——'Women and Sexual Ambivalence in *Sefer Ḥasidim*', *Jewish Quarterly Review*, 91/1 (2006), 1–8.

BAUMGARTEN, ELISHEVA, *Mothers and Children: Jewish Family Life in Medieval Europe* (Princeton, NJ: Princeton University Press, 2004).

——*Practicing Piety in Medieval Ashkenaz: Men, Women, and Everyday Religious Observance* (Philadelphia: University of Pennsylvania Press, 2014).

——'A Tale of a Christian Matron and Sabbath Candles: Religious Difference, Material Culture and Gender in Thirteenth-Century Germany', *Jewish Studies Quarterly*, 20 (2013), 83–99.

BEN-SASSON, HAYIM H., 'The German Pietists on the Distribution of Material Possessions and Spiritual Assets among People' (Heb.), *Zion*, 25 (1970), 62–79.

——'The "Northern" European Jewish Community and Its Ideals', in Haim H. Ben-Sasson and Shmuel Ettinger (eds.), *Jewish Society through the Ages* (Jerusalem: Schocken Books, 1971), 208–19.

BERGER, DAVID, *Cultures in Collision and Conversation: Essays in the Intellectual History of the Jews* (Boston, Mass.: Academic Studies Press, 2011).

——(ed. and trans.), *The Jewish–Christian Debate in the High Middle Ages: A Critical Edition of the Nizzahon Vetus* (Philadelphia: Jewish Publication Society, 1979).

——'Judaism and General Culture in Medieval and Early Modern Times', in Jacob J. Schacter (ed.), *Judaism's Encounter with Other Cultures: Rejection or Integration?* (Northvale, NJ: Jason Aronson, 1997), 57–141.

——*Persecution, Polemic, and Dialogue: Essays in Jewish–Christian Relations* (Boston, Mass.: Academic Studies Press, 2010).

BERNSTEIN, ALAN, *Hell and Its Rivals: Death and Retribution among Christians, Jews, and Muslims in the Early Middle Ages* (Ithaca, NY: Cornell University Press, 2017).

——Review of *La Naissance du Purgatoire*, *Speculum*, 59 (1984), 179–83.

BIELER, LUDWIG, 'An Austrian Fragment of a Life of St. Patrick', *Irish Ecclesiastical Record*, 95 (1961), 176–81.

——*Four Latin Lives of St. Patrick* (Dublin, 1971).

BINCHY, DANIEL A., 'A Pre-Christian Survival in Medieval Irish Hagiography', in Dorothy Whitelock, Rosamond McKitterick, and David Dumville (eds.), *Ireland in Early Mediaeval Europe: Studies in Memory of Kathleen Hughes* (Cambridge: Cambridge University Press, 1982), 165–78.

BINSKI, PAUL, *Medieval Death: Ritual and Representation* (Ithaca, NY: Cornell University Press, 1996).

BITEL, LISA M., 'Ascetic Superstars', Christian History Institute website (accessed 12 Aug. 2019).

——'Saints and Angry Neighbors: The Politics of Cursing in Irish Hagiography', in Sharon Farmer and Barbara H. Rosenwein (eds.), *Monks and Nuns, Saints and*

Outcasts: Religion in Medieval Society: Essays in Honor of Lester K. Little (Ithaca, NY: Cornell University Press, 2000), 123–52.

BOHAK, GIDEON, 'Conceptualizing Demons in Late Antique Judaism', in Siam Bhayro and Catherine Rider (eds.), *Demons and Illness from Antiquity to the Early Modern Period* (Leiden: Brill, 2017), 111–33.

——'Expelling Demons and Attracting Demons in Jewish Magical Texts', in Gert Melville and Carlos Ruta (eds.), *Experiencing the Beyond: Intercultural Approaches* (Berlin: De Gruyter, 2018), 170–85.

The Book of the Dun Cow: An Irish Precursor of Dante, trans. Charles S. Boswell (London: David Nutt, 1908).

BOWKER, J. W., 'Intercession in the Qur'an and the Jewish Tradition', *Journal of Semitic Studies*, 11/1 (1966), 69–82.

BOWYER, R. A., 'The Role of the Ghost-Story in Medieval Christianity', in Hilda R. E. Davidson and William M. S. Russell (eds.), *Folklore of Ghosts* (Bury St Edmunds: Folklore Society, 1981), 177–92.

BOYARIN, DANIEL, *Dying for God: Martyrdom and the Making of Christianity and Judaism* (Stanford, Calif.: Stanford University Press, 1999).

BRAET, HERMAN, 'Les Visions de l'invisible, VIe–XIIIe siècles', in Claude Kappler (ed.), *Apocalypses et voyages dans l'au-delà* (Paris: Cerf, 1987), 405–19.

BRANDON, SAMUEL G. F., *The Judgment of the Dead: An Historical and Comparative Study of the Idea of a Post-Mortem Judgment in the Major Religions* (London: Weidenfeld & Nicolson, 1967).

BRATU, ANCA, 'Fin des temps et temps du Purgatoire dans quelques jugements derniers de la fin du Moyen Âge', in *Fin des temps et temps de la fin dans l'univers médiéval* (Aix-en-Provence: Presses Universitaires de Provence, 1993), 69–80.

BRAY, DOROTHY A., *A List of Motifs in the Lives of Early Irish Saints* (Helsinki: Suomalainen Tiedeakatemia, 1992).

——'Malediction and Benediction in the Lives of the Early Irish Saints', *Studia Celtica*, 36 (2002), 47–58.

——'Miracles and Wonders in the Composition of the Lives of the Early Irish Saints', in Jane Cartwright (ed.), *Celtic Hagiography and Saints' Cults* (Cardiff: Wales University Press, 2003), 136–47.

BROWN, PETER, 'The Decline of the Empire of God: Amnesty, Penance, and the Afterlife from Late Antiquity to the Middle Ages', in Caroline W. Bynum and Paul Freedman (eds.), *Last Things: Death and Apocalypse in the Middle Ages* (Philadelphia: University of Pennsylvania Press, 2000), 41–59.

——*The Ransom of the Soul: Afterlife and Wealth in Early Western Christianity* (Cambridge, Mass.: Harvard University Press, 2015).

——'The Rise and Function of the Holy Man', *Journal of Roman Studies*, 61 (1971), 80–101; repr. in id., *Society and the Holy in Late Antiquity* (London, 1982), 103–52.

——'Vers la naissance du Purgatoire: Amnistie et pénitence dans le Christianisme occidental de l'antiquité tardive au haut Moyen Âge', *Annales. Histoire, Sciences Sociales*, 52/6 (1997), 1247–61.

Bull, Marcus G. (ed.), *The Miracles of Our Lady of Rocamadour: Analysis and Translation* (Woodbridge, Suffolk: Boydell, 1999).

Butler, Cuthbert, *Benedictine Monachism: Studies in Benedictine Life and Rule* (London: Longmans, Green, 1919).

Bynum, Caroline W., *The Resurrection of the Body in Western Christianity, 200–1336*, Lectures on the History of Religions (New York: Columbia University Press, 1995).

Caciola, Nancy M., *Afterlives: The Return of the Dead in the Middle Ages* (Ithaca, NY: Cornell University Press, 2016).

——'Wraiths, Revenants and Ritual in Medieval Culture', *Past and Present*, 152 (1996), 3–45.

Caesarius of Heisterbach, *Dialogue on Miracles*, trans. Henry von Essen Scott and Charles Cooke Swinton Bland (London: Routledge, 1929).

Carey, John, Máire Herbert, and Padraig Ó Riain (eds.), *Studies in Irish Hagiography: Saints and Scholars* (Dublin: Four Courts Press, 2001).

Carozzi, Claude, *Le Voyage de l'âme dans l'au-delà d'après la littérature latine (Ve–XIIIe siècle)* (Rome: École Française de Rome, 1994).

Catalogue of Romances in the Department of Manuscripts in the British Museum, vols. i and ii, ed. Harry L. D. Ward; vol. iii, ed. John A. Herbert (London: British Museum, 1893).

Chadwick, Nora K., 'Norse Ghosts: A Study in the *Draugr* and the *Haugbúi*', *Folklore*, 56 (1946), 50–65.

Chazan, Robert, 'The Early Development of Hasidut Ashkenaz', *Jewish Quarterly Review*, 75 (1985), 199–211.

——*European Jewry and the First Crusade* (Berkeley: University of California Press, 1987).

Chiffoleau, Jacques, *La Comptabilité de l'au-delà: Les Hommes, la mort, et la religion dans la région d'Avignon à la fin du Moyen Âge (vers 1320–vers 1480)* (Rome: École Française de Rome, 1980).

Clarke, Peter, and Tony Claydon (eds.), *The Church, the Afterlife, and the Fate of the Soul*, Studies in Church History 45 (Woodbridge, Suffolk: Boydell, 2009).

Clayton, Mary, *The Cult of the Virgin Mary in Anglo-Saxon England* (Cambridge: Cambridge University Press, 1990).

Cohen, Aryeh, '"Do the Dead Know?": The Representation of Death in the Bavli', *AJS Review*, 24/1 (1999), 45–71.

Cohen, Jeremy, *Sanctifying the Name of God: Jewish Martyrs and Jewish Memories of the First Crusade* (Philadelphia: University of Pennsylvania Press, 2004).

Costa, José, *L'Au-Delà et la résurrection dans la littérature rabbinique ancienne* (Paris: Peeters, 2004).

Dagan, Itamar (ed.), *Essays in Jewish Studies in Honour of Rivka Dagan* [Vehineh rivkah yotset: iyunim bemada'ei hayahadut likhvod rivkah dagan] (Jerusalem: Tsur ot, 2017).

Dan, Joseph, '*Ashkenazi Hasidim*, 1941–1991: Was There Really a Hasidic Movement in Medieval Germany?', in Peter Schäfer and Joseph Dan (eds.), *Gershom*

Scholem's Major Trends in Jewish Mysticism *50 Years After* (Tübingen: J. C. B. Mohr, 1993), 89–101.

——'Demonological Stories from the Writings of R. Judah the Pious' (Heb.), in Ivan Marcus (ed.), *The Religious and Societal Ideas of the Jewish Pietists in Medieval Germany* [Dat veḥevrah bemishnatam shel ḥasidei ashkenaz: leket ma'amarim] (Jerusalem: Merkaz Zalman Shazar, 1987), 165–81.

——*The Esoteric Theology of Ashkenazi Hasidism* [Torat hasod shel ḥasidut ashkenaz] (Jerusalem: Mosad Bialik, 1968).

——'The Problem of Martyrdom in the Ideological Programme of the German Pietist Movement' (Heb.), in *Holy War and Martyrology* [Milḥemet kodesh umartirologyah betoledot yisra'el uvetoledot ha'amim] (Jerusalem: Hahevrah Hahistorit Hayisra'elit, 1967), 121–9.

——*Rabbi Judah the Pious* [Rabi yehudah heḥasid] (Jerusalem: Merkaz Zalman Shazar, 2006).

——'Rabbi Judah the Pious and Caesarius of Heisterbach: Common Motifs in their Stories', *Scripta Hierosolymitana*, 22 (1971), 18–27.

——*The 'Unique Cherub' Circle: A School of Mystics and Esoterics in Medieval Germany*, Texts and Studies in Medieval and Early Modern Judaism 15 (Tübingen: Mohr Siebeck, 1999).

DAVIDSON, HILDA R. E., 'The Restless Dead: An Icelandic Ghost Story', in Hilda R. E. Davidson and William M. S. Russell (eds.), *The Folklore of Ghosts* (Cambridge: D. S. Brewer, 1981), 155–75.

DAVIES, WENDY, 'Anger and the Celtic Saint', in Barbara H. Rosenwein (ed.), *Anger's Past: The Social Uses of an Emotion in the Middle Ages* (Ithaca, NY: Cornell University Press, 1998), 191–202.

——'The Place of Healing in Early Irish Society', in Donnechadh Ó Corráin, Liam Breatnach, and Kim McCone (eds.), *Sages, Saints, and Storytellers: Celtic Studies in Honour of Professor James Carney* (Maynooth: An Sagart, 1989), 43–55.

DAVILA, JAMES, *Hekhalot Literature in Translation: Major Texts of Merkavah Mysticism*, Supplements to the Journal of Jewish Thought and Philosophy 20 (Leiden: Brill, 2013).

DAVIS, NATALIE Z., 'Ghosts, Kin, and Progeny: Some Features of Family Life in Early Modern France', *Daedalus*, 106/1 (1977), 87–114.

——Review of *The Birth of Purgatory*, *New York Review of Books*, 32/12 (18 July 1985), 31–3.

DELMAS, MARIE-CHARLOTTE, *Fantômes et revenants: Le Monde de l'au-delà* (Paris: Omnibus, 2006).

DELORT, ROBERT, *Le Commerce des fourrures en Occident à la fin du Moyen Âge (vers 1300–vers 1450)*, 2 vols. (Rome: École Française de Rome, 1978).

DENNY, DON, 'The Date of the Conques Last Judgment and Its Compositional Analogues', *The Art Bulletin*, 66/1 (1984), 7–14.

DEREGNAUCOURT, JEAN-PIERRE, 'Autour de la mort à Douai: Attitudes, pratiques et croyances, 1250/1500' (Ph.D. diss., Université Charles de Gaulle-Lille III, 1993).

DIDRON, ADOLPHE N., *Christian Iconography: A History of Christian Art in the Middle Ages*, trans. Ellen J. Millington, 2 vols. (London, 1886; repr. New York: Frederick Ungar, 1965).

DIEM, ALBRECHT, 'Monks, Kings, and the Transformation of Sanctity: Jonas of Bobbio and the End of the Holy Man', *Speculum*, 82/3 (2007), 521–59.

DOUDET, ESTELLE, *La Mort écrite: Rites et rhétoriques du trépas au Moyen Âge*, Cultures et Civilizations Médiévales 30 (Paris: Presses de l'Université Paris-Sorbonne, 2005).

DRIVER, SAMUEL R., and ADOLF NEUBAUER, *The 'Suffering Servant' of Isaiah, According to the Jewish Interpreters*, vol. ii (Oxford, 1877; repr. New York: Hermon Press, 1969).

DUBY, GEORGE, *The Age of the Cathedrals: Art and Society 980–1240* (Chicago: University of Chicago Press, 1981).

——*The Three Orders: Feudal Society Imagined*, trans. Arthur Goldhammer (Chicago: University of Chicago Press, 1980).

DUNN, MARILYN, *The Christianization of the Anglo-Saxons c.597–c.700: Discourses of Life, Death, and Afterlife* (London: Continuum, 2009).

——'Gregory the Great, the Vision of Fursey and the Origins of Purgatory', *Peritia*, 14 (2000), 238–54.

DUTTON, MARSHA L., 'Intimacy and Imitation: The Humanity of Christ in Cistercian Spirituality', in John R. Sommerfeldt (ed.), *Studies in Medieval Cistercian History*, xi: *Erudition at God's Service* (Kalamazoo: Cistercian Publications, 1987), 33–70.

EDREI, ARYEH, 'Atonement for the Dead' (Heb.), in Moshe Bar-Asher, Yehoshua Levinson, and Berakhyahu Lifshitz (eds.), *Studies in Talmud and Midrash: Memorial Volume for Tirzah Lifshitz* [Meḥkarim betalmud uvemidrash: sefer zikaron letirtsah lifshitz] (Jerusalem: Mosad Bialik, 2005), 1–27.

——'"When a Soul Sins Unintentionally"—Responsibility Without Guilt? On the Responsibility of an Unintentional Sinner in Scripture and in Rabbinic Literature' (Heb.), *Shenaton hamishpat ha'ivri*, 24 (2007), 1–62.

EDWARDS, GRAHAM R., 'The Idea of Post Mortem Purgation in the Western Church to the End of the Middle Ages' (Ph.D diss., University of Exeter, 1983).

——'Purgatory: "Birth" or Evolution?', *Journal of Ecclesiastical History*, 36/4 (1985), 634–66.

EHRLICH, DROR, 'The Theory of Retributive Punishment in Discussions about Gehenna in Rabbinic Thought' (Heb.), *Jewish Studies, an Internet Journal*, 13 (2015), 1–20.

EIDELBERG, SHLOMO (trans. and ed.), *The Jews and the Crusaders: The Hebrew Chronicles of the First and Second Crusades* (Madison: University of Wisconsin Press, 1977).

EINBINDER, SUSAN, *Beautiful Death: Jewish Poetry and Martyrdom in Medieval France* (Princeton, NJ: Princeton University Press, 2002).

ELBAUM, YAAKOV, *Repentance and Self-Flagellation in the Writings of the Sages of Germany and Poland 1348–1648* [Teshuvat halev vekabalat yisurim: iyunim beshitot hateshuvah shel ḥakhmei ashkenaz upolin] (Jerusalem: Magnes Press, 1992).

ELEAZAR OF WORMS, *Perushei sidur hatefilah laroke'aḥ*, ed. Moshe Hershler and Yehuda Hershler, 2 vols. (Jerusalem: Makhon Harav Hershler Lamehkar, 1992).
——*Sefer haroke'aḥ hagadol*, ed. Barukh S. Shneerson (Jerusalem: Otsar Haposekim, 1967).
——*Sefer ḥokhmat hanefesh* (Safed, 1913).
——*Sefer roke'aḥ: hilkhot teshuvah hashalem*, ed. Yeruham E. Rosenfeld (New York: Y. E. Rosenfeld, 2000).
——*Sifrei harabi eleazar migermayza ba'al haroke'aḥ*, 2 vols. (Jerusalem: Makhon Sodei Rezaya, 2006).
ELIEZER B. SAMUEL OF METZ, *Sefer yere'im al mitsvot hatorah*, ed. Avraham A. Shiff (Vilna: Romm, 1891–1902).
EPSTEIN, ABRAHAM, 'The History of Ashkenazic Kabbalah' (Heb.), in *Collected Essays of Abraham Epstein* [Kitvei avraham epstein], ed. A. M. Haberman (Jerusalem: Mosad Harav Kook, 1957), ii. 226–48.
EVANS, JOAN, *Monastic Life at Cluny: 910–1157* (London: Oxford University Press, 1931).
Eyrbyggja Saga, trans. H. Pálsson and P. Edwards (Harmondsworth: Penguin Books, 1989).
FARMER, SHARON, *Communities of Saint Martin: Legend and Ritual in Medieval Tours* (Ithaca, NY: Cornell University Press, 1991).
——'Personal Perceptions, Collective Behavior: Twelfth-Century Suffrages for the Dead', in Richard C. Trexler (ed.), *Persons in Groups: Social Behavior as Identity Formation in Medieval and Renaissance Europe* (Binghampton, NY: Medieval & Renaissance Texts & Studies, 1985), 231–9.
FENTON, PAUL, 'Deux écoles piétistes: Les Hasidei Ashkenaz et les soufis juifs d'Egypte', in Shmuel Trigano, *La Société juive à travers l'histoire: La Fabrique du peuple* (Paris: Fayard, 1992), i. 200–25.
FISHMAN, TALYA, *Becoming the People of the Talmud: Oral Tradition as Written Tradition in Medieval Jewish Cultures* (Philadelphia: University of Pennsylvania Press, 2011).
——'The Penitential System of *Ḥasidei Ashkenaz* and the Problem of Cultural Boundaries', *Journal of Jewish Thought and Philosophy*, 8 (1999), 201–29.
FOOT, SARAH, 'Anglo-Saxon "Purgatory"', in Peter Clarke and Tony Claydon (eds.), *The Church, the Afterlife, and the Fate of the Soul*, Studies in Church History 45 (Woodbridge, Suffolk: Boydell, 2009), 87–96.
FORQUIN, GUY, *Lordship and Feudalism in the Middle Ages*, trans. Iris and A. L. Lytton Sells (London: Allen & Unwin, 1976).
FRANTZEN, ALLEN J., *The Literature of Penance in Anglo-Saxon England* (New Brunswick, NJ: Rutgers University Press, 1983).
FREEHOF, SOLOMON, 'Hazkarath Neshamoth', *HUCA*, 36 (1965), 179–89.
FULTON, RACHEL, *From Judgment to Passion: Devotion to Christ and the Virgin Mary, 800–1200* (New York: Columbia University Press, 2002).
GAGE, JOHN, *Color and Meaning: Art, Science, and Symbolism* (Berkeley: University of California Press, 1999).

GALINSKY, JUDAH, 'Charity and Prayer in the Ashkenazi Synagogue' (Heb.), in Itamar Dagan (ed.), *Essays in Jewish Studies in Honour of Rivka Dagan* [Vehineh rivkah yotset: iyunim bemada'ei hayahadut likhvod rivkah dagan] (Jerusalem: Tsur ot, 2017), 163–74.

GALOOB, ROBERT P., '*Post hoc propter hoc*: The Impact of Martyrdom on the Development of *Hasidut Ashkenaz*' (Ph.D. diss., Graduate Theological Union, Berkeley, Calif., 2017).

GARDNER, EILEEN (ed.), *Visions of Heaven and Hell before Dante* (New York: Italica Press, 1989).

GASTER, MOSES (ed.), *Ma'aseh Book: Book of Jewish Tales and Legends* (Philadelphia: The Jewish Publication Society of America, 1934).

GEARY, PATRICK J., 'Humiliation of Saints', in Stephen Wilson (ed.), *Saints and Their Cults: Studies in Religious Sociology, Folklore and History* (Cambridge: Cambridge University Press, 1983), 123–40.

——*Living with the Dead in the Middle Ages* (Ithaca, NY: Cornell University Press, 1994).

GEULAH, AMOS, 'Lost Aggadic Midrashim Known Only from Ashkenaz: *Abkir*, *Asufah*, and *Devarim Zuta*' [Midreshei agadah avudim hayedu'im me'ashkenaz bilevad: abkir, asufah, udevarim zuta] (Ph.D. diss., Hebrew University, 2007).

GILCHRIST, JOHN, 'The Perception of Jews in the Canon Law in the Period of the First Two Crusades', *Jewish History*, 3/1 (1988), 9–24.

GINZBURG, LOUIS (ed.), *Ginzei shekhter*, 3 vols. (New York: Jewish Theological Seminary, 1928–9).

GLICK, SHMUEL, *Light Has Dawned: The Link between Marriage and Mourning Customs in Jewish Tradition* [Or nagah aleihem: hazikah shebein minhagei nisu'in leminhagei avelut bemasoret yisra'el] (Efrat: Keren Ori, 1997).

——*A Light Unto the Mourner: The Development of Major Customs of Mourning in the Jewish Tradition, from After the Burial until the End of Shiva* [Or la'avel: lehitpatḥutam shel ikarei minhagei avelut bemasoret yisra'el mile'aḥar hakevurah ad tom hashivah] (Efrat: Keren Ori, 1991).

GOLD, PENNY S., *The Lady and the Virgin: Image, Attitude and Experience in Twelfth-Century France* (Chicago: University of Chicago Press, 1985).

GOLDBERG, SYLVIE-ANNE, 'The Contribution of the Study of Death to Jewish Studies', *Proceedings of the Eleventh World Congress of Jewish Studies* (Jerusalem: World Union of Jewish Studies, 1994), i. 159–64.

——*Crossing the Jabbok: Illness and Death in Ashkenazi Judaism in Sixteenth- through Nineteenth-Century Prague*, trans. Carol Cosman (Berkeley: University of California Press, 1996).

GOLDIN, SIMHA, *The Ways of Jewish Martyrdom*, trans. Yigal Levin, ed. C. Michael Copeland (Turnhout: Brepols, 2008).

GORRINGE, TIMOTHY, *God's Just Vengeance: Crime, Violence and the Rhetoric of Salvation* (Cambridge: Cambridge University Press, 1996).

GOUREVITCH, EDOUARD, 'La Mort chez les Hassidim au Moyen Âge allemand', in Daniel Tollet (ed.), *La Mort et ses représentations dans le Judaïsme* (Paris: Champion, 2000), 71–5.

GRIMM, JAKOB, *Teutonic Mythology*, trans. James Steven Stallybrass, 4 vols. (London, 1883–8; repr. Gloucester, Mass.: Peter Smith, 1976).

——and WILHELM GRIMM, *The German Legends of the Brothers Grimm*, ed. and trans. Donald Ward, 2 vols. (Philadelphia: Institute for the Study of Human Issues, 1981).

GROSS, DALIA, 'The Bond Between the Living and the Dead in *Sefer ḥasidim*' [Hakesher bein haḥayim vehametim besefer ḥasidim] (MA thesis, Bar-Ilan University, 2010).

GROSSMAN, AVRAHAM, *The Early Sages of Ashkenaz: Their Lives, Leadership and Works (900–1096)* [Ḥakhmei ashkenaz harishonim: koroteihem, darkam behanhagat hatsibur, yetsiratam haruḥanit], 2nd edn. (Jerusalem: Magnes Press, 1989).

——*Pious and Rebellious: Jewish Women in Medieval Europe* [Ḥasidot umoredot: nashim yehudiyot be'eiropah biymei habeinayim] (Jerusalem: Merkaz Zalman Shazar, 2001).

——'Prayer in the Teachings of the German Pietists' (Heb.), in Michael Shashar (Sharshavsky) (ed.), *Yeshurun: 75th Anniversary of the Yeshurun Organization* [Yeshurun: bimelot shivim veḥamesh shanim lehistadrut yeshurun] (Jerusalem: Shashar, 1999), 27–56.

GÜDEMANN, MORITZ, *The Torah and Life in Western Lands during the Middle Ages* [Hatorah vehaḥayim be'artsot hama'arav biymei habeinayim], trans. Abraham S. Friedberg (Warsaw: Hotsa'at Ahi-Asaf, 1896–9).

GUIBERT OF NOGENT, *A Monk's Confession: The Memoirs of Guibert of Nogent*, trans. Paul J. Archambault (University Park: Penn State University Press, 1996).

GUREVICH, ARON, 'Die Darstellung von Persönlichkeit und Zeit in der mittelalterlichen Kunst und Literatur', *Archiv für Kulturgeschichte*, 71/1 (1988), 1–44.

——*Historical Anthropology of the Middle Ages*, ed. Jane Howlett (Chicago: University of Chicago Press, 1992).

——*Medieval Popular Culture: Problems of Belief and Perception*, trans. János M. Bak and Paul A. Hollingsworth (Cambridge: Cambridge University Press, 1988).

——'Oral and Written Culture of the Middle Ages: Two "Peasant Visions" of the Late Twelfth to the Early Thirteenth Centuries', in Jana Howlett (ed.), *Historical Anthropology of the Middle Ages* (Chicago: University of Chicago Press, 1992), 50–64.

——'Popular and Scholarly Medieval Cultural Traditions: Notes in the Margin of Jacques Le Goff's Book', *Journal of Medieval History*, 9 (1983), 71–90.

HABERMANN, ABRAHAM M., *Persecutions in Medieval Germany and France: Memoirs from Contemporaries of the Period of the Crusades and a Selection of Their Liturgical Poems* [Gezerot ashkenaz vetsarefat: divrei zikhronot mibenei hadorot shebitkufat masa'ei hatselav umivḥar piyuteihem] (Jerusalem: Tarshish and Mosad Harav Kook, 1945).

HALBERSTAM, DAVID, *The Amateurs: The Story of Four Young Men and their Quest for an Olympic Gold Medal* (New York: William Morrow, 1985).

HALEVI, LEOR, *Muhammad's Grave: Death Rites and the Making of Islamic Society* (New York: Columbia University Press, 2007).

HARRIS, MANFORD, 'Dreams in *Sefer Ḥasidim*', *Proceedings of the American Academy for Jewish Research*, 31 (1963), 51–81.

HAVERKAMP, ALFRED, 'Jews and Urban Life: Bonds and Relationships', in Christoph Cluse (ed.), *The Jews of Europe in the Middle Ages (Tenth to Fifteenth Centuries)* (Turnhout: Brepols, 2004), 55–69.

HAVERKAMP, EVA, *Hebräische Berichte über die Judenverfolgungen während des Ersten Kreuzzugs*, Monumenta Germaniae Historica, Hebräische Texte aus dem mittelalterlichen Deutschland (Hanover: Hahnsche Buchhandlung, 2005).

HAZAN, JACOB B. JUDAH OF LONDON, *Ets ḥayim: halakhot, pesakim uminhagim*, ed. Israel Brody, 3 vols. (Jerusalem: Mosad Harav Kook, 1962).

HAZAN-ROKEM, GALIT, *Web of Life: Folklore and Midrash in Rabbinic Literature*, trans. Batya Stein (Stanford, Calif.: Stanford University Press, 2000).

HEALY, JOHN, *Insula Sanctorum et Doctorum or Ireland's Ancient Schools and Scholars* (Dublin: Sealy, Bryers, and Walker, 1908).

Hebrew–English Edition of the Babylonian Talmud, 'Berakhot', trans. Maurice Simon, ed. Isidore Epstein (London: Soncino Press, 1972).

HELLER, BERNARD, 'Notes de Folklore Juif', *Revue des études juives*, 82 (1926), 301–16.

HELVÉTIUS, ANNE-MARIE, 'Le Récit de vengeance des saints dans l'hagiographie franque (VIe–IXe siècle)', in D. Barthélemy, F. Bougard, and R. Le Jan (eds.), *La Vengeance, 400–1200* (Rome: École Française de Rome, 2006), 421–50.

Ḥidushei haritva al bava metsia, ed. Shiloh Rafa'el (Jerusalem: Shiloh Rafa'el, 1992).

HIEBERT, PAUL G., *Transforming Worldviews: An Anthropological Understanding of How People Change* (Grand Rapids, Mich.: Baker Academic, 2008).

HILDBURGH, W. L., 'An English Alabaster Carving of St. Michael Weighing a Soul', *Burlington Magazine for Connoisseurs*, 89/530 (May 1947), 128–31.

——'Iconographical Peculiarities in English Medieval Alabaster Carvings: Part I', *Folklore*, 44/1 (Mar. 1933), 32–56.

HIMMELFARB, MARTHA, *Tours of Hell: An Apocalyptic Form in Jewish and Christian Literature* (Philadelphia: University of Pennsylvania Press, 1983).

HIRSCH, WOOLF, *Psychology in Our Ancient Literature in the Written and Oral Laws* [Hapsikhologyah besifrutenu ha'atikah betorah shebikhtav veshebe'al peh] (Tel Aviv: Devir, 1959).

HO, CYNTHIA, '*Corpus Delicti*: The Edifying Dead in the Exempla of Jacques De Vitry', in Jacqueline Hamesse et al. (eds.), *Medieval Sermons and Society: Cloister, City, University*, Textes et Études du Moyen Âge 9 (Louvain-la-Neuve: Fédération Internationale des Instituts d'Études Médiévales, 1998), 203–18.

HOLLENDER, ELISABETH, *Clavis Commentariorum of Hebrew Liturgical Poetry in Manuscript*, Clavis Commentariorum Antiquitatis et Medii Aevi 4 (Leiden: Brill, 2005).

HOROWITZ, ELLIOT, 'Regarding Kissing the Dead in the Mediterranean Region' (Heb.), *Tarbiz*, 67 (1998), 131–4.

——'Speaking to the Dead: Cemetery Prayer in Medieval and Early Modern Jewry', *Journal of Jewish Thought and Philosophy*, 8 (1999), 310–35.

Huizinga, Johan, *The Waning of the Middle Ages: Study of the Forms of Life, Thought and Art in France and the Netherlands in the Fourteenth and Fifteenth Centuries*, trans. F. Hopman (London: E. Arnold, 1937).

Hunt, Noreen, *Cluniac Monasticism in the Central Middle Ages* (Hamden, Conn.: Archon, 1971).

——*Cluny Under St. Hugh: 1049–1109* (London: Edward Arnold, 1967).

Hyams, Paul, *Rancor and Reconciliation in Medieval England* (Ithaca, NY: Cornell University Press, 2003).

Idel, Moshe, 'Gazing at the Head in Ashkenazi Hasidism', *Journal of Jewish Thought and Philosophy*, 6 (1997), 265–300.

——'On *She'elat Ḥalom* in Ḥasidei Ashkenaz: Sources and Influences', *Materia Giudaica*, 10/1 (2005), 99–109.

——'Regarding the Identity of the Authors of two Ashkenazi Commentaries on the Liturgical Poem "Ha'aderet veha'emunah" and on R. Eleazar of Worms's Conception of the Theurgy and the Kavod' (Heb.), *Kabbalah*, 29 (2013), 67–208.

Idelman Smith, Jane, and Yvonne Yazbeck Haddad, *The Islamic Understanding of Death and Resurrection* (Albany, NY: SUNY Press, 1981).

Iogna-Prat, Dominique, and Jean-Charles Picard, 'Les Morts dans la comptabilité céleste des clunisiens de l'an mil', in Dominique Iogna-Prat (ed.), *Religion et culture autour de l'an mil: Royaume capétien et lotharingie* (Paris: Picard, 1990), 55–69.

——*Order and Exclusion: Cluny and Christendom Face Heresy, Judaism and Islam: 1000–1150*, trans. Graham R. Edwards (Ithaca, NY: Cornell University Press, 2002).

Ireland, Colin, 'Penance and Prayer in Water: An Irish Practice in Northumbrian Hagiography', *Cambrian Medieval Celtic Studies*, 34 (1997), 51–66.

The Irish Penitentials. Scriptores Latini Hibernae, trans. and ed. Ludwig Bieler, vol. v (Dublin: Dublin Institute for Advanced Studies, 1963).

Isaac b. Joseph of Corbeil, *Sefer amudei golah*, ed. Dovid Harfenis (Satmar, 1935; repr. Jerusalem: Mefitsei Or, 1958).

Isaac of Vienna, *Or zarua*, ed. Yaakov Farbshtain, 3 vols. (Jerusalem: Mekhon Yerushalayim, 2010).

Jacobus de Voragine, *The Golden Legend: Readings on the Saints*, trans. William G. Ryan, 2 vols. (Princeton, NJ: Princeton University Press, 1993).

Jacques de Vitry, *The Exempla or Illustrative Stories from the Sermones Vulgares of Jacques de Vitry*, ed. Thomas F. Crane (London, 1890; repr. New York: Burt Franklin, 1971).

James, M. R., 'Twelve Medieval Ghost Stories', *English Historical Review*, 37 (1922), 413–22.

Jellinek, Adolf (ed.), *Beit hamidrash*, vol. i (Leipzig, 1853; repr. Jerusalem: Wahrman, 1967).

Johnson, Máire, '"Vengeance Is Mine": Saintly Retribution in Medieval Ireland', in Susanna A. Throop and Paul R. Hyams (eds.), *Vengeance in the Middle Ages: Emotion, Religion and Feud* (Farnham, Surrey: Ashgate, 2010), 5–37.

JOHNSON, PENELOPE D., *Prayer, Patronage, and Power: The Abbey of la Trinité, Vendôme, 1032–1187* (New York: NYU Press, 1981).

JOSEPH B. MOSES, *Sefer leket yosher*, ed. Jacob Freimann (Frankfurt am Main: Mekitsei Nirdamim, 1903/4).

JOYNES, ANDREW (ed.), *Medieval Ghost Stories: An Anthology of Miracles, Marvels, and Prodigies* (Woodbridge, Suffolk: Boydell, 2001).

JUDAH HEHASID (the Pious), *Perushei hatorah lerabenu yehudah heḥasid*, ed. Yitshak S. Lange (Jerusalem: Lange, 1975).

——*Sefer gematriyot lerabenu yehudah heḥasid*, ed. Ya'akov Y. Stahl, 2 vols. (Jerusalem: Leor, 2005).

——*Sefer ḥasidim*, ed. Reuven Margaliot (Jerusalem: Mosad Harav Kook, 1957).

——*Sefer ḥasidim*, ed. Judah Wistinetzky (Berlin, 1891; repr. Jerusalem: Mekitsei Nirdamim, 1998).

——'The Testament of R. Judah the Pious' [Tsava'at rabenu yehudah heḥasid], in *Sefer ḥasidim*, ed. Margaliot (Jerusalem: Mosad Harav Kook, 1957), 10–34.

KAEUPER, RICHARD W., *Holy Warrior: The Religious Ideology of Chivalry* (Philadelphia: University of Pennsylvania Press, 2009).

KAHANA, MAOZ, 'Sources of Knowledge and the Vicissitudes of Time: The Will of R. Judah the Pious in Modern Times' (Heb.), in Hayim Kreisel, Boaz Huss, and Uri Ehrlich (eds.), *Spiritual Authority: Struggles over Cultural Power in Jewish Thought* [Samkhut ruḥanit: ma'avakim al ko'aḥ tarbuti behagut hayehudit] (Beer Sheva: Ben-Gurion University Press, 2009), 223–62.

KAMELHAR, YEKUTIEL, *The First Pietists* [Haḥasidim harishonim] (Waizen, 1917).

KANARFOGEL, EPHRAIM, *Jewish Education and Society in the High Middle Ages* (Detroit: Wayne State University Press, 2008).

——*Peering through the Lattices: Mystical, Magical, and Pietistic Dimensions in the Tosafist Period* (Detroit: Wayne State University Press, 2000).

——'Rabbinic Attitudes toward Non-Observance in the Medieval Period', in Jacob J. Schacter (ed.), *Jewish Tradition and the Nontraditional Jew* (Northvale, NJ: Jason Aronson, 1992), 3–35.

——'The Scope of Talmudic Commentary in Europe during the High Middle Ages', in Sharon L. Mintz and Gabriel M. Goldstein (eds.), *Printing the Talmud: From Bomberg to Schottenstein* (New York: Yeshiva University Museum, 2005), 37–52.

KASHER, MENAHEM, and YAAKOV MANDELBAUM (eds.), *The Officers of Thousands: A Millennium of Hebrew Authors, 500–1500 CE: A Complete Bibliographical Compendium of Hebraica Written during the Thousand-Year Period between the Close of the Talmud and the Beginning of the Shulḥan Arukh* [Sarei ha'elef: reshimat hasefarim shebidfus umeḥabreihem sheḥayu batekufah bat elef shanim mizman ḥatimat hatalmud ad tekufat hashulḥan arukh], 2 vols. (Jerusalem: Torah Shelemah, 1984).

KATZ, JACOB, *Exclusiveness and Tolerance: Studies in Jewish–Gentile Relations in Medieval and Modern Times* (London: Oxford University Press, 1961).

KATZENELLENBOGEN, ADOLF, *The Sculptural Programs of Chartres Cathedral: Christ, Mary, Ecclesia* (Baltimore: Johns Hopkins University Press, 1959).

KELLY, FERGUS, *A Guide to Early Irish Law*, Early Irish Law Series 3 (Dublin: Dublin Institute for Advanced Studies, 1988).

KIMHI, JOSEPH, *The Book of the Covenant of Joseph Kimḥi*, trans. Frank Talmage (Toronto: Pontifical Institute of Medieval Studies, 1972).

KLAPHOLZ, ISRAEL, *Stories of Elijah the Prophet: A Collection of Stories and Traditions Gathered from the Babylonian and Palestinian Talmuds, Midrashim and Books of Early and Later Sages*, trans. Abigail Nadav, 3 vols. (Benei Berak: Pe'er Hasefer, 1970–3).

KLEINIG, JOHN, *Punishment and Desert* (The Hague: Martinus Nijhoff, 1973).

KOHEN, NAFTALI, *Otsar hagedolim, alufei ya'akov*, 9 vols. (Haifa: Hakohen, 1967–70).

KOHLER, KAUFMANN, *Heaven and Hell in Comparative Religion: With Special Reference to Dante's Divine Comedy* (New York: Macmillan, 1923).

KOSMAN, ADMIEL, 'Kissing the Dead: Regarding the Shifts and Vicissitudes of a Custom' (Heb.), *Tarbiz*, 65 (1996), 483–503.

KOZMA, EMESE, 'The Practice of *Teshuvah* (Penance) in the Medieval Ashkenazi Jewish Communities' (Ph.D. diss., Eötvös Loránd University, Budapest, 2012).

KUPFER, EPHRAIM, 'The History of the Family of R. Moses b. Yom Tov, "Knight of the World" of London' (Heb.), *Tarbiz*, 40/3 (1971), 384–7.

KUSHELEVSKY, RELLA, *Penalty and Temptation: Hebrew Tales in Ashkenaz: MS Parma 2295, De Rossi 563* [Sigufim ufituyim: hasipur ha'ivri be'ashkenaz, ketav yad parma 2295, derossi 563] (Jerusalem: Magnes Press, 2010).

——'Rabbi Joshua b. Levi and the Angel of Death' (Heb.), in Yoav Elstein, Avidav Lipsker, and Rella Kushelevsky (eds.), *Encyclopedia of the Jewish Story: A Story Following a Story* [Entsiklopedyah shel hasipur hayehudi: sipur okev sipur] (Ramat Gan: Bar-Ilan University Press, 2004), 261–79.

LARSON, ATRIA A., *Master of Penance: Gratian and the Development of Penitential Thought and Law in the Twelfth Century*, Studies in Medieval and Early Modern Canon Law 11 (Washington, DC: Catholic University of America Press, 2014).

LAUWERS, MICHEL, *La Mémoire des ancêtres. Le Souci des morts. Morts, rites et société au Moyen Âge* (Paris, 1997).

——*Naissance du cimetière: Lieux sacrés et terre des morts dans l'Occident médiéval* (Paris: Aubier, 2005).

LECOUTEUX, CLAUDE, *Chasses fantastiques et cohortes de la nuit au Moyen Âge* (Paris: Imago, 1999).

——*Fantômes et revenants au Moyen Âge*, 2nd edn. (Paris: Imago, 1996).

——*The Return of the Dead: Ghosts, Ancestors, and the Transparent Veil of the Pagan Mind*, trans. Jon E. Graham (Rochester, Vt.: Inner Traditions, 2009).

——and PHILIPPE MARCQ (eds.), *Les Esprits et les morts, croyances médiévales* (Paris: Honoré Champion, 1990).

LE GOFF, JACQUES, *The Birth of Purgatory* (Chicago: University of Chicago Press, 1984).

——*La Bourse et la vie: Économie et religion au Moyen Âge* (Paris: Hachette, 1986).

Le Goff, Jacques, 'Christianity and Dreams (Second to Seventh Century)', in id., *The Medieval Imagination*, trans. Arthur Goldhammer (Chicago: University of Chicago Press, 1988), 193–231.

——'Dreams in the Culture and Collective Psychology of the Medieval West', in Jacques Le Goff (ed.), *Time, Work, and Culture in the Middle Ages*, trans. Arthur Goldhammer (Chicago: University of Chicago Press, 1980), 201–4.

——'Gestures in Purgatory', in id., *The Medieval Imagination*, trans. Arthur Goldhammer (Chicago: University of Chicago Press, 1988), 86–92.

——'The Learned and Popular Dimensions of Journeys in the Otherworld in the Middle Ages', in Steven L. Kaplan (ed.), *Understanding Popular Culture: Europe from the Middle Ages to the Nineteenth Century* (Berlin: Mouton, 1984), 19–37.

——'The Time of the Exemplum (Thirteenth Century)', in id., *The Medieval Imagination*, trans. Arthur Goldhammer (Chicago: University of Chicago Press, 1988), 78–82.

——'The Time of Purgatory (Third to Thirteenth Century)', in id., *The Medieval Imagination*, trans. Arthur Goldhammer (Chicago: University of Chicago Press, 1988), 67–77.

——*Your Money or Your Life: Economy and Religion in the Middle Ages*, trans. Patricia Ranum (New York: Zone, 1988).

Lekai, Louis J., *The Cistercians: Ideals and Reality* (Kent State, Ohio: Kent State University Press, 1977).

——*The White Monks: A History of the Cistercian Order* (Okauchee, Wis.: Cistercian Fathers, Our Lady of Spring Bank, 1953).

Lerner, Meron B., 'The Story of the Tanna and the Dead: Its Literary and Halakhic Vicissitudes' (Heb.), *Asufot*, 2 (1988), 29–70.

Lévi, Israel, 'La Commémoration des âmes dans le Judaïsme', *Revue des études juives*, 29 (1894), 43–60.

——'Le Repos sabbatique des âmes damnées', *Revue des études juives*, 25 (1892), 1–13.

Liber exemplorum ad usum praedicantium, ed. Andrew George Little, British Society of Franciscan Studies 1 (Aberdoniae: Typis Academicis, 1908).

Lichtenstein, Yechezkel, 'From the Impurity of the Dead to Their Sanctification' [Mitumat hamet lehakdashato] (Ph.D. diss., Bar-Ilan University, 1997).

——*From Impurity to Sanctity: Prayer and Ritual Objects in Cemeteries and Pilgrimage to the Graves of the Righteous* [Mitumah likdushah: tefilah veḥeftsei mitsvah bevatei kevarot ve'aliyah lekivrei tsadikim] (Tel Aviv: Hakibutz Hame'uhad, 2007).

Lieberman, Saul, 'On Sins and Their Punishment', in id., *Texts and Studies* (New York: Ktav, 1974), 29–51.

——'Some Aspects of After Life in Early Rabbinic Literature', in id., *Texts and Studies* (New York: Ktav, 1974), 235–72.

Little, Lester K., 'Anger in Monastic Curses', in Barbara H. Rosenwein (ed.), *Anger's Past: The Social Uses of an Emotion in the Middle Ages* (Ithaca, NY: Cornell University Press, 1998), 9–33.

——*Benedictine Maledictions: Liturgical Cursing in Romanesque France* (Ithaca, NY: Cornell University Press, 1993).

——'Pride Goes Before Avarice: Social Change and the Vices in Latin Christendom', *American Historical Review*, 76 (1971), 16–49.

——'Romanesque Christianity in Germanic Europe', *Journal of Interdisciplinary History*, 23/3 (1993), 453–74.

LIVINGSTONE, ELIZABETH A. (ed.), *The Concise Oxford Dictionary of the Christian Church*, 2nd edn., abridged (Oxford: Oxford University Press, 1977).

MCGUIRE, BRIAN P., 'The Cistercians and the Rise of the *Exemplum* in Early Thirteenth-Century France: A Reevaluation of Paris BN MS Lat. 15912', *Classica et Mediaevalia*, 34 (1983), 211–67.

——'Purgatory, the Communion of Saints, and Medieval Change', *Viator*, 20 (1989), 61–9.

MCLAUGHLIN, MEGAN, 'Consorting with Saints: Prayer for the Dead in Early Medieval French Society' (Ph.D. diss., Stanford University, 1985).

——*Consorting with Saints: Prayer for the Dead in Medieval France* (Ithaca, NY: Cornell University Press, 1994).

MCNEILL, JOHN T., *The Celtic Penitentials and Their Influence on Continental Christianity* (Paris: É. Champion, 1923).

——and HELENA M. GAMER, *Medieval Handbooks of Penance: A Translation of the Principal 'Libri Poenitentiales' and Selections from Related Documents* (New York: Columbia University Press, 1938).

MAIMONIDES, MOSES, *Rambam le'am: sefer mada*, ed. Shmuel T. Rubenstein (Jerusalem: Mosad Harav Kook, 1993).

MÂLE, ÉMILE, *The Gothic Image: Religious Art in France of the Thirteenth Century*, trans. Dora Nussey (New York: Harper, 1958).

——*Religious Art in France. The Twelfth Century: A Study in the Origins of Medieval Iconography* (Princeton, NJ: Princeton University Press, 1978).

MANSFIELD, MARY C., *The Humiliation of Sinners: Public Penance in Thirteenth-Century France* (Ithaca, NY: Cornell University Press, 1995).

MAP, WALTER, *De Nugis Curialium: Courtiers' Trifles*, trans. and ed. Montague R. James (Oxford: Clarendon Press, 1983).

MARCUS, IVAN G., 'From Politics to Martyrdom: Shifting Paradigms in the Hebrew Narratives of the 1096 Crusade Riots', *Prooftexts*, 2/1 (1982), 40–52.

——'Hasidei Ashkenaz Private Penitentials: An Introduction and Descriptive Catalogue of Their Manuscripts and Early Editions', in Joseph Dan and Frank Talmage (eds.), *Studies in Jewish Mysticism* (Cambridge, Mass.: Association for Jewish Studies), 57–83.

——'The Penitentials of the German Jewish Pietists' (Heb.), in Joseph Dan and Joseph Hacker (eds.), *Studies in Jewish Mysticism, Philosophy, and Ethical Literature: Presented to Isaiah Tishby on his 75th Birthday* [Meḥkarim bekabalah, befilosofyah yehudit uvesifrut hamusar vehahagut: mugashim liyshayah tishbi bimlot lo shivim veḥamesh shanim] (Jerusalem: Magnes Press, 1986), 369–84.

——*Piety and Society: The Jewish Pietists of Medieval Germany*, Études sur le Judaïsme Médiéval 10 (Leiden: Brill, 1981).

——'The Recensions and Structure of "Sefer Ḥasidim"', *Proceedings of the American Academy for Jewish Research*, 45 (1978), 131–53.

MARCUS, IVAN G., *Rituals of Childhood: Jewish Acculturation in Medieval Europe* (New Haven: Yale University Press, 1996).

——*Sefer Ḥasidim and the Ashkenazic Book in Medieval Europe* (Philadelphia: University of Pennsylvania Press, 2018).

MARMORSTEIN, ARTHUR, *The Doctrine of Merits in Old Rabbinical Literature* (London: Oxford University Press, 1920).

MARTIN, J. D., 'Law and the (Un)Dead: Medieval Models for Understanding the Hauntings in *Eyrbyggja Saga*', *Saga-Book: Viking Society for Northern Research*, 19 (2005), 67–82.

'Masekhet gehinom', in Adolf Jellinek (ed.), *Beit hamidrash* (Leipzig, 1853; repr. Jerusalem: Wahrman, 1967), i. 147–9.

MATSUDA, TAKAMI, *Death and Purgatory in Middle English Didactic Poetry* (Cambridge: D. S. Brewer, 1997).

MEIR OF ROTHENBURG, *Hilkhot semaḥot hashalem*, ed. Akiva D. and Yaakov A. Landau (Jerusalem: n.p., 1976).

——*Sefer minhagim devei maharam mirotenburg*, ed. Yisrael S. Alfenbein (New York: n.p., 1967).

——*She'elot uteshuvot maharam bar barukh* [responsa], ed. Mosheh A. Bloch (Budapest: Y. Sternberg, 1894/5).

——*Teshuvot, pesakim uminhagim*, ed. Yitshak Z. Kahana, vol. iii (Jerusalem: Mosad Harav Kook, 1957).

METZGER, THÉRÈSE, and MENDEL METZGER, *Jewish Life in the Middle Ages: Illuminated Hebrew Manuscripts of the Thirteenth through the Sixteenth Centuries* (New York: Alpine Fine Arts Collection, 1982).

'Midrash aseret hadibrot', in Adolf Jellinek (ed.), *Beit hamidrash* (Leipzig, 1853; repr. Jerusalem: Wahrman, 1967), i. 62–90.

Midrash bemidbar rabah, ed. Ephraim Halevi Epstein (Tel Aviv: Hotsa'at Mehabrot Lesifrut, 1963).

Midrash bereshit rabah, ed. J. Theodor and Hanokh Albeck, 3 vols. (Berlin, 1903–29; repr. Jerusalem: Wahrman, 1965).

Midrash bereshit rabati nosad al sifro shel rabi mosheh hadarshan, ed. Hanokh Albeck (Jerusalem: Mekitsei Nirdamim, 1940).

Midrash shemot rabah, ed. Avigdor Shinan (Jerusalem: Dvir, 1984).

Midrash tanḥuma hakadum vehayashan, meyuḥas lerabi tanḥuma berabi aba, al ḥamishah ḥumshei torah, ed. Salomon Buber (Vilna: Romm, 1913; repr. New York: Sefer, 1946).

Midrash tanḥuma hamefo'ar, 2 vols. (Jerusalem, 1998).

Midrash tehilim hamekhuneh shoḥer tov, ed. Salomon Buber (Jerusalem: n.p., 1965/6).

Midrash vayikra rabah: al pi kitvei yad useridei hagenizah, im ḥilufei nusḥaot vehe'arot, ed. Mordekhai Margaliot, 4 vols. (Jerusalem: Misrad Hahinukh Vehatarbut shel Medinat Yisra'el, 1953–60).

MILIKOWSKY, HAYM, 'Gehenna and Jewish Sinners according to the *Seder Olam*' (Heb.), *Tarbiz*, 55 (1986), 311–43.

Millénaire monastique du Mont Saint-Michel, iii: *Culte de Saint Michel et pèlerinages au mont*, Bibliothèque d'Histoire et d'Archéologie Chrétiennes (Paris: P. Lethielleux, 1971).

MILLER, DEAN A., *The Epic Hero* (Baltimore: Johns Hopkins University Press, 2000).

MILLER, WILLIAM I., *Bloodtaking and Peacemaking: Feud, Law, and Society in Saga Iceland* (Chicago: University of Chicago Press, 1990).

——'Choosing the Avenger: Some Aspects of the Bloodfeud in Medieval Iceland and England', *Law and History Review*, 1/2 (Autumn 1983), 159–204.

——*Humiliation and Other Essays on Honor, Social Discomfort and Violence* (Ithaca, NY: Cornell University Press, 1993).

MOORE, GEORGE F., *Judaism in the First Centuries of the Christian Era: The Age of the Tannaim*, 2 vols. (1927, 1930; repr. Cambridge, Mass.: Harvard University Press, 1958).

MORDECAI B. HILLEL HAKOHEN, *Sefer hamordekhai*, printed in standard editions of the Babylonian Talmud.

MOSES OF COUCY, *Sefer mitsvot gadol*, ed. Elyakim Schlesinger, 3 vols. (Jerusalem: Elyakim Schlesinger, 1989).

MOSES OF ZURICH, *Sefer hasemak mitsurikh*, ed. Yitshak Y. Har-Shoshanim-Rozenberg, 3 vols. (Jerusalem: n.p., 1973).

MURPHY, JEFFRIE G., *Getting Even: Forgiveness and Its Limits* (Oxford: Oxford University Press, 2003).

NAGY, PIROSKA, and ALAIN BOUREAU, *Le Don des larmes au Moyen Age: Un instrument spirituel en quête d'institution (Xe-XIIIe siècle)* (Paris: A. Michel, 2000).

NAHMANIDES, MOSES, *Torat ha'adam*, in *Kitvei ramban*, ed. Chaim D. Chavel, vol. ii (Jerusalem: Mosad Harav Kook, 1964), 9–311.

NEUBAUER, ADOLF R., 'Le Memorbuch de Mayence: Essai sur la littérature des complaints', *Revue des études juives*, 4 (1882), 1–30.

NOZICK, ROBERT, *Philosophical Explanations* (Cambridge, Mass.: Harvard University Press, 1981).

NTEDIKA, JOSEPH, *L'Évocation de l'au-delà dans la prière pour les morts: Étude de patristique et de liturgie latines IVe–VIIIe s.*, Recherches Africaines de Théologie 2 (Leuven: Editions Nauwelaerts, 1971).

ODEBERG, HUGO (trans. and ed.), *3 Enoch or The Hebrew Book of Enoch* (New York: Ktav, 1973).

O'HANLON, JOHN, *Lives of the Irish Saints*, vol. vi (Dublin: James Duffy and Sons, 1873).

ORDERIC VITALIS, *The Ecclesiastical History of England and Normandy*, trans. Thomas Forrester, vol. ii (London: Henry G. Bohn, 1854).

Orḥot ḥayim lerav aharon hakohen milunel, vol. ii (Berlin: Mekitsei Nirdamim, 1902).

Ó RIAIN, DIARMUID, 'The *Magnum Legendarium Austriacum*: A New Investigation of One of Europe's Richest Hagiographical Collections', *Analecta Bollandiana*, 133 (2015), 87–165.

Ó Riain, Diarmuid, '*Schottenklöster*: The Early History and Architecture of the Irish Benedictine Monasteries in Medieval Germany' (Ph.D. diss., School of Archaeology, University College Dublin, 2008).

Ó Riain-Raedel, Dagmar, 'Aspects of the Promotion of Irish Saints' Cults in Medieval Germany', *Zeitschrift für Celtische Philologie*, 39/1 (1982), 220–34.

——'Cashel and Germany: The Documentary Evidence', in Damian Bracken and Dagmar Ó Riain-Raedel (eds.), *Ireland and Europe in the Twelfth Century: Reform and Renewal* (Dublin: Four Courts Press, 2006), 176–217.

——'Ireland and Austria in the Middle Ages: The Role of the Irish Monks in Austria', in id., *Austro-Irish Links through the Centuries* (Vienna: Diplomatische Akadamie Wien, 2002), 11–40.

——'The Travel of Irish Manuscripts from the Continent to Ireland', in Toby Barnard, Dáibhí Ó Cróinín, and Katharine Simms (eds.), *A Miracle of Learning: Studies in Manuscripts and Irish Learning in Honor of William O'Sullivan* (Aldershot, Hants.: Ashgate, 1998), 52–67.

Otsar hage'onim: teshuvot ge'onei bavel uferusheihem al pi seder hatalmud: yom tov, ḥagigah, mashkin (mo'ed katan), ed. B. M. Levin (Jerusalem: Hebrew University Press, 1931/2).

Palmer, Barbara D., 'The Inhabitants of Hell: Devils', in C. Davidson and T. H. Seiler (eds.), *The Iconography of Hell* (Kalamazoo: Medieval Institute Publications, 1992), 20–36.

Palmer, Nigel F., *'Visio Tnugdali': The German and Dutch Translations and Their Circulation in the Later Middle Ages* (Munich: Artemis, 1982).

Patch, Howard R., *The Other World According to Descriptions in Medieval Literature* (Cambridge, Mass.: Harvard University Press, 1950).

Paxton, Frederick S., *Christianizing Death: The Creation of a Ritual Process in Early Medieval Europe* (Ithaca, NY: Cornell University Press, 1990).

Payen, Jean Charles, *Le Motif de repentir dans la littérature française médiévale* (Geneva: Droz, 1967).

Pelikan, Jaroslav, *Mary through the Centuries: Her Place in the History of Culture* (New Haven, Conn.: Yale University Press, 1996).

Perez, Ido, 'The Dead in the World of the Living: Ghost Stories in the Medieval Hebrew Narrative' [Metim be'olam haḥayim: sipurei ruḥot basipur ha'ivri biymei habenayim] (MA thesis, Tel Aviv University, 2005).

Perry, Mary P., 'On the Psychostasis in Christian Art—I', *Burlington Magazine for Connoisseurs*, 22/116 (Nov. 1912), 94–105.

——'On the Psychostasis in Christian Art—II', *Burlington Magazine for Connoisseurs*, 22/118 (Jan. 1913), 208–18.

Perry, Micha, 'Jewish Heaven and Christian Hell: Rabbi Joshua ben Levi's Vision of the Afterlife', *Journal of Medieval History*, 43/2 (2017), 212–27.

——*Tradition and Change: The Transmission of Knowledge amongst the Jews of Western Europe in the Middle Ages* [Masoret veshinui: mesirat yeda bekerev yehudei ma'arav eiropah biymei habeinayim] (Tel Aviv: Hakibutz Hame'uhad, 2010).

Pesikta rabati, ed. M. Ish-Shalom (Vienna, 1880).

Piskei harosh al masekhet mo'ed katan, Babylonian Talmud, any standard edn.

PLANTINGA, ALVIN, *Essays in the Metaphysics of Modality*, ed. M. Davidson (New York: Oxford University Press, 2003).

——and MICHAEL TOOLEY, *Knowledge of God* (Oxford: Blackwell Publishing, 2008).

PLATELLE, HENRI, 'Crime et châtiment à Marchiennes', in H. Platelle, *Présence de l'Au-delà: Une vision médiévale du monde* (Paris: Septentrion, 2004), 159–88.

POZNANSKY, SAMUEL, *An Introduction to the Commentary of Eliezer Beaugency on Ezekiel and the Minor Prophets* [Mavo leferush al yeḥezkel utrei asar lerabi eli'ezer beaugency] (Warsaw, 1931).

——'Megilat setarim' (Heb.), *Hatsofeh leḥokhmat yisra'el*, 5 (1921), 177–93.

RASPE, LUCIA, 'A Medieval Sage in Early Modern Folk Narrative: The Case of Rashi and Godfrey of Bouillon', in D. Krochmalnik, H. Liss, and R. Reichman (eds.), *Raschi und sein Erbe: Internationale Tagung der Hochschule für Jüdische Studien mit der Stadt Worms* (Heidelberg: Heidelberg University Press, 2007), 125–61.

——'Sacred Space, Local History, and Diasporic Identity: The Graves of the Righteous in Medieval and Early Modern Ashkenaz', in Ra'anan S. Boustan, Oren Kosansky, and Marina Rustow (eds.), *Jewish Studies at the Crossroads of Anthropology and History: Authority, Diaspora, Tradition, Jewish Culture and Contexts* (Philadelphia: University of Pennsylvania Press, 2011), 147–63.

REICH, E., 'Sacrifice for Mitsvah Observance: Ideologies and Shifts from Rabbinic Literature to Early Ashkenaz' [Mesirat hanefesh al kiyum hamitsvot: ide-'ologyot utemurot misifrut ḥazal ad ashkenaz hakedumah] (Ph.D. diss., Bar-Ilan University, 2012).

REIF, STEFAN C., ANDREAS LEHNARDT, and AVRIEL BAR-LEVAV (eds.), *Death in Jewish Life: Burial and Mourning Customs among Jews of Europe and Nearby Communities* (Berlin: De Gruyter, 2014).

REINACH, S., 'L'Origine des prières pour les morts', *Revue des études juives*, 41–42 (1900), 161–73.

REINER, AVRAHAM (RAMI), 'The Dead as Living History: On the Publication of *Die Grabsteine vom jüdischen Friedhof in Würzburg 1147–1346*', in Stefan C. Reif, Andreas Lehnardt, and Avriel Bar-Levav (eds.), *Death in Jewish Life: Burial and Mourning Customs among Jews of Europe and Nearby Communities* (Berlin: De Gruyter, 2014), 199–211.

——'From "Paradise" to "Bound in the Bonds of Life": Blessings for the Dead on Tombstones in Medieval Ashkenaz' (Heb.), *Zion*, 76 (2011), 5–28.

RICHARDS, PETER, *The Medieval Leper and His Northern Heirs* (Cambridge: D. S. Brewer, 2000).

RIDER, CATHERINE, 'Agreements to Return from the Afterlife in Late Medieval Exempla', in P. Clarke and T. Claydon (eds.), *The Church, the Afterlife, and the Fate of the Soul*, Studies in Church History 45 (Woodbridge, Suffolk: Boydell, 2009), 174–84.

ROCHE, THOMAS, 'The Way Vengeance Comes: Rancorous Deeds and Words in the World of Orderic Vitalis', in S. A. Throop and P. R. Hyams (eds.), *Vengeance in the Middle Ages: Emotion, Religion, and Feud* (Farnham, Surrey: Ashgate, 2010), 115–36.

ROSENTHAL, JOEL THOMAS, *The Purchase of Paradise: Gift-Giving and the Aristocracy, 1307–1485* (London: Routledge, 1972).

ROSENWEIN, BARBARA H., THOMAS HEAD, and SHARON FARMER, 'Monks and Their Enemies: A Comparative Approach', *Speculum*, 66/4 (1991), 764–96.

ROSEN-ZVI, ISHAY, *Demonic Desires: 'Yetzer Hara' and the Problem of Evil in Late Antiquity* (Philadelphia: University of Pennsylvania Press, 2011).

ROTH, ABRAHAM Z. N., 'Memorial Prayer, Haftarah, and the Orphan's Kaddish' (Heb.), *Talpiyot*, 7/2–4 (1961), 369–81.

ROTHWAGER, JOY, '*Sefer Pa'aneah Raza* and Biblical Exegesis in Medieval Ashkenaz' (MA thesis, Touro College, 2000).

ROTMAN, DAVID, 'The Marvellous in the Medieval Hebrew Narrative' [Hamufla basipur ha'ivri biymei habeinayim] (Ph.D. diss., Tel Aviv University, 2011).

RUBIN, ASHER, 'The Concept of Repentance among *Hasidey 'Ashkenaz*', *Journal of Jewish Studies*, 16/3 (1965), 161–76.

RUBIN, NISSAN, *The End of Life: Rites of Burial and Mourning in the Talmud and Midrash* [Kets haḥayim: tiksei kevurah ve'evel bimkorot ḥazal] (Tel Aviv: Hakibutz Hame'uhad, 1997).

RUSSELL, JAMES, *The Germanization of Early Medieval Christianity: A Socio-Historical Approach to Religious Transformation* (Oxford: Oxford University Press, 1994).

RYAN, SALVADOR, 'Fixing the Eschatological Scales: Judgement of the Soul in Late Medieval and Early Modern Irish Tradition', in P. Clarke and T. Claydon (eds.), *The Church, the Afterlife, and the Fate of the Soul*, Studies in Church History 45 (Woodbridge, Suffolk: Boydell, 2009), 184–95.

SALDARINI, ANTHONY J., 'Last Words and Deathbed Scenes in Rabbinic Literature', *Jewish Quarterly Review*, 68/1 (1977), 28–45.

SALLER, RICHARD P., *Personal Patronage under the Early Empire* (Cambridge: Cambridge University Press, 1982).

SCHÄFER, PETER, 'The Ideal of Piety of the Ashkenazi Hasidim and Its Roots in Jewish Tradition', *Jewish History*, 4/2 (1990), 9–23.

——'In Heaven as It Is in Hell', in Ra'anan S. Boustan and Annette Y. Reed (eds.), *Heavenly Realms and Earthly Realities in Late Antique Religions* (Cambridge: Cambridge University Press, 2004), 233–74.

——*Synopse zur Hekhalot-Literatur* (Tübingen: J. C. B. Mohr, 1981).

SCHMIDT, GARY D., *The Iconography of the Mouth of Hell: Eighth-Century Britain to the Fifteenth Century* (Selinsgrove, Pa.: Susquehanna University Press, 1995).

SCHMITT, JEAN-CLAUDE, *Conversion of Herman the Jew: Autobiography, History, and Fiction in the Twelfth Century*, trans. Alex J. Novikoff (Philadelphia: University of Pennsylvania Press, 2010).

——*Ghosts in the Middle Ages: The Living and the Dead in Medieval Society*, trans. Teresa L. Fagan (Chicago: University of Chicago Press, 1998).

——'Les Images des revenants', in Danièle Alexandre-Bidon and Cécille Treffor (eds.), *À réveiller les morts: La Mort au quotidien dans l'Occident médiéval* (Lyon: Presses Universitaires de Lyon, 1993), 287–93.

——'The Liminality and Centrality of Dreams in the Medieval West', in David Shulman and Guy G. Stroumsa (eds.), *Dream Cultures: Toward a Comparative History of Dreaming* (New York: Oxford University Press, 1989), 281–6.

SCHOLEM, GERSHOM, *Major Trends in Jewish Mysticism* (New York: Schocken Books, 1941).

SCHREMER, A., 'Regarding the Commentaries on Tractate *Mo'ed Katan* Attributed to Rashi' (Heb.), in Daniel Boyarin et al. (eds.), *A Crown for the Living: Studies in Talmudic and Rabbinic Literature in Honor of Professor Hayim Zalman Dimitrovsky* [Atarah leḥayim: meḥkarim basifrut hatalmudit veharabanit likhvod profesor ḥayim zalman dimitrovski] (Jerusalem: Magnes Press, 2000), 534–54.

SCHUR, YECHIEL, 'The Care for the Dead in Medieval Ashkenaz, 1000–1500' (Ph.D. diss., New York University, 2008).

——'When the Grave Was Searched, the Bones of the Deceased Were Not Found', in Stefan C. Reif, Andreas Lehnardt, and Avriel Bar-Levav (eds.), *Death in Jewish Life: Burial and Mourning Customs among Jews of Europe and Nearby Communities* (Berlin: De Gruyter, 2014), 171–86.

SED-RAJNA, GABRIELLE, *Le Maḥzor enluminé: Les Voies de formation d'un programme iconographique* (Leiden: Brill, 1983).

Sefer dikdukei soferim, ed. Raphael N. N. Rabinowitz, vol. i: *Berakhot* (1877; repr. Jerusalem: Or Hahokhmah, 2002); vol. ix: *Bava kama*, *Bava metsia* (1882–3; repr. Jerusalem: Or Hahokhmah, 2001).

Sefer ma'aseh hage'onim, ed. Abraham Epstein (Berlin, 1910; repr. Jerusalem: Mekitsei Nirdamim, 1981).

Sefer ma'asiyot:ḥibur yafeh min hayeshuah (Benei Berak: Mishor, 1985).

Sefer megilat setarim, in *Rabbi Nisim Gaon: Five Books* [Rav nisim ga'on: ḥamishah sefarim], ed. Shraga Abramson (Jerusalem: Mekitsei Nirdamim, 1965).

Sefer moshav zekenim al hatorah: kovets perushei raboteinu ba'alei tosafot, ed. Solomon D. Sassoon (London: S. D. Sassoon, 1959).

Sefer sha'arei tsedek: teshuvot hage'onim, ed. M. Safra (1792; repr. Jerusalem: Kelal Uferat, 1966).

Sefer tana devei eliyahu: seder eliyahu rabah veseder eliyahu zuta im perush shay lamorah, ed. Shmuel Y. Weinfeld (Jerusalem: Eshkol, 1989/90).

SEGAL, ELIEZER, 'Judaism', in Harold Coward (ed.), *Life after Death in World Religions* (New York: Orbis, 1997), 11–30.

SEYMOUR, JOHN D., *Irish Visions of the Other World: A Contribution to the Study of Medieval Visions* (London: Society for Promoting Christian Knowledge, 1930).

SHALOM OF NEUSTADT, *Hilkhot uminhagei rabenu shalom minoyshtat: derashot maharash*, ed. Shlomo Y. Spitzer (Jerusalem: Mekhon Yerushalayim, 1977).

SHARPE, RICHARD, *Medieval Irish Saints' Lives: An Introduction to Vitae Sanctorum Hiberniae* (Oxford: Clarendon Press, 1991).

SHEPKARU, SHMUEL, 'From After Death to Afterlife: Martyrdom and Its Recompense', *AJS Review*, 24/1 (1999), 1–44.

——*Jewish Martyrs in the Pagan and Christian Worlds* (Cambridge: Cambridge University Press, 2006).

——'To Die for God: Martyrs' Heaven in Hebrew and Latin Crusade Narratives', *Speculum*, 77/ 2 (2002), 311–41.

Shibolei haleket hashalem, ed. Salomon Buber (Vilna: Romm, 1886).

SHOHAM-STEINER, EPHRAIM, 'Burial *ad sanctos* for a Jewish Murderer? Alexander Wimpfen and Rabbi Meir of Rothenburg', *Jewish Quarterly Review*, 23/2 (2016), 124–41.

——'"For a Prayer in that Place would be Most Welcome": Jews, Holy Shrines, and Miracles—A New Approach', *Viator*, 37 (2006), 369–95.

——'From Speyer to Regensburg: The Wanderings of the Hasid's Family from the Rhineland to the Danube Basin' (Heb.), *Zion*, 81 (2016), 149–76.

——'Jews and Healing at Medieval Saints' Shrines: Participation, Polemics and Shared Cultures', *The Harvard Theological Review*, 103/1 (Jan. 2010), 111–29.

——*On the Margins of a Minority: Leprosy, Madness, and Disability among the Jews of Medieval Europe* (Detroit: Wayne State University Press, 2014).

——'An Ultimate Pariah? Jewish Social Attitudes toward Jewish Lepers in Medieval Western Europe', *Social Research*, 70/1 (2003), 237–68.

SHOSHAN, BOAZ, 'High Culture and Popular Culture in Medieval Islam', *Studia Islamica*, 73 (1991), 67–107.

SHYOVITZ, DAVID I., '"He Has Created a Remembrance of His Wonders": Nature and Embodiment in the Thought of the *Ḥasidei Ashkenaz*' (Ph.D. diss., University of Pennsylvania, 2011). Published as *A Remembrance of His Wonders: Nature and the Supernatural in Medieval Ashkenaz* (Philadelphia: University of Pennsylvania Press, 2017).

——'Response', lecture at the conference '*Sefer Ḥasidim* in Context' (Jerusalem, Mar. 2017).

——'"You Have Saved Me from the Judgment of Gehenna": The Origins of the Mourner's Kaddish in Medieval Ashkenaz', *AJS Review*, 39/1 (2015), 49–73.

Sidur rashi, ed. Solomon Buber and Jacob Freimann (Berlin: Mekitzei Nirdamim, 1911).

Sifrei al sefer devarim, ed. Louis Finkelstein and Saul Horovitz (1939; repr. New York: Jewish Theological Seminary, 2001).

Sifrei devei rav: maḥberet rishonah sifrei al sefer bemidbar vesifrei zuta, ed. Hayim S. Horovitz (Leipzig, 1917; repr. Jerusalem: Wahrman, 1966).

SIMHAH B. SAMUEL OF VITRY, *Maḥzor vitry*, ed. Aryeh Goldschmidt, 4 vols. (Jerusalem: Mekhon Otsar Haposekim, 2003/4).

SIMPSON, JACQUELINE, 'Repentant Soul or Walking Corpse? Debatable Apparitions in Medieval England', *Folklore*, 114 (2003), 389–402.

SMITH, JANE I., 'Concourse between the Living and the Dead in Islamic Eschatological Literature', *History of Religions*, 19/3 (1980), 224–36.

——and YVONNE Y. HADDAD, *The Islamic Understanding of Death and Resurrection* (Albany: State University of New York, 1981).

SMITH, JULIA M. H., 'Oral and Written: Saints, Miracles, and Relics in Brittany, *c*.850–1250', *Speculum*, 65/2 (1990), 309–43.
SMYTH, MARINA, 'The Origins of Purgatory through the Lens of Seventh-Century Irish Eschatology', *Traditio* (2003), 91–132.
SOLOVEITCHIK, HAYM, 'Halakhah, Hermeneutics, and Martyrdom in Medieval Ashkenaz: Part I', *Jewish Quarterly Review*, 94/1 (2004), 77–108.
——'Halakhah, Hermeneutics, and Martyrdom in Medieval Ashkenaz: Part II', *Jewish Quarterly Review*, 94/2 (2004), 278–99.
——'The Midrash, *Sefer Ḥasidim* and the Changing Face of God', in Rachel Elior and Peter Schäfer (eds.), *Creation and Re-creation in Jewish Thought: Festschrift in Honor of Joseph Dan on the Occasion of His Seventieth Birthday* (Tübingen: Mohr Siebeck, 2005), 165–77.
——'On Dating *Sefer ḥasidim*' (Heb.), in Reuven Bonfil, Menahem Ben-Sasson, and Joseph Hacker (eds.), *Culture and Society in Medieval Jewry: A Collection of Articles in Memory of Hayim Hillel Ben-Sasson* [Tarbut veḥevrah betoledot yisra'el biymei habeinayim: kovets ma'amarim lezikhro shel ḥayim hilel ben-sason] (Jerusalem: Merkaz Zalman Shazar, 1989), 383–98.
——*Pawnbroking: A Study of the Relationship between Halakhah, Economic Activity and Communal Self-Image* [Halakhah, kalkalah vedimui atsmi: hamashkona'ut biymei habeinayim] (Jerusalem: Hebrew University, 1985).
——'Piety, Pietism and German Pietism: *Sefer Ḥasidim I* and the Influence of *Ḥasidei Ashkenaz*', *Jewish Quarterly Review*, 92/3–4 (Jan.–Apr. 2002), 455–93.
——'Rabbi Menahem Hameiri's *Bet habeḥirah* and Its Fate' (Heb.), in Yaron Ben-Na'eh et al. (eds.), *Studies in Jewish History Presented to Joseph Hacker* [Asufah leyosef: kovets meḥkarim shai leyosef hacker] (Jerusalem: Merkaz Zalman Shazar, 2014), 253–9.
——'Religious Law and Change: The Medieval Ashkenazic Example', *AJS Review*, 12/2 (1987), 205–21.
——'Three Themes in *Sefer Ḥasidim*', *AJS Review*, 1 (1976), 311–57.
——'Topics in the *Ḥokhmat ha-Nefesh*', *Journal of Jewish Studies*, 18 (1967), 65–78.
——'Two Notes on the "Commentary on the Torah" of R. Yehudah he-Ḥasid', in Michael A. Shmidman (ed.), *Turim: Studies in Jewish History and Literature Presented to Dr. Bernard Lander* (New York: Touro College Press, 2008), ii. 242–52.
——*Wine in Ashkenaz in the Middle Ages: 'Yein Nesekh'—A Study in the History of Halakhah* [Hayayin biymei habeinayim—yein nesekh: perek betoledot ha-halakhah be'ashkenaz] (Jersualem: Merkaz Zalman Shazar, 2008).
SOUTHERN, RICHARD W., 'Medieval Humanism', in Richard W. Southern, *Medieval Humanism and Other Studies* (New York: Harper and Row, 1970), 29–60.
——*Saint Anselm: A Portrait in a Landscape* (Cambridge: Cambridge University Press, 1990).
Le Speculum laicorum: Édition d'une collection d'exempla, composée en Angleterre à la fin du XIIIe siècle, ed. J. Th. Welter (Paris: A. Picard, 1914).
SPITZER, SHLOMO Y., 'Responsa of R. Judah the Pious on Matters of Penitence' (Heb.), in Y. Buksboim (ed.), *Memorial Volume in Honour and in Memory of*

R. Shemuel Barukh Verner [Sefer hazikaron likhvodo ulezikhron r. shemuel barukh verner] (Jerusalem: Mekhon Yerushalayim, 1996), 199–207.

STAHL, YAAKOV Y., 'New Passages from the Manuscripts of the Bible Commentary of R. Judah the Pious: In Honour of the 800th *Yahrzeit* of R. Judah the Pious, 1217–2017' (Heb.), *Ḥizei giborim-peletat soferim*, 10 (Apr. 2017), 134–51.

——'The Prayer of Dead Souls in the Synagogue' (Heb.), *Yerushatenu*, 3 (1999), 177–236.

——'Repentance in the Matter of Judgement according to Our Rabbi Isaac Alfasi' (Heb.), *Hama'ayan*, 49/2 (2009), 39–43.

STEINFELD, ZEVI A., 'Atonement for the Dead' (Heb.), *Sidra*, 17 (2002), 217–28.

STEMBERGER, GÜNTER, *Introduction to the Talmud and Midrash*, 2nd edn., trans. and ed. Markus Bockmuehl (Edinburgh: T. and T. Clark, 1996).

SUTTO, CLAUDE (ed.), *Le Sentiment de la mort au Moyen Âge* (Montreal: L'Aurore, 1979).

SWANSON, R. N., 'Ghosts and Ghostbusters in the Middle Ages', in P. Clarke and T. Claydon (eds.), *The Church, the Afterlife, and the Fate of the Soul*, Studies in Church History 45 (Woodbridge, Suffolk: Boydell, 2009), 143–73.

TA-SHMA, ISRAEL, *Early Franco-German Ritual and Custom* [Minhag ashkenaz hakadmon] (Jerusalem: Magnes Press, 1992).

——'The Notebook *Zekher asah lenifle'otav* of R. Judah the Pious' (Heb.), *Kovets al yad*, 12 (1994), 121–46.

——'A Remark on the Topic of the Mourner's Kaddish and Its Customs' (Heb.), *Tarbiz*, 53/4 (1984), 559–68.

'Ten Martyrs of the Empire' (Heb.), in Yehudah D. Eisenstein (ed.), *A Treasury of Midrash: A Bound Volume of 200 Small Midrashim, Agadot, and Stories Arranged Alphabetically* [Otsar midrashim: beit eked lematayim midrashim ketanim ve'a-gadot uma'asiyot beseder alpha beta] (1915; repr. New York: E. Grossman, 1956), ii. 439–50.

THROOP, SUSANNA A., and PAUL R. HYAMS (eds.), *Vengeance in the Middle Ages: Emotion, Religion, and Feud* (Farnham, Surrey: Ashgate, 2010).

TOCH, MICHAEL, 'The Economic Activities of German Jews', in Yom Tov Assis et al. (eds.), *Facing the Cross: The Persecutions of 1096 in History and Historiography* [Yehudim mul hatselav: gezerot tatnu behistoryah uvehistoriografyah] (Jerusalem: Magnes Press, 2000), 32–54.

——'The Jews in Europe: 500–1050', in Paul Fouracre (ed.), *The New Cambridge Medieval History*, i: *c.500–c.700* (Cambridge: Cambridge University Press, 1995), 547–70.

Tosefot harashba al masekhet pesaḥim merabenu shimshon ben rav avraham mishants, ed. Mordecai Y. Fromm (Jerusalem: Mosad Haga'on Aderet, 1955/6).

Tosefot harosh al hashas: ḥagigah, ed. David Metzger (Jerusalem: Mosad Harav Kook, 2010).

Tosefot harosh al hashas: megilah, ed. David Metzger (Jerusalem: Mosad Harav Kook, 2010).

Tosefot harosh al masekhet rosh hashanah, ed. Hayim B. Ravits (Benei Berak: n.p., 1968).

Tosefot harosh: masekhet berakhot lerabenu asher b. r. yeḥiel, ed. Shmuel Udvin (Melbourne: Shmuel Udvin, 1990).

Tosefot rabenu perets lemasekhet bava metsi'a, lerabenu perets b. r. eliyahu mikorbil, ed. H. Ben-Tsiyon Hershler (Jerusalem: H. Ben-Tsiyon Hershler, 1969/70).

Tosefot rabenu perets lemasekhet berakhot, lemasekhet beitsah, lemasekhet sukah, lerabenu perets b. r. eliyahu mikorbil. Tosafot yeshanim, lemasekhet rosh hashanah leraboteinu ba'alei hatosafot, ed. Mosheh Hershler (Jerusalem: Makhon Shalem, Tsefunot Kadmonim, Mekhon Regensberg, 1984).

Tosefot rabenu yehudah sirleon al masekhet berakhot, ed. Nisan Zaks (Jerusalem: Yad Harav Herzog, 1972).

Tosefta al pi kitvei yad erfurt uvinah, ed. Moses S. Zuckermandel (1937; repr. Jerusalem: Wahrman, 1975).

TRACHTENBERG, JOSHUA, *Jewish Magic and Superstition: A Study in Folk Religion* (1939; repr. New York: Athenaeum, 1982).

The Tractate Mourning (Semaḥot), trans. Dov Zlotnick (New Haven, Conn.: Yale University Press, 1966).

TUBACH, FREDERIC C., *Index Exemplorum: A Handbook of Medieval Religious Tales* (Helsinki: Suomalainen Tiedeakatemia, 1969).

URBACH, EPHRAIM E., 'Asceticism and Afflictions in the Teachings of the Rabbis' (Heb.), in E. E. Urbach, *From the World of the Sages: A Collection of Studies* [Me'olamam shel ḥakhamim: kovets meḥkarim], 2nd edn. (Jerusalem: Magnes Press, 2002), 437–58.

——*The Sages: Their Concepts and Beliefs*, trans. Israel Abrahams (Cambridge, Mass.: Harvard University Press, 1979).

——*The Tosafists: Their History, Writings, and Methods* [Ba'alei hatosafot: toledoteihem, ḥibureihem, shitatam], 2 vols. (Jerusalem: Bialik Institute, 1986).

VAN ENGEN, JOHN, 'The "Crisis of Cenobitism" Reconsidered: Benedictine Monasticism in the Years 1050–1150', *Speculum*, 61/2 (Apr. 1986), 269–304.

VAN GENNEP, ARNOLD, *The Rites of Passage*, trans. Monika B. Vizedom and Gabrielle L. Caffee (Chicago: University of Chicago Press, 1960).

VAUCHEZ, ANDRÉ, *Sainthood in the Later Middle Ages*, trans. Jean Birrell (Cambridge: Cambridge University Press, 1997).

VISFISH, ELIEZER, *Book of Ramot Gilad: Topics Relating to Elijah the Prophet Gathered from the Books of the Sages and Early Authorities* [Sefer ramot gilad: inyanei eliyahu hanavi melukatim midivrei ḥazal, rishonim vekadmonim mesudarim berubam al seder hapiyut hanafuts eliyahu hanavi], 2 vols. (Jerusalem: E. Visfish, 2005).

VOVELLE, MICHELLE, *Ideologies and Mentalities*, trans. Eamon Ó'Flaherty (Chicago: University of Chicago Press, 1990).

WACHTEL, DAVID, 'The Ritual and Liturgical Commemoration of Two Medieval Persecutions' (MA thesis, Columbia University, 1997).

WARD, BENEDICTA, *Miracles and the Medieval Mind: Theory, Record and Event 1000–1215*, rev. edn. (Philadelphia: University of Pennsylvania Press, 1987).

WATKINS, CARL S., *History and the Supernatural in Medieval England* (Cambridge: Cambridge University Press, 2007).

WATKINS, CARL S., 'Sin, Penance, and Purgatory in the Anglo-Norman Realm: The Evidence of Visions and Ghost Stories', *Past and Present*, 175 (2002), 3–33.

WEBER, MAX, 'The Social Psychology of the World Religions', in Hans H. Gerth and Charles W. Mills (eds.), *From Max Weber: Essays in Sociology* (New York: Oxford University Press, 1953), 267–301.

WEINGARTEN, SUSAN, 'The *Quederah*: The Everyday Cooking Pot of Talmudic Times', in Mark McWilliams (ed.), *Food and Material Culture. Proceedings of the Oxford Symposium on Food and Cookery 2013* (Totnes: Prospect Books, 2014), 344–53.

WERSES, SHMUEL, 'Towards the Identification of the Structural and Genre-Related Characteristics of the Stories of *Sefer ḥasidim*' (Heb.), in Joseph Dan and Joseph Hacker (eds.), *Studies in Jewish Mysticism, Philosophy, and Ethical Literature Presented to Isaiah Tishby on His 75th Birthday* [Meḥkarim bekabalah, befilosofyah yehudit uvesifrut hamusar vehehagut mugashim liyshayah tishbi bimlot lo shivim veḥamesh shanim] (Jerusalem: Magnes Press, 1986), 349–68.

WERTHEIMER, ABRAHAM (ed.), *Houses of Study: Twenty-Five Midrashim Published for the First Time from Manuscripts Discovered in the Genizot of Jerusalem and Egypt* [Batei midrashot: esrim veḥamishah midreshei ḥazal al pi kitvei yad migenizat yerushalayim umitsrayim], 2 vols. (Jerusalem: Ketav Vesefer, 1986).

WIESELTIER, LEON, *Kaddish* (New York: Knopf, 1998).

YALON, HENOCH, *Phrases* [Pirkei lashon] (Jerusalem: Mosad Bialik, 1971).

YASSIF, ELI, 'The Exemplum Tale in *Sefer ḥasidim*' (Heb.), *Tarbiz*, 57/2 (1988), 217–55.

——*The Hebrew Folktale: History, Genre, Meaning*, trans. Jacqueline S. Teitelbaum (Bloomington: Indiana University Press, 1999).

——*Ninety-Nine Tales: The Jerusalem Manuscript Cycle of Legends in Medieval Jewish Folklore* [Me'ah sipurim ḥaser eḥad: agadot ketav yad yerushalayim befolklor yehudi shel yemei habeinayim] (Tel Aviv: Tel Aviv University Press, 2013).

——'The Overturned Story: Orpheus in the Medieval Hebrew Story' (Heb.), in Eliezer Papo et al. (eds.), *Dametah letamar: Studies in Honor of Tamar Alexander* [Dametah letamar: meḥkarim likhvodah shel tamar aleksander] (Be'er Sheva: Moshe David Gaon Latarbut Haladino, 2015), 275–89.

YUVAL, YISRAEL Y., *Sages in Their Time: The Spiritual Leadership of Medieval German Jewry in the Late Middle Ages* [Ḥakhamim bedoram: hamanhigut haruḥanit shel yehudei germanyah beshilhei yemei habeinayim] (Jerusalem: Magnes Press, 1989).

ZIMMER, ERIC (ITZHAK), 'The Persecutions of 1096 in the Customs Manuals of Medieval and Modern Times: Creation and Expansion of Mourning Rituals' (Heb.), in Yom Tov Assis et al. (eds.), *Jews Facing the Cross: 1096 in History and Historiography* [Yehudim mul hatselav: gezerot tatnu behistoryah uvehistoriografyah] (Jerusalem: Magnes Press, 2000), 157–70.

ZOHARI, HAYIM, *Aggadic Tales and Rabbinic Halakhah in Rashi's Commentary on the Torah* [Midreshei agadah vehalakhah beferush rashi latorah], 2 vols. (Jerusalem: H. Zohari, 1980).

INDEX

A

Aaron ben R. Yosi Hakohen, R. 370n.
Aaron Berakhyah of Modena, R. 51
Abraham, patriarch:
  'bosom of' 92, 160n.
  burial of wife 30n.
  release of souls from Gehenna 241, 248
  son Ishmael 272, 308, 321, 356
Abraham b. Azriel, R.:
  calculations on posthumous judgement 343–5, 351, 381n.
  views compared with R. Judah's 10, 343–5, 351, 371, 380
Abraham bar Hiya 316n.
afterlife:
  corporeality in 122–9
  fears surrounding death and the role of the World to Come in rabbinic sources 153–9, 167–8
  gravity of sin in 171–80
  individual (Christian background) 159–64
  individual (in *Sefer ḥasidim*) 164–8
  Pietist concern with 205–7
  see also dead; Gehenna; Heaven; Hell; Paradise; punishment; Purgatory; souls
Aha bar Hanina, R. 85
Ahai b. R. Yoshiyah, R. 154
Akiva, R.:
  burial 87n.
  commemoration 94
  death 90n.
  debate over sanctity of the sabbath 243n.
  entering *pardes* 55n.
  opinion on duration of Gehenna sentence 208–9, 211–12
  story of Akiva and the dead man 328–33, 366–7, 375, 377, 379
  story of Akiva and the faithful woman 201n.
Alber, priest 247–8
Alexander, Tamar 7n., 204n.
Alfasi, R. Isaac 270n.
All Souls' Day 163, 197, 282, 284
alms for the dead:
  Christian accounts 162, 224, 228, 229, 277, 279, 282, 285, 286, 324, 327
  geonic view 274–5, 276, 293
  halakhic sources 293
  Pietist positions 271, 293, 296n., 299–301, 317–18, 319, 325, 333–9, 367, 379
Alphabetum Narrationum 102–3, 104, 107, 178, 312n.
Amiens, monumental art 313, 355
Anan, R. 20
Angel of Death 54–5, 151–3, 155–6
angels of torment 180–2, 187, 317, 337n.
Anselm of Canterbury 216, 352–4
Apocalypse of Joshua b. Levi 63
Apocalypse of Paul 105n., 178n.
Asher, Rabbenu (Rosh) 237, 252n.
Ashkenaz, medieval:
  ascetic practices 392
  beliefs and practices 8
  burial customs 132, 144
  cemetery status 112
  conception of God 344, 380, 394
  cultural milieu and territory 6
  fasting 258n.
  Germano-Christian influences 9, 373
  kissing the dead 50
  martyrs as holy dead 91–4, 113, 375–6
  Perek gehinom 183
  practices of prayer and charity for the dead 301–5
  'promise of two friends' motif 166
  sabbath rest of souls 243
  study of death-related material 54, 58
  talit-wearing 130
  tefilin-wearing 212n.
  tosafists 391

Ashkenaz, medieval (*cont.*):
views on posthumous judgement 10, 345–7
Asolf, hermit 98–100, 102, 103, 104
atonement:
Anselm's theory of 353–4
charitable acts of others 293, 300
Christian theories 255, 353, 382, 384
Divine severity 192
paying for rabbi's burial 111n.
Pietist doctrine 2, 201–2, 219–20, 232–3, 234n., 254, 258, 262, 265, 293, 300, 322, 333, 378–9, 382, 384, 389
rabbinic positions on 272–3, 308, 320
ransom theory 255
release from Gehenna 211, 320, 322
restitution of stolen goods 316n.
returning sinners 67–8, 71
suicide as 204–5n.
venial sin 216
vicarious 256, 258, 265, 378–9
Yom Kippur 301–2
Augustine, St:
on body and soul 128
on categories of soul 163n., 213, 277, 278n., 337, 367, 370
influence 379
on posthumous purgation 160, 213
on prayer for the dead 277–8, 283n.
on the returning dead 25, 41
Autun, cathedral sculptures 185n., 314n., 315n., 346n., 348n., 354
Avigdor Kohen Tsedek, R. 273n.

B

Bachrach, R. Shimshon 111
Bahya ben Asher 145
Barzilai Hagiladi 292n.
Baschet, Jérôme 26, 128, 185n., 186n., 246n., 354n., 355n.
Baumgarten, Elisheva 7n., 9n., 44–5, 178
Bede the Venerable 42n., 75n., 161n., 162, 183, 278n., 279n.
Ben-Sasson, Haim Hillel 10, 378
Benedict, St 121, 127n., 141, 312n., 358n.
Benedictine order:
ascetic penitential practices 350, 384
claustration 386
communal prayer service 197
communities in southern Germany 382–3
community in Regensburg 247, 260, 383, 384
prayer for the dead 197–8, 350
Berger, David 3n., 386
Bernard of Clairvaux, St 203n., 251n., 290n., 297, 328
Bernstein, Alan 129
Binom, gravedigger 193
Book of Enoch 63
Bowker, J. W. 271n.
Brandon, Samuel 312n., 315n.
Bratu, Anca 186
Brown, Peter 355n., 390
Brunhild, monastic benefactor 363
Bull, Marcus 192
Burchard of Worms 23, 219
burial:
appearance of returning dead in cemetery 56
archaeological excavations of cemeteries 23, 64, 124n.
averting posthumous attacks 29–30
care of graves in cemetery 36–7
in cemetery of city where person died 33n.
cemetery outskirts 95
churchyards 95n., 98n., 102
clothing for the dead 115–20, 122–9, 139–42, 146, 375
coffins 23, 29–30, 33–5, 57, 145, 158, 375
in consecrated ground 98–9, 107, 110
conversation of spirits in cemetery 115–18, 267–9
decomposition of corpse 24, 124, 154
desecration of graves 38
exhumation 32, 57, 66–7, 106, 374
graves in cemetery 47, 52
Icelandic practices 23, 24, 64, 95, 97–100
improper burial of the wicked 85–9, 113
inappropriate burial in *Sefer ḥasidim* 94–7
Jewish customs 29–31, 52–3

martyrs 85–6, 87–90, 93, 107, 111–12, 113–14, 144–5, 376
monastic 137n.
motif of improper burial (pre-Christian roots and Christian origins) 97–104, 113
motif of improper burial in *Sefer ḥasidim* 85–6, 104–6, 113
near the altar 98, 99, 103n., 106
near the saints 102, 103, 105–6, 110
north European 23–4
Pietist customs 52–3
position of graves in cemetery 95–6, 96n., 110, 111n., 375
rabbinic attitudes 85–7, 88–91, 113, 157–8
role of cemetery in Jewish life 8n., 95, 107–8, 112–13, 142, 271, 292, 376
shrouds 23, 32, 53–4, 97n., 118–23, 127, 136n., 137, 146
in a *talit* with *tsitsit* 12, 129–39, 142–7, 375
tombstones 248–9
treatment of the corpse 157–8
in unconsecrated ground 27, 98, 100, 103
of the wicked 85–7, 95

C
Caciola, Nancy 26, 30n., 44, 128
Caesarius of Arles 162n.
Caesarius of Heisterbach:
belief in corporeal post-mortem punishment 83
categories of the dead 337–8, 367, 380
on Cistercians in Heaven 198
on clothes of the dead 120, 127, 129, 137n., 140–1
Dialogus miraculorum (*Dialogue on Miracles*) 7n., 26–7, 42–3, 120, 129, 146, 165, 169n., 178, 202, 230, 312n., 348
stories of the dead summoning the living 42–3, 45–7
stories of hellfire 189
stories of posthumous punishments 169, 172, 192, 230
stories of substitutions 49
stories of the Virgin 290n., 311, 348
story of condemned criminal 101
story of fathers haunting children 26–7
story of the promise of two friends 165
story of scribe's hand 231n.
story of usurer's ghost 327
story of wandering dead knight 76–8, 80, 226–7, 228
on sweet smell of the righteous 194n.
capuchon 141, 206, 384
charity for the dead, *see* alms
Christianity:
absolution 65n., 66, 101, 126, 285–6
appearances of the holy dead 57
attitudes to belief in returning dead 25–6
Benedictine order, *see* Benedictine order
burial concerns 160
burial in holy ground 112–13
Celtic penitential system 214
choral singing 197, 206
Christianizing pagan beliefs 38, 41n., 64–6, 72, 83, 100–1, 141, 176, 223
Cistercian order, *see* Cistercian order
Cluniac cult of the dead, *see* Cluny
Communion 45n., 169–70, 276n.
concept of posthumous purgation 160–2
concept of vicarious penance 285–6, 291, 306, 379
death rite (Roman) 276–7
doctrine of penance 215–16
doctrine of Purgatory 163–4, 264
doctrine of vicarious atonement 256, 378
early medieval models of prayer for dead 284–7, 306
exempla, *see* exempla literature
fasting 162, 219, 229, 258n., 259, 286
flagellation 202, 219, 259, 384, 385
Harrowing of Hell 255, 280
individual afterlife 159–64
influences on Pietism 2–3, 9–11, 84, 247–8, 265–6, 378–9
intercession, *see* intercession
Irish monasticism, *see* Ireland
Last Judgement 159–60, 215n., 217n., 277, 279, 283, 348n.

Christianity (*cont.*):
Last Judgement scenes 126–7, 185–7, 269n., 289n., 290n., 312n., 314n., 315n., 354–5
martyr-saints 91, 92, 106, 112–13
miracle stories 196–7, 284, 287, 289n., 290–1, 310–11, 366
monastic clothing 141, 146, 206, 384
monastic tales of the dead 191–2, 197–8, 206–7
mortification of the flesh 206–7, 219, 385
notions of posthumous penance and purgation 213–17
Original Sin 255, 265, 378, 388
posthumous purgation 160–1
prayer for the damned 280–1
prayer for the dead (early medieval models) 284–7
prayer for the dead (institutionalization under the Carolingians) 162–3, 281–3
prayer for the dead (origins) 276–80
prayer for the dead (role of suffrages in high medieval period) 288–91
problem of corporeality 189, 206
ransom theory of atonement 255
role of suffrages in high medieval period 288–91
Roman emperor as model for power of mercy 214
visionary literature 26n., 105n., 129, 161, 183–4, 187–8, 206, 207, 214, 215n., 217, 251, 279–80, 312n., 373, 377, 379
visual images of Hell 185–7, 245–6, 354–5
vitae (lives of the saints) 260–2, 284, 362–4
Christina Mirabilis 45, 178–9
Cistercian order:
belief in posthumous corporeal punishment 83
belief in proper clothing for the dead 121, 126, 129, 145, 146
belief in return of corporeal dead 83, 99n., 129
devotion to the Virgin 290n.
image of humanity of Christ 365
miracle stories 196–9, 207
'The Promise of Two Friends' 165
views on sins and punishments 172, 191, 192, 293n.
Cluny, monasteries:
All Souls' Day 163, 197, 282, 284
communal prayer service with choral singing 197, 206
cult of the dead 6
'economy of salvation' 197–8, 350
miracle stories 196, 197–8, 203, 207
power to save souls 163, 197–8, 284–5, 324n.
prayer for the dead 281–3
prayer on St Michael's Day 269n.
Coemgen, St 260
Cohen, Aryeh 20n.
Columba, St 215, 260, 279
Columbanus, St 214, 363, 391
Conques, sculptures 127n., 185, 245n., 289n., 348n., 354
cuculla 141, 146, 206, 384
Crusades 7n., 88, 91–2, 110, 145, 249, 302

D

Dan, Joseph 3n., 7n., 94n.
Daniel, book of 138, 236–7
David, King:
music 101n., 194, 387
penance in aid of 201n.
prayer for Absalom 308, 320–2
purging his soul 257n., 349–50
dead, the:
amount of flesh on corpse 30n., 154n.
appearance in dreams, *see* dreams
belief in the dangerous dead 22–7, 64–5, 75–6, 374
blessings on tombstones 249
burial, *see* burial
charity for (in Jewish legal tradition and practice) 272–4
charity for (in medieval Ashkenaz) 301–5
charity for (R. Judah the Pious on) 299–301
Christian background (origins of medieval suffrages for the dead) 276–80
clothing 115–20, 122–9, 139–42, 146, 375

conversations overheard by the living 267–9
corporeal punishment in the afterlife 169–71, 173, 175, 180
corporeal torture in the afterlife 181, 183–8
corporeality in the afterlife 122–9, 146, 154, 377
dangerous dead (Germano-Christian beliefs) 44, 50
dangerous dead (medieval European beliefs) 58, 67–8, 71–2, 76–7, 206, 374
dangerous dead (medieval Jewish beliefs) 40, 374, 377
dangerous dead (pre-Christian beliefs) 22–5, 39, 51, 57, 60–1, 64–6, 70–1, 76, 83, 292
dangerous dead in *Sefer ḥasidim* 11, 28–32, 39, 83–4, 206
decomposition of corpse 24, 124, 154
deserving and undeserving 316–28
disease caused by 32, 41, 84
encounters with 17–18, 56–8
encounters with in rabbinic sources 19–22
exhumation 32, 57, 66–7, 106, 374
'false dead' 65n., 101
fear of 12, 57–8
geonic model of prayer for 274–6, 306
intercession 271n., 274–6
holy dead (Christian notions) 38, 88, 112, 113, 114, 310, 312, 314, 338, 362, 376, 377, 380
holy dead (Jewish memorialization) 302–3
holy dead (martyrs as) 12, 91–4, 106–13, 376
holy dead in rabbinic era 21, 56, 87, 113, 114, 271, 305, 373–4
holy dead in *Sefer ḥasidim* 56–7, 87, 106–13, 114, 376
kissing 49–52, 374
knowledge of events in the world of the living 115–17
limitation on prayer and alms for the deserving dead 333–9
loci of punishment in rabbinic and post-rabbinic sources 61–3
medieval attitudes to the returning dead 374, 377
memorialization of 7n., 282–3, 301, 302–3, 305
miraculous preservation of body 231–2
neutral dead 11, 12, 116, 119, 146, 154n.
passage to the hereafter 139–46, 147
practices of prayer and charity for the dead in medieval Ashkenaz and R. Judah's position 301–5
prayer for (in Jewish legal tradition and practice) 272–4
prayer for (in medieval Ashkenaz) 301–5
prayer for (R. Judah's model) 291–8, 306
prayer for the damned 280–1
prayer for the dead by the dead 307–16
praying for the living 269–71
pre-Christian notions 7, 28, 51, 57, 64–8, 75–6, 83, 292, 373, 375
rabbinic attitudes to the returning dead 374
resurrection, *see* resurrection of the dead
separation of body and soul on death 124–6
sinful dead 11, 12, 61–3, 65, 72, 80, 83, 244, 318, 374
summoning power of the dead 41–56
terrestrial post-mortem purgation 64–8
vengeful dead in *Sefer ḥasidim* 32–41
death:
fears about 151–3, 376
fears about death and the role of the world to come in rabbinic sources 153–9
foreknowledge of 45, 46
individual afterlife (Christian background) 159–64
pain after dying 154
demonic agents 180–8, 206, 207, 209, 246, 377
demons:
beating sinners with rods of fire 170n.
depictions of 354
dream of burning by 175

demons (*cont.*):
early medieval consciousness 25
in Gehenna 245–6
ghosts as 21–2, 40–1, 71, 77, 82–3, 153, 374
Hellequin's Hunt 71
observing the sabbath 82
in Purgatory 141
rabbinic fear of 40–1, 374
rescue from 279, 285, 311, 314n., 348
Divine name 18, 28, 29, 71, 72n.
dreams, appearances of the dead in:
Augustine's account 25, 41
burial issues 85–6, 96–100, 104, 106, 107n., 109–10, 119n., 120–2, 137, 179n.
concern over death of body 154
Icelandic and north European stories 37, 51, 98–100
kissing by the dead 50
presaging death 41–8
'promise of two friends' 151–3
stories in *Sefer ḥasidim* 34–7
summoning the living 43–8
telling stories of the afterlife 168, 173, 198, 200, 205n., 313–14
warning the living 167, 292
Dresden *mahzor* 346
Drythelm, monk 162, 225n.

E

Eadmer of Canterbury 290n.
Edrei, Aryeh 273n.
Ekkehard, chronicler 68, 69, 224n.
Eleazar, R. 322–3
Eleazar ben Arakh, R. 54–5
Eleazar ben Azaryah, R. 275, 308, 320n., 323n.
Eleazar ben Kalir 345
Eleazar b. Shimon, R. 200, 256
Eleazar of Worms, R.:
burial concerns 95
on burial in *tsitsit* 134–5, 143
on charity for the dead 298, 301–2, 320
on clothing of the dead 119n., 120, 122
on custom of burning spices 194n.
on dead praying for the living 270–1
on deserving and undeserving dead 319–20, 333
on duration of punishment 209n., 235–6, 252
on favouritism in the afterlife 294, 341
on fire of Gehenna 234n., 244
on harmful dead 31
Hasidei Ashkenaz role 4
on kissing the dead 50–1
manual of penance 262–4
on Paradise 171n.
on penance for adultery 263, 389
perception of sin 262–4
on posthumous judgement 294, 341–2, 345, 368
on post-mortem punishment 63n., 81–3, 187–9, 375
on prayer for the dead 303, 330n., 333
problem of corporeality 125–6, 188–9
on punishment of detractors of Pietism 319, 360n.
on returning after death 167
on sabbath rest of souls 244
Sefer haroke'aḥ 81, 95, 134, 135n., 142, 143n., 301n., 341
Sefer ḥasidim role 5–6, 11
Sefer ḥokhmat hanefesh 31, 32, 51, 63n., 81, 95, 119n., 120, 122, 125, 126, 138n., 167n., 171n., 187, 234n., 270, 328n., 331, 333, 341
story of Akiva and the dead man 375
students 10, 343
on *talit* 131, 137–8
on *tsitsit* in afterlife 137–8
on vicarious penance 298
view of Divine judgement 371
views compared with R. Judah's 5–6, 10–11, 341–2, 368, 378, 380
Eliezer ben Joel Halevi (Ravyah) 131, 132, 137
Eliezer of Metz, R. 166
Eligius of Noyon 367
Elijah:
ascent to Heaven in chariot of fire 17n., 63, 125n.
posthumous appearances 17–20, 21, 56, 123, 373–4

role in Paradise 309
Elijah, R. 134n.
Elisha the prophet 17n., 85, 86, 89, 95, 108
Elisha ben Avuyah 62, 222, 275, 307, 309, 320n., 335
1 Enoch 181
3 Enoch 36n., 181
Ephraim of Bonn 109n., 111
exempla literature:
aid from living to dead 329
burial concerns 88, 97, 102, 103, 104–7, 113–14
clothes for the dead 120–1, 126, 145, 146, 375
Cluniac tales 197, 203, 350
collections 7n., 190, 384
concern with afterlife 206–7
dangerous dead 31
dead warning the living 292
depictions of usurers 26n., 185
duration of punishment 229–32, 252, 264
encounters with ghosts 39
'false dead' 65n., 101
ghosts changing shape 22n.
grateful ghosts 109
Gregory the Great's work 25, 278, 323
influence on *Sefer ḥasidim* 168, 175–6, 178, 180, 190–1, 206–7, 218, 373
intercession 312n., 323–4
invocation of Divine name 28
Liber exemplorum 169–70
posthumous purgation 161, 164
prayer for the damned 328
'The Promise of Two Friends' 165
punishment in Paradise 169–71
Purgatory 217, 251
signum use 227
sin and punishment 171–2, 174, 175, 178, 185, 189, 190–1
substitutions in 49, 51
torture of the damned 377
transfer of merits 297, 298n.
value of indulgences 325
vicarious penance 335
on the Virgin 290–1
visions of holy dead 57

F

fasting:
Akiva story 331n.
Christian practices 162, 219, 229, 259, 286, 384
geonic views 295
in Pietism 46, 195n., 201, 218n., 219, 334n., 388
in rabbinic era 20, 174n.
tosafist position 263
Faustinius, St 102–3, 104
Finian, St 223, 259, 260
flagellation:
Christian practices 202, 219, 259, 384, 385
Pietist penitential system 219, 258
in *Sefer ḥasidim* 201n., 202, 257n.
Freehof, Solomon 304n.
Fursey, St 75n., 161, 183, 214–15, 279

G

Gan Eden 92–3, 171n.
Gehenna:
angels of torment 181–3
categories of sinners 211–12
cold and darkness 61n.
colour of sinners' faces 177n., 181, 208
corporeal torture by demonic agents 180–8, 207, 246, 377
duration of punishment 208–9, 211–13, 221, 225, 229–30, 233–6, 264–5, 331n., 377
fire and smoke 60, 61–2, 210
foul smell of 244n.
levels and compartments 63, 156, 182
location 60, 61, 168, 209–10
name 61–2
Original Sin and Pietist sin 252–64
Pietist accounts 124, 125, 137, 171n., 187–90, 196, 208–9, 213, 221–3, 225, 228, 229–30, 233–6, 264–5, 340n., 351, 362, 382
Pietist approaches to prayer for the dead 291, 295–7, 299, 304–6, 307–10, 317, 320, 328, 330, 333–5
Pietist versus tosafist teaching 236–52, 321–2
post-rabbinic accounts 62–3

Gehenna (*cont.*):
- posthumous punishment of the wicked 59–60, 124
- punishment outside 81
- punishments in 122, 155, 172, 174, 182, 187–9, 207
- rabbinic accounts 61–2, 83, 105n., 157, 158, 168, 171, 180–1, 209–13, 264, 272, 275, 303, 307–8, 375
- release from 31, 242, 250, 264, 272, 275, 281, 305, 306, 309, 320, 322n., 333, 335, 377
- sabbath rest of souls 8, 12, 31, 40, 82, 243–4, 265, 374
- sins and merits 80, 196, 228, 248, 251–2, 264, 308, 320, 343–4, 351

Gerald of Wales 363

Germanic beliefs and customs:
- black colour 99n.
- burial concerns 23, 64, 97
- Christianization 12, 176, 269n., 373
- clothing for the dead 67, 129, 139–41, 142
- corporeal ghost 25, 26, 29, 58, 76, 83
- corporeality in the afterlife 129, 146, 154
- dangerous dead 26, 28, 50, 51, 56, 292
- disease caused by dead 32, 41
- dreams 35
- Germano-Christian beliefs 9, 11, 12, 28, 50, 56, 57, 83, 373
- goddess Holle 176
- *Hellekeppelin* 141–2, 145, 146–7, 375
- Hellequin's Hunt 70, 83, 224n.
- *Helskór* 140, 142, 145, 146, 147, 375
- influence on Ashkenazi Jews 375
- influence on Pietism 12, 28, 29, 83, 229, 264
- January 1st 71n.
- omens 49n.
- public penance 285n.
- suicides 24
- summoning power of the dead 142
- wagon legends 73
- wandering corporeal dead 154n., 226

Glaber, Raoul 68, 224n., 285

Glam, *draugr* 23, 33

Glick, Shmuel 273n.

Godfrey, canon 175

Godfrey, monk 202n.

Gregory, abbot of St James monastery 260

Gregory, St 102

Gregory the Great:
- influences on 215
- on personal merit 287
- on posthumous purgation 160–1, 213, 215n.
- on prayer for the dead 278–9
- praying for soul of Trajan 323–4
- tales of dead in Roman baths 65, 67, 68, 76
- use of ghost tales 25

Gregory of Tours 38

Grettir 37–8

Güdemann, Moritz 2

Guibert of Nogent 105n., 165

Gur, Inbal 5

Gurevich, Aron 186

H

Hai Gaon, R. 274, 275n., 293–5, 297, 299, 320–1

Hanina, R. 238, 239, 241n.

Hanina ben Dosa, R. 171n.

Hanina bar Hama, R. 222n.

Hanina b. Papa, R. 156

Hanina b. Tradyon, R. 90n., 91, 94, 310

Hasidei Ashkenaz, *see* Pietists

Hazan, Jacob ben Judah, R. 143

Heaven:
- Academy of 21, 299, 309, 335
- ascent of soul to 29, 270n., 276, 283
- Christian accounts 162, 176, 197, 198, 247, 260, 276, 284
- clothing in 126–8, 198
- Elijah's ascent to 63
- medieval Jewish view 250
- Pietist views 189, 198, 203, 256, 294, 390
- role of archangel Michael 269n.
- status in 155, 201n., 256, 390
- tosafist belief 377
- 'upside-down world' 154–5
- Virgin Mary's ascent to 289n.

Heavenly Chariot 54–5

heikhalot literature 36n., 174, 177n., 181, 182n., 194n., 229n.

Helinand of Froidmont 71, 74, 165
Hell:
- angels of destruction 183, 187
- clothing in 126–7
- demonic agents 184–7, 377
- descriptions 183–4, 247
- distinction between Hell and Purgatory 216–17
- duration of sentence 160, 189, 225, 314n.
- fire 105, 161–2, 183, 189
- Harrowing of Hell 255, 280
- images of 354–5, 377
- medieval monumental depictions 185–7, 245–6, 354–5
- non-Jews 249–50, 338n.
- numbers sent to 250–1
- punishments 63, 174–5, 184–7, 225, 331n.
- rescue from 109n., 221, 229, 265, 279–81, 284–5, 287, 297, 310–11, 312n., 323–4, 327, 333, 366, 380
- sins and punishments 191, 216
- smell 105
- tortures 162, 184–5, 247
- tortures depicted 185–7, 377
- tours of 62–3, 162, 174, 178, 181–2, 188, 249–50, 260

Hellekeppelin 141–2, 145, 146–7, 375
Hellequin 70, 73, 141
Hellequin's Hunt:
- Akiva tale comparison 331, 332
- army of the dead 68–72
- Christian and pre-Christian roots 68–72
- first mentioned 68
- name 68
- versions in *Sefer ḥasidim* 60–1, 72–9, 83, 223–8, 264–5, 375

Heller, Bernard 329n.
Helskór 140, 142, 145, 146, 147, 375
Herbert of Clairvaux 70
Herla, King 70, 374–5
Hincmar of Reims 178n., 287
Hiya, R. 21, 88, 157
Ho, Cynthia 105n.
Honorius Augustodunensis 189
Honorius of Autun 105n., 184–5
Hoshana Rabah 116–17, 268–9, 312
Hrapp, *draugr* 23, 24
Hugh of Lincoln 66
Hugh of Pisa 217n.
Hugh of St Victor 216
Huna, R. 19n., 21n., 88
Huna bereih derav Yehoshua, R. 155

I

Icelandic sagas:
- belief in the dangerous dead 22–3, 24, 26, 35, 37, 39, 64, 70, 71n., 76
- burial practices 24, 64, 95, 97–100, 107
- *draugr* stories 22–3, 27, 29, 31, 33, 58, 67n., 101
- dream appearances 51
- 'false ghosts' 98, 101
- role of the dead 102–3
- shared motifs 104, 107, 113
- story of Asolf 98–100, 102, 104
- story of dead magician 99–100, 107

Ilai, Rav 89
intercession:
- Akiva stories 332–3, 366–7
- Augustine's position 283n.
- Christian exempla accounts 121, 323
- Christian pastoral model 285, 287, 306
- by Christian saints 279, 284, 289, 306
- geonic views 274–5, 306, 308
- Gregory the Great accounts 65, 278, 323–4
- monastic prayer for the dead 282
- Muslim teaching 276
- pastoral model 306
- Pietist views 306, 310–11, 332, 349, 350, 366–7, 370, 380, 394
- rabbinic views 275, 307–8, 310, 368
- by the Virgin Mary 281, 289–91, 311–12, 315, 347, 348n., 380

Ireland, Colin 259n.
Ireland, religious traditions:
- ascetic practices 219, 259–60, 261, 262, 266, 383–4
- attitudes to sin and penance 214
- choral singing of psalms 386–7
- Christ as a vengeful lord 365n.
- concept of judgement 215n.
- confession and penance 215n., 218–19, 285n.

Ireland, religious traditions (*cont.*):
druids 363
Irish Benedictine houses in Austria and southern Germany (*Schottenklöster*) 185, 247–8, 260–2, 265–6, 382–3
missionaries from 215, 258, 260–1, 383
monastic penitential system 218–21, 256–7, 259–60, 265, 350, 384, 388
notion of punishment in Paradise 247n.
penitential manuals 215, 219, 220, 221, 223, 258n., 259, 279
role of St Michael 348n.
St Patrick's Purgatory 141n., 184
saints 261, 266, 362–4, 369, 384, 389–90
tariffed penance 214, 215n., 217, 285n.
visionary literature 64n., 75n., 161, 214, 247, 251, 279, 384
vitae (lives of the saints) 260–2, 362–4, 383
Isaac, patriarch 90n., 308, 321, 356
Isaac, R. 34, 154
Isaac, son of R. Eleazar of Worms 4n., 369
Isaac ben Abraham of Dampierre, R. (Ritsba) 134n.
Isaac ben Asher Halevi of Speyer, R. 135n., 143n.
Isaac of Dampierre, R. (Ri) 10n., 130n., 132, 134n., 391
Isaac ben Hayim, R. 93n.
Isaac ben Joseph of Corbeil, R. 134n.
Isaac b. Judah, R. 142–3
Isaac ben Malki Tsedek, R. 134n.
Isaac of Vienna, R. 95–6, 131, 132, 192–3, 243–4n., 303, 330n.
Islam:
burial customs 119n.
intercessory prayer 276
Israel Bruna of Regensburg, R. 145

J

Jacob, patriarch 50, 253, 272
Jacob b. Moses Moelin, R. (Maharil) 28, 112
Jacob ben Solomon, R. 145
Jacobus de Voragine 67, 292n., 298n., 311, 336n., 337n.
Jacques de Vitry 27, 101, 105n., 185
Jeremiah, prophet 209–10
Jeremiah, R. 139
Jonas of Bobbio 363, 391
Jonas of Orléans 367
Joseph, biblical 50, 51, 356
Joseph ben Moses 29
Joseph son of R. Joshua b. Levi, Rav 154–5
Joshua, biblical 253
Joshua b. Levi, R. 19n., 63, 155–6, 182, 250n.
Jotsald, monk of Cluny 324n.
Judah b. Bava, R. 19n., 94
Judah ben Kalonymus of Mainz, R. 135n., 143n.
Judah the Pious, R.:
ascetic lifestyle 258
authorship of *Sefer ḥasidim* 5–6, 11, 378
belief in 'double-body' phenomenon 29, 58
belief in terrestrial post-mortem punishment 79–83, 375
burial concerns 30, 34, 94–6, 108, 130, 136–7, 141
categories of the dead 337–8
cemetery story 117, 118
character 370
on charity for the dead 13, 293, 299–301, 333–4
Christian influences on 2, 9–11, 84, 190, 247–8, 378–9
on clothing the dead 119–20, 122, 130, 136–7, 141
concept of inevitable sin 255–6, 265
conception of God 13, 294, 352–3, 355, 368–9, 362, 365–6, 368, 380–1, 394
conception of Paradise 309n.
confidence in his knowledge of Divine justice 359–60, 381
on corporeality of souls and ghosts 125, 129, 209
on demonic agents 180, 187, 209
on determining time of one's own death 49n.
on Divine judgement 10, 177, 294, 348–50, 366, 368, 378
on Divine justice 360, 368, 380–1
on Divine punishments 13, 177, 355–6, 366, 380

on duration of punishment 208, 213, 225, 228–9, 232–4, 242–4, 252, 265, 379
on enemies of the Pietists 361, 382
on favouritism in the afterlife 308–10, 323, 339, 340n., 350, 381
feelings towards monasticism 262n., 384–9
ghost tales to frighten listener into repentance 168–70, 192
hatred of Christian worship and images 387–8
home 185, 247–8, 261–2, 383, 389–90
on importance of personal merit 291
on importance of singing 193, 194
on intercession 349–50, 365, 366–7, 368, 370, 379–81, 390n.
on kissing the dead 50
leadership of Pietists 1, 4
on martyrs 108, 110
miracle stories 4–5, 248n., 261n., 390n.
monastic perspective 190–2, 206, 265–6, 350, 381–90
omission of story of Akiva and the dead man 328–33, 375, 379
opposition to 392–3
on penance by the living for the dead 337
portrayal of Pietist master (*ḥakham*) 256
on posthumous judgement 339–41, 350–1, 380
on posthumous punishment 10, 12, 124, 206, 246, 351, 365, 379
on posthumous reward 124, 192–3, 196, 204n., 206, 351
on prayer for the dead 13, 228, 291–8, 301–5, 333–4, 350–1, 367, 379
on prayer of the dead for the dead 306, 307–8, 310, 312n., 366
on prayer of the dead for the living 269–70, 307
on prayer for the deserving dead 291, 306, 316–17, 320, 337–8, 367, 379
on prayer of the living for the dead 306, 307, 366
on prayer for the undeserving dead 291, 317–20, 321–8, 332–3, 337–8, 366–7, 370, 379
on prayer for the undeserving dead (question of authorship) 369–72
problem of corporeality 188, 189
on promise to return after death 151–3, 165
on protection from the dead 18
on protracted Pietist prayer ritual 195–6, 206
on punishment in Paradise 168–71, 178–80, 209, 351
on punishment of the righteous 177
on punishment as vengeance 359–60
on retributive justice 173n.
on returning dead 154n., 166–7
on saving the public from unknown sin 222
on shoes of the dead 140
on sin and accountability 13, 296n., 315, 338, 351, 352, 365, 368, 380
on sins and merits 295–6, 311, 349–50, 351, 367, 368, 380, 381
on sins and punishments 171–2, 190–2, 225–6, 234, 245–6, 251–4, 349–50, 356, 368
students 31, 95, 131, 368, 375, 380
on study of death-related talmudic law 54–6
on substitution 48n.
on summons to death 46
swearing in God's name 18
on taxpaying 314n.
'Testament of R. Judah the Pious' 29, 33, 46, 50, 52–3, 143
on vengeful dead 34–5
on vicarious atonement 256, 257n., 265, 378–9
on vicarious penance 258–9, 285–6, 291, 294–8, 306, 334–5, 338, 379
views compared with other Pietists 5–6, 10–11, 341–6, 368, 378, 380
views compared with rabbinic teachings 9, 84, 209, 252
views compared with tosafists 9, 10, 241–2
on voluntary suffering 201n., 202, 206, 221, 235, 256–7, 334–6, 378, 382
on wearing the *talit* 131, 136–7, 141, 198–9, 206

Judah the Pious, R. (*cont.*):
world-view 10, 265, 350, 370, 371, 378
Judah the Prince:
benefits of his suffering 200, 256
deathbed 157
posthumous appearances 20, 21, 56, 123, 373–4
Judah Sirleon, R. 131n., 132, 133n.
judgement:
duration of sentence 208–9, 236–7
fear of God's 156–7, 163, 289
Final Judgement at the End of Days 181–2, 210, 236, 237–8
Judgement Day 68n., 106, 161, 214, 278, 287
Last Judgement 159–60, 213, 215n., 217n., 277, 279, 283, 348n.
Last Judgement scenes 126–7, 185–7, 269n., 289n., 290n., 312n., 314n., 315n., 354–5
personal judgement after death 6, 215, 238, 289
Pietist attitudes 2, 10, 167, 177, 202, 221, 223, 233, 294, 315–16, 334, 339–51, 365–6, 368, 371, 378, 380, 394
Rosh Hashanah 117, 238, 270, 346, 347
tosafist views 237–40
Weighing of Souls 311–16
Julian Pomerius 162n., 278n.
Julian of Toledo 162n.

K

Kaddish:
emergence 8, 303, 375, 377
establishment as intercessory prayer 303–4, 306
orphan sons reciting 303, 328n., 329n., 330
punishment for speaking during 177
Kedushah prayer 168, 170
Kimhi, Joseph 383
Korah, assembly of 59–61, 234n., 275n.
Kushelevsky, Rella 7n., 193n., 201n., 203n.

L

Landri of Orbec 332
Le Goff, Jacques 45n., 105n., 163n., 164n., 215n., 289n.
Lecouteux, Claude 22n., 70n., 97n., 98n., 101n., 140n.
Lévi, Israel 7n., 208n., 273n., 274n.
Liber exemplorum 169–70
Liber miraculorum sancta Fidis 69
Lotharingia 132, 133n., 144, 243n.

M

Ma'aseh bukh 4–5, 248n., 261n.
McLaughlin, Megan 160n., 162n., 213n., 282n., 283n., 284n., 286n.
Magnum Legendarium Austriacum 261, 389
Maḥzor vitry:
on burial clothing 134n.
on charity for the dead 301, 322
ghost tale 328n., 332
on harmful dead 40, 374
on mass assemblage of dead 57
on mourners' Kaddish 303, 330
on posthumous punishment 377
on prayers for dead 303, 330
Maimonides 345n.
manuscript illumination 4, 346–8, 349, 368, 380
Map, Walter 27, 70, 102, 104, 224n.
Marcus, Ivan 5, 10, 93n., 247n., 378
Marcus, monk 247, 260
Marianus Scotus 261
martyrs:
burial issues 85–6, 87–8, 93, 107, 111–12, 113–14, 144–5, 376
Christian 91, 92, 106, 113, 160, 337n.
Christian concepts of holy dead 12
clothing 127
expiation for communal sins 256n.
in ghost tales in *Sefer ḥasidim* 376
as holy dead in Ashkenaz 91–4, 113, 114, 302, 375–6, 393
as holy dead in *Sefer ḥasidim* 106–13, 114
rabbinic attitudes 90–2, 113, 375–6
Rhineland 88, 92–4, 107, 111–12, 113, 302, 376
Roman period 87, 90–1, 92, 310
voluntary martyrdom 93, 94
mazikin (harmful demons) 31, 40, 374

Mefiboshet 201n., 257n.
Meir, R. 20n., 307–8, 347
Meir of Rothenburg, R. 110, 111n., 134n., 136n., 343
memorbukhs 7, 302
Menahem ben Meir Tsiyon, R. 29
merits, transfer of 295–7, 298n., 305
Meshulam of Melun, R. 243n.
Michael, archangel:
  care of souls 193n., 315n., 348
  cult of 269n.
  interaction with Satan 269n., 314, 348
  weigher of souls 269n., 312n., 313, 314n., 346n., 348, 350
Milḥamot hashem 255
Mordecai ben Hillel Hakohen 134n., 243n., 244
Moses 59, 112, 234n., 253, 275, 309n.
Moses of Coucy, R. 130n.
Moses Zaltman (Zalman), R. 369
Moses of Zurich, R. 134n.
Munnu, St 364

N

Nahman, R. 151, 152, 154n.
Nahmanides 89n., 238, 351, 380
Nicholas de Flavigny 103
Nisim, Rabbenu 325–6
Nisim Gaon, R. 274–5, 293–4, 308, 320, 323n., 343

O

Odilo, abbot of Cluny 163, 197, 282, 285, 324n.
Orderic Vitalis:
  story of three brothers 360–1, 362n.
  on troop of the dead 69, 71, 72–3, 75, 78, 80, 224–5, 226n., 227–8, 331–2
  on women's feud 357n.
Otloh of St Emmeram 75n., 77n., 102, 104

P

Paradise:
  Akiva story 330n.
  blessing of 249
  chased out of 80, 228, 317, 337n.
  Cistercian view 197
  clothing in 120–2, 125–7, 129, 137–9, 141, 143–7, 375
  descriptions 155–6, 246n.
  geonic view 320–1
  martyrs in 92–3, 110
  number sent to 251
  Pietist view 124–5, 192–6, 203–4, 295–7, 309–10, 322–3, 324–7, 339, 350, 367, 381
  punishment in 168–71, 175, 178–80, 191, 207, 209, 247, 351
  rabbinic views 155–7
  sections of 200, 201n., 203, 204, 309
  sins and merits 313–14, 317, 343
  summons to 46
  sweet smell 192, 193n., 201n.
  tosafist view 237n., 321–2
  tours 62–3, 182, 187, 260
Patrick, St 259
patronage:
  geonic model of prayer for the dead 274–6, 294, 306, 379
  monastic tradition 283, 284
  pastoral model 285
  patron saints 102–3, 278, 280, 284, 289, 312n., 358–9
  R. Judah's position 293, 294, 338, 351, 352, 365, 368
  Roman model 214, 274, 275–6, 278, 284, 352
penance:
  Christian doctrine 12, 215–16
  Christian manuals 176n., 177n., 219
  Christian notions of posthumous penance and purgation 162, 213–17, 280n., 285–7
  commutation of 218n., 220, 221, 239, 288–9
  medieval Ashkenazi manuals 192n.
  monastic agenda 202, 259–62, 265, 382, 384
  origins of Christian system 277
  Pietist agenda 265
  Pietist doctrine 1–2, 10–11, 190, 192, 201–3, 205n., 253–9, 265, 334, 337, 368, 378, 382, 393n.
  Pietist drive for perfection 389
  Pietist manuals 170n., 191n., 247, 262
  post-mortem on Earth 67–9, 72, 78, 178, 223–4, 226–7, 374, 377

penance (*cont.*):
  pre-purgatorial notions in *Sefer ḥasidim* 218–23
  role of Pietist master 365, 381
  for sin of entering church courtyard 388
  system of 'tariffed penances' 214, 215n., 217, 218, 285n.
  table of commutations 220, 221
  vicarious 286–7, 291, 294–8, 306, 334–6, 338, 379
Perek gehinom 183, 187–8
Peter of Cluny 292n.
Peter Damian 197n., 285, 324n.
Peter Lombard 216
Pietists (Hasidei Ashkenaz):
  accountability 177, 315, 338, 371, 381
  ascetic behaviour 219, 258, 384
  attitude towards women 2, 253
  belief in terrestrial post-mortem punishment 79–83
  burial practices 12, 53, 87–8, 95–7, 104–6, 113–14, 376
  burial in a *talit* with *tsitsit* 12, 129, 130–9, 143–5, 146
  choral singing 194–5, 206
  Christian influences 2–3, 9–11, 207, 265–6
  clothing 130–1, 141–2, 146, 198–9, 206, 384
  clothing the dead 12, 118–19, 129, 142, 146, 268
  concept of corporeality 122, 125–6, 129, 146, 175, 206
  concept of God's 'unspoken law' (*retson haborê*) 1, 32n., 201n., 222, 258, 293, 339, 360, 378, 384, 390–1, 392
  concept of unknowing sin 253, 255–8, 265, 339
  concept of vicarious penance 334
  conception of God 353, 394
  concern with afterlife 206–7
  deathbed testaments 45n.
  demise 2, 11, 393–4
  Divine defence of 359, 362, 364, 366, 369, 382, 391, 394
  doctrine of atonement 2, 201–2, 219–20, 232–3, 234n., 254, 258, 262, 265, 293, 300, 322, 333, 378–9, 382, 384, 389
  doctrine of Inevitable Sin 256, 265, 378, 388
  doctrine of repentance and penance 1–2, 190, 192, 201–3, 205n., 218–20, 222, 235, 247, 258, 265, 334, 337, 368, 378, 382
  dreams 153n.
  elitism 1, 106, 138, 139n.
  enemies of Pietists 319, 359, 361–2, 364, 366, 367
  fasting 195n., 201, 219, 259
  fear of omnipresent sin 253–4
  flagellation 219, 258, 259
  ghost tales 29, 60, 73, 75–8, 180, 206–7
  ghost tales on posthumous reward (validation of Pietist values) 192–204
  humility 156, 168n., 390
  leadership 4, 5, 371
  manuals of penance 170n., 191n.
  martyrs as holy dead 88, 94, 106–7, 111, 113–14, 376
  monastic features 206–7, 218–20, 259–60, 262, 265–6, 381, 383–4
  mortification of the flesh 201–3, 206–7, 219, 258–9
  movement 1–2, 13, 221–2, 393–4
  mystical tradition 1, 10, 36n., 174, 194, 343
  observation of all injunctions 171n.
  Original Sin and Pietist sin 252–64, 265, 378
  prayer ritual 194–6, 197, 206, 219n., 359, 386
  problem of corporeality 188–9, 206
  punishment in Paradise 206–7
  religious virtuosi 390–3
  reward in the hereafter 204, 326–7, 381
  ridiculed and shamed 319, 359, 392–3
  role of Pietist master (*ḥasid ḥakham*) 10, 36, 218, 221–2, 256, 265, 293–4, 350–1, 368, 381, 382, 391
  Sefer ḥasidim, see *Sefer ḥasidim*
  severity of Divine punishment in the afterlife 172–3, 177
  sin of swearing in God's name 18
  stories of returning dead 63, 225, 226–9

teaching on posthumous punishment compared with tosafists 236–52
theories of sin and punishment 2, 171n., 177, 190, 229–30, 232, 254–9
views compared with rabbinic thought 10, 57, 147, 209, 263–4
views on duration of punishment 225, 229, 234–5
views on intercession 394
views on kissing the dead 50, 52
views on martyrdom 2, 113–14
views on posthumous judgement 209, 339, 341–50
views on prayer for the dead 365
views on retributive justice 173n.
views on the wicked dead 31, 87–8, 171n., 225, 326–7
voluntary suffering 201–3, 206–7, 221, 258–9, 265, 368
world-view 4, 7n., 209
piyut commentary 4, 345–6, 349, 350, 368, 380
Pontius, abbot 203n., 297
Preida, R. 322–3
punishment:
Akiva story 328–33
anxiety over punishments in afterlife 376, 377
of average man 356
in both worlds 319n.
capital 85, 87, 95, 205n.
demonic agents 180–8
described to encourage repentance 166–7
duration of posthumous punishment 208–9, 211–13, 221, 225, 229–30, 233–7, 264–5, 331n., 376, 379
duration of punishment in exempla literature 229–32, 252
duration of punishment in *Sefer ḥasidim* 232–6, 265
eternality in *Sefer ḥasidim* (the Hunt narratives) 223–9
fitting the crime 225–6
groups of sinners 59–60
in the hereafter 168–71
immediacy 359
loci of punishment in rabbinic and post-rabbinic sources 61–3
miracle stories 196
in Paradise 168–71, 178–80, 207, 247n., 351
Pietist doctrine of repentance 201–1
Pietist versus tosafist teaching on posthumous punishment 236–52, 321–2
Pietist views 10, 342–4, 351, 368, 378
posthumous punishment in *Sefer ḥasidim* (monastic affinity) 190–2, 206, 381
problem of corporeality 188–9
rabbinic views of posthumous punishment 155–6, 158–9, 209–13, 236, 264, 376, 379
release from 162–3, 274–5, 278, 307, 320, 324n., 329–30, 334, 377, 379
as retribution 355, 357–8, 361, 362
role of clothing 122, 125–6, 131, 137
terrestrial post-mortem punishment 60–1, 64–5, 68–83, 375, 379
severity of 171–3, 176n., 191–2, 225, 229–30, 265, 355–6, 381, 390
sins and punishments 171–80, 206, 216, 220, 253–64, 342–3, 349–51, 354–6, 382
as vengeance 355–66, 368
voluntary suffering to reduce 221–2, 334, 336–7
purgation:
Christian notions of posthumous 160–4, 183–4, 213–17, 278–9, 285–6
demonic agents 183–4
doctrine of 280n.
duration 212, 214–15, 223, 224, 244, 283, 287, 294
fire 189
in Gehenna 177
Pietist position 228, 230, 244, 252, 264–5
pre-purgatorial notions in *Sefer ḥasidim* 218–23
rabbinic teaching 229–30, 264
terrestrial post-mortem 64–8, 72
Purgatory:
clothes in 127, 141
conceptions of 216–17, 249

Purgatory (*cont.*):
  demonic agents 184
  descriptions 246n.
  doctrine 68n., 164, 218, 228, 264, 336
  duration of punishment 288–9, 336
  fires 105, 161
  ghosts returning from 231, 250
  individual 68n.
  legend of St Patrick's Purgatory 141n., 184
  location 161, 163, 280n.
  numbers sent to 250–1
  origins 7, 12, 45n., 160, 163–4, 223, 249, 280n., 303
  popularization of 161, 164, 217, 376, 377
  release from 316n., 324n., 325n., 332
  sentence to 186
  sins and punishments 172, 191
  smell 105
  suffering in 38, 105, 184, 187, 227–8, 247, 293n., 327
  tour 247, 260

R

Rabah b. Bar Hanah 59–60
Rabah son of Avuha 19
Rami, *see* Reiner, Avraham
Rashbam, *see* Samuel ben Meir
Rashi:
  authorship issues 40, 54n.
  burial concerns 123, 136n., 142
  conception of God 394
  on Gehenna 240
  on sabbath rest of souls 243n.
  on *tsitsit* 136n., 143n.
  use of Midrash 275
Ravyah, *see* Eliezer ben Joel Halevi
Regensburg:
  Honorius of Autun in 185
  Irish Benedictine community 247, 260, 384
  Irish *vitae* 261, 262, 362, 383, 389–90
  R. Judah's home in 247–8, 261–2, 383, 389–90, 393n.
  monastery of St James 247, 260–1, 266, 383
  tombstone inscriptions 249
  'Visio Tnugdali' 247–8, 260, 384
Reiner, Avraham (Rami) 249
Reish Lakish 17n., 239–40, 241, 252n.
resurrection of the dead:
  Christian views 159–60
  clothing 135–6, 139, 147
  dead to remain in grave until 28, 57
  period following 63, 126–7, 137, 139, 181, 210, 233
  rabbinic concern 158–9, 205, 376
  reunification of soul with body 26n., 127
  sin of denying 212
retson haboré (God's 'unspoken law'):
  compared with monasticism 384
  Pietist theology 1, 32n., 258, 360, 390–1, 392
  role of Pietist master (*ḥasid ḥakham*) 293, 391
  unwitting sin 201n., 222, 258, 339, 378
Roger of Wendover 105n.
Roman period:
  Christian death rite 276–7
  Christian martyrs 106
  destruction of the Temple 157
  emperors 62, 214, 274, 323–4, 352, 355n.
  funerary rites 97
  Jewish captive children 159
  Jewish martyrs 87, 90, 310
  model of patronage 214, 274, 275–6, 278, 284, 285, 352
  pagan cult of the dead 25
  tales of the dead in the Roman baths 65
Rosh Hashanah 117, 238, 269–70, 345–7
Rubin, Asher 2n.
Rubin, Nissan 108n., 124n., 218n.
Rudolf von Schlettstadt 103, 107

S

saints:
  asceticism 259–60, 261, 262, 266, 383, 389, 391
  bodies of 194n., 231
  burial 99, 102, 105–6, 107, 112, 376
  clothing 127
  communion of 164n., 289
  'humiliation of the' 358n.

intercession by 102, 213, 214, 278–81, 284, 287, 289, 306, 394
Irish 259–61, 266, 362–4, 369, 384, 389–90
martyr-saints 91, 92, 106, 112–13
miracle tales 192, 287, 289n., 310, 311, 362–4, 369, 382, 389, 390n., 391
patron saints 102–3, 104, 278, 280, 284, 289, 312n., 358–9, 362
powers of 38, 160–2, 287, 364
visions of 25, 57, 102, 104, 161
vitae (lives of the saints) 260–2, 284, 362–4, 383, 389–90

Samuel, prophet 122
Samuel, talmudic sage 20–1, 51n., 133n., 135n., 136n., 299, 309n., 335
Samuel ben Meir, R. (Rashbam) 387
Samuel the Pious, R.:
authorship of *Sefer ḥasidim* 5n., 222
on compulsion of others 222
home 247n.
leadership of Pietists 4, 252
miracle stories 4
on sin and punishment 222, 234–5, 252, 254, 255n.
on voluntary suffering 235

Satan 255n., 269n., 291, 342, 347, 349–50
Schmitt, Jean-Claude 3, 26n., 38, 39n., 128
Schur, Yechiel 30
Seder yetsirat havalad 187–8
Sefer hagan 4n., 369–71
Sefer ḥasidim (Book of the Pious):
absence of appearances of holy dead 56–7, 373–4
afterlife 12, 164–8
aim of text 382
appearances of the dead 166–7
appearances of the dead in dreams 168–9, 374
ascetic penitential practices 384
authorship 4, 5–6, 11, 371–2, 378
burial (improper) 94–7, 104–6, 376
burial of martyrs 85–6, 87–8, 144–5, 376
burial practices 30–2
burial in *talit* and *tsitsit* 130–1, 136–9
burial of the wicked 85–6, 87, 97
categories of repentance 219–20
character of R. Judah 370
'characters' of the dead 11
Christian influences 2–3, 164–5, 264–6
clothing the dead 12, 118–20, 121–2, 125–7, 129, 140, 146
concept of corporeality 125–6
conception of God 352–66, 372
dangerous dead 11, 12, 28–32, 39, 57–8, 84, 375
demonic tales 180–8
demons in 21, 22n.
depiction of Pietists 391
descriptions of torture 206
Divine vengeance 356–60, 361–2, 364–5, 369
doctrine of atonement 219
doctrine of penance 2, 219
duration of punishment 208–9
encounters with the dead 17–19, 56–8
eternality of punishment (the Hunt narratives) 223–9, 264–5, 375
examples of excessive punishment 356
fasting 46, 218n., 219, 258n., 300n., 334n., 384
fear of the dead 12, 18, 21
flagellation 202, 384
Germano-Christian beliefs 9, 375
ghost tales 3, 12
ghost tales on posthumous reward (validation of Pietist values) 192–204
ghosts in 21–2
gravity of sin in the afterlife 171–80
hatred of Christianity 255, 387–8
Hellequin's Hunt in 60–1, 72–9, 83, 375
holy dead 11, 12, 21, 56–7, 114
identification of the wicked 382
individual afterlife in 164–8, 205
individual confession 219
influence of doctrine of Purgatory 164
intercessors 293n., 301
kissing the dead 50–1
martyrs as holy dead in 87–8, 94, 106–13, 114, 376
neutral dead 11, 12, 119, 146
omission of story of Akiva and the dead man 328, 330, 332–3, 366–7, 375
Paradise and Gehenna 124

Sefer ḥasidim (*cont.*):
parallels with exempla 373
Pietist pronouncements in 232–6
'The Pious Sinner' 203, 204n.
portrayal of Pietist master 256
posthumous judgement 339–51
posthumous punishment 379, 390
posthumous punishment of group of sinners 59–61, 63, 72–3, 375
posthumous punishment (monastic affinity) 190–2
posthumous reward 192–204
prayer for the dead 267, 291–4, 300–1, 305, 308–10
prayer of the dead for the dead 307
prayer of the dead for the living 270, 305
pre-Christian notions 28, 57, 58, 75–6, 83–4, 97, 113, 218, 373, 375
pre-purgatorial notions 218–23
problem of corporeality 188, 206
promise to return after death ('promise of two friends') 151–2, 376–7
punishment of average man 356
punishment in hereafter 168–71
punishment in Paradise 168–71, 178–80, 207, 247n.
retributive punishment 174, 356–7, 362, 364
severity of justice in afterlife 173–4, 177
shoes of the dead 140
sin, Pietist 252, 256, 258–9, 265, 378
sin and penance 378–9
sin and punishment 206, 265, 378
summoning powers of dead 43–9, 57
'Tale of the Herdsman' 203, 204n., 290n.
'The Tale of the Three Confessors' 203, 204n.
tales of status in the hereafter 381
terrestrial post-mortem punishment 79–83
undeserving dead 318–19, 370
vengeful dead 32–4
views compared with Christian literature 206–7, 373, 381
views compared with rabbinic literature 9, 205, 209, 270–1, 373–4
views compared with tosafist teaching 236–52
violent dead 30–1, 57–8
voluntary suffering 333–4
Sefer havikuaḥ, teshuvah leminim 246, 255
Sefer nitsaḥon yashan 255, 324, 383
Sefer yosef hamekane 255
Shalom of Neustadt, Rabbi 28, 48, 95–6n.
Shaul, Abba 133n., 135n.
She'ilta 270
Shemuel Hakatan 123
Sherira Gaon, R. 274, 321n.
Shimon b. Isaac, R. 111n.
Shimon b. Yohai, R. 20n., 156, 322, 323, 335, 344n.
Shneur Kohen Tsedek, R. 293
Shoham-Steiner, Ephraim 9n., 247n.
Shulḥan arukh 177n.
Shyovitz, David I. 5n., 303n., 330n.
sin:
accountability for 13, 339n., 351, 365, 368, 380, 381
atonement, *see* atonement
burial concerns 86, 89
cardinal 216
categories of sinners 225–6, 238–41, 251–2, 263, 265, 337
Christian absolution 286
Christian influences 10, 84, 265–6, 368
Christian notions of posthumous penance and purgation 213–17
colour black 99n.
deserving and undeserving dead 318–20
disproportion between sin and punishment 171–80, 206
Divine judgement 294, 339–41, 348–50, 355–6
duration of punishment 208–9, 289
duration of punishment in exempla literature 229–32
eternality of punishment in *Sefer ḥasidim* 223–9
gravity in the afterlife 171–80
inevitable 256, 265, 378, 388
intentional 216
length of purgation 161
merits and sins 196, 251–2, 264, 294–7,

311, 313–14, 317, 340–4, 346–7, 349–50, 351, 367–8, 380–1
monastic agenda 265
Original Sin 255n., 265, 378, 388
Original Sin and Pietist sin 252–64
penance during lifetime 163
Pietist agenda 265
Pietist doctrine of repentance 201–2
Pietist pronouncements in *Sefer ḥasidim* 232–6
Pietist sins 196
Pietist versus tosafist teaching on posthumous punishment 236–52
Pietist views 10, 342–4
pre-purgatorial notions in *Sefer ḥasidim* 218–23
punishment connected with 122, 183–4
punishment in Paradise 168–70
rabbinic view of posthumous punishment 209–13, 264
rabbinic views on duration of punishment 208–9, 263
returning dead expiating sin 64–8
sin as affront to God's honour 354, 364, 365, 368
sin offerings 272, 293n.
swearing in God's name 18
terrestrial post-mortem punishment 68, 72, 74–83
unknown sin revealed 253, 255–8
unwitting 201n., 255–8, 339, 357
venial 216
weighing of sins and merits 340–50
Soloveitchik, Haym 10, 57
souls:
All Souls' Day 163, 197, 282, 284
categories of 124, 163, 182, 236–7, 277, 278n.
Christian beliefs 127–9, 159–64, 213–15, 284–5
corporeal punishment in afterlife 175, 180–9, 209
problem of corporeality 125–6, 146, 188–9
in rabbinic literature 124, 154, 159, 212, 222
sabbath rest in Gehenna 8, 12, 31, 40, 82, 243–4, 265, 374
separation of body and soul on death 124–6
Weighing of Souls 269n., 311–15, 346–50
Speyer 73, 107n., 247, 248n., 261, 369, 393
Stahl, Y. Y. 40n., 194n., 234n., 270n.
Suibne mac Domnaill, King 364
suicide:
as an act of penance 204–5n.
ascetic practices 200, 202, 203
burial concerns 95n., 102, 159
dangerous dead 22, 24
returning dead 64
voluntary martyrdom 93

T

Ta-Shma, Israel 273n., 300n., 303n., 329n.
Talmud:
on angels of torment 180–2
attitudes to the returning dead 20–1, 374
burial concerns 85–8, 89, 95–7, 113, 123, 143, 155, 158
on categories of souls 236, 343
on cemeteries 108, 112, 271
on the dead's knowledge of the living 33–4, 115–18, 267–9
death-related tractates 54–5
deathbed scenes 157
on duration of punishment in Gehenna 208, 211–12, 236–42
on Elijah's posthumous appearances 17–20, 56, 123
on encounters with the ordinary dead 20–1, 56
on fear of harmful demons 40
on foetus in the womb 187
on funeral procedure 52, 56
on Gehenna 61
holy dead 56, 113
on Judah the Prince's posthumous appearances 20, 56, 123
on kissing the dead 50
on martyrs 89–91, 92, 113
on posthumous punishment 62, 81, 173–4, 188, 234n., 264
on posthumous punishment of a group of sinners 59–60

Talmud (*cont.*):
on prayer for dead 273–4, 275, 299, 309, 320–1, 322–3
on prayer of dead for dead 307–8, 310
on prayer of dead for living 112n., 270–1
prohibition on entering churches 388
'promise of two friends' motif 152–3, 376–7
on punishment and reward in hereafter 155–6, 159, 170, 171–2, 295–6, 297n.
on rescue from Gehenna 222, 248, 250, 274, 307–8, 309, 320–1, 335
on resurrection 59, 136, 139, 159, 211n., 212, 237
on separation of body and soul 124, 154
on sin offering 293n.
on sin and repentance 262
on sins and merits 341
on study of the Heavenly Chariot 54–5
on suffering of the righteous 256
on *talit* and *tsitsit* 130–1, 133, 135–6, 138–9, 147
on voluntary suffering 200n., 335
talmudic tractates:
Avodah zarah 130n., 310
Berakhot 17, 20, 34, 115, 153, 156, 267, 335
Eduyot 208, 209, 211
Eruvin 61, 238, 240, 274, 308, 327
Gitin 62, 159
Ḥagigah 55, 238, 239, 248, 262–3, 274, 295, 298, 307–10, 327, 335
Horayot 272n., 273n.
Mo'ed katan 21, 54–5, 88–9, 95–6, 151, 153–4
Nedarim 61
Rosh hashanah 212, 236, 237, 239, 242, 248n., 343–4, 346
Sanhedrin, 59, 85, 89, 95, 321–2
Semaḥot 95n., 108n., 123, 132n., 133n., 135n.
Sotah 60n., 308, 320, 321–2, 327
Sukah 335
Tamid 61
Tam, Rabbenu 132, 133n., 144, 166, 243n.
Theuderic, King 363
Thietmar of Merseburg 44–5
Thomas Aquinas 26n., 184n.
Thomas of Canterbury 290n.
Thomas of Cantimpré 21n., 316n.
Thorolf l'Estropié 23, 25, 101n.
Titus, Roman emperor 62
Tnugdalus 247–8, 260
Tosafot, tosafists:
on angel from the fire 55
on burial in *talit* with *tsitsit* 132–6, 144
on categories of sinner 239–42, 248n.
on duration of posthumous punishment 209n., 236–7, 238–42, 377
on judgement of individuals 237–8
Pietist versus tosafist teaching on posthumous punishment 10, 236–52, 254, 321–2, 326
on prayer for the dead 308, 321–2, 326
on praying at cemetery 112n.
on 'promise of two friends' 166
on repentance 262–4
on *talit*-wearing 130–1
on *tefilin*-wearing 212n.
tosafists as intellectual virtuosi 391–2
on *tsitsit* 133n., 144
on viewing church sculpture 387
Trachtenberg, Joshua 2, 53n.
Tsidkiyah Harofé of Rome, R. 273n., 299n., 301, 304n., 305
Tsidkiyah b. Kena'anah 86
Tur 177n.

U

Urbach, Ephraim 173, 273n., 296n., 355n.

V

van Gennep, Arnold 144n.
Vespasian, Roman general 157
Virgin Mary:
in art 312–13, 314
cult 289–91
intercessory power 281, 289–91, 311–12, 315, 347, 377
miracles 65, 176, 290–1, 310, 348, 358n.
portrayal in Last Judgement scenes 290n.
role 176, 289, 315n.
subverting judicial process 313, 314–15n., 380

summons to death 42–3n.
vengeance-type tales 362
'Visio Pauli' 215
'Vision of Adamnán' 64n., 214n., 251
'Vision of Bernoldus' 178n., 279–80
'Vision of Charles the Fat' 280n., 312n.
'Vision of Drythelm' 162, 225n.
'Vision of Fursey' 75n., 161, 183, 214, 215, 279
'Vision of Rotcharius' 280
'Vision of Tundale' (Visio Tnugdali) 184, 186n., 217n., 247, 260, 384

W
Walkelin, priest 71, 73–5, 224–5, 227–8, 331–2
Watkins, Carl S. 67n., 217n., 224n.
Weighing of Souls:
balance image 312n., 313–14
in exempla 311–12, 314, 348
in *mahzor* illumination 346–7, 349, 350
in medieval art 312–13, 314n., 315n., 347–8, 349, 350
in *piyut* commentary 345–6, 349, 350
in *Sefer hasidim* 313–15, 380
Wieseltier, Leon 303n.
William, count of Julich 175, 327n.
William, monk 169
William of Auvergne 26, 189, 216
William of Glos 71, 75, 224n.
William of Nassyngton 328n.
William of Newburgh 27, 32, 33n., 66, 67n.
Wimpfen, Alexander 110, 111n.

Y
Yassif, Eli 4, 7n., 168n., 174
Yeruham b. Meshulam, R. 50
Yizkor service 7, 302, 303n.
Yohanan, R.:
on burial with *tsitsit* 135n.
on freedom of dead from *mitsvot* 13
rescuing master Elisha 222n., 275, 307–8, 309–10, 320n., 335
Yohanan ben Zakai, R. 54, 55, 156–7, 329n.
Yom Kippur 81, 271n., 301–2, 304, 341, 359
Yom Tov, R. 204–5n.
Yom Tov al-Sevilli, R. (Ritva) 130n., 238n.
Yosi, R. 17–19

Z
Ze'iri, R. 20, 123

www.ingramcontent.com/pod-product-compliance
Lightning Source LLC
Chambersburg PA
CBHW071508081225
36481CB00011B/332
* 9 7 8 1 8 0 2 0 7 1 9 9 3 *